T0236151

Lecture Notes in Artificial Intelligence 10350

Subseries of Lecture Notes in Computer Science

LNAI Series Editors

Randy Goebel
University of Alberta, Edmonton, Canada
Yuzuru Tanaka
Hokkaido University, Sapporo, Japan
Wolfgang Wahlster
DFKI and Saarland University, Saarbrücken, Germany

LNAI Founding Series Editor

Joerg Siekmann
DFKI and Saarland University, Saarbrücken, Germany

More information about this series at http://www.springer.com/ser

Editors
Salem Benferhat
Artois University
Lens
France

Karim Tabia
Artois University
Lens
France

Moonis Ali
Texas State Uni
San Marcos, TX
USA

ISSN 0302-9743   ISSN 1611-3349 (electr
Lecture Notes in Artificial Intelligence
ISBN 978-3-319-60041-3   ISBN 978-3-319-60042-0
DOI 10.1007/978-3-319-60042-0

Library of Congress Control Number: 2017943043

LNCS Sublibrary: SL7 – Artificial Intelligence

Printed on acid-free paper

This Springer imprint is published by Springer Nature
The registered company is Springer International Publishing AG
The registered company address is: Gewerbestrasse 11, 6330 Cham,

Preface

In many industrial applications, there is a real need to develop intelligent systems that deal with complex, open, and dynamic information systems. These information systems often involve a huge amount of data that may be incomplete, heterogeneous, pervaded with uncertainty, and inconsistent with available ontologies or expert knowledge.

This volume, entitled *Advances in Artificial Intelligence: From Theory to Practice*, contains the papers presented at the 30th International Conference on Industrial, Engineering, and Other Applications of Applied Intelligent Systems (IEA/AIE 2017) which was held in Arras (France), during June 27–30, 2017. This edition continues the tradition of emphasizing applications of applied intelligent systems to solve real-life problems in all areas including engineering, science, industry, automation and robotics, business and finance, health care, agronomy, anomaly detection, human–machine interactions, etc.

In this 30th year of the IEA/AIE conference, we received 180 papers for the main and the special tracks. We accepted 70 papers as full papers and 45 papers as short papers. All accepted papers were carefully reviewed by Program Committee members. The accepted papers cover a wide array of applied artificial intelligence topics including knowledge representation and reasoning, machine learning, argumentation systems, ontological reasoning, computer animation, non-monotonic and uncertainty-based reasoning, graphical models, decision support systems, recommendation systems, meta-heuristics, planning and scheduling, practical problem solving, etc.

In addition to the list of accepted papers, the conference greatly benefited from invited lectures by three world-leading researchers in applied artificial intelligence: (a) Jian J. Zhang (Professor of Computer Graphics at the National Centre for Computer Animation, Bournemouth University, UK), who gave a talk on "Creativity for Research – An Analogy Model"; (b) Umberto Straccia (Senior Researcher at the Istituto di Scienza e Tecnologie dell' Informazione (ISTI) of the Italian National Council of Research CNR), who gave a talk on "Fuzzy Semantic Web Languages and Beyond"; and (c) Leendert van der Torre (Professor of Computer Science at University of Luxembourg, Luxembourg), who gave a talk on "Rational Enterprise Architecture."

In addition to the main track, the following special tracks were organized:

- Agronomy and Artificial Intelligence
- Anomaly Detection
- Applications of Argumentation
- Conditionals and Non-monotonic Reasoning
- De Finetti's Heritage in Uncertainty and Decision-Making
- Computational Intelligence in Databases
- Graphical Models: From Theory to Applications
- Innovative Applications of Textual Analysis Based on AI
- Intelligent Systems in Health Care and mHealth for Health Outcomes

Additionally, two affiliated workshops were also organized:

- Workshop on ASP Technologies for Querying Large-Scale Multiple-Source Heterogeneous Web Information, WASPIQ 2017 (co-chairs Odile Papini, Salem Benferhat, Laurent Garcia, and Marie-Laure Mugnier)
- Computer Animation and Artificial Intelligence, CAnimAI (co-chairs The Duy Bui, Sylvain Lagrue, Hongchuan Yu, Huu-Hoa Nguyen, Pradorn Sureephong, Mohd Shafry Mohd Rahim, and Karim Tabia)

We would like to thank the following organizations/projects for their support of the conference:

- International Society of Applied Intelligence (ISAI)
- University of Artois, France
- Centre Nationale de la Recherche Scientifique (CNRS), France
- The ANR (French National Research Agency) project ASPIQ (ASP Technologies for Querying Large-Scale Multisource Heterogeneous Web Information)
- The European RISE (Research and Innovation Staff Exchange) project AniAge (High-Dimensional Heterogeneous Data-Based Animation Techniques for Southeast Asian Intangible Cultural Heritage Digital Content).

We would like to thank all the members of the Program Committees (from the main and the special tracks), as well as the additional reviewers, who devoted their time for the reviewing process. We thank all the authors of submitted papers, the invited speakers, and the participants for their scientific contributions to the conference. Finally, we would like to thank all the Organizing Committee members (with a special thanks to Sylvain Lagrue, from CRIL, CNRS-University of Artois) for their excellent local organization, which made the IEA/AIE-2017 conference a success.

May 2017

Salem Benferhat
Karim Tabia
Moonis Ali

Organization

Executive Committee

General Chair

Moonis Ali, USA

International Advisory Committee

Hamido Fujita, Japan (Chair)
Enrique Herrera-Viedma, Spain
Francisco Chiclana, UK
Yinglin Wang, China
Love Ekenberg, Sweden
Imre Rudas, Hungary
Shiliang Sun, China
Vincenzo Loia, Italy
Ali Selamat, Malaysia
Bipin Indurkhya, Poland
Chris Bowman, Australia
Jun Sasaki, Japan
Ligang Zhou, Macao
Rajendra Acharya, Singapore
Levente Kovacs, Hungary

Program Co-chairs

Salem Benferhat, France
Karim Tabia, France

Local Co-chairs

Salem Benferhat, France
Sylvain Lagrue, France

Special Sessions Co-chairs

Zied Bouraoui, UK
Steven Schockaert, UK

Workshop Co-chairs

Jianbing Ma, UK
Hongchuan Yu, UK

Social Events and Local Arrangements Co-chairs

Fahima Cheikh-Alili, France
Nathalie Chetcuti-Sperandio, France
Karim Tabia, France

Web Co-chairs

Jérôme Delobelle, France
Fabien Delorme, France
Amélie Levray, France

Publicity Chair

Farid Nouioua, France

Registration and Financial Chair

Virginie Delahaye, France

Local Organizing Committee

François Chevallier, France
Jérôme Delobelle, France
Yacine Izza, France
Amélie Levray, France
Emmanuel Lonca, France
Valentin Montmirail, France
Imen Ouled Dlala, France
Éric Piette, France
Nicolas Szczepanski, France

Program Committee (Main Track)

Carole Adam, France
Mario Alviano, Italy
Youngchul Bae, South Korea
Edurne Barrenechea, Spain
Fevzi Belli, Germany
Nahla Ben Amor, Tunisia
Sadok Ben Yahia, Tunisia
Jamal Bentahar, USA
Mehul Bhatt, Germany
Isabelle Bloch, France
Leszek Borzemski, Poland
Thouraya Bouabana Tebibel, Algeria
Imen Boukhris, Tunisia

Mustapha Bourahla, Algeria
Zied Bouraoui, UK
Narhimene Boustia, Algeria
Patrick Brezillon, France
The Duy Bui, Vietnam
Stephane Cardon, France
Tristan Cazenave, France
Martine Cebiero, USA
Michael C.W. Chan, Hong Kong,
    SAR China
Darryl Charles, UK
Shyi-Ming Chen, Taiwan
Laurence Cholvy, France

Paul Chung, UK
Mike Cook, UK
Fabio Cozman, Brazil
José Valente de Oliveira, Portugal
Georgios Dounias, Greece
Florence Dupin De Saint Cyr, France
Zied Elouedi, Tunisia
Roberta Ferrario, Italy
Philippe Fournier-Viger, China
Hamido Fujita, Japan
Eric Jacopin, France
Laurent Garcia, France
Lluis Godo, Spain
Maciej Grzenda, Poland
Allel Hadjali, France
Jun Hakura, Japan
Shyamanta M. Hazarika, India
Bipin Indurkhya, Poland
He Jiang, China
Bian Jiang, USA
Vicente Julian, Spain
Gabriele Kern-Isberner, Germany
Faiza Khellaf, Algeria
Frank Klawonn, Germany
Vladik Kreinovich, USA
Amruth Kumar, USA
Bora Kumova, Turkey
Sylvain Lagrue, France
Jean-Charles Lamirel, France
Jooyoung Lee, USA
Chang-Hwan Lee, South Korea
Mehdi Kaytoue, France
Arnaud Lallouet, France
Eric Lefevre, France
Philippe Leray, France
Mark Sh. Levin, Russia
Amélie Levray, France
Vincenzo Loia, Italy
Bouzar Lydia, Algeria
Jianbing Ma, UK
Thi Chau Ma, Vietnam
Francesco Marcelloni, Italy
Joao Marques-Silva, Portugal
Arnaud Martin, France
Philippe Mathieu, France
Kishan Mehrotra, USA

Carlos Mencia, Spain
Engelbert Mephu Nguifo, France
Enrique Miranda, Spain
François Modave, USA
Yasser Mohammad, Egypt
Mohd Shafry Mohd Rahim, Malaysia
Aïcha Mokhtari, Algeria
Malek Mouhoub, USA
Thanhthuy Nguyen, Vietnam
Ngoc-Thanh Nguyen, Poland
Farid Nouioua, France
Jae Oh, USA
Santiago Ontanon, USA
Meltem Ozturk, France
Gregorio Sainz Palmero, Spain
Odile Papini, France
Rafael Peñaloza, Italy
Eric Piette, France
Don Potter, USA
Nico Potyka, Germany
Henri Prade, France
Guilin Qi, China
Chedy Raissi, France
Srini Ramaswamy, USA
Florian Richoux, France
Abdallah Saffidine, Australia
Giuseppe Sanfilippo, Italy
Paulo E. Santos, Brazil
Steven Schockaert, UK
Karima Sedki, France
Michael Spranger, France
Pradorn Sureephong, Thailand
Armando Tacchella, Italy
Choh Man Teng, USA
Le Thanh Ha, Vietnam
Ruck Thawonmas, Japan
Marco Valtorta, USA
Barbara Vantaggi, Italy
Ivan Varzinczak, France
Zsolt Janos Viharos, Hungary
Marco Viviani, Italy
Martijn Warnier, The Netherlands
Mary-Anne Williams, Australia
Safa Yahi, France
Don-Lin Yang, Taiwan
Lei Zhang, USA

Program Committees (Special Tracks)

Agronomy and Artificial Intelligence

Madalina Croitoru, France (Co-chair)
Pierre Bisquert, France (Co-chair)
Abdallah Arioua, France
Estelle Chaix, France
Liliana Ibanescu, France
Wim Laurier, Belgium
Alexandru Mihnea Moisescu, Romania
Claire Nedelec, France
Nir Oren, UK
Alun Preece, UK
Danai Symeonidou, France
Rallou Thomopolous, France
Jan Top, The Netherlands

Anomaly Detection

Ryan McConville, UK (Co-chair)
Weiru Liu, UK (Co-chair)
Frans Coenen, UK
Masud Moshtaghi, Australia
Nico Görnitz, Germany
Jun Hong, UK
Michael Davis, Switzerland
Paul Miller, UK
Zhanyu Ma, China
Jen Houle, UK
Hanghang Tong, USA
Florian Skopik, Austria

Applications of Argumentation

Federico Cerutti, UK (Co-chair)
Richard Booth, UK (Co-chair)
Leila Amgoud, France
Pietro Baroni, Italy
Ringo Baumann, Germany
Stefano Bistarelli, Italy
Claudette Cayrol, France
Wolfgang Faber, UK
John Fox, UK
Sarah Gaggl, Germany
Massimiliano Giacomin, Italy
Tom Gordon, Germany

Matti Jarvisalo, Finland
Antonis Kakas, Cyprus
Jean-Guy Mailly, France
Nir Oren, UK
Sylwia Polberg, UK
Alun Preece, UK
Guillermo Simari, Argentina
Nikos Spanoudakis, Greece
Christian Stab, Germany
Manfred Stede, Germany
Hannes Strass, Germany
Matthias Thimm, Germany
Mauro Vallati, UK
Srdjan Vesic, France
Serena Villata, France
Johannes Wallner, Finland
Stefan Woltran, Austria

Conditionals and Non-monotonic Reasoning

Gabriele Kern Isberner, Germany (Co-chair)
Christian Eichhorn, Germany (Co-chair)
Ofer Arieli, Israel
Christoph Beierle, Germany
Giovanni Casini, Luxembourg
Lupita Estefania Gazzo Castañeda, Germany
Laura Giordano, Italy
Tommie Meyer, South Africa
Odile Papini, France
Marco Ragni, Germany
Gavin Rens, South Africa
Gerhard Schurz, Germany
Niels Skovgaard Olsen, Germany
Matthias Thimm, Germany
Stefan Woltran, Austria
Renata Wassermann, Brazil
Anna Zamansky, Israel

De Finetti's Heritage in Uncertainty and Decision-Making

Giualianella Coletti, Italy (Co-chair)
Davide Petturiti, Italy (Co-chair)
Barbara Vantaggi, Italy (Co-chair)
Giuseppe Sanfilippo, Italy
Giualianella Coletti, Italy
Davide Petturiti, Italy
Barbara Vantaggi, Italy

Gernot Kleiter, Austria
Romano Scozzafava, Italy
Vladik Kreinovich, USA

Computational Intelligence in Databases

Guy De Trév, Belgium (Co-chair)
Allel Hadjali, France (Co-chair)
Mohamed Anis Bach, Tunisia
Belkasmi Djamal, Algeria
Stephane Jean, France
Karima Akli Astouati, Algeria
Zied Elouedi, Tunisia
Slawomir Zadrozny, Poland
Mourad Ouziri, France
Djamal Benslimane, France
Ludovic Lietard, France
Gloria Bordogna, Italy
Ahmed Mostefaoui, France
Arnaud Martin, France
Daniel Rocacher, France
Anne Laurent, France
Peter Dolog, Denmark
Maria Rifqi, France

Graphical Models: From Theory to Applications

Christophe Gonzales, France (Co-chair)
Philippe Leray, France (Co-chair)
Alexandre Aussem, France
Concha Bielza, Spain
Andrés Cano, Spain
Luis M. De Campos, Spain
Julia Flores, Spain
Jan Lemeire, Belgium
Anders L. Madsen, Denmark
Jose Luis Molina Gonzales, Spain
Thomas D. Nielsen, Denmark
Agnieszka Onisko, Poland
Silja Renooi, The Netherlands
Pierre-Henri Wuillemin, France

Innovative Applications of Textual Analysis-Based on AI

Yinglin Wang, China (Chair)
Xin Lin, China
Lei Duan, China

Deqing Yang, China
Hongtao Lu, China
Min Liu, China
Jian Cao, China

Intelligent Systems in Health Care and mHealth for Health Outcomes

François Modave, USA (Co-chair)
Jiang Bian, USA (Co-chair)
William Hogan, USA
Zhe He, USA
Yi Guo, USA
Xia Hu, USA
Remzi Seker, USA
Juan Antonio Lossio-Ventura, USA
Jiawei Yuan, USA
Mengjun Xie, USA
Tanja Magoc, USA
Kenji Yoshigoe, USA
Olac Fuentes, USA
Enrico Pontelli, USA
Doug Talbert, USA
Yanming Gong, USA
Yonghui Wu, USA
Lixia Yao, USA
Ramzi Salloum, USA

Sponsoring Institutions

IEA/AIE 2017 was organized by the Centre de Recherche en Informatique de Lens (UMR CNRS 8188) of Artois University, Arras, France.

Sponsored by

International Society of Applied Intelligence (ISAI)
University of Artois, France
Centre Nationale de la Recherche Scientifique (CNRS), France
The ANR (French National Research Agency) project ASPIQ (ASP Technologies for Querying Large-Scale Multisource Heterogeneous Web Information)
The European RISE (Research and Innovation Staff Exchange) project AniAge (High Dimensional Heterogeneous Data-Based Animation Techniques for Southeast Asian Intangible Cultural Heritage Digital Content)

Organized in cooperation with

Association for the Advancement of Artificial Intelligence (AAAI)
Association for Computing Machinery (ACM/SIGART)

Catalan Association for Artificial Intelligence (ACIA)
International Neural Network Society (INNS)
Italian Artificial Intelligence Association (AI*IA)
Japanese Society for Artificial Intelligence (JSAI)
Lithuanian Computer Society - Artificial Intelligence Section (LIKS-AIS)
Spanish Society for Artificial Intelligence (AEPIA)
Society for the Study of Artificial Intelligence and the Simulation of Behaviour (AISB)
Taiwanese Association for Artificial Intelligence (TAAI)
Taiwanese Association for Consumer Electronics (TACE)
Centre Nationale de la Recherche Scientifique (CNRS)
Texas State University, USA
Artois University, France

Creativity for Research - An Analogy Model (Invited Talk)

Jian Jun Zhang

National Centre for Computer Animation,
Bournemouth University, Poole, UK
jzhang@bmth.ac.uk

Abstract. Scientific creativity and innovation is at the heart of scientific research which represents the essential driving force for economic growth. In this talk, I will talk about the latest development of a European Commission funded project, called the Dr Inventor, whose objective is to develop a prototype of scientific creativity model for enhancing scientific innovation. It is built on the vision that technologies have great potential to supplement and elevate human ingenuity by overcoming the limitations that people suffer in pursuing scientific discoveries. By exploiting the rich availability of web-based research resources, our research develops a virtual personal research assistant, utilising machine-empowered search and cognitive computation to bring scientific researchers novel and thought-provoking perspectives for scientific develop-ment. Dr Inventor is built on a cognitive model of the human ability to reason using analogies. An analogy is a comparison between two seemingly different ideas, which highlights some previously unnoticed similarities. Many scientists are familiar with the notion that a development in one field can have significant implications in another field, which suggests that an approach developed to solve a problem in one domain may be just as (or even more) applicable to another discipline. The project has been developed with an initial focus on the discipline of computer graphics, which can be extended to other disciplines.

Contents – Part I

Data Mining and Machine Learning

Sensors, Signal Processing and Data Fusion

Recommender Systems

Decision Support Systems

Knowledge Representation and Reasoning

Navigation, Control and Autonomous Agents

Sentiment Analysis and Social Media

Contents – Part II

Graphical Models: From Theory to Applications

Anomaly Detection

Agronomy and Artificial Intelligence

Applications of Argumentation

Intelligent Systems in Healthcare and mHealth for Health Outcomes

Innovative Applications of Textual Analysis Based on AI

Invited Talks

Fuzzy Semantic Web Languages and Beyond

Umberto Straccia[✉]

ISTI - CNR, Pisa, Italy
straccia@isti.cnr.it

Abstract. The aim of this talk is to present the state of the art in representing and reasoning with fuzzy knowledge in Semantic Web Languages such as triple languages RDF/RDFS, conceptual languages of the OWL 2 family and rule languages. We further show how one may generalise them to so-called annotation domains, that cover also e.g. temporal and provenance extensions.

1 Introduction

Reasoning under fuzziness is growing in importance in Semantic Web research as recognised by a large number of research efforts in this direction [16,18]. *Semantic Web Languages* (SWL) are the languages used to provide a formal description of concepts, terms, and relationships within a given domain, among which the *OWL 2 family* of languages [10], *triple languages* RDF & RDFS [4] and *rule languages* (such as RuleML [6], Datalog$^{\pm}$ [5] and RIF [11]) are major players. While their syntactic specification is based on XML [22], their semantics is based on logical formalisms: briefly,

- RDFS is a logic having intensional semantics and the logical counterpart is ρdf;
- OWL 2 is a family of languages that relate to *Description Logics* (DLs);
- rule languages relate roughly to the *Logic Programming* (LP) paradigm, specifically *Datalog*;
- both OWL 2 and rule languages have an extensional semantics.

Fuzzyness. We recap that under *fuzziness* fall all those approaches in which statements (for example, "heavy rain") are true to some *degree*, which is taken from a truth space (usually $[0, 1]$). For instance, the grade of the sentence "heavy rain" may depend on the amount of rain is falling.[1] Often we may find rough definitions about rain types, such as:[2]

Rain. Falling drops of water larger than 0.5 mm in diameter. In forecasts, "rain" usually implies that the rain will fall steadily over a period of time;

---

[1] More concretely, the intensity of precipitation is expressed in terms of a precipitation rate R: volume flux of precipitation through a horizontal surface, i.e. $m^3/m^2 s = ms^{-1}$. It is usually expressed in mm/h.

[2] http://usatoday30.usatoday.com/weather/wds8.htm.

© Springer International Publishing AG 2017
S. Benferhat et al. (Eds.): IEA/AIE 2017, Part I, LNAI 10350, pp. 3–8, 2017.
DOI: 10.1007/978-3-319-60042-0_1

Light rain. Rain falls at the rate of 2.6 mm or less an hour;
Moderate rain. Rain falls at the rate of 2.7 mm to 7.6 mm an hour;
Heavy rain. Rain falls at the rate of 7.7 mm an hour or more.

It is evident that such definitions are quite harsh and resemble a bivalent (two-valued) logic: e.g. a precipitation rate of 7.7 mm/h is a heavy rain, while a precipitation rate of 7.6 mm/h is just a moderate rain. This may be unsatisfactory, as quite naturally the more rain is falling, the more the sentence "heavy rain" is true and, vice-versa, the less rain is falling the less the sentence is true. A more fine grained way to define the various types of rains is illustrated in Fig. 1.

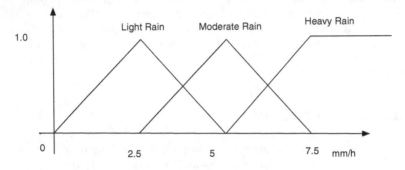

Fig. 1. Light, Moderate and Heavy Rain.

Light rain, moderate rain and heavy rain are called *Fuzzy Sets* in the literature and are characterised by the fact that membership is a matter of degree. Of course, the definition of fuzzy sets is frequently context dependent and subjective: e.g. the definition of heavy rain is quite different from heavy person and the latter may be defined differently among human beings.

From a logical point of view, a propositional interpretation maps a statement ϕ to a truth degree in $[0,1]$, i.e. $\mathcal{I}(\phi) \in [0,1]$. Fuzzy statements are truth-functional, that is, the degree of truth of every statement can be calculated from the degrees of truth of its constituents. For the sake of illustrative purpose, an example of truth functional interpretation of propositional statements is as follows:

$$\mathcal{I}(\phi \wedge \psi) = \min(\mathcal{I}(\phi), \mathcal{I}(\psi))$$
$$\mathcal{I}(\phi \vee \psi) = \max(\mathcal{I}(\phi), \mathcal{I}(\psi))$$
$$\mathcal{I}(\neg\phi) \quad = 1 - \mathcal{I}(\phi) \ .$$

Fuzzy statements have the form $\langle \phi, r \rangle$, where $r \in [0,1]$, which encodes that the degree of truth of ϕ is *greater or equal* r, i.e. fuzzy interpretation $\mathcal{I}$ *satisfies* a fuzzy statement $\langle \phi, r \rangle$, or $\mathcal{I}$ is a *model* of $\langle \phi, r \rangle$, denoted $\mathcal{I} \models \langle \phi, r \rangle$, iff $\mathcal{I}(\phi) \geq r$. A *fuzzy knowledge base* is a set of fuzzy statements and an interpretation $\mathcal{I}$ *satisfies* (is a *model* of) a knowledge base, denoted $\mathcal{I} \models \mathcal{K}$, iff it satisfies each element in it. The *best entailment degree* of ϕ w.r.t. $\mathcal{K}$ (denoted $bed(\mathcal{K}, \phi)$), i.e. $bed(\mathcal{K}, \phi) = \sup \{r \mid \mathcal{K} \models \langle \phi, r \rangle\}$.

Annotation Domains. We have seen that fuzzy statements extend statements with an *annotation* $r \in [0,1]$. Interestingly, we may further generalise this by allowing a statement being annotated with a value λ taken from a so-called *annotation domain* [23], which allow to deal with several domains (such as, fuzzy, temporal, provenance) and their combination, in a uniform way. Formally, let us consider a non-empty set L. Elements in L are our annotation values. For example, in a fuzzy setting, $L = [0, 1]$, while in a typical temporal setting, L may be time points or time intervals. In the annotation framework, an interpretation will map statements to elements of the annotation domain. Now, an *annotation domain* is an idempotent, commutative semi-ring $D = \langle L, \oplus, \otimes, \bot, \top \rangle$, where $\oplus$ is $\top$-annihilating. That is, for $\lambda, \lambda_i \in L$

1. $\oplus$ is idempotent, commutative, associative;
2. $\otimes$ is commutative and associative;
3. $\bot \oplus \lambda = \lambda$, $\top \otimes \lambda = \lambda$, $\bot \otimes \lambda = \bot$, and $\top \oplus \lambda = \top$;
4. $\otimes$ is distributive over $\oplus$, i.e.$\lambda_1 \otimes (\lambda_2 \oplus \lambda_3) = (\lambda_1 \otimes \lambda_2) \oplus (\lambda_1 \otimes \lambda_3)$.

We refer the reader to [23] for more details about annotation domains.

Talk Overview. We present here some salient aspects in representing and reasoning with fuzzy knowledge in Semantic Web Languages (SWLs) such as *triple languages* [4] (see, e.g. [17]), *conceptual languages* [10] (see, e.g. [9]) and *rule languages* (see, e.g. [13,15]). We refer the reader to [18,19] for an extensive presentation concerning fuzziness and semantic web languages. We then further show how one may generalise them to so-called annotation domains, that cover also e.g. temporal and provenance extensions (see, e.g. [23]).

2   Fuzzy Logic and Semantic Web Languages

We have seen in the previous section how to "fuzzyfy" a classical language such as propositional logic and FOL, namely fuzzy statements are of the form $\langle \phi, r \rangle$, where ϕ is a statement and $r \in [0, 1]$. The natural extension to SWLs consists then in replacing ϕ with appropriate expressions belonging to the logical counterparts of SWLs, namely ρdf, DLs and LPs, as we will illustrate next.

2.1   Fuzzy RDFS

The basic ingredients of *RDF* are *triples* of the form (s, p, o), such as $(umberto, likes, tomato)$, stating that *subject* s has *property* p with *value* o. In *RDF Schema* (RDFS), which is an extension of RDF, additionally some special keywords may be used as properties to further improve the expressivity of the language. For instance we may also express that the class of 'tomatoes are a subclass of the class of vegetables', $(tomato, \mathsf{sc}, vegetables)$, while Zurich is an instance of the class of cities, $(zurich, \mathsf{type}, city)$.

In *Fuzzy RDFS* (see [17] and references therein), triples are annotated with a degree of truth in $[0, 1]$. For instance, "Rome is a big city to degree 0.8" can be represented with $\langle (Rome, \mathsf{type}, BigCity), 0.8 \rangle$. More formally, *fuzzy triples* are expressions of the form $\langle \tau, r \rangle$, where τ is a RDFS triple (the truth value r may be omitted and, in that case, the value $r = 1$ is assumed).

Annotation Domains and RDFS. The generalisation to annotation domains is conceptual easy, as now one may replace truth degrees with annotation terms taken from an appropriate domain. For further details see [23].

2.2 Fuzzy DLs

Description Logics (DLs) [1] are the logical counterpart of the family of OWL languages. So, to illustrate the basic concepts of fuzzy OWL, it suffices to show the fuzzy DL case (see [2,9,18], for a survey). We recap that the basic ingredients are the descriptions of classes, properties, and their instances, such as

– $a{:}C$, meaning that individual a is an instance of concept/class C (here C is seen as a unary predicate);
– $(a, b){:}R$, meaning that the pair of individuals $\langle a, b \rangle$ is an instance of the property/role R (here R is seen as a binary predicate);
– $C \sqsubseteq D$, meaning that the class C is a subclass of class D.

In general, fuzzy DLs allow expressions of the form $\langle a{:}C, r \rangle$, stating that a is an instance of concept/class C with degree at least r, i.e. the FOL formula $C(a)$ is true to degree at least r. Similarly, $\langle C_1 \sqsubseteq C_2, r \rangle$ states a vague subsumption relationships. Informally, $\langle C_1 \sqsubseteq C_2, r \rangle$ dictates that the FOL formula $\forall x. C_1(x) \rightarrow C_2(x)$ is true to degree at least r. Essentially, *fuzzy DLs* are then obtained by interpreting the statements as fuzzy FOL formulae and attaching a weight n to DL statements, thus, defining so *fuzzy DL statements*.

So far, several *fuzzy* variants of DLs have been proposed: they can be classified according to (see [2,18])

– the description logic resp. ontology language that they generalize;
– the allowed fuzzy constructs;
– the underlying fuzzy logic;
– their reasoning algorithms and computational complexity results.

Annotation Domains and OWL. The generalisation to annotation domains is conceptual easy, as now one may replace truth degrees with annotation terms taken from an appropriate domain (see, e.g. [3,14]).

2.3 Fuzzy Rule Languages

The foundation of the core part of rule languages is *Datalog* [21], i.e. a Logic Programming Language (LP) [7] without n-ary function symbols ($n \geq 1$). In LP, the management of imperfect information has attracted the attention of many researchers and numerous frameworks have been proposed. Addressing all of them is almost impossible, due to both the large number of works published in this field (early works date back to early 80-ties [12]) and the different approaches proposed (see, e.g. [16,18,19]).

Basically, a Datalog program $\mathcal{P}$ is made out by a set of rules and a set of facts. *Facts* are ground *atoms* of the form $P(\boldsymbol{c})$. On the other hand rules are of the form

$$A(\boldsymbol{x}) \leftarrow \exists \boldsymbol{y}.\varphi(\boldsymbol{x}, \boldsymbol{y}) \ ,$$

where $\varphi(\boldsymbol{x}, \boldsymbol{y})$ is a conjunction of n-ary predicates. A *query* is a rule and the *answer set* of a query q w.r.t. a set $\mathcal{K}$ of facts and rules is the set of tuples $\boldsymbol{t}$ such that there exists $\boldsymbol{t}'$ such that the instantiation $\varphi(\boldsymbol{t}, \boldsymbol{t}')$ of the query body is true in *minimal model* of $\mathcal{K}$, which is guaranteed to exists.

In the *fuzzy* case, rules and facts are as for the crisp case, except that now a predicate is annotated. An example of fuzzy rule defining good hotels may be the following:

$$\langle GoodHotel(x), s \rangle \leftarrow Hotel(x), \langle Cheap(x), s_1 \rangle, \langle CloseToVenue(x), s_2 \rangle,$$
$$\langle Comfortable(x), s_3 \rangle, s := 0.3 \cdot s_1 + 0.5 \cdot s_2 + 0.2 \cdot s_3 \quad (1)$$

A *fuzzy query* is a fuzzy rule and, informally, the *fuzzy answer set* is the ordered set of weighted tuples $\langle \boldsymbol{t}, s \rangle$ such that all the fuzzy atoms in the rule body are true in the minimal model and s is the result of the scoring function f applied to its arguments. The existence of a minimal is guaranteed if the scoring functions in the query and in the rule bodies are *monotone* [18].

A rising problem is the problem to compute the top-k ranked answers to a query, without computing the score of all answers. This allows to answer queries such as "find the top-k closest hotels to the conference location". Solutions to this problem can be found in e.g. [8,15,20].

Annotation Domains and Rule Languages. The generalisation of fuzzy rule languages to the case in which an annotation $r \in [0, 1]$ is replaced with an annotation value λ taken from an annotation domain is straightforward and proceeds as for the other SWLs.

References

1. Baader, F., Calvanese, D., McGuinness, D., Nardi, D., Patel-Schneider, P.F. (eds.): The Description Logic Handbook: Theory, Implementation, and Applications. Cambridge University Press, Cambridge (2003)
2. Bobillo, F., Cerami, M., Esteva, F., García-Cerdaña, À., Peñaloza, R., Straccia, U.: Fuzzy description logics in the framework of mathematical fuzzy logic. In: Cintula, C.N.P., Fermüller, C. (eds.) Handbook of Mathematical Fuzzy Logic, Volume 3. Studies in Logic, Mathematical Logic and Foundations, vol. 58, pp. 1105–1181. College Publications (2015). Chapter 16
3. Borgwardt, S., Peñaloza, R.: Description logics over lattices with multi-valued ontologies. In: Proceedings of the Twenty-Second International Joint Conference on Artificial Intelligence (IJCAI-11), pp. 768–773 (2011)
4. Brickley, D., Guha, R.V.: RDF Vocabulary Description Language 1.0: RDF Schema. W3C Recommendation, W3C (2004). http://www.w3.org/TR/rdf-schema/

5. Calì, A., Gottlob, G., Lukasiewicz, T.: A general datalog-based framework for tractable query answering over ontologies. J. Web Seman. **14**, 57–83 (2012)
6. The rule markup initiative. http://ruleml.org/index.html
7. Lloyd, J.W.: Foundations of Logic Programming. Springer, Heidelberg (1987)
8. Lukasiewicz, T., Straccia, U.: Top-k retrieval in description logic programs under vagueness for the semantic web. In: Prade, H., Subrahmanian, V.S. (eds.) SUM 2007. LNCS, vol. 4772, pp. 16–30. Springer, Heidelberg (2007). doi:10.1007/978-3-540-75410-7_2
9. Lukasiewicz, T., Straccia, U.: Managing uncertainty and vagueness in description logics for the semantic web. J. Web Seman. **6**, 291–308 (2008)
10. OWL 2 Web Ontology Language Document Overview. W3C (2009). http://www.w3.org/TR/2009/REC-owl2-overview-20091027/
11. Rule Interchange Format (RIF). W3C (2011). http://www.w3.org/2001/sw/wiki/RIF
12. Shapiro, E.Y.: Logic programs with uncertainties: a tool for implementing rule-based systems. In: Proceedings of the 8th International Joint Conference on Artificial Intelligence (IJCAI-83), pp. 529–532 (1983)
13. Straccia, U.: Query answering in normal logic programs under uncertainty. In: Godo, L. (ed.) ECSQARU 2005. LNCS, vol. 3571, pp. 687–700. Springer, Heidelberg (2005). doi:10.1007/11518655_58
14. Straccia, U.: Description logics over lattices. Int. J. Uncertainty Fuzziness Knowl. Based Syst. **14**(1), 1–16 (2006)
15. Straccia, U.: Towards top-k query answering in deductive databases. In: Proceedings of the 2006 IEEE International Conference on Systems, Man and Cybernetics (SMC-06), pp. 4873–4879. IEEE (2006)
16. Straccia, U.: Managing uncertainty and vagueness in description logics, logic programs and description logic programs. In: Baroglio, C., Bonatti, P.A., Małuszyński, J., Marchiori, M., Polleres, A., Schaffert, S. (eds.) Reasoning Web. LNCS, vol. 5224, pp. 54–103. Springer, Heidelberg (2008). doi:10.1007/978-3-540-85658-0_2
17. Straccia, U.: A minimal deductive system for general fuzzy RDF. In: Polleres, A., Swift, T. (eds.) RR 2009. LNCS, vol. 5837, pp. 166–181. Springer, Heidelberg (2009). doi:10.1007/978-3-642-05082-4_12
18. Straccia, U.: Foundations of Fuzzy Logic and Semantic Web Languages. CRC Studies in Informatics Series. Chapman & Hall (2013)
19. Straccia, U., Bobillo, F.: From fuzzy to annotated semantic web languages. In: Pan, J.Z., Calvanese, D., Eiter, T., Horrocks, I., Kifer, M., Lin, F., Zhao, Y. (eds.) Reasoning Web 2016. LNCS, vol. 9885, pp. 203–240. Springer, Cham (2017). doi:10.1007/978-3-319-49493-7_6
20. Straccia, U., Madrid, N.: A top-k query answering procedure for fuzzy logic programming. Fuzzy Sets Syst. **205**, 1–29 (2012)
21. Ullman, J.D.: Principles of Database and Knowledge Base Systems, vol. 1, 2. Computer Science Press, Potomac, Maryland (1989)
22. XML: W3C. http://www.w3.org/XML/
23. Zimmermann, A., Lopes, N., Polleres, A., Straccia, U.: A general framework for representing, reasoning and querying with annotated semantic web data. J. Web Seman. **11**, 72–95 (2012)

Rational Enterprise Architecture

Leendert van der Torre[1(✉)] and Marc van Zee[2]

[1] University of Luxembourg, Luxembourg City, Luxembourg
leon.vandertorre@uni.lu
[2] Google Research, Zurich, Switzerland
marcvanzee@google.com

Abstract. We are interested in formal foundations for enterprise decision support. In this perspective, enterprise architecture is characterised by highly uncertain plans in a changing environment, and translates strategic goals into an IT strategy. Typically there are a large number of stakeholders with conflicting views, communicating plans of action, and explaining decisions instead of making them. An enterprise architecture considers qualitative before quantitative data, has stronger business focus than other disciplines, and politics, emotions, and soft skills play a bigger role than in other areas. We view a plan abstractly as a sequence of commitments in time, and each commitment in the plan may come with a number of underlying assumptions. If these underlying assumptions change, then parts of the plan may require revision, which in turn may invalidate other parts of the plan, and so on. Therefore, assumptions have an inherently *non-monotonic* character: they are assumed to be true, unless it becomes clear they are false. This is related to the resource-boundedness of enterprise architecture: an enterprise architect cannot always know all of the assumptions, especially for long term plans.

1 Enterprise Architecture

We use the following definition of an enterprise architecture:

"Those properties of an enterprise that are necessary and sufficient to meet its essential requirements" [6].

A commonly used metaphor for an enterprise architect is a city planner. City planners work on long-term visions, providing the roadmaps and regulations that a city uses to manage its growth and provide services to citizens. Using this analogy, we can differentiate the role of the system architect, who plans one or more buildings; software architects, who are responsible for the HVAC (Heating, Ventilation and Air Conditioning) within the building; network architects, who are responsible for the plumbing within the building, and the water and sewer infrastructure between buildings or parts of a city. The enterprise architect however, like a city planner, both frames the city-wide design and other activities into the larger plan.

There are a large number of responsibilities and skills that can potentially be associated with an enterprise architect. One way to frame these responsibilities and skills is to distinguish two main roles of an enterprise architect (Fig. 1).

© Springer International Publishing AG 2017
S. Benferhat et al. (Eds.): IEA/AIE 2017, Part I, LNAI 10350, pp. 9–18, 2017.
DOI: 10.1007/978-3-319-60042-0_2

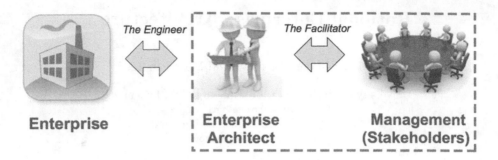

Fig. 1. Two roles of an enterprise architect, and our scope (red dashed line)

1. *The engineer.* The architect (usually a group of architects) develops models of business and IT. These models can be UML-like diagrams, specialised enterprise architecture diagrams, risk analysis tools, textual descriptions, or any other representation that the architect feels comfortable with.
2. *The facilitator.* The architect (usually the lead architect) is intermediator between IT and business. Often, the architect attends business meetings and serves as an IT expert, consulted by managers on what specific IT solutions to use.

   Enterprise architects often work on large projects with a long duration, and try to steer the enterprise such that the long-term goals and visions of the enterprise are reached, with an emphasise on the IT part of the enterprise. Let us illustrate this through a simple example.

Example 1 (University of Luxembourg). The University of Luxembourg is in the process of merging three separate campuses into a single campus on a new location. This process takes several decades, and requires a complete re-design of the IT landscape. The university would like to ensure that their long-term strategy and vision is aligned with their overall IT strategy, so they hire a team of enterprise architects. The lead architect discusses and refines the strategic goals and vision of the university with the executive board. She then works together with the other architects to develop a long-term IT strategy. This plan involves modelling the current business-IT landscape in ArchiMate, a specialised enterprise architecture modelling language, performing risk analysis on various alternatives, etc. The board, not having expertise nor time to understand the technical details of this problem, are then presented a simplified version of these plans. The members of the board have different – and changing – concerns, discuss these plans with each other and with the architect, who then brings this input back to his team of architects. This process may be repeated any number of times.

   Although the example above is (purposely) simplified, it does give an idea of the large number of varying tasks an enterprise architect should be able to carry out. The enterprise architect is responsible for ensuring the IT strategy and planning are aligned with the company's business goals, and must optimise information management through understanding evolving business needs (*facilitator*), but it also must ensure projects do not duplicate functionality or diverge from each other, and work with solution architects to provide a consensus based enterprise solution that is scalable and adaptable (*engineer*). As a result, an enterprise architect should have a large number of skills, from technical skills such as comprehensive knowledge of hardware, software, application, and systems engineering, to soft skills such as communication skills and the ability to explain complex technical issues in a way that non-technical people understand it, to managerial skills such as project and program management planning, time management and prioritisation.

2   ArchiMate

There are a large number of definitions of enterprise architecture in existence. The many existing definitions of enterprise architecture each have their own focus. For example, the definitions of enterprise architecture provided by IEEE [20], TOGAF [21], ArchiMate [8] and Giachetti [5], tend to focus on the elements of an enterprise architecture. The Zachman framework [31] and the GERAM framework [2] also have their focus more on the possible elements (in particular the relevant viewpoints) of an enterprise architecture. Dietz and Hoogervorst [4, 7] define enterprise architecture primarily in terms of its meaning. The definition provided by Ross et al. [16] touches both on the purpose and elements aspects, while Op 't Land, et al. [11] put the focus more on its purpose as a means for informed governance for enterprise transformations.

In line with the different definitions, various languages and techniques for enterprise architecture have been developed in the last decades. In the ArchiMate project [10], a language for the representation of enterprise architectures was developed, together with visualisation and analysis techniques. The resulting ArchiMate language is an Open Group standard [8, 21], and the TOGAF/ArchiMate combination of standards is playing an increasing role in the marketplace [30]. ArchiMate distinguishes itself from other languages such as Unified Modelling Language and Business Process Modelling and Notation (BPMN) by its scope on enterprise modelling as a whole. It is a language for describing the construction and operation of business processes, organisational structures, information flows, IT systems, and technical infrastructure. This is comparable to an architectural drawing in classical building where the architecture describes the various aspects of the construction and use of a building. This insight helps the different stakeholders to design, assess, and communicate the consequences of decisions and changes within and between these business domains.

The Archimate framework divides the enterprise architecture into a business, application and technology layer. In each layer, three aspects are considered: active elements that exhibit behaviour (e.g. Process and Function), an internal structure and elements that define use or communicate information. One of the main objectives of the ArchiMate language is to define the relationships between concepts in different architecture domains.

Initial research for the capturing of architectural design decisions was done during the ArchiMate project as well [10,29]. Following this preliminary work, Plataniotis et al. [12–14] develop a framework for the capturing and rationalisation of enterprise architecture decisions called EA Anamnesis. This framework formalises enterprise architecture decisions through meta models.

3 Rational Enterprise Architecture

Besides the preliminary attempts we described about, there is currently little research on enterprise architecture decision support. We provide an abstract overview of the evolution of decision support for enterprise architecture in Fig. 2. In the early days, that is, in the time before desktop computers were available to the common man, the tasks of enterprise architects were done on paper (left image, coaster). At the next stage of the evolution, the introduction of the desktop computer made available general tools such as Microsoft Powerpoint (second image from the left, Powerpoint). As the field of enterprise architecture matured, specialised languages and tool support were developed for enterprise architects, such as the ArchiMate language [9] (third image from the left, ArchiMate). In this thesis, we aim to lie the foundations for the next step (right image, question mark).

Fig. 2. Evolution of enterprise architecture decision support. From coasters (left), to Powerpoint (second left), to ArchiMate (second right), to the future (right)

We contribute to the development of enterprise architecture decision support by focusing on the *facilitator* role (Fig. 1, red dashed line) of the enterprise architect. This means we focus on the interactions and dynamics between the enterprise architect (the facilitator) and management. Our aim is to formalise this using logical frameworks that store important commitments, or high-level decisions, made during discussions or meetings. Such decisions are based on underlying assumptions. Assumptions may pertain to the goals of stakeholders, strategic directions of the enterprise, architecture principles, requirements, arguments put forward in discussions, etc. In practice, enterprises are confronted with frequent changes and challenges to these assumptions. Even more, the assumptions, and their relative priority, also depend on the specific stakeholders that are involved in creating the architecture of the future enterprise, as well as the actual transformation.

4 Characterizing Decision Making in Enterprise Architecture

The state of the art research in enterprise architecture is diverse with many different definitions emphasising different parts of the field. Therefore, one of our first activities has been to understanding the field of enterprise architecture better by identifying important characteristics of enterprise architecture. We did this in various ways, and we briefly discuss two main approaches.

Empirical study. We performed an empirical study on how the practice of high-level decision making (i.e., decisions in the role of the *facilitator* of Fig. 1) in enterprise architecture is perceived by professional enterprise architects. We did so through a questionnaire incorporating qualitative and quantitative questions, targeting enterprise architects around the world, in order to determine what they consider to be the important characteristics of enterprise architecture decision making, and whether these characteristics differ considerably from those in closely related fields such as software architecture [22].

The most important characteristics of enterprise architecture we found are:

1. Translating strategic goals into an IT strategy
2. Communicating plans of action
3. Explaining decisions instead of making them
4. Qualitative before quantitative data
5. Stronger business focus than other disciplines
6. Politics, emotions, and soft skills play a bigger role than in other disciplines
7. Large number of stakeholders with conflicting views
8. Highly uncertain plans in a changing environment

We use these eight characteristics as yardsticks for a formal theory to support enterprise architects. We observe that approaches based on the idea of *classical rationality* may be less appropriate that those based on *bounded rationality*, which is motivated by the observation that our study shows architects often work with incomplete data and face many types of uncertainty. We propose to use logical theories based on practical reasoning, since such theories have rich concepts for motivational attitudes such as goals and intentions, which appear to be playing an important role.

Determining an ontology. We analyzed an existing framework for capturing enterprise architecture design decisions called *EA Anamnesis* and recognize various ambiguities and flaws in the specification. We proposed a more precise formalisation of EA Anamnesis using first-order logic, and used this first-order logic to develop an enterprise architecture ontology. Our main conclusion is that our formalism does not offer much support for the type of reasoning processes specific to enterprise architecture we found in the previous chapter. More notably, it is not directly possible to reason about the *dynamics* of decisions in a principled way.

5   Reasoning About Enterprise Dynamics

One of the earlier practitioners in system architecture Steven H. Spewak defined *enterprise architecture planning* as "the process of defining architectures for the use of information in support of the business and the plan for implementing those architectures" [19]. An important lesson from the ArchiMate project [10] was that it is inherently difficult to plan architectural design. TAFIM, an enterprise architecture model by and for the United States Department of Defence recommends that in a typical five-year plan, only the first year is detailed, and the other steps are described only in a very abstract way. At each step in the plan, not only must the future abstract plans be further detailed, but architectural designs also have to be reconsidered and possibly revised.

This is a complicated picture, and developing a logical framework for this type of reasoning may seem daunting. We view a plan abstractly as a sequence of commitments in time, and each commitment in the plan may come with a number of underlying assumptions. If these underlying assumptions change, then parts of the plan may require revision, which in turn may invalidate other parts of the plan, and so on. Therefore, assumptions have an inherently *non-monotonic* character: they are assumed to be true, unless it becomes clear they are false. This is related to the resource-boundedness of our problem domain: an enterprise architect cannot always know all of the assumptions, especially for long term plans.

6   Formal Methods for Rational Enterprise Architecture

Motivated by our empirical findings which indicated that the enterprise architecture domain is very complex, with many types of uncertainty, we choose to apply a *separation of concerns* approach when developing our formal theory. We make a distinction between the *enterprise architect* and an *intelligent database*.

- The *enterprise architect* and the *stakeholders* form plans, have discussions, change preferences, pursue goals, etc.
- The *intelligent database* stores temporal commitments made by the architect and the stakeholders, and reasons about the consistency of these commitments with underlying assumptions.

As such, the intelligent database is a tool to assist the enterprise architect in dealing with high cognitive load of the enterprise architecture domain. Indeed, our intelligent database is very similar to an *intelligent calendar* (See [17] for conceptual underpinnings). Such a *database perspective* has proven itself useful in the consumer domain already: Yoav Shoham developed these ideas with Jacob Banks, one of his PhD students, and behavioral economist Dan Ariely into the intelligent calendar application Timeful, which attracted over $6.8 million in funding and was acquired by Google in 2015[1], who aim to integrate it into their

---

[1] http://venturebeat.com/2015/05/04/google-acquires-scheduling-app-timeful-and-plans-to-integrate-it-into-google-apps/.

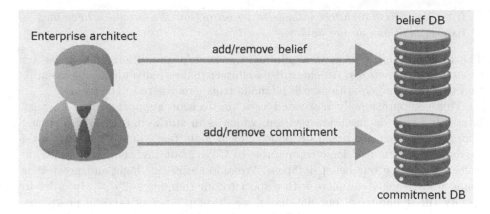

Fig. 3. We view consistency of commitments and beliefs as a database management problem.

Calendar applications. As Shoham [18] says himself: "The point of the story is there is a direct link between the original journal paper and the ultimate success of the company (Fig. 3)." (p. 47)

In our system, an enterprise architect is in the process of making plans, possibly with a group of stakeholders, and stores commitments and beliefs in two database. We focus on two main sources for the databases to change:

1. The enterprise architect forms a new beliefs, e.g. from discussions with stakeholders, or from a piece of data. If the new belief is inconsistent with the existing beliefs, these beliefs will have to be revised to accommodate it. We give general conditions on a single revision with new information that the database has already committed to incorporating using ideas from the classical AGM postulates [1] approach.
2. The enterprise adds a commitment. We formalise these tasks as *future directed atomic intentions*, understood as time-labeled actions pairs (a, t) that might make up a plan. It is assumed the enterprise architect has already committed to the intention, so it must be accommodated by any means short of revising beliefs. The force of the theory is in restricting how this can be accomplished. The job of the database is to maintain consistency and coherence between intentions and beliefs.

In order to formalise this, we develop a logic for beliefs about actions in time. We associate pre-and postconditions with actions. A key element in our approach is the asymmetry we put on assumptions about preconditions and postconditions of actions. First of all, we assume that

If an enterprise architect intends to do an action, she assumes the consequences of this action hold.

However, for preconditions we add a weaker requirement:

If an enterprise architect intends to do an action she cannot believe that its preconditions do not hold.

The result of this weakened requirement is that preconditions of actions are treated as *assumptions*: An enterprise architect makes plans under the assumption that these preconditions will be made true somewhere in the future.

This computationally motivated view on decision support leads to a very interesting take on intention revision, which is in stark contrast with existing approaches which are based on philosophical logic (e.g., [3,15]). In our work, we develop a temporal logic comparable to CTL*, but slightly less complex, in order to describe our belief database. We axiomatise our logic and prove it is sound and strongly complete with respect to our semantics [25,28]. In order to specify the dynamics of our databases, we develop a set of revision postulates comparable to the well-known AGM postulates for belief revision [1]. We prove that our revision postulates correspond to a preorder over semantical models, such that revising beliefs and intentions corresponds to selecting minimal models in some preorder [23,26,27].

7   Conclusion

While decision support systems have found their way in many domains such as software architecture and information architecture, they have not been adopted in enterprise architecture. We report on the past four years of our effort in analysing the domain of enterprise architecture, and developing logical foundations that can be used as a starting point for such enterprise decision support systems. The results and insights in this paper are further elaborated in the PhD thesis of Marc van Zee [24].

References

1. Alchourrón, C.E., Gärdenfors, P., Makinson, D.: On the logic of theory change: partial meet contractions and revision functions. J. Symbolic Logic **50**, 510–530 (1985)
2. Bernus, P., Nemes, L., Schmidt, G. (eds.): Handbook on Enterprise Architecture. International Handbooks on Information Systems. Springer, Heidelberg (2003)
3. Cohen, P.R., Levesque, H.J.: Intention is choice with commitment. Artif. Intell. **42**(2–3), 213–261 (1990)
4. Dietz, J.: Architecture - Building Strategy into Design. Netherlands Architecture Forum. Academic Service - SDU, The Hague (2008)
5. Giachetti, R.: Design of Enterprise Systems: Theory, Architecture, and Methods. CRC Press, Boca Raton (2010)
6. Greefhorst, D., Proper, E.: Architecture Principles: The Cornerstones of Enterprise Architecture, 1st edn. Springer Publishing Company Incorporated, Heidelberg (2011)
7. Hoogervorst, J.: Enterprise Governance and Enterprise Engineering. Springer, Berlin (2009)

8. Iacob, M.-E., Jonkers, H., Lankhorst, M., Proper, H.: ArchiMate 1.0 Specification. The Open Group (2009)
9. Iacob, M.-E., Jonkers, H., Lankhorst, M., Proper, H.: ArchiMate 2.0 Specification. The Open Group (2012)
10. Lankhorst, M. (ed.): Enterprise Architecture at Work: Modelling, Communication and Analysis. Springer, Berlin (2005)
11. Op 't Land, M., Proper, H., Waage, M., Cloo, J., Steghuis, C.: Enterprise Architecture - Creating Value by Informed Governance. Enterprise Engineering Series, Germany (2008)
12. Plataniotis, G., Kinderen, S., Proper, H.A.: Capturing decision making strategies in enterprise architecture – a viewpoint. In: Nurcan, S., Proper, H.A., Soffer, P., Krogstie, J., Schmidt, R., Halpin, T., Bider, I. (eds.) BPMDS/EMMSAD -2013. LNBIP, vol. 147, pp. 339–353. Springer, Heidelberg (2013). doi:10.1007/ 978-3-642-38484-4_24
13. Plataniotis, G., de Kinderen, S., Proper, H.A.: Relating decisions in enterprise architecture using decision design graphs. In: 2013 17th IEEE International Enterprise Distributed Object Computing Conference (EDOC), pp. 139–146. IEEE (2013)
14. Plataniotis, G., De Kinderen, S., Proper, H.A.: Ea anamnesis: an approach for decision making analysis in enterprise architecture. Int. J. Inf. Syst. Model. Des. (IJISMD) **5**(3), 75–95 (2014)
15. Rao, A., Georgeff, M.: Modeling rational agents within a BDI-architecture. In: KR (1991)
16. Ross, J., Weill, P., Robertson, D.: Enterprise Architecture as Strategy: Creating a Foundation for Business Execution. Harvard Business School Press, Boston (2006)
17. Shoham, Y.: Logical theories of intention and the database perspective. J. Philos. Logic **38**, 633–647 (2009)
18. Shoham, Y.: Why knowledge representation matters. Commun. ACM **59**(1), 47–49 (2016)
19. Spewak, S.H., Hill, S.C.: Enterprise Architecture Planning: Developing a Blueprint for Data, Applications and Technology. QED Information Sciences Inc. (1993)
20. The Architecture Working Group of the Software Engineering Committee. Recommended Practice for Architectural Description of Software Intensive Systems. Technical report IEEE P1471: 2000, ISO/IEC 42010: 2007, Standards Department, IEEE, Piscataway, New Jersey, September 2000
21. The Open Group. TOGAF Version 9. Van Haren Publishing, Zaltbommel (2009)
22. van der Linden, D., van Zee, M.: Insights from a study on decision making in enterprise architecture. In: PoEM (Short Papers), CEUR Workshop Proceedings, vol. 1497, pp. 21–30 (2015)
23. van Zee, M.: Rational architecture = architecture from a recommender perspective. In: Proceedings of the International Joint Conference on Artificial Intelligence (2015)
24. van Zee, M.: Rational Architecture: Reasoning about Enterprise Dynamics. Ph.D. thesis, University of Luxembourg (2017, to appear). 5
25. van Zee, M., Dastani, M., Doder, D., van der Torre, L.: Consistency conditions for beliefs and intentions. In: Twelfth International Symposium on Logical Formalizations of Commonsense Reasoning (2015)
26. van Zee, M., Dastani, M., Shoham, Y., van der Torre, L.: Collective intention revision from a database perspective. In: Collective Intentionality Conference, July 2014

27. van Zee, M., Doder, D.: AGM-style revision of beliefs and intentions. In: Proceedings of the 22nd European Conference on Artificial Intelligence (ECAI 2016), September 2016
28. van Zee, M., Doder, D., Dastani, M., van der Torre, L.: AGM revision of beliefs about action and time. In: Proceedings of the International Joint Conference on Artificial Intelligence (2015)
29. Veldhuijzen van Zanten, G., Hoppenbrouwers, S., Proper, H.: System development as a rational communicative process. J. Systemics Cybern. Inform. $2(4)$, 47–51 (2004)
30. Wilson, C., Short, J.: Magic Quadrant for Enterprise Architecture Tools. Technical Report ID Number: G00207406, Gartner, October 2010
31. Zachman, J.: A framework for information systems architecture. IBM Syst. J. $26(3)$, 276–292 (1987)

Constraints, Planning and Optimization

Cluster-Specific Heuristics
for Constraint Solving

Seda Polat Erdeniz$^{(\boxtimes)}$, Alexander Felfernig, Muesluem Atas$^{(\boxtimes)}$,
Thi Ngoc Trang Tran, Michael Jeran, and Martin Stettinger

Institute of Software Technology, Graz University of Technology,
Inffeldgasse 16b/II, 8010 Graz, Austria
{spolater,alexander.felfernig,muesluem.atas,ttrang,mjeran,
martin.stettinger}@ist.tugraz.at
http://ase.ist.tugraz.at/

Abstract. In Constraint Satisfaction Problems (CSP), variable ordering heuristics help to increase efficiency. Applying an appropriate heuristic can increase the performance of CSP solvers. On the other hand, if we
apply specific heuristics for similar CSPs, CSP solver performance could
be further improved. Similar CSPs can be grouped into same clusters.
For each cluster, appropriate heuristics can be found by applying a local
search. Thus, when a new CSP is created, the corresponding cluster can
be found and the pre-calculated heuristics for the cluster can be applied.
In this paper, we propose a new method for constraint solving which
is called *Cluster Specific Heuristic (CSH)*. We present and evaluate our
method on the basis of example CSPs.

Keywords: Configuration · Constraint satisfaction problems · Variable
and value ordering heuristics · Clustering · Performance optimization

1 Introduction

Configuration systems [3,7] are used to find solutions for problems which have
many variables and constraints. An example of a configuration problem can
be *the customization of cars* where many hardware and software modules exist
and all of them should work together without any conflicts. Configuration problems can be formulated as a constraint satisfaction problem (*CSP*) [19] which is
defined as a triple *(V,D,C)* where *V* is a set of variables, *D* is set of domains for
each variable, and *C* is a set of constraints. The constraint set may also include
the user requirements (*R*) if available.

In this paper, we propose a new method for constraint solving which is called
Cluster Specific Heuristics (CSH).[1] Figure 1 shows the main contribution of CSH
in constraint solving. CSH creates clusters of similar instances of a CSP which

---

[1] The work presented in this paper has been conducted within the scope of the
European Union Horizon 2020 research project AGILE (Adoptive Gateways for
dIverse MuLtiple Environments – www.agile-project-iot.eu.).

© Springer International Publishing AG 2017
S. Benferhat et al. (Eds.): IEA/AIE 2017, Part I, LNAI 10350, pp. 21–30, 2017.
DOI: 10.1007/978-3-319-60042-0_3

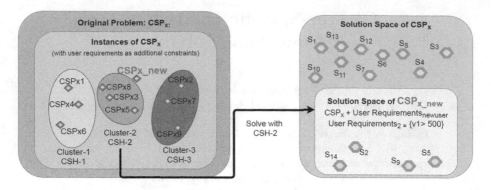

Fig. 1. Contribution of CSH in CSP solving. K-Means clustering is applied on the cluster elements $CSPx1, CSPx2, .., CSPx9$. 3 clusters are generated. Specific variable ordering heuristics are learned for each cluster as CSH-1, CSH-2 and CSH-3 where CSH-i stands for the learned variable ordering heuristic for the Cluster-i. Whenever we get a new instance of the original problem $CSPx$ as $CSPx\_new$, we can solve $CSPx\_new$ by using the calculated variable ordering heuristics. In this example, we use CSH-2, since the most similar CSPs to $CSPx\_new$ are in Cluster-2. The CSP solver finds a solution faster by using CSH compared to other global heuristics.

can be exploited to learn and generate specific search heuristics for each cluster. Whenever a new instance of the original configuration problem occurs, CSH finds the most relevant cluster for this CSP and it applies the pre-calculated cluster-specific heuristic to solve this CSP. We show that, compared to other heuristics, CSH increases the performance of CSP solving in many scenarios.

The remainder of this paper is organized as follows. We first provide an overview of the used algorithms in Sect. 3. We then state the problem definition and our solution in Sects. 3.1 and 3.2. Finally, we present our experimental results and comparisons with state-of-the-art heuristics in Sects. 4 and 5. Finally, in Sect. 6, we discuss issues for future work and conclude the paper.

2 Background

CSP Solvers solve a CSP defined as *(V,D,C)* by generating search trees among different instances of variables and search for satisfactory solutions based on the constraints of the problem. There exist different open source libraries for solving CSPs, for example, Choco Solver [17]. To improve the performance of such solvers, search is guided by so-called variable and value ordering heuristics. Variable and value ordering heuristics are generally used in problems such as *configuration, job shop scheduling*, and *integrated circuit design* [18].

Our CSH approach uses *K-Means clustering* [10] to cluster different instances of the same CSP. K-Means clustering is applied to the user requirements included in the CSPs. For example, if two CSPs include similar values for their variables, then these two CSPs can be grouped in the same cluster. K-Means clustering is popular for cluster analysis in data mining. It creates k clusters by minimizing the sum of squares of distances between cluster elements.

Formula 1 shows the minimization function of k-Means clustering where k is the number of target clusters, S is a cluster set, μi is the average value of cluster elements in the Si and x is a cluster element in Si.

$$min \sum_{i=1}^{k} \sum_{x \in Si} \|x - \mu i\|^2 \tag{1}$$

If there is more than one variable in the cluster elements that will be clustered, then the difference between x and μi can be calculated based on the *Euclidean n-distance* as shown in Formula 2 where xj is the jth variable in the cluster element x and μij is the average value of jth variables of the cluster elements in the ith cluster.

$$x - \mu i = \sqrt{\sum_{j=1}^{n} (xj - \mu ij)^2} \tag{2}$$

As an example, we can consider clustering 6 elements with 2 variables into 2 clusters (k $=$ 2) after 4 iterations (i $=$ 4). Before clustering starts, two clusters can be created randomly. In every iteration, we calculate a cluster element's total distance to both clusters. In the first iteration, we randomly take a cluster element, $x = (x1 = 100, x2 = 200)$ and compare it with the clusters $S1$ with a mean value $\mu 1 = (\mu 1 = 300, \mu 2 = 400)$ and $S2$ with a mean value $\mu 2 = (\mu 2 = 0, \mu 2 = 400)$. The distance between x and the clusters is calculated based on Formula 2 which gives 282.84 for $S1$ and 223.60 $S2$. Based on Formula 1, putting x into the cluster $S2$ minimizes the total distance between cluster elements. In follow-up iterations, we take another cluster element and apply the same distance calculations and put it into a more similar cluster to minimize total distances. After 4 iterations, we obtain 2 clusters with a low distance between the elements in the same cluster. If we increase the number of iterations, it is often possible to determine even lower total distances.

CSH applies a *genetic algorithm* [14] to generate cluster-specific variable ordering heuristics.

3 Cluster-Specific Heuristics

In this work, we aim to find an answer to the question: "If we cluster instances of the a CSP and apply a cluster-specific variable ordering heuristic, could we increase the overall performance of a CSP solver for solving a new instance of the same CSP?".

We implemented Algorithms 1 and 2, using the Java libraries Choco Solver [17] (for CSP solving) and Java Machine Learning [10] (for K-Means clustering). Besides, we implemented the "Simple Genetic Algorithm"[2]. The genetic

---

[2] www.theprojectspot.com.

algorithm applies mutations and crossover operations on variable order arrays (individuals). *Fitness value* is the execution time of the CSP solver with this order. Consequently, a smaller fitness value indicates a better variable order.

Algorithm 1. Learn Cluster-Specific Heuristics

Input: *OriginalCSP*, *sampleInstancesOfOriginalCSP*
Output: *clusters*, *heuristics*
1 Cluster *sampleInstancesOfOriginalCSP* based on K-Means and Euclidean n-distance algorithms
2 Learn *heuristics* based on Simple Genetic Algorithm
3 Return *clusters* and *heuristics*

Algorithm 1 takes *OriginalCSP* and *sampleInstancesOfOriginalCSP* as input and returns *clusters* and the corresponding specific variable ordering *heuristics* as output. Algorithm 2 takes the output of Algorithm 1 and the new instance of the original CSP *CSPnew* as input.

Algorithm 2. Solve the CSP with learned CSH

Input: *CSPnew*, *clusters*, *heuristics*
Output: *solution*
1 Find *mostSimilarCluster* for *CSPnew*
2 Solve the *CSPnew* with related learned *heuristic*
3 Return *solution*

To explain our approach, we introduce a CSP with 5 variables as shown in Table 1. In the subsections below, we provide more details of the main steps of CSH which are "Clustering", "Learning Heuristics", and "Solving a new CSP".

Table 1. A simple CSP definition (CSP_{cars} as an abstract representation of a car customization problem).

CSPcars	Definitions
Variables	v1, v2, v3, v4, v5
Domains	DomainRangeforAllVariables=[0..1000]
Constraints	C1: $(v1 \leq 200) \implies (v5 \geq 600)$
	C2: $(v4 = v5) \implies (v2 \geq 1000)$
	C3: $(v3 \geq 20000) \implies (v4 = 80)$

3.1 Clustering

If we do not have instances of an original CSP in terms of historical data (e.g. log files), we need to generate some sample instances to create clusters and learn specific heuristics. For our example we generated 10 different sample instances of the original CSP as depicted in Table 2. We combine CSPcars with different user constraints to generate new instances of the same problem which are denoted as CSPcarsInstance1 - CSPcarsInstance10.

Table 2. Sample instances of the car customization problem CSPcars

Instances of the problem CSPcars	Different user requirements (R)
CSPcarsInstance1 = CSPcars ∧ R1	R1: (v2 = 2000 ∧ v5 = 500)
CSPcarsInstance2 = CSPcars ∧ R2	R2: (v2 = 7000 ∧ v5 = 700)
CSPcarsInstance3 = CSPcars ∧ R3	R3: (v2 = 1000 ∧ v5 = 300)
CSPcarsInstance4 = CSPcars ∧ R4	R4: (v4 = 80)
CSPcarsInstance5 = CSPcars ∧ R5	R5: (v4 = 70)
CSPcarsInstance6 = CSPcars ∧ R6	R6: (v4 = 50)
CSPcarsInstance7 = CSPcars ∧ R7	R7: (v1 = 100 ∧ v2 = 500)
CSPcarsInstance8 = CSPcars ∧ R8	R8: (v1 = 800 ∧ v2 = 250)
CSPcarsInstance9 = CSPcars ∧ R9	R9: (v3 = 10)
CSPcarsInstance10 = CSPcars ∧ R10	R10: (v3 = 80000)

The CSP solver tries to find satisfactory values for the non-initialized variables (all variable domains are represented as integers which have positive values). Since we are trying to find a variable ordering heuristic for similar CSPs, it is reasonable to group the same non-initialized variables into the same cluster. Therefore, before clustering, non-initialized variables in the CSP problems are assigned to "−1000", since all initialized variables should have positive values due to the domain definitions (DomainRangeforAllVariables=[0..1000]) where the minimum value is 0. This assignment decreases the similarity between the CSPs which have different initialized variables. The similarity between two CSPs (using only the user requirements inside the CSPs) is calculated based on the Formula 2. JavaML's K-Means calculates the distance between x and μ based on *Euclidean n-space distance*. We used JavaML K-Means with its default constructor which applies 100 iterations (i = 100) during the K-Means clustering and creates 4 clusters (k = 4) in our case.

K-Means clustering is applied to the instances of the original CSP given in Table 2. After running JavaML K-Means clustering with its default constructor as mentioned in [1], we obtained 4 clusters as can be seen in Table 3. For example, CLcarsInstance1=(CSPcarsInstance1, CSPcarsInstance2, CSPcarsInstance3), where all CSPs have the same initialized variables which are v2 and v5. This means, for all these CSPs, the CSP solver will find solutions by assigning satisfactory values for the same non-initialized variables v1, v3 and v4. For the CSPs in CL1, the CSP solver will search in the same solution set. Therefore, it is applicable to use similar heuristics for these CSPs.

3.2 Learning Heuristics

After finding clusters, using the *Simple Genetic Algorithm* for each cluster, variable ordering heuristics are calculated as shown in Table 3.

Table 3. Clusters and corresponding heuristics. Based on the similar instances of the same problem in the clusters, CSH finds the variable ordering that will be used for solving the new instances of the same problem.

Clusters	CSPs	Variable ordering
CL1	CSPcarsInstance1, CSPcarsInstance2, CSPcarsInstance3	v1, v2, v5, v4, v3
CL2	CSPcarsInstance4, CSPcarsInstance5, CSPcarsInstance6	v4, v2, v5, v3, v1
CL3	CSPcarsInstance7, CSPcarsInstance8	v1, v5, v2, v3, v4
CL4	CSPcarsInstance9, CSPcarsInstance10	v1, v5, v4, v2, v3

In line 2 of Algorithm 1, the *Simple Genetic Algorithm* is used to learn the heuristics based on the clustered sample CSPs. We applied some adaptations during the implementation of this algorithm. In our implementation, *individuals* are variable orders (an array of variable names such as: *[v4,v5,v1,v3,v2]*) rather than the binary arrays as in the original implementation.

When an individual is created by the algorithm, the corresponding *fitness* values are also calculated. The fitness of an individual is described by the execution time of the CSP solver using the corresponding variable ordering heuristic. After all, the genetic algorithm selects the best individual according to the execution time. Shorter execution time implies a better individual. In our genetic algorithm, we set the target of fitness to 1000 ms. This means the population evolution loop can be executed until the target fitness value is reached or 10 s are exceeded.

3.3 Solving a new CSP

A new user activates the configuration system and defines his/her own requirements as *Rnew: (v2 = 500 ∧ v5 = 100)*. Rnew is combined with the original

Table 4. The CSP solver finds a solution for this CSP where the solution is consistent with all constraints and the domain values defined in the CSP.

Solution of CSPnew				
v1	v2	v3	v4	v5
500	7000	30000	80	100

CSP which is CSPcars and a new instance is created as CSPnew. First, the most similar cluster to CSPnew is retrieved by CSH. The most similar cluster is CL1 because the CSPs in the CL1 and CSPnew have the same variables in the user requirements(v2 and v5). The CSP Solver applies the variable ordering heuristic of CL1 (v1, v2, v5, v4, v3) (this heuristic is given as an input to the constructor of the Choco Solver) to find a solution as seen in Table 4.

Table 5. Runtime performance (given in seconds) of the Choco solver with Choco's built-in heuristics compared to CSH. CSH is the fastest heuristic for solving a new instance of a known CSP.

Test results				
Heuristics	4 Different Original CSPs			
	CSP1 100 variables D:[0..100]	CSP2 100 variables D:[0..1000]	CSP3 1000 variables D:[0..100]	CSP4 1000 variables D:[0..1000]
Largest	276.302	311.875	2316.203	2192.573
Smallest	164.918	212.154	9573.073	9481.634
ActivityBased	66.480	71.612	265,688	226.500
FirstFail	48.869	32.657	125.613	109.634
AntiFirstFail	40.821	95.055	115,699	125.146
Cyclic	36509	28.691	88.640	79.543
Random	45.486	32.307	80.010	77.560
MaxRegret	58.082	53.417	172.266	171.682
Occurrence	41.871	39.422	99.137	100.070
Input Order	32.307	32.657	76.277	86.074
DomOverDweg	25.076	44.203	63.448	75.136
ImpactBased	63.448	73.362	247.027	283.766
Generalized MinDomain	39.188	32.657	75.927	76.011
CSH	**24.959**	**24.026**	**23.443**	**74.995**

4   Experimental Results

We tested and measured the performance of CSH and compared it with the heuristics available in the Choco Solver.[3] Choco Solver [11] comes with built-in variable and value ordering heuristics.[4] To solve a constraint satisfaction problem, a built-in heuristic can be chosen for a specific search problem. In this context, we generated our specific variable ordering that can be given to the Choco solver as an input during the solver initialization.

We tested 13 built-in variable ordering heuristics of Choco Solver and compared these with CSH. We ran our tests over 4 CSPs as shown in Table 5. Each CSP has a different number of variables and domain ranges (domains are the same for each variable in a CSP). For example, in CSP1 there are 100 variables with domain D:[0..100]. Sample instances of the original CSP are generated by selecting the variables randomly and assigning random values with respect to their domain definitions.

To be able to find the clusters and heuristics, we created 100 instances (to create clusters) of these 4 CSPs. During the instance creation, we selected some variables of the CSP instance randomly and each selected variable is assigned with a value randomly in the defined domain. These 4 CSPs and their generated instances are similar to the working example in Tables 1 and 2.

Table 5 shows the performance comparison between Choco's built-in heuristics and CSH. We made the comparison with respect to runtime performance (average of the runtime of 40 new instances for each CSP). It can be observed that CSH is the fastest heuristic for solving a new instance of a known CSP.

5   Related Work

Jannach [9] proposes a learning solution for domain specific heuristics. In this work, it is mentioned that solving complex configuration problems often requires the usage of domain-specific search heuristics which have to be explicitly modeled by domain experts and knowledge engineers. This work significantly differs from ours since no cluster-specific heuristics are taken into account.

Li et al. [12] apply a clustering approach to divide a search problem into subproblems. The authors apply a variable and value ordering heuristic over these clusters. In our approach, we cluster similar problems to be able to determine cluster-specific search heuristics. We do not divide a problem into sub-problems.

O'Sullivan et al. [16] use a constraint solver and decision tree learning to solve a CSP query of a user. The overall goal of this work is also to improve the overall efficiency of search.

Balduccini et al. [2] implemented domain specific heuristics for Answer Set Programming Solvers. Heuristics are learned by the proposed platform. This

---

[3] Our experiments have been conducted on an Intel Core i5-5200U PC, 2.20 GHz processor, 8 GB RAM, and 64 bit Windows 7 Operating System and Java Run-time Environment 1.8.0.

[4] choco-solver.org.

work is similar to ours but does not take into account clustering mechanisms. It learns heuristics for domains as *Domain-Specific Heuristics* but does not cluster the underlying problems.

Epstein et al. [5] postulate several types of crucial sub-problems and show how local search can be harnessed to solve them before global search is triggered. A variety of heuristics and metrics are then used to guide (global) solution search.

Liu et al. [13] generate a variable ordering strategy for solving Disjunctive Temporal Problems (DTPs) which are an essential aspect for building systems that reason about time and actions. DTP model events and their relationships (as distances between events) and provide the means to specify the temporal elements of an episode with a temporal extent.

Ciccio et al. [4] introduce techniques which guarantee the consistency of the discovered models and keep the most interesting constraints in the pruned set. The level of interestingness is dictated by user-specified prioritization criteria. Merhej et al. [15] introduce an approach to assign weights to rules of thumb by sampling in a particular way from a pool of possible repairs.

6   Future Work and Conclusion

In this paper, we proposed *CSH* (Cluster Specific Heuristics) which is an intelligent method that can be used to support the inclusion of search heuristics in CSP solving. With this method, the performance of the CSP solver can be improved compared to other built-in heuristics. *CSH* can be useful for CSP scenarios such as *product configuration* where different CSP instances reoccur. As *future work* we plan to apply specific clustering methods for different CSP types rather than using K-Means clustering for every CSP type. With this, we expect to increase the similarities within clusters and increase the efficiency of CSP search. We will also work on generating cluster-specific value ordering heuristics and cluster-specific heuristics for diagnosis tasks [8]. We also plan to use optimization functions to decide on the number of clusters. Thus, the number of clusters can vary depending on the underlying CSPs. We will also apply *CSH* in our ongoing European Union Horizon 2020 project AGILE which focuses a.o. on the development of efficient recommendation [6] and configuration technologies [7,20] for different types of Internet of Things scenarios.

References

1. Abeel, T., de Peer, Y., Saeys, Y.: Java-ML: a machine learning library. J. Mach. Learn. Res. **10**, 931–934 (2009)
2. Balduccini, M.: Learning and using domain-specific heuristics in ASP solvers. AI Commun. **24**(2), 147–164 (2011)
3. Benavides, D., Felfernig, A., Galindo, J.A., Reinfrank, F.: Automated analysis in feature modelling and product configuration. In: Favaro, J., Morisio, M. (eds.) ICSR 2013. LNCS, vol. 7925, pp. 160–175. Springer, Heidelberg (2013). doi:10. 1007/978-3-642-38977-1_11

4. Di Ciccio, C., Maggi, F.M., Montali, M., Mendling, J.: Resolving inconsistencies and redundancies in declarative process models. Inf. Sys. **64**, 425–446 (2017)
5. Epstein, S.L., Wallace, R.J.: Finding crucial subproblems to focus global search. In: 18th IEEE International Conference on Tools with Artificial Intelligence (ICTAI 2006), pp. 151–162 (2006)
6. Falkner, A., Felfernig, A., Haag, A.: Recommendation technologies for configurable products. AI Mag. **32**(3), 99–108 (2011)
7. Felfernig, A., Hotz, L., Bagley, C., Tiihonen, J.: Knowledge-Based Configuration: From Research to Business Cases, 1st edn. Morgan Kaufmann Publishers Inc., San Francisco (2014)
8. Felfernig, A., Schubert, M., Zehentner, C.: An efficient diagnosis algorithm for inconsistent constraint sets. Artif. Intell. Eng. Des. Anal. Manufact. (AIEDAM) **26**(1), 53–62 (2012)
9. Jannach, D.: Toward automatically learned search heuristics for CSP-encoded configuration problems - results from an initial experimental analysis. In: Proceedings of the 15th International Configuration Workshop, Vienna, Austria, pp. 9–13, 29–30 August 2013
10. Jin, X., Han, J.: K-means clustering. In: Sammut, C., Webb, G.I. (eds.) Encyclopedia of Machine Learning, pp. 563–564. Springer, Boston (2010)
11. Jussien, N., Rochart, G., Lorca, X.: Choco: an open source Java constraint programming library. In: CPAIOR 2008 Workshop on Open-Source Software for Integer and Contraint Programming (OSSICP 2008), Paris, France, pp. 1–10 (2008)
12. Li, X., Epstein, S.L.: Learning cluster-based structure to solve constraint satisfaction problems. Ann. Math. AI **60**(1–2), 91–117 (2010)
13. Liu, Y., Jiang, Y., Qian, H.: Topology-based variable ordering strategy for solving disjunctive temporal problems. In: 15th International Symposium on Temporal Representation and Reasoning, pp. 129–136. IEEE (2008)
14. Man, K.F., Tang, K.S., Kwong, S.: Genetic algorithms: concepts and applications. IEEE Trans. Ind. Electron. **43**(5), 519–534 (1996)
15. Merhej, E., Schockaert, S., De Cock, M.: Repairing inconsistent answer set programs using rules of thumb: a gene regulatory networks case study. Int. J. Approximate Reasoning **83**, 243–264 (2017)
16. O'Sullivan, B., Ferguson, A., Freuder, E.C.: Boosting constraint satisfaction using decision trees. In: 16th IEEE International Conference on Tools with Artificial Intelligence (ICTAI 2004), pp. 646–651 (2004)
17. Prud'homme, C., Fages, J.G., Lorca, X.: Choco Solver Documentation (2017)
18. Sadeh, N., Fox, M.S.: Variable and value ordering heuristics for the job shop scheduling constraint satisfaction problem. AI J. **86**(1), 1–41 (1996)
19. Tsang, E.: Foundations of Constraint Satisfaction. Academic Press, London (1993)
20. Walter, R., Felfernig, A., Küchlin, W.: Constraint-based and SAT-based diagnosis of automotive configuration problems. J. Intell. Inf. Syst. (JIIS), 1–32 (2016)

Car Pooling Based on a Meta-heuristic Approach

Fu-Shiung Hsieh[(⊠)], Fu-Min Zhan, and Yi-Hong Guo

Department of Computer Science and Information Engineering,
Chaoyang University of Technology, 41349 Taichung, Taiwan
fshsieh@cyut.edu.tw

Abstract. The high use of private cars increases the load on the environment and raises issues of high levels of air pollution in cities, parking problems, congestion and low transfer velocity. Car pooling is a collective transportation model based on shared use of private cars to reduce the number of cars in use by grouping people. By exploiting car pooling model, it can significantly reduce congestion, fuel consumption, parking demands and commuting costs. An important issue in car pooling systems is to develop a car pooling algorithm to match passengers and drivers. The goals of this paper are to propose a model and a solution methodology that is seamlessly integrated with existing geographic information system to facilitate determination of drivers/passengers for ride sharing. In this paper, we formulate a car pooling problem and propose a solution algorithm for it based on a meta-heuristic approach. We have implemented our solution algorithm and conduct experiments to illustrate the effectiveness of our proposed method by examples.

Keywords: Car pooling · Meta-heuristic algorithm · Particle swarm optimization

1 Introduction

The high use of private cars increases the load on the environment and raises issues of high levels of air pollution in cities, parking problems, congestion and low transfer velocity. A solution to the problem of the increasing passengers and transport demands is to improve the efficiency of transport systems based on car pooling. The objectives of car pooling are to reduce the number of vehicles in use and overall travel distance in transporting people by grouping people. There are several papers that provide a good survey of the studies on car pooling problem. Please refer to [1, 2]. Car pooling can be operated in two main ways: Daily Car Pooling Problem (DCPP) [3] or Long-term Car Pooling Problem (LCPP) [4]. In the case of DCPP [3], each day a number of drivers declare their availability for picking up and later bringing back passengers on that particular day. The problem is to assign passengers to drivers and to identify the routes to be driven by the drivers in order to minimize costs and a penalty due to unassigned passengers, subject to time window and car capacity constraints. In the case of LCPP [4], the objectives are to maximize pool sizes and minimize the total distance traveled by all users subject to car capacity and time window constraints. Several prototype

© Springer International Publishing AG 2017
S. Benferhat et al. (Eds.): IEA/AIE 2017, Part I, LNAI 10350, pp. 31–40, 2017.
DOI: 10.1007/978-3-319-60042-0_4

systems or simulation studies for car pooling are also available. For example, paper [5] presents an ongoing project to design and implement a car pooling system. Paper [6] considers the problem of matching drivers and riders in a dynamic setting. In [7], the authors present a methodology based on the extraction of suitable information from mobility traces to identify rides along the same trajectories that are amenable for ride sharing. In [8], the authors propose a new approach to design demand responsive transport systems in multi-agent system architecture and use the tree search algorithm to solve it.

The goals of this paper are to propose an algorithm to facilitate determination of drivers/passengers for ridesharing and develop a solution algorithm to improve the efficiency of the transport system and reduce costs and total system-wide travel distance of vehicles. We formulate the problem to match passengers with drivers taking into account requirements of drivers and passengers, capacity constraints of vehicles and efficiency constraints. The efficiency constraints impose the conditions that the overall cost with car pooling is less than that without car pooling. In our pooling system, passengers place bids according to their need and requirements and drivers submit bids according to their preference and constraints. A bid generation algorithm is used to generate the potential routes for drivers to pick up and drop passengers. Based on the car pooling problem formulation, we propose our solution algorithm. The problem to determine the drivers and passengers for car pooling is notoriously difficult to solve from a computational point of view due to the exponential growth of the number of combinations as the problems grow. In this paper, we propose a meta-heuristic method to solve the above mentioned problem based on a Particle Swarm Optimization (PSO) approach [9], a population based optimization method developed based on observations of the social behavior of animals such as bird flocking, fish schooling and swarm theory. PSO has been applied successfully to nonlinear constrained optimization problems [10], neural networks [11], scheduling problems [12], etc. As the decision variables of the car pooling problem is discrete binary variables, we apply the method proposed in [13] to the car pooling problem. We have also implemented our solution algorithm and conduct experiments to verify its practicality by examples.

The remainder of this paper is organized as follows. In Sect. 2, we describe and formulate the car pooling problem. Our solution algorithm will be presented in Sect. 3. In Sect. 4, we verify our method by examples. In Sect. 5, we conclude this paper.

2 Problem Formulation

In this section, we present the car pooling problem formulation. In a car pooling system, there are a set of passengers, a set of drivers and a set of cars own by the drivers. Let P denote the set of all passengers in the system. A passenger is represented by p, where $p \in P$. Let D denote the set of all drivers in the system. A driver is represented by d, where $d \in D$. We will also use d to refer to the car of driver $d \in D$.

The requirement of driver $d \in D$ is described by $R_d = (Lo_d, Le_d, EDT_d, LAT_d)$, where Lo_d denotes the origin of driver $d \in D$, Le_d denotes the destination of driver $d \in D$, EDT_d is the earliest departure time and LAT_d is the latest arrival time. The requirement of passenger $p \in P$ is described by $R_p = (Lo_p, Le_p, EDT_p, LAT_p)$, where

Lo_p denotes the origin, Le_p denotes the destination, EDT_p is the earliest departure time and LAT_p the latest arrival time of passenger p. To formulate the car pooling problem, we define the following notations.

Let Π_d denote the set of all feasible routes satisfying the requirements R_d of driver d. Each route $\pi \in \Pi_d$ starts with Lo_d, ends with Le_d and the car departs Lo_d after EDT_d and arrives at Le_d before LAT_d. If π, where $\pi \in \Pi_d$, visits the origin Lo_p and destination Le_p of at least one passenger, p, and satisfies the time constraints of EDT_p and EDT_p, π is called a candidate route for driver d. Let Π_d^c, where $\Pi_d^c \subseteq \Pi_d$, denote the set of all candidate routes selected by driver d. Let $J_d = \left| \Pi_d^c \right|$. Driver d will submit J_d bids. Let b_{dj}^D denote the $j - th$ bid associated with a candidate route $\pi_{dj} \in \Pi_d^c$ of driver d. A bid b_{dj}^D is called a winning bid if π_{dj} is selected by the car pooling system to transport passengers. A passenger p submits bids based on R_p. Let b_p^P denote the bid submitted by passenger p based on R_p. We assume that each passenger p submits only one bid. A bid b_p^P is called a winning bid if passenger p is selected by the car pooling system to share ride with some driver.

Notation:

K: the number of all pick-up locations of passengers,
k: the index of pick-up location or dropped off location, $k \in \{1, 2, \ldots, K\}$
LOC_k: the k-th location, $k \in \{1, 2, \ldots, K\}$
P: the number of different passengers
p: a passenger. Each $p \in \{1, 2, 3, \ldots P\}$ represents the index of a certain passenger
D: the number of drivers in the car pooling system
d: a driver. Each $d \in \{1, 2, 3, \ldots, D\}$ represents the index of a driver
s_{pk}: the number of seats requested by passenger p for location k, where $k \in \{1, 2, 3, \ldots, K\}$. If $s_{pk} > 0$, it represents the requested number of seats for picking up the passengers. If $s_{pk} < 0$, it represents the number of seats released due to dropping off the passengers
J_d: the number of bids placed by driver $d \in \{1, 2, \ldots, D\}$ in the car pooling system
j: the $j - th$ bid submitted by a driver, where $j \in \{1, 2, \ldots, J_d\}$
c_{dj}: a real positive number that denotes the routing cost for transporting the bundle of passengers in the $j - th$ bid submitted by driver d
o_{dj}: the original travel cost of driver d without transporting any passengers. That is, o_{dj} is the cost that driver d travels alone
q_{djk}: a nonnegative integer that denotes the quantity of seats available at location k in the bid submitted by driver d
b_{dj}^D: a vector to represent the $j - th$ bid submitted by driver d. $b_{dj}^D = (q_{dj1}, q_{dj2}, q_{dj3}, \ldots, q_{djK}, \ldots, c_{dj})$
f_p: the original price paid by passenger p if he travels alone
$b_p^P = (s_{p1}, s_{p2}, s_{p3}, \ldots, s_{pK}, f_p)$ a vector to represent the bid submitted by passenger p. The bid b_p^P is actually an offer to pay the price f_{ph} for transporting s_{pk} passengers for each $k \in \{1, 2, 3, \ldots, K\}$
x_{dj}: the variable to indicate the $j - th$ bid placed by driver d i s a winning bid ($x_{dj} = 1$) or not ($x_{dj} = 0$)

y_p: the variable to indicate the bid placed by passenger p is a winning bid ($y_p = 1$) or not ($y_p = 0$)

In our car pooling problem, each passenger $p \in P$ and each driver $d \in D$ submits bids to the system to describe their requirements. The objective of the car pooling problem is to assign passengers to drivers to such that the reduction in overall travel cost/distance is maximized.

The fitness function is defined as follows:

$$F(x, y) = \left(\sum_{p=1}^{P} y_p f_p \right) + \left(\sum_{d=1}^{D} \sum_{j=1}^{J_d} x_{dj} o_{dj} \right) - \left(\sum_{d=1}^{D} \sum_{j=1}^{J_d} x_{dj} c_{dj} \right)$$

The car pooling problem is formulated as follows:

$$\max_{x,y} \ F(x, y) \tag{1}$$

s.t.
$$\sum_{d=1}^{D} \sum_{j=1}^{J_d} x_{dj} q_{djk} \geq \sum_{p=1}^{P} y_p s_{pk} \ \forall k \in \{1, 2, \ldots, K\} \tag{2}$$

$$\sum_{p=1}^{P} y_p f_p + \sum_{d=1}^{D} \sum_{j=1}^{J_d} x_{dj} o_{dj} \geq \sum_{d=1}^{D} \sum_{j=1}^{J_d} x_{dj} c_{dj} \tag{3}$$

$$\sum_{j=1}^{J_d} x_{dj} \leq 1 \ \forall d \in \{1, \ldots, D\}, \forall j \in \{1, 2, \ldots, J_d\} \tag{4}$$

$$x_{dj} \in \{0, 1\} \ \forall d, \forall j$$
$$y_p \in \{0, 1\} \ \forall p$$

3   Discrete Particle Swarm Algorithm

In this section, we present our discrete particle swarm algorithm for the car pooling problem. A brief introduction to the standard particle swarm optimization method is given first.

With the standard particle swarm optimization, each particle of the swarm adjusts its trajectory according to its own flying experience and the flying experiences of other particles within its topological neighborhood in a N-dimensional space S. The velocity and position of particle i are represented as $v_i = (v_{i1}, v_{i2}, v_{i3}, \ldots, v_{iN})$ and $z_i = (z_{i1}, z_{i2}, z_{i3}, \ldots, z_{iN})$, respectively. Its best historical position is recorded as z_i^{best}. The best historical position that the entire swarm has passed is denoted as z_g. The velocity and position of particle i on dimension n, where $n \in \{1, 2, 3, \ldots, N\}$, in iteration $t+1$ are updated as follows:

$$v_{in}^{t+1} = \omega v_{in}^{t} + c_1 r_1 (p_{in}^{t} - x_{in}^{t}) + c_2 r_2 (p_{gn}^{t} - x_{in}^{t})$$

$$z_{in}^{t+1} = z_{in}^{t} + v_{in}^{t}$$

where ω is a parameter called the inertia weight, c_1 and c_2 are positive constants referred to as cognitive and social parameters, respectively, and r_1 and r_2 are random numbers generated from a uniform distribution in the region of [0, 1].

In the carpool problem formulated previously, the decision variables x_{dj} and y_p can be represented by a two dimensional binary vector z, which consists of two vectors z_x and z_y:

$$z_x(d,j) = x_{dj}$$

$$z_y(p) = y_p$$

We may concatenate each row of z_x and each row of z_y to obtain an one dimensional binary vector z. Te resulting one dimensional binary vector z is used to describe each particle in discrete particle swarm algorithm. The length of z is $N = \sum\limits_{d=1}^{D} J_d + P$. The component $z(n)$ of the vector is either 0 or 1, where 1 denotes that bid is a winning bid and 0 denotes that bid is not a winning bid. Consider a car pooling problem with 3 drivers and 5 passengers. Suppose each driver and each passenger submits only one bid. In this case, N is equal to 8.

Fitness Function

For our problem, the fitness function is $F(x, y)$, which can be described by $F(z)$:

$$F(z) = \left[\left(\sum_{p=1}^{P} z_y(p) f_p \right) - \left(\sum_{d=1}^{D} \sum_{j=1}^{J_d} z_x(d,j)(c_{dj} - o_{dj}) \right) \right]$$

The carpooling problem formulated previously is an optimization problem with binary decision variables and constraints. These constraints must be handled properly in the proposed algorithm. In existing literature, there are several ways to handle constraints, including methods based on preserving feasibility of solutions, methods based on penalty functions and methods based on biasing feasible over infeasible solutions. Two popular constraint handling methods are the methods of penalty function [14, 15] and the methods based on biasing feasible over infeasible solutions [16]. In this paper, we adopt a method based on biasing feasible over infeasible solutions [16].

Let S_f: $S_f = \{(x, y)|(x, y)$ is a solution in the current population, (x, y) satisfies constraints $(2-2) \sim (2-4)\}$ is the set of all feasible solutions in the current population. $S_{f\,min}$: $S_{f\,min} = \min\limits_{(x,y) \in S_f} F(x, y)$, the object function value of the worst feasible solution in the current population.

The fitness function $F_1(x, y)$ is defined as follows:

$$F_1(x, y) = \begin{cases} F(x, y) & if \quad (x, y) \ satisfies \ (2-2) \sim (2-4) \\ U_1(x, y) & otherwise \end{cases},$$

Where

$$U_1(x, y) = S_{fmin} + \sum_{k=1}^{K}(\min(\sum_{d=1}^{D}\sum_{j=1}^{J_d} x_{dj}q_{djk} - \sum_{p=1}^{P} y_p s_{pk}, 0.0)) +$$

$$\min(\sum_{p=1}^{P} y_p f_p - \sum_{d=1}^{D}\sum_{j=1}^{J_d} x_{dj}(c_{dj} - o_{dj}), 0.0) + \sum_{d=1}^{D}\sum_{j=1}^{J_d} \min(1 - \sum_{k=1}^{K} x_{dj}, 0.0)$$

To describe the discrete particle swarm optimization (DPSO) algorithm, we define the required notations as follows.

Notation:

S^t: the set of all particles at time t

I: the number of particles in the population, $I = |S^t|$

N_x: the number of bids placed by all drivers, $N_x = \sum_{d=1}^{D} J_d$

N_y: the number of bids placed by all drivers, $N_x = P$

Z_i^t: the position of particle i at time t, where $i \in \{1, 2, \ldots, I\}$, and $Z_i^t = (x_i^t, y_i^t)$, where x_i^t is a N_x-dimensional vector corresponding to decision variables x_{dj} and y_i^t is a N_y-dimensional vector corresponding to decision variables y_p

PZ_i^t: the personal best of particle i at time t, where $i \in \{1, 2, \ldots, I\}$, and $PZ_i^t = (Px_i^t, Py_i^t)$, where Px_i^t is the personal best position (a N_x-dimensional vector) corresponding to decision variables x_{dj} and Py_i^t is the personal best position (a N_y-dimensional vector) corresponding to decision variables y_p

GZ^t: the global best at time t, and $GZ^t = (Gx^t, Gy^t)$, where Gx^t is the global best position (a N_x-dimensional vector) corresponding to decision variables x_{dj} and Gy^t is the global best position (a N_y-dimensional vector) corresponding to decision variables y_p

c_1: a non-negative real parameter less than 1

c_2: a non-negative real parameter less than 1

r_1: a random variable with uniform distribution $U(0, 1)$

r_2: a random variable with uniform distribution $U(0, 1)$

V_{max}: A maximum value of velocity

$s(vx_{in}^t)$: the probability of the bit x_{in}^t

$s(vy_{in}^t)$: the probability of the bit y_{in}^t

The DPSO) algorithm proposed in this paper is as follows:

Discrete Particle Swarm Optimization (DPSO) Algorithm

Input: $P, D, b_{ph}^P, b_{dj}^D, a_{dj}, T_m^D, T_m^P$

Output: GZ^t

Step 0: $t \leftarrow 0$

    Generate Z_i^t for each particle $i \in \{1,2,...,I\}$ in the initial population of swarm, S^t

Step 1:

While (stopping criteria is not satisfied)

    $t \leftarrow t+1$

    Evaluate each particle Z_i^t in S^t according to the fitness function $F_1(x,y)$

    Determine the personal best of each particle in S^t

    Determine the global best of swarm, G^t

    For each $i \in \{1,2,...,I\}$

        Calculate the velocity of particle i as follows

        Generate r_1, a random variable with uniform distribution $U(0,1)$

        Generate r_2, a random variable with uniform distribution $U(0,1)$

$$vx_{in}^t = vx_{in}^{t-1} + c_1 r_1 (Px_{in}^t - x_{in}^t) + c_2 r_2 (Gx_{in}^t - x_{in}^t)$$

$$vx_{in}^t \in [-V_{max}, V_{max}]$$

$$vy_i^t = vy_{in}^{t-1} + c_1 r_1 (Py_{in}^t - y_{in}^t) + c_2 r_2 (Gy_{in}^t - y_{in}^t)$$

$$vy_{in}^t \in [-V_{max}, V_{max}]$$

        Apply a sigmoid limiting transformation to vx_{in}^t to obtain $s(vx_{in}^t)$.

        Apply a sigmoid limiting transformation to vy_{in}^t to obtain $s(vy_{in}^t)$.

        Update particle i as follows

        Generate $rsid$, a random variable with uniform distribution $U(0,1)$

$$x_{in}^t = \begin{cases} 1 \; rsid < s(vx_{in}^t) \\ 0 \; otherwise \end{cases}$$

        Generate $rsid$, a random variable with uniform distribution $U(0,1)$

$$y_{in}^t = \begin{cases} 1 \; rsid < s(vy_{in}^t) \\ 0 \; otherwise \end{cases}$$

    End While

4 Numerical Results

In this section, we present the simulation results by applying the proposed method to an application scenario. In this example, there are 7 passengers and 3 drivers. Therefore, $P = 7$ and $D = 3$. Each passenger submits only one bid. Hence $H_p = 1$. However, a driver may submit multiple bids, each bid reflecting different way to pick up different combination of passengers selected for ride sharing. Table 1 shows the location of 7 passengers in this example. The price of each bid for each passenger generated by our bid generation algorithm is also shown in Table 1. Table 2 shows the location

Table 1. Requirements of passengers

p	h	Origin		Destination		f_p
1	1	24.1783294	120.7385673	24.14891	120.66295	20
2	1	24.13425	120.5539	24.14416	120.69092	36
3	1	24.14702	120.67257	24.114	120.69139	9
4	1	24.114	120.69139	24.11775	120.6274	17
5	1	24.20052	120.65714	24.16989	120.6762	8
6	1	24.12434	120.65873	24.13075	120.66168	2
7	1	24.254705	120.7246715	24.12751	120.69479	33

Table 2. Requirements of drivers

d	j	Origin		Destination	
1	1	24.254705	120.7246715	24.11009	120.64146
2	1	24.23115	120.57268	24.14443	120.70454
3	1	24.20195	120.56815	24.02302	120.69638

information of the 3 drivers in this example. We set the filter parameter to 1.7 to filter the passengers for each driver. The price of each bid for each driver generated by the bid generation algorithm is also shown in Table 3.

For this example, $x_{1,3} = 1$, $x_{2,2} = 1$, $x_{3,1} = 1$, $y_{1,1} = 1$, $y_{2,1} = 1$, $y_{6,1} = 1$, $y_{7,1} = 1$. The total routing distance with carpooling for this solution is 125.11. The total routing distance without carpooling is 152.10. Therefore, the total routing distance is reduced

Table 3. Requirements of drivers

d	j	q_{dj1}	q_{dj2}	q_{dj3}	q_{dj4}	q_{dj5}	q_{dj6}	q_{dj7}	c_{dj}	o_{dj}
1	1	1	0	0	0	0	0	0	27.192	24.661
1	2	0	0	0	0	1	0	0	25.51	24.661
1	3	0	0	0	0	0	0	1	23.322	24.661
2	1	0	0	1	0	0	0	0	25.396	27.936
2	2	0	1	0	0	0	1	0	34.361	27.936
3	1	1	0	0	0	0	0	0	49.302	34.903
3	2	0	1	0	0	0	0	0	48.26	34.903

Table 4. Results

Case	D	P	Overall distance/ cost (without carpooling)	Overall distance/cost (with carpooling)	Reduction in overall distance
1	3	6	104.38/144.82	79.92/84.26	23.43%
2	3	7	152.10/216.70	125.11/143.24	17.74%
3	4	6	143.02/183.53	111.67/128.86	21.92%
4	4	7	118.14/167.62	109.03/143.20	7.71%
5	2	5	100.62/153.76	85.34/97.93	15.19%

by 17.74% with carpooling. Table 4 shows the simulation results for several cases. It indicates that significant reduction in overall travel distance can be obtained by applying our proposed algorithms.

5 Conclusions

Car pooling is a viable way to reduce air pollution, parking problems, fuel consumption and commuting costs based on shared use of private cars or vehicles. In this paper, we study the car pooling problem and develop a solution algorithm car pooling system to realize ridesharing. To study the car pooling problem, we formulate the problem as a discrete optimization problem. We propose a method to facilitate determination of drivers/passengers for ridesharing based on swarm intelligence to improve efficiency of transport systems and reduce costs. Our solution methodology combines geographic information system, meta-heuristic algorithms and information technology. We adopt discrete particle swarm algorithm to solve the car pooling problem. We have implemented our solution algorithm and conduct experiments to verify its practicality by examples. The numerical results of our experiments indicate that significant reduction in total distance can be achieved through car pooling based on the proposed car pooling algorithm.

Acknowledgement. This paper was supported in part by Ministry of Science and Technology, Taiwan, under Grant MOST-105-2410-H-324-005.

References

1. Furuhata, M., Dessouky, M., Ordóñez, F., Brunet, M.-E., Wang, X., Koenig, S.: Ridesharing: the state-of-the-art and future directions. Transp. Res. Part B: Meth. **57**, 28–46 (2013)
2. Agatz, N., Erera, A., Savelsbergh, M., Wang, X.: Optimization for dynamic ride-sharing: a review. Eur. J. Oper. Res. **223**(2), 295–303 (2012)
3. Baldacci, R., Maniezzo, V., Mingozzi, A.: An exact method for the car pooling problem based on lagrangian column generation. Oper. Res. **52**(3), 422–439 (2004)
4. Maniezzo, V., Carbonaro, A., Hildmann, H.: An ants heuristic for the long-term car pooling problem. In: Onwubolu, G., Babu, B.V. (eds.) New Optimization Techniques in Engineering, pp. 412–429 (2004)
5. Bruglieri, M., Ciccarelli, D., Colorni, A., Luè, A.: PoliUniPool: a carpooling system for universities. Procedia – Soc. Behav. Sci **20**, 558–567 (2011)
6. Agatz, N.A.H., Erera, A.L., Savelsbergh, M.W.P., Wang, X.: Dynamic ride-sharing: a simulation study in metro Atlanta. Transp. Res. Part B: Meth. **45**(9), 1450–1464 (2011)
7. Bicocchi, N., Mamei, M.: Investigating ride sharing opportunities through mobility data analysis. Pervasive Mob. Comput. **14**, 83–94 (2014)
8. Satunin, S., Babkin, E.: A multi-agent approach to intelligent transportation systems modeling with combinatorial auctions. Expert Syst. Appl. **41**(15), 6622–6633 (2014)
9. Kennedy, J., Eberhart, R.C.: Particle swarm optimization. In: Proceedings of IEEE International Conference on Neural Networks, Piscataway, NJ, pp. 1942–1948 (1995)

10. El-Galland, A.I., El-Hawary, M.E., Sallam, A.A.: Swarming of intelligent particles for solving the nonlinear constrained optimization problem. Eng. Intell. Syst. Electr. Eng. Commun. **9**, 155–163 (2001)
11. Van den Bergh, F., Engelbrecht, A.P.: Cooperative learning in neural network using particle swarm optimizers. S. Afr. Comput. J. **26**, 84–90 (2000)
12. Tasgetiren, M.F., Sevkli, M., Liang, Y.C., Gencyilmaz, G.: Particle swarm optimization algorithm for single machine total weighted tardiness problem. In: Proceedings of the IEEE Congress on Evolutionary Computation, Oregon, Portland, vol. 2, pp. 1412–1419 (2004)
13. Kennedy, J., Eberhart, R.C.: A discrete binary version of the particle swarm algorithm. In: 1997 IEEE International Conference on Systems, Man, and Cybernetics: Computational Cybernetics and Simulation, vol. 5, pp. 4104–4108 (1997)
14. Ravindran, A., Ragsdell, K.M., Reklaitis, G.V.: Engineering Optimization: Methods and Applications, 2nd edn. Wiley, New York (2007)
15. Kalyanmoy, D.: Optimization for Engineering Design: Algorithms and Examples. Prentice-Hall, Upper Saddle River (2004)
16. Deb, K.: An efficient constraint handling method for genetic algorithms. Comput. Methods Appl. Mech. Eng. **186**(2–4), 311–338 (2000)

Reactive Motion Planning with Qualitative Constraints

Domen Šoberl[✉] and Ivan Bratko

Faculty of Computer and Information Science, University of Ljubljana,
Večna pot 113, 1000 Ljubljana, Slovenia
{domen.soberl,ivan.bratko}@fri.uni-lj.si

Abstract. Qualitative modeling tends to be closer to human type of reasoning than traditional numerical modeling and proved to be very useful in certain branches of cognitive robotics. However, due to the lack of precise numerical relations, planning with qualitative models has been achieved to a limited extent. Typically, it is bound to predicting possible future behaviors of the system, and demands additional exploration of numerical relations, before constructed plans can be executed. In this paper we show how qualitative models can be interpreted in terms of reactive planning, to produce executable actions without the need for additional numerical learning. We demonstrate our method on two classical motion planning problems – pursuing and obstacle avoidance, and a complex problem of pushing objects.

1 Introduction

A common way to model a dynamic system is to use a set of differential equations to specify numerical relations between its continuous variables. In cases when such relations are not known or are difficult to measure, the system can be described qualitatively. In artificial intelligence, first qualitative approaches to solving physical and mechanical problems were proposed in the 1980s [3, 4], when the notion of *Qualitative Differential Equations* (QDEs), as qualitative abstractions of traditional differential equations, was introduced. Kuipers proposed and implemented a qualitative simulation algorithm QSIM [5], which can predict possible future behaviors of a system by resolving its qualitative constraints.

In recent years, qualitative reasoning gained more attention in cognitive robotics. Algorithms such as QUIN [2] and Padé [12], which can induce qualitative models from existing numerical data, were introduced. Autonomously exploring agents were now able to build qualitative theories of their surroundings and hand out to people clearer, more intuitive explanations of their findings, sometimes intuitive enough to be deemed agent's *insights* [1].

Motivation to use qualitative modeling in cognitive robotics is clear, hence the question of their usefulness for planning is relevant. Lacking numerical information, exact future states of the system are hard to predict, therefore qualitative planning is often coupled with numerical learning. Using STRIPS-like notation, Sammut and Yik [6] devised an abstract qualitative plan for a humanoid robot

© Springer International Publishing AG 2017
S. Benferhat et al. (Eds.): IEA/AIE 2017, Part I, LNAI 10350, pp. 41–50, 2017.
DOI: 10.1007/978-3-319-60042-0_5

to walk. Using this plan, the robot was able to fine-tune the needed numerical parameters using reinforcement learning. Willey et al. [10,11] took a similar approach to train their terrain climbing vehicle robot. They used QSIM as a symbolic planner that reduced the search space for trial-and-error learning.

We take a somewhat different approach to qualitative planning. We show that by continuous observation of environmental parameters, the robot can reactively be guided to complete its task without the need for additional learning. Our view on the given qualitative model is that of an instinctive knowledge, suggesting the robot the most prominent action at a given moment. We indicated this trend of research in our previous work [7], where we trained a robot to push objects of various shapes. The solution, however, was problem-specific and the feasibility of using such an approach in general, was unclear.

In this paper we show how to interpret and systematically resolve qualitative constraints, typically used in qualitative simulation, in the context of reactive planning. We demonstrate our method on two classical motion planning problems of pursuing objects and avoiding obstacles, and a complex problem of pushing objects.

2   Qualitative Modeling

The state of a system at time t is described in terms of values of a set of variables, each being a continuous function of time. Relationships between these variables are expressed by qualitative constraints. In QSIM, seven types of constraints are defined, which we list in Table 1.

Table 1. Types of qualitative constraints

Constraint	Definition	Constraint	Definition
`const(x)`	$\dot{x}(t) = 0$	`add(x, y, z)`	$x(t) + y(t) = z(t)$
`M+(x, y)`	$\frac{dy}{dx} > 0$, at all times t	`minus(x, y, z)`	$x(t) - y(t) = z(t)$
`M-(x, y)`	$\frac{dy}{dx} < 0$, at all times t	`mult(x, y, z)`	$x(t) \cdot y(t) = z(t)$
`deriv(x, y)`	$y(t) = \dot{x}(t)$		

Constraints `M+(x, y)` and `M-(x, y)` respectively represent classes of monotonically increasing and decreasing functions, stating that x monotonically increases/decreases with y and vice versa, for all t. We also use the multivariate version [9]; e.g. constraint `M+-+(u, [x, y, z])` states that u increases with x and z, decreases with y, and is not dependent on any other variable. If, for instance, x and y both increase, u can increase, decrease or stay unchanged. In such cases an unambiguous prediction cannot be made.

A variable can assume any real value, unless its range is limited by optional *minimum* or *maximum* landmarks. Those are determined by inequality statements, e.g. `x > 0` or `0 < x < 1`, which hold at all times t. We allow circular topologies, declared by predicate `circ`, e.g. `circ(a, [0, 360])` to state that $a \in [0, 360]$ and $a : 0 \cong 360$. Rotations are typically handled this way. Knowing the current state of the system, we consider its future dynamics, which is expressed qualitatively, in the form of *qualitative directions*.

Definition 1 (Qualitative direction). Qualitative direction *and* negative qualitative direction *of variable x at time t, are respectively:*

$$\hat{x}(t) = \begin{cases} inc, \ \dot{x}(t) > 0; \\ dec, \ \dot{x}(t) < 0; \\ std, \ \dot{x}(t) = 0, \end{cases} \qquad -\hat{x}(t) = \begin{cases} inc, \ \dot{x}(t) < 0; \\ dec, \ \dot{x}(t) > 0; \\ std, \ \dot{x}(t) = 0. \end{cases}$$

3   Planning with Qualitative Models

Qualitative constraints listed in Table 1 suffice for simulation. To allow planning, the notion of *action* and *goal* must also be introduced. We define actions qualitatively and state the goal numerically.

Definition 2 (Qualitative action). *Qualitative action A is a subset of variables with their corresponding qualitative directions, denoted $A = [x_1 : qdir_1, \ldots, x_k : qdir_k]$, where $qdir_i \in \{inc, std, dec\}$.*

Qualitative action determines its effect on the system in terms of setting qualitative directions directly to a subset of variables called *controlled variables*. The duration of such an effect depends on the controller and is not known to the planner in advance. Action $A = [x_1 : inc, x_2 : dec, x_3 : std]$ executed at time t_0 and lasting until time t_1, asserts the property $\hat{x}_1(t) = inc$, $\hat{x}_2(t) = dec$, and $\hat{x}_3(t) = std$, for all $t \in [t_0, t_1]$. A special case is the *trivial action* $T = [x_i : std]$, which holds steady all controlled variables x_i. The effect of an action on non-controlled variables is propagated through the system of given qualitative constraints (which we discuss in Sect. 3.1). Not knowing numerical relations between variables, exact future value of any variable x at time t under action A, denoted $x_A(t), t \in (t_0, t_1]$, cannot be computed (with the exception of x being a constant). We are therefore interested in *relative qualitative effects* of actions.

Definition 3 (Relative qualitative effect). *Let qualitative action A and trivial qualitative action T be executed independently on equal configurations in time interval $[t_0, t_1]$, and let x be any variable. Relative qualitative effect of A on x is defined as*

$$\hat{A}(x) = \begin{cases} inc, \ x_A(t) - x_T(t) > 0; \\ dec, \ x_A(t) - x_T(t) < 0; \quad \forall t \in (t_0, t_1]. \\ std, \ x_A(t) - x_T(t) = 0; \end{cases}$$

At time t_0 it holds $x_A(t_0) = x_T(t_0)$, therefore we may omit the action symbol and write simply $x(t_0)$. Executing a proper sequence of actions, a favorable dynamics should be induced for the system to eventually reach a goal state.

Definition 4 (Goal). *Goal G is a set of variables $g_1, \ldots, g_m$ with their corresponding numerical values, denoted $G = [g_1 = V_1, \ldots, g_m = V_m]$, where $V_i \in \mathbb{R}$.*

We specify a goal using the `goal` predicate, e.g. `goal(x = 0, y = 0)` to state that the goal is to reach $x = y = 0$. To the planner, such a statement represents a tendency to move the goal variables closer to their goal values. Goal values should eventually be reached, but a variable may temporarily also move away from it. Additionally, minimum and maximum landmarks, if set to a non-goal variable, assert a tendency to keep the bounded variable away from its extremes. The `circ` predicate gives the planner the freedom to plan the movement of a variable in either direction. Statements can be guarded by additional landmarks, e.g. `(0 < x < 1): M+(x, y)` to state that the right-hand monotonic relation holds when $0 < x < 1$.

Let $x_1, \ldots, x_k$ be goal variables, and $g_1, \ldots, g_k$ their corresponding goal values. Let $x_{k+1}, \ldots, x_n$ be non-goal variables with the tendency to avoid a left extreme ($x_i > a_i$), a right extreme ($x_i < b_i$), or both ($a_i < x_i < b_i$). Let action A be considered at time t_0. Denote by $\max(|\dot{x}_i|)$ the maximal speed of x_i observed before t_0. Action A is evaluated according to its relative qualitative effect $\hat{A}(x_i)$ on each x_i, and assigned the weight:

$$\Gamma(A) = \sum_{i=1}^{k} N(\hat{A}(x_i)) \cdot \frac{g_i - x_i}{\max(|\dot{x}_i|)} + \sum_{i=k+1}^{n} N(\hat{A}(x_i)) \cdot T(x_i) \cdot \max(|\dot{x}_i|), \quad (1)$$

where function N maps inc $\mapsto 1$, dec $\mapsto -1$, std $\mapsto 0$. Function $T(x_i)$ sets the tendency factor, which needs to rise quickly when variable x_i approaches an extreme. We use:

$$T(x_i) = \begin{cases} \cos\left(\frac{\pi}{b_i - a_i} \cdot \left(x_i - \frac{a_i + b_i}{2}\right)\right)^{-1} - 1, & a_i < x_i < b_i; \\ (x - a_i)^{-1}, & x_i > a_i; \\ (b_i - x)^{-1}, & x_i < b_i. \end{cases} \quad (2)$$

Equation (1) represents a kind of greedy heuristic towards the goal state. Its value is the sum of individual votes by each variable under action A. The farther a variable is removed from its goal value, the higher the weight of its vote. The vote will be positive if the effect $\hat{A}(x_i)$ is the most favorable amongst the three, negative if the least, and zero otherwise. Different metric could be used for different variables, therefore their speeds are used to normalize their values. If due to an ambiguity in stated qualitative relations the effect of an action on a variable cannot be determined, the vote of that variable is omitted, that is $N(\hat{A}(x_i) = ?) = 0$.

3.1 Resolving Qualitative Constraints

The relative qualitative effect $\hat{A}(x_i)$ of each variable x_i must be known before action A can be evaluated using Eq. (1). Effects are propagated through qualitative constraints listed in Table 1. The following propositions state the rules for their resolution. Recall the notation $\hat{x}(t)$ for qualitative direction of x at time t (Definition 1).

Proposition 1. *Let action A be executed in time interval $[t_0, t_1]$ and work directly on controlled variable x. Then $\hat{A}(x) = \hat{x}(t), \forall t \in (t_0, t_1]$.*

Proof. The value of x at any time $t_i \in (t_0, t_1]$ under action A is $x_A(t_i) = x(t_0) + \int_{t_0}^{t_i} \dot{x}_A(t)\, dt$, and its value under the trivial action is $x_T(t_i) = x(t_0)$. By definition, relative qualitative effect $\hat{A}(x)$ is determined by the sign of $x_A(t_i) - x_T(t_i) = \int_{t_0}^{t_i} \dot{x}_A(t)\, dt$. Action A asserts a consistent sign to $\dot{x}_A(t)$ for all $t \in (t_0, t_i]$. As $\dot{x}_A(t)$ is integrated over time $t \in (t_0, t_i]$, the same sign is inferred to $x_A(t_i) - x_T(t_i)$.□

Proposition 2. *Qualitative constraint* `const(x)` *implies $\hat{A}(x) =$ std for any action A.*

Proof. Let A be any action executed in time interval $[t_0, t_1]$. The value of x under A at any time $t_i \in (t_0, t_1]$ is $x_A(t_i) = x(t_0) + \int_{t_0}^{t_i} \dot{x}_A(t)\, dt$. Constraint `const(x)` asserts $\dot{x}_A(t) = 0$ for all t, therefore $x_A(t_i) = x_T(t_i) = x(t_0)$. From $x_A(t_i) - x_T(t_i) = 0, \forall t_i \in (t_0, t_1]$, it follows $\hat{A}(x) =$ std by definition.   □

Proposition 3. *Let action A be executed in time interval $[t_0, t_1]$ and have a non-steady relative qualitative effect on variable x, i.e. $\hat{A}(x) \neq$ std. Constraints* `M+(x, y)` *and* `M-(x, y)` *imply $\hat{A}(y) = \hat{A}(x)$ and $\hat{A}(y) = -\hat{A}(x)$, respectively.*

Proof. Suppose the trivial action T has been executed in time interval $[t_0, t_1]$, and values $x_T(t), y_T(t)$ observed at arbitrary time $t \in (t_0, t_1]$. Independently, action A has been executed on an equal configuration in time interval $[t_0, t_1]$, and values $x_A(t), y_A(t)$ observed at the same time t. Consider differentials $dx = x_A(t) - x_T(t)$ and $dy = y_A(t) - y_T(t)$. By definition, $\hat{A}(x)$ is determined by the sign of dx, and $\hat{A}(y)$ by the sign of dy. Since action A has a non-steady effect on x, $dx \neq 0$. (i) Constraint `M+(x, y)` asserts $\frac{dy}{dx} > 0$ for all t, which holds if and only if $\text{sgn}(dy) = \text{sgn}(dx), dx \neq 0$. Therefore $\hat{A}(y) = \hat{A}(x)$. (ii) Constraint `M-(x, y)` asserts $\frac{dy}{dx} < 0$ for all t, which holds if and only if $\text{sgn}(dy) = -\text{sgn}(dx), dx \neq 0$. Therefore $\hat{A}(y) = -\hat{A}(x)$.   □

The above rule can be extended to multivariate monotonic qualitative constraints, e.g. `M+-+(u, [x, y, z])`. If at least one of the independent variables (x, y or z) is non-steady and all non-steady variables agree on the direction of the dependent variable u, the prediction is unambiguous.

Proposition 4. *Let action A be executed in time interval $[t_0, t_1]$, and have a relative qualitative effect on variable y. Constraint* `deriv(x, y)` *implies $\hat{A}(x) = \hat{A}(y)$.*

Proof. By definition, the value of $\hat{A}(x)$ is determined by the consistent sign of $x_A(t_i) - x_T(t_i)$, for all $t_i \in (t_0, t_1]$. The values of x at time $t_i \in (t_0, t_1]$ under actions A and T are respectively $x_A(t_i) = x(t_0) + \int_{t_0}^{t_i} \dot{x}_A(t)\, dt = x(t_0) + \int_{t_0}^{t_i} y_A(t)\, dt$ and $x_T(t_i) = x(t_0) + \int_{t_0}^{t_i} \dot{x}_T(t)\, dt = x(t_0) + \int_{t_0}^{t_i} y_T(t)\, dt$. Therefore $x_A(t_i) - x_T(t_i) = \int_{t_0}^{t_i} y_A(t)\, dt - \int_{t_0}^{t_i} y_T(t)\, dt = \int_{t_0}^{t_i} (y_A(t) - y_T(t))\, dt$. By definition, $\hat{A}(y)$ asserts a consistent sign to $y_A(t) - y_T(t)$, for all $t \in (t_0, t_1]$. By integrating $y_A(t) - y_T(t)$ over time $t \in (t_0, t_i]$, the same sign is inferred to $x_A(t_i) - x_T(t_i)$. $\qquad\Box$

Proposition 5. *Let qualitative action A be executed in time interval $[t_0, t_1]$ and have a known effect on variables x and y. Relative qualitative effect on z through qualitative constraints* add(x, y, z) *and* minus(x, y, z) *are given in below tabulations, where possible values $\hat{A}(x)$ are listed as rows and $\hat{A}(y)$ as columns. Ambiguity is denoted by question mark.*

$+$	inc	std	dec
inc	inc	inc	?
std	inc	std	dec
dec	?	dec	dec

$-$	inc	std	dec
inc	?	inc	inc
std	dec	std	inc
dec	dec	dec	?

Here we provide the proof for rules add(inc, inc, inc) and minus(inc, inc, ?). All other rules can be verified following the same manner of deduction.

Proof. Define $X(t) = x_A(t) - x_T(t)$ and $Y(t) = y_A(t) - y_T(t)$. From $\hat{A}(x) = $ inc and $\hat{A}(y) = $ inc it follows by definition $X(t) > 0$ and $Y(t) > 0$, for all $t \in (t_0, t_1]$. Relative qualitative effect $\hat{A}(z)$ is determined by the sign of $z_A(t) - z_T(t)$, at all $t \in (t_0, t_1]$. (i) With constraint add(x, y, z) we deduce: $z_A(t) - z_T(t) = (x_A(t) + y_A(t)) - (x_T(t) + y_T(t)) = (x_A(t) - x_T(t)) + (y_A(t) - y_T(t)) = X(t) + Y(t)$. Since $X(t)$ and $Y(t)$ are both positive over $t \in (t_0, t_1]$, $\hat{A}(z) = $ inc. (ii) With constraint minus(x, y, z) we deduce: $z_A(t) - z_T(t) = (x_A(t) - y_A(t)) - (x_T(t) - y_T(t)) = (x_A(t) - x_T(t)) - (y_A(t) - y_T(t)) = X(t) - Y(t)$. Since $X(t)$ and $Y(t)$ are both positive over $t \in (t_0, t_1]$, all cases $\hat{A}(z) \in \{$inc, std, dec$\}$ are possible. $\qquad\Box$

The multiplication constraint mult(x, y, z) is useful only when additional numerical restrictions are considered, e.g. $x, y \in [0, \inf)$. The derived rules are specific to each case and too vast to cover them all here. Note that in the experiments presented in this paper we do not use the multiplication constraint.

4   Experiments in Robotics

We demonstrate our planning approach in a robotic motion planning domain, using a simple planar two-wheeled robot. The problems we choose are *pursuing*, *obstacle avoidance*, and *pushing*. All three experiments were done in a simulator, assuming an overhead camera and object recognition system as sensory input. Locations and orientations of objects were captured and passed to the planner whenever a change was observed. Actions received from the planner were in the form v, w $\in \{$inc, std, dec$\}$, where v is translational and w angular velocity of the robot. These actions were then translated to numerical outputs using a constant numerical step by which v and w were increased, decreased, or kept steady.

4.1   Pursuing

The goal of this task is to follow and eventually catch an arbitrarily moving object. The observed attributes are Euclidean distance D and angular distance phi (see Fig. 1a). The model can be described intuitively using the following qualitative constraints:

```
(0 <= phi < 90): M--(D', [v, w])          circ(phi, [-180, 180])
(-90 <= phi < 0): M-+(D', [v, w])         deriv(D, D')
(90 <= phi < 180): M+-(D', [v, w])        action(v, w)
(-180 <= phi -90): M++(D', [v, w])        goal(D = 0)
```

Increasing or decreasing v and w does not directly affect the distance D, but rather its speed D', which is its time derivative. In relation to that we recognize four distinct qualitative states and therefore four distinct ways in which D' is increased or decreased: the target is *front left* (phi $\in [0, 90)$), *front right* (phi $\in [-90, 0)$), *back left* (phi $\in [90, 180)$) or *back right* (phi $\in [-180, 90)$). The goal is to reach D = 0.

(a) Relation of the robot to a target.   (b) Trajectory made by the robot.

Fig. 1. Robot pursuing a moving target.

We initially positioned the robot facing away from the target which started moving from the left to the right with a constant speed. The trajectory made by the robot during one of the trials is shown in Fig. 1b. We observed the robot first making a back turn and then proceed forward towards the target. We find such a maneuver visually very intuitive from a human perspective. Being slightly faster than the target, the robot managed to catch it and declare the goal reached.

4.2   Obstacle Avoidance

The general idea to modeling obstacle avoidance is to introduce an additional constraint to the second object, to which the role of an obstacle is now given, and let the robot still pursue the first object. The additional constraint is D2 > 0, where D2 is the distance between the robot's and obstacle's bodies. So we have combined the task of pursuing with the task of avoiding, since avoiding alone would drive the robot away from the obstacle with no specific target to reach.

We managed to achieve the desired behavior by slightly altering the model of pursuing as shown by the first three lines in the model below, while the succeeding four lines represent the added model of avoidance, which is depicted in

Fig. 2a. Such model allows the robot to balance between the orientation towards
the target and away from the obstacle. Note the `abs(phi1)` function, which
returns the absolute value of `phi1`.

```
(abs(phi1) <= 90): M-(D', v)        deriv(D1, D1')
(abs(phi1) > 90): M+(D', v)         deriv(D2, D2')
M-(phi1', w)                        deriv(phi1, phi1')
(0 <= phi2 < 90): M--(D2, [v, w])   D2 > 0
(-90 <= phi2 < 0): M-+(D2, [v, w])  action(v, w)
(90 <= phi2 < 180): M+(D2, v)       goal(D1 = 0, phi1 = 0)
(-180 <= phi2 -90): M+(D2, v)
```

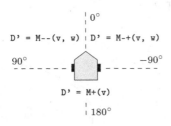

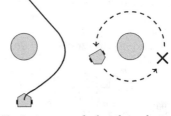

(a) The qualitative model of avoidance with three qualitative states.

(b) Trajectory made by the robot avoiding an obstacle while pursuing a stationary target (left) and chasing a moving target around the obstacle (right).

Fig. 2. Robot avoiding an obstacle.

Results of planning are shown in Fig. 2b. With a stationary target the robot
managed to circumvent the obstacle and catch the target. If the target was
moving around the obstacle, the robot was chasing it without colliding with the
obstacle.

4.3 Pushing

It has been demonstrated [8] that the problem of pushing represents a complex
numerical problem. Using the methods described in this paper we were able
to reproduce the pushing experiment presented in [7]. In the original work, a
problem-specific planning method was used and the possibility of a more general
solution left unaddressed. With successful reproduction we now provide a more
universal approach to qualitative pushing.

The task of the robot is to push a convex polygonal object to a designated
location and orientation using a single point contact. Domain attributes are
depicted in Fig. 3a. All the values are given relative to the robot's position: position of the object (x, y), orientation of the object `beta`, goal position $(x1, y1)$,
goal orientation `gamma`, orientation of the robot `theta`, the point of contact

tau ∈ [−1, 1] and the angle of pushing phi ∈ [−30°, 30°]. Qualitative behavior of pushing was induced by autonomous robot exploration and its detailed interpretation is given in the original work. It is comprised of the following six monotonically increasing relations:

```
M--(x', [tau, w])        M--(tau', [w, phi])
M+(y', v)                M+(theta', w)
M+(phi', w)              M+--(beta', [tau, phi, w])
```

The possibility to use the same qualitative model without the need to consider possible quantitative differences between the two experiments, demonstrates the main advantage of qualitative approach to motion planning. We complete the model with the following constraints, previously hard-coded with the planner:

```
-30 < phi < 30                    deriv(x, x')
-1 < tau < 1                      deriv(y, y')
circ(beta, [0, 360])             deriv(beta, beta')
circ(gamma, [0, 360))            deriv(phi, phi')
circ(theta, [0, 360))            deriv(tau, tau')
action(v, w)                      deriv(theta, theta')
goal(x = x1, y = y1, beta = gamma)   y' > 0
```

Constraint y' > 0 votes out actions that try to *pull* the object. In the original work, no pulling experiments were performed to discover their ineffectiveness, so the induced model assumes such possibility.

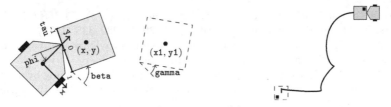

(a) Attributes of the pushing domain.   (b) Trajectory made by the object.

Fig. 3. Robot pushing a rectangular object.

The robot needs to handle three difficulties simultaneously: push the object towards the goal location, rotate it towards the goal orientation, and balance the angle of pushing to sustain the single point contact. Typically, a repositioning of the robot is needed a few times to complete the task. This takes place when no available action reaches a positive weight, meaning that no action exists to improve the overall configuration. A resulting trajectory of pushing a square objects is shown in Fig. 3b. It is interesting to note that the lengths of trajectories obtained by such qualitative approach in many cases come close to the lengths of calculated optimal geometric solutions, as shown in [7].

5 Conclusions

We have shown that qualitative models can contain enough information to allow basic motion planning without the need for additional numerical learning. We proposed a novel framework for planning with qualitative constraints that enables a high level of abstraction and the possibility of expressing different planning problems in a general way. We demonstrated the simplicity of describing a robotic domain and the robot's task qualitatively, or reuse existing qualitative models, without the need to consider numerical properties of the system. Results show high responsiveness of the system to dynamic changes and the usefulness of qualitative modeling in real-time environments.

One shortcoming of our planning algorithm is its short-sightedness due to its greedy approach. Certain actions might seem prominent at the moment, but may lead to suboptimal solutions. We believe this also makes it inadequate for more complex tasks. The problem could be tackled by combining reactive planning with qualitative simulation to test possible long-term effects of actions and search the state space for possible optimal solutions.

References

1. Bratko, I.: An assessment of machine learning methods for robotic discovery. In: 30th International Conference on Information Technology Interfaces, ITI 2008, pp. 53–60, Dubrovnik (2008)
2. Bratko, I., Šuc, D.: Learning qualitative models. AI Mag. **24**(4), 107–119 (2003)
3. De Kleer, J., Brown, J.S.: A qualitative physics confluences. Artif. Intell. **24**(1–3), 7–83 (1984)
4. Forbus, K.D.: Qualitative process theory. Artif. Intell. **24**(1–3), 85–168 (1984)
5. Kuipers, B.: Qualitative simulation. Artif. Intell. **29**(3), 289–338 (1986)
6. Sammut, C., Yik, T.: Multistrategy learning for robot behaviours. In: Advances in Machine Learning I, Chap. 5, pp. 457–476. Springer, Heidelberg (2010)
7. Šoberl, D., Žabkar, J., Bratko, I.: Qualitative planning of object pushing by a robot. In: Foundations of Intelligent Systems. LNCS, vol. 9384, pp. 410–419. Springer (2015)
8. Troha, M., Bratko, I.: Qualitative learning of object pushing by a robot. In: 25th International Workshop on Qualitative Reasoning, pp. 175–180, Barcelona (2011)
9. Wellman, M.P.: Qualitative simulation with multivariate constraints. In: Second International Conference on Principles of Knowledge Representation and Reasoning, pp. 547–557. Morgan Kaufmann (1991)
10. Wiley, T., Bratko, I.: A Multi-strategy architecture for on-line learning of robotic behaviours using qualitative reasoning. In: Proceedings of the Third Annual Conference on Advances in Cognitive Systems, vol. 2015, pp. 1–16, Atlanta, USA (2015)
11. Wiley, T., Sammut, C., Hengst, B., Bratko, I.: A planning and learning hierarchy using qualitative reasoning for the on-line acquisition of robotic behaviors. Adv. Cogn. Syst. **4**, 93–112 (2016)
12. Žabkar, J., Bratko, I., Demšar, J.: Learning qualitative models through partial derivatives by Padé. In: Proceedings of the 21st Annual Workshop on Qualitative Reasoning, pp. 193–202 (2007)

A New System for the Dynamic Shortest Route Problem

Eisa Alanazi[1], Malek Mouhoub[2(✉)], and Mahmoud Halfawy[3]

[1] Department of Computer Science, College of Computers and Information Systems,
Umm Alqura University, Makkah, Saudi Arabia
eaanazi@uqu.edu.sa
[2] Department of Computer Science, University of Regina,
Regina, SK S4S 0A2, Canada
mouhoubm@uregina.ca
[3] IDS Infrastructure Data Solutions,
Inc. 2 Research Drive, Suite 150 E, Regina, SK S4S 7H9, Canada
halfawym@gmail.com

Abstract. The Shortest Route Problem concerns routing one vehicle to one customer while minimizing some objective functions. The problem is essentially a shortest path problem and has been studied extensively in the literature. We report a system with the objective to address two dynamic aspects of the Shortest Route Problem. The first aspect corresponds to handing incremental changes during the routing plan. The second one is about finding the most probable shortest path i.e. the path with the highest probability of being not congested. We describe how each of these two aspects has been implemented in the system as well as the other features and components of this latter.

1 Introduction

The Shortest Route (or Path) Problem [1,2] is an essential daily problem for transportation companies and organizations. Informally, the problem is to find a shortest route to reach a given customer from a particular source, while minimizing a set of objective functions including the customer waiting time and distance. The problem has been extensively studied in the literature and many variants have been proposed [1,3–6] (see [5] for a taxonomic review on variants of the shortest path problem) to address different scenarios, notably, the ones that consider the dynamic nature of the problem [7–9]. The Dynamic Shortest Route Problem concerns any sudden change to the environment while the vehicle is routing. For example, a truck can have imprecise information over the time it would take to traverse over a specific road and we wish to find a route where this imprecise information is taken into account. Usually, a *planner* is responsible for suggesting such routes to vehicles. This can be any entity responsible for suggesting the routes: an expert, an expert aided by a routing software or a fully automated routing software. Solving the Shortest Route Problem can be solved by the Dijkstra algorithm. Classic Shortest Route Problem planners assume the

© Springer International Publishing AG 2017
S. Benferhat et al. (Eds.): IEA/AIE 2017, Part I, LNAI 10350, pp. 51–60, 2017.
DOI: 10.1007/978-3-319-60042-0_6

graph information, i.e., the road segments and their weights, fixed in advance and one needs to start from scratch re-doing all the computations in case any change happened to the graph while routing.

In this paper, we consider a dynamic variant of the shortest route problem that we aim to tackle in an incremental way. The road network we consider is simply a directed (possibly cyclic) graph where each edge corresponds to a road segment. Each road segment includes information such as distance, speed limit, horizontal, vertical and tunnel clearance, bridge strength and other road restrictions such as the type of goods allowed, time constraints, ..., etc. An example of time constraints can be as follows: *"According to the city's paving schedule, road x is unavailable from Sunday midnight until 3:00 pm on the next Tuesday"*. In addition, information about the truck (dimensions, weight, fuel consumption, ..., etc.), the goods and the driver are provided. The driver's information include the behavior (fuel cost sensitive, slow driver, ..., etc.) in addition to other information (working hours, experience, ..., etc.). The goal here is to find a route for the vehicle starting from point s until reaching another point t in the road network, respecting all the constraints while optimizing a given objective function. This latter can be one of the following.

1. Find the shortest route: distance-based cost.
2. Find the quickest route: time-based cost.
3. Find the cheapest route: money-based cost (considering fuel consumption, toll fees, driver's hours).
4. Find the eco-friendliest route: fuel efficient (gas emission)-based cost.

We propose a system that tackles two dynamic aspects of the shortest route problem. In the first one, changes are due to user interaction. The planner, i.e., the one whose in charge of suggesting routes, interacts with the system and changes some of the problem information (truck, driver, ..., etc.) or objective functions after the optimal path is returned. This change is handled by modifying the weights and information of some edges in the graph before updating the optimal route in an incremental way by reusing as much information as possible from the previous computations. This allows for faster responses to changes. In the second dynamic aspect, changes are due to uncontrollable external events such as accidents, weather conditions and natural disasters. This is addressed using a probability distribution $\mathbf{P}$ over the road segments of the network where $\mathbf{P}(e)$ is the probability that the road segment e is *not* congested. The goal here is to find the most robust route maximizing the probabilities while minimizing the objective functions. Furthermore and as described above, the system is expressive to consider specific information about the roads, drivers and trucks. To our best knowledge, there is no available system that allows such information to be augmented into the planner.

2   Dynamic Shortest Route Problem

2.1   Problem Definition

We have a road network that represents a set of intersections $V = \{v_1, v_2, \ldots, v_n\}$ along with the possible roads leading from one to another. Consider the directed graph $G = (V, E)$ where every intersection is represented by a vertex $v_i \in V$ and an edge $(v_i, v_j) \in E$ iff there is a road that *directly* connects v_i to v_j. We further assume the existence of a real-valued function $f : E \to \mathbb{R}^+$ where the cost of a path $p = v_1, v_2, \ldots, v_k$, denoted as $c(p)$, is $\sum_{i=1}^{k-1} f(e_i)$ where $e_i = (v_i, v_{i+1}) \in E$. The problem is then to solve: $\min_{p \in B} c(p)$ where B is the set of all paths from s to t.

2.2   Dynamic Due to User Changes

Consider $v_1, v_2, \ldots, v_k$ to be the path from $s = v_1$ to $t = v_k$ with the minimum cost $c_{min}(s, t)$. Such path can be found by running Dijkstra and we denote it as R_{org}. Assume some changes happen to the weighted graph, i.e., the cost of some edges have changed, some edges were removed/added or possibly some vertices were added. We can run Dijkstra again over the new graph and get a new path with a new cost $c_{min}(s, t)'$. This, however, uses no information from the previous run R_{org}. The main motivation for incremental algorithms is to re-use the previous results. Note that there is a not-very-known incremental variant of Dijkstra that does exactly this. In this section, we consider the dynamic nature of user interactions. This is done by implementing an incremental variant of Dijkstra called DynamicSWSF-FP [10]. In particular, the implementation coincides with the Lifelong Planning A* (LPA*) as described in [11] where we set the heuristic function h to return zero for every possible state during the search. LPA* is an incremental search for A* where setting $h(u) = 0$, for any state u, turn it into the DynamicSWSF-FP algorithm [11]. Here, we informally describe the algorithm referring the reader to [10, 11] for more information. Let G be a digraph with non-negative weights and $s, t \in G$ respectively the source and target nodes. Let G' be an update of the graph G after some changes happen. DynamicSWSF-FP tries to re-use the previous computations of G to find the new shortest path in G'. Informally, DynamicSWSF-FP splits the graph nodes into consistent and inconsistent ones and then try to "fix" the inconsistent ones until all nodes are consistent. This is done by associating a new value $rhs(u)$ to each node $u \in G'$ and u is said to be consistent if and only if $f(u) = rhs(u)$ where $f(u)$ is the minimum distance found so far from s to u. An inconsistent node u i.e., $rhs(u) \neq f(u)$ is either over-consistent $rhs(u) > f(u)$ or under-consistent $rhs(u) < f(u)$. If a node u is under-consistent, the algorithm assigns $rhs(u)$ to ∞ and thus turn all under-consistent nodes to over-consistent ones.

2.3   Most Probable Shortest Path

Let $G = (V, E)$ be a weighted directed graph representing the road map of a given area. Let $\mathbf{P}$ be a probability distribution over the set of edges E where

$\mathbf{P}(e)$ is the probability that there is *no* congestion in the road segment from u to v for $e = (u, v)$. By congestion, we mean a slower traffic than usual and $\mathbf{P}(e)$ is assumed to be taken from experts and historical data. Moreover, it is assumed that the probability of a not congested road segment is independent from the probability of other roads. As a result, every edge e in the graph is associated with two non-negative values $w(e)$ and $\mathbf{P}(e)$ where $w(e)$ is the weight associated with the edge e. The *most probable path* from s to t is the path $v_1, v_2, \ldots, v_k$ where $\prod_{i=1}^{k-1} \mathbf{P}(e_i)$ is maximized such that $s = v_1$, $t = v_k$ and $e_i = (v_i, v_{i+1}) \in E$. So far we have discussed two criteria of finding a path from s to t:

- Most probable path: the path from s to t with the highest probability of being not congested.
- Shortest path: the path from s to t with the minimum cost.

What we are interested in is *the most probable shortest path*. Such path should respect both the probability of routing over a not congested path and minimizing the cost of routing. In essence, the problem can be viewed as a multi objective optimization problem with two conflicting objectives. Let p_1 be the most probable path and p_2 be the shortest path. Recall that the latter can be found by running Dijkstra's algorithm. Certainly, the most probable shortest path *mpsp* does not necessary (and actually should not) equal p_1 neither p_2. We use the logarithm trick to convert the problem of finding the most probable path into a shortest path problem. In particular, $\mathbf{P}(e)$ is converted into $L(e) = -log(\mathbf{P}(e))$. Then finding the most probable path corresponds to the shortest path where $L(e)$ is the cost of each edge; which can be solved by running Dijkstra's algorithm as well. To see why the shortest path corresponds to the most probable path, recall that maximizing $\prod_{i=1}^{k-1} \mathbf{P}(e_i)$ is equivalent to maximizing its log $log(\prod_{i=1}^{k-1} \mathbf{P}(e_i)) = \sum_{i=1}^{k-1} log(\mathbf{P}(e_i))$ as log is an increasing function; which in turn is equivalent to minimizing $\sum_{i=1}^{k-1} -log(\mathbf{P}(e_i))$. As $0 < \mathbf{P}(e_i) < 1$, we have $log(\mathbf{P}(e_i)) < 0$ for every edge e_i and, therefore, $-log(\mathbf{P}(e_i))$ is always non-negative. Thus, we convert the problem into a single objective as follows: we obtain another graph G' with the same vertex and edge sets as of G but now $w(e) = w_0(e) + L(e)$ where $w_0(e)$ is the original weight of the edge e. The problem can now be solved by Dijkstra's algorithm as a shortest path problem and the output respects both the probability distribution and the costs.

3   System Overview

Data Structure Used: It is known that the choice of data structure in implementing Dijkstra affects the algorithm complexity. In particular, there are two ways in implementing Dijkstra: (i) standard priority queues (min heaps) with only `insert` and `delete-min` operation; (ii) Fibonacci heap where we allow an operation called `decrease-key` that is responsible for changing the position of a node v in the queue without removing it. Recent studies [12] suggest that using standard priority queue outperforms the Fibonacci heap in road networks graphs. As a result, we adopt the standard priority queue when implementing Dijkstra.

Road Network Data Source: Open Street Map (OSM) and Google are the main providers of maps in the web. Usually, maps are represented in a standardized format. Such format is not available freely from Google. In contrast, OSM constitutes an open source alternative which allows anyone to contribute in adding more information about a spatial point or an area. Many research works and mature applications have used OSM as their data source. On the other hand, a great deal of work is based on using whatever Google Maps API returns and tweaks it to follow the spirit of the original purpose. Given that our goal is to handle dynamic Shortest Route Problem along with high expressive power, we prefer to have access to the actual road network. This allows us to build highly customized techniques tailored into our purposes without worrying about what a third party API could give as a result. Therefore, we adopt OSM as a data source for the system. In particular, we use the TAREEG [13] to extract the road network from a certain spatial area. TAREEG is a web service with which one is able to extract spatial features of a certain area in the map.

1. Data Source: We use TAREEG to extract the road network of the area under consideration, pre-processes it for any inconsistency like redundant edges, and then associate the following information with each edge in the network: distance, speed limit, time, height, weight, width and hazmat where hazmat is a flag indicating whether the road allows carrying hazard items.
2. Road Availability: Such data assert that some roads are not available during particular time.
3. Driver Profile: Every driver has a profile that shows some information on the driver. This aims to suggesting routes taking into account the drivers' preferences and style of driving. So far, we have simplified the profile as follows: some drivers prefer not to speed up during their commute while other like to drive up to the speed limit.
4. Vehicle Profile: This profile contains truck information like height, weight, width and whether the truck contains hazardous items or not.

4 Case Study

In the following, we show the results of our system along with screenshots for different scenarios. The first scenario we consider is the static Shortest Route Problem. The area of interest is the city of Regina which has roughly 15,000 nodes and 33,000 edges when using OSM. In this scenario, we report the system results on different criteria and constraints. Constraints correspond to a set of requirements that the driver, truck and the road must satisfy. For instance, if the edge represents an actual bridge or tunnel, then the vehicle height, weight and width need not to exceed the limit. Another example is the hazardous items. If the truck contains hazardous items then we need to make sure every edge or road segment of the suggested route allows vehicles carrying such items.

Figure 1 shows the result that OSM and Google Maps respectively return for a given source and destination. Note that the path returned by Google Maps is different than the one returned by our system using OSM. This is due to the fact that Google Maps does not have the ability to take into consideration the requirements we mentioned above regarding the driver, truck and road.

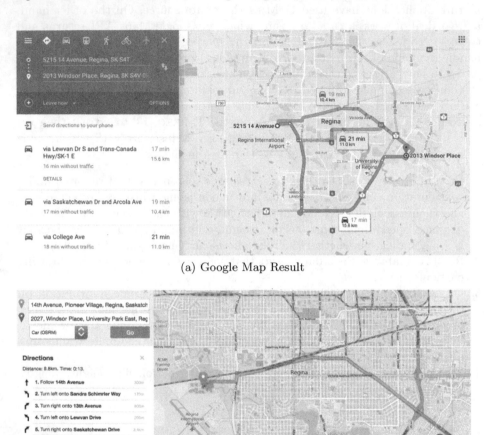

(a) Google Map Result

(b) Open Street Maps Result

Fig. 1. The result of Google Maps and Open Street Maps when trying to find a route from source to destination.

Figure 2 shows the system output w.r.t. three different objective functions: distance, time and fuel efficiency.

(a) Shortest distance.

(b) Quickest path.

(c) Most fuel-efficient path.

Fig. 2. Shortest paths based distance, time and fuel respectively and with no constraints.

Figure 3 shows the shortest path in terms of distance when the vehicle contains hazardous items, i.e., this requires applying the hazard constraint to make sure every road segment in the route allows such items.

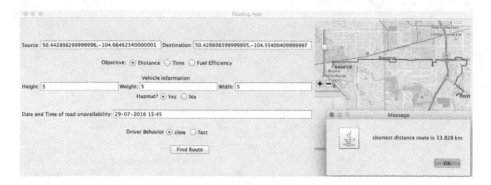

Fig. 3. The shortest distance road for a truck with hazard items when 3% of the roads are unavailable.

Finally, we show screenshots for two more scenarios. These are scenarios corresponding to the two dynamic aspects we mentioned earlier in this paper. The first one corresponds to changes due to the interaction with the user. In this regard, after returning the shortest path as depicted in the top screen shot of Fig. 4, the user decides to change about 30% of the graph information. This is done by clicking the "make some changes" button. Note that we only allow the changes of objectives and edges information. The user updates some of the edges information and submits these changes in order to get the new shortest path. This is shown in screen shot (b) of Fig. 4. The second dynamic aspect corresponds to changes due to external events. In this regard, the graph is updated with a probability (of each edge not been congested) distribution over all its edges. The goal here is to find the most probable shortest path i.e. the one maximizing the joint probability over the graph while minimizing the distance. The bottom screen shot of Figure 4 shows this most probable shortest path.

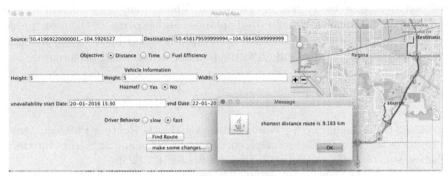

(a) Original graph result

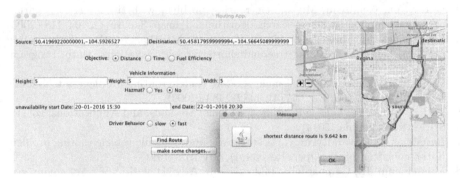

(b) New shortest path returned after randomly changing 30% of the graph information (by clicking on the "make some changes" button)

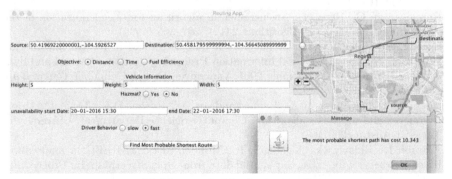

(c) Most probable shortest path

Fig. 4. Screenshots for the incremental change and the most probable shortest path.

5   Conclusion and Future Work

In this work, we have addressed two variants of the shortest route problem and developed an interactive system in this regard. The system in its current format requires lots of interaction with the route planner and experts. In the near future, we plan to have more comprehensive driver profiles and apply some machine learning techniques to learn and elicit the planner criteria and preferences.

References

1. Golden, B.L., Raghavan, S., Wasil, E.A.: The Vehicle Routing Problem: Latest Advances and New Challenges. Operations Research/Computer Science Interfaces Series, vol. 43. Springer Science & Business Media, US (2008)
2. Laporte, G.: The vehicle routing problem: an overview of exact and approximate algorithms. Eur. J. Oper. Res. **59**(3), 345–358 (1992)
3. Bräysy, O., Gendreau, M.: Vehicle routing problem with time windows, part i: route construction and local search algorithms. Transp. Sci. **39**(1), 104–118 (2005)
4. Christofides, N., Mingozzi, A., Toth, P.: Exact algorithms for the vehicle routing problem, based on spanning tree and shortest path relaxations. Math. Program. **20**(1), 255–282 (1981)
5. Eksioglu, B., Vural, A.V., Reisman, A.: The vehicle routing problem: a taxonomic review. Comput. Ind. Eng. **57**(4), 1472–1483 (2009)
6. Toth, P., Vigo, D.: Vehicle Routing: Problems, Methods, and Applications, vol. 18. SIAM, Philadelphia (2014)
7. Bertsimas, D.J., Van Ryzin, G.: A stochastic and dynamic vehicle routing problem in the euclidean plane. Oper. Res. **39**(4), 601–615 (1991)
8. Montemanni, R., Gambardella, L.M., Rizzoli, A.E., Donati, A.V.: Ant colony system for a dynamic vehicle routing problem. J. Comb. Optim. **10**(4), 327–343 (2005)
9. Psaraftis, H.N.: Dynamic vehicle routing: status and prospects. Ann. Oper. Res. **61**(1), 143–164 (1995)
10. Ramalingam, G., Reps, T.: An incremental algorithm for a generalization of the shortest-path problem. J. Algorithms **21**(2), 267–305 (1996)
11. Koenig, S., Likhachev, M.: Incremental a*. In: Advances in Neural Information Processing Systems 14. Neural Information Processing Systems: Natural and Synthetic, NIPS 2011, 3–8 December 2001, Vancouver, British Columbia, Canada, pp. 1539–1546 (2001)
12. Chen, M., Chowdhury, R.A., Ramachandran, V., Roche, D.L., Tong, L.: Priority queues and dijkstra's algorithm. Computer Science Department, University of Texas at Austin (2007)
13. Alarabi, L., Eldawy, A., Alghamdi, R., Mokbel, M.F.: TAREEG: a mapreduce-based web service for extracting spatial data from OpenStreetMap. In: Proceedings of the 2014 ACM SIGMOD International Conference on Management of Data, SIGMOD 2014, pp. 897–900. ACM, New York (2014)

M-NSGA-II: A Memetic Algorithm for Vehicle Routing Problem with Route Balancing

Yuyan Sun, Yuxuan Liang, Zizhen Zhang[(✉)], and Jiahai Wang

School of Data and Computer Science,
Sun Yat-Sen University, Guangzhou, Guangdong, China
zhangzizhen@gmail.com

Abstract. The vehicle routing problem with route balancing (VRPRB) is a variant of classical VRPs. It is a bi-objective optimization problem which considers the total length of routes and the balance issue among different routes. In this paper, the balance objective we introduce is the minimization of the maximal route length, which can effectively avoid the occurrence of distorted solutions. We develop an NSGA-II based memetic algorithm (M-NSGA-II) for the VRPRB. The M-NSGA-II algorithm combines the NSGA-II algorithm with a local search procedure which consists of four local search operators. To evaluate our algorithm, we test it on the standard benchmarks and compare our results with the referenced approach. Moreover, we analyze the effect of different local search operators on M-NSGA-II algorithm. Computational results indicate that our M-NSGA-II algorithm is able to produce better solutions.

Keywords: Vehicle routing problem · Route balancing · Bi-objective · Memetic algorithm

1 Introduction

The vehicle routing problem (VRP) is one of the most popular combinatorial optimization problems in the past several decades. It can be described as the problem of designing an optimal set of routes such that all customers' requirements and the operational constraints are satisfied. In this paper, we consider an extension of the VRP, called the vehicle routing problem with route balancing (VRPRB). The VRPRB we study is to optimize the following two objectives simultaneously.

1. Minimization of the total length of routes.
2. Minimization of the maximal route length.

The first objective comes from the classical VRP and the second objective aims at balancing the length of different vehicle routes. The goal of the problem is to find a set of non-dominated solutions to approximate all the Pareto-optimal solutions of the VRPRB. A solution is called Pareto-optimal, if it is not dominated by any other solutions in the solution space.

© Springer International Publishing AG 2017
S. Benferhat et al. (Eds.): IEA/AIE 2017, Part I, LNAI 10350, pp. 61–71, 2017.
DOI: 10.1007/978-3-319-60042-0_7

In literature, the VRPRB has been receiving more and more attention in recent years. [5] solved VRPRB by adding an elitist diversification mechanism and a parallel model into a meta-heuristic method. The balancing objective they used is the minimization of the difference between the maximal and minimal route length. With the same balancing objective in [5,6] proposed an algorithm called Multi-Start Split-based Path Relinking (MSSPR) to solve VRPRB and compared their results with [5]. Moreover, [8] also used the same balancing objective to solve VRPRB with their proposed algorithm. [7] developed a heuristic algorithm to minimize the travel path and balance drivers' load simultaneously. The proposed balancing objective is to minimize the sum of the working time difference between each vehicle and the vehicle with the shortest working time. [9] introduced an algorithm based on the scatter search meta-heuristic to solve the problem from a Spanish company. The used balancing objective is to minimize the difference between the maximum and minimum route length regarding time. [10] devised a new algorithm, which combines local search and a variant of a greedy randomized adaptive search procedure (GRASP), to find VRPRB solutions. They tried to achieve route balancing by minimizing the difference between the longest and the shortest route. [11] did research on bus routing problem and formulated it as a bi-objective optimization model that deals with the minimization of both the longest route length and the total route length. Tabu search within Multiobjective Adaptive Memory Programming framework was proposed to solve it.

As can be seen from the aforementioned literature, the most commonly used balance objective is the minimization of the difference between the maximal and the minimal route length. However, we find that this objective may lead to distorted solutions, which will be expressed in detail in Sect. 2. This motivates us to modify the landscape of the problem to minimize the maximal route length.

In order to solve the VRPRB, we develop an NSGA-II [3] based memetic algorithm (M-NSGA-II). A route splitting method and a local search procedure are main ingredients of our M-NSGA-II. The contributions of our works include two parts. Firstly, we introduce an effective balance objective (i.e., the minimization of the maximal route length) for the VRPRB to eliminate distorted Pareto-optimal solutions. Secondly, our solution method can provide competitive benchmark results which can serve as baseline for future research on this topic.

2   Problem Definition, Formulation and Properties

The VRPRB is defined on a complete and undirected graph $G = (N, E)$, where $N = \{0, 1, \ldots, n\}$ is the node set and $E = \{(i, j) | i, j \in N\}$ is the edge set. The set N consists of depot 0 and n customers. The following notations are useful to explain our work.

$c_{i,j}$: The length of the edge $(i, j) \in E$;
d_i: The demand for each customer $i \in N \setminus \{0\}$ $(d_0 = 0)$;
V: The collection of m homogeneous vehicles;
C: The capacity of a vehicle in the set V;
Ω: The collection of all the feasible solutions.

A feasible solution $s \in \Omega$ requires that each customer is visited by exactly one route and the vehicle capacity constraint is satisfied. Let $s = \{r_1, r_2, ..., r_m\}$, each route r_i is written by a customer visiting sequence, i.e., $r_i = (v_0^i, v_1^i, v_2^i, ..., v_{n_i}^i, v_{n_i+1}^i)$, where $v_0^i = v_{n_i+1}^i = 0$ and n_i is the number of nodes visited for the i-th route. Let $c(r_i) = \sum_{j=0}^{n_i} c_{v_j^i, v_{j+1}^i}$ be the length of the i-th route. The first objective function is defined as:

$$f_1(s) = \sum_{i=1}^{m} c(r_i) \tag{1}$$

The second objective function defines the balance among different vehicle routes. It can be written as:

$$f_2(s) = \max_{i=1,...,m} c(r_i) \tag{2}$$

$f_2(s)$ is to be minimized. Another commonly used objective function $\bar{f}_2(s)$ is the minimization of the difference between the maximal route length and the minimal route length, namely,

$$\bar{f}_2(s) = \max_{i=1,...,m} c(r_i) - \min_{i=1,...,m} c(r_i) \tag{3}$$

However, minimizing $\bar{f}_2(s)$ may result in *distorted* solutions. A solution s is called *distorted*, if it is Pareto-optimal but some route(s) is not optimal in terms of the route length.

Figure 1 shows two vehicle routes marked in solid lines. The square represents the depot and the circle represent the customers. Routes 1 and 2 have the same total traveling length, which is equal to 6. The difference between the maximal and the minimal route length is 0. When the second objective is defined by Expression (3), the two objectives of this solution can be represented by (12, 0). If we replace Route 2 with the route indicated by the dash lines, then the length of Route 2 becomes 5 and the two objectives of the solution become (11, 1). Both of these two solutions are Pareto-optimal. However, it is obvious that the previous one is *distorted* because Route 2 takes a detour with a larger route length to achieve the balance.

When the second objective is defined by Expression (2), we call it min-max fairness. The min-max fairness will not distort the Pareto-optimal solutions. For example, in Fig. 1, whether Route 2 is marked with the solid lines (the objective values can be represented by (12, 6)) or the dash lines (the objective values can be represented by (11, 6)), the corresponding solutions have the same value of f_2, which is equal to 6. Therefore, (11, 6) is the only Pareto-optimal solution. Route 2 denoted in solid lines is dominated by the route in dash lines and will not appear in the Pareto-optimal solutions.

To sum up, the model of VRPRB can be written as:

$$(\min f_1(s), \min f_2(s)) \tag{4}$$

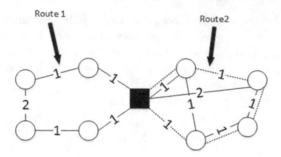

Fig. 1. An example of the distorted solution.

3   Solution Approaches

Our solution method makes changes on NSGA-II [3] to approximate the Pareto-optimal solutions. The mutation process in NSGA-II is replaced by a Local Search (LS) procedure. LS can help to improve the solution quality locally. The main framework of our proposed M-NSGA-II algorithm is shown in Algorithm 1. At the beginning, an initial population P is generated. Thereafter, the recombination is conducted on P to generated P'. We use the tournament selection to select a solution and optimize it $Iter_{ls}$ times with local search operators. Totally, $Iter$ solutions are selected to be optimized. The population P is updated with methods originated from NSGA-II. The algorithm terminates when the number of generations exceeds N_{gen}. The final parameter settings are: population size $|P| = 200$, $Iter_{ls} = 3000$, $Iter = 40$, $N_{gen} = 12000$.

3.1   Solution Encoding and Decoding

We encode a solution of the VRPRB by a giant tour [1] representation. A giant tour is a tour starting from the depot and visiting around all the customers. That is, a giant tour is represented by a permutation of the node set N where 0 (the depot) is always the first node of the permutation.

Given a giant tour, we need to split it into a set of feasible vehicle routes according to the vehicle numbers. Suppose that a giant tour $(0, \pi_1, \pi_2, \ldots, \pi_n)$ is to be split into m routes, where each π_i corresponds to a customer index. Because a solution is associated with two objectives, we implement two kinds of splitting methods as follows.

The first splitting method aims at finding a splitting that minimizes the total route length. $L[k][i]$ represents the minimum distance for k vehicles to visit customers $(\pi_1, \pi_2, \ldots, \pi_i)$. The dynamic programming recursion is:

$$L[k][i] = \min_{0 \leqslant j \leqslant i \ and \ cap(j+1,i) \leqslant C} \{L[k-1][j] + cost(j+1, i)\}, \tag{5}$$

where $cost(j, i)$ and $cap(j, i)$ correspond to the traveling distance and the required capacity of route $(0, \pi_j, \ldots, \pi_i, 0)$.

Algorithm 1. The NSGA-II based memetic algorithm (M-NSGA-II).

1: Generate an initial population P;
2: **while** the number of generations does not exceed N_{gen} **do**
3:     $P' = $ **recombination**(P);
4:     **for** $l = 1$ to $Iter$ **do**
5:         $s \leftarrow$ **tournament**$(P \cup P')$; //select a solution
6:         **for** $ls = 1$ to $Iter_{ls}$ **do**
7:             $k \leftarrow$ generate a random integer in the range $[1, K]$;
8:             $s \leftarrow$ **LS**$_k(s)$;
9:         **end for**
10:    **end for**
11:    $P = $ **update**(P, P');
12: **end while**
13: **return** P;

The second splitting method aims at finding a splitting that minimizes the maximal route length. $F[k][i]$ represents the minimum maximal route length for k vehicles to visit customers $(\pi_1, \pi_2, \ldots, \pi_i)$. The dynamic programming recursion is:

$$F[k][i] = \min_{0 \leqslant j \leqslant i \ and \ cap(j+1, i) \leqslant C} \{\max\{F[k-1][j], cost(j+1, i)\}\} \qquad (6)$$

The above descriptions show that a giant tour can be decoded into two VRPRB solutions s_1 and s_2 according to different splitting methods.

3.2 Population Initialization

Each solution in the initial population is generated in a random way. Specifically, a random permutation is generated to form a giant tour and the corresponding two solutions are obtained by applying two giant tour splitting methods.

3.3 Recombination

A population P' is generated from the original population P through the recombination procedure. Two solutions are iteratively selected as parents from population P and are mated with a probability p_m. The first parent is selected randomly, while the second parent is selected randomly or according to route similarity (The probability of using route similarity is set to 0.01). The similarity between two solutions to VRPRB, according to the Jaccards similarity coefficient, simply as the ratio of the number of shared arcs to the number of total arcs used in both solutions [4]. Readers are referred to [4] for more details of the route similarity method. Every solution is associated with a similarity value, which indicates its similarity with the rest of the population P. The solution with the smallest similarity value and has not been chosen yet will be chosen as the second parent.

The giant tours of two selected parents are recombined to generate two offspring giant tours, where the Order Crossover (OX) operator is applied. For each offspring giant tour, two splitting methods are used to generate two VRPPB solutions. The solution that is non-dominated by the other is added to the population set P'.

3.4   Local Search Operators

The following four local search operators are used in the LS procedure.

1. $exchange(i, j)$. Customer i in route r_1 is replaced by customer j in route r_2. Customer j in route r_2 is replaced by customer i in route r_1.
2. $relocate(i, j)$. Customer i in route r_1 is removed and inserted into the position after customer j in route r_2.
3. $2 - opt(i, j)$. All the customers after position i in route r_1 are removed and inserted into the position after customer j in route r_2. All the customers after position j in route r_2 are removed and inserted into the position after customer i in route r_1.
4. $reverse(i, j)$. Different from the above operators, the reverse operator is used for a single route. Customers from position i to position j are reversed, changing a part of the route from $(i, i + 1, \ldots, j - 1, j)$ to $(j, j - 1, \ldots, i + 1, i)$.

To apply them, two different customers i and j are first drawn from the solution s. Then, the corresponding operator is performed according to the index k (line 7 of Algorithm 1). All the operators must guarantee the feasibility of their resultant solutions.

3.5   Solution Selection and Population Updating

At each iteration of local search, a solution is selected from the population $P \cup P'$. The selection method we used is the tournament selection. In terms of population updating, the non-dominated sorting approach and crowding-distance approach are used. These methods are originated from NSGA-II [3]. The crowding-distance of a solution is calculated as the sum of individual distance values corresponding to each objective. The new population P is updated from $P \cup P'$ using these two methods.

4   Computational Results

We conducted a series of experiments to evaluate the proposed M-NSGA-II approach. For each instance in all experiments conducted, we executed the algorithm 10 independent runs with different random seeds. The first experiment is to compare the performance of M-NSGA-II with another evolutionary approach given by Jozefowiez et al. [5]. The balance objective they considered is the difference between the maximal and minimal route length (see Expression (3)). Seven benchmark instances from [5] were used to evaluate the approach. They reported the best-known value for the total traveling distance, the best found value for the total traveling distance associated with its route balance and the

Table 1. Performance comparison between Jozefowiez et al. (2009)'s method and the M-NSGA-II on VRPRB instances (Minimization of the total traveling distance).

| Instance | Minimizing the total traveling distance | | | | |
| | Best-known | Results from Jozefowiez et al. (2009) | | Our results | |
		Best found	Associated route balance	Best found	Associated route balance
E51-05e	524.61	524.61	20.07	**524.61**	20.07
E76-10e	835.26	835.32	78.10	**835.32**	78.10
E101-08e	826.14	827.39	67.55	**826.14**	97.89
E101-10c	819.56	819.56	93.43	**819.56**	93.43
E121-07c	1042.11	1042.11	146.67	**1042.11**	146.67
E151-12c	1028.42	1047.35	74.78	**1042.32**	82.10
E200-17c	1291.45	1352.46	76.60	**1324.48**	75.64

Table 2. Performance comparison between Jozefowiez et al.(2009)'s method and the M-NSGA-II on VRPRB instances (Minimization of the difference).

| Instance | Minimizing the difference | | | |
| | Results from Jozefowiez et al. (2009) | | Our results | |
	Best found	Associated total traveling distance	Best found	Associated total traveling distance
E51-05e	0.24	618.22	**0.013**	791.05
E76-10e	0.59	1203.98	**0.075**	1142.93
E101-08e	0.29	1871.06	**0.042**	1297.47
E101-10c	1.15	1429.90	**0.029**	1378.36
E121-07c	0.10	2388.30	**0.004**	1598.49
E151-12c	0.80	1484.48	**0.040**	1526.14
E200-17c	1.38	1902.64	**0.070**	1889.03

best found route balance associated with its total length. In order to compare with their results, the second objective function of our M-NSGA-II approach is modified to Expression (3).

The experimental results are shown in Tables 1 and 2. The name of each instance has the form $Ei - jk$, where E indicates that the distance metric is Euclidean, i is the number of customers, j is the number of vehicles and k is an identifier. The column "Best-known" gives the optimal total traveling distance found by existing VRP approaches. In both tables, we mark the numbers in bold if the best found value of M-NSGA-II is better than (or equal to) that of the other. The tables show that M-NSGA-II always wins in terms of either minimizing the total traveling distance or minimizing the difference. Moreover, Table 2 reveals that M-NSGA-II dominates the approach by Jozefowiez et al. [5] on five out of seven instances (E76-10e, E101-08e, E101-10c, E121-07c and E200-17c).

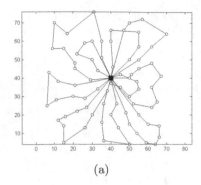   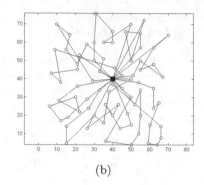

(a)   (b)

Fig. 2. (a) The solution for instance $E76 - 10e$ with the minimum traveling distance. (b) The solution for instance $E76 - 10e$ with the minimum difference.

Table 3. The proposed M-NSGA-II on VRPRB instances.

Instance	Solely minimizing the total traveling distance		Solely minimizing the maximal route length	
	Best found	Associated maximal route length	Best found	Associated total traveling distance
E51-05e	524.61	118.52	111.37	537.89
E76-10e	835.32	119.32	93.04	891.22
E101-08e	827.39	126.90	110.25	871.88
E101-10c	819.56	137.02	120.53	1046.81
E121-07c	1042.11	213.63	200.56	1256.18
E151-12c	1034.81	118.61	100.75	1152.11
E200-17c	1318.98	118.50	99.88	1450.29

We also depict two extreme solutions produced by M-NSGA-II on instance $E76 - 10e$ in Fig. 2(a) and (b), respectively. One solution corresponds to solely minimizing traraling distance and the other corresponds to solely minimizing the difference. Observe from Fig. 2(b) that when the second objective is defined by Expression (3), many routes take detours for achieving route balancing and thus, a *distorted* solution is produced.

We thereby used Expression (2) to define the route balancing and re-executed our approach. The extreme solutions produced are reported in Table 3. Table 3 shows that the proposed algorithm can produce solutions well performing on both goals. In addition, we plot in Fig. 3(a) the non-dominated solutions found by M-NSGA-II for the instance $E76 - 10e$. Among 18 non-dominated solutions found in total, the best solutions corresponding to solely optimizing the first and the second objectives are given by the points (835.3, 119.3) and (891.2, 93.04), respectively. The detailed routes of these two extreme solutions are illustrated

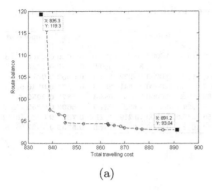
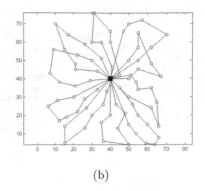

(a)   (b)

Fig. 3. (a) The 13 non-dominated solutions found by M-NSGA-II for instance $E76 -$
$10e$. (b) The solution for instance $E76 - 10e$ with the minimum maximal route length.

in Figs. 2(a) and 3(b). The figures demonstrate that the occurrence of detours
can be effectively avoided.

The second experiment is to analyze the impact of local search operators.
To do so, we set k in line 7 of Algorithm 1 to the fixed index corresponding to
a particular operator. To numerically evaluate the performance of M-NSGA-II
with different operators, the following two indicators are introduced.

1. *Inverted generational distance (IGD)*. The concept of IGD indicator [2] is
   used to estimate the distance of the elements in the approximate Pareto front
   towards those in the true Pareto front. A smaller IGD indicates a better
   approximate Pareto set.
2. *Hypervolume (HV)*. For a bi-objective minimization problem, the HV [12]
   value is given by the area of the union of all rectangles covered by the Pareto
   optimal solutions. Both convergence and diversity of the non-dominated solutions can be reflected from the HV value. The larger the HV value is, the
   closer the corresponding non-dominated solutions are to the Pareto front.

The above two indicators require the true Pareto front. However, it is difficult
to obtain the true Pareto front, so it is set to the front of all the non-dominated
solutions obtained by M-NSGA-II with exchange, relocate, 2-opt, reverse and
a mix of four operators, respectively. For each algorithm, 10 independent runs
with different random seeds were carried out. Table 4 shows the HV values, the
IGD values and the running times by the five algorithms on seven VRPRB
instances, where the best IGD and HV values are marked in bold. Among the
five algorithms, M-NSGA-II with a mix of four operators has the best HV value
and IGD value. It takes advantages of different neighborhood structures and
thus the local search process has more chances to escape from local minima.

Table 4. The performance comparison between different local search operators.

Instance	Exchange			Relocate			2-opt			Reverse			Mixed four operators		
	HV	IGD	Time	HV	IGD	Time	HV	IGD	Time	HV	IGD	Time	HV	IGD	Time
E51-05e	0.0174	1.4593	501.1	0.0000	4.2060	450.7	0.0791	1.1220	616.4	0.0000	10.7666	421.7	**0.3620**	**0.0546**	585.3
E76-10e	0.0701	0.7869	605.3	0.0000	2.3357	537.5	0.2111	0.5724	739.4	0.0000	8.8106	530.8	**0.7165**	**0.1425**	715.2
E101-08e	0.0841	0.5630	745.6	0.3098	0.2576	720.8	0.2284	0.3395	914.5	0.0000	7.7232	630.3	**0.5062**	**0.0975**	860.2
E101-10c	0.6060	0.2602	770.6	0.7504	0.1348	728.7	0.8301	0.1047	944.1	0.0000	3.2641	650.6	**0.8567**	**0.0540**	926.8
E121-07c	0.0002	0.8688	808.5	0.0003	1.5510	749.2	0.0415	0.4769	999.8	0.0000	7.3153	688.4	**0.1875**	**0.2059**	924.7
E151-12c	0.1921	0.5283	1055.0	0.3068	0.3760	1012.9	0.2959	0.3851	1229.0	0.0000	7.6202	924.9	**0.6693**	**0.0860**	1158.7
E200-17c	0.2422	0.4831	1465.6	0.2805	0.4499	1436.9	0.1416	0.6056	1647.0	0.0000	10.2199	1421.4	**0.7354**	**0.0784**	1611.6
Average	0.1731	0.7071	850.2	0.2354	1.3301	805.2	0.2611	0.5152	1012.9	0.0000	7.9600	752.6	**0.5762**	**0.1027**	968.9

5 Conclusions

This paper proposes an NSGA-II based memetic algorithm (M-NSGA-II) for vehicle routing problem with route balancing (VRPRB). We introduce a min-max balance objective for VRPRB and demonstrate its effectiveness in preventing distorted solutions. Experimental results show that M-NSGA-II can attain promising solutions for VRPRB.

To further improve the performance of M-NSGA-II on VRPRB, more advanced search strategies, e.g., large neighborhood search, can be introduced into M-NSGA-II. Moreover, adding more practical constraints, such as multi-depot and time windows into VRPRB is one of the subsequent studies.

Acknowledgments. This research was partially supported by Guangdong Natural Science Funds (No. 2014A030310312, No. 2016A030313264) and National Natural Science Foundation of China (No. 61673403).

References

1. Beasley, J.E.: Route firstcluster second methods for vehicle routing. Omega **11**(4), 403–408 (1983)
2. Coello, C.A.C., Cortés, N.C.: Solving multiobjective optimization problems using an artificial immune system. Genet. Program. Evolvable Mach. **6**(2), 163–190 (2005)
3. Deb, K., Pratap, A., Agarwal, S., Meyarivan, T.: A fast and elitist multiobjective genetic algorithm: Nsga-ii. IEEE Trans. Evol. Comput. **6**(2), 182–197 (2002)
4. Garcia-Najera, A., Bullinaria, J.A.: Bi-objective optimization for the vehicle routing problem with time windows: using route similarity to enhance performance. In: Ehrgott, M., Fonseca, C.M., Gandibleux, X., Hao, J.-K., Sevaux, M. (eds.) EMO 2009. LNCS, vol. 5467, pp. 275–289. Springer, Heidelberg (2009). doi:10.1007/978-3-642-01020-0_24
5. Jozefowiez, N., Semet, F., Talbi, E.G.: An evolutionary algorithm for the vehicle routing problem with route balancing. Eur. J. Oper. Res. **195**(3), 761–769 (2009)
6. Lacomme, P., Prins, C., Prodhon, C., Ren, L.: A multi-start split based path relinking (MSSPR) approach for the vehicle routing problem with route balancing. Eng. Appl. Artif. Intell. **38**, 237–251 (2015)
7. Lee, T.R., Ueng, J.H.: A study of vehicle routing problems with load-balancing. Int. J. Phys. Distrib. Logistics Manage. **29**(10), 646–657 (1999)

8. Mandal, S.K., Pacciarelli, D., Lkketangen, A., Hasle, G.: A memetic NSGA-II for the bi-objective mixed capacitated general routing problem. J. Heuristics **21**(3), 359–390 (2015)
9. Melián-Batista, B., De Santiago, A., AngelBello, F., Alvarez, A.: A bi-objective vehicle routing problem with time windows: a real case in tenerife. Appl. Soft Comput. **17**, 140–152 (2014)
10. Oyola, J., Løkketangen, A.: Grasp-ASP: an algorithm for the CVRP with route balancing. J. Heuristics **20**(4), 361–382 (2014)
11. Pacheco, J., Caballero, R., Laguna, M., Molina, J.: Bi-objective bus routing: an application to school buses in rural areas. Transp. Sci. **47**(3), 397–411 (2013)
12. Zitzler, E., Laumanns, M., Thiele, L., et al.: SPEA2: improving the strength pareto evolutionary algorithm. In: Eurogen, vol. 3242, pp. 95–100 (2001)

A Matrix-Based Implementation of DE Algorithm: The Compensation and Deficiency

Jeng-Shyang Pan[1], Zhenyu Meng[2(✉)], Huarong Xu[3], and Xiaoqing Li[4]

[1] Fujian Provincial Key Lab of Big Data Mining and Applications,
Fujian University of Technology, Fuzhou, China
[2] Department of Computer Science and Technology,
Harbin Institute of Technology Shenzhen Graduate School, Shenzhen, China
mzy1314@gmail.com
[3] Department of Computer Science and Technology,
Xiamen University of Technology, Xiamen, China
[4] Shenzhen Institute of Advanced Technology, Chinese Academy of Sciences,
Shenzhen, China

Abstract. Differential Evolution has become a very popular continuous optimization algorithm since its inception as its simplicity, easy coding and good performance over kinds of optimization problems. Difference operator in donor vector calculation is the key feature of DE algorithm. Usually, base vector and difference vectors selection in calculating a donor usually cost extra lines of condition judgement. Moreover, these vectors are not equally selected from the individual population. These lead to more perturbation in optimization performance. To tackling this disadvantage of DE implementation, a matrix-based implementation of DE algorithm is advanced herein this paper. Three commonly used DE implementation approaches in literature are also presented and contrasted. CEC2013 test suites for real-parameter optimization are used as the test-beds for these comparison. Experiment results show that the proposed matrix-based implementation of DE algorithm performs better on optimization performance than the common implementation schemes of DE algorithm with similar time complexity.

Keywords: Benchmark function · Differential evolution · Global optimization · Matrix-based implementation

1 Introduction

Optimization algorithm is proposed to tackle kinds of complex problems in real-world applications. The key criterion is that the algorithm itself should not be complicated. Differential Evolution is such a simple but powerful algorithm, and it was first introduced by Storn [1] in 1995. The canonical DE algorithm is originated from Genetic Annealing algorithm which can be considered as a hybrid algorithm of Genetic Algorithm (GA) [2] and Simulated Annealing (SA) [3]. Therefore, operations such as mutation, crossover and selection used in GA

© Springer International Publishing AG 2017
S. Benferhat et al. (Eds.): IEA/AIE 2017, Part I, LNAI 10350, pp. 72–81, 2017.
DOI: 10.1007/978-3-319-60042-0_8

are also inherited into DE algorithm, though the sequence of the operations is different. Consequently, mutation and crossover play important roles in the performance of DE algorithm when tackling different objective functions. Price et al. in [5] introduced 10 working strategies including 5 mutation strategies and 2 crossover strategies, and the general convention "DE/x/y/z" was used to differ these DE variants. DE denotes the different evolution algorithm, x denotes the base vector in calculation of the mutant vector, y denotes the number of difference pairs used in the calculation of mutant vector and z denotes one of the different crossover schemes. Therefore, the five mutation strategies can be written as "DE/$rand$/1", "DE/$best$/1", "DE/$target - to - best$/1", "DE/$rand$/2" and "DE/$best$/2", and the two crossover strategies are binomial crossover "DE/x/y/bin" and exponential crossover "DE/x/y/exp". Table 1 gives the related mutant vectors of all these DE variants. $X_{i,G}$ denotes the target/current vector of the ith individual in the population of the Gth generation. $X_{r_k,G}, k \in [0, 4]$ denotes a vector of a randomly chosen individual from the population in the Gth generation. $X_{gbest,G}$ denotes the global best vector of which individual finds the best solution of the objective function in the Gth generation. $V_{i,G}$ is the corresponding donor vector of target vector $X_{i,G}$ for mutation.

Table 1. The corresponding mutant vector $V_{i,G}$ of these five DE mutant schemes

No.	DE/x/y	Equation
1	DE/$rand$/1	$V_{i,G} = X_{r0,G} + F * (X_{r1,G} - X_{r2,G})$
2	DE/$best$/1	$V_{i,G} = X_{gbest,G} + F * (X_{r1,G} - X_{r2,G})$
3	DE/$target -$ $to - best$/1	$V_{i,G} = X_{i,G} + F * (X_{gbest,G} - X_{i,G}) + F * (X_{r1,G} - X_{r2,G})$
4	DE/$rand$/2	$V_{i,G} = X_{r0,G} + F * (X_{r1,G} - X_{r2,G}) + F * (X_{r3,G} - X_{r4,G})$
5	DE/$best$/2	$V_{i,G} = X_{gbest,G} + F * (X_{r1,G} - X_{r2,G}) + F * (X_{r3,G} - X_{r4,G})$

There are also three control parameters used in DE algorithm, the scale factor F of difference pair $X_{r1,G} - X_{r2,G}$ in the mutant vector, the crossover rate Cr used in the crossover operation, and the population size ps restricting the number of individuals used in the population. Usually, F is restricted in the range $[0.4, 0.9]$, also a constant initial value of $F = 0.5$ is a good choice [4]. The recommend value of Cr is in $[0.1, 0.9]$, a smaller Cr value, e.g. $Cr = 0.1$, usually performs better on uni-modal and separable objective functions while a larger Cr value, e.g. $Cr = 0.9$, usually performs better on multi-modal and nonseparable objective functions [6], and an initial value of $Cr = 0.9$ is a good choice. The population size ps defines how many individuals are there in the population, and it is usually to be set a 5–10 integral multiple number of objective function dimensions, e.g., $ps = 10 \cdot D$. Moreover, if there are D dimensions in objective function, there are D parameters in the current vector $X_{i,G}$, $X_{i,G} = (x_{i1,G}, x_{i2,G}, ..., x_{ij,G}, ..., x_{iD,G})$, $j \in [1, D]$, $x_{ij,G}$ is the jth parameter of ith vector $X_{i,G}$ in the population. For consistency, $x_{ij,G}$ in the paper is used to denote the jth parameter of $X_{i,G}$, $X_{i,G}$ is to denote the vector of the ith individual in the population. $\widehat{X_G}$, with the equation $\widehat{X_G} = [X_{1,G}, X_{2,G}, ..., X_{i,G}, ..., X_{ps,G}]^T$, $i \in [1, ps]$, is used to denote the population matrix of all the individuals in G^{th} generation.

As we know, different coding styles for tackling the same problem consume different time. The default DE algorithm is coded in a parameter-by-parameter way, and the selection of base vector and difference vectors in calculation of donor vector usually cost extra lines of condition judgement. Moreover, the selection of base vector and difference vectors are not equally chosen from the individual population. These cause more perturbation in optimization performance of DE algorithm. In this paper a matrix-based implementation of DE algorithm is proposed to tackle the above mentioned weakness. Several canonical DE implementation schemes are contrasted with the proposed matrix-based implement scheme. CEC2013 test suites for real-parameter optimization are used for the verification of the new proposed implement scheme. The rest of the paper is organized as follows: some commonly used implementation scheme of DE are presented first in Sect. 2. Then a new matrix-based implementation approach of DE algorithm is advanced in Sect. 3. CEC2013 benchmarks for real-parameter optimization are described in Sect. 4 and the deficiency and compensation of these different implementation approaches are also discussed and presented in this section. Finally, conclusion is given in Sect. 5.

2   The Common Implementation of Canonical DE Algorithm

For the default canonical DE algorithm, the mutation and binomial crossover equations are given in Eqs. 1 and 2 respectively. The donor vector can be written as $V_{i,G} = [v_{i1,G}, v_{i2,G}, ..., v_{ij,G}, ..., v_{iD,G}]$, $j \in [1, D]$ and the trial vector written as $U_{i,G} = [u_{i1,G}, u_{i2,G}, ..., u_{ij,G}, ..., u_{iD,G}]$, $j \in [1, D]$. Crossover starts at a random number $J = rnbr(i)$ indexed parameter in donor vector $V_{i,G}$, and this parameter is inherited into the trial vector $U_{i,G}$. Then the index cursor goes to the next parameter (if J is the last parameter in $V_{i,G}$, when the index cursor goes next, it points to the first parameter of the $V_{i,G}$.), and a new random number $randb(j) \in (0, 1)$ is generated and measured with crossover rate Cr. If $randb(j) \leq Cr$, parameter of the donor vector is inherited into the trial vector, otherwise parameter of the target vector is inherited into the trial vector.

$$Mutation : V_{i,G} = X_{r_0,G} + F * (X_{r_1,G} - X_{r_2,G}) \tag{1}$$

$$Crossover : u_{ij,G} = \begin{cases} v_{ij,G} & if(randb(j) \leq Cr)\, or\, J = rnbr(i) \\ x_{ij,G} & if(randb(j) > Cr)\, or\, J \neq rnbr(i) \end{cases} \tag{2}$$

In the mutation equation, three vectors with the corresponding individuals are selected from the population, and they are $X_{r_0,G}$, $X_{r_1,G}$ and $X_{r_2,G}$.

The selection of these individuals can be separated into two parts, the based vector $X_{r_0,G}$ selection and difference vectors selection $(X_{r_1,G}, X_{r_2,G})$. For the base vector selection, there are mainly three schemes in literature. The first selection scheme is called "Random Selection Without Restriction". Each individual in the population needs a randomly chosen base vector $X_{r_0,G}$, and the index r_0 is generated according to Eq. 3.

$$r_0 = ceil(rand(0, 1) \cdot ps) \tag{3}$$

As the base indices are selected without restriction, some vectors may be picked more than once per generation while others are omitted in the generation [5]. The second selection scheme of base vector $X_{r_0,G}$ is called "Permutation Selection". A randomly chosen sequence from $ps!$ permutations is used for the base vector of $V_{i,G}$. If the chosen sequence is $s = [s_1, s_2, ..., s_{ps}]$, then the index of the base vector for the calculation of $V_{i,G}$ satisfies $r_0 = s[i]$. The third selection scheme of base vector in the mutant calculation is called "Random Offset Selection". A random offset number "os" is used for the calculation of the index in the base vector, and the calculation equation is shown in Eq. 4. All these three base vector selection schemes are illustrated in Fig. 1.

$$os = ceil(rand(0, 1) \cdot ps)$$
$$r_0 = (i + os - 1)\%ps + 1 \tag{4}$$

For the difference vectors selection, $X_{r_1,G}$ and $X_{r_2,G}$, there are usually two different schemes with respect to base vector selection. When the "Random Selection Without Restriction" is used for base vector selection, the indices of difference vectors and base vector are selected according to Algorithm 1, and the indices of r_0, r_1 and r_2 are implemented exclusively.

When the "Permutation Selection" is used for the base vector selection, the indices of $X_{r_1,G}$ and $X_{r_2,G}$ satisfies $r_1 = s[i\%ps + 1]$ and $r_2 = s[(i + 1)\%ps + 1]$.

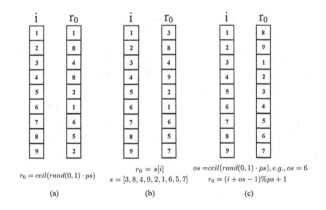

Fig. 1. Three selection of base vector selection in the mutation operation of DE algorithm. (a) is the illustration of "Random Selection Without Restriction"; (b) is the "Permutation Selection"; (c) is the "Random Offset Selection".

Algorithm 1. Pseudo code of indices r_0, r_1 and r_2 selection utilizing random scheme

For the index selection of donor vector $V_{i,G}$
repeat
    $r_0 = ceil(rand(0, 1) \cdot ps)$
until $r_0 \neq i$
repeat
    $r_1 = ceil(rand(0, 1) \cdot ps)$
until $r_1 \neq r_0 \& \& r_1 \neq i$
repeat
    $r_2 = ceil(rand(0, 1) \cdot ps)$
until $r_2 \neq r_0 \& \& r_2 \neq r_1 \& \& r_2 \neq i$

Algorithm 2. Pseudo code of indices r_0, r_1 and r_2 selection utilizing offset scheme

$os = ceil(rand(0, 1) \cdot ps)$
$r_0 = (i + os - 1)\% ps + 1$
repeat
    $os_1 = ceil(rand(0, 1) \cdot ps)$
until $os_1 \neq os$
$r_1 = (i + os_1 - 1)\% ps + 1$
repeat
    $os_2 = ceil(rand(0, 1) \cdot ps)$
until $os_2 \neq os \ \& \& \ os_2 \neq os_1$
$r_2 = (i + os_2 - 1)\% ps + 1$

The permutation s in each generation is different. When the "Random Offset Selection" is used for base vector selection, the indices of difference vectors and base vectors are selected according to Algorithm 2.

3   The Matrix-Based Implementation of DE

In this section, a matrix-based implementation of DE is advanced. Also, $\widehat{X_G}$ is used to denote the population matrix of all individuals in G^{th} population with the equation shown in Eq. 5. $X_{i,G}$ denotes the vector of ith individual in the population and $X_{i,G}$ is also the ith row vector of matrix $\widehat{X_G}$. $\widehat{V_G}$ is used to denote the donor matrix with the equation shown in Eq. 6. $V_{i,G}$ denotes the donor vector of ith individual in the population and $V_{i,G}$ is also the ith row vector of matrix $\widehat{V_G}$. $\widehat{U_G}$ is used to denote the trial matrix with the equation shown in Eq. 7. $U_{i,G}$ denotes the trial vector of the ith individual in the population and it is also the ith row vector of matrix $\widehat{U_G}$.

$$\widehat{X_G} = [X_{1,G}, X_{2,G}, ..., X_{i,G}, ..., X_{ps,G}]^T, i \in [1, ps] \tag{5}$$

$$\widehat{V_G} = [V_{1,G}, V_{2,G}, ..., V_{i,G}, ..., V_{ps,G}]^T, i \in [1, ps] \tag{6}$$

$$\widehat{U_G} = [U_{1,G}, U_{2,G}, ..., U_{i,G}, ..., U_{ps,G}]^T, i \in [1, ps] \tag{7}$$

Then $\widehat{U_G}$ can be calculated by Eq. 8. $\bigotimes$ is to denote element-wise multiplication, same as ".*" in Matlab software. M is the crossover matrix, and it can be calculated according to Eq. 9, the result of element-wise binary "OR" operation between binary matrix M_{tmp} and binary matrix One. M_{tmp} is initialized according to Eq. 10. rnd_{ij} is a random number in the range $(0, 1)$, and expression $rnd_{ij} \leq Cr$ return a binary value "0" or "1" with regard to the value of crossover rate Cr. Matrix One is initialized according to Eq. 11, the elements in the first column of One_{tmp} are all set to 1, and all the left elements are set to "0". Symbol $\rightarrow$ is to denote the permutation operation, elements in each row vector of One_{tmp} is randomly permutated, and each row is dealt separately, then we can get matrix One. $\overline{M}$ means a element-wise binary inverse operation of matrix M, the inverse value of 1-element is 0, and the inverse value of 0-element is 1. Crossover matrix M as well as element-wise multiplication $\bigotimes$ operation together implements the crossover operation in canonical DE algorithm.

$$\widehat{U_G} = \overline{M} \bigotimes \widehat{X_G} + M \bigotimes \widehat{V_G} \tag{8}$$

$$M = M_{tmp} | One \tag{9}$$

$$M_{tmp} = \begin{bmatrix} rnd_{11} \leq Cr & rnd_{12} \leq Cr & \cdots & rnd_{1D} \leq Cr \\ rnd_{21} \leq Cr & rnd_{22} \leq Cr & \cdots & rnd_{2D} \leq Cr \\ \vdots & \vdots & \vdots & \vdots \\ rnd_{i1} \leq Cr & rnd_{i2} \leq Cr & rnd_{ij} \leq Cr & rnd_{iD} \leq Cr \\ \vdots & \vdots & \vdots & \vdots \\ rnd_{ps,1} \leq Cr & rnd_{ps,2} \leq Cr & \cdots & rnd_{ps,D} \leq Cr \end{bmatrix} \tag{10}$$

$$One_{tmp} = \begin{bmatrix} 1 & 0 & \cdots & 0 \\ 1 & 0 & \cdots & 0 \\ \vdots & \vdots & \cdots & \vdots \\ 1 & 0 & \cdots & 0 \end{bmatrix} \rightarrow \begin{bmatrix} 0 & 1 & \cdots & 0 \\ 0 & \cdots & 0 & 1 \\ \vdots & \vdots & \cdots & \vdots \\ 0 & \cdots & 1 & 0 \end{bmatrix} = One \tag{11}$$

For the calculation of donor matrix $\widehat{V_G}$, a new approach is proposed in the matrix-based implementation of DE. It is somewhat similar with the "Permutation Selection", but the new approach is of different thought. The indices of r_0, r_1 and r_2 are generated all by permutation, and each index is selected with an independent sequence. Three randomly chosen sequences s, s' and s'' are from $ps!$ permutations. r_0 utilizes sequence s for base vector section of $V_{i,G}$ ($r_0 = s[i]$), r_1 utilizes sequence s' ($r_1 = s'[i]$) and r_2 utilizes sequence s'' ($r_2 = s''[i]$) for difference vectors selection. The Matlab code of donor matrix $\widehat{V_G}$ calculation is shown in Fig. 2. After the calculation of donor matrix $\widehat{V_G}$, selection is finally made between $\widehat{U_G}$ and $\widehat{X_G}$. If the ith row vector $U_{i,G}$ in matrix $\widehat{U_G}$ secures a better fitness value of the objective function than the target vector $X_{i,G}$ in $\widehat{X_G}$, then $X_{i,G+1} = U_{i,G}$, otherwise $X_{i,G+1} = X_{i,G}$.

```
%pos is the population matrix
posr0 = pos(randperm(size(pos,1))',:);
posr1 = pos(randperm(size(pos,1))',:);
posr2 = pos(randperm(size(pos,1))',:);
%vmat is the donor matrix
vmat = posr0+F*(posr1-posr2);
```

Fig. 2. Illustration of Matlab code for donor matrix calculation. *pos* in the above Matlab code is to denote the population matrix $\widehat{X_G}$, *posr0* denotes individual sequence randomly permutated matrix according to sequence *s*, *posr1* denotes individual sequence randomly permutated matrix according to s', and *posr2* denotes the corresponding permutated matrix to s''.

4   Benchmark Functions and Experiment Analysis

Performance evaluation of optimization algorithm is difficult as the limit theory, so benchmark function play important role in the algorithm analysis. Here in this section, CEC2013[1] test suite for real-parameter optimization is used for performance evaluation of these different implementation of DE algorithm. The three canonical DE implementation is notated as "Rand-DE", "Permutate-DE" and "Offset-DE", and the new proposed matrix-based implementation of DE is notated as "Matrix-DE". CEC2013 benchmarks suggest a fix-cost evaluation criterion, and totally $100 \times D \times ps$ function evaluations are allowed and set as the termination with $100 \times D$ generation for each individual in the evolution. The crossover rate Cr is set to $Cr = 0.9$ and the fluctuation coefficient F is set to $F = 0.5$ as recommended for uncertain optimization problems, the same control parameter setting of F and Cr as [6–8].

Optimization performance and time consumption are two aspects of our evaluation for the matrix-based approach in contrast with three canonical implementations. Table 2 shows the contrasts among the three implementation schemes of canonical DE algorithm, and we can see that "Permutation Selection" (Permutate-DE) secures the best implementation approach of DE algorithm. Table 3 shows the comparison between the best implementation of DE algorithm "Permutate-DE" and the new proposed matrix-based approach "Matrix-DE". We can see that the new proposed matrix-based DE implementation approach has an overall better performance on CEC2013 real-parameter optimization test suite, and the "Matrix-DE" performs very well on function f_1–f_7, f_9–f_{20}, f_{22}–f_{26} and f_{27}. For the time consumption evaluation, computation time just for function f_{14} in the CEC2013 test suite is contrasted in this section. The total time consumption can be separated into two parts, one part T_1 is the time consumed for generating trial vectors $U_{i,G}$ (or trial matrix in the matrix-based implementation $\widehat{U_G}$). The other part T_2 is the time consumed in the calculation of fitness values for the objective function. A base time T_0 is used for the evaluation. T_0 denotes time consumption for the calculation of sequent expressions including $x = 0.55 + double(i)$, $x = x + x$, $x = x./2$, $x = x*x$, $x = sqrt(x)$, $x = log(x)$,

---

[1] http://www3.ntu.edu.sg/home/epnsugan/ EA benchmark/CEC Competitions.

Table 2. Best value (minimum), mean and standard deviation of 20–run fitness error comparisons among different kinds of DE implementation schemes including "Rnd-DE", "Permutate-DE" and "Offset-DE". The population size $ps = 100$ and generation of particles $gen = 100$ are the same with totally Number of Function Evaluations NFEs$= 100 \cdot ps \cdot D$. The best results of the comparisons are emphasized in **BOLD-FACE**.

10D	Rnd-DE			Permutate-DE			Offset-DE		
No.	best	mean	std	best	mean	std	best	mean	std
f_1	0	0	0	0	0	0	0	0	0
f_2	3.8881E-11	3.3591E-10	4.2589E-10	5.8435E-11	**2.5941E-10**	2.3899E-10	**1.1141E-11**	4.4961E-10	5.5046E-10
f_3	3.6558E-04	1.8614E-01	2.3875E-01	**9.7595E-07**	**1.1347E-01**	8.5355E-02	7.1491E-04	1.1129E+00	2.2459E+00
f_4	**2.2737E-13**	**1.9668E-12**	1.6549E-12	6.8212E-13	2.9331E-12	2.2724E-12	4.5475E-13	3.5584E-12	3.0239E-12
f_5	0	0	0	0	0	0	0	0	0
f_6	0	9.0438E-11	2.7522E-10		1.6627E-11	6.9156E-11	0	5.1170E-11	2.2642E-10
f_7	1.1778E-04	**4.4796E-04**	3.6589E-04	2.0778E-04	6.8388E-04	9.6039E-04	**9.8420E-05**	4.9735E-04	2.9058E-04
f_8	**2.0185E+01**	2.0355E+01	6.9194E-002	2.0268E+01	2.0362E+01	5.3706E-02	2.0198E+01	**2.0350E+01**	6.5405E-02
f_9	2.9997E-07	7.0557E-01	7.7929E-01	**8.4759E-08**	**4.3433E-01**	3.8604E-01	5.6146E-04	4.5209E-01	6.4022E-01
f_{10}	**1.4795E-02**	3.8502E-01	1.4657E-01	2.2128E-02	**3.7626E-01**	1.4121E-01	2.4640E-02	3.7939E-01	1.3356E-01
f_{11}	**9.8852E+00**	1.7209E+01	3.1343E+00	1.2044E+01	**1.6759E+01**	3.0977E+00	1.2151E+01	1.8564E+01	3.4448E+00
f_{12}	2.0016E+01	2.6773E+01	3.0158E+00	**1.0991E+01**	2.5647E+01	5.8164E+00	1.6471E+01	**2.4573E+01**	3.4991E+00
f_{13}	1.7328E+01	2.6334E+01	3.9748E+00	1.8067E+01	2.7007E+01	4.8699E+00	**1.5519E+01**	**2.4899E+01**	4.9885E+00
f_{14}	8.9451E+02	1.0407E+03	8.0574E+01	7.9776E+02	8.9983E+02	1.3395E+02	**5.8240E+02**	**6.9988E+02**	1.7903E+02
f_{15}	1.0926E+03	**1.2861E+03**	1.0297E+02	**9.6334E+02**	1.3221E+03	1.6822E+02	1.1722E+03	1.3222E+03	9.7849E+01
f_{16}	**5.1122E-01**	**1.0118E+00**	2.0018E-01	5.1498E-01	1.0453E+00	2.2742E-01	8.4118E-01	1.0405E+00	1.5569E-01
f_{17}	2.2318E+01	2.9321E+01	3.0795E+00	**2.1931E+01**	**2.8733E+01**	3.8426E+00	2.5468E+01	2.9775E+01	2.6595E+00
f_{18}	2.7723E+01	**3.5728E+01**	4.2339E+00	**2.6266E+01**	3.6034E+01	4.5454E+00	2.6386E+01	3.6037E+01	3.8690E+00
f_{19}	1.5216E+00	2.1227E+00	2.5868E-01	**1.2552E+00**	**2.0079E+00**	3.1822E-01	1.6149E+00	2.1302E+00	2.6954E-01
f_{20}	1.9158E+00	2.5874E+00	2.8104E-01	2.0670E+00	2.5752E+00	2.4094E-01	**1.8476E+00**	**2.5385E+00**	2.3572E-01
f_{21}	1.0000E+02	3.4515E+02	9.9953E+01	**1.0000E+02**	**3.3514E+02**	1.0409E+02	2.0000E+02	3.4014E+02	9.4124E+01
f_{22}	**2.9552E+02**	1.0184E+03	2.5266E+02	6.4565E+02	**9.7015E+02**	1.7972E+02	7.2195E+02	1.0422E+03	1.4313E+02
f_{23}	9.7253E+02	1.2896E+03	2.3088E+02	**8.3693E+02**	1.2732E+03	1.8485E+02	8.7380E+02	**1.2590E+03**	1.7975E+02
f_{24}	**1.1811E+02**	**1.9342E+02**	2.4962E+01	1.2853E+02	1.9739E+02	1.6374E+01	2.0000E+02	2.0199E+02	3.1134E+00
f_{25}	2.0000E+02	2.0091E+02	1.8629E+00	**1.2873E+02**	**1.9712E+02**	1.6182E+01	1.3345E+02	1.9735E+02	1.5133E+01
f_{26}	1.1806E+02	**1.5121E+02**	3.6888E+01	**1.1664E+02**	1.5834E+02	3.8768E+01	1.1881E+02	1.6336E+02	3.7699E+01
f_{27}	3.0000E+02	**3.0000E+02**	4.0084E-04	3.0000E+02	3.0500E+02	2.2361E+01	3.0000E+02	3.0500E+02	2.2361E+01
f_{28}	1.0000E+02	2.8000E+02	6.1559E+01	1.0000E+02	**2.3000E+02**	9.7872E+01	1.0000E+02	2.7000E+02	7.3270E+01

$x = exp(x)$, $y = x/x$, with variable i from $i = 1$ to $i = 1000000$. As time consumption T_1 for the trial vector calculation is usually a relative small value, 1000000 times calculation of T_1 is collected for comparison. $\frac{T_2}{T_0}$ is used as a criterion for computation time evaluation, because if the time for the calculation of fitness value counts for a large proportion in T_2, time consumption comparison may have little sense in the evaluation, and optimization performance play the key role in algorithm evaluation.

Table 4 shows the time comparison, both T_1 and T_2 are the average value of 20 runs. We can see from the table that "Offset-DE" implementation scheme consumes the least time and all these four implementation schemes including the proposed matrix-based implementation have similar performance for the time consumption evaluation. But, the new proposed matrix-based implementation scheme of DE algorithm secure the best optimization performance in all these comparisons. Moreover, the whole cover selection of the base vector in donor calculation show bad effect on the optimization performance, and the allowance of zero vectors in the difference pair $X_{r_1,G} - X_{r_2,G}$ shows good effect on the optimization performance. The new proposed matrix-based implementation scheme of DE only uses four lines of code for the donor vector calculation, and shows better performance than the common three implementation schemes of DE. This implementation is a very simple and easy coding approach for kinds of application. Also, the permutation operation is a new way to tackle the inborn weakness

Table 3. Best value (minimum), mean and standard deviation of 20–run fitness error comparisons between the best DE implementation scheme "Permutate-DE" and the new proposed matrix-based implementation "Matrix-DE". The population size $ps = 100$ and generation of particles $gen = 100$ are the same with totally Number of Function Evaluations NFEs $= 100 \cdot ps \cdot D$. The best results of the comparisons are emphasized in **BOLDFACE**.

10D	Permutate-DE				Matrix-DE			
No.	best	median	mean	std	best	median	mean	std
f_1	0	0	0	0	0	0	0	0
f_2	5.8435E-11	1.5712E-10	2.5941E-10	2.3899E-10	**2.2737E-13**	**1.4779E-12**	**1.5689E-12**	**1.2711E-12**
f_3	9.7595E-07	1.2090E-01	1.1347E-01	8.5355E-02	**2.0145E-10**	**4.6360E-02**	**1.0335E-01**	**1.4701E-01**
f_4	6.8212E-13	1.9327E-12	2.9331E-12	2.2724E-12	**0**	**0**	**0**	**0**
f_5	0	0	0	0	0	0	0	0
f_6	0	0	1.6627E-011	6.9156E-011	0	0	1.0067E-09	4.5012E-09
f_7	2.0778E-04	5.2457E-04	6.8388E-04	9.6039E-04	**2.4677E-05**	**8.1219E-05**	**1.0148E-04**	**7.0291E-05**
f_8	**2.0268E+01**	**2.0354E+01**	**2.0362E+01**	**5.3706E-02**	2.0286E+01	2.0441E+01	2.0430E+01	7.5537E-02
f_9	8.4759E-08	5.0895E-01	**4.3433E-01**	**3.8604E-01**	2.3874E-12	8.2989E-02	5.9103E-01	7.2119E-01
f_{10}	2.2127E-02	3.8862E-01	3.7626E-01	1.4121E-01	**0**	5.7789E-02	**6.7577E-02**	**8.2772E-02**
f_{11}	1.2044E+01	1.5877E+01	1.6759E+01	3.0977E+00	**0**	**0**	**1.7359E-01**	**3.7023E-01**
f_{12}	1.0991E+01	2.6927E+01	2.5647E+01	5.8164E+00	**1.9899E+00**	**6.9454E+00**	**8.0788E+00**	**4.3558E+00**
f_{13}	1.8067E+01	2.7614E+01	2.7007E+01	4.8699E+00	**1.9899E+00**	**9.5863E+00**	**1.0851E+01**	**6.0133E+00**
f_{14}	7.9776E+02	9.9642E+02	9.8983E+02	1.3395E+02	**3.6023E+00**	**2.5157E+01**	**2.9344E+01**	**2.5162E+01**
f_{15}	9.6334E+02	1.3076E+03	1.3221E+03	1.6822E+02	**1.2554E+02**	**1.0541E+03**	**1.0016E+03**	**3.4018E+02**
f_{16}	5.1498E-01	1.0604E+00	1.0453E+00	2.2742E-01	**3.5837E-01**	**1.0332E+00**	1.0666E+00	3.0073E-01
f_{17}	2.1931E+01	2.9138E+01	2.8733E+01	3.8426E+00	**1.0373E+01**	**1.1347E+01**	**1.1538E+01**	**8.0462E-01**
f_{18}	2.6266E+01	3.6070E+01	3.6034E+01	4.5454E+00	**1.7028E+01**	**2.9149E+01**	**2.8212E+01**	**5.4803E+00**
f_{19}	1.2552E+00	2.0425E+00	2.0079E+00	3.1822E-01	**2.2073E-01**	**5.9760E-01**	**6.1002E-01**	**1.7505E-01**
f_{20}	2.0670E+00	2.5717E+00	2.5752E+00	2.4094E-01	**1.7433E+00**	**2.5499E+00**	**2.4892E+00**	4.5520E-01
f_{21}	**1.0000E+02**	4.0019E+02	**3.3514E+02**	1.0409E+02	2.0000E+02	4.0019E+02	3.4014E+02	9.4124E+01
f_{22}	6.4565E+02	1.0006E+03	9.7015E+02	1.7972E+02	**1.5886E+01**	**6.6862E+01**	**8.3986E+01**	**6.6537E+01**
f_{23}	8.3693E+02	1.2855E+03	1.2732E+03	1.8485E+02	**3.8965E+02**	**9.4140E+02**	**9.4798E+02**	2.5429E+02
f_{24}	1.2853E+02	2.0000E+02	1.9739E+02	1.6374E+01	**1.0855E+02**	2.0000E+02	**1.8762E+02**	3.3120E+01
f_{25}	1.2873E+02	2.0000E+02	1.9712E+01	1.6182E+01	**1.0744E+02**	2.0000E+02	**1.9583E+02**	2.0851E+01
f_{26}	1.1664E+02	1.2877E+02	1.5834E+02	3.8768E+01	**1.0199E+02**	**1.0597E+02**	**1.1819E+02**	**2.9135E+01**
f_{27}	3.0000E+02	3.0000E+02	3.0500E+02	2.2361E+01	3.0000E+02	3.0000E+02	**3.0000E+01**	3.2636E-06
f_{28}	1.0000E+02	3.0000E+02	**2.3000E+02**	9.7872E+01	1.0000E+02	3.0000E+02	2.8000E+02	6.1559E+01

Table 4. Time consumption comparison under 10D function f_{14} in CEC2013 test suite.

Algorithms	T_0	T_1	T_2	$\frac{T_2}{T_0}$
Rnd-DE	0.1226	$\frac{19.1132}{1000000}$	1.0913	8.9160
Permutate-DE	0.1226	$\frac{27.6438}{1000000}$	1.1010	8.9804
Offset-DE	0.1226	$\frac{15.4053}{1000000}$	1.0885	8.8785
Matrix-DE	0.1226	$\frac{37.7647}{1000000}$	1.1130	9.0783

of DE, the positional bias, and a new structure can be proposed by utilizing permutation operation with much better optimization performance which can be found in literature [9–12].

5   Conclusion

In this paper, we propose a matrix-based implementation scheme of DE algorithm. The commonly three implementation schemes are also illustrated and contrasted in the paper. Optimization performance as well as time complexity is also contrast among all these different schemes. CEC2013 test suite for real-parameter optimization is used as the test-bed for these comparison. Experiment results shows that the new proposed matrix-based implementation scheme of DE is much easier for coding, similar time complexity for implementation and of much better optimization performance. Moreover, the permutation operation can be a new attempt to tackle the inborn positional bias weakness of DE, which will be discussed in a future paper.

Acknowledgement. This work is funded by Shenzhen Innovation and Entrepreneurship Project with the project number: GRCK20160826105935160.

References

1. Storn, R., Price, K.: Differential evolution a simple and efficient adaptive scheme for global optimization over continuous spaces. International Computer Science Institute, Berkeley, CA, Technical report TR-95-012 (1995)
2. Holland, J.H.: Adaptation in Natural and Artificial Systems: An Introductory Analysis with Applications to Biology, Control, and Artificial Intelligence. U Michigan Press, Ann Arbor (1975)
3. Kirkpatrick, S.C., Gelatt, D., Vecchi, M.P.: Optimization by simmulated annealing. Science **220**(4598), 671–680 (1983)
4. Storn, R., Price, K.: Differential Evolution - a simple and efficient heuristic for global optimization over continuous spaces. J. Global Optim. **11**(4), 341–359 (1997)
5. Price, K., Storn, R.M., Lampinen, J.A.: Differential Evolution: A Practical Approach to Global Optimization. Springer, New York (2006)
6. Mezura-Montes, E., Velázquez-Reyes, J., Coello Coello, C.A.: A comparative study of differential evolution variants for global optimization. In: Proceedings of the 8th Annual Conference on Genetic and Evolutionary Computation, pp. 485–492. ACM (2006)
7. Liu, J., Lampinen, J.: A fuzzy adaptive differential evolution algorithm. Soft Comput. Fusion Found. Methodologies Appl. **9**(6), 448–462 (2005)
8. Rahnamayan, S., Tizhoosh, H.R., Salama, M.M.A.: Opposition-based differential evolution. IEEE Trans. Evol. Comput. **12**(1), 64–79 (2008)
9. Meng, Z., Pan, J.S., Xu, H.: QUasi-Affine TRansformation Evolutionary (QUATRE) algorithm: a cooperative swarm based algorithm for global optimization. Knowl. Based Syst. **109**, 104–121 (2016)
10. Meng, Z., Pan, J.S., QUasi-affine TRansformation Evolutionary (QUATRE) algorithm: a parameter-reduced differential evolution algorithm for optimization problems. In: IEEE Congress on Evolutionary Computation (CEC), pp. 4082–4089. IEEE (2016)
11. Meng, Z., Pan, J.S.: Monkey King Evolution: a new memetic evolutionary algorithm and its application in vehicle fuel consumption optimization. Knowl. Based Syst. **97**, 144–157 (2016)
12. Meng, Z., Pan, J.-S.: A Competitive QUasi-Affine TRansformation Evolutionary (C-QUATRE) Algorithm for global optimization. In: 2016 IEEE International Conference on Systems, Man, and Cybernetics (SMC). IEEE (2016)

A Bayesian Model of Game Decomposition

Hanqing Zhao[1,2], Zengchang Qin[1](✉), Weijia Liu[2], and Tao Wan[3](✉)

[1] Intelligent Computing and Machine Learning Lab, School of ASEE,
Beihang University, Beijing 100191, China
zcqin@buaa.edu.cn
[2] École Centrale de Pékin, Beihang University, Beijing 100191, China
[3] School of Biological Science and Medical Engineering, Beihang University,
Beijing 100191, China
taowan@buaa.edu.cn

Abstract. In this paper, we propose a Bayesian probabilistic model to describe collective behavior generated by a finite number of agents competing for limited resources. In this model, the strategy for each agent is a binary choice in the Minority Game and it can be modeled by a Binomial distribution with a Beta prior. The strategy of an agent can be learned given a sequence of historical choices by using Bayesian inference. Aggregated micro-level choices constitute the observable time series data in macro-level, therefore, this can be regarded as a machine learning model for time series prediction. To verify the effectiveness of the new model, we conduct a series of experiments on artificial data and real-world stock price data. Experimental results demonstrate the new proposed model has a better performance comparing to a genetic algorithm based decomposition model.

Keywords: Collective behaviour · Bayesian inference · Stock prediction

1 Introduction

Collective Intelligence (CI) is a shared or group intelligence that emerges from the interactions of individual agents and appears in consensus decision making. The interactions could be either cooperative or competitive in different multi-agent systems (MAS). Agent-based experimental games have attracted much attention in different areas, especially in economics and social science. For example, Pipattanasomporn et al. [10] proposed a network based MAS for designing a distributed smart grid. For economic problems, Tesauro and Kephart [15] simulates price evolution in an artificial market with fixed strategies. For social problems, Sabater and Sierra [12] analyzed reputation of agents in a social network. Researchers from different areas aim to model the systems where involving agents with similar capability are competing for a limited resource. That provides invaluable insight into the highly non-trivial collective behavior of a population of agents. We can find a substantial amount of references of MAS in different practical areas that study how complex behavior emerges from simple rules.

© Springer International Publishing AG 2017
S. Benferhat et al. (Eds.): IEA/AIE 2017, Part I, LNAI 10350, pp. 82–91, 2017.
DOI: 10.1007/978-3-319-60042-0_9

In this paper, we turn our focus on the prediction power of the agent-based system by decomposing the collective behavior into micro-level actions of agents.

In an agent-based complex system, agents may share global information and learn from past experience. If we assume that every agent in the market knows the historical information, the key problem is to how to decide to act based on this global information. Such a problem has been studied intensively in physics [8] and applied mathematics. For example, Szolnoki et al. [13] find that the wisdom of groups could promote cooperation in evolutionary social dilemmas. Nowak [8] summaries five rules of evolution of cooperation and even puts *natural cooperation* as the third fundamental principle of evolution beside mutation and natural selection. Most related research in evolutionary games is focused on the evolution of the system dynamics [9]. and different tools are applied study emergence of the collective behavior from interacting agents [11].

Recently, the study of decision making follows a Bayesian process is becoming increasingly popular [14], where human decision-making is affected by both statistical learning and constraints from existing knowledge. Inspired by this idea, we assume that agent processes a probabilistic strategy on decision making in this paper. Such a probabilistic strategy is more intuitive and appropriate to describe human behavior of decision making comparing to the classical assumption of fixed strategies in previous works [5,6,11]. The strategies are governed by prior distributions and that can be learned through the Bayesian inference by maximizing the likelihood of historical collective behavior data.

The rest of the paper is structured as follows: in Sect. 2, we construct the multi-agent model in which each agent is with a binomial strategy. A Bayesian learning algorithm is used to update the strategy given a time series data. In Sect. 3 the effectiveness of the new proposed model is verified on an artificial data set. In Sect. 4 the performance of the new model is evaluated and compared to a Genetic Algorithm based model on real world stock data. Finally, the results are discussed and the conclusion are given in Sect. 5.

2 Minority Game Model

Previous works [3,5,7,11] show that complex collective behavior can be decomposed into the aggregation of simple actions following the minority game. Each individual agent's action can be modeled by a deterministic strategy (e.g. a lookup table) given a series of historical data. However, in the real-world, uncertainty always exists in decision making and hardly for agents to follow never-changed deterministic strategies. Though, some works introduced the dynamic strategy [7] that could be changed based on its current winning situation, but such dynamic change is essentially a transition from one fixed strategy to the other, the decision making is still deterministic. In this paper, we assume that the agent behavior follows its own *probabilistic* strategy. In each decision making process, it is uncertain and may follow a particular probabilistic distribution.

2.1   Collective Behavior

In this paper, the *collective behavior* is generated sequentially by finite number of agents in a *minority game* [2]. The minority game is a simplified version of the El-Farol Bar [1] problem: in each round of the game, an odd number of agents must choose one of the two choices independently. The agents who end up in the minority side win the game. In the game, every agent is assigned with a strategy by which the agent make choice based on observed collective behavior [4].

Formally, in round $t \in \mathbb{T}$ of the game, an agent $a_i \in \mathbb{A}$ has to make a choice from a binary choice $\mathbb{E} = \{0, 1\}$. Thus, a choice C can be defined by:

$$C(a_i, t) = 1 \qquad \textit{Agent i choose 1 in round t}$$
$$C(a_i, t) = 0 \qquad \textit{Agent i choose 0 in round t} \qquad (1)$$

The outcome $h(t) \in [0, |\mathbb{A}|]$ can be obtained by summing up the choices in each round of the game.

$$h(t) = \sum_{i=0}^{|\mathbb{A}|} C(a_i, t) \qquad (2)$$

In the minority game, the group of agents who make the minority choice wins, such a group of agent belongs wining side of the game. The wining side in each round of game denoted by $w(t)$, when $w(t) = 1$ agents who make choice 1 wins and when $w(t) = 0$ agents who make choice 0 wins. Given a threshold $\theta \in [0, 1]$, where:

$$w(t) = 1 \; iff \; \frac{h(t)}{|\mathbb{A}|} > \theta$$
$$w(t) = 0 \; iff \; \frac{h(t)}{|\mathbb{A}|} \leq \theta \qquad (3)$$

When $\theta = 0.5$, the game is the pure minority game.

2.2   Probabilistic Strategy of Agent

In the real world, people are used to make decisions through their past experience, thus, we assume that agents in each round of game make choice reference to a finite length of *memory*. The memory in round t can be defined as a vector $m(t) \in \{0, 1\}^l$ composed by wining Outcomes in previous l rounds of games.

$$m(t) = [w(t - l), ..., w(t - 1)] \qquad (4)$$

For each piece of memory, an agent possesses a *trategy* by which generate its choice in the next round of game, such strategy can be represented by a set of rules, a function or a look-up table. In this paper, the strategy of each agent is modeled by a Bernoulli distribution on a binary event space. Therefore, each choice of agent can be regarded as a random variable follows a Bernoulli distribution. For an agent, we can have:

$$P(C(a_i, t) = 1) = p_t$$
$$P(C(a_i, t) = 0) = 1 - p_t \tag{5}$$

where the selective probability $p_t \in [0,1]$ is the probability this agent choose 1. This could be different for each agent, each history, and each time point. From a Bayesian perspective, this probability can be regarded as a value sampled from a random variable subject to a prior Beta distribution $p_t \sim Be(b_1, b_2)$, which reflects the agent's prior knowledge, the density function of the prior distribution is shown in Eq. (6).

$$\pi_t(p_t) = \frac{p_t^{b_1-1}(1-p_t)^{b_2-1}}{\int_0^1 s^{b_1-1}(1-s)^{b_2-1}ds} \tag{6}$$

Where b_1, b_2 are two parameters of prior Beta distribution of agent, their values are different for each agent, each history, and each time point. Given memory length $l = 3$ and wining threshold $\theta = 0.5$, the process of time series wining outcome generation is illustrated in Fig. 1.

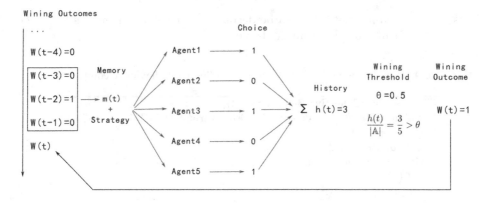

Fig. 1. Wining outcome generation in t round of game by a group of 5 agents.

2.3   Bayesian Inference of Strategy

In order to modify agent's behavior, and make the group of agents' collective behavior more similar to real collective data (e.g. stock movement, population evolution). The Bayesian inference method can be applied to regulate a agents' Strategies, specifically to modify the parameters b_1, b_2 of each agent. So as to obtain a similar history generated by the group of agents. Given a finite time series collective data $d(t), t \in [1, T]$, e.g. for the stock data, the corresponding history data can be generated as:

$$d(t) = P(t) - P(t-1) \tag{7}$$

By mapping these data to the interval $[0, |\mathbb{A}|]$ we can obtain the actual history denoted $h_a(t)$ as the training data to infer agent's strategies.

$$h_a(t) = round\left(\frac{d(t) - d_{min}}{d_{max} - d_{min}} \times |\mathbb{A}|\right)$$
$$d_{min} = -\max\{|d(t)| \ t \in [1,T]\}$$
$$d_{max} = \max\{|d(t)| \ t \in [1,T]\} \tag{8}$$

where $h_a(t)$ is referred to the volatility of the prices and it is from re-scaling the original prices into $[0,1]$. On step further, in order to infer the two parameters b_1, b_2 of posterior distribution govern agents' Strategies, the macro actual history $h_a(t)$ has to be decomposed into micro *Actual Choice* of each agent denoted $C_a(a_i, t) \in \{0, 1\}$. We suppose that the probability of each agent becomes the actor of Actual Choice 1 at round t is proportional to its Selective Probability $p_t(m(t), a_i)$. Supposing that $X_{a,t}$ is a random variable defined on set $\mathbb{A}$, subjected to a Multinomial distribution $multi_t(\mathbb{A})$ on $\mathbb{A}$ where:

$$P(X_{a,t} = a_i) = \frac{p_t(m(t), a_i)}{\sum_{j=1}^{|\mathbb{A}|} p_t(m(t), a_j)} \ \forall i \in [1, |\mathbb{A}|] \tag{9}$$

Thus, each actual history $h_a(t)$ can be decomposed into actual choices $C_a(a_i, t)$ of each agent using the algorithm in Table 1.

Table 1. Pseudo-code of the algorithm for collective behavior decomposition

Given Actual Collective Behavior $h_a(t)$;
Initialing $C_a(a_i, t) = 0, \forall i \in [1, |\mathbb{A}|]$, Flag variable $F(a_i) = 0, \forall a_i \in \mathbb{A}$;
Set *counter* = 0;
While *counter* < $|\mathbb{A}|$:
Generate a random number from distribution $x \sim multi_t(\mathbb{A})$;
If $F(x) = 0$:
$C_a(x, t) = 1, F(x) = 1, counter + +$;

Where the flag variable $F(x)$ indicates whether an agent $x \in \mathbb{A}$ is assigned an actual choices. Based on the Bayes theorem, because of the Beta distribution is the conjugate prior distribution of Bernoulli distribution, the density function of prior distribution in $t + 1$ round of game can be modified reference to the decomposed Actual Choices $C_a(a_i, t)$ in t round of game.

$$\pi_{t+1}(p(m(t), a_i)) = \pi_t(p(m(t), a_i)|C_a(a_i, t)) = \frac{L(C_a(a_i, t)|p(m(t), a_i))\pi_t(p(m(t), a_i))}{\int_0^1 L(C_a(a_i, t)|\theta)\pi_t(\theta)d\theta}$$
$$L(C_a(a_i, t)|p(m(t), a_i)) = p(m(t), a_i)^{C_a(a_i, t)}(1 - p(m(t), a_i))^{1-C_a(a_i, t)}$$
$$\pi_t(p(m(t), a_i)) = \frac{p(m(t), a_i)^{b_1(m(t), a_i, t)-1}(1 - p(m(t), a_i))^{b_2(m(t), a_i, t)-1}}{\int_0^1 \theta^{b_1(m(t), a_i, t)-1}(1 - \theta)^{b_2(m(t), a_i, t)-1}d\theta} \tag{10}$$

From Eq. (10), we have:

$$\pi_{t+1}(p(m(t),a_i)) = \frac{p(m(t),a_i)^{b_1(m(t),a_i,t)+C_a(a_i,t)-1}(1-p(m(t),a_i))^{b_2(m(t),a_i,t)-C_a(a_i,t)-1}}{\int_0^1 \theta^{b_1(m(t),a_i,t)-1}(1-\theta)^{b_2(m(t),a_i,t)-1}d\theta}$$

(11)

Intuitively, function $\pi_{t+1}(p(m(t),a_i))$ is the density function of Beta distribution $Be(b_1(m(t),a_i,t+1),b_2(m(t),a_i,t+1))$, where:

$$b_1(m(t),a_i,t+1) = b_1(m(t),a_i,t) + C_a(a_i,t)$$
$$b_2(m(t),a_i,t+1) = b_2(m(t),a_i,t) + 1 - C_a(a_i,t)$$

(12)

So that the parameters of agents' prior distributions in round $t+1$ have been amended according to previous information. The remaining parameters in $t+1$ round correspond to Memories in addition to $m(t)$ are simply inherited from t round.

$$b_j(k,a_i,t+1) = b_j(k,a_i,t) \quad \forall k \in \{0,1\}^l \setminus \{m(t)\}, \ j \in \{1,2\}, \ i \in [1,|\mathbb{A}|] \quad (13)$$

3 Simulation of Artificial Collective Behavior

In order to evaluate the validity of the new proposed model, we firstly consider the collective data generated by a generator group of 31 agents with fixed prior distributions. For all the agents in the generator group $\mathbb{G}$, their prior distributions are the same $Be(a,a)$ and does not change with the number of rounds. In each round t of game, each agent samples a Selective Probability $p_t(m(t),a_i)$ from prior Beta distribution $Be(a,a)$, then generates its Choice in this round $C_a(a_i,t)$ through the Bernoulli distribution $B(p_t(m(t),a_i),1-p_t(m(t),a_i))$, thereby forming an artificially generated collective behavior sequence $h_a(t)$ and related Wining Outcomes $w_a(t)$ given Wining Threshold $\theta = 0.5$.

Given a predictor group $\mathbb{P}$ of 31 agents where their prior distributions are randomly generated, at each round of game, agents in the predictor group generate

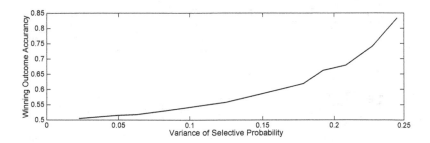

Fig. 2. Changes of wining outcome accuracy with variances of selective probabilities of agents in generator group.

a collective behavior $h_p(t)$ and related Wining Outcome

$$w_p(t) = round\left(\frac{h_p(t)}{|\mathbb{P}|}\right)$$

and then trained by the actual collective behavior $h_a(t)$ through the method shown in Sect. 2.3. At each round of game, agents repeat their selections for X times, we use the *Wining Outcome Accuracy* in X times of selections to evaluate the model.

$$w_a(t) = \frac{\sum_{i=1}^{X} \Delta(w_a(t,i), w_p(t,i))}{X} \tag{14}$$

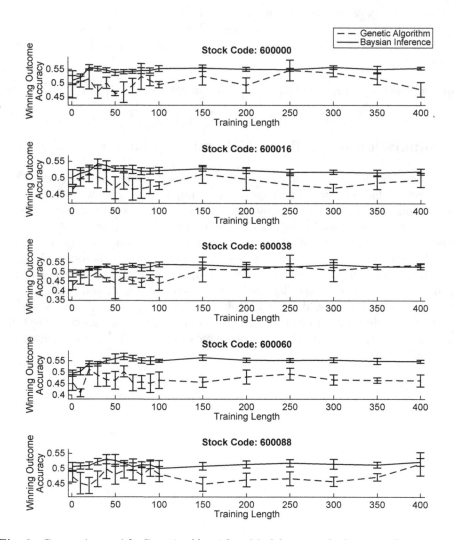

Fig. 3. Comparison with Genetic Algorithm Model on stock data simulation given $\theta = 0.5$.

where $\Delta(\bullet, \bullet)$ is a truth function, we have $\Delta(x, y) = 1$ iff $x = y$ else, $\Delta(x, y) = 0$. Given $X = 1000$ and prior distribution of agents in generator group $Be(a, a)$, the changes of averaged wining outcome accuracy between 200 and 300 rounds of games with the variances of generators' selective probability. The results are shown in Fig. 2.

$$var[p(m(t), a_i)] = \frac{1}{8a + 4} \qquad (15)$$

As we can see from Fig. 2, when the variance is very small, the selective probability of all agents in generator group are close to $\frac{a}{2a} = 0.5$, as a result, their choices have no obvious rules to follow, so that the Wining Outcome Accuracy is very low. As the variance increases, the Wining Outcome Accuracy increases gradually.

4   Simulation on Real Market Data

4.1   Accuracy Evaluation

In order to evaluate the adaptability of our new model on real collective behavior data, we consider stock price data preprocessed by the method shown in Sect. 2.3. Our evaluation is based on the Wining Outcome Accuracy in 100 times of selections (as introduced in Eq. (14)), given Wining Threshold $\theta = 0.5$. For each stock, we construct a test set of 100 consecutive trading days prior to 1 August 2016. The averaged Wining Outcome Accuracy for all the 100 days in the test set is used as the evaluation indicator. The Wining Outcome Accuracy of each day is calculated after using a specified length of prior data to train the model. The variations in averaged Wining Outcome Accuracy of 5 stocks listed on the Shanghai Stock Exchange over the length of training days are shown in Fig. 3, these results are the average of 10 experiments. As shown in Fig. 3, the new proposed model has a more accurate and more stable performance in the simulation of the collective behavior of stock market participants than a Genetic Algorithm based model [11].

4.2   ROC Evaluation

The Receiver Operating Characteristic Curve (ROC) is an effective implement for comparing performances between two classifiers. Considering the stock data testing set of 100 days introduced in Sect. 4.1. Given a training length and a testing stock set, considering the price raising dates as positive simples and price plummeting dates as negatives simples. By changing the Wining Threshold from 0 to 1, an ROC and its related the *Area Under ROC Curve* (AUC) can be generated respectively for each classifier. The maximum AUC values and related training lengths of collective behavior model and a Genetic Algorithm based model [11] on each stock set are listed in Table 2.

Table 2. AUC & related training length comparisons between collective behavior model and Genetic Algorithm model.

Stock code	Collective behavior		Genetic algorithm	
	Maximum AUC	Training length	Maximum AUC	Training length
600000	**0.606**	70 days	0.591	100 days
600016	**0.618**	70 days	0.522	3 days
600028	**0.592**	80 days	0.529	40 days
600038	**0.561**	350 days	0.547	40 days
600056	0.565	60 days	**0.608**	20 days
600060	**0.609**	300 days	0.527	150 days
600088	**0.642**	4 days	0.633	30 days
600619	0.567	7 days	**0.583**	20 days
600900	**0.647**	200 days	0.596	20 days

5   Conclusion

In this paper, we proposed a novel model to simulate the collective behavior generated by a finite number of agents in a series of game. In each round of the game, one agent has to generate a choice from a binary choice space, based on its probabilistic strategy described by a Binomial distribution with a Beta prior. In each round of the game, a group of agents generate a wining outcome as a consequence of collective behavior. In our experimental studies, we compare the new proposed model to the Genetic Algorithm based decomposition model on a stock price database in Shanghai Stock Exchange. We found that the new model has a better accuracy in terms of AUC value.

Acknowledgement. This work is funded by the National Science Foundation of China No. 61401012.

References

1. Arthur, W.B.: Bounded rationality and inductive behavior (the El Farol problem). Am. Econ. Rev. **84**, 406–411 (1994)
2. Challet, D., Zhang, Y.-C.: Emergence of cooperation and organization in an evolutionary game. Physica A **246**, 407–418 (1997)
3. Challet, D., Marsili, M., Zecchina, R.: Statistical mechanics of systems with heterogeneous agents: minority games. Phys. Rev. Lett. **84**, 1824–1827 (2000)
4. Challet, D., Marsili, M., Zhang, Y.-C.: Minority Games: Interacting Agents in Financial Markets. Oxford University Press, Oxford (2004)
5. Du, Y., Dong, Y., Qin, Z., Wan, T.: Exploring market behaviors with evolutionary mixed-games learning model. In: Jędrzejowicz, P., Nguyen, N.T., Hoang, K. (eds.) ICCCI 2011. LNCS, vol. 6922, pp. 244–253. Springer, Heidelberg (2011). doi:10.1007/978-3-642-23935-9_24

6. Li, G., Ma, Y., Dong, Y., Qin, Z.: Behavior learning in minority games. In: Guttmann, C., Dignum, F., Georgeff, M. (eds.) CARE 2009-2010. LNCS, vol. 6066, pp. 125–136. Springer, Heidelberg (2011). doi:10.1007/978-3-642-22427-0_10

7. Ma, Y., Li, G., Dong, Y., Qin, Z.: Minority game data mining for stock market predictions. In: Cao, L., Bazzan, A.L.C., Gorodetsky, V., Mitkas, P.A., Weiss, G., Yu, P.S. (eds.) ADMI 2010. LNCS, vol. 5980, pp. 178–189. Springer, Heidelberg (2010). doi:10.1007/978-3-642-15420-1_15

8. Nowak, M.: Five rules for the evolution of cooperation. Science **314**, 1560–1563 (2006)

9. Perc, M., Szolnoki, A.: Coevolutionary games—A mini review. BioSystems **99**, 109–125 (2010)

10. Pipattanasomporn, M., Feroze, H., Rahman, S.: Multi-agent systems in a distributed smart grid: design and implementation. In: Power Systems Conference and Exposition, PSCE 2009, pp. 1–8. IEEE Press (2009)

11. Qin, Z., Wan, T., Dong, Y., Du, Y.: Evolutionary collective behavior decomposition model for time series data mining. Appl. Soft Comput. **26**, 368–377 (2015)

12. Sabater, J., Sierra, C.: Reputation and social network analysis in multi-agent systems. In: Proceedings of the First International Joint Conference on Autonomous Agents and Multiagent Systems, Part 1 (2002)

13. Szolnoki, A., Wang, Z., Perc, M.: Wisdom of groups promotes cooperation in evolutionary social dilemmas. Sci. Rep. **2**, 576 (2012)

14. Tenenbaum, J., Griffiths, T., Kemp, C.: Theory-based Bayesian models of inductive learning and reasoning. Trends Cogn. Sci. **10**(7), 309–318 (2006)

15. Tesauro, G., Kephart, J.: Pricing in agent economies using multi-agent Q-learning. Auton. Agent. Multi-Agent Syst. **5**(3), 289–304 (2002)

Two-Timescale Learning Automata for Solving Stochastic Nonlinear Resource Allocation Problems

Anis Yazidi[✉], Hugo Lewi Hammer, and Tore Møller Jonassen

Department of Computer Science,
Oslo and Akershus University College of Applied Sciences, Oslo, Norway
anis.yazidi@hioa.no

Abstract. This papers deals with the Stochastic Non-linear Fractional Equality Knapsack (NFEK) problem which is a fundamental resource allocation problem based on incomplete and noisy information [2,3]. The NFEK problem arises in many applications such as in web polling under polling constraints, and in constrained estimation. The primary contribution of this paper is a *continuous* Learning Automata (LA)-based, *optimal*, efficient and yet simple solution to the NFEK problem. Our solution reckoned as the Two-timescale based Learning Automata (T-TLA) solves the NFEK problem by performing updates on two different timescales. To the best of our knowledge, this is the first tentative in the literature to design an LA that operates with two-time scale updates. Furthermore, the T-TLA solution is distinct from the first-reported optimal solution to the problem due to Granmo and Oommen [2,3] which resorts to utilizing multiple two-action discretized LA, organized in a hierarchical manner, so as to be able to tackle the case of multi-materials. Hence, the T-TLA scheme mitigates the complexity of the state-of-the-art solution that involves partitioning the material set into two subsets of equal size at each level. We report some representative experimental results that illustrate the convergence of our scheme and its superiority to the state-of-the-art [2,3].

Keywords: Continuous Learning Automata · Two-timescale learning · Stochastic Non-linear Fractional Equality Knapsack · Resource allocation

1 Introduction

This paper deals with the Stochastic Non-linear Fractional Equality Knapsack (NFEK) Problem which is the central underlying problem pertinent to allocating

A. Yazidi—The author gratefully acknowledges the assistance of his PhD supervisor, Dr. John Oommen, a *Chancellor's Professor* from Ottawa, Canada. John helped a lot with the style and language of this paper. He also very graciously provided me with some of the text when it concerned the introductory sections and the background material. These portions have been included here, in some cases *verbatim*, with his kind permission. Thank you John!!.

© Springer International Publishing AG 2017
S. Benferhat et al. (Eds.): IEA/AIE 2017, Part I, LNAI 10350, pp. 92–101, 2017.
DOI: 10.1007/978-3-319-60042-0_10

resources based on incomplete and noisy information. Such situations are not merely hypothetical – rather, they constitute the vast majority of allocation problems in the real-world. Resource allocation problems which involve such incomplete and noisy information are particularly intriguing. They cannot be solved by traditional optimization techniques, rendering them ineffective.

The NFEK problem, that was first solved optimally in [4], is not merely of academic interest. Indeed, it is found in many settings, for example, in the web polling problem and constrained estimation [2]. More specifically, in the case of web polling, the decision maker attempts to choose web pages in a manner that maximizes the number of changes detected, and the optimal allocation of the resources again involves "trial and error". Web pages may change with varying frequencies (that are unknown to the decision maker), and changes appear more or less randomly. Furthermore, as argued elsewhere [4], the probability that an individual web page poll uncovers a change on its own *decreases monotonically* with the polling frequency used for that web page. The NFEK also has applications in determining the optimal sample size required for estimation purposes. This paper briefly addresses these problems as application domain problems – they are discussed, in more detail, elsewhere [4].

The NFEK problem has two main peculiarities:

- First, the unit volume values of each material are treated as *stochastic* variables whose distributions are *unknown*.
- The expected value of a material may decrease after each addition to the knapsack.

The first optimal solution to the NFEK problem is due to Granmo and Oommen [2,3], and resorts to the invoking a hierarchy of two-action discretized Learning Automata (LA). The solution was generalized using a hierarchical scheme in order to tackle the case of multi-materials. Although the solution proposed in [4] is elegant, its implementation is, unfortunately, complex because it involves updates at different levels of a balanced binary tree.

1.1   Formal Problem Formulation

The Stochastic NFEK Problem: The generalization of the nonlinear equality knapsack problem is due to Granmo and Oommen [2,3]. First of all, we let the material value per unit volume for any x_i be a *probability* function $p_i(x_i)$. Furthermore, we consider the distribution of $p_i(x_i)$ to be *unknown*. That is, each time an amount x_i of material i is placed in the knapsack, we are only allowed to observe an instantiation of $p_i(x_i)$ at x_i, and not $p_i(x_i)$ itself. Given this stochastic environment, we seek a solution to the Stochastic NFEK problem that is on-line and incremental, and that learns the mix of materials of maximal *expected* value, through a series of informed guesses. Thus, to clarify issues, we are provided with a knapsack of fixed volume c, which is to be filled with a mix of n different materials. However, unlike the NFEK, in the Stochastic NFEK Problem the unit volume value of a material i, $1 \leq i \leq n$, is a random quantity

— it takes the value 1 with probability $p_i(x_i)$ and the value 0 with probability $1 - p_i(x_i)$, respectively. As an additional complication, $p_i(x_i)$ is nonlinear in the sense that it decreases monotonically with x_i, i.e., $x_{i_1} \leq x_{i_2} \Leftrightarrow p_i(x_{i_1}) \geq p_i(x_{i_2})$.

Since the unit volume values are random, we operate with expected unit volume values rather than the actual unit volume values themselves. With this understanding, and the above perspective in mind, the expected value of the amount x_i of material i, $1 \leq i \leq n$, becomes $f_i(x_i) = \int_0^{x_i} p_i(u)du$. Accordingly, the expected value per unit volume[1] of material i becomes $f_i'(x_i) = p_i(x_i)$. In this stochastic and non-linear version of the FK problem, the goal is to fill the knapsack so that the expected value $f(\boldsymbol{x}) = \sum_1^n f_i(x_i)$ of the material mix contained in the knapsack is maximized. Thus, we aim to:

$$\text{maximize } f(\boldsymbol{x}) = \sum_1^n f_i(x_i),$$

$$\text{where} f_i(x_i) = \int_0^{x_i} p_i(u)du, \text{ and } p_i(x_i) = f_i'(x_i),$$

$$\text{subject to } \sum_1^n x_i = c \text{ and } \forall i \in \{1, \ldots, n\}, x_i \geq 0.$$

A fascinating property of the above problem is that the amount of information available to the decision maker is limited — the decision maker is only allowed to observe the current unit value of each material (either 0 or 1). That is, each time a material mix is placed in the knapsack, the unit value of each material is provided to the decision maker. The actual outcome probabilities $p_i(x_i), 1 \leq i \leq n$, however, remain *unknown*. As a result of the latter, the expected value of the material mix must be maximized by means of trial-and-failure, i.e., by experimenting with different material mixes and by observing the resulting random unit value outcomes.

1.2   The Hierarchy of Twofold Resource Allocation Automaton (H-TRAA) Solution

The stochastic NFEK problem was first addressed in the literature in [4]. The first reported generic treatment of the stochastic NFEK problem itself can be found in [4]. The state-of-the-art scheme for hierarchically solving n-material problems [2,3] involves a primitive module, namely the Twofold Resource Allocation Automaton (TRAA) for the *two-material* problem, that has been proven to be asymptotically optimal. The authors of [2,3] demonstrated a mechanism by which the primitive TRAAs can be arranged in a hierarchy so as to solve *multi-material* Stochastic NFEK Problems.

The hierarchy of TRAAs, referred to as H-TRAA, assumes that $n = 2^\gamma, \gamma \in \mathbb{N}^+$. If the number of materials is less than this, one trivially assumes the existence of additional materials whose values are "zero", and which thus are not

---

[1] We hereafter use $f_i'(x_i)$ to denote the derivative of the expected value function $f_i(x_i)$ with respect to x_i.

able to contribute to the final optimal solution. The hierarchy is organized as a balanced binary tree with depth $D = \log_2(n)$. Each node in the hierarchy can be related to three entities: (1) a set of materials, (2) a partitioning of the material set into two subsets of equal size, and (3) a dedicated TRAA that allocates a given amount of resources among the two subsets. At depth D, then, each individual material can be separately assigned a fraction of the overall capacity by way of recursion, using a subtle mechanism described, in detail, in [3]. The principal theorem that guarantees the convergence of the H-TRAA [2,3] has cleverly shown that if all the individual TRAAs converge to their *local* optimum, then the global optimum is attained.

1.3   Contributions of This Paper

The contributions of this paper are the following:

1. We report an optimal solution to the stochastic NFEK problem based on the bridging the theory of LA with the theory two-timescale separation [1,5]. To the best of our knowledge, this paper provides the first attempt in the literature to bridge the latter two fields: LA on one hand and two-time scale scheme on the other hand.
2. In contrast to the H-TRAA solution [2,3], our T-TLA solution does not involve a hierarchy, and it is thus easier to implement. This is because, in fact, TRAAs must be arranged in a hierarchy in order for them to be able to solve a *multi-material* Stochastic NFEK Problems. Further, through empirical experiments, we confirm that the T-TLA provides desirable convergence properties that makes it competitive to the H-TRAA.

As a result of the above contributions, we believe that the T-TLA is a viable realistic strategy for solving demanding real-world knapsack-like problems such as the optimal allocation of sampling resources [2], and other problems related to the world wide web [4].

1.4   Paper Organization

The paper is organized as follows. In Sect. 2 we present the T-TLA for the *n-material* problem. We proceed in Sect. 3 to empirically verify that the T-TLA solution provides competitive convergence results to the H-TRAA while being, at the same time, simpler to implement. Finally, we offer suggestions for further work and conclude the paper in Sect. 4.

2   A T-TLA Solution to Resource Allocation

The *Stochastic Environment* for the n materials case can be characterized by:

1. The capacity c of the knapsack, which is normalized in this case;
2. $n - material$ unit volume value probability functions $[p_1(x_1), \ldots, p_n(x_n)]$.

In brief, if the amount x_i of material i is suggested to the Stochastic Environment, the Environment replies with a unit volume value $\delta_i = 1$ with probability $p_i(x_i)$ and a unit volume value $\delta_i = 0$ with probability $1 - p_i(x_i)$. To render the problem both interesting and non-trivial, we assume that $p_i(x_i)$ is unknown to the LA.

We shall first characterize the optimal solution to a Stochastic NFEK Problem provided in [2,3].

Lemma 1. *The material mix $\boldsymbol{x}^* = [x_1^*, \dots, x_n^*]$ is a solution to a given Stochastic NFEK Problem if (1) the derivatives of the expected material amount values are all equal at $\boldsymbol{x}^*$, (2) the mix fills the knapsack, and (3) every material amount is positive, i.e.:*

$$f_1'(x_1^*) = \cdots = f_n'(x_n^*)$$
$$\sum_1^n x_i^* = c \text{ and } \forall i \in \{1, \dots, n\}, x_i^* \geq 0.$$

The above lemma is based on the well-known principle of Lagrange Multipliers, and its proof is therefore omitted here for the sake of brevity.

Now, we shall present our solution to the stochastic NFEK [3].

The idea behind our T-TLA is to resort to a two-timescale based approach, where the polling probabilities x_i are updated on the "slower timescale" while $p_i(x_i)$ are estimated on a "faster timescale". In practice, the updating parameter (in this case λ) used for updating the probabilities x_i should be much smaller than the corresponding updating parameter θ for the task of estimation of the p_i. Thus, we can say that the fast-evolving dynamics of p_i sees x_i as "almost constant", while the slowly evolving dynamics of x_i given sees p_i as "almost equilibrated" [1,5].

Another possible manner to to implement a two-time scale approach is to execute one update on the slower timescale loop for every few iterations on the faster timescale loop, i.e., the slower timescale loop is run less frequently.

We denote the decision variable for selecting an action at time instant t, $\alpha(t)$ that is, for $i \in [1..n]$. We say that the event $\{\alpha(t) = i\}$ has occurred if the action i is polled.

Once the action i is polled, the estimate $\hat{p}_i(t+1)$ of the reward probabilities is immediately updated using an exponential moving averaging based estimator:

$$\hat{p}_i(t+1) = \hat{p}_i(t) + \theta(\delta_i(t) - \hat{p}_i(t)) \tag{1}$$

where $\delta_i(t)$ is a random variable that takes a value 1 with $p_i(x_i(t))$ and 0 with $1 - p_i(x_i(t))$.

The reward estimates for the other actions are left unchanged, i.e.,

$$\hat{p}_j(t+1) = \hat{p}_j(t) \text{ for } j \neq i, j \in [1, n]$$

Thus, the evolution of the reward estimates can be described by the following set of stochastic iterative equations for $i \in [1..n]$:

$$\hat{p}_i(t+1) = \hat{p}_i(t) + \theta I_{\{\alpha(t)=i\}}(\delta_i(t) - \hat{p}_i(t)) \tag{2}$$

Now, we are ready to present the update equations for the polling probabilities x_i for $i \in [1..n]$.

The complete algorithm is described as follows:

1. Poll an action at time instant t denoted by $\alpha(t)$ according to the probability vector $[x_1, x_2, \ldots, x_n]$ and observe $\delta_i(t)$.
2. Update the reward probabilities estimates of the n actions according to the following equation, for $i \in [1..n]$:

$$\hat{p}_i(t+1) = \hat{p}_i(t) + \theta I_{\{\alpha(t)=i\}}(\delta_i(t) - \hat{p}_i(t)) \tag{3}$$

3. Update the polling probabilities for the next time instant $t+1$ according to:

$$x_1(t+1) = x_1(t) - \lambda \left(\frac{1}{n} \sum_{i=1}^{n} \hat{p}_i(x_i(t)) - \hat{p}_1(x_1(t)) \right)$$

$$x_2(t+1) = x_2(t) - \lambda \left(\frac{1}{n} \sum_{i=1}^{n} \hat{p}_i(x_i(t)) - \hat{p}_2(x_2(t)) \right)$$

$$\vdots$$

$$x_n(t+1) = x_n(t) - \lambda \left(\frac{1}{n} \sum_{i=1}^{n} \hat{p}_i(x_i(t)) - \hat{p}_n(x_n(t)) \right)$$

$$\tag{4}$$

Idea behind the proof. The proof of the optimality of the above algorithm is quite involved and so we include only the overall behind the proof in the interest of space and brevity. The complete proof is included in the unabridged version of this paper [6]. According to Lemma 1, the optimal solution equalizes the reward probabilities $p_i(x_i^*)$.

Following the proof of two-timescale separation provided in [1], $\hat{p}_i(x_i(t))$ approximates $p_i(x_i(t))$ whenever λ is much smaller than θ reflecting the fact that the fast-evolving dynamics of p_i sees x_i as "almost constant". Moreover, the system of Eq. 4 can be proved to converged to the fixed point described by Lemma 1 using the theory of dynamical systems.

3 Experimental Results

We have conducted our experiments for one objective function (referred to as $E_i(x_i)$) being optimized. The function can be seen as representative for the class of concave objective functions that we address. We have also conducted experiments with a number of other objective functions, including those found in [2,3] that are not reported here due to space limitations and can be found in [6]. However, it turns out that $E_i(x_i)$ is particularly useful in the sense that they permit us to appropriately model a large range of distinct material unit value functions.

More specifically, these objective functions have been given below for a material with index i as:

$$E_i = \frac{0.9}{i}(1 - \exp(-ix_i)) \tag{5}$$

In the above, the constants are based on the boundary conditions due the contributions of x_i at the boundary values. These constants, however, are not crucial in the optimization because the corresponding unit value functions are obtained as their respective derivatives. These are two probability functions given below for a material with index i as $E_i'(x_i)$, which fall exponentially as per Eq. (6) below:

$$E_i'(x_i) = 0.9 \cdot \exp(-ix_i) \tag{6}$$

To clarify how these functions work, consider the functions $E_i'(x_i)$. Then the relative profitability of material i decreases with x_i, its presence in the mixture, exponentially. Thus, if $x_2 = 0.3$ (i.e., material 2 fills 30% of the knapsack), the marginal profitability of increasing the amount of x_2 is $exp(-2 \cdot (0.3)) = exp(-0.6)$. Observe that with the notation, the profitability of materials that have a smaller index decreases *slower* than the profitability of materials that have a higher index.

Given the above considerations, our aim is to find x^*, the amounts of the materials that have to be included in the knapsack so as to maximize its value. Note that in general application domains, we may not able to observe $f_i'(x_i)$ directly — examining a potential solution may be the only way to reveal the success of the chosen allocation.

We will present some experimental results that compare our T-TLA to H-TRAA solution for binary and quaternary stochastic knapsacks. We performed ensembles of 1000 simulations each consisting of 5000 time steps.

Stochastic knapsack with 2 resources. Figure 1a and b depict the evolution of the polling probability for the case of two-resources $n = 2$ for our T-TLA and for the legacy H-TRAA solution respectively.

For the T-TLA solution we chose $\lambda = 0.001$ and $\theta = 0.01$. We chose the resolution of H-TRAA to be $N = 1000$, which corresponds here to $\frac{1}{\lambda}$ so that to allow fair comparison via an equal update parameters of both schemes. We observe from Fig. 1a and b that both approaches are able to converge to the optimal value $x^* = (2/3, 1/3)$ which is seen too from Lemma 1. This takes place after approximately more than 4000 time instants. Furthermore, Fig. 2 reports the estimate of the reward probability which evolves at a faster timescale than the polling probabilities for our T-TLA solution. We observe from Fig. 2 that the T-TLA solution successfully equalizes $\hat{p}_1(x_1(t))$ and $\hat{p}_2(x_2(t))$ after approximately more than 4000 time instants.

Stochastic Knapsack with 4 resources. Similarly, Fig. 3a and b depict the evolution of the polling probability for the case of two-resources $n = 4$ for our T-TLA and for the legacy H-TRAA solution respectively. The T-TLA scheme was characterized by parameters $\lambda = 0.001$ and $\theta = 0.01$. We chose the resolution of

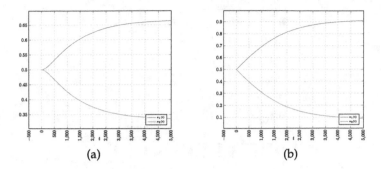

Fig. 1. Evolution of the polling probabilities for $n = 2$ for (a) the T-TLA solution and (b) the H-TRAA solution

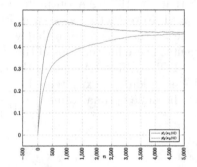

Fig. 2. Evolution of the reward probability estimates for $n = 2$.

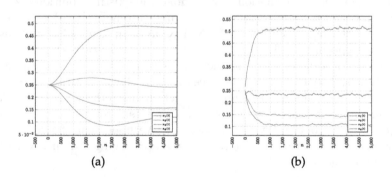

Fig. 3. Evolution of the polling probabilities for $n = 4$ for (a) the T-TLA solution and (b) the H-TRAA solution.

H-TRAA to be $N = 31$. Please note that $\lambda = \approx \frac{1}{N^2}$ which reflects an equal "update steps" for both schemes when the number of levels in H-TRAA is 2.

We see from Fig. 3a and b that the polling probability vector converges to the optimal vector $x^* = (0.48, 0.24, 0.16, 0.12)$ which is also confirmed by Lemma 1.

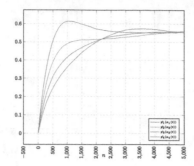

Fig. 4. Evolution of the reward probability estimates for $n = 4$

However, we observe too that the H-TRAA outperforms the T-TLA solution in terms of convergence speed. Nevertheless, as seen in Fig. 3b, the H-TRAA is unable to get of rid of some fluctuations despite that we are averaging over an ensemble of 1000 experiments. These fluctuations of the H-TRAA merely reflect a larger variance than the T-TLA. Figure 4 reports the estimate of the reward probability for our T-TLA solution. As expected, the estimates get equalized over time and converge to the same optimal value.

4   Conclusion

In this paper, we have presented an optimal and efficient solution to Stochastic NFEK Problem, which is a fundamental resource allocation problem based on incomplete and noisy information [2,3]. Unlike the existing solutions [2,3], our primary contribution is a *two-timescale* Learning Automata (LA)-based, *optimal*, efficient and yet simple solution to the NFEK problem. Our solution is distinct from the one reported in solutions [2,3] that uses multiple two-action discretized LA, organized in a hierarchical manner, so as to be able to tackle the case of multi-materials. The T-TLA does not need a hierarchical partitioning, and does not require us to maintain dedicated two-action discretized LA that allocate a given amount of resources among the two subsets. Preliminary experimental results confirm the optimality of the solution. We hope that the current work will pave the way towards more development in bridging LA theory with the theory of two-time scale separation.

References

1. Benveniste, A., Métivier, M., Priouret, P.: Adaptive Algorithms and Stochastic Approximations, vol. 22. Springer, Heidelberg (2012)
2. Granmo, O.-C., Oommen, B.J.: Optimal sampling for estimation with constrained resources using a learning automaton-based solution for the nonlinear fractional knapsack problem. Appl. Intell. **33**(1), 3–20 (2010)

3. Granmo, O.-C., Oommen, B.J.: Solving stochastic nonlinear resource allocation problems using a hierarchy of twofold resource allocation automata. IEEE Trans. Comput. **59**(4), 545–560 (2010)
4. Granmo, O.-C., Oommen, B.J., Myrer, S.A., Olsen, M.G.: Learning automata-based solutions to the nonlinear fractional knapsack problem with applications to optimal resource allocation. IEEE Trans. Syst. Man Cybern. Part B Cybern. **37**(1), 166–175 (2007)
5. Sastry, P.S., Magesh, M., Unnikrishnan, K.P.: Two timescale analysis of the alopex algorithm for optimization. Neural Comput. **14**(11), 2729–2750 (2002)
6. Yazidi, A., Hammer, L.H., Jonassen, T.M.: On two-timescale approach for solving resource allocation problems. Unabridged Journal version of this paper (2017). (To be submitted for publication)

A Hybrid of Tabu Search and Simulated Annealing Algorithms for Preemptive Project Scheduling Problem

Behrouz Afshar-Nadjafi[(⊠)] , Mehdi Yazdani, and Mahyar Majlesi

Faculty of Industrial and Mechanical Engineering, Qazvin Branch,
Islamic Azad University, Qazvin, Iran
afsharnb@alum.sharif.edu, m_yazdani@qiau.ac.ir,
mahyar_industrial_engineer@yahoo.com

Abstract. In this paper, the resource constrained project scheduling problem with preemption is studied in which fixed setup time is needed to resume the preempted activities. The project entails activities with finish-to-start precedence relations, which need a set of renewable resources to be done. A mathematical model is presented for the problem and a hybrid of Tabu Search (TS) and Simulated Annealing (SA) with tuned parameters is developed to solve it. In order to evaluate the performance of the proposed TS/SA a set of 100 test problems is applied. Comprehensive statistical analysis shows that the proposed algorithm efficiently solves the problem. Furthermore, the benefits of preemption with setup times and its justifiability is demonstrated numerically.

Keywords: Project scheduling · Simulated annealing · Tabu search · Preemption · Set up time

1 Introduction

The resource constrained project scheduling problem (RCPSP) is a challenging optimization problem because of its application and NP-hardness [1]. The objective of RCPSP is minimization of project duration preserving the precedence and resources constraints. There are many solution methods to solve the RCPSP [2–5]. In classic scheduling problems it is supposed that each activity once started, will be continued nonstop. Preemptive project scheduling problem addresses the problem which relax this constraint and lets activities to be preempted and resumed later. To solve the preemptive case of project scheduling problems we can find some algorithms in the literature [6–8].

Considering setup times, it is a common assumption in machine scheduling [9–11], while this is not true in the context of project scheduling. Setup is defined as preparedness of all perquisites for the accomplishment of an activity. The required time for this preparedness is named setup time. When set up time is considerably small in comparison with processing time of activity, set up time can be merged into processing time. However, when activities require relatively long setup times, formulating and solving the problem as a traditional RCPSP, may culminate in poor solutions especially when preemption is permitted [12].

© Springer International Publishing AG 2017
S. Benferhat et al. (Eds.): IEA/AIE 2017, Part I, LNAI 10350, pp. 102–111, 2017.
DOI: 10.1007/978-3-319-60042-0_11

Motivation of this work is modelling the setup times in the preemptive case and solving the model. In doing so, a mixed integer formulation is proposed for the preemptive RCPSP with setup times. We call this problem PRCPSP-ST. Then, an efficient hybrid of TS/SA is developed to solve this NP-hard problem. Finally, the proposed algorithm is evaluated to solve the PRCPSP-ST and effect of setup time on project duration is analyzed. The rest of the paper is organized as follows: in Sect. 2 the PRCPSP-ST is described and formulated. In Sect. 3 the steps of the proposed algorithm are explained. Section 4 is devoted to the experimental results and validation of the proposed TS/SA. Finally, conclusion of the paper in presented in Sect. 5.

2 Problem Description

In preemptive resource constrained project scheduling problem with setup times (PRCPSP-ST), each activity i is performed in a single mode with deterministic duration of d_i. There is a max number K of renewable resource types where each activity i requires r_{ik}^{ρ} units of renewable resource type k $(k = 1, \ldots, K)$ per time unit. Availability of the renewable resource type k, R_k^{ρ}, is constant throughout the project. The project is represented in activity on node, AON, style by $G = \{N, A\}$ in which, N, denoted activities (nodes) and, A, denotes finish to start precedence relations (arcs). The activities are numbered from the dummy start activity 0 to the dummy end activity $n + 1$. When an activity i is preempted, a setup time ST_i is needed to resume the preempted activity. In modelling PRCPSP-ST, we assume that:

- Preemption of the activities is in discrete time points.
- A setup time is needed to resume a preempted activity.
- Duration of an activity contains the initial setup time.
- Setup times are known and constant.
- Each activity is restarted immediately after its setup.
- Setups require same resources as process of activities.

The objective of the PRCPSP-ST is minimization of the project duration. A feasible schedule S is defined by a vector of activities start times satisfying all perquisite relations and resources constraints. Let $f_{i,j}$ represents the finish time of jth unit of activity i. Also let $f_{i,0}$ denotes start time of activity i. By defining $x_{ij} = 1$ if j^{th} unit $(1 \leq j \leq d_i - 1)$ of an activity i is preempted; $x_{ij} = 0$ otherwise, PRCPSP-ST can be conceptually modelled as follows:

$$Min \; C_{max} = f_{n+1,0} \tag{1}$$

$$f_{i,d_i} \leq f_{j,0}; \qquad for \; (i,j) \in A \tag{2}$$

$$f_{i,j-1} + 1 \leq f_{i,j} - x_{i,(j-1)}(1 + ST_i); \qquad for \; i = 0, \ldots, n+1 \; and \; j = 0, \ldots, d_i \tag{3}$$

$$f_{i,j} - x_{i,(j-1)}(1 + ST_i) \leq f_{i,j-1} + 1 + Mx_{i,(j-1)}; \qquad for \; i = 0, \ldots, n+1 \; and \; j = 0, \ldots, d_i \tag{4}$$

$$f_{0,0} = 0 \tag{5}$$

$$\sum_{i \in S_t} r_{ik}^\rho \leq R_k^\rho; \qquad for \ k = 1, \ldots, K \ and \ t = 1, \ldots, f_{n+1,0} \tag{6}$$

$$x_{i,j} \in \{0, 1\}, \ f_{i,j} \in Integer; \qquad for \ i = 0, \ldots, n+1 \ and \ j = 0, \ldots, d_i \tag{7}$$

The objective in Eq. (1) minimizes the project duration. Equation (2) preserves the finish to start precedence relations. Equations (3) and (4) impose a setup time after any preemption. Parameter M is a big positive number. Equations (3) and (4) maintains the logical relation between x_{ij} and f_{ij}. Equation (5) guarantees that start activity 0 be started at time 0. Equation (6) take care of the renewable resources availability. S_t denotes the set of activities which are in progress or their setups are in progress at time interval $[t - 1, t]$. Equation (7) specifies that f_{ij} are integers, while x_{ij} are binary.

3 Proposed Hybrid TS/SA

In this work a hybrid algorithm based on Tabu Search (TS) and Simulated Annealing (SA) is developed to solve PRCPSP-ST. The proposed algorithm uses both advantages of TS and SA. Tabu search applies an intelligent local (http://en.wikipedia.org/wiki/Local_search_(optimization)) search procedure to iteratively move from one potential solution to an improved one by using memory structures that describe the visited solutions or user-provided sets of rules [13]. Simulated annealing is a random search method that is initially proposed by Kirkpatrick et al. [14]. SA algorithm starts by generating an initial solution and by initializing the temperature parameter T. Then, at each iteration a solution S' is randomly generated in the neighborhood of the current solution S and if it is an improvement upon the current solution, it replaces the current solution, else it replaces the current solution with a probability generally computed following the Boltzmann distribution:

$$p = \exp\left(-\frac{f(s') - f(s)}{T}\right) \tag{8}$$

where T is the current temperature and $f(s') - f(s)$ is the change in objective function value obtained by moving from previous solution to new solution. Tabu search and simulated annealing are successfully applied to a noticeable number of project scheduling problems. Solution representation, starting solution and neighborhood generation and tabus are the basic elements of TS/SA.

3.1 Solution Representation

Random-key (RK) and activity-list (AL) are two important representations for solutions in project scheduling. It is proved that AL representation outperform the others [15]. Herein the AL representation is applied to encode a schedule and a revised version of serial schedule generation scheme (SSGS) followed by a double justification is used to decode the codes to schedules. An activity i with duration of d_i is replaced by d_i activities with duration of 1 and the same resource requirements as the original activity. Then a feasible solution is represented by an $N' = \sum_{i=1}^{n} d_i$ elements vector (I). In this structure, each unit $j = 1, \ldots, d_i$ of an activity i is successor of the previous unit $(j-1)$.

$$I = (J^1, J^2, \ldots, J^{N'})$$ (9)

When a feasible solution represented by the above mentioned vector obtained, the start times of all activities is determined by a revised SSGS followed by a double justification. The SSGS sequentially adds activities to the partial schedule till a complete feasible schedule is achieved. In each step, the first un-scheduled activity in the AL is selected and the first possible start time is devoted to it preserving precedence and resource constraints. In the revised SSGS applied in this work, setup time after preemptions is embedded.

The double justification is an improvement procedure with two steps which is implemented on a schedule generated by the revised SSGS. In the first step, except for the first and the last dummy activities all activities are shifted to the right in the schedule which culminates in a right active schedule; a schedule where no activity can be finished later without delaying some other activities or increasing the makespan. In the second step, except for the initial activity; all activities are shifted to the left which results to a left active schedule; a schedule where no activity can be started earlier without violating the precedence or resource constraints.

3.2 Starting Solution

An initial solution is constructed by a Greedy Randomized Adaptive Search Procedure (GRASP) which is a two phase iterative procedure: construction and improvement [16]. The construction mechanism consists of two main components: a dynamic constructive heuristic and randomization. A solution is constructed by adding one new element from a set of elements at a time. The next element is selected randomly from a *candidate list* (*CL*). CL contains the activities that have all their predecessors already scheduled. The elements are prioritized based on a heuristic criterion that gives them a rank as a function of their insertion benefits. The second phase is a local search, which may be a basic or an advanced technique.

3.2.1 Construction Phase

At each stage, starting from the partial schedule assembled thus far, the *CL* is calculated. For each activity $j \in CL$, a priority *cost(j)* is calculated which is duration of the schedule resulted by adding the activity j to the partial schedule assembled thus far. Then activities with the lowest *cost(j)* are filtered to restricted candidate list (*RCL*). Length of *RCL* is controlled by a parameter $0 \leq \alpha \leq 1$. An activity is selected from *RCL* at random and inserted to partial schedule. This procedure continues until a complete schedule is reached.

3.2.2   Local Search Phase

After constructing the greedy randomized solution, the local search is employed on solution using the following Insertion procedure. First, an integer a is randomly selected from set $\{1, \ldots, N'\}$. Let J_e^a denotes the last predecessor and J_w^a denotes the first successor of activity J^a in activity list of the current solution I. Then, an integer h different from a is randomly selected from set $\{e + 1, \ldots, w - 1\}$. Finally, the activity in position a is moved to position h. This operator preserves the feasibility of the new solution. Local search procedure is continued until a predetermined number of iterations *max_neighbor* is reached. After the local search is done, the fitness of neighbor schedules is calculated and if the best neighbor schedule is better than current schedule, it replaces the schedule.

3.3   Main Structure of the Proposed TS/SA

Starting from the initial feasible solution S generated by GRASP, number of *max_subiteration* neighbor solutions is considered. Main structure of the proposed algorithm is based on SA, while neighborhood structure is based on TS. In regular TS, one must evaluate the objective for every element of the neighborhood $N(S)$ of the current solution. An alternative is to instead consider only a random sample $N'(S)$ of $N(S)$, thus reducing the computational effort. This sample must be large enough to get a better solution with a fair probability at the next search stage. In our implementation, the size of $N'(S)$ is set equal to the square root of the number of activities N'. Finally, the best neighbor solution generated by TS will be subject of acceptance criterion of SA. The choice of an appropriate cooling schedule is crucial for the performance of the SA. In proposed TS/SA a geometric law $T_{k+1} = \beta T_k; 0 \leq \beta \leq 1$ is used which corresponds to an exponential decay of the temperature. The procedure is continued until a predetermined number of schedules, *max_schedules*, are produced. We obtained good results by indexing the number of produced schedules to the size of the problem, i.e. use of the small number of produced schedules for small problems and large number of produced schedules for larger problems. Therefore after some trials to obtain reasonable results, we fixed the number of produced schedules limited to $100N'$.

3.4   Neighborhood Structure (Moves)

The neighbor generation operators (moves) utilized in TS/SA is defined as follows:

  i. Insertion: As described in Subsect. 3.2.2.
 ii. Swap: Two random integers, c and d are drawn from set $\{1, \ldots, N'\}$ with $c < d$. Then the positions of activities J^c and J^d in the activity list are exchanged. Also, some activities between these positions are shifted to left or right such that feasibility of resulting solution is preserved.

3.5   Tabu List

The tabu list is managed as follows: Whenever a feasible move performed, its reverse move is added to the tabu list and the oldest existing move is removed from the front of the list according to the First-in-First-out (FIFO) rule. All moves on the tabu list are forbidden. However, if a tabu move can generate a solution better than the best found so far its tabu status may be cancelled in the light of the aspiration criterion so that the algorithm can move to this solution.

3.6   Calibrating

Value of the meta-heuristics parameters and operators are crucial factors in their performance. Herein the Taguchi experimental design is applied to calibrate the parameters of the proposed TS/SA. The Taguchi method determines the optimal level of controllable factors and minimizes the effect of noise [17]. In the proposed GRASP, the factors that should be tuned are RCL control parameter, α, number of GRASP iterations, GRASPit, and number of neighbors, Nmax. A randomly generated problem with 30 non-dummy original activities and 102 sub-activities with duration of 1 is utilized for parameters tuning. Using MINITAB software version 16, a L9 orthogonal array design is applied. To obtain more reliable data each experiment executed 4 times and the best result is considered. Also, same selection and reproduction scheme is used for all 36 runs.

However, we used the Taguchi design to calibrate the number of neighbors (subiteration), length of Tabu list, initial temperature and cooling rate considering three levels for each of these parameters. With tuned values for GRASP parameters and using a L27 orthogonal array design, the randomly generated problem is considered again. The number of produced schedules limited to 10000 as stopping criterion. We found optimal levels of α, GRASPit and Nmax as 0.3, 20, and 10, respectively, while tuned values for number of neighbors (subiteration), length of Tabu list, initial temperature and cooling rate are 10, 0.3, 20 and 0.7, respectively (Fig. 1).

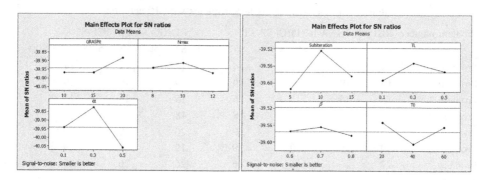

Fig. 1. The mean S/N ratio plot for the parameters

4 Performance Evaluation

4.1 Validation of Proposed Algorithm

In order to validate the proposed TS/SA algorithm for the PRCPSP-ST, a set of 10 problems with 10 non-dummy activities is generated by the generator ProGen developed by Drexl et al. [18] using the parameters given in Table 1.

Table 1. The parameter settings for the problem set

Control parameter	Value
Activity durations	Integer [1, 5]
Number of initial activities	Integer [1, 3]
Number of terminal activities	Integer [1, 2]
Maximal number of successors and predecessors	3
Number of renewable resources	2
Activity renewable resource demand (per period)	Integer [1, 10]
Resource factor (RF)	0.5
Resource strength (RS)	0.2
Network complexity (NC)	1.5

The proposed TS/SA were coded in Borland C++ 5.02 and executed on a personal computer with an Intel Core i5, 2.4 GHz processor and 4000 MB memory. Table 2 presents the computational results of the proposed algorithm. For problems with 10 activities, the results are compared with the optimal solutions obtained by LINGO 11. In Table 2, set up time ST of an activity is defined as a percent of its duration. Table 2 shows that when the number of activities is equal to 10, the results obtained by proposed TS/SA and LINGO are identical.

Also, Table 2 reveals that for problems 2, 3, 6, 8 and 10, makespan of the project in the preemptive RCPSP is same as the non-preemptive case. In problem 1, makespan of

Table 2. Comparison results for problems with 10 activities

Problem number	RCPSP	TS/SA for PRCPSP-ST			LINGO for PRCPSP-ST		
		ST = 0%	ST = 25%	ST = 50%	ST = 50%	ST = 50%	ST = 50%
Problem 1	14	13	14	14	14	14	14
Problem 2	19	19	19	19	19	19	19
Problem 3	15	15	15	15	15	15	15
Problem 4	18	17	17	18	18	18	18
Problem 5	20	19	19	20	20	20	20
Problem 6	19	19	19	19	19	19	19
Problem 7	27	26	26	26	26	26	26
Problem 8	22	22	22	22	22	22	22
Problem 9	24	23	23	23	23	23	23
Problem 10	19	19	19	19	19	19	19

PRCPSP without setup time (ST = 0%) is less than non-preemptive RCPSP, while when setup time is ST = 25% and 50%, preemption has no improving effect. In problems 4 and 5, a setup time up to ST = 25% and in problems 7 and 9, a setup time up to ST = 50% has improving effect on makespan of the project.

4.2 Experimental Results

In order to evaluate the proposed TS/SA for problems with more activities which LINGO is unable to solve the problem optimally in a reasonable time, a set of 90 project networks is considered. These project networks contain 30, 60 and 90 activities which are randomly chosen from the PSPLIB. The proposed TS/SA executed 10 times for each problem to obtain more reliable data. The results are reported in Table 3. In Table 3, Max.imp.(%) and Avr.imp.(%) denotes the maximum and average percentage of improvement in project makespan compared to non-preemptive RCPSP, respectively. Also, Imp.Inst.(%) denotes the percentage of improved problems compared to non-preemptive RCPSP. These measures in Table 3 reveal that when the number of activities or setup time is increased, the justifiability of preemption is reduced. This is

Table 3. Comparison of the results for problems with 30, 60 and 90 activities obtained by the TS/SA

ST(%)	Max.imp. (%)	Avr.imp. (%)	Imp.Inst. (%)	ARD (%)	Avr.CPU
0	6.4	1.18	30	0.08	163.586
25	4.7	0.34	10		106.549
50	2	0.18	6.66		77.648
0	8.1	0.82	16.66	0.19	1250.73
25	3.9	0.27	13.33		712.734
50	1.9	0.06	3.33		466.666
0	4.2	0.35	16.66	0.20	545.476
25	1.3	0.04	3.33		339.097
50	0.00	0.00	0.00		213.137

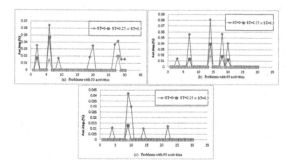

Fig. 2. Average improvement PRCPSP-ST to RCPSP

demonstrated in Fig. 2 based on Avr.imp.(%). Avr.CPU denotes the average CPU-time for the TS/SA (in seconds). Average CPU-time for TS/SA indicates when the number of activities is increased the complexity of problem is increased, too. Also, average CPU-time is a decreasing function of setup time ST%. ARD(%) denotes the average relative deviation percentages from the best found solution by the TS/SA. ARDs for the TS/SA algorithm are not high. This means that proposed TS/SA gives robust solutions. These results show that when the number of activities is large, while the LINGO is unable to solve the problem, there is a satisfying solution by the proposed TS/SA in a reasonable CPU time.

5 Conclusions

In this paper, we formulated and solved the preemptive resource constrained project scheduling problem with setup time to resume preempted activities. The objective is to schedule the activities in order to minimize of project duration subject to the precedence relations and renewable resource constraints. The problem was conceptually formulated, and then a hybrid of tabu search and simulated annealing (TS/SA) was designed to solve it. The parameters of proposed TS/SA were calibrated based on Taguchi experimental design. The evaluation of the proposed algorithm is done on 100 test problems with 10, 30, 60 and 90 activities. From the computation results, we found that the TS/SA algorithm could efficiently solve optimally the problems with 10 activities. Also, for problems with more activities which LINGO was unable to solve the problem optimally, we could find out that the proposed TS/SA is capable to find a satisfying solution in a reasonable CPU time. However results showed that the justifiability of preemption is a decreasing function of the number of activities and setup time.

References

1. Blazewicz, J., Lenstra, J., Rinnooy Kan, A.: Scheduling subject to resource constraints: classification and complexity. Discrete Appl. Math. **5**, 11–24 (1983)
2. Hartmann, S., Briskorn, D.A.: Surveys of variants and extensions of the resource constrained project scheduling problem. Eur. J. Oper. Res. **207**(1), 1–14 (2010)
3. Fang, C., Wang, L.: An effective shuffled frog-learning algorithm for resource constrained project scheduling problem. Comput. Oper. Res. **39**(5), 890–901 (2012)
4. Kone, O.: New approaches for solving the resource constrained project scheduling problem. 4OR **10**(1), 105–106 (2012)
5. Paraskevopoulos, D.C., Tarantilis, C.D., Ioannou, G.: Solving project scheduling problems with resource constraints via an event list-based evolutionary algorithm. Expert Syst. Appl. **39**(4), 3983–3994 (2012)
6. Van Peteghem, V., Vanhoucke, M.: A genetic algorithm for the preemptive and non-preemptive multi-mode resource constrained project scheduling problem. Eur. J. Oper. Res. **201**(2), 409–418 (2010)

7. Afshar-Nadjafi, B., Majlesi, M.: Resource constrained project scheduling problem with setup times after preemptive processes. Comput. Chem. Eng. **69**, 16–25 (2014)
8. Moukrim, A., Quilliot, A., Toussaint, H.: An effective branch-and-price algorithm for the preemptive resource constrained project scheduling problem based on minimal interval order enumeration. Eur. J. Oper. Res. **244**, 360–368 (2015)
9. Roshanaei, V., Naderi, B., Jolai, F., Khalili, M.: A variable neighborhood search for job shop scheduling with setup times to minimize makespan. Future Gener. Comput. Syst. **25**, 654–661 (2009)
10. Nagano, M.S., Silva, A.A., Lorena, L.A.N.: A new evolutionary clustering search for a no-wait flow shop problem with setup times. Eng. Appl. Artif. Intell. **25**(6), 1114–1120 (2012)
11. Liao, C.J., Chao, C.W., Chen, L.C.: An improved heuristic for parallel machine weighted flow time scheduling with family setup times. Comput. Math. Appl. **63**(1), 110–117 (2012)
12. Kolisch, R.: Project Scheduling Under Resource Constraints - Efficient Heuristics for Several Problem Classes. Physica, Heidelberg (1995)
13. Glover, F., Laguna, M.: Tabu Search. Kluwer Academic Publishers, Norwell (1997)
14. Kirkpatrick, S., Gelatt, C., Vecchi, M.: Optimization by simulated annealing. Science **220**, 671–680 (1983)
15. Hartmann, S., Kolisch, R.: Experimental evaluation of state-of-the-art heuristics for the resource constrained project scheduling problem. Eur. J. Oper. Res. **127**, 394–407 (2000)
16. Pitsoulis, L.S., Resende, M.G.C.: Greedy randomized adaptive search procedure. In: Pardalos, P., Resende, M. (eds.) Handbook of Applied Optimization, pp. 168–183. Oxford University Press, Oxford (2002)
17. Taguchi, G.: Introduction to Quality Engineering. Asian Productivity Organization, Tokyo (1986)
18. Drexl, A., Nissen, R., Patterson, J.H., Salewski, F.: ProGen/πx - an instance generator for resource constrained project scheduling problems with partially renewable resources and further extensions. Eur. J. Oper. Res. **125**, 59–72 (2000)

Elitist Ant System for the Distributed Job Shop Scheduling Problem

Imen Chaouch[1,2(✉)], Olfa Belkahla Driss[1,3], and Khaled Ghedira[1,4]

[1] COSMOS Laboratory, Université de la Manouba, Manouba, Tunisia
imen.chaouch@ensi.rnu.tn, {olfa.belkahla,khaled.ghedira}@isg.rnu.tn
[2] Ecole Nationale des Sciences de l'Informatique,
Université de la Manouba, Manouba, Tunisia
[3] Ecole Supérieure de Commerce de Tunis,
Université de la Manouba, Manouba, Tunisia
[4] Institut Supérieur de Gestion de Tunis,
Université de Tunis, Tunis, Tunisia

Abstract. In this paper, we are interested in industrial plants geographically distributed and more precisely the Distributed Job shop Scheduling Problem (DJSP) in multi-factory environment. The problem consists of finding an effective way to assign jobs to factories then, to generate a good operation schedule. To do this, a bio-inspired algorithm is applied, namely the Elitist Ant System (EAS) aiming to minimize the makespan. Several numerical experiments are conducted to evaluate the performance of our algorithm applied to the Distributed Job shop Scheduling Problem and the results show the shortcoming of the Elitist Ant System compared to developed algorithms in the literature.

Keywords: Elitist Ant System · Job shop · Makespan · Multi-factory · Scheduling

1 Introduction

The manufacturing industry has undergone an important evolution these recent years due to the trend of globalisation. Owing to this evolution, there have been significant changes in the structure of production plants. Industrial companies are increasingly merging to distributed ones and thus, the structure of their shops changes from simple configurations to distributed ones. In this paper, we focus on the Distributed Job shop Scheduling Problem (DJSP), which can be considered as an extension of the simple Job shop Scheduling Problem (JSP). It can be treated as a set of f factories, which are geographically distributed in different areas. Distributed Scheduling problems in multi-factory production are much more complicated than classical scheduling problems [2] since two decisions have to be taken: allocating jobs to suitable factories and sequencing the operations on machines so that yield a feasible schedule aiming to minimize one or more predefined performance criteria.

© Springer International Publishing AG 2017
S. Benferhat et al. (Eds.): IEA/AIE 2017, Part I, LNAI 10350, pp. 112–117, 2017.
DOI: 10.1007/978-3-319-60042-0_12

In this work, we seek to minimize the maximum completion time (makespan, denoted as C_{max}) of DJSP, which is the maximum makespan among all factories using the Elitist Ant System (EAS) and assuming that all factories are identical due to the complexity of the problem in such a system.

Garey et al. [5] proved that the JSP is strongly NP-hard. Hence, the DJSP is ordinarily NP-hard and the case of the simple JSP can be obtained when $f = 1$.

The rest of the paper is organized as follows. Section 2 gives the specifications of the DJSP and a short literature review of the limited existing literature on DJSP is provided. Section 3 proposes an effective way to assign jobs to factories and sketches the proposed Elitist Ant System algorithm. Section 4 conducts the numerical experiments. Finally, Sect. 5 concludes the paper and suggests few future research directions.

2   Problem Statement and State-of-the-Art

The DJSP can be stated as follows: a set $J = \{j_1...j_n\}$ of independent jobs, each of which consists of an ordered set of operations. Each operation must be executed on a specific machine from a set $M = \{i_1...i_m\}$ of machines geographically distributed on f identical factories. The main objective of the problem is to find an optimal scheduling minimizing a specified criterion which is generally time related such as makespan, maximum tardiness or total tardiness. In our case, we are aiming to minimize the maximum completion time (makespan) among all factories. There are various constraints on both jobs and machines. Each operation needs to be processed during an uninterrupted time of a fixed processing period and a given machine. A job can be processed by at most one machine at a time and a machine can process at most one job at a time. Furthermore, there are no precedence constraints among the operations of different jobs. In addition, it is assumed that a job does not visit the same machine twice and neither the release times nor due dates are specified. In the DJSP all operations of a job should be assigned to the same factory.

Researchers are beginning to study the DJSP recently. We can find [6–8] which have studied the DJSP and proposed a Genetic Algorithm approach in order to facilitate collaboration between geographically distributed plants. Recently, the problem of DJS have been mathematically formulated by [9] and six heuristics were adapted to the problem. In their next paper [10] have differently treated the problem using a simulated annealing algorithm and two additional mechanisms of local search.

3   The Proposed Ant System Algorithm

3.1   Job-Factory Assignment

A crucial step in solving the DJS problem is the allocation of jobs to suitable factory. The objective is to partition jobs into factories so as to equilibrate the workload in different factories. In our approach, we use the *job-facility assign-ment rule* introduced in [9]. As first step, the workload on each machine is separately calculated using the following rule:

$$workload(j,i) = \left(\sum_{k \in R_{j,i}} p_{j,k} \right) + p_{j,i} \quad \forall_{i,j} \tag{1}$$

where $R_{j,i}$ is the set of all machines preceding machine i in the processing of job j and $P_{j,i}$ is the processing time of job j on machine i. The Workload of each operation is calculated and regarding the total workloads, the jobs are ranked in descending order, from highest workload to the lowest ones. Suppose that we have f factories. The n first jobs are assigned to factories $\{1...n\}$, respectively. The workload of machines on different factories becomes equal to those of the assigned jobs and the maximum workload in the f factories is determined. To assign the next job, the maximum workload is calculated if the job is assigned to a factory. All the possibilities should be enumerated and the workload is calculated at each time. Then, the job is assigned to the factory with minimum of the maximum workload. The procedure repeats for subsequent jobs until all jobs are assigned. This method proved to be efficient to well equilibrate workloads in different factories.

3.2   Elitist Ant System Applied to the DJSP

Once all jobs are affected to their corresponding factory, they need to be sequenced. To do this, an improved version of the classic Ant System algo-rithm introduced by [3, 4] is applied, namely the Elitist Ant System (EAS). As the name suggests, ant algorithms have been inspired by the behavior of real ant colonies, in particular, by their collective foraging behaviour. The first Ant Colony System (ACS) was introduced by Dorigo's Ph.D. [3], which is called Ant System (AS). The basic idea in AS is to imitate the cooperative behavior of real ants to solve optimization problems [12]. In the nature, ants are able to find the shortest path between a food source and their nest according to their collective behaviour. During their move, they lay down a chemical trail (pheromone) on the ground, which guides other ants towards best path. In DJSP, the aim is to find the best path giving the minimum makespan among all possible paths.

The difference between AS and our employed EAS is the pheromone updates rule. In the AS algorithm, every ant has the same "weight" in contributing to the pheromone trail, but in EAS the best ant contributes more than other ants. Main steps of proposed EAS algorithm are listed below:

Step 1: Constructing solutions by ants
The first procedure consists of a probabilistic construction of solutions by all the ants according to the State Transition Rule. The probability for an ant to choose its next node is directed by both the amount of pheromone on the route

and heuristic distance from its current location to the next one.

$$s = \begin{cases} argmax_{u \in AllowedNodes} \left[\tau_{i,j}(t)\right]^{\alpha} \times \left[\frac{1}{d_{i,j}}\right]^{\beta}, if\, q <= q_0 \\ S,\, otherwise(biased\, exploitation) \end{cases} \tag{2}$$

with

- $\tau_{i,j}$ quantity on pheromone between the $node_i$ and $node_j$
- $d_{i;j}$ heuristic distance between $node_i$ and $node_j$. In our case, $d_{i;j}$ is the processing time of the operation.
- q is a random number uniformly distributed in $[0, 1]$
- q_0 is a user-defined parameter with $(0 <= q_0 <= 1)$
- $p_{i;j}$ probability to branch from $node_i$ to $node_j$
- The parameters α and β tune the relative importance in probability of the amount of pheromone versus the heuristic distance.
- S is a random variable selected according to the probability distribution given below:

$$P(i, s)(t) = \begin{cases} \dfrac{\left[\tau_{i,s}(t)\right]^{\alpha} \times \left[\frac{1}{d_{i,s}}\right]^{\beta}}{\sum_{j \in AllowedNodes} \left[\tau_{i,j}(t)\right]^{\alpha} \times \left[\frac{1}{d_{i,j}}\right]^{\beta}} \\ 0,\, otherwise \end{cases} \tag{3}$$

Step 2: Local Updating pheromone

While constructing its solution, an ant will modify the amount of pheromone on the visited edges by applying the local updating rule.

$$\tau_{i,s}(t + n) = (1 - \rho) \times \tau_{i,s}(t) + \rho \times \tau_0(t + n) \tag{4}$$

where ρ is the coefficient representing pheromone evaporation (note: $0 < \rho < 1$). The purpose of the local pheromone update rule is to make the visited edges less and less attractive as they are visited by ants, indirectly favouring the exploration of not yet visited edges. As a consequence, ants tend not to converge to a common path [1].

Step 3 : Global Updating pheromone

Once all ants have generated a solution, the global updating rule is applied in two phases: *An evaporation phase* where a fraction of the pheromone evaporates and decreases automatically, so as to diversify the search procedure into larger solution spaces and *a reinforcement phase* where each ant deposits an amount of pheromone which is proportional to the generated solutions

$$\tau_{i,s}(t + n) = (1 - \xi) \times \tau_{i,s}(t) + \xi \times \Delta\tau_{i,s}(t + n) \tag{5}$$

$$\Delta\tau_{i,s}(t + n) = \frac{Q}{BestC_{max_{ant}}} \tag{6}$$

Here: $0 < \xi < 1$ is the pheromone decay parameter and Q is a constant.

The process is repeated until a termination condition has been reached which is a fixed number of iterations.

4   Numerical Experiments

To test the performance of the EAS applied to the DJSP on large instances, we use those of Taillard benchmark for job shops [11]. This benchmark includes 8 combinations for n and m, and 10 instances for each combination. It sums up to 80 instances. Each instance is solved by different levels of $f(f = 2, 3, 4, 5)$; thus, there are 320 instances. First, the EAS parameters are tuning and the best results are obtained with the parameters initialized as $\alpha = 1, \beta = 1, \rho = 0.7, \xi = 0.7, Q_0 = 0.8$, the number of iterations is fixed at 1000. The results described in the following sections have been obtained on a personal computer with 3.4 GHz Intel Core i7 and 8 GB of RAM memory. The performance measure used in this research is Relative Percentage Deviation (RPD). It can be calculated as follows:

$$RPD = \frac{Alg - Min}{Min} \times 100 \qquad (7)$$

where Alg is the makespan obtained by any of the algorithm and Min is the lowest makespan obtained for a given instance.

Table 1. The RPD of the EAS compared with other algorithms

n	m	Algorithms					
		EAS	HSA	SA	GSA	GA	GH3
15	15	11.48	0.42	0.34	0.79	2.35	5.37
20	15	13.55	0.76	0.92	2.06	3.85	9.69
	20	27.58	0.2	0.31	1.30	6.36	8.79
30	15	19.10	0.4	1.35	2.65	6.07	11.73
	20	45.60	0.14	0.95	2.00	9.09	13.97
50	15	38.75	1.68	3.42	3.45	10.17	20.46
	20	84.25	0.12	3.19	2.44	12.81	19.40
100	20	117	0.00	6.89	8.52	20.77	61.09
Average		44.29	0.46	2.17	2.90	8.93	18.81

Results are compared with six available algorithms, GH3 proposed in [9], Simulated Annealing (SA), Hybridized Simulated Annealing (HAS), Greedy Simulated Annealing (GSA) in [10] and Genetic Algorithm (GA) in [7]. Table 1 shows the results averaged by the combinations of (n, m). We should mention that in our algorithm we consider the optimal of [11] as best makespan, however the other authors considered their own best makespan as optimum solution.

As we can see from Table 1, for larger instances EAS gives a very poor solution quality compared to state-of-the-art algorithms with average RPD of 44.29. This is due to randomized character of the EAS algorithm which makes probabilistic decisions in the construction of the solution. EAS gives better results than the classic AS but still poor compared to the existed state-of-the-art.

5 Conclusion and Perspectives

In this work, we have applied the Elitist Ant System algorithm for the first time to solve the Distributed Job shop Scheduling Problem with makespan minimization criterion. The algorithm is compared with other algorithms in literature. Results are very poor for large instances and show that the EAS is not competitive at all comparing to other methods.

For future work, it will be interesting to investigate on the different variations of Ant System and maybe the integration of local search leads to a possible improvement of the results. Also, we can study the problem aiming to optimize other objectives. And finally, we can consider the case of a DJSP with non identical factories. Because somewhere, considering that the factories are the same, can be an idealization to the real problem, since it is rarely the case.

References

1. Bonabeau, E., Dorigo, M., Theraulaz, G.: Swarm Intelligence: from Natural to Artificial Systems, vol. 1. Oxford University Press, New York (1999)
2. Chung, S.H., Lau, H.C., Ho, G.T., Ip, W.: Optimization of system reliability in multi-factory production networks by maintenance approach. Expert Syst. Appl. **36**(6), 10188–10196 (2009)
3. Dorigo, M.: Optimization, learning and natural algorithms. Ph.D. thesis, Politecnico di Milano, Italy (1992)
4. Dorigo, M., Maniezzo, V., Colorni, A.: Ant system: optimization by a colony of cooperating agents. IEEE Trans. Syst. Man Cybern. Part B (Cybern.) **26**(1), 29–41 (1996)
5. Garey, M.R., Johnson, D.S., Sethi, R.: The complexity of flowshop and jobshop scheduling. Math. Oper. Res. **1**(2), 117–129 (1976)
6. Jia, H., Fuh, J.Y., Nee, A.Y., Zhang, Y.: Web-based multi-functional scheduling system for a distributed manufacturing environment. Concurrent Eng. **10**(1), 27–39 (2002)
7. Jia, H., Fuh, J.Y., Nee, A.Y., Zhang, Y.: Integration of genetic algorithm and gantt chart for job shop scheduling in distributed manufacturing systems. Comput. Ind. Eng. **53**(2), 313–320 (2007)
8. Jia, H., Nee, A.Y., Fuh, J.Y., Zhang, Y.: A modified genetic algorithm for distributed scheduling problems. J. Intell. Manufact. **14**(3–4), 351–362 (2003)
9. Naderi, B., Azab, A.: Modeling and heuristics for scheduling of distributed job shops. Expert Syst. Appl. **41**(17), 7754–7763 (2014)
10. Naderi, B., Azab, A.: An improved model and novel simulated annealing for distributed job shop problems. Int. J. Adv. Manufact. Technol. **81**, 1–11 (2015)
11. Taillard, E.: Benchmarks for basic scheduling problems. Eur. J. Oper. Res. **64**(2), 278–285 (1993)
12. Talbi, E.G.: Metaheuristics: from Design to Implementation, vol. 74. Wiley, New York (2009)

Fuzzy Reinforcement Learning for Routing in Multi-Hop Cognitive Radio Networks

Jerzy Martyna[✉]

Faculty of Mathematics and Computer Science, Institute of Computer Science,
Jagiellonian University, ul. Prof. S. Lojasiewicza 6, 30-348 Cracow, Poland
jerzy.martyna@gmail.com

Abstract. Cognitive radio networks (CRNs) are composed of cognitive, spectrum-agile devices capable of changing their configuration on the fly, based on the spectrum assignment policy. Moreover, the CRNs technology allows sharing of licensed spectrum band in an opportunistic and non-interfering manner. Routing and the spectrum management are the challenges in these networks. To solve these problems, in this paper, a fuzzy reinforcement learning method is proposed, where a new fuzzy reinforcement learning procedure is built in each secondary user (SU). The proposed procedure learns the best routing with a guarantee that the interference at the primary receivers is below the threshold and focuses on the problem of effective routing solutions in multi-hop CRNs.

1 Introduction

The cognitive radio (CR) technology is a wireless network technology based on intelligent radio equipments. Thus, the CR technology allows sharing of a wireless channel with licensed users in an opportunistic manner. The networks built with the CR technology, referred as cognitive radio networks (CRNs), provide high bandwidth to mobile users through heterogeneous wireless architectures.

For routing in traditional wireless networks, the same frequencies for communication are deployed. Only the transmission power and the topology of nodes are affected for the routing. In CR networks, routing is a combination of traditional routing and spectrum management, since spectrum availability is also dependent on the activity of the PUs. Thus, routing and spectrum management in the CR networks can be considered by the cross-layer approach and the decoupled approach. The first approach and spectrum management are treated jointly. In the decoupled approach, the route is performed independently of spectrum management by the use several path algorithms. After finding some candidate paths through an analysis of the spectrum availability, the solution, with respect to channels is determined. The cross-layer approach is more beneficial for the CR networks [2].

For routing, decision in the CR networks and spectrum management must be solved a.o. the following problems [4]:

© Springer International Publishing AG 2017
S. Benferhat et al. (Eds.): IEA/AIE 2017, Part I, LNAI 10350, pp. 118–123, 2017.
DOI: 10.1007/978-3-319-60042-0_13

(1) Due to lack of broadcasting or global broadcast messages, specific functionalities, such as neighbour discovery, route discovery and route establishment, are not possible to obtain.
(2) The network connectivity in the CR network depends on the spectrum availability. Therefore, the intermittent connectivity in CRNs may frequently change under the influence of the spectrum availability and PUs activity.
(3) Primary user (PU) activity affects routing in such a way as the bandwidth, delay, energy efficiency, achievable throughput, etc.

In this paper, a new fuzzy reinforcement learning method for routing in multi-hop cognitive radio networks is introduced. This method provides on-demand route discovery method, which also takes into consideration the PUs activity as well as a new route metric of link quality in CRN. Thus, the cognitive route cost and the route metric is determined. Finally, the proposed method allows us to obtain the proper route.

The rest of paper is organized as follows. Section 2 gives the system model. Section 3, includes the fuzzy reinforcement learning method for routing in the CR networks and all fuzzy rules used in this approach. Simulation results are outlined in Sect. 4. Finally, this paper is concluded in Sect. 5.

2 The System Model

In this section, the statement of system for routing in multi-hop cognitive radio networks is presented.

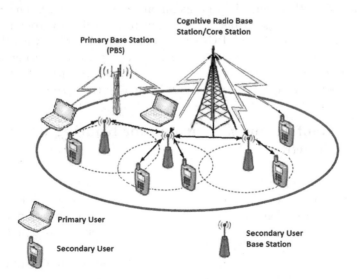

Fig. 1. Basic architecture of downlink/uplink cognitive radio network.

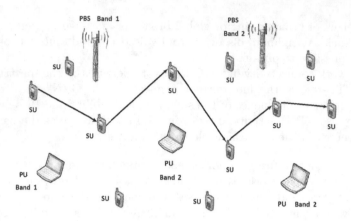

Fig. 2. Multi-hop routing in cognitive radio network.

A cognitive radio network (CRN) with one or more PUs and some number of SUs can be illustrated in Fig. 1. Typically, each PU is assigned with licensed bands by a centralized primary base station (PBS). All SUs who have not been allocated spectrum-usage rights can utilize the temporally unused licensed bands owned by PUs. In the CRN architecture, the components include both a secondary network and primary network. Therefore, all SUs have evaluation of the spectrum white space (free bands, free transmission slots, etc.) to trade own transmission.

The problem of routing in multi-hop CRNs requires the creation and the maintenance of wireless multi-hop paths among SUs (see Fig. 2). The SUs may have different views of the available spectrum bands gained through the local spectrum process. Typically the PUs are immobile and interfere with the transmission of data between SUs, which can change their positions during transmission. Thus, the multi-hop routing in CRNs requires constant analysis of link-quality, topology changes and connectivity broken by the activities of PUs.

3   Fuzzy Reinforcement Learning for Routing in Cognitive Radio Networks

We assume that a single SU station is equipped with three detectors: one to detect the current SINR, the second to indicate usefulness of remote SU station, and the third to denote the value of the indicator to specify whether the secondary system is generating an aggregated interference above or below the threshold of the primary receivers [3].

For a two-dimensional environment, all the information obtained by the j-th SU about the current SINR is defined by the membership functions μ_x, μ_y, namely

A membership function defining the fuzzy state of the usefulness k-th SU defining possible data transmission for a two-dimensional environment is as follows:

$$\mu_{state}^{(j)}(usefulness^{(k)}) = \mu_x^{(j)}(usefulness^{(k)}) \cdot \mu_y^{(j)}(usefulness^{(k)}) \qquad (1)$$

A membership function defining the fuzzy state of the indicator for the j-th SU specifying whether the secondary system is generating an aggregated interference above or below the given threshold of the primary receivers is as follows:

$$\mu_{state}^{(j)}(I) = \mu_x^{(j)}(I) \cdot \mu_y^{(j)}(I) \qquad (2)$$

The system model is described by the multidimensional membership function, which can be treated as a multidimensional hypercube. The fuzzy state for the j-th SU can be defined by the fuzzy pair (s_n, a_n) for the n-th fuzzy variable, where s and a are the state and action respectively.

Using the aggregation of the fuzzy state, we can achieve:

$$Q_{state}^{(j)}(s, a) \leftarrow Q_{state}^{(j)}(s, a) + \sum_{n=1}^{N} \alpha_n^{(j)} \cdot \mu_{state}^{(j)}(s_n, a_n) \qquad (3)$$

where N is the total number of fuzzy variables.

For the three exemplary fuzzy variables we have the Q-function for j-th SU, namely

$$Q_{state}^{(j)} \leftarrow Q_{state}^{(j)}(s, a)$$
$$+ \sum_{k=1}^{K} (\alpha_k^{(j)} \mu_{state}^{(j)}(SINR) + \alpha_k^{(j)} \mu_{state}^{(j)}(usefulness^{(k)}))$$
$$+ \sum_{k=1}^{K} (\alpha_k^{(j)} \mu_{state}^{(j)}(I)) \qquad (4)$$

where $\alpha_n^{(j)}$ is the learning rate for SU j with respect to n-th fuzzy variable, K is the total number of SUs, l-th $(1 \leq l \leq L)$ is the nearest PU for j-th SU, L is the total number of PU.

Let the radio transmitting range of the SU be equal to R. Thus, we can again define the Q-function value as follows:

$$Q_{state}^{(j)}(s_{t+1}, a_{t+1}) \leftarrow \begin{cases} 0 & \text{if } j \notin \{J\} \\ Q_{state}^{(j)}(s_t, a_t) + \alpha_{state}^{(j)}(s_t, a_t) & \text{if } j \in \{J_{0<r\leq 0.5R}\} \\ Q_{state}^{(j)}(s_t, a_t) + \beta^{(j)} Q_{state}^{(j)}(s_t, a_t) & \text{if } j \in \{J_{0.5R<r\leq R}\} \end{cases} \qquad (5)$$

where $\{J\}$ is the set of SUs and PUs in the range of the SU observation with the radius equal to R, $\{J_{0<r\leq 0.5 \cdot R}\}$ and $\{J_{0.5 \cdot R<r\leq R}\}$ are the sets of SUs and

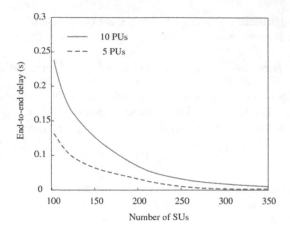

Fig. 3. Average end-to-end delay versus the number of SUs.

PUs in the range of the SU observation with the radius equal to $0 < r \le 0.5 \cdot R$ and $0.5 \cdot R < r \le R$, respectively. $\beta^{(j)}$ are learning rate factors.

The state space in reinforcement learning can be treated as a stochastic problem. In the standard approach, we can generalise the Q-value across states using the function approximation $Q(s, a, f)$ for approximating $Q(s, a)$, where f is the set of all learned fuzzy logic mechanisms [1].

4   Simulation Results

This section complements the previous sections with simulation studies. The objective of the simulations is to check the validity of the solution approaches: we validate the basic model of fuzzy reinforcement learning for routing in multi-hop CR networks, and get an insight on when it performs well.

In our simulation, a model of multi-hop CR network, based on the IEEE 802.11 standard, was performed, in which nodes are randomly distributed in an area of $1000 \times 1000 \, \text{m}^2$. Only one PU base station was applied in all of the experiments. The transmission range of each node is equal to $200 \, \text{m}$. For each node, the transmission interval equal to $100 \, \text{ms}$.

A following assumption was made that initially all the values of Q-function had an identical Q-value equal to 0.5. The learning rates are $\alpha = 0.5$ and $\gamma = 0.7$, respectively. It was also established that the threshold value of $SINR_{Th}$ is equal to $25 \, \text{dB}$.

At first, the impact of the SUs density on the end-to-end delay has been studied. Figure 3 shows the average end-to-end delay versus the number of SUs in the CR network for various value of PUs. The graphs in Fig. 3 show that the growth of the PU number gives the greater value of the delay.

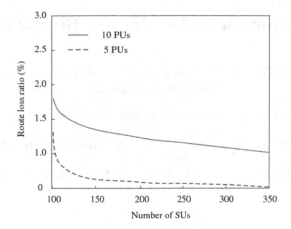

Fig. 4. Route loss ratio in dependence of the SUs number.

Next, the impact of the SUs density on the route loss ratio has been the subject of analysis. Figure 4 shows the dependence of route loss ratio in dependence of the SUs number for different value of PUs. It is evident that the increased number of PUs increases route loss ratio.

5   Conclusion

Here, a new routing method in the multi-hop CR networks is presented in detail. This method combines two simple yet powerful features: integration of spectrum and route discovery to establish communications across areas of spectrum availability and the fuzzy reinforcement learning approach. Moreover, the proposed method exploits the joint path and spectrum diversity in routing in order to provide multi-path routes with an aim to offer route discovery in appearance of path failures caused by PU activities during data delivery. The simulation results have confirmed that the proposed method is comparable to the classical routing methods in the CR networks.

References

1. Beon, H.R., Chen, H.S.: A sensor-based navigation for a mobile robot using fuzzy-logic and reinforcement learning. IEEE Trans. Syst. Man Cybern. **25**(3), 467–477 (1995)
2. Cesana, M., Cuomo, F., Ekici, E.: Routing in cognitive radio networks: challenges and solutions. Ad Hoc Netw. **9**(3), 228–248 (2011)
3. Galindo-Serrano, A., Giupponi, L.: Distributed Q-learning for aggregated interference control in cognitive radio networks. IEEE Trans. Veh. Technol. **59**(4), 1823–1834 (2010)
4. Hadawale, K., Barve, S.: Routing solutions in cognitive radio network using local network state information. Int. J. Emerg. Technol. Comput. Appl. Sci. (IJETCAS 13-112) **4**(1), 72–76 (2013)

FJS Problem Under Machine Breakdowns

Rim Zarrouk[1]([⊠]), Imed Bennour[1], Abderrazak Jemai[2],
and Abdelghani Bekrar[3]

[1] Labo NOCCS, National Engineering School of Sousse, Sousse, Tunisia
rima.zarrouk@gmail.com
[2] Labo LIP2, Faculty of Sciences of Tunis, University of Tunis El Manar,
Tunis, Tunisia
[3] LAMIH, University of Valenciennes and Hainaut-Cambrésis, UVHC,
Valenciennes, France

Abstract. One of the most challenging problems in manufacturing field is to solve the flexible job shop (FJS) problem subject to machines breakdown. In this paper, we propose two rescheduling solutions to handle machine breakdowns: a PSO-based solution and a shifting-based solution. The first solution aims to improve the robustness while the second solution aims to improve the stability.

Keywords: Flexible job shop · Machine breakdowns · Particle swarm optimization · Scheduling

1 Introduction

The FJS Problem consists in scheduling a set of operations forming jobs on a limited set of machines such that the maximal completion time of all operations is minimized. FJS problem is a strongly NP-hard problem and handling random machine breakdowns further complicates the problem. In the context of machines breakdown, there are two phases: a prescheduling phase (before the breakdown) and a rescheduling phase (after the breakdown). The quality of a rescheduling solution is often measured by three criteria: completion time of all jobs, robustness and stability comparing to the prescheduling solution [2]. Machines breakdown can be handled at priori (preventive) [1], at posteriori (curative) [5–7] or at both stages [3]. In [1] a genetic algorithm with idle-time insertions is proposed. In [5, 6], a genetic algorithm combining right shift strategy (RSS) and route is proposed as a curative solution. In [3] authors use the particle swarm optimization (PSO) and RSS to handle machine breakdowns.

In this paper, two curative solutions are presented: PSO historic route changing (PSO-HRC) and modified shifting strategy (MSS). The first aims to improve the robustness while the second aims to improve the stability. Two assumptions are used: a single machine breakdown and non-resumable mode (i.e. affected operations have to be restarted).

© Springer International Publishing AG 2017
S. Benferhat et al. (Eds.): IEA/AIE 2017, Part I, LNAI 10350, pp. 124–130, 2017.
DOI: 10.1007/978-3-319-60042-0_14

This paper is organized as follows. Sections 2 and 3 define respectively the FJS problem under breakdown machine, and the PSO meta-heuristic. Sections 4 and 5 present respectively the proposed curative solutions and the experimental results. Section 6 concludes the paper.

2 The FJS Problem with Stability and Robustness Criteria

The FJS problem is defined by:

$J = \{J_1, J_2 \ldots J_n\}$ *a set of n independent jobs,* $M = \{m_1, m_2 \ldots m_k\}$ *a set of machines and* $O = \{(O_{11}, O_{12}, \ldots), (O_{21}, O_{22}, \ldots) \ldots (O_{n1}, O_{n2}, \ldots)\}$ *the set of operations, where* O_{ji} *is operation i of job j.*

The goal is to find a schedule of operations that minimizes the completion times of all jobs (MakeSpan of the schedule), where, C_j *is the completion time of job J:*

$$MS = Minimize\left[Max\left(C_1, C_2, \ldots C_j\right)\right] \tag{1}$$

We will use the same definitions of robustness and stability of the rescheduling solution as in [1, 8]. Two formulas are used to measure robustness:

$$RM1 = \frac{MS_r - MS_p}{MS_p} \times 100\% \tag{2}$$

where, MS_p is the makespan of the prescheduling solution and MS_r is the makespan of the rescheduling solution. A schedule is robust if RM1 is low.

$$RM2 = \sum_{i=1}^{o} \frac{Load_m}{Load_{tot}} Pt_i \tag{3}$$

$$Load_{tot} = \sum_{m=i}^{k} Load_m \tag{4}$$

where, Pt_i is the processing time of the i and $Load_m$ is the workload of theMachine handling operation i. A schedule is robust if RM2 is high.

Three formulas are used to measure stability:

$$SM1 = \sum_{j=1}^{n} \sum_{i=1}^{qj} \left|c_{O_{jip}} - c_{O_{jir}}\right| \tag{5}$$

$$SM2 = \frac{\sum_{j=1}^{n} \sum_{i=1}^{qj} \left|C_{O_{jir}} - C_{O_{jir}}\right|}{\sum_{j=1}^{n} Oj} \tag{6}$$

$$SM3 = \frac{\sum_{j=1}^{n} \sum_{i=1}^{qj} |C_{O_{jio}} - C_{O_{jir}}|}{\sum_{i=1}^{n} \sum_{j=1}^{qi} AO_j} \tag{7}$$

where, n is the number of jobs, q_j is the number of operations in job j, $c_{O_{jiP}}$ the completion time of O_{ji} in the pre-schedule, $c_{O_{jir}}$ the completion time of O_{ji} in the re-schedule, and O_j the total number of operations of job j and, AO_i the total number of operations in jobs j affected by the breakdown.

3   The PSO Meta-heuristic

The PSO [3] works by having a population of candidate solutions that are moving around in the search space in order to improve their current solutions. The movements of particles are guided by their own best-known position in the search-space as well as the entire swarm's best-known position. At each instant, each particle p takes a new position vector noted $X_p(t)$, and new velocity vector noted $V_p(t)$, are computed using:

$$V_{p,d}(t+1) = w.V_{p,d}(t) + K_1.r_1 \left(Xbest_{p,d}(t) - X_{p,d}(t) \right) + K_2.r_2 \left(Xgbest_{p,d}(t) - X_{p,d}(t) \right) \tag{8}$$

$$X_{p,d}(t+1) = X_{p,d}(t) + V_{p,d}(t+1) \tag{9}$$

Where, d is the dimension of vectors, $Xbest_p(t-1)$ is the best position reached by the particle up to time $t-1$, $Xgbest_p(t)$ is the best position ever found by the whole swarm. r_1 and r_2 are random numbers in the interval [0, 1], K_1 and K_2 are positive constant called respectively the coefficient of the self-recognition component, and the coefficient of the social component. w a dynamic inertia coefficient varying over time [7].

4   The Proposed Rescheduling Solutions

This section presents the two rescheduling approaches (MSS and PSO-HRC). We use the PSO metaheuristic to determine the prescheduling solution that minimizes the total workload and the makespan.

Let X_{pt} be the set of operations that are already triggered before the breakdown and X_{pr} the set of operations not triggered yet. The MSS approach starts by determining: the operation AO_{jim} directly affected by the breakdown, the indirectly affected operations $O_{j(i+1)m'}$ of the same job, and the indirectly affected operations $O_{j'i'm}$ mapped to machine m. Then the MSS performs a guided right shift according to Algorithm_1.

Algorithm_1: MSS

-Prescheduling: run the PSO for solving FJS problem.
-Occurrence of a breakdown on machine m.
-Rescheduling
    For each operation affected AO_{jim} in X_{pr} **do**
      a. Move AO_{jim} right to a time period = repair time
      b. Update the start time and the end time of AO_{jim}
      c. **If** ($O_{j'i'm}$ exist) **then**
          If (there is an idle time after AO_{jim} that can
          absorb the repair time) **then** go to (d)
          Else $AO_{jim} \leftarrow O_{j'i'm}$, go to (a) **End if**
      End if
      d. **If** ($O_{j(i+1)m'}$ exist) **then**
          Get the start time denote as $Next_{st}$ of $O_{j(i+1)m'}$
          If (completion of AO_{jim} > $Next_{st}$) **then**
            $AO_{jim} \leftarrow O_{j(i+1)m'}$, go to (a)
          End if
      End if
    End for

In the PSO-HRC approach, a leader historic table is maintained during the prescheduling phase. This table contains the best scheduling solutions reached by leading particles. Once a machine is broken down, the position vector X_p is divided into two parts X_{pt} and X_{pr}, then a search of X_{pt} in the historic_table is performed followed by an update of X_{pr}. Algorithm_2 presents the main steps of PSO-HRC.

Algorithm_2: PSO-HRC

-Prescheduling: run the PSO for solving FJS problem and
save the best schedules in the historic_table.
-Occurrence of a breakdown on machine m.
-Rescheduling
    For each position vector HX_p in the historic_table **do**
      Split HX_p into 2 vectors HX_{pt} and HX_{pr}
      if (HX_{pt} == X_{pt}) **then**
        $X_{pr} \leftarrow HX_{pr}$;
        Calculate the new MS.
        if (new MS < old MS) **then** update the solution **End if**
      End if
    End for

5 Experimental Results

In this section we present the simulation results of the proposed rescheduling algorithms then we compare them to those obtained by the idle time insertion (ITI) [1] and the random route changing (RRC). The comparison criteria are robustness RM1 (Eq. 2) and RM2 (Eq. 3), stability SM1, SM2 and SM3 (Eqs. 5, 6 and 7), the makespan MS (Eq. 1) and the total workload (Eq. 4). Due to lack of space we present the experimental results only for two FJS problem instances: an instance of 10 machines and 10 jobs with a total flexibility, and an instance of 8 machines and 8 jobs with a partial flexibility. The probability of machine breakdowns, the machine repair period, the occurrence time of the breakdown and the four disruption scenarios are chosen in a similar manner as in [1]. These scenarios are listed in Table 1. Figure 1 shows the prescheduling solutions (i.e. before breakdown) obtained by the PSO algorithm after 20 trials using 500 particles and 500 iterations.

Tables 2, 3 and 5 compare the fitness, the workload and the robustness of the four scheduling algorithms. We notice the out performance of PSO-HRC. RRC and ITI give best result if there is only one affected operation with a short repair time (as in SN2 and SN4). Tables 4 and 6 compares the stability of the four rescheduling algorithms. We notice that MSS gives the best stability but not the best fitness.

Table 1. Breakdown scenarios

FJS problem instance	Problem1: 8*8				Problem2: 10*10	
Broken machine m	1				2	
Disruption scenarios	SN_1	SN_2	SN_3	SN_4	SN_1	SN_2
Occurrence time	1	5	3	5	2	2
Repair period	2	2	5	5	1	4
Directed AO_{jim}	$O_{8,1,1}$	$O_{6,3,1}$	$O_{5,1,1}$	$O_{6,3,1}$	$O_{4,2,2}$	$O_{4,2,2}$
Number of AO_{ij}	13	1	8	1	16	16

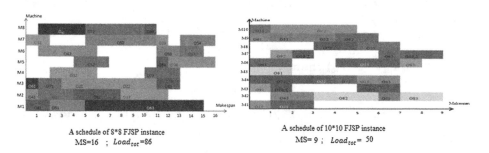

A schedule of 8*8 FJSP instance
MS=16 ; $Load_{tot}$ =86

A schedule of 10*10 FJSP instance
MS=9 ; $Load_{tot}$ = 50

Fig. 1. Prescheduling schedules of the FJS instances

Table 2. Problem 8*8, SN_1 & SN_2: fitness, robustness, workload and slack time

	SN_1				SN_2			
	MS	$Load_{tot}$	RM1	RM2	MS	$Load_{tot}$	RM1	RM2
PSO-HRC	**17**	**73**	**6.25**	**9.84**	**16**	**75**	**0**	**9.84**
RRCA	**17**	**73**	**6.25**	**9.84**	17	73	6.25	9.84
MSS	19	86	18.75	11.3	17	86	6.25	11.3
ITI	27	86	68.75	11.3	17	86	6.25	11.3

Table 3. Problem 8*8, SN_3 & SN_4: fitness, robustness, workload and slack time

	SN_3				SN_4			
	MS	$Load_{tot}$	RM1	RM2	MS	$Load_{tot}$	RM1	RM2
PSO-HRC	**20**	**77**	**25**	**9.84**	**16**	**76**	**0**	**9.84**
RRCA	21	73	31.25	9.84	17	73	6.25	9.84
MSS	22	86	37.5	11.3	20	86	25	11.3
ITI	37	86	131.25	11.3	20	86	25	11.3

Table 4. Problem 8*8: stability

	SN_1			SN_2			SN_3			SN_4		
	SM1	SM2	SM3	SM1	SM2	SM3	SM1	SM2	SM3	SM1	SM2	SM3
PSO-HRC	60	2.22	4.61	20	0.74	20	59	2.18	7.37	12	0.44	12
RRCA	60	2.22	4.01	28	1.03	28	71	2.62	7.88	25	0.92	25
MSS	29	1.07	1.93	2	0.07	2	48	1.77	5.33	5	0.18	5
ITI	86	3.18	5.73	2	0.07	2	123	4.55	13.66	5	0.18	5

Table 5. Problem 10*10, SN_1 & SN_2: fitness, robustness, workload and slack time

	SN_1				SN_2			
	MS	$Load_{tot}$	RM1	RM2	MS	$Load_{tot}$	RM1	RM2
PSO-HRC	**9**	**41**	11.11	5.5	**11**	**47**	**11.11**	**5.5**
RRCA	15	41	66.66	6.9	12	41	20	6.9
MSS	10	50	22.22	4.7	18	50	80	4.7
ITI	13	50	30	4.7	28	50	211.11	4.7

Table 6. Problem 10*10: stability

	SN_1			SN_2		
	SM1	SM2	SM3	SM1	SM2	SM3
PSO-HRC	23	0.76	3.27	31	1.03	4.42
RRCA	46	1.53	7.66	68	2.26	8.5
MSS	8	0.86	1.33	24	0.8	3
ITI	15	0.5	2.5	76	2.53	9.5

6 Conclusions

In this paper, we proposed two rescheduling solutions (PSO-HRC and MSS) to solve the FJS problem under machine breakdowns. Comparing to other solutions, the PSO-HRC provides better makespan, better workload and better robustness. While the MSS offers a better stability. In our future work we will target other types of machine breakdowns such as the partial breakdowns and the breakdowns causing changes on the durations of operations.

References

1. Nasr, A.-H., El Mekkawy, T.Y.: Robust and stable flexible job shop scheduling with random machine breakdowns using a hybrid genetic algorithm. Int. J. Prod. Economics **132**, 279–291 (2011)
2. Xiong, J., Xing, L., Chen, Y.: Robust scheduling for multi-objective flexible job-shop problems with random machine breakdowns. Int. J. Prod. Economics **141**, 112–126 (2013)
3. Singh, M.R., Mahapatra, S.S.: Robust scheduling for flexible job shop problems with random machine breakdowns using a quantum behaved particle swarm optimization. Int. J. Serv. Oper. Manage. **20**(1), 1–20 (2015)
4. He, W., Sun, D.: Scheduling flexible job shop problem subject to machine breakdown with route changing and right-shift strategies. Int. J. Adv. Manuf. Technol. **66**, 501–514 (2012)
5. He, W., Sun, D.: Scheduling flexible job shop problem subject to machine breakdown with game theory. Int. J. Prod. Res. **52**(13), 3858–3876 (2013)
6. Yahyaoui, A., Fnaiech, N., Fnaiech, F.: New shifting method for job shop scheduling subject to invariant constraints of resources availability. In: 35th Annual Conference of IEEE Industrial Electronics, pp. 3211–3216 (2009)
7. Modares, H., Alfi, A., Sistani, M.B.N.: Parameter estimation of bilinear systems based on an adaptive particle swarm optimization. Eng. Appl. Artif. Intell. **23**(7), 1105–1111 (2010)
8. Xiong, J., Xing, L.N., Chen, Y.W.: Robust scheduling for multi-objective flexible job-shop problems with random machine breakdowns. Int. J. Prod. Economics **141**(1), 112–126 (2013)

A Dijkstra-Based Algorithm for Selecting the Shortest-Safe Evacuation Routes in Dynamic Environments (SSER)

Angely Oyola, Dennis G. Romero$^{(\boxtimes)}$, and Boris X. Vintimilla

Faculty of Electrical and Computer Engineering, Escuela Superior Politécnica del Litoral, Km 30.5 via Perimetral, P.O. Box 09-01-5863, Guayaquil, Ecuador
{ajoyola,dgromero,boris.vintimilla}@espol.edu.ec

Abstract. In this work is proposed an approach for addressing the problem to find the shortest-safe routes in buildings with many evacuation doors and where the accessibility of internal areas could be changed by different kind of sensors. We present two advantages over the common use of Dijkstra's algorithm, related to the problem of obtaining evacuation routes: (1) Fast search of the shortest-safe evacuation route to multiple exits with a backward approach and (2) Support to dynamic environments (graph with variable vertex availability). Four Dijkstra-based algorithms were considered in order to evaluate the performance of the proposed approach, achieving short times in evacuation to multiple exits.

Keywords: Dijkstra · Dynamic environments · Shortest-safe

1 Introduction

In the scope of evacuation systems, algorithms based on *Dijkstra* have been developed to calculate evacuation routes, seeking to optimize resources, simplifying methods and obtaining acceptable response times even with large amounts of data, addressing problems where is necessary to analyze all possible evacuation routes, indicating a single exit as destination [1,2]. However, traditional implementations of these algorithms are impractical in dynamic environments, where the availability of evacuation routes may vary suddenly, for example, in applications requiring continuous monitoring.

2 Related Work

Techniques like Dijkstra [3], Floy-Warshall [4] and Bellman Ford [5] are the most commonly used algorithms for evaluating shortest paths, considering their simplicity, being Dijkstra the one with the best run-time on extensive graphs [1,2]. These algorithms have been used to propose novel approaches for route planning in different application contexts such as buildings, sensor networks,

© Springer International Publishing AG 2017
S. Benferhat et al. (Eds.): IEA/AIE 2017, Part I, LNAI 10350, pp. 131–135, 2017.
DOI: 10.1007/978-3-319-60042-0_15

vehicle congestion, among others. In this sense, we review some studies related to the problem of route planning which includes finding the shortest path, reducing resource consumption, processing times and getting safe suggestions. In [6], the Dijkstra's approach has served on the development of algorithms to find short routes in buildings with a single evacuation door and with always-available areas. However, nowadays it's not enough to find short routes but also finding routes that take less time to be followed, less effort or resource consumption and safer. There are some situations according to the size and building configuration that requires several exit doors, as well as areas that can be temporarily or permanently disabled. Other studies have been conducted to develop systems that could exclude unsafe paths and calculate the shortest-safe path from multiple starting points to multiple exit points during an emergent situation [1,7].

3   Proposed Approach

To overcome the difficulties associated with dynamic environments (variable availability of escape doors and evacuation routes), the SSER approach (*Safe and Short Evacuation Routes*) uses its own structures to represent different areas of the building, aisles and evacuation doors. In this sense, two main structures are used: *vertex*, corresponding to escape areas of the building (offices or places with access to the main aisles or escape routes) and the *edges* or aisles connecting these areas. Considering the structures and properties of the vertices, adjacent arcs, evacuation routes and how the graph is examined, we can mention two main advantages over the common use of Dijkstra's algorithm, related to the problem of obtaining evacuation routes [1]:

(1) Fast search of the shortest-safe evacuation route to multiple exits with a *backward* approach: SSER uses a backward approach, which involves to consider evacuation doors as the starting point of the route, towards the different vertices representing evacuation areas, resulting in a time complexity of $O(m \times n^2)$, where m is the number of target vertices (exit doors) and n represents all the source vertices (areas to be evacuated).

(2) Support to dynamic environments: Dijkstra's common use works with a static graph (where the vertices and edges, established at the beginning, are always available). If the application requires to modify the connections in the graph, it is necessary stop processing, modify the graph, load the graph and execute the process again. All these steps when applied on large graphs, involves waste of time, specially by considering emergency situations. For this, the SSER approach includes the initially defined "Accessibility Status" property in each vertex, in order to label the vertices as available or unavailable. It should be noted that updating the accessibility status is performed in real time without having to stop processing. The status information is sent by sensors housed in different building areas, the kind of sensors used depends on the situation to monitor (fire, smoke, toxic gases, among others). Based on the current status of the vertex, the SSER approach will only consider the available vertices to obtain the evacuation routes in the building. In this way, people are not addressed by escape routes

involving dangerous areas. In this context, the proposed approach is able to find the shortest-safe evacuation route, considering the access availability of vertices.

4 Experimental Results

The SSER algorithm's runtime was compared with 4 other Dijkstra-based algorithms (Fibonacci, BGL, Lemon and OrTool) [8] with focus on graphs analysis using different data structures. One of the main considerations for testing was to use the same programming language in the implementation of the mentioned methods to compare, in order to avoid discrepancies due to compiler or code interpreter.

For testing purposes were considered 3 graphs randomly-generated, each one with 10.000 vertices (n), density (d) and different arcs (m). The equation used to determine the graphs is: $\frac{2m}{n(n-1)}$ [8]. Following this, the algorithm SSER was applied to each graph, where were generated randomly 50 evacuation doors (vertices as destination). The algorithm analyzed evacuation routes to all vertices in the graph. This was not done with the other 4 methods (Fibonacci, BGL, Lemon and OrTool) because these are focused on determining the shortest path between two vertices. Subsequently, we proceeded to calculate the execution time of the SSER algorithm. The results are detailed in Table 1, where can be observed the execution time of the SSER algorithm compared with the other four methods, which is positioned in third place among the analyzed algorithms. One of the causes of its performance is due to its goals of seeking the safe evacuation of all areas (represented by vertices in the graph), so it focused on finding evacuation routes considering all vertices from each of the 50 evacuation doors randomly selected for the test.

Table 1. Comparing runtimes

Graph	Fibonacci	BGL	Lemon	OrTools	SSER
Rand1	0.052	0.0059	0.0074	1.2722	0.0177
Rand2	0.0134	0.0535	0.0706	1.6128	0.0459
Rand3	0.0705	0.5276	0.7247	4.2535	0.3704

Although SSER did not get the best runtime, the results are enhanced by the selection of safe routes considering all escape doors. With this it could be justified how the SSER algorithm has an effective role in situations involving finding the shortest safe routes, where is required to consider all selected vertices in the graph to specific ones.

It should be mentioned that each vertex stores information about segments around vertices that make up different evacuation routes. In a particular emergency, illustrated in Fig. 1, the vertices stored only one evacuation route to E_1. After that V_3 is enabled, the evacuation routes to E_1 are recalculated toward

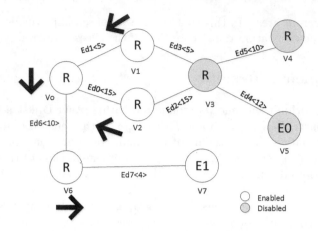

Fig. 1. Illustration of an Emergency in $v3$

the two evacuation doors. Each vertex considered between the two options the shortest one.

5   Conclusions

This paper tackles the challenging problem of computing evacuation routes in buildings with multiple exits, seeking the safe option before the shortest one. In order to fulfill this goal, the SSER approach considers variations on the graph by storing meta-data into vertices, in order to be able to select another alternative when some connection into the graph is broken, this can prevent evacuation systems to suggest routes involving blocked or dangerous areas. This approach makes the algorithm suitable to be applied on dynamic environments where the availability status of internal areas can be modified by different kind of sensors.

Acknowledgement. This work has been supported by the ESPOL under Project G4-DI-2014.

References

1. Cho, J., Lee, G., Won, J., Ryu, E.: Application of dijkstra's algorithm in the smart exit sign. In: The 31st International Symposium on Automation and Robotics in Construction and Mining (ISARC 2014) (2014)
2. Santos Navarrete, M.E., et al.: Estudio y simulación de algoritmos para la evacuación de personas en situaciones de emergencia sobre una estructura similar al rectorado de la espol. RTE (2015)
3. Dijkstra, E.W.: A note on two problems in connexion with graphs. Numer. Math. 1(1), 269–271 (1959)
4. Floyd, R.W.: Algorithm 97: shortest path. Commun. ACM 5(6), 345 (1962)

5. Bellman, R.: On a routing problem. Technical report, DTIC Document (1956)
6. Randell, B.: Edsger dijkstra. In: The Ninth IEEE International Workshop on Object-Oriented Real-Time Dependable Systems, WORDS 2003 Fall, p. 3, October 2003
7. Kim, D.O., Mun, H.W., Lee, K.Y., Kim, D.W., Gil, H.J., Kim, H.K., Chung, Y.S.: The development of the escape light control system. J. Korean Inst. Illum. Electr. Install. Eng. **23**(6), 52–58 (2009)
8. Gualandi, I.: Dijkstra, Dantzig, and shortest paths. (2012). http://stegua.github.io/blog/2012/09/19/dijkstra/. Accessed 18 Jun 2015

Replication in Fault-Tolerant Distributed CSP

Fadoua Chakchouk[1,2(✉)], Julien Vion[1], Sylvain Piechowiak[1], René Mandiau[1],
Makram Soui[2], and Khaled Ghedira[2]

[1] LAMIH UMR CNRS 8201, University of Valenciennes, Valenciennes, France
{Fadoua.Chakchouk,Julien.Vion,Sylvain.Piechowiak,
Rene.Mandiau}@univ-valenciennes.fr
[2] ENSI, University of Manouba, Manouba, Tunisia
souii_makram@yahoo.fr, khaled.ghedira@anpr.tn

Abstract. Real life problems can be solved by a distributed way, in
particular by multi-agent approaches. However, the fault tolerance is
not guarantee when an agent, for example, does not have any activity
(e.g. it dies). This problem is very crucial, when the interactional model
is based on a Distributed CSP. Many algorithms have been proposed in
the literature, but they give wrong results if an agent dies. This paper
presents an approach which is based on a replication principle: each local
CSP is replicated in another agent.

1 Introduction

A Distributed Constraint Satisfaction Problem (DisCSP) presents a set of agents
that cooperate with each other to solve a Constraint Satisfaction Problem (CSP).
This kind of models varied problems such as timetabling/meeting problems, road
traffic, multi-robot exploration [4]. During a DisCSP solving, different unexpected events can influence the final result such an agent failure; a such event
produces a wrong result. To detect this failure, Tanenbaum et al. [5] proposed to
send checking activity message to different agents. In existing studies, to improve
the robustness and fault tolerance of multi-agent system. A method based on the
concept of duplication was proposed by Guessoum et al. [1] to identify critical
agents in the system and duplicate them. Another one is proposed by Fedoruk
et al. [3] based on a transparent agent replication. According to our knowledge,
few approaches studied in MAS context, but there do not badly exist approaches
for DisCSPs. In this paper we present an approach to solve a DisCSP in presence
of a failed agent.

2 Solving DisCSP Process in Presence of Failed Agent

In this paper, we present an approach based on the local CSP replication. The
general process starts by a distribution local CSP process executed by a particular agent called *Dispatcher Agent*. This distribution aims to assign a duplicate
of each local CSP to another agent. It guarantees that an agent can have one

© Springer International Publishing AG 2017
S. Benferhat et al. (Eds.): IEA/AIE 2017, Part I, LNAI 10350, pp. 136–140, 2017.
DOI: 10.1007/978-3-319-60042-0_16

or more copies of CSPs, but a local CSP is copied only once, to ensure that the local CSP of failed agent will be supported by a single agent.

During the DisCSP solving, and in case of a failure of an agent, when an agent does not send any message from a time interval, it receives a checking activity message from one of its neighbors. If this agent does not respond to this message, the sender considers it as a failed agent, and informs other agents of this failure by sending a message to its neighbors.

Receiving the failure information, each agent transmits the message to its neighbors and so on, to guarantee that all failed agent neighbors are aware of the agent failure. Then, the agent having the replicate of the failed agent CSP starts the merging CSPs process which aims to merge two different CSPs to obtain a single one. So, the agent merges the copy with its own local CSP to obtain a new one. This merging concerns variables and constraints: (i) inter-agent constraints which interconnect the failed agent with the delegate one became intra-agent constraints of the delegate agent, and (ii) the rest of inter-agent constraints of the failed agent became inter-agent constraints of the delegate one. After merging CSPs, the delegate agent informs the failed agent neighbors that it supports the CSP of the failed agent, so they can update their neighbours' lists.

3   Experiments

This section describes different assumptions used in our experiments (Sect. 3.1), and presents obtained results (Sect. 3.2).

3.1   Assumptions

To validate our approach, different DisCSPs are randomly generated according to parameters $<m, n, d, p>$ where:

- m is the number of agents of the system
- n is the number of each agent variables with a domain of d values
- p is the hardness of each constraint in the system.

To evaluate proposed failure handling, obtained results of handling failure are compared with those obtained if the failure is not detected, and if there is no failure. This comparison is done according to evaluation criteria proposed by Mandiau et al. [4]: The number of exchanged messages, total CPU calculated from the beginning of Multi-ABT execution to the end of slower agent behavior, and the Non Concurrent Constraints NCCC.

For each instance, one agent chosen randomly fails. The failure is simulated just after sending its first solution. To do this, we used JADE multi-agent platform [2]. Results of these simulations were obtained on a computer equipped with 2.4 GHz Intel Core i7 and 8 GB of RAM. Results concern instances having as parameters $<m, 1, 6, 0.4>$.

3.2 Results

Figure 1(a) illustrates results of solving DisCSPs having failed agent with and without applying our approach. The y-axis presents the percentage of results that gives a solution. This figure presents only instances giving solutions because, in absence of an agent, and if the result is wrong, the system displays automatically that there is no solution. The figure shows the number of expected results obtained by solving DisCSP in presence of failed agent decreases if the number of agents increases. But if our approach is applied, the same results as those obtained by applying Multi-ABT without failed agent are obtained (all instances giving solutions with Multi-ABT provide also solutions by applying our approach). Our single-variable context becomes multi-variable problem after merging CSPs.

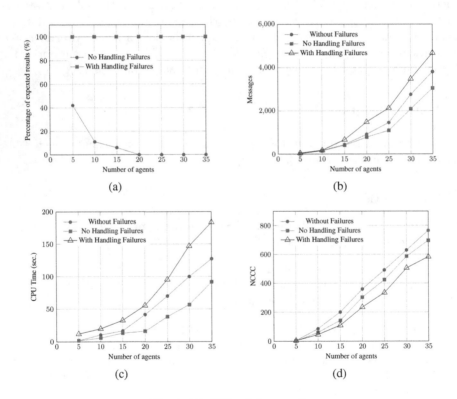

Fig. 1. DisCSP solving results

Figure 1(b) presents the variation of exchanged messages to solve the DisCSP. The number of exchanged messages decreases if the system loses an agent. This decreasing is due to the loss of messages sent by the failed agent. Also, applying our approach, the number of exchanged messages increases. This is due to the addition of exchanged messages after detecting the failed agent. In fact, since some agents resume the resolution from the beginning after detecting the failure, they sent same messages before and after the failure detection. Additional messages present less than 3% of the total number of exchanged messages.

Figure 1(c) presents the CPU time spent by each resolution method. A decreasing of 40% is observed in DisCSPs with 30 agents which is due to the elimination of the failed agent behavior. On the other hand, an increasing of the CPU time is observed, when applying our approach, which is due to the added information to handle. In fact, the time spent to detect failed agent, to merge the CSPs and to transmit different information, is an extra time that added to the initial CPU time: the time spent by *Dispatcher Agent* to distribute CSPs present less than 0.1% of the global CPU time. Also, the CPU time for detection and merging processes present less than 1.7% of the global CPU time.

Figure 1(d) presents the number of NCCCs with and without agent failure. Its values decreases slightly if a failure is not handled, and this is due to the loss of some inter-agent constraints checking (which belongs to the failed agent). The number of solutions of the merged CSP is also reduced. In fact, more the agent has intra-agent constraints, more the number of its solutions decreases. Then, during the resolution, the agent has less solutions to check.

The variation of these values does not affect the final result. In fact, this paper is interested to the final solution of the DisCSP, to obtain the same result as that obtained without died agent. In spite of the variation of exchanged message number, of NCCCs number and of spent CPU time, the proposed method can solve a global DisCSP having a failed agent by giving the same result as the one given without died agent (one solution or no solution).

4 Conclusion

This paper describes a method, which is applied on Multi-ABT, to solve a DisCSP if an agent fails. This method is based on the replication of the local CSP of each agent. To improve it, it can be applied with multi-variable case, i.e. each agent encapsulates more than a single variable. Also, it can be adapted to be applied with other algorithms than Multi-ABT such as Multi-AWC and Multi-DBS. The downside of this method is that not respect the privacy of each agent, since the local CSP of each agent should be copied in another one. This problem remains open and underlines the compromise between the industrial needs for robustness and data privacy.

References

1. Ductor, S., Guessoum, Z., Ziane, M.: Adaptive replication in fault-tolerant multi-agent systems. In: Proceedings of the 2011 IEEE/WIC/ACM International Conference on Intelligent Agent Technology, pp. 304–307 (2011)
2. Trucco, T., Bellifemine, F., Caire, G.: Jade programmer's guide. Technical report, Telecom Italia (2000)

3. Fedoruk, A., Deters, R.: Improving fault-tolerance by replicating agents. In: Proceedings of the First International Joint Conference on Autonomous Agents and Multiagent Systems: Part 2, pp. 737–744. ACM (2002)
4. Mandiau, R., Vion, J., Piechowiak, S., Monier, P.: Multi-variable distributed backtracking with sessions. Appl. Intell. **41**(3), 736–758 (2014)
5. Tanenbaum, A.S., Steen, M.V.: Distributed Systems: Principles and Paradigms, 2nd edn. Prentice-Hall Inc., Upper Saddle River (2006)

Optimal Route Prediction as a Smart Mobile Application of Gift Ideas

Veronika Nemeckova[1], Jan Dvorak[1], Ali Selamat[1,2],
and Ondrej Krejcar[1(✉)]

[1] Faculty of Informatics and Management,
Center for Basic and Applied Research, University of Hradec Kralove,
Rokitanskeho 62, 500 03 Hradec Kralove, Czech Republic
{veronika.nemeckova, jan.dvorak}@uhk.cz,
Ondrej@Krejcar.org
[2] Faculty of Computing, Universiti Teknologi Malaysia,
81310 Johor Baharu, Johor, Malaysia
aselamat@utm.my

Abstract. Searching for gifts' inspirations for relatives is becoming increasingly difficult. A person can collect ideas on the internet, ask the relatives or get inspiration from gifts, which the person received in the past. This study focuses on the suggestion and development of an algorithm for the calculation of the optimal route between searched shops, which is a part of the mobile application for Android platform. The results of this study are summarised in the article's conclusion.

Keywords: Google maps API · Google places API · Minimum spanning tree

1 Introduction

The shopping for gifts is a task, which is relevant during the whole year – for occasions such as birthday, name day and other. The search for the most suitable gift becomes more difficult each year. With the upcoming Christmas, more users search online for the gifts' inspirations for relatives. This is shown in the numbers of search results for the terms "gift ideas" [2], which are available on Google Trends. The graph of interest for such related topics (gifts, gifts for women, gifts for men, etc.) increases in values. By using the Google Trends [3] it is possible to study the trends for search for various topics on Google.

Nowadays, it is very common to use the mobile phones for resolving various matters. Therefore, the rich usability of this mobile application for gift ideas search is undisputable. This application could simplify the selection of gifts for relatives and reduce possible stress caused by searching for the most suitable presents for the given occasion. There are many ways, how can the user plan the route between stores. In order to solve this issue, two solutions arise: use the principle of Hamiltonian

© Springer International Publishing AG 2017
S. Benferhat et al. (Eds.): IEA/AIE 2017, Part I, LNAI 10350, pp. 141–145, 2017.
DOI: 10.1007/978-3-319-60042-0_17

path search in the graph or to use one of the algorithms for search of minimum spanning tree. These algorithms are applied even by authors in [4–6] for the problems' solutions based on the route search, radius, or minimum spanning tree in the evaluated graph.

2 Optimal Route Prediction Algorithm

The aim of this study is to suggest a suitable algorithm for the optimal route search between found shops that will be based on the principle of searching for the minimum spanning tree in the evaluated graph. Therefore, the focus of the following chapters will concentrate on the algorithm which will be based on the algorithm of searching for the minimum spanning tree of the evaluated graph. However, the resulting path between the found shops will be the Hamilton's path. The calculation of the optimal path between found shops will be based on the distance between the individual shops.

The application will show the user a list of stores according to the entered parameters which correspond to the user's requirements. These found stores are then shown on the map with the possibility of also displaying the calculated path between these shops.

The store search according to the given parameters will be implemented using the Google Places API service [7] while to display the found shops on the map, the Google Maps API service is used [8]. The main part of the application is the route calculation between the found shops. In order to build the optimal route, it is necessary at first to obtain the distances between the individual shops. The distance between the stores can be found on the basis of a query to the Google Maps Directions API that must contain the coordinates of the starting and target destination. The service, similarly as in the previous case, returns data in the JSON format that also contain the needed distance. These data will be used for the calculation of the optimal route [9]. The developed algorithm for the purpose of this survey will be based on the principle of Kruskal's algorithm for minimum spanning tree search in the evaluated graph. It is not wanted for the result path to contain points, to which the user would have to come back in order to continue to the next stores. Therefore, it will be controlled that the resulting path is a path between stores. This means that within one calculated route, there will be only one path to the store, as well as one path from the store (except border points). This will be achieved by the addition of a condition that will control the number of paths to/from the shop. Suggested algorithm in pseudo-code:

- Calculation of the routes between individual stores:
  - o Input: list of stores with saved coordinates
  - o Create empty list of routes between individual stores
    - For each store in the list
      - Find out from the coordinates of the store the distance to all other shops in the list
      - Save calculated routes into the list
  - o Return a list with calculated routes between individual stores
- Calculation of the result route:
  - o Input: list of routes between individual stores
  - o Create an empty list for resulting route
  - o Create an empty map into which the added stores will be added
  - o Order routes between stores according to the distance from shortest to longest
  - o For each route from the November
    - If the circle creates by adding the route
      - Continue with the next route
    - If one of the stores from planned route has already two saved routes that lead to the given store
      - Continue with the next route
    - Add the path to the resulting route
    - Add stores from the resulting path into the map
- Return the calculated route

3   Testing of Developed Solution

The testing is focused on the optimisation of the process for obtaining the distance between individual stores, calculation of the optimal route and acquiring the list of coordinates for depicting the route between the stores. This part of the algorithm takes the longest. In the first test, the calculation time and the route depiction is to be tested. Here it is necessary to first obtain the distances between individual stores and the list of the coordinates for the route depiction is only acquired for those routes that were returned by the algorithm for the optimal route calculation.

The second test focuses on the improved algorithm with which it is possible to save the coordinates at the time of distance determination between the stores. However, this is done in the form of symbols chain which is decoded into coordinates only until those paths that were included into the optimal route between stores.

The algorithm in the last test is able to decode the text chain, where the coordinates for the future route are saved, immediately during the recognition of the distance between the stores for all routes. This list is then saved. This test is focused on the time calculation and route depiction. Here was for each route saved only the distance and the values for the route depiction were acquired for the paths which were part of the optimal route. The results of the measuring can be found in the Table 1 below.

Table 1. Results of the measurement of the calculation and route depiction without the saving of the route's coordinates between individual stores throughout the process (1), without decoding (2), with decoding (3)

Attempt	Number of stores	Duration (1)	Duration (2)	Duration (3)
1	10	00:09,81	00:03,38	00:03,57
2	10	00:08,76	00:03,75	00:03,87
3	10	00:08,85	00:02,42	00:02,56
4	10	00:09,61	00:02,88	00:02,34
5	10	00:09,54	00:02,95	00:02,38
6	10	00:09,11	00:03,11	00:02,47
7	10	00:08,67	00:03,07	00:03,02
8	10	00:08,25	00:02,54	00:03,26
9	10	00:08,61	00:02,81	00:03,18
10	10	00:09,06	00:03,12	00:03,14

The tests proved that the most suitable option is to directly save the list of coordinates that create the path between the two stores, and that applies as well for the paths that in the end will be included in the final optimal route between stores. At the same time, it was shown that there is not such a large difference between the access, during which the coordinates' list is directly decoded or the one during which the data are left in the text form and then transferred into the coordinates list only for the paths that are depicted in the result. The aim of this testing was to optimise the suggested algorithm in order to achieve calculation and depiction of the obtained route in the shortest possible time. This was successfully achieved.

4 Conclusions

The aim of this study was to suggest and implement an algorithm for optimal route search between searched stores. However, the requirement was to achieve calculation and depiction of the obtained route in the shortest possible time. This was successfully achieved. The advantage of this new algorithm is that it is possible to use it for the search of any points of interest, as far as the coordinates of this place are available. By using a simple modification, it can be achieved that the resulting route must not be the path between the chosen points, but the real minimum spanning tree of the evaluated graph.

Acknowledgement. This work and the contribution were supported by project "SP-2102-2017 - Smart Solutions for Ubiquitous Computing Environments" Faculty of Informatics and Management, University of Hradec Kralove, Czech Republic.

References

1. Google Trends - Tipy na dárky. Google Trends. https://www.google.com/trends/explore#q=tipy%20na%20d%C3%A1rky. Accessed 28 Dec 2015
2. Google Trends – Gift ideas. Google Trends. https://www.google.com/trends/explore#q=gift%20ideas.. Accessed 28 Dec 2015
3. Google Trends (2016). https://www.google.cz/trends/. Accessed 28 Dec 2015
4. Contreas-Bolton, C., Gatica, G., Barra, C.R., Parada, V.: A multi-operator genetic algorithm for the generalized minimum spanning tree problem. Expert Syst. Appl. **50**, 1–8 (2016). doi:10.1016/j.eswa.2015.12.014
5. Moncla, L., Gaio, M., Nogueras-Iso, J., Mustiere, S.: Reconstruction of itineraries from annotated text with an informed spanning tree algorithm. Int. J. Geogr. Inf. Sci. **30**(6), 1137–1160 (2016)
6. Shangin, R., Pardalos, P.: Heuristics for the network design problem with connectivity requirements. J. Comb. Optim. **31**(4), 1461–1478 (2016)
7. Nemeckova, V., Dvorak, J., Krejcar, O.: Mobile application for calculation of optimal route between searched points of interest. In: Król, D., Nguyen, N.T., Shirai, K. (eds.) ACIIDS 2017. SCI, vol. 710, pp. 537–547. Springer, Cham (2017). doi:10.1007/978-3-319-56660-3_46
8. Google Places API. https://developers.google.com/places/. Accessed 23 Mar 2017
9. Google Maps API. https://developers.google.com/maps/. Accessed 23 Mar 2017
10. Google Maps Directions API. https://developers.google.com/maps/documentation/directions/. Accessed 23 Mar 2017

Data Mining and Machine Learning

Machine Learning Approach to Detect Falls on Elderly People Using Sound

Armando Collado-Villaverde, María D. R-Moreno, David F. Barrero$^{(\boxtimes)}$, and Daniel Rodriguez

Universidad de Alcalá, Departamento de Automática Crta. Madrid-Barcelona, Alcalá de Henares, Madrid, Spain
david@aut.uah.es

Abstract. One of the most notable consequences of aging is the loss of motor function abilities, making elderly people specially susceptible to falls, which is of the most remarkable concerns in elder care. Thus, several solutions have been proposed to detect falls, however, none of them achieved a great success mainly because of the need of wearing a recording device. In this paper, we study the use of sound to detect fall events. The advantage of this approach over the traditional ones is that the subject does not require to wear additional devices to monitor his or her activities. Here, we apply *machine learning* techniques to process sound simulated the most common type of fall for the elderly, i.e., when the foot collides with an obstacle and the trunk hits the ground before using his/her hands to absorb the fall. The results show that high levels of accuracy can be achieved using only a few signal processing techniques.

Keywords: Fall detection · Feature extraction · Machine learning · Classification · Supervised learning · Care for the elderly

1 Introduction

Falls are one of the most important health problems for the elderly [1]. They are a significant source of problems mainly because the great damage that they can cause which usually leads to hip injuries. Falls in this group of people have two main sources, the loss of motor functions making them prone to accidental falls and loss of consciousness as a symptom of a hearth attack or other diseases.

The problem has been approached from different angles [2]. During the last few years a wide variety of solutions have been proposed, the majority of them use recorded accelerations from an accelerometer [3] to detect fall events as well as monitoring home rehabilitation [4]. One of the main advantages of this approach is the accelerometer's small size and availability in most modern cell phones, also, they respect the people privacy, unlike other systems. Some systems exploit smartphone's popularity which are used by a lot of elderly people nowadays [5,6], few others prefer the use of dedicated devices which are usually placed on the trunk [7].

© Springer International Publishing AG 2017
S. Benferhat et al. (Eds.): IEA/AIE 2017, Part I, LNAI 10350, pp. 149–159, 2017.
DOI: 10.1007/978-3-319-60042-0_18

Another interesting approach is the processing of images captured by a camera [8,9], however, this system has an inherent problem, which is the invasion of privacy. People are usually not willing to have cameras in their private spaces, even if they do not transmit the recorded images. Furthermore, the need to cover every blind spot and all angles is also a problem worth mentioning.

In order to overcome the usage disadvantages of previous devices, we propose the use of a microphone. An important advantage of this approach is that there is no need to wear any device, by getting rid of this need its adoption resistance will be reduced by a large margin, since wearing additional devices to monitor the healthcare of the elders was one the major factor by which other systems were refused. The invasiveness of a microphone in some areas of the house is way lower than having a camera, since with one microphone we can entirely cover an area whereas with cameras we need to cover several blind spots depending on the house distribution.

Many researches have tried to detect events, falls included, by processing sound. Some approaches use human mimicking dolls in the data acquisition tasks to achieve a high accuracy [10]. Other projects use the floor vibrations in addition to the data collected through the microphone achieving a significant accuracy increase [11]. Another interesting approach has its foundation on the difference of the recorded sound depending on the height, in order to exploit that we can use two microphones placed at different heights, considering the difference between both heights of the recorded sound to determine if a fall has happened [12]. Many more projects use sound but only as a secondary source of data, while they use the data obtained using an accelerometer as the main source [13]. We present a Machine Learning (ML) fall detection system which uses only one microphone achieving high accuracy of the classifiers used over the datasets generated under the supervision of professionals in the field.

Other recent works in this field can also be mentioned: ambient assisted living using audio sensing technology [14]; advances on the exploitation of the use of more than one microphone and comparing the sound at different heights [15]; the use of even more microphones, specifically four, in order to detect the 3-D sound source location [16], this approach also uses floor sensors in combination with the microphones to classify the recorded events.

The rest of the paper is structured as follows. First, we address the problem of the data acquisition and its subsequent preprocessing, then we present an explanation of the features analyzed and extracted from the sound waves is described, later on we apply ML algorithms to create a classifier with the obtained data, we also evaluate the selected features and its predictive value. The paper finishes with conclusions and future work.

2   Data Acquisition

One of the most critical problems in any ML process is the acquisition of high quality datasets. Recording falls using elderly people was not a reasonable option, since the risk of injuring an actual elder subject was too high considering their fragile physical condition, so we decided to simulate the falls as realistically as possible. A typical fall in an elderly is originated by a trip over, i.e. the collision of a foot with an object while the person is walking, losing the equilibrium and falling over. Then, the trunk bends forward, and given the increased reaction time of elderly, they hits the ground without using their hands for cushioning, resulting in very dangerous falls. We recorded the sound of several falls using a microphone, with a sampling frequency of 44.1 kHz.

Using a healthy subject we recorded falls with all possible realism while also trying to avoid risks. We consulted geriatric experts who informed us about the general fall process of elderly people, which involves an increased reaction time, unnatural to the subject we initially planned to use, to overcome that adversity, the experts trained the subject to fall like an older person would.

Therefore, the trained subject was placed on a tatami for safety. Using a thick pad to simulate the obstacle the subject will trip over with as well as serving as a safety method to avoid any damage. The subject started walking and after a couple of steps he would hit the pad with a foot and fell over the pad. The experts supervised all falls recorded, validating only the ones that were similar to the falls that an elderly person would experience. Considering that the recorded data may differ considering which foot hit the pad, the process was repeated to record the same number of falls with each foot.

The volunteer simulated 47 falls in total, but the geriatric experts validated only 40, 20 for each feet. Figure 1(a) shows the sound wave of a recorded fall. We can easily appreciate when the fall starts, as the first major variation in the wave, when the foot collides with the pad and the moment when the trunk falls and hits the pad as the biggest peak of the wave.

In order to create a classifier using ML algorithms we also need to use sound where no falls happen, that sound will be compared to the recorded sound from the falls. We extracted the sound from two different sources. The first one was a conversation, which had several moments without sound in between each phrase from the speakers. The second one were war sounds extracted from an action video game, this clip had fewer silent moments since there were constant background sounds, the first wave has much more time between each sounds while the second one has its sounds much more closer to each other.

3 Data Preprocessing

Data needs some preprocessing in order to apply the machine learning classifier. First of all, we need to cut the recorded sound from the falls, since it contains a lot of absence of sound before and after the fall, otherwise we would consider the absence of sound as falls.

Once the cut was performed, after some initial tests we faced another problem. The classifier exploited the high amount of silence contained in the fall, so they were easy to differentiate from the conversation and other sounds. To avoid this problem we mixed the sound from the falls, adding either the conversation or the game sounds as background. In the Fig. 1(b) and (c) we can see the wave

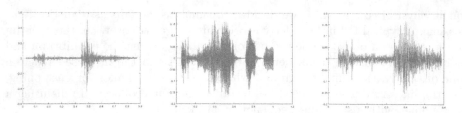

(a) Example of the sound (b) Mix of the fall sound (c) Mix of the fall sound with
wave of a fall after the cut.   with the conversation   the war sounds

Fig. 1. Original and mixed fall sound waves.

sounds of the fall after the mix, they are much more similar to the waves with
which we are going to compare them. We also had to cut the '*no fall*' sounds so
their duration would similar to the fall sounds.

An important issue about dataset is that it is unbalanced. Since falls are
hard to simulate, there were much more data coming from conversations and
game sounds than from simulated falls. To face this issue we undersampled the
'not-fall' class, getting the same number of instances for each class.

4   Feature Extraction by Processing the Signal

We need to process the recorded sound. Using different processing techniques
we were able to extract 10 features from each audio signal. As our first step we
need to process the signal, we will separate each audio clip into portions with
less duration, we will use frames of 2048 samples, if we consider the sampling frequency of 44.1 kHz, each frame will contain 46.3 ms of sound. This duration has
not been chosen arbitrarily, because of the aleatory and non-stationary nature
of the sound we need to use small frames to analyze the spectrum created by
the sound properly. By using such an small frame, we will obtain a practically stationary signal, facilitating the posterior feature extraction. In addition,
by separating the sound into frames, we will obtain two features per equation
applied, since we can calculate the mean and standard deviation of all the frames
generated from the original sound wave.

The feature extraction is a mathematical process which can characterize an
audio signal, we will group our features into two main groups: (i) temporal
and (ii) spectral features. When analyzing *temporal features* we will consider
frequency and level (decibels), these features include the energy of the signal and
the zero-crossing feature. *Spectral features* which will be extracted by computing
the Fast Fourier Transform, which will consist on the spectral centroid, the
Rolloff factor and the spectral flux, all of them apply mathematical equations to
the discrete-time signal $x[n]$ of each sound frame:

- **Energy of the signal** (E_k): the energy is calculated as the squared mod of
  the window as shown in the Eq. (1), it basically informs about the strength of

the signal. In addition, we introduced a threshold of 9.2376^{-6} Joules, which eliminates the windows whose energy does not surpass it.

$$E_k = \sum_{n=0}^{N} |x[n]|^2 \tag{1}$$

- **Zero-crossing** (Z_k): this parameter informs about the amount of noise contained in the signal by counting the amount of times where the sign of the signal changes from positive to negative. The higher its value, the more noisy the signal is. We will use the Eq. (2) to count the amount of times each window changes its sign, as shown in the equation we need to halve our result since we are only interested in the changes from positive to negative.

$$Z_k = \frac{1}{2} \cdot \sum_{n=0}^{N-1} |sign(x[n]) - sign(x[n+1])| \tag{2}$$

We used the following spectral features:

- **Spectral centroid** (C_k): the centroid is the middle point of the spectrum, the frequency that divides the spectrum into two equal parts, sound signals formed by mainly high frequency samples have higher centroid values. The centroid is calculated by the average frequency weighted by amplitudes, divided by the sum of the amplitudes, as shown in the Eq. (3).

$$C_k = \frac{\sum_{n=0}^{N} F_k[n] \cdot n}{\sum_{n=0}^{N} F_k[n]} \tag{3}$$

Where $F_k[n]$ is the amplitude of the fast Fourier transform of the n frequency applied to the k window.

- **Rolloff factor** R: R frequency below which is 85% of the spectrum, this feature informs about the form of the signal spectrum as a whole, in order to calculate it we will use the Eq. (4).

$$\sum_{n=0}^{R} F_k[n] = 0.85 \cdot \sum_{n=0}^{N} F_k[n] \tag{4}$$

- **Spectral flux** (F_k): this feature indicates how quickly the energy of the spectrum changes calculated by comparing the squared difference of the module of spectrum for one frame against the power spectrum from the previous frame, as illustrated in the Eq. (5).

$$F_k = \sum_{n=0}^{N} (F_k[n] - F_{k-1}[n])^2 \tag{5}$$

Where $F_k[n]$ and $F_{k-1}[n]$ are the module of the fast Fourier transform of the k and k-1 window.

Once we have obtained all of the features from all the frames created by dividing the original sound wave, we will calculate the mean and standard deviation of each feature considering the values obtained by processing each frame, in addition, each sample was labeled as 'fall' or 'not-fall' depending of the analyzed sound, the combination of the extracted features and the class label will serve as input for the classifier.

5   Detection of Fall Events

Detection of fall events can be summarized as a binary classification problem: Considering the extracted features we classify each sound sample as '*fall*' or '*non-fall*', thus we used some classical classification algorithms implemented in Weka such as C4.5 (J48), 1-NN, Logistic regression, Naïve Bayes, PART, Random Forest and Support Vector Machines (SVMs). Some of them did not achieve a high performance, but we included them for comparison purposes. The performance of these algorithms can be seen as a benchmark given their high performance without requiring an excessive training or evaluation time. The features that feed the classifiers are summarized in Table 1. The evaluation of the classifiers was carried out using 10-fold cross-validation.

We performed three experiments, we compared the recorded sound from the falls with war ambient sounds and a recorded conversation and later on we mixed the fall sounds with the war and conversation sounds using the two last ones as background sound. First, we compared the fall sounds with one conversation sounds representing the 'fall' class, and sounds from other conversation as the 'non-fall' class. The performance of the previously listed algorithms using this dataset is summarized Table 2 including the precision, recall and F-measure for each class respectively and the overall performance which is quite high, achieving in all cases more than 75%, the highest performance algorithm is the Random Forest, in which we used 100 iterations of the algorithm.

In the second case we mixed the fall sounds with fragments from the war sounds clip representing the 'fall' class, while fragments which were not used previously in the mixing part represent the 'not-fall' class. We analyzed the dataset using the same algorithms that we used previously, we can see the performance in the Table 3. The performance in this case is higher than in the previous one, mainly because the sounds in the conversation are more intermittent, similar to the falls, while the war sounds are more continuous, contrary to the falls case.

Table 1. Features used to detect fall sounds.

Energy mean	Energy standard deviation (Std)
Number of zeros mean	Number of zeros std
Spectral flux mean	Spectral flux std
Roll off factor mean	Roll off factor std
Spectral centroid mean	Spectral centroid std

Table 2. Evaluation of the classifiers using the falls sound mixed with the conversation as 'falls' and sounds from another conversation as 'non-falls' dataset.

Parameter	Class	C4.5	1-NN	Log reg	Naïve Bayes	PART	Random forest	SVM
Precision	Fall	78.9%	77.5%	79.5%	79.1%	86.5%	87.5%	83.3%
Recall	Fall	75.0%	77.5%	87.5%	85.0%	80.0%	87.5%	87.5%
F-Measure	Fall	76.9%	77.5%	83.3%	81.9%	83.1%	87.5%	85.4%
Precision	NonFall	76.2%	77.5%	86.1%	83.8%	81.4%	87.5%	86.8%
Recall	NonFall	80.0%	77.5%	77.5%	77.5%	87.5%	87.5%	82.5%
F-Measure	NonFall	78.0%	77.5%	81.6%	80.5%	84.3%	87.5%	84.66%
Overall	Both	77.5%	77.5%	82.5%	81.25%	83.75%	**87.5%**	85.0%

Table 3. Evaluation of the classifiers using the falls sound mixed with the war as 'falls' and other war sounds as 'non-falls' dataset.

Parameter	Class	C4.5	1-NN	Log reg	Naïve Bayes	PART	Random forest	SVM
Precision	Fall	87.2%	87.8%	97.4%	91.9%	82.2%	87.5%	94.3%
Recall	Fall	85.0%	90.0%	95.0%	85.0%	92.5%	87.5%	82.5%
F-Measure	Fall	86.1%	88.9%	96.2%	88.3%	87.1%	87.5%	88.0%
Precision	NonFall	86.4%	90.5%	95.5%	87.0%	92.1%	88.4%	85.4%
Recall	NonFall	88.4%	88.4%	97.7%	93.0%	81.4%	88.4%	95.3%
F-Measure	NonFall	87.4%	89.4%	96.6%	89.9%	86.4%	88.4%	0.91%
Overall	Both	86.7%	89.1%	**96.3%**	89.1%	86.7%	87.9%	89.15%

We can highlight the Logistic Regression algorithm whose performance is the highest among all the analyzed algorithms, achieving an overall performance of 96.3%.

Finally we mixed the two datasets that were analyzed individually previously to get a better generalization. Performance will be a bit lower than the classifier created mixing the fall sounds with the war ones. The required time to create the classifiers and the time to perform the classifications will also be higher. Table 4 shows the performance is higher than the conversation only dataset, and lower than the war only dataset. All the algorithms have a similar performance, the Logistic Regression and Random forest are still the best performing algorithms but the difference is not as high as it was previously, although they have the same overall performance. The logistic regression missclassifies less 'falls' instances, classifying them as 'non falls' and the main source of mistakes is the missclasification of 'non falls' instances, while in the random forest algorithm it goes the other way. Finally, the worst performing algorithm is Naïve Bayes.

Table 4. Evaluation of the classifiers using the dataset mixing the falls sounds with the war and conversation as 'falls' and other war and conversation sounds as 'not falls'.

Parameter	Class	C4.5	1-NN	Log reg	Naïve Bayes	PART	Random forest	SVM
Precision	Fall	82.3%	83.6%	85.4%	72.7%	89.6%	87.2%	76.5%
Recall	Fall	81.3%	76.3%	87.5%	90.0%	75.0%	85.0%	77.5%
F-Measure	Fall	81.8%	79.7%	86.4%	80.4%	81.6%	86.1%	77.0%
Precision	NonFall	82.1%	78.9%	87.7%	87.5%	79.2%	85.9%	78.0%
Recall	NonFall	83.1%	85.5%	85.5%	67.5%	91.6%	88.0%	77.1%
F-Measure	NonFall	82.6%	82.1%	86.6%	76.2%	84.9%	86.9%	77.6%
Overall	Both	82.2%	80.9%	**86.5%**	78.5%	83.4%	**86.5%**	77.3%

6   Overview of Attributes Classification Power

Although the number of used attributes is low, we estimated the predictive power of each attribute in order to determine which features perform the best. We ranked the attributes using the Information Gained per Attribute Evaluator/ which evaluates the worth of an attribute by measuring the information gain with respect to the class, afterwards, we ranked them according to their individual evaluations.

Following Table 5, the best attributes are the ones which measure the standard deviation of the analyzed features. The most powerful one is the standard deviation of the spectral centroids, if we consider that, this feature gives us information about the overall shape of the sound wave its value is logical; the second best attribute is the standard deviation of the energy of the signal. After this two features, the other ones have a significant fewer predictive power, if we consider the group that the two top features belong to, we can deduce that both temporal and spectral features are important and that we can not exclude either one of them.

Table 5. Ranking of the worth of information gained per attribute with respect to the class.

% Inf	Attrib	% Inf	Attrib
0.441	Centroid std	0.136	Number of zeros std
0.291	Energy std	0.119	Flux mean
0.186	Flux std	0	Centroid mean
0.168	Rolloff std	0	Rolloff mean
0.146	Energy mean	0	Number of zeros mean

Table 6. Evaluation of the classifiers using the dataset mixing the two previous ones after removing the less informative attributes.

Parameter	Class	C4.5	1-NN	Log reg	Naïve Bayes	PART	Random forest
Precision	Fall	85.5%	82.7%	81.2%	72.4%	92.3%	87.2%
Recall	Fall	81.3%	77.5%	86.3%	88.8%	75.0%	85.0%
F-Measure	Fall	83.3%	80.0%	83.6%	79.8%	82.8%	86.1%
Precision	NonFall	82.8%	79.5%	85.9%	79.6%	79.2%	85.9%
Recall	NonFall	86.7%	84.3%	80.7%	67.5%	94.0%	88.0%
F-Measure	NonFall	84.7%	81.9%	83.2%	75.7%	86.2%	86.9%
Overall	Both	84.0%	80.9%	83.4%	77.9%	**84.6%**	**86.5%**
Impact of the selection		**+1.8%**	±0%	**-3.0%**	-0.6%	**+1.2%**	±0%

Table 6 shows the performance of the algorithms if we remove the three attributes less correlated to the class according to the previous analysis (see Table 5). The 'Impact of the selection' row calculates the difference in *overall performance* with respect to the Table 4. We can observe that some algorithms, 1-NN and Random Forest, have their performance intact, since they did not use the removed attributes, however, the PART and C4.5 algorithms experience a minor improvement, increasing their overall performance by 1.2% and 1.8% respectively. The performance of the Logistic regression and Naïve Bayes algorithms has suffered a loss of performance by 3% and 0.6% respectively.

It can be concluded that we will need to remove those algorithms with a poor contribution of information if we plan to use either the C4.5 or PART algorithms. It is advisable to remove them if the plan to use the 1-NN or Random Forest algorithms, since we will relive some computational load by reducing the number of attributes that need to be evaluated. However, if we are planning to use either the Naïve Bayes or Logistic regression algorithms, we must not remove them since it would lead to a loss of performance.

7   Conclusions and Future Work

In this paper we described a ML application to detect falls by analyzing the produced sound. The aim is to implement a fall detection system oriented to the care of the elderly. This population group is prone to suffer the analyzed type of fall that we simulated and recorded. Data, along with recordings from a conversation and war ambient sound were divided into window frames and then five features were extracted from each window, allowing us to calculate the mean and standard deviation of all the windows in each sound sample. Those served as input for the ML classifiers that we used to create the classifiers.

In the near future we expect to expand the detection with new kind of falls and new features to improve the classifiers accuracy.

Acknowledgements. The authors thank the contribution of Isabel Pascual Benito, Francisco López Martínez and Helena Hernández Martínez, from Department of Nursing and Physiotherapy of the University of Alcalá, for their help designing and supervising the simulated falls procedure as well as Diego López Pajares and Enrique Alexandre Cortizo for their help regarding the signal processing tasks. This work is supported by UAH (2015/00297/001), JCLM (PEII-2014-015-A) and EphemeCH (TIN2014-56494-C4-4-P) Spanish Ministry of Economy and Competitivity projects.

References

1. Sadigh, S., Reimers, A., Andersson, R., Laflamme, L.: Falls and fall-related injuries among the elderly: a survey of residential-care facilities in a swedish municipality. J. commun. Health **29**, 129–140 (2004)
2. Blasco, J., Chen, T.M., Tapiador, J., Peris-Lopez, P.: A survey of wearable biometric recognition systems. ACM Comput. Surv. **49**, 43:1–43:35 (2016)
3. Noury, N., Fleury, A., Rumeau, P., Bourke, A.K., Laighin, G.O., Rialle, V., Lundy, J.E.: Fall detection - principles and methods. In: 2007 29th Annual International Conference of the IEEE Engineering in Medicine and Biology Society, pp. 1663–1666 (2007)
4. Tao, Y., Hu, H., Zhou, H.: Integration of vision and inertial sensors for 3d Arm motion tracking in home-based rehabilitation. Int. J. Robot. Res. **26**, 607–624 (2007)
5. Luštrek, M., Kaluža, B.: Fall detection and activity recognition with machine learning. Informatica **33**, 205–212 (2008)
6. Albert, M.V., Kording, K., Herrmann, M., Jayaraman, A.: Fall classification by machine learning using mobile phones. PLoS ONE **7**, 3–8 (2012)
7. Gibson, R.M., Amira, A., Ramzan, N., Casaseca-de-la-Higuera, P., Pervez, Z.: Multiple comparator classifier framework for accelerometer-based fall detection and diagnostic. Appl. Soft Comput. J. **39**, 94–103 (2016)
8. Miaou, S.G., Sung, P.H., Huang, C.Y.: A customized human fall detection system using omni-camera images and personal information. In: Conference Proceedings - 1st Transdisciplinary Conference on Distributed Diagnosis and Home Healthcare, D2H2 2006, pp. 39–42 (2006)
9. Auvinet, E., Multon, F., Saint-Arnaud, A., Rousseau, J., Meunier, J.: Fall detection with multiple cameras: an occlusion-resistant method based on 3-D silhouette vertical distribution. IEEE Trans. Inf. Technol. Biomed. **15**, 290–300 (2011)
10. Zigel, Y., Litvak, D., Gannot, I.: A method for automatic fall detection of elderly people using floor vibrations and sound—proof of concept on human mimicking doll falls. IEEE Trans. Biomed. Eng. **56**, 2858–2867 (2009)
11. Litvak, D., Zigel, Y., Gannot, I.: Fall detection of elderly through floor vibrations and sound. In: Conference Proceedings Annual International Conference of the IEEE Engineering in Medicine and Biology Society, IEEE Engineering in Medicine and Biology Society, Annual Conference 2008, pp. 4632–4635 (2008)
12. Popescu, M., Member, S., Li, Y., Skubic, M., Rantz, M.: Information to reduce the false alarm rate, pp. 4628–4631 (2008)
13. Doukas, C., Maglogiannis, I.: Advanced patient or elder fall detection based on movement and sound data. In: Proceedings of the 2nd International Conference on Pervasive Computing Technologies for Healthcare 2008, PervasiveHealth, pp. 103–107 (2008)

14. Vacher, M., Portet, F., Fleury, A., Noury, N.: Development of audio sensing technology for ambient assisted living: applications and challenges. In: Digital Advances in Medicine, E-Health, and Communication Technologies, p. 148 (2013)
15. Li, Y., Ho, K., Popescu, M.: A microphone array system for automatic fall detection. IEEE Trans. Biomed. Eng. **59**, 1291–1301 (2012)
16. Chaudhuri, S., Thompson, H., Demiris, G.: Fall detection devices and their use with older adults: a systematic review. J. Geriatr. Phys. Ther. **37**(2014), 178 (2001)

A Novel k-NN Approach for Data with Uncertain Attribute Values

Asma Trabelsi[1,2(✉)], Zied Elouedi[1], and Eric Lefevre[2]

[1] Institut Supérieur de Gestion de Tunis, LARODEC,
Université de Tunis, Tunis, Tunisia
trabelsyasma@gmail.com, zied.elouedi@gmx.fr
[2] Univ. Artois, EA 3926, Laboratoire de Génie Informatique
et d'Automatique de l'Artois (LGI2A), 62400 Béthune, France
eric.lefevre@univ-artois.fr

Abstract. Data uncertainty arises in several real world domains, including machine learning and pattern recognition applications. In classification problems, we could very well wind up with uncertain attribute values that are caused by sensor failures, measurements approximations or even subjective expert assessments, etc. Despite their seriousness, these kinds of data are not well covered till now. In this paper, we propose to develop a machine learning model for handling such kinds of imperfection. More precisely, we suggest to develop a new version of the well known k-nearest neighbors classifier to handle the uncertainty that occurs in the attribute values within the belief function framework.

Keywords: Evidential k-nearest neighbors · Uncertainty · Belief function theory · Classification

1 Introduction

The k Nearest Neighbor (k-NN) classifier, firstly proposed by Fix and Hodges [4], is regarded as one of the well commonly used classification techniques in the fields of machine learning and pattern recognition. The original k-NN version consists of assigning a query pattern to the majority class of its k nearest neighbors. The major shortcoming of this technique arises from learning a k-NN classifier with skewed class distributions, meaning that training instances with the most prevalent class may dominate the prediction of new query patterns due a large value of k. From this, numerous researchers have proven that the uncertainty about the class label of a given test pattern can be modeled through various uncertainty theories such as the possibilistic theory [8], the fuzzy theory [15], the belief function theory [9], etc. This latter, also referred to as evidence theory, has shown a great success in several pattern recognition problems, notably for representing and managing the uncertainty relative to the label class of new patterns to be classified. In [2], Denoeux has proposed an evidence theoretic k-NN (Ek-NN) method relied on the belief function theory where each neighbor of a pattern to be classified is regarded as a piece of evidence supporting

© Springer International Publishing AG 2017
S. Benferhat et al. (Eds.): IEA/AIE 2017, Part I, LNAI 10350, pp. 160–170, 2017.
DOI: 10.1007/978-3-319-60042-0_19

some hypothesis concerning its class membership. The basic belief assignments obtained by all the k nearest neighbors are then merged through the Dempster rule to identify the class label relative to each test pattern. An extended version of the Ek-NN, denoted by EEk-NN, has been introduced in [5], where the label class of each training instance will be represented by an evidential label to handle the uncertainty that occurs in the training data. Its is worth noting that, in several real world data, the attribute values may also contain some noise and outliers that can make erroneous classification results. Thus, evidential databases where attributes' values are represented using the evidence theory have been introduced over the past few years. Despite their accuracy, neither the Ek-NN nor the EEk-NN are able to handle such kinds of data. Inspired from both Ek-NN and EEk-NN, in this paper, we suggest to develop a new k-NN version for dealing with data described by uncertain attribute values, particularly where the uncertainty is represented within the belief function framework. The reminder of this paper is organized as follows: Sect. 2 is devoted to highlighting the basic concepts of the belief function theory as explained by the Transferable Belief Model framework, one interpretation of the belief function theory. In Sect. 3, we present our novel k-NN version for handling evidential databases. Our experimentation on several synthetic databases are described in Sect. 4. Finally, in Sect. 5, we draw our conclusion and our main future work directions.

2 Belief Function Theory: Background

The belief function theory, originally pointed out by Dempster [1] and Shafer [9], has shown a great success for modeling uncertain knowledge. In what follows, we recall the main concepts of this theory.

2.1 Frame of Discernment

The frame of discernment, denoted by Θ, is the set of all possible answers for a given problem which should be mutually exhaustive and exclusive:

$$\Theta = \{H_1, \ldots, H_N\} \tag{1}$$

From the frame of discernment Θ, one can deduce the set 2^Θ containing all subsets of Θ:

$$2^\Theta = \{\emptyset, H_1, H_2, \ldots, H_N, H_1 \cup H_2, \ldots, \Theta\} \tag{2}$$

2.2 Basic Belief Assignment

A basic belief assignment (bba), denoted by m, is a mapping function m: $2^\Theta \rightarrow [0, 1]$, such that:

$$\sum_{A \subseteq \Theta} m(A) = 1 \tag{3}$$

Each subset A of 2^Θ fulfilling $m(A) > 0$ is called a focal element.

2.3 Combination Operators

Several combination rules have been introduced to merge reliable independent information sources issued from independent information sources. The conjunctive operator, proposed within the Transferable Belief Model (TBM) [11], is a well known one. For two information sources S_1 and S_2 having respectively the bbas m_1 and m_2, the conjunctive rule, denoted by $\bigcirc$, will be written in the following form:

$$m_1 \bigcirc m_2(A) = \sum_{B \cap C = A} m_1(B)m_2(C), \quad \forall A \subseteq \Theta. \tag{4}$$

The belief committed to the empty set is called conflictual mass. A normalized version of the conjunctive operator, proposed by Dempster [1], manages the conflict by redistributing the conflictual mass over all focal elements. The Dempster rule is defined as follows:

$$m_1 \oplus m_2(A) = \frac{1}{1-K} \sum_{B \cap C = A} m_1(B)m_2(C), \quad \forall A \subseteq \Theta \tag{5}$$

where K $(K \neq 1)$, representing the conflictual mass between the two bbas m_1 and m_2, is set as:

$$K = \sum_{B \cap C = \emptyset} m_1(B)m_2(C) \tag{6}$$

2.4 Decision Making

To make decisions within the belief function framework, Smets, in [10], has proposed the so-called pignistic probability denoted by $BetP$ which transforms the beliefs held into probability measures as follows:

$$BetP(A) = \sum_{B \cap A = \emptyset} \frac{|A \cap B|}{|B|} m(B), \quad \forall A \in \Theta \tag{7}$$

2.5 Dissimilarity Between bbas

In the literature, there have been several measures allowing the computation of the degree of dissimilarity between two bodies of evidence [6,12]. One of the commonly used measures is the Jousselme distance which is set as follows for two given bbas m_1 and m_2:

$$dist(m_1, m_2) = \sqrt{\frac{1}{2}(m_1 - m_2)^T D(m_1 - m_2)} \tag{8}$$

where D is the Jaccard similarity measure defined by:

$$D(X,Y) = \begin{cases} 1 & \text{if } X = Y = \emptyset \\ \dfrac{|X \cap Y|}{|X \cup Y|} & \forall X, Y \in 2^\Theta \end{cases} \tag{9}$$

3 Nearest Neighbor Classifiers for Uncertain Data

In what follows, we address classification problems with uncertain data. More precisely, we get inspired from the Evidential k-NN classifier and its extended version [2,5] to handle the uncertainty that occurs in the attribute values and is represented within the belief function framework. Let $X = \{x^i = (x_1^i,\ldots,x_n^i)|i=1,\ldots,N\}$ be a set of N n-dimensional training samples, and let $\Theta = \{H_1,\ldots,H_M\}$ be a set of M classes. Each sample x^i is described by n uncertain attribute values represented within the belief function framework and a class label $L^i \in \{1,\ldots,M\}$ expressing with certainty its membership to one class in Θ. Assume that L is the set of labels, we denote by $T = \{(x^1, L^1), \ldots (x^N, L^N)\}$ the training set that will be used to classify new objects. Suppose that y is a new pattern to be classified based on the information contained in the training set T. The idea consists of computing the distance between the test pattern y and each pair (x^i, L^i) in T using a distance metric $d_{y,i}$ which is calculated as the sum of the absolute differences between the attribute values. More specifically, we have resorted to the Jousselme distance metric to cope with the uncertainty that arises in the attribute values. Thus, $d_{y,i}$ is set as follows:

$$d_{y,i} = \sum_{j=1}^{n} \sqrt{\frac{1}{2}(x_j^i - y_j)^T D_j (x_j^i - y_j)} \tag{10}$$

where D_j is the Jaccard similarity measure defined by:

$$D(X,Y) = \begin{cases} 1 & \text{if } X = Y = \emptyset \\ \dfrac{|X \cap Y|}{|X \cup Y|} & \forall\, X,Y \in 2^{\Theta_j} \end{cases} \tag{11}$$

A small value of $d_{y,i}$ reflects the situation that both instances y and x^i have the same label class L^i. On the contrary, a large value of $d_{y,i}$ may reflect the situation of almost complete ignorance concerning the label class of y. The information concerning the label class of the pattern query y can be modeled through the belief function theory. Thus, for the test sample y, each training instance x^i provides an item of evidence $m^{(i)}(.|x^i)$ over Θ as follows:

$$m^{(i)}(H_q|x^i) = \alpha \Phi_q(d_{y,i}) \tag{12}$$

$$m^{(i)}(\Theta|x^i) = 1 - \alpha \Phi_q(d_{y,i})$$

$$m^{(i)}(A|x^i) = 0, \forall A \in 2^{\Theta}\backslash\{\Theta, H_q\}$$

where H_q is the class label of the instance x^i and α is a parameter such that $0 < \alpha < 1$. Author in [2] has proven that setting α to 0.95 can yield good results. The decreasing function Φ_q, verifying $\Phi_q(0) = 1$ and $lim_{d\to\infty}\Phi_q(d) = 0$, should be set as:

$$\Phi_q(d) = exp(-\gamma_q d^2), \tag{13}$$

where γ_q be a positive parameter relative to the class H_q that can be optimized using either an exact method relying on a gradient search procedure for medium or small training sets or a linearization method for handling large training sets [16]. For both exact and approximated methods, the best values of γ are determined by minimising the mean squared classification error over the whole training set T of size N. The final bba m^y regarding the class of the query pattern y can be obtained by merging the N bbas issued from the different training instances. We ultimately resorted to the Dempster rule, one of the well-known rules used for ensuring fusion. It is set as follows:

$$m^y = m^{(1)}(.|x^1) \oplus m^{(2)}(.|x^2) \oplus \ldots \oplus m^{(N)}(.|x^N) \tag{14}$$

As some training instances may be too far from y, only the k nearest neighbors of the test sample y should be considered to determinate its class membership. The final bba will be set as follows:

$$m^y = m^{(1)}(.|x^1) \oplus m^{(2)}(.|x^2) \oplus \ldots \oplus m^{(k)}(.|x^k) \tag{15}$$

To make a decision about the label class of the query pattern y, the pignistic probability $BetP$ should be computed based on the combined bba m^y as shown in Eq. 7. The test pattern is then assigned to the class with the maximum pignistic probability:

$$L^y = argmax_{H_q} BetP(H_q) \tag{16}$$

where $BetP(H_q)$ corresponds to the pignistic probability of the hypothesis H_q associated to the bba m^y.

4   Experimentations

In this Section, we present our carried out experimentations to assess the performance of our proposed k-NN classifiers.

4.1   Experimentation Settings

For checking the performance of our proposed k-NN classifier, we have performed experimentations on several synthetic databases obtained by adding uncertainty to some real world databases acquired from the well known UCI machine learning repository. As we only deal with categorical attributes, in this paper, we have resorted to only symbolic databases. A brief description of these databases is presented in Table 1. We have managed various uncertainty levels according to certain degrees of uncertainty denoted by P:

- No uncertainty: $P = 0$
- Low Uncertainty: $0 < P < 0.4$
- Middle Uncertainty: $0.4 \leq P < 0.7$
- High Uncertainty: $0.7 \leq P \leq 1$

Table 1. Description of databases

Databases	#Instances	#Attributes	#Classes
Voting records	435	16	2
Heart	267	22	2
Tic-Tac-Toe	958	9	2
Monks	195	23	2
Balloons	16	4	2
Hayes-Roth	160	5	3
Balance	625	4	3
Lenses	24	4	3

Given a database described by N objects x^i ($i \in \{1, \ldots, N\}$), n attributes x^i_j ($j \in \{1, \ldots, n\}$) for each instance x^i and a specific degree of uncertainty P. Suppose that Θ_j is the frame of discernment relative to the attribute j. Let us denote by $|\Theta_j|$ the cardinality of Θ_j, each attribute value $v^i_{j,t}$ corresponds to an instance x^i such that $v^i_{j,t} \in \Theta_j$ ($t \in \{1, \ldots, |\Theta_j|\}$) will be represented through the belief function framework as follows:

$$m^{\Theta_j}\{x^i\}(\{v^i_{j,t}\}) = 1 - P \quad \text{and} \quad m^{\Theta_j}\{x^i\}(\Theta_j) = P \qquad (17)$$

To evaluate the performance of our proposed k-NN classifier, we have relied on a distance criterion that measures the error rate between the test instance's bba and its real label class. It is set as follows where M corresponds to the number of classes, $P_i = \{BetP_i(H_1), \ldots, BetP_i(H_M)\}$ is the output vector of the pignistic probabilities of the bba obtained by Eq. 15 and δ_{iq} equals 1 when L^i represents the real class of the test instance x^i, and 0 otherwise:

$$Distance_i = Distance(P_i, L^i) = \sum_{q=1}^{M} (BetP_i(H_q) - \delta_{iq})^2 \qquad (18)$$

Then, we just have to calculate the average distance obtained by all test instances to get a final error rate. Note that the final distance should satisfy the following property:

$$0 \leqslant Distance_i \leqslant 2 \qquad (19)$$

In the way, the lower the distance metric the better the classification performance can be obtained.

4.2 Experimentation Results

For assessing the results, we have performed the 10-fold cross-validation technique that divides randomly a given dataset into ten equal sized parts where one part is used as a testing set and the remaining parts are used as training sets. This process will be repeated ten times where each part should be used exactly once as a test set. The distance results yielded by our new k-NN classifier are given from Figs. 1, 2, 3, 4, 5, 6, 7 and 8 for $k \in [1,15]$. We can remark from Figs. 1, 2, 3, 4, 5, 6, 7 and 8 that our proposed classifier has yielded interesting results for the different uncertainty levels. In fact, the distance results obtained for the mentioned benchmark data sets with the different uncertainty degrees are almost in the range [0.04,0.775]. For instance, the distance results yielded by the balance-scale database for the best values of k with No, Low, Middle and high uncertainties are respectively equal to 0.405, 0.397, 0.372 and 0.543. As well, there are equal to 0.642, 0.583 0.574 and 0.615 for the worst values of k. These encouraging results may be explained by the fact that our novel k-NN classifier has a great power for predicting the label classes of instances to be classified. We have suggested to evaluate the performance of our novel k-NN classifier against other evidential classifiers dealing also with uncertainty that arises in the attribute values. In our previous works [13,14], we have proposed extensions of the decision tree classifiers inspired from the belief decision tree paradigm [3] to handle such kind of imperfection. Precisely, we have tackled the case of uncertainty that occurs in both construction and classification phases.

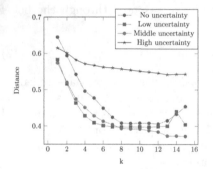

Fig. 1. Distances for Balance database

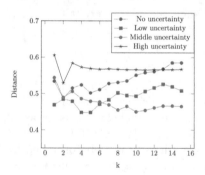

Fig. 2. Distances for Hayes-Roth database

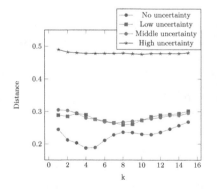

Fig. 3. Distances for Monks database

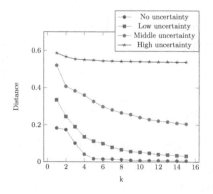

Fig. 4. Distances for Balloons database

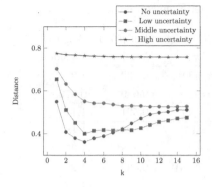

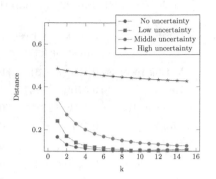

Fig. 5. Distances for Lenses database

Fig. 6. Distances for Voting Records database

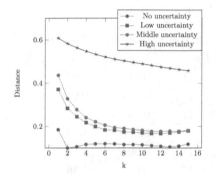

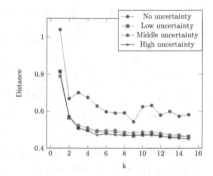

Fig. 7. Distances for Tic-Tac-Toa database

Fig. 8. Distances for Heart database

For the construction step, we have mainly relied on the ratio *Gain Ratio* criterion proposed by Quinlan [7] to construct decision trees in [13], while in [14], we have relied on a *Diff Ratio* criterion based on distance that calculates the difference before and after the partitioning process has been performed using a such attribute. It is worth noting have both versions have yielded interesting results. The performance of our proposed k-NN classification technique for best and worst values of k will then be compared to [13] and [14]. The comparative results are given from Tables 2, 3, 4 and 5 where *Belief DT Version1* and *Belief DT Version2* correspond to our extended decision trees published respectively in [13] and [14]. From the distance results, given in Tables 2, 3, 4 and 5, we can remark that our proposed k-NN classifier has given mostly distance results smaller than those yielded in [13] and [14] for both best values of k (the values of k that yield the lowest distances) and worst values of k (the values of k that yield the highest distances). From this, we can conclude that our k-NN is the best performance classification technique compared with the two other ones within the framework of uncertain data represented by the evidence theory.

Table 2. Comparative results: no uncertainty

Bases	New k-NN Best values of k	New k-NN Worst values of k	Belief DT Version 1	Belief DT Version 2
Voting records	0.103 ($k = 8$)	0.167 ($k = 1$)	0.832	1.04
Heart	0.570 ($k = 14$)	1.04 ($k = 1$)	0.649	0.972
Tic-Tac-Toa	0.1 ($k = 2$)	0.185 ($k = 1$)	0.521	1.11
Monks	0.187 ($k = 4$)	0.286($k = 15$)	0.726	1.18
Balloons	0.0049 ($k = 15$)	0.183 ($k = 1$)	0.468	1.35
Hayes-Roth	0.487 ($k = 2$)	0.586 ($k = 13$)	0.449	1.22
Balance-Scale	0.406 ($k = 12$)	0.645 ($k = 1$)	0.71	1.37
Lenses	0.362 ($k = 4$)	0.511 ($k = 14$)	0.45	1.15

Table 3. Comparative results: low uncertainty

Bases	New k-NN Best values of k	New k-NN Worst values of k	Belief DT Version 1	Belief DT Version 2
Voting records	0.104 ($k = 8$)	0.241 ($k = 1$)	0.914	1.09
Heart	0.461 ($k = 13$)	0.815 ($k = 1$)	0.713	0.998
Tic-Tac-Toa	0.167 ($k = 13$)	0.372 ($k = 1$)	0.654	1.21
Monks	0.259 ($k = 8$)	0.301 ($k = 15$)	0.817	1.13
Balloons	0.0315 ($k = 15$)	0.335 ($k = 1$)	0.59	1.15
Hayes-Roth	0.469 ($k = 1$)	0.526 ($k = 13$)	0.624	1.16
Balance-Scale	0.397 ($k = 9$)	0.583($k = 1$)	0.62	1.28
Lenses	0.400 ($k = 4$)	0.654($k = 1$)	0.581	1.14

Table 4. Comparative results: middle uncertainty

Bases	New k-NN Best values of k	New k-NN Worst values of k	Belief DT Version 1	Belief DT Version 2
Voting records	0.130 ($k = 13$)	0.341 ($k = 1$)	0.927	1.17
Heart	0.462 ($k = 15$)	0.789 ($k = 1$)	0.802	1.01
Tic-Tac-Toa	0.177 ($k = 13$)	0.437 ($k = 1$)	0.897	1.32
Monks	0.270 ($k = 9$)	0.303($k = 2$)	0.901	1.01
Balloons	0.205 ($k = 15$)	0.520($k = 1$)	0.9304	1.02
Hayes-Roth	0.450 ($k = 10$)	0.544($k = 1$)	0.946	1.04
Balance-Scale	0.372 ($k = 15$)	0.574($k = 1$)	0.94	1.25
Lenses	0.526 ($k = 4$)	0.703($k = 1$)	0.925	1.028

Table 5. Comparative results: high uncertainty

Bases	New k-NN Best values of k	New k-NN Worst values of k	Belief DT Version 1	Belief DT Version 2
Voting records	0.426 ($k = 15$)	0.485 ($k = 1$)	0.987	1.23
Heart	0.45($k = 15$)	0.813 ($k = 1$)	0.868	1.21
Tic-Tac-Toa	0.485 ($k = 15$)	0.608 ($k = 1$)	0.986	1.35
Monks	0.476 ($k = 10$)	0.490($k = 1$)	0.985	1
Balloons	0.537 ($k = 14$)	0.586($k = 1$)	1	1
Hayes-Roth	0.529 ($k = 2$)	0.606($k = 1$)	0.95	1.03
Balance-Scale	0.543 ($k = 13$)	0.615($k = 1$)	1	1.08
Lenses	0.757 ($k = 15$)	0.775($k = 1$)	0.998	1

5   Conclusion

In this paper, we have developed a new version of the well-known k-NN classifier to handle the case of the uncertainty that exists in the attribute values and is represented with the belief function framework. Our novel k-NN technique has been compared to other belief decision tree classifiers that deal with the same kind of uncertainty. The experimental results in terms of the distance criterion have proven the efficiency of our proposed k-NN classifier compared with the two other evidential ones. As a future work, we intend to extend our proposed k-NN in order to handling numerical and mixed databases.

References

1. Dempster, A.P.: Upper and lower probabilities induced by a multivalued mapping. Ann. Math. Stat. **38**, 325–339 (1967)
2. Denoeux, T.: A k-nearest neighbor classification rule based on Dempster-Shafer theory. IEEE Trans. Syst. Man Cybern. **25**(5), 804–813 (1995)
3. Elouedi, Z., Mellouli, K., Smets, P.: Belief decision trees: theoretical foundations. Int. J. Approximate Reasoning **28**(2), 91–124 (2001)
4. Fix, E., Hodges Jr., J.L.: Discriminatory Analysis-Nonparametric Discrimination: Consistency Properties. Technical report, DTIC Document (1951)
5. Jiao, L., Denœux, T., Pan, Q.: Evidential editing K-nearest neighbor classifier. In: Destercke, S., Denoeux, T. (eds.) ECSQARU 2015. LNCS, vol. 9161, pp. 461–471. Springer, Cham (2015). doi:10.1007/978-3-319-20807-7_42
6. Jousselme, A., Grenier, D., Bossé, E.: A new distance between two bodies of evidence. Inf. Fusion **2**(2), 91–101 (2001)
7. Quinlan, J.R.: Induction of decision trees. Mach. Learn. **1**(1), 81–106 (1986)
8. Sgarro, A.: Possibilistic information theory: a coding theoretic approach. Fuzzy Sets Syst. **132**(1), 11–32 (2002)
9. Shafer, G.: A Mathematical Theory of Evidence, vol. 1. Princeton University Press, Princeton (1976)

10. Smets, P.: Decision making in the TBM: the necessity of the pignistic transformation. Int. J. Approximate Reasoning **38**(2), 133–147 (2005)
11. Smets, P., Kennes, R.: The transferable belief model. Artif. Intell. **66**(2), 191–234 (1994)
12. Tessem, B.: Approximations for efficient computation in the theory of evidence. Artif. Intell. **61**(2), 315–329 (1993)
13. Trabelsi, A., Elouedi, Z., Lefevre, E.: Handling uncertain attribute values in decision tree classifier using the belief function theory. In: Dichev, C., Agre, G. (eds.) AIMSA 2016. LNCS, vol. 9883, pp. 26–35. Springer, Cham (2016). doi:10.1007/978-3-319-44748-3_3
14. Trabelsi, A., Elouedi, Z., Lefevre, E.: New decision tree classifier for dealing with partially uncertain data. In: 25eme Rencontres francophones sur la Logique Floue et ses Applications (LFA 2016), pp. 57–64 (2016)
15. Zadeh, L.A.: Fuzzy sets. Inf. Control **8**(3), 338–353 (1965)
16. Zouhal, L.M., Denoeux, T.: An evidence-theoretic k-NN rule with parameter optimization. IEEE Trans. Syst. Man Cybern. Part C (Appl. Rev.) **28**(2), 263–271 (1998)

On Combining Imputation Methods
for Handling Missing Data

Nassima Ben Hariz[1(✉)], Hela Khoufi[2], and Ezzeddine Zagrouba[1]

[1] LIMTIC Laboratory, Research Team SIIVA, Institut Supérieur d'Informatique,
Université de Tunis El Manar, 2 Rue Abou Rayhane Bayrouni, 2080 Ariana, Tunisia
nassima.benhariz@gmail.com
[2] Faculty of Computing and Information Technology,
Khulais King Abdulaziz University, Jeddah, Kingdom of Saudi Arabia

Abstract. In real-world problems, data are generally characterized by
their imperfection. One of the most common forms of imperfection is
missing data. In fact, dealing with missing data remains a very important issue in data mining and knowledge discovery researches. A panoply
of methods, addressing this problem, is proposed in the literature handling different types of data. In this work, we focus our study towards
three methods which are KNN, MissForest, and EM algorithm. These
methods are considered among the most efficient in different imputation
problems. In the first part of this work, we present a brief state of the
art of the used imputation methods and the strategy that we propose
to use. In the second part, we provide a comparative study based on
different criterion showing the efficiency of MissForest compared to the
other methods and we demonstrate that the combination is preferable to
improve the imputation of continuous data instead of using them individually.

Keywords: Missing data · Imputation methods · KNN · MissForest ·
EM algorithm · Combination

1 Introduction

Among the most relevant problems effecting the quality of data is the presence
of missing data. Different sources can be the origin of the existence of missing
data in databases citing for instance the death of patients in medical domain,
equipment malfunctions in industrial field, refusal of respondents to answer certain questions in surveys, loss of files, etc. This problem has gained a growing
interest in recent researches in data mining trying to reduce the risk of incorrect
estimates and results. In fact, a variety of methods addressing the management
of missing data have been developed. Choosing the appropriate method to handle missing data during the analysis and decision making process is considered
as one of the most challenges confronting researchers.

Appropriately, dealing with missing requires a careful examination of the data
in order to be able to identify the type and the mechanism of missingness, and

© Springer International Publishing AG 2017
S. Benferhat et al. (Eds.): IEA/AIE 2017, Part I, LNAI 10350, pp. 171–181, 2017.
DOI: 10.1007/978-3-319-60042-0_20

a clear understanding of how the different imputation methods work. According to Rubin and Little [10], there are three types of missing data distributions (or mechanisms): Missing Completely At Random (MCAR), Missing At Random (MAR) and Missing not at Random (MNAR). In the MCAR mechanism, the probability of a missing value depends only on some unknown parameters. It does not computed by the observed or unobserved values. For the MAR mechanism, the probability of a missing value depends on the observed values and on unknown parameters but not on the missing value itself. For example, the probability of missing data of the age variable depends only on the observed variable sex. Concerning the MNAR mechanism, the probability of missing values is related to the unobserved values themselves. For the income variable, for example, the probability of missing data is determined according to the same income variable [15].

In this work, we are particularly interested in three methods which are KNN, MissForest, and EM algorithm for the MCAR mechanism. In the case of continuous variables, we don't know which method is the best. Thus, our first objective consists in analyzing the performance of these methods for continuous data by varying the rate of missing values to be able to determine the suitable method for each case.

In machine learning domain, it is demonstrated that the combination of algorithms can provide a better performance than the use of each algorithm separately. Moreover, according to our knowledge there is no study that use the combination of imputation methods. For these reasons, we discuss the conditions under which the combination of the three mentioned methods is most effective.

This work is organized as follows: Sect. 2 describes the imputation problem. Section 3 surveys the most used methods for missing data treatment. Section 4 presents a brief overview of combination methods. Section 5 presents a comparative study using different datasets. Finally, the concluding discussion and remarks are provided in Sect. 6.

2   Imputation Problem

Assume that $X = (X_1, X_2, ..., X_p)$ is a $n \times p$ dimensional database with n rows representing the observations $(i_1, ..., i_n)$ and p columns representing the variables $(v_1, v_2, ..., v_p)$. In a database, missing values are modeled by empty cases or by other notations such as '?' or 'NA'. If X_{comp} is a matrix of complete data, we can artificially introduce missing data for X_{comp} and we obtain a matrix with missing values denoted by X_{mis}. Imputation methods for missing values replace missing cases X_{mis} with a plausible values to obtain an imputed matrix denoted by X_{imp}. Figure 1 shows an example of X_{mis} from iris dataset [6].
For an arbitrary variable $X_s (s = 1, ..., p)$ from X with missing values at entries $i_{mis}^s \in \{1, ..., n\}$ the dataset can be divided into four parts:

1. The observed values of X_s, denoted y_{obs}^s;
2. The missing values of X_s, denoted y_{mis}^s ;

X₁	X₂	X₃	X₄	Class
4,6	3,4	1,4	0,2	NA
5	NA	1,5	0,4	setosa
NA	3,1	1,5	0,1	setosa
5,4	3,7	1,5	0,2	setosa
4,4	2,9	1,4	NA	setosa
NA	3,1	1,5	0,1	setosa
6,5	2,8	4,6	NA	versicolor
NA	2,8	4,5	1,4	versicolor
6,7	2,5	5,8	1,8	virginica
7,2	3,6	6,1	NA	Virginica

X₁	X₂	X₃	X₄	Class
4,6	3,4	1,4	0,2	NA
5	NA	1,5	0,4	setosa
NA	3,1	1,5	0,1	setosa
5,4	3,7	1,5	0,2	setosa
4,4	2,9	1,4	NA	setosa
NA	3,1	1,5	0,1	setosa
6,5	2,8	4,6	NA	versicolor
NA	2,8	4,5	NA	versicolor
6,7	2,5	5,8	1,8	virginica
7,2	3,6	6,1	2,1	Virginica

Legend:

x^4_{obs}

x^4_{mis}

y^4_{obs}

y^4_{mis}

Fig. 1. Example of instances with missing values from iris dataset

Fig. 2. Different parts of the example of instances from iris dataset

3. The variables other than X_s with observations $i^s_{obs} \in \{1, ..., n\} \backslash i^s_{mis}$, denoted x^s_{obs} ;
4. The variables other than X_s with observations i^s_{mis} , denoted x^s_{mis}.

Figure 2 presents four parts of the dataset described above, for variable X_4.

A variable X_s can be continuous or discrete. The continuous variables are not countable, they can be measured with infinitive possible values. For example: width, length, size and temperature are continuous variables.

The discrete variables can take a finite number of numerical values, categories or codes. It can be classified into the following categories:

- Nominal: nominal variable is one that has two or more categories, but there is no intrinsic ordering to the categories. For example, hair color is a nominal variable having a number of categories (blonde, brown, brunette, red, etc.);
- Ordinal: discrete ordinal variable is a nominal variable, but its different states are ordered in a meaningful sequence. For example, satisfaction is a ordinal variable having the following values: unsatisfied, satisfied, very satisfied and very much satisfied;
- Binary: binary variable is a nominal variable with two possible values. For example, gender is a binary variable having two categories (male and female).

3 Literature Review

For handling missing data, many techniques are proposed in the literature [4,9,10,13]. According to Rubin and Little [10] there are different strategies for dealing with missing data. The simplest solution is the deletion of any observation with missing values. This method can be applied only with few number of missing data and with MCAR mechanism. Another solution consists in imputation strategy that replaces each missing case with a plausible value (single imputation) or with a vector of plausible values (multiple imputation [9]). For single imputation, the most popular methods are the mean imputation which replaces missing values of a variable with the mean of all known values of that variable, the regression imputation and the K-Nearest Neighbors (KNN) imputation [4,10]. Another category includes iterative methods based on iterative algorithms such as MissForest [13] and Expectation Maximization (EM) algorithm [5]. From different existing methods, we are specially interested in studying the behavior of the last three cited techniques considered among the most efficient methods [8].

3.1   KNN Imputation

Thanks to its simplicity, KNN imputation is the most well-known method for continuous datasets [4]. The goal of this method is to replace the missing values with the value of k nearest neighbors in the dataset. For each observation x_i with missing values, k nearest values are selected by calculating the distances between x_i and the other observations $x_j (i, j = 1, ..., n, j \neq i)$. The most used distance measure is the Euclidean distance, that is calculated by the following equation:

$$Euclidean\ Distance(x_j, x_i) = \sqrt{\sum_{s=1}^{p}(x_j^s - x_i^s)^2} \qquad (1)$$

For continuous variables, imputed value is the weighted average of the k neighbor values. This method preserves the distribution and the correlation between variables.

Troyanskaya et al. [14] compared the performance of the KNN to the performance of two other methods such as Singular Value Decomposition SVD and row average. These methods were evaluated using different real datasets from microarray experiments and varying the rate of missing data from 1% to 20%. Troyanskaya et al. demonstrated that KNN is more robust for missing value estimation than SVD and row average.

Batista et al. [2] present a comparative study of KNN with two well known Machine Learning algorithms named CN2 and C4.5. Evaluation is performed using three datasets from UCI repository [6] such as Bupa, Cmc and Pima with artificially introduced missing values ranging from 10% to 60% under MCAR condition. The missing values were replaced by the estimated values using 1, 3, 5, 10, 20, 30, 50 and 100 nearest neighbors. Analysis results indicate that missing data imputation based on the KNN outperformed the internal methods used by C4.5 and CN2. This method provided very good results, even when the datasets had a large amount of missing data.

3.2   MissForest

Proposed by Stekhoven and Bühlmann [13], this method is based on the algorithm of Random Forest (RF) [3]. Indeed, it begins with an initial 'naive' imputation to obtain a complete sample and continues with a sequence of random forests until the first degradation of the model. The Algorithm 1 presents the missForet method proposed in [13].

Algorithm 1. MF Algorithm

Inputs: X an $n \times p$ matrix and stopping criterion ν
Make initial estimation for missing values;
$k \leftarrow$ vector of sorted indices of columns in X (with respect to increasing the rate of missing values);
while not ν **do**
   $X_{imp}^{old} \leftarrow$ store previously imputed matrix
   for s in k **do**
      Pick a random forest using y_{obs}^s and x_{obs}^s
      Estimate y_{mis}^s using x_{mis}^s
      $X_{imp}^{new} \leftarrow$ update imputed matrix using estimated y_{mis}^s
   end for
   update ν.
end while
return the imputed matrix X_{imp}^{new}

The principal of MissForest (MF) can be described as follows [13]: Initially, estimate missing values using mean imputation or any other imputation method. Then, sort all the variables $X_s(s = 1, \ldots, p)$ starting with the variables having the lowest rate of missing values. For each variable X_s, pick a RF with response y_{obs}^s and predictors x_{obs}^s and estimate the missing values y_{mis}^s by applying the trained RF to x_{mis}^s (see Sect. 2). The process continue until a stopping criterion ν is reached. Indeed, the stopping criterion ν is obtained when the difference between the newly imputed data matrix X_{imp}^{new} and the previous one X_{imp}^{old} increases for the first time. For continuous variables N, this difference is defined as:

$$\Delta_N = \frac{\sum_{j \in N} \left(X_{imp}^{new} - X_{imp}^{old} \right)^2}{\sum_{j \in N} \left(X_{imp}^{new} \right)^2} \tag{2}$$

For continuous variables, Stekhoven and Bühlmann [13] compared the miss-Forest method to KNN imputation [14] and to Missingness Pattern Alternating Lasso algorithm (MissPALasso) [12]. These methods were evaluated using multiple datasets coming from biological fields. Missing data was inserted completely at random (MCAR) with different rates of missing data (10% to 30%) of the total of instances. Stekhoven and Bühlmann showed that MissForest outperformed the other imputation methods in all cases of the missing rates.

The performance of the method was assessed using Normalized Root Mean Squared Error (NRMSE) proposed by [7]. For continuous variables this measure is defined by the Eq. (3) where μ, σ^2 are the empirical mean and the variance computed over the continuous missing values.

$$NRMSE = \sqrt{\frac{\mu \left((X_{comp} - X_{imp})^2 \right)}{\sigma^2 (X_{comp})}} \tag{3}$$

MissForest is a nonparametric method which not require assumptions about distribution of data. Moreover, this method can be used in data with complex interaction, non-linear relation or high dimensional datasets.

3.3 EM Algorithm

The EM algorithm is a probabilistic approach to estimate missing values [5]. It is an iterative method for maximizing the observed likelihood. The principle of this method is illustrated in the Algorithm 2. Indeed, this method has two steps:

1. Expectation step: computing expected values for the missing data given the current parameter estimates P.
2. Maximization step: estimating new parameter values by maximizing the observed likelihood after substituting the values estimated in step 1 into the likelihood equation.

Algorithm 2. EM Algorithm

Random initialization for parameters P
while the algorithm not converge **do**
    Estimation of X_{miss} according to X_{obs} and the value of P
    Maximizing the likelihood using the estimated X_{miss} performed in the previous step.
    Updating the value of P
end while

Afshari Safavi et al. [1] compared the EM algorithm to other imputation approaches (mean imputation, mode imputation and linear regression imputation) addressing missing data in the questionnaires. In this study, 500 questionnaires were used for self-medication in diabetic patients. It is shown that the EM algorithm was the most accurate method.

4   Proposed Approach

The technique of combination is a classical approach that has proved its efficiency in several problems with machine learning and pattern recognition researchers as the combination of classifiers [11]. The idea is to combine the results obtained by two or more methods or classifiers to obtain a single and relevant result.

The most commonly used combination methods are: weighted mean, minimum, maximum and product for numerical data, and majority vote for categorical data [11]. According to our knowledge from the literature, there is no study dedicated to the problem of missing data using combination of imputation methods. Thus, we proposed to combine the outputs of the used imputation methods in order to improve imputation results. In this paper, we are interested in three methods dealing with numerical data which are:

- Minimum: this rule always chooses the minimum imputed value among the set of values provided by the different methods $m_i(i = 1, ..., l)$, we denote l the number of combined methods.

$$min_{comb} = MIN(X_{imp}^{m_1}, ..., X_{imp}^{m_l})$$ (4)

- Maximum: this rule has the same principle as the previous rule by choosing the maximum imputed value.

$$max_{comb} = MAX(X_{imp}^{m_1}, ..., X_{imp}^{m_l})$$ (5)

- Weighted mean: we calculate the mean between the values imputed by the different methods m_i with respect to the rate of accurate imputed values $(K_i = 1 - NRMSE_i)$ in the imputed dataset.

$$mean_{comb} = \frac{\sum_{i=1}^{l} \left(X_{imp}^{m_i} \times K_i\right)}{\sum_{i=1}^{l} K_i}$$ (6)

The main steps of the combination approach using these methods are presented in the following Algorithm 3.

Algorithm 3. Combination Algorithm

Inputs: X_{imp} : imputed datasets by different methods.
$l \leftarrow$ number of methods for combination;
for i in 1 to l **do**
    $X_{imp} \leftarrow (X_{imp}^{m_1}, ..., X_{imp}^{m_l})$;
end for
calculate X_{comb} for X_{imp} using respectively the Eqs. 4, 5 or 6;
return X_{comb};

---

5   Experimental Results

The main objective of the experiments conducted in this work is to evaluate the efficiency of the three methods: KNN, MissForest and EM Algorithm as imputation methods to treat missing data.

The experiments were carried using four continuous datasets extracted from UCI [6] such as iris, glass, vertebral column and yeast. We choose these datasets because they have no missing values. This means that we have access to a complete matrix X_{comp}. The main reason for this choice is that we want to have total control over the missing data in the dataset. For instance, we would like that the test sets do not have any missing data. Table 1 summarizes the datasets used in this study. For each dataset, we present the number of instances, the number of attributes and the number of classes.

In our experiments, missing values were artificially generated with different rates and attributes. From each original dataset, we derived five incomplete

Table 1. Description of the datasets used in the experiments

Datasets	Number of instances	Number of attributes (all continuous)	Number of classes
Iris plants database	150	4	3
Glass identification database	214	9	2
Vertebral column database	310	5	2
Yeast database	1484	8	10

datasets, removing 10%, 20%, 30%, 40% and 50% of values completely at random. For each rate, we perform 100 independent runs by randomly generating missingness patterns (see Fig. 3). We imputed the missing datasets using the three different approaches.

To assess the performance of each imputation approach, we calculated a Normalized Root Mean Squared Error, by comparing the original dataset with the imputed datasets (Eq. 3). The final NRMSE is averaged over 100 repetitions. Lower values of NRMSE indicate better estimates of the variables.

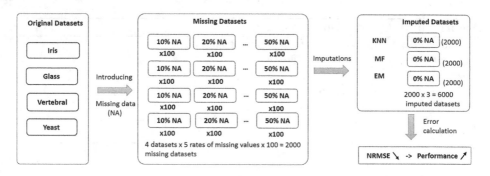

Fig. 3. Main steps used in experimental study.

The imputation errors of different methods are given in Figs. 4, 5, 6 and 7. Overall, our analysis showed that bias was lower when the rate of missing values was lower. We can also see that missForest performs better than the other two methods in all datasets, sometimes reducing the average NRMSE by up to 20%. For glass dataset (Fig. 5), EM algorithm has a slightly smaller NRMSE than missForest only when the rate of missing values is lower than 15%. But for vertebral column dataset and yeast dataset, EM performed less well due to the increase of number of instances.

To improve these results, we proposed to combine the outputs of methods and compare combination results to missForest. Combination was carried using three methods of combination : weighted mean (mean), min and max. In the following Table 2 we summarize some results for the three combination methods

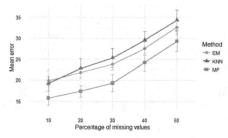

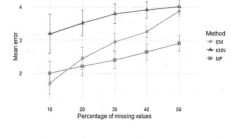

Fig. 4. Results of imputation methods for iris dataset

Fig. 5. Results of imputation methods for glass dataset

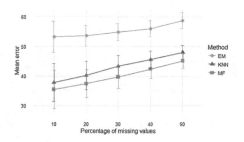

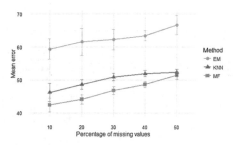

Fig. 6. Results of imputation methods for vertebral column dataset

Fig. 7. Results of imputation methods for yeast dataset

for iris dataset and vertebral column dataset by showing the error rates for each method.

From Table 2, we can see that in all cases weighted mean performed well than the two other combination methods. Therefore, in the rest part of experiments, we are especially interested in results of the weighted mean.

Figures 8, 9, 10 and 11 present the results of all possible combinations of the three imputation methods. In these figures, the worst result is obtained by the combination of KNN with EM. This combination didn't improve the performance of missForest. The combination of the three methods performs well for the four datasets especially for higher missing rates. For iris dataset, the best result is obtained by combining the outputs of missForest and EM. These results are better than those provided by the single missForest especially when the rate

Table 2. Average imputation error (NRMSE in %) of the combination methods

Dataset	Missing rate	10%			30%			50%		
	Methods	Min	Max	Mean	Min	Max	Mean	Min	Max	Mean
Iris	MF+EM	16.94 ± 2.09	17.52 ± 2.53	**15.84 ± 1.13**	21.28 ± 2.30	21.52 ± 2.12	**18.82 ± 1.38**	29.97 ± 2.81	30.23 ± 2.11	**26.37 ± 1.54**
	KNN+MF+EM	18.14 ± 1.24	18.97 ± 2.47	**15.54 ± 1.02**	20.72 ± 2.33	21.22 ± 2.11	**18.70 ± 1.31**	27.8 ± 1.81	29.21 ± 2.34	**25.32 ± 1.21**
Vertebral	MF+KNN	37.10 ± 5.30	36.28 ± 6.51	**35.02 ± 6.71**	42.53 ± 3.80	40.63 ± 3.63	**39.04 ± 4.03**	47.60 ± 2.22	45.64 ± 2.75	**43.40 ± 2.75**
column	KNN+MF+EM	45.69 ± 5.91	47.11 ± 5.14	**36.13 ± 6.41**	50.11 ± 3.15	49.27 ± 2.22	**39.58 ± 3.75**	54.67 ± 2.01	53.80 ± 2.02	**43.75 ± 2.61**

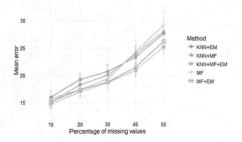

Fig. 8. Combination results for iris database

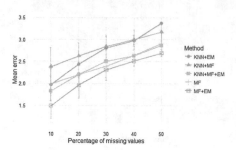

Fig. 9. Combination results for glass database

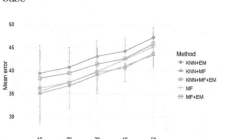

Fig. 10. Combination results for vertebral column database

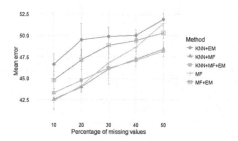

Fig. 11. Combination results for yeast database

of missing values is more than 20%. For glass database, the combination of the ensemble composed by missForest and EM is higher than the performance of the single missForest. For vertebral column dataset, in most cases the performance of missForest and KNN combination and the performance of the three methods combination are superior to single missForest and other combinations.

We remark then that to improve imputation results it is preferable to use combination of missForest with another method such as EM or EM and KNN than to use the missForest individually especially when the rate of missing values is greater than 20%.

6   Conclusion

In this work, the behavior of three imputation methods is analyzed according to the rate of missing data into different attributes of four real datasets. The results are very promising. The missForest method provides very good results, even when the training sets had a large amount of missing data. This confirms the results obtained by [14]. The combination of this method with other methods significantly improves the results obtained by single missForest especially for high rates of missing data. In the future, we can use other combination approaches such as combination based on OWA (Ordered Weighted Average). Also, it is interesting to study the behavior of the imputation methods for datasets with more instances and with other attribute types as nominal and mixed types. Moreover, we should emphasize that we assumed the variables are missing completely at random. Our future work will also explore the case of dependent variables.

References

1. Afshari Safavi, A., Kazemzadeh Gharechobogh, H., Rezaei, M.: Comparison Of EM algorithm and standard imputation methods for missing data: a questionnaire study on diabetic patients. Iran. J. Epidemiol. **11**(3), 43–51 (2015)
2. Batista, G.E., Monard, M.C.: A study of K-Nearest neighbour as an imputation method. HIS **87**(251–260), 48 (2002)
3. Breiman, L.: Random forests. Mach. Learn. **45**(1), 5–32 (2001)
4. Chen, J., Shao, J.: Nearest neighbor imputation for survey data. J. Official Stat. **16**(2), 113 (2000)
5. Dempster, A.P., Laird, N.M., Rubin, D.B.: Maximum likelihood from incomplete data via the EM algorithm. J. R. Stat. Soc. Ser. B (Meth.) **39**, 1–38 (1977)
6. Merz, C.J., Murphy, P.M.: UCI repository of machine learning databases. University of California, Irvine, Department of Information and Computer Science (1998). http://www.ics.uci.edu/~mlearn/MLRepository.html
7. Oba, S., Sato, M.A., Takemasa, I., Monden, M., Matsubara, K.I., Ishii, S.: A Bayesian missing value estimation method for gene expression profile data. Bioinformatics **19**(16), 2088–2096 (2003)
8. Penone, C., Davidson, A.D., Shoemaker, K.T., Di Marco, M., Rondinini, C., Brooks, T.M., Young, B.E., Graham, C.H., Costa, G.C.: Imputation of missing data in life-history traits datasets: which approach performs the best? Meth. Ecol. Evol. **5**, 961–970 (2014)
9. Rubin, D.B.: Basic ideas of multiple imputation for nonresponse. Surv. Methodol. **12**(1), 37–47 (1986)
10. Rubin, D.B., Little, R.J.: Statistical Analysis with Missing Data. Wiley, Hoboken (2002)
11. Shipp, C.A., Kuncheva, L.I.: Relationships between combination methods and measures of diversity in combining classifiers. Inf. Fusion **3**(2), 135–148 (2002)
12. Stdler, N., Bühlmann, P.: Pattern alternating maximization algorithm for high-dimensional missing data. Arxiv preprint arXiv, 1005 (2010)
13. Stekhoven, D.J., Bühlmann, P.: MissForestnon-parametric missing value imputation for mixed-type data. Bioinformatics **28**(1), 112–118 (2012)
14. Troyanskaya, O., Cantor, M., Sherlock, G., Brown, P., Hastie, T., Tibshirani, R., Botstein, D., Altman, R.B.: Missing value estimation methods for DNA microarrays. Bioinformatics **17**(6), 520–525 (2001)
15. Zhu, X.P.: Comparison of four methods for handing missing data in longitudinal data analysis through a simulation study. Open J. Stat. **4**(11), 933 (2014)

Supervised Feature Space Reduction
for Multi-Label Nearest Neighbors

Wissam Siblini[1,2]([⊠]), Reda Alami[1], Frank Meyer[1], and Pascale Kuntz[2]

[1] Orange Labs, Avenue Pierre Marzin, 22300 Lannion, France
wissam.siblini@univ-nantes.fr,
{wissam.siblini,reda1.alami,franck.meyer}@orange.com
[2] Laboratoire des Sciences du Numérique de Nantes (LS2N),
44300 Nantes Cedex, France
pascale.kuntz@univ-nantes.fr

Abstract. With the ability to process many real-world problems, multi-label classification has received a large attention in recent years and the instance-based ML-kNN classifier is today considered as one of the most efficient. But it is sensitive to noisy and redundant features and its performances decrease with increasing data dimensionality. To overcome these problems, dimensionality reduction is an alternative but current methods optimize reduction objectives which ignore the impact on the ML-kNN classification. We here propose ML-ARP, a novel dimensionality reduction algorithm which, using a variable neighborhood search meta-heuristic, learns a linear projection of the feature space which specifically optimizes the ML-kNN classification loss. Numerical comparisons have confirmed that ML-ARP outperforms ML-kNN without data processing and four standard multi-label dimensionality reduction algorithms.

Keywords: Multi-label classification · k-nearest neighbors · Dimensionality reduction

1 Introduction

In the traditional single-label classification paradigm, the objective is to associate each instance to one label only. However, in various real-world applications (e.g. music annotation, image categorization, text mining), objects are intrinsically describable with multiple labels. Consequently, multi-label classification has received a large attention in recent years and many algorithms have been proposed [10,14,19]. Among them, the multi-label adaptation of the well-known k-nearest neighbor algorithm (ML-kNN [18]) is probably one of the most successful. Based on the maximum a posteriori principle, ML-kNN operates instance-based learning. Numerical comparisons with many model-based methods have confirmed the high quality of its results.

However, instance-based algorithms such as ML-kNN have two major shortcomings [2]. First, as they rely on a distance function, they are very sensitive to noisy, redundant and irrelevant features. Second, they encounter the explosion of

© Springer International Publishing AG 2017
S. Benferhat et al. (Eds.): IEA/AIE 2017, Part I, LNAI 10350, pp. 182–191, 2017.
DOI: 10.1007/978-3-319-60042-0_21

their computational complexity when dealing with high-dimensional data where numerous instances are described by numerous variables. In practice these serious issues are brought to the fore today with the expansion of online labeling services which produce massive raw data of varying quality.

By appearing as a promising lever for these problems, dimensionality reduction encounters a renewed interest. Roughly speaking, the reduction approaches used in multi-label classification can be divided into two families: (i) the unsupervised methods that reduce the feature space independently of any label information [1] and (ii) supervised methods that benefit from the labeling information with an objective that is either independent [12,13,20] or dependent on the classifier [7,9]. The last type of method seems more promising as the final objective is to optimize the classification quality. However, the joint problem between classification and dimensionality reduction is generally set in the form of a multi-objective optimization which is hard to solve even heuristically.

In this article, we skirt the explicit multi-objective formulation with a novel linear reduction method for optimizing the ML-kNN classification performances. Our approach, called Multi-Label Adaptative Random Projection (ML-ARP), initializes a random linear projection and iteratively adapts it with a reduced variable neighborhood search in order to increase the ML-kNN performances on the projected feature space. Numerical comparisons on twelve classical multi-label datasets have confirmed that, while reducing the dimensionality of data and the neighborhood search complexity up to 90%, ML-ARP is not only better on average than ML-kNN without data processing but it also outperforms a simple random projection technique and four standard multi-label dimensionality reduction algorithms from the literature (Principal Component Analysis [1], Canonical Correlation Analysis [13], Multi-label Dimensionality reduction via Dependence Maximization [20] and the Orthonormal version of Partial Least Squares [12]).

The remainder of this paper is organized as follows. Section 2 reviews previous approaches for multi-label dimensionality reduction. We describe our new algorithm ML-ARP in Sect. 3 and present the experimental comparisons in Sect. 4.

2 Multi-label Feature Space Dimensionality Reduction

We here present the two main families of dimensionality reduction methods: the unsupervised methods which do not take label information into account and the supervised methods which use it to guide the reduction.

2.1 Unsupervised Dimensionality Reduction

The unsupervised methods can themselves be organized into two classes: methods based on random projection and methods based on feature information. The first type has been investigated in multi-label classification to reduce both label [16] and feature space [11]. In the classical context, it is known to be the fastest way to reduce the dimensionality and the Johnson-Lindenstrauss lemma

[6] has proved that it accurately preserves the pairwise l_2 distances between the instances in the projected space. However, the result quality declines with the reduced space dimensionality.

The second type usually tends to reduce the feature space while keeping a maximum of its structural information (e.g. feature covariance or co-occurrence). It has a long history dating back to the inception of data analysis. The most popular method still remains the Principal Component Analysis [1] but several variants have been proposed [4]. However, these approaches do not consider some useful information contained in the links between the features and the labels.

2.2   Supervised Dimensionality Reduction

Supervised approaches guide the reduction with constraints or label information. The reduction can be done independently or dependently of the classifier criterion.

The most prevalent methods ignore the classifier objective and usually aim at strengthening the link between the projected features and the labels (e.g. with a dependence or covariance criterion). In the multi-label context, among the most popular are the Canonical Correlation Analysis (CCA) [8,13], the Partial Least Square (PLS) [3] and the Multi-label Dimensionality reduction via Dependence Maximization (MDDM) [20]. CCA seeks the directions in both label and feature spaces which maximize the correlations between each other. PLS seeks the directions in the feature space that maximize the covariance with the label space. A variant of PLS (Orthonormal PLS [12]) introduces orthogonality constraints between the computed directions. MDDM computes a projection of the feature space that minimizes the Hilbert-Schmidt independence criterion between the projected data features and the labels. In studies previously published, all these approaches have been applied at a pre-processing stage before the ML-kNN classifier. The experimental results are promising but, by only optimizing their own criteria (covariance, dependence and co-occurrence), these methods can degrade the performances of the classifier.

Recent researches have confirmed that the best dimensionality reduction method can vary with the choice of the classifier [20]. These results stimulate the development of approaches which integrate a coupling between dimensionality reduction and classification in a global optimization problem. They usually resort to an SVM classifier [9] or a large margin classifier [7]. However, in both cases the optimization process tries to combine explicitly two different objectives. In [7] the expressed loss function is a sum of two reconstruction errors: dimensionality reduction and classification. In [9] the combination of the two formulations leads to a two-parameter optimization problem where each parameter is computed alternatively. This multi-objective strategy may converge to a poor quality solution for the classifier. Moreover, these previous approaches do not consider a coupling with the ML-kNN classifier which is, with its intrinsic multi-label nature, its powerful classification rules and its potential for an online adaptation, the center of our attention in this study.

To overcome these limits, we here propose a novel approach where the projection of the reduced space is the unique parameter and the optimization of the ML-kNN performance is the unique objective.

3   Description of the ML–ARP Algorithm

In the following we consider a d_x - dimensional feature space $\mathcal{X}$ and a d_y - dimensional label space $\mathcal{Y}$. Each instance (x_i, y_i) is represented by a feature vector x_i and its associated binary label vector y_i where the jth component $(y_i)^j$ is equal to 1 if the instance is described by the jth label and 0 otherwise. In the learning scenario, data are partitioned in two sets: the training set $\mathcal{L} = \{(x_i, y_i) \in \mathcal{X} \times \mathcal{Y} \mid i \in \{1, ..., N_{\mathcal{L}}\}\}$ of cardinality $N_{\mathcal{L}}$ used to train the model and the testing set $\mathcal{T} = \{(x_i, y_i) \in \mathcal{X} \times \mathcal{Y} \mid i \in \{1, ..., N_{\mathcal{T}}\}\}$ of cardinality $N_{\mathcal{T}}$ used to compute the performances of the model.

3.1   The Algorithm ML-kNN

Let us recall that ML-kNN [18] combines the principle of the k-nearest neighbor algorithm with a powerful multi-label decision rule. More precisely, for a given feature vector $x \in \mathcal{X}$ it first determines its neighborhood in $\mathcal{L}$ using the Euclidean l_2 distance. Next, it predicts a real-valued output $\widehat{y_{int}} \in \mathbb{R}^{d_y}$ by summing the labels of the k-nearest neighbors. Then, it converts its prediction into classification with a maximum a posteriori rule; this rule benefits from the labeling pattern embodied in the instance neighborhood. This operation requires a training phase where two quantities are computed for each label l: (i) the prior probability of the presence (resp. the absence) of the label l which is its frequency (resp. the complementary) in $\mathcal{L}$ and (ii) the likelihood in $\mathcal{L}$ that an instance associated with the label l has exactly j neighbors with the label l, for j in $\{0, ..., k\}$. With these two pieces of information and $\widehat{y_{int}}$, ML-kNN determines the posterior probability for the presence/absence of each label with a Bayes rule. If the presence probability is higher than the absence probability, the label is set to 1 in the final predicted label vector $\widehat{y} \in \mathcal{Y}$.

In the original ML-kNN, a Laplace smoothing is optionally applied to prevent events which do not occur in the training set $\mathcal{L}$ from having a likelihood or a prior probability equal to zero. In our experiments, without any prior knowledge about the data, we prefer to avoid using this smoothing. Moreover, as ML-kNN is here applied for each method of our benchmark, the smoothing parameter would only affect absolute performances and not relative comparisons.

3.2   ML-ARP: Multi-Label Adaptative Random Projection

Our objective is to build a projection which explicitly optimizes the ML-kNN performances Θ in the reduced feature space (of dimensionality r). This is likely to correct the two previously-cited shortcomings by (i) implicitly filter the features that are irrelevant for classification and (ii) reducing the complexity of distance evaluation from d_x operations to r operations. The performances are here measured with the Hamming Loss (HL) which is a global reconstruction error widely used in the multi-label context. The minimization problem over the objective $\Theta(P)$ is then defined by:

$$\min_{P \in \mathbb{R}^{d_x \times r}} \Theta(P) = \min_{P \in \mathbb{R}^{d_x \times r}} \sum_{i=1}^{N_{\mathcal{L}}} HL(y_i, \widehat{y_i} = \text{ML-}k\text{NN}(\mathcal{L}^P, x_i)) \qquad (1)$$

where $\text{ML-}k\text{NN}(\mathcal{L}^P, x_i)$ denotes the prediction for x_i of ML-kNN applied in the P-projected training set.

As the variation of $\text{ML-}k\text{NN}(\mathcal{L}^P, x_i)$ in function of P is hard to express, standard optimization approaches are impracticable and we resort to a Reduced Variable Neighborhood Search (RVNS) heuristic [17] to compute a solution to the problem (1). Our implementation of the RVNS changes the projection parameter P iteratively and randomly and selects the changes which improve the objective Θ. More precisely, the different steps of the algorithm are the following:

1. Initialize P with a random projection drawn from a zero-mean, unit-variance Gaussian distribution.
2. Make a slight modification of the solution P into a new solution P' using a speed matrix ΔP: $P' = P + \Delta P$.
3. Evaluate the loss $\Theta(P')$ of the new parameter P'.
4. If $\Theta(P')$ is lower than $\Theta(P)$, then consider P' as the new current solution; otherwise keep P.
5. If the new solution is P', repeat the steps 2, 3 and 4 with the same speed matrix ΔP; otherwise, repeat these steps with a new sparse speed matrix (The speed matrix is chosen to be sparse so that only a few parameters are changed at each RVNS iteration) generated with the following process:
   Randomly select a mutation rate α in $[0, 1]$. Then, for each term of the matrix ΔP, run a coin toss with a probability of α. If the result is negative, the term is set to 0; otherwise, the term is randomly generated from a zero-mean Gaussian distribution.

The process stops after a fixed number of iterations or a maximum computation time. Let us remark that the conditions of the Johnson-Lindenstrauss lemma are not valid here: by selecting specific modifications, the ML-ARP algorithm produces a final solution P which is no longer a random projection. Consequently, the initial distances in the original space $\mathcal{X}$ are not preserved; they are modified in order to improve the ML-kNN performances.

Let us remark that a non linear reducing mapping could also be a candidate. However, without any further information on the search spaces, we have here favoured the simplest choice of a linear mapping. The non linearity is indirectly tackled by the combination of the mapping with the non linear classifier ML-kNN.

4   Experiments

We first describe the experimental protocol and then present the comparisons obtained with six different approaches on twelve data sets of various sizes.

4.1   Experimental Settings

Datasets. We have conducted our experimental comparisons on twelve real-world datasets from various domains: music annotation (Emotions), image annotation (Scene, Corel5k), video (Mediamill), text mining (Enron, Bibtex, Delicious, Bookmarks, Reuters) and medical mining (Yeast). Their main statistical properties are described in Table 1 and we refer to Mulan [15] for details.

Table 1. Description of the twelve datasets: application domain, training set cardinality ($N_{\mathcal{L}}$), testing set cardinality ($N_{\mathcal{T}}$), feature space dimensionality (d_x), label space dimensionality (d_x), label space density (r_y).

	Domain	# instances	$N_{\mathcal{L}}$	$N_{\mathcal{T}}$	d_x	d_y	r_y
Yeast	Genetic	2417	2173	244	103	14	0.3
Emotions	Audio	593	533	60	72	6	0.31
Mediamill	Video	43907	39516	4391	120	101	0.043
Scene	Images	2407	2166	241	294	6	0.18
Corel5k	Images	5000	4500	500	499	374	0.0094
Delicious	Text(tags)	16105	14495	1610	500	983	0.019
Enron	Text	1702	1531	171	1001	53	0.064
Genbase	Biology	662	595	67	1186	27	0.05
Medical	Health	978	880	98	1449	45	0.0027
Bibtex	Text	7395	6656	739	1836	159	0.015
Bookmarks	Text	87856	79070	8786	2150	208	0.0098
Reuters	Text	6000	5400	600	47229	101	0.026

Algorithms. The new algorithm ML-ARP has been compared to four other dimensionality reduction approaches from the state-of-the-art (PCA [1], CCA [13], MDDM [20], OPLS [12]) coupled to ML-kNN. We have added two other comparisons which play the role of yardsticks: one with a normalized random projection (RP) drawn from a zero-mean, unit-variance Gaussian distribution and another with the original ML-kNN classifier without dimensionality reduction. In our experiments, the dimensionality r of the reduced feature space is of the same order of magnitude as those classically used in the literature: 128 or 64 if the dimensionality of the original feature space is smaller than 128. The higher the reduced space dimensionality r, the more expressive the projection. Fixing the same value for every method therefore allows an equal comparison. The chosen baseline systematically predicts the labels frequencies computed on

$\mathcal{L}$, for any $x \in \mathcal{T}$. The real values of the frequency vector are binarized with a threshold of 0.5. As we here restrict ourselves to the comparison of the different approach performances, we have not explored the impact of the neighbor number. We have followed the recommendation of [18] and fixed k = 5. As well as for the smoothing parameter, changing k would mostly affect absolute performances. The maximal computation time was fixed to two hours to meet our operational constraints.

Quality evaluation. To evaluate the performances of the algorithms on each dataset, we have performed a 10-fold evaluation and computed the mean performance and standard deviation of 11 different measures [10,14,19] evaluating ranking performances, classification accuracies and global reconstruction errors: Ranking Loss, One Error, Coverage, Jaccard Loss, Hamming Loss, Accuracy, Recall, Precision, Subset Accuracy, Average Precision, F1-Score.

Further analysis with statistical tests on Hamming Loss have been carried out to evaluate the significative differences and similarities between the algorithms. Using the R *scmamp* package [5], we have applied the Friedman test with $\alpha = 0.1$ (90% confidence) and completed it with the Nemenyi post-hoc test.

4.2   Results

The results obtained with the Hamming Loss for the different approaches are summarized in Table 2. Firstly, they show that ML-ARP outperforms the other dimensionality reduction approaches (MDDM, PCA, OPLS, CCA) for three datasets (Yeast, Emotions, Delicious) and that it is very close to the best values for the other datasets. Secondly, they suggest that ML-ARP is better than ML-kNN, RP and the baseline but the statistical significance of the dominance is only

Table 2. Hamming Loss performances (with N/A for unavailable values)

		ML-ARP	Baseline	ML-kNN	RP	MDDM	PCA	OPLS	CCA
Yeast	$r = 64$	**0.191**	0.232	0.195	0.202	0.227	0.194	0.203	0.204
Emotions	$r = 64$	**0.226**	0.313	0.262	0.261	0.31	0.262	0.256	0.252
Scene	$r = 128$	0.091	0.179	**0.088**	0.108	0.089	0.097	0.166	0.162
Enron	$r = 128$	0.05	0.062	0.051	0.053	**0.049**	**0.049**	0.067	0.064
Genbase	$r = 128$	0.047	0.047	0.047	0.047	0.047	0.047	0.047	N/A
Corel5k	$r = 128$	0.009	0.009	0.009	0.009	0.009	0.009	0.009	N/A
Delicious	$r = 128$	**0.014**	0.019	**0.014**	0.020	0.018	0.018	N/A	N/A
Medical	$r = 128$	0.017	0.028	0.015	0.018	**0.013**	0.015	N/A	N/A
Bibtex	$r = 128$	0.014	0.015	0.014	0.014	**0.012**	0.013	N/A	N/A
Mediamill	$r = 64$	0.027	0.035	0.027	0.028	N/A	N/A	**0.025**	N/A
Bookmarks	$r = 128$	0.008	0.009	0.008	0.008	N/A	N/A	N/A	N/A
Rcv1	$r = 4000$	0.026	0.028	0.026	0.026	N/A	N/A	N/A	N/A

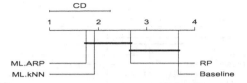

Fig. 1. Results of the Nemenyi test for ML-ARP, RP, ML-kNN and the baseline on all the datasets.

confirmed against the baseline by the Nemenyi test (Fig. 1). Thirdly, the performances of the original ML-kNN are always improved by at least one dimensionality reduction approach. But, for some datasets, the independent dimensionality reduction may lead to degraded results (e.g. MDDM for Emotions and CCA for Scene). MDDM, CCA, OPLS, PCA are not applied on some datasets (N/A values) either because their complexity (spatial and temporal) is too high or because they require an inversion of a non invertible matrix.

For the four datasets where all the algorithms have been applied (Emotions, Scene, Enron and Yeast) ML-ARP obtains the highest mean rank for a majority of performance measures (Table 3). For the global reconstruction error measures (Hamming Loss, Jaccard Loss, Accuracy), it is always the best. For some ranking sensitive measures (Coverage, One Error, Precision, Ranking Loss), it is slightly surpassed by ML-kNN and PCA with very close performances but the differences are not statistically significant (Fig. 2). Moreover, if a closer examination of the convergence time goes beyond the objective of this paper, we have observed that,

Table 3. Ranks regarding all performance measures on four datasets (Emotions, Scene, Enron and Yeast).

	ML.ARP	Baseline	ML-kNN	RP	MDDM	PCA	OPLS	CCA
Accuracy	**2.00**	8.00	3.25	4.75	4.00	3.00	6.5	4.5
Average precision	**2.00**	7.75	3.375	5.00	4.25	2.875	6.125	4.625
Coverage	3.25	6.75	**2.375**	4.375	4.00	3.00	6.5	5.75
F1	**2.5**	8.00	3.00	5.25	4.00	2.625	6.125	4.5
Hamming loss	**2.00**	7.5	3.375	4.5	4.375	3.25	5.75	5.25
Jaccard loss	**2.5**	8.00	3.00	4.75	4.00	2.75	6.5	4.5
One error	2.75	8.00	**2.625**	5.00	5.00	**2.625**	5.75	5.25
Precision	3.375	5.75	4.375	4.625	3.75	**3.125**	6.00	5.00
Ranking loss	3.00	8.00	**2.75**	4.25	4.00	**2.75**	6.5	4.75
Recall	**2.625**	8.00	3.875	5.25	4.00	3.00	5.5	3.75
Subset accuracy	**2.00**	8.00	3.25	4.25	4.00	3.5	6.00	5.00
Mean	**2.55**	7.52	3.2	4.73	4.13	2.95	6.11	4.81
Global rank	**1.64**	7.91	2.64	5.41	4.05	1.91	7.09	5.36

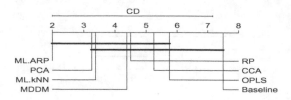

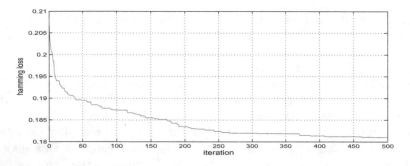

Fig. 2. Results of the Nemenyi test for all the algorithms on four datasets (Yeast, Emotions, Scene, Enron).

Fig. 3. Evolution of Hamming loss training error for ML-ARP on Emotions (mean curve for 10 runs)

on average, ML-ARP optimization converges fast enough after several hundreds of iterations (Fig. 3).

5   Conclusions and Future Works

Whatever the dataset, it has been observed that there exists a reduced space for which ML-kNN performances are improved or maintained. Thus, dimensionality reduction approaches not only have the advantage of reducing the number of features and speeding up the neighborhood search but also have the potential of improving the ML-kNN classification. However, in practice, classical reduction approaches have obtained poor performances for some datasets and have deteriorated the classification on average because their independent objective does not guarantee an effective neighborhood for ML-kNN.

In contrast, ML-ARP presents two advantages. From a statistical point of view, it is more stable than the other methods: as a wrapper designed to specifically target the ML-kNN objective, it presents the most regular performances and the best mean rank when facing a wide variety of problems. From a technological point of view, it is easily implementable, anytime and more scalable.

To accelerate the algorithm in the big data scenario we plan in the next future to explore a sampling strategy (random, clustering, condensation) and a GPU implementation for the nearest neighbor search.

References

1. Abdi, H., Williams, L.J.: Principal component analysis. Wiley Interdisc. Rev. Comput. Stat. **2**(4), 433–459 (2010)
2. Bellet, A., Habrard, A., Sebban, M.: A survey on metric learning for feature vectors and structured data. arXiv preprint arXiv:1306.6709 (2013)
3. Bishop, C.M.: Pattern Recognition and Machine Learning. Springer, New York (2006)
4. Burges, C.J.: Geometric methods for feature extraction and dimensional reduction-a guided tour. In: Maimon, O., Rokach, L. (eds.) Data Mining and Knowledge Discovery Handbook, pp. 53–82. Springer, New York (2009)
5. Calvo, B., Santafe, G.: scmamp: statistical comparison of multiple algorithms in multiple problems. R J. **8**(1), 248–256 (2015)
6. Dasgupta, S., Gupta, A.: An elementary proof of a theorem of johnson and lindenstrauss. Random Struct. Algorithms **22**(1), 60–65 (2003)
7. Guo, Y., Schuurmans, D.: Semi-supervised multi-label classification. In: Flach, P.A., Bie, T., Cristianini, N. (eds.) ECML PKDD 2012. LNCS, vol. 7524, pp. 355–370. Springer, Heidelberg (2012). doi:10.1007/978-3-642-33486-3_23
8. Hotelling, H.: Relations between two sets of variates. Biometrika **28**(3/4), 321–377 (1936)
9. Ji, S., Ye, J.: Linear dimensionality reduction for multi-label classification. In: IJCAI, vol. 9, pp. 1077–1082. Citeseer (2009)
10. Madjarov, G., Kocev, D., Gjorgjevikj, D., Džeroski, S.: An extensive experimental comparison of methods for multi-label learning. Pattern Recogn. **45**(9), 3084–3104 (2012)
11. Ran, R., Oh, H.: Adaptive sparse random projections for wireless sensor networks with energy harvesting constraints. EURASIP J. Wirel. Commun. Networking **2015**(1), 113 (2015)
12. Rosipal, R., Krämer, N.: Overview and recent advances in partial least squares. In: Saunders, C., Grobelnik, M., Gunn, S., Shawe-Taylor, J. (eds.) SLSFS 2005. LNCS, vol. 3940, pp. 34–51. Springer, Heidelberg (2006). doi:10.1007/11752790_2
13. Sun, L., Ji, S., Ye, J.: Canonical correlation analysis for multilabel classification: a least-squares formulation, extensions, and analysis. IEEE Trans. Pattern Anal. Mach. Intell. **33**(1), 194–200 (2011)
14. Tsoumakas, G., Katakis, I.: Multi-label Classification: An Overview. Department of Informatics, Aristotle University of Thessaloniki, Greece (2006)
15. Tsoumakas, G., Spyromitros-Xioufis, E., Vilcek, J., Vlahavas, I.: Mulan: a JAVA library for multi-label learning. J. Mach. Learn. Res. **12**(Jul), 2411–2414 (2011)
16. Wan, S., Mak, M.W., Kung, S.Y.: Sparse regressions for predicting and interpreting subcellular localization of multi-label proteins. BMC Bioinformatics **17**(1), 97 (2016)
17. Xiao, Y., Kaku, I., Zhao, Q., Zhang, R.: A reduced variable neighborhood search algorithm for uncapacitated multilevel lot-sizing problems. Eur. J. Oper. Res. **214**(2), 223–231 (2011)
18. Zhang, M.L., Zhou, Z.H.: Ml-knn: a lazy learning approach to multi-label learning. Pattern Recogn. **40**(7), 2038–2048 (2007)
19. Zhang, M.L., Zhou, Z.H.: A review on multi-label learning algorithms. IEEE Trans. Knowl. Data Eng. **26**(8), 1819–1837 (2014)
20. Zhang, Y., Zhou, Z.H.: Multilabel dimensionality reduction via dependence maximization. ACM Trans. Knowl. Discov. Data (TKDD) **4**(3), 14 (2010)

Stock Volatility Prediction Using Recurrent Neural Networks with Sentiment Analysis

Yifan Liu[1], Zengchang Qin[1(✉)], Pengyu Li[1,2], and Tao Wan[3(✉)]

[1] Intelligent Computing and Machine Learning Lab,
School of ASEE Beihang University, Beijing 100191, China
zcqin@buaa.edu.cn
[2] School of Mechanical Engineering and Automation Beihang University,
Beijing 100191, China
[3] School of Biological Science and Medical Engineering Beihang University,
Beijing 100191, China
taowan@buaa.edu.cn

Abstract. In this paper, we propose a model to analyze sentiment of online stock forum and use the information to predict the stock volatility in the Chinese market. We have labeled the sentiment of the online financial posts and make the dataset public available for research. By generating a sentimental dictionary based on financial terms, we develop a model to compute the sentimental score of each online post related to a particular stock. Such sentimental information is represented by two sentiment indicators, which are fused to market data for stock volatility prediction by using the Recurrent Neural Networks (RNNs). Empirical study shows that, comparing to using RNN only, the model performs significantly better with sentimental indicators.

Keywords: Natural language processing · Stock volatility prediction · Sentimental analysis · Sentimental score

1 Introduction

In time-series data mining, stock market is notoriously difficult to analyze, even be totally unpredictable based on the famous Efficient Market Hypothesis (EMH). As early as 1900s, Bachelier [2] applied statistical methods to analyze stock data, and found that the mathematical expectation of the stock fluctuation tends to be zero. In the 1970s, Fama [7] formally put forward the EMH, which stated that under the condition of market with complete information, investors couldn't gain more than fifty percent of the profits only with the past price, or simply, no one could 'beat' the market' continuously. The Random Walk Theory (RWT) proposed by Osborne [14] also suggested same conclusion that the stock prices were unpredictable. But all these theories are based on the same assumption that investors are rational and complete market information is available.

© Springer International Publishing AG 2017
S. Benferhat et al. (Eds.): IEA/AIE 2017, Part I, LNAI 10350, pp. 192–201, 2017.
DOI: 10.1007/978-3-319-60042-0_22

Paul Hawtin[1] once said "For years, investors have widely accepted that financial markets are driven by fear and greed." In the actual market, investors cannot be completely rational. They may be influenced by their emotions and make impulsive decisions [16]. Therefore, the basic assumption of EMH and RWT is not impregnable. Many researchers have tried to study the correlation between sentiment and stock market volatility to challenge the classical theories. For example, researchers found that some factors, e.g. weather and sports games, can affect public emotion and also the stock market. The sunny weather and the rising stock index had certain correlations [10]. There would be a significant market decline after the soccer lost [5]. In recent years, the rapid development of social networks (Facebook, Twitter, Weibo) opens a new door to measure the public emotion. Bollen et al. [3] analyzed the text content of daily Twitter by using two mood tracking tools: OpinionFinder (OF) and Google-Profile of Mood States (GPOMS). The authors then used self-organizing fuzzy neural network (SOFNN) to predict the volatility of the Dow Jones Industrial Average (DJIA). By considering the sentimental information from Twitter, the prediction accuracy has raised up by 13%. The results were very encouraging and this direction was followed by some other similar research. Zhang et al. [19] found that a burst of public emotion no matter positive or negative, heralded the falling of the index. There were also some research on the individual stock, Si et al. [17] proposed a technique to leverage topic based sentiment from Twitter to help predict the stock price while O'Connor [13] found that the popularity of a brand was much related to related tweets and its stock price.

But there are still some problems remained. First, Twitter users are predominantly English speakers, or even worse the investors of a particular market may not use Twitter to discuss their finance [3]. Second, popular sentiment analysis dictionary can not entirely measure the emotion of the stock investors [11]. Sprenger et al. [18] selected tweets which mentioned the company in the Standard & Poor's 100 index, and labeled the tweets with *buy*, *hold* or *sell* signals. With the labeled training data, they used a Naive Bayes classifier to extract the signals from the tweets automatically and calculated the bullishness through these signals. Finally, they found that a strategy based on bullishness signals could earn substantial abnormal returns.

Above all, a great amount of focus has been placed on the correlation between the investors' sentiment and the U.S. stock market. While limited by the Chinese expression complexity, little attention has been paid to the relevant research on Chinese stock market. According to the World Federation of Exchanges database[2], Chinese market capitalization ranked the second in 2015 in the world. That's the reason we focus on our study of Chinese stock market. In this paper, based on Sprenger's [18] approach, we propose a model to study Chinese stock market. The sentiment of Chinese investors are from the East Money Forum[3],

---

[1] The founder of Derwent Capital Markets and one of early pioneers in the use of social media sentiment analysis to trade financial derivatives.

[2] http://www.indexmundi.com/facts/indicators/CM.MKT.LCAP.CD/rankings.

[3] http://guba.eastmoney.com/.

which is one of the biggest and specified stock forum in China, but it is not public forums like Facebook or Twitter. Each stock has its individual sub-forum which ensures that most posts from the sub-forums are published by the investors who hold or sell this particular stock. In order to avoid the problem that the ordinary dictionary often makes misunderstanding in recognizing investors sentiment, we use a machine learning method to generate our own dictionary and then calculate the sentiment score of the posts based on the dictionary automatically. To study the correlation between Chinese stock market and Chinese investor sentiment, we propose sentiment indicators for the stock volatility prediction model using the Recurrent Neural Networks (RNNs) to obtain a better performance.

2   Sentiment Analysis

Bollen et al. [3] proposed a dictionary-based method for sentiment analysis of the financial contexts. However, Loughran and Mcdonald [11] found that three-fourths of the words identified as negative by the Harvard Dictionary are not typically considered as negative in financial contexts. The same problem also occurs in Chinese sentiment analysis. We find that Chinese posts in stock forums have some special expressions containing strong emotions. But these expressions rarely appear in common sentiment analysis dictionary. So in this research, we first need a practical dataset from which we can obtain a dictionary of financial words, we also develop a simple but effective tool to generate sentimental weights for the words.

2.1   Data Processing

East Money Forum is one of the most influential Internet financial media in China. It has more than 3000 sub-forums for each individual stock. We randomly select 10 stocks as well as the sub-forum of the posts from 25th Sept., 2015 to 30th Sept., 2016 with a web crawler "Bazhuayu (means "Octopus")"[4]. Nearly 96000 pieces of posts are obtained, and most of them are short and colloquial. They do not follow any strict syntax but contain strong sentiment. We randomly sampled 3427 stock posts from 10 different stocks to do the manual annotation[5]. If the post expresses an optimistic attitude towards the stock market and suggests to buy, we label it as positive, otherwise, we label it as negative. We have annotated 2067 negative posts and 1360 positive posts manually. The original Chinese texts need to be preprocessed by segmentation, and a classical Chinese text segmentation tool called "Jieba" (Chinese for "to stutter") in Python[6] is chosen for this.

---

[4] http://www.bazhuayu.com.
[5] http://dsd.future-lab.cn/members/2016/LiuYFProject/data.xlsx.
[6] https://github.com/fxsjy/jieba.

2.2   Polarity Model of Sentiment

The polarity model of sentiment is trained by a collection of texts labelled only by positive or negative. Emotional words are extracted and each one has an associated sentiment weight. Weights can be learned from the labeled training dataset [9]. The sum of weighted sentiment scores of all terms determines the sentiment polarity (positive or negative) of the post. If the sum is greater than 0, it is positive and vice versa. The sentiment score $h_{\mathbf{w}}(\mathbf{x})$ of a given post is computed as follows:

$$h_{\mathbf{w}}(\mathbf{x}) = f\left(\sum_{i=1}^{N} w^{(i)} x^{(i)}\right) = f(\mathbf{w}^T \mathbf{x}); 1 \leq i \leq N \tag{1}$$

where N is the number of all the terms in the corpus, a term could be uni-gram or bi-gram model. $w^{(i)}$ is the sentimental weight for each term $t^{(i)}$, $x^{(i)}$ is the term frequency or tf-idf value of the given term $t^{(i)}$. Function $f(\cdot)$ is a sigmoid function to compress the linear combination of sentimental weight into 0 and 1, and make it smooth.

$$f(z) = \frac{1}{1 + e^{-z}} \tag{2}$$

By using the logistic regression, the target label y is 1 for positive posts and 0 for negative ones. So that $h_{\mathbf{w}}(\mathbf{x})$ represents the probability of a post being positive. If we take the threshold value as 0.5, the prediction of the sentiment is:

$$y = \begin{cases} 1 \ h > 0.5 \\ 0 \ h \leq 0.5 \end{cases} \tag{3}$$

Given a training corpus with M text posts, $\mathbf{x}^{(k)}$ denotes the kth $(1 \leq k \leq M)$ post feature value vector. We can derive the cost function and its logarithmic likelihood function based on the maximum likelihood estimation. The loss function $J(\cdot)$ is:

$$J(h_{\mathbf{w}}(\mathbf{x}), y) = \begin{cases} -\log(h_{\mathbf{w}}(\mathbf{x})) & if \ y = 1 \\ -\log(1 - h_{\mathbf{w}}(\mathbf{x})) & if \ y = 0 \end{cases} \tag{4}$$

The average loss for the entire data set is (for $1 \leq k \leq M$):

$$\begin{aligned} J(\mathbf{w}) &= -\frac{1}{M} \sum_{k=1}^{M} J(h_{\mathbf{w}}(\mathbf{x}), y) \\ &= -\frac{1}{M} \left[\sum_{k=1}^{M} y^{(k)} \log(h_{\mathbf{w}}(\mathbf{x}^{(k)})) + (1 - y^{(k)}) \log(1 - h_{\mathbf{w}}(\mathbf{x}^{(k)})) \right] \end{aligned} \tag{5}$$

In order to minimize $J(\mathbf{w})$, we can update $\mathbf{w}$ using the Gradient Descent algorithm with a learning rate α: $\mathbf{w}_{j+1}^{(k)} = \mathbf{w}_j^{(k)} - \alpha(h^{(k)} - y^{(k)})\mathbf{x}^{(k)}$. The values of the sentimental weight can be obtained. The term with a higher sentimental weight indicates a stronger positive sentiment and vice versa. We use the weights and the corresponding terms to build a sentimental dictionary. The sentiment score of a post can be calculated by weighted sum of weights of all consisting terms based on Eq. (1).

3   Emotion Model for Stock Prediction

3.1   Sentimental Indicators

Some literatures in finance [18] suggest that individual investors have a herd mentality when they make decisions. For example, if they find that most of people are not optimistic in the outlook of the stock price, they will trade on the advice and move the price. What's more, a larger quantity of the posts on a forum indicates a larger amount of attention which may lead to a severe price volatility. Therefore, we propose an emotion model (EMM) according to the following two important assumptions: (1) Increased bullishness of stock posts is associated with higher stock price. (2) Increased posts volume suggests a more substantial volatility. The index of bullishness of online posts can be defined on a daily basis according to [1]:

$$B_t = \ln \frac{1 + N_t^p}{1 + N_t^n} \tag{6}$$

where $N_t^p (N_t^n)$ represents the number of positive (negative) posts on the day t. This indicator reflects both the expectations of the rise in price and the total number of posts. When the posts have a continuous sentimental score instead of a binary label, the index of bullishness becomes

$$B_t = \ln \frac{\varepsilon + S_t^p}{\varepsilon + |S_t^n|} = \ln \frac{\varepsilon + \sum_{k=1}^{N_t^p} h_{\mathbf{w}}(\mathbf{x})^{(k)}}{\varepsilon + \left| \sum_{i=1}^{N_t^n} h_{\mathbf{w}}(\mathbf{x})^{(i)} \right|} \tag{7}$$

where $S_t^p (S_t^n)$ represents the sum of positive (negative) sentimental score of the posts on the day t and $h_{\mathbf{w}}(\mathbf{x})^{(k)}$ $(h_{\mathbf{w}}(\mathbf{x})^{(i)})$ represents the positive (negative) sentimental score of the kth (i^{th}) post on the day t. $\varepsilon(\varepsilon > 0)$ is a tiny number for smoothing, and we set $\varepsilon = 0.0001$ in our research. The reason we use absolute value is because the score of negative sentiment is always less than zero.

The total number of the posts N_t on the day t is $N_t = N_t^p + N_t^n$. To enable fair comparison for B_t and N_t, we use the z-score to normalize data based on the mean and standard deviation within a sliding window of length l (we average the data of l days before and after the current date t). The z-scores for B_t and N_t are:

$$Z_B^{(t)} = \frac{B_t - \mu(B_{t \pm l})}{\sigma(B_{t \pm l})} \tag{8}$$

$$Z_N^{(t)} = \frac{N_t - \mu(N_{t \pm l})}{\sigma(N_{t \pm l})} \tag{9}$$

where $\mu(B_{t \pm l})$ and $\mu(N_{t \pm l})$ are the means and $\sigma(B_{t \pm l})$ and $\sigma(N_{t \pm l})$ are the standard deviations with $2l$ days around the current day t. The correlations of Z_B and stock price (Fig. 1-(a)), Z_N and stock volatility (Fig. 1-(b)) given a particular stock are shown in Fig. 1 We can see they are positively correlated and satisfy the two assumptions on sentimental indicators we previously gave.

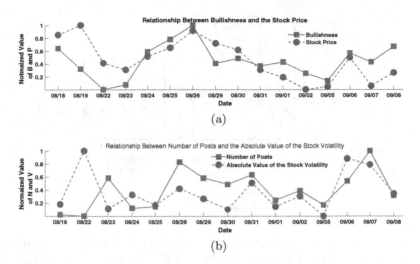

Fig. 1. Relationship between sentimental indicators and the stock information

3.2 Stock Prediction with Recurrent Neural Network

The stock price for a day is the weighted average price of all transactions on that day. In the Chinese market, it is calculated by the last minute of the trading day, so it is also referred to as the closing price [12]. In the actual stock market, profit-driving investors only care about the volatility of a stock instead of the exact price. The stock volatility V_t is defined based on the closing price P_t on the current day t and the previous day $t-1$:

$$V_t = \frac{P_t - P_{t-1}}{P_{t-1}}; V_t \in [-0.1, 0.1] \tag{10}$$

In order to regulate the stock market from any malicious manipulations, any stock has the volatility more than 10% will be forced to quit the market on that trading day, therefore, V_t always lies in the range of $[-0.1, 0.1]$. In our experiment, we normalize the volatility into a time series between 0 and 1 based on mini-max normalization method, and generate the normalized time series **V**. At the same time, we set 0.5 as the threshold in order to obtain a binary label (0 for price going down, and 1 for price rising).

$$F_t = \begin{cases} 1 & V_t > 0.5 \\ 0 & otherwise \end{cases} \tag{11}$$

A stock market is highly complex in the control of "invisible hands". However, there are still loads of research on statistical modeling and machine learning approaches to learn from history data. The key to predict the stock market is to fit a latent nonlinear relation between the history data and the future stock volatility. The traditional statistical models used for financial forecasting were simple and suffered from several shortcomings. Machine learning methods

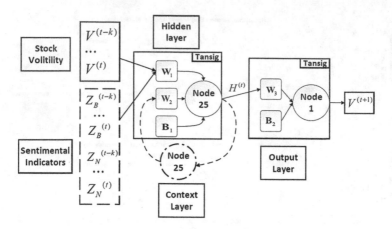

Fig. 2. The structure of the RNN model with sentimental indicators. The input values are stock volatility (V) and sentimental indicators (Z), we use the inputs of previous k trading days to predict the stock volatility of the next trading day $(V^{(t+1)})$. There are 25 hidden nodes used in our model.

like Multi-Layer Perception (MLP), Recurrent Neural Networks, Support Vector Machine (SVM) [15] have an increasing popularity in this area. RNN is incorporated in our fundamental prediction model due to its appropriateness to address time series problem. The context layer stores the outputs of the state neurons from the previous time step and outputs to the next time step for computation. In this paper, we employ Elman Network [6] in the following experiments. If we denote the output of hidden layer at time t by $H^{(t)}$, the final prediction can be made by:

$$V^{(t+1)} = f(H^{(t)}W_3 + B_2) \tag{12}$$

$$H^{(t)} = f([V, Z]W_1 + H^{(t-1)}W_2 + B_1) \tag{13}$$

where $f(\cdot)$ is the activation function and B is bias. The structure of our proposed model[7] is show in Fig. 2.

4   Experimental Studies

In order to verify the effectiveness of the new proposed model, we test it on the stock data introduced in Sect. 2.1. The stock data of 250 consecutive trading days is downloaded from the DaZhiHui (DZH)[8] software. In order to evaluate the quality of the model, we define the concept of accuracy based on the binary label F. F^* is the predict label of the test data while F is the real label. Define *counter* as the total number if $F_t^* = F_t$, accuracy $Acc = \frac{counter}{\|F\|}$.

We choose one stock (000573) as an example, we extract the volatility data and run RNN on it, and then compare to the RNN with sentimental indicators

---

[7] github link: https://github.com/irfanICMLL/EMM-for-stock-prediction.
[8] It can be downloaded from http://www.gw.com.cn.

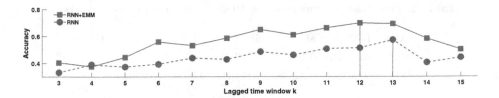

Fig. 3. Comparison results with different k.

$Z_B{}^{(t)}$ and $Z_N{}^{(t)}$ (RNN+EMM). We vary k from 3 to 15 to test the best length of history for predicting the future. The experiments are replicated for 50 times. Comparison results are shown in Fig. 3. We can see that sentimental indicators help to improve the accuracy significantly, and the parameter k will affect the prediction accuracy, the optimal length is around 10 based on different data sets. For the stock 000573, the best accuracy of the EMM with RNN is 69.85%($k = 12$) while the best accuracy without sentimental information is 57.33%($k = 13$), and the accuracy is significantly better than 0.5. Another 9 stocks are selected randomly to test the model, that increase the credibility of the conclusion.

As for each particular stock, we can obtain better performance for 8 datasets in 10 and the detailed result comparisons are shown in Table 1. To make it more intuitive, we draw the histogram in Fig. 4. From the results, we can see that the stock 000573 performs better than others. The reason may be that most of the training posts of the emotion classifier come from its sub-forum during the chosen period. In other words, if the actual sentimental indicators are obtained, the accuracy of the model can be better.

Table 1. Accuracy and the best k for RNN+EMM and RNN

Stock number	000573	000733	000703	300017	600605	300333	000909	601668	000788	600362
RNN+EMM	0.6985	0.6187	0.6757	0.6927	0.7355	0.6491	0.6154	0.5626	0.5917	0.7092
RNN	0.5733	0.524	0.605	0.6455	0.6982	0.6232	0.6029	0.5543	0.6017	0.7344
k (RNN+EMM)	12	13	11	14	3	4	11	15	13	11
k (RNN)	13	5	5	14	14	6	10	3	13	6

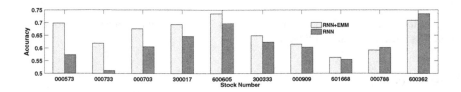

Fig. 4. Accuracy for RNN+EMM and RNN on 10-stocks dataset

Table 2 shows the comparison results of four learning models: MLP [8], SVM [4], RNN, EMM+RNN and the baseline is a random guesser (RAND). On the 10

Table 2. Performance comparisons on 10 stocks from the Chinese market.

Method	RAND	MLP	SVM	RNN	RNN+EMM
MEAN	0.500168	0.559257	0.602339	0.61623	0.6549
STD	0.003846	0.028681	0.111318	0.06347	0.05640

datasets with online discussions, the accuracy of RNN is higher than MLP and SVM, because it contains information about the previous states. When considering sentimental indicators, the prediction performance improves nearly 4% on the average which verifies the assumptions about the sentimental indicators. We only test 10 stocks, because the posts are not so easy to be obtained and labeled. We need roughly 20 h to collect one sub-forum. And then extract the sentimental indicators through the method introduced in Sect. 2. In order to make the results more credible, we do repetition under various of the initial parameters to make sure that the improved accuracy is thus most likely not the result by chance nor the selection of a specifically favorable test period.

5   Conclusions

In this research, we investigated the relationship between the stock volatility and sentimental information obtained from an online stock forum. We employed a RNN model to consider sentimental information, experimental results show that the new model can boost the prediction accuracy. The main contribution of our research are as follows: (1) Generate a sentimental weight dictionary of Chinese stock posts. (2) Propose sentimental indicators and investigate the relationship between the stock volatility and the information from the stock forums. (3) Build a RNN model considering sentimental information for stock prediction and verifies the information from forums can help to predict the stock market of China. (4) We construct a benchmark dataset of labeled financial posts and make it public available for comparison studies. Finally, it's worth mentioning that our analysis doesn't take into account many factors. The posts from the forums may contains a lot of fake messages that confuse the public. We will consider that in our future work.

Acknowledgement. This work is supported by the National Science Foundation of China Nos. 61401012 and 61305047.

References

1. Antweiler, W., Frank, M.Z.: Is all that talk just noise? The information content of internet stock message boards. J. Finan. **59**(3), 1259–1294 (2004)
2. Bachelier, L.: Théorie de la spéculation. Ann. Scientifiques De L École Normale Supérieure **3**, 21–86 (1900)

3. Bollen, J., Mao, H., Zeng, X.: Twitter mood predicts the stock market. J. Comput. Sci. **2**(1), 1–8 (2010)
4. Burges, C.J.C.: A tutorial on support vector machines for pattern recognition. Data Min. Knowl. Disc. **2**(2), 121–167 (1998)
5. Edmans, A., García, D., Norli, Ø.: Sports sentiment and stock returns. J. Finan. **62**(4), 1967–1998 (2007)
6. Elman, J.L.: Finding structure in time. Cogn. Sci. **14**(2), 179–211 (1990)
7. Fama, E.: Efficient market hypothesis: a review of theory and empirical work. J. Finan. **25**, 383–417 (1970)
8. Frank, R.J., Davey, N., Hunt, S.P.: Input window size and neural network predictors. In: IEEE-INNS-ENNS International Joint Conference on Neural Networks, vol. 2, pp. 237–242 (2000)
9. Guo, T., Li, B., Fu, Z., Wan, T., Qin, Z.: Learning sentimental weights of mixed-gram terms for classification and visualization. In: Booth, R., Zhang, M.-L. (eds.) PRICAI 2016. LNCS (LNAI), vol. 9810, pp. 116–124. Springer, Cham (2016). doi:10.1007/978-3-319-42911-3_10
10. Hirshleifer, D., Shumway, T.: Good day sunshine: stock returns and the weather. J. Finan. **58**(3), 1009–1032 (2003)
11. Loughran, T., Mcdonald, B.: When is a liability not a liability? ČFA Dis. **41**(2), 57–59 (2011)
12. Ma'Aji, M.M., Abdullahi, S.R.: Market reaction to international cross-listing: evidence from nigeria. Int. J. Inf. Technol. Bus. Manage. **27**(1), 13–25 (2014). Social Science Electronic Publishing
13. O'Connor, A.: The power of popularity: an empirical study of the relationship between social media fan counts and brand company stock prices. Soc. Sci. Comput. Rev. **31**(2), 229–235 (2013)
14. Osborne, M.: Browing motion in the stock market. Oper. Res. **7**(2), 145–173 (1959)
15. Rout, A.K., Dash, P.K., Dash, R., Bisoi, R.: Forecasting financial time series using a low complexity recurrent neural network and evolutionary learning approach. J. King Saud Univ. - Comput. Inf. Sci. (2015)
16. Rzepczynski, M.: Beyond Greed and Fear: Understanding Behavioral Finance and the Psychology of Investing, vol. 78, pp. 99–101. OUP Catalogue (2007)
17. Si, J., Mukherjee, A., Liu, B., Li, Q., Li, H., Deng, X.: Exploiting topic based twitter sentiment for stock prediction. In: Proceedings of ACL, pp. 24–29 (2013)
18. Sprenger, T.O., Tumasjan, A., Sandner, P.G., Welpe, I.M.: Tweets and trades: the information content of stock microblogs. Eur. Financ. Manage. **20**(5), 926–957 (2010)
19. Zhang, X., Fuehres, H., Gloor, P.A., Zhang, X., Fuehres, H.: Predicting stock market indicators through twitter "I hope it is not as bad as I fear". Soc. Behav. Sci. **26**(26), 55–62 (2011)

Incremental Quantiles Estimators for Tracking Multiple Quantiles

Hugo Lewi Hammer[(⊠)] and Anis Yazidi

Department of Computer Science,
Oslo and Akershus University College of Applied Sciences, Oslo, Norway
hugo.hammer@hioa.no

Abstract. In this paper, we investigate the problem of estimating multiple quantiles when samples are received online (data stream). We assume that we are dealing with a dynamical system, i.e. the distribution of the samples from the data stream changes with time. A major challenge arises when simultaneously maintaining multiple quantile estimates using *incremental* type of estimators. In fact, a naive implementation where multiple incremental quantile estimators are updated in *isolation* might lead to violation monotone property of quantiles, i.e., an estimate of a lower target quantile might erroneously overpass that of a higher one. Surprisingly, the related work on countering those violations is extremely sparse [1,3] and almost absent.

Our work tries to fill this literature gap by proposing two solutions to the problem that build on the deterministic update based multiplicative incremental quantile estimator (DUMIQE) recently proposed by Yazidi and Hammer [5], which was shown to be the most efficient incremental quantile estimator in the literature.

Experimental results show that the modified DUMIQE methods perform very well and have a superior performance to the DUMIQE. Moreover, our proposed methods satisfy the monotone property of quantiles. The methods outperform the state of the art multiple incremental quantile estimator of Cao et al. [1,3].

1 Introduction

Quantiles are key indicators for monitoring the performance of a system in an online fashion. For instance, system administrators are interested in monitoring the 95% response time of a web-server so that to hold it under a certain threshold. Quantile tracking is also useful for detecting abnormal events and in intrusion detection systems in general.

In the context of large data streams, quantile estimators have a major computational and memory complexity disadvantage as even linear computational complexity is not affordable. Several algorithms have been proposed to deal with this challenges.

The most efficient and lightweight quantile estimator reported in the literature are the so-called incremental estimators [2,4]. An incremental quantile

© Springer International Publishing AG 2017
S. Benferhat et al. (Eds.): IEA/AIE 2017, Part I, LNAI 10350, pp. 202–210, 2017.
DOI: 10.1007/978-3-319-60042-0_23

estimator by definition resorts to only the last data sample in order to update the current estimate. The informed reader will observe that the exponential moving average is a type of incremental estimator but rather for the average and not the quantile where the current estimate is a weighted average of the old estimate and the last observation.

From a practical point of view it is often useful to estimate many quantiles of the dynamic data stream. A simple approach is to estimate the different quantiles independent of each other by running incremental estimators in parallel, one for each quantile to be estimated. Unfortunately, such an approach often leads to unrealistic estimates as the monotone property of quantiles might be violated, e.g. that the estimate of a lower quantile can at some time instants overpasses the estimate of a higher quantile. As a way of illustration, we know that 50% quantile can not overpass 70% quantile due to the monotone property of the cumulative distribution and consequently the respective estimates of both quantities should maintain this monotone property too.

Please note that the latter major disadvantage is inherent in any incremental quantile estimator without exception since, by design, they do not enforce the monotone property.

To the best of our knowledge, Cao et al. [3] is the only solution found in the literature. The main idea is to rather resort to linear interpolation to yield an increasing approximate of the cumulative function. Consequently, updated quantile estimates are obtained from the approximate cumulative distribution. Unfortunately, such operation is usually expensive.

In this paper, we tackle the problem of estimating multiple quantiles from a dynamically changing data stream. To achieve this, we extend the DUMIQE method proposed by Yazidi and Hammer [5]. The choice of DUMIQE method as a core for our current work is deliberate since it was shown to be the most performant method in the literature. In this paper, we thus focus on extending the DUMIQE method in order to accommodate the case of tracking multiple quantiles. DUMIQE presents an efficient extension of randomized update based multiplicative incremental quantile estimator (RUMIQE) proposed in [6].

It is worth mentioning that the algorithms presented in this paper are not limited to the incremental quantile estimator developed in [5] and their essence can be easily transferred and generalized for other types of incremental estimators.

The reminder of the article is organized as follows. In Sect. 2, we present two different algorithms for designing parallel incremental quantile estimates satisfying the monotone property. Section 3 presents some thorough experimental results where we catalogue the performance of the two proposed algorithms and compare them to the state-of-art. Section 4 concludes the article.

2   Estimation of Multiple Quantiles

Let X_n denote a stochastic variable denoting the possible outcomes from the data stream at time n and let x_n denote a random sample of X_n. We assume that X_n is distributed according to some distribution $f_n(x)$ that varies dynamically with time n. Further let $Q_n(q)$ denote the quantile associated with probability q at time n, i.e. $Q_n(q) = F_X(q) = P(X_n \leq q)$.

In this paper we focus on simultaneously estimating the quantiles for K different probabilities $q_1, q_2, \ldots, q_K$ at each time step. We assume an increasing order of the probabilities, i.e. $q_1 < q_2 < \cdots < q_K$. The straight forward approach to estimate the quantiles would be to simply run DUMIQE (or some other online estimation procedure) for every target quantile

$$
\begin{aligned}
\widehat{Q_{n+1}}(q_k) &\leftarrow (1 + \lambda q_k)\widehat{Q_n}(q_k) & \text{if } \widehat{Q_n}(q_k) < x_n \\
\widehat{Q_{n+1}}(q_k) &\leftarrow (1 - \lambda(1 - q_k))\widehat{Q_n}(q_k) & \text{if } \widehat{Q_n}(q_k) \geq x_n
\end{aligned}
\tag{1}
$$

for $k = 1, 2, \ldots, K$. Unfortunately, this may lead to a violation of the monotone property of quantiles, i.e. we may not satisfy

$$
\widehat{Q_{n+1}}(q_1) \leq \widehat{Q_{n+1}}(q_2) \leq \cdots \leq \widehat{Q_{n+1}}(q_K)
\tag{2}
$$

In order to further shed the light on the eventuality of violating the monotone property, we provide a simple example. Assume at time n that the monotone property is satisfied and that the sample x_n gets a value between $\widehat{Q_n}(q_k)$ and $\widehat{Q_n}(q_{k+1})$, i.e.

$$
\widehat{Q_n}(q_1) \leq \cdots \leq \widehat{Q_n}(q_k) < x_n < \widehat{Q_n}(q_{k+1}) \leq \cdots \leq \widehat{Q_n}(q_K)
\tag{3}
$$

Then according to (1) the estimates are updated as follows

$$
\begin{aligned}
\widehat{Q_{n+1}}(q_j) &\leftarrow (1 + \lambda q_j)\widehat{Q_n}(q_j) & \text{for } j = 1, 2, \ldots, k \\
\widehat{Q_{n+1}}(q_j) &\leftarrow (1 - \lambda(1 - q_j))\widehat{Q_n}(q_j) & \text{for } j = k+1, \ldots, K
\end{aligned}
\tag{4}
$$

which means that the estimates are increased for the quantiles with an estimate below x_n and decreased for the estimates above x_n. Consequently, the monotone property may be violated in this case. Next we present present two modifications of the DUMIQE such that the monotone property will be satisfied.

2.1   Sorting Based Approach

The first approach we propose in this paper is simple and intuitive. It is based on sorting the quantile estimates. Every time we receive a new sample x_n the procedure consists of the three following steps:

1. Update the quantile estimates according to (1) and get the estimates $\widehat{Q_{n+1}}(q_k), k = 1, 2, \ldots, K$
2. Sort the updated estimates and denote them $\widetilde{Q_{n+1}}(q_k), k = 1, 2, \ldots, K$. The estimates after sorting naturally will satisfy the monotone property, but will also contain less (or equal) estimation error than the original estimates. In other words, this is a win-win solution, but at the computational cost of sorting the quantiles, $O(K \log(K))$.

3. We have two alternatives for update at the subsequent time instant $n + 1$. Upon receiving the sample (x_{n+1}), we may update according to Eq. (1) using
   (a) the estimates from before the sorting, i.e. $\widehat{Q_{n+1}}(q_k), k = 1, 2, \ldots, K$
   (b) or the estimates after the sorting, i.e. $\widehat{Q_{n+1}}(q_k), k = 1, 2, \ldots, K$

Alternative (a) means that we do *not* feed the information from the sorting back into the estimation process, while in (b) we do. Using alternative (a) means that we only use sorting to "repair" the estimates from the original estimation process based on Eq. (1). The overall computational complexity of this approach thus is $O(K \log(K))$ in every iteration.

2.2 Adjusting the Size λ

The next strategy is based on reducing the value of λ in a given iteration if the updates result in monotone property violation. Assume that we are in the situation where the sample x_n gets a value between $\widehat{Q_n}(q_k)$ and $\widehat{Q_n}(q_{k+1})$ as given by (3). The first observation is that after the update, the monotone property always will be satisfied on each side of x_n, i.e.

$$\widehat{Q_{n+1}}(q_1) \leq \widehat{Q_{n+1}}(q_2) \leq \cdots \leq \widehat{Q_{n+1}}(q_k) \text{ and}$$
$$\widehat{Q_{n+1}}(q_{k+1}) \leq \widehat{Q_{n+1}}(q_{k+2}) \leq \cdots \leq \widehat{Q_{n+1}}(q_K)$$

This follows from Eq. (4). Therefore a sufficient criterion to satisfy the monotone property is to make sure to use a sufficiently small λ such that permits to satisfy the following inequality: $\widehat{Q_{n+1}}(q_k) \leq \widehat{Q_{n+1}}(q_{k+1})$. We derive such a λ, denoted $\tilde{\lambda}$, by making sure that the distance between $\widehat{Q_{n+1}}(q_k)$ and $\widehat{Q_{n+1}}(q_{k+1})$ is some portion, α, of the distance from the previous iteration, i.e.

$$\widehat{Q_{n+1}}(q_{k+1}) - \widehat{Q_{n+1}}(q_k) = \alpha \left(\widehat{Q_n}(q_{k+1}) - \widehat{Q_n}(q_k) \right)$$

$$(1 - \tilde{\lambda}(1 - q_{k+1}))\widehat{Q_n}(q_{k+1}) - (1 + \tilde{\lambda}q_k)\widehat{Q_n}(q_k) = \alpha \left(\widehat{Q_n}(q_{k+1}) - \widehat{Q_n}(q_k) \right)$$

$$(5)$$

with $\alpha \in [0, 1)$. Solving (5) with respect to $\tilde{\lambda}$ we get

$$\tilde{\lambda} = (1 - \alpha)\frac{\widehat{Q_n}(q_{k+1}) - \widehat{Q_n}(q_k)}{(1 - q_{k+1})\widehat{Q_n}(q_{k+1}) + q_k\widehat{Q_n}(q_k)}$$

$$= (1 - \alpha)H\left(\widehat{Q_n}(q_k), \widehat{Q_n}(q_{k+1}) \right)$$

$$(6)$$

We substitute λ with $\tilde{\lambda}$ in (1) if using the originally chosen λ results into the violation of the monotone property. We then obtain the following updates

$$\widehat{Q_{n+1}}(q_k) \leftarrow (1 + \lambda q_k)\widehat{Q_n}(q_k) \quad \text{if } \widehat{Q_n}(q_k) < x_n \cap \widehat{Q_n}(q_{k+1}) < x_n \tag{7}$$

$$\widehat{Q_{n+1}}(q_k) \leftarrow (1 + \lambda q_k)\widehat{Q_n}(q_k)$$
$$\text{if } \widehat{Q_n}(q_k) < x_n \cap \widehat{Q_n}(q_{k+1}) \geq x_n \cap \lambda < H\Big(\widehat{Q_n}(q_k), \widehat{Q_n}(q_{k+1})\Big) \tag{8}$$

$$\widehat{Q_{n+1}}(q_k) \leftarrow \Big(1 + (1-\alpha)H\Big(\widehat{Q_n}(q_k), \widehat{Q_n}(q_{k+1})\Big) q_k\Big)\widehat{Q_n}(q_k)$$
$$\text{if } \widehat{Q_n}(q_k) < x_n \cap \widehat{Q_n}(q_{k+1}) \geq x_n \cap \lambda > H\Big(\widehat{Q_n}(q_k), \widehat{Q_n}(q_{k+1})\Big) \tag{9}$$

$$\widehat{Q_{n+1}}(q_k) \leftarrow (1 - \lambda(1-q_k))\widehat{Q_n}(q_k) \quad \text{if } \widehat{Q_n}(q_k) \geq x_n \cap \widehat{Q_n}(q_{k-1}) \geq x_n \tag{10}$$

$$\widehat{Q_{n+1}}(q_k) \leftarrow (1 - \lambda(1-q_k))\widehat{Q_n}(q_k)$$
$$\text{if } \widehat{Q_n}(q_k) \geq x_n \cap \widehat{Q_n}(q_{k-1}) < x_n \cap \lambda < H\Big(\widehat{Q_n}(q_{k-1}), \widehat{Q_n}(q_k)\Big) \tag{11}$$

$$\widehat{Q_{n+1}}(q_k) \leftarrow \Big(1 - (1-\alpha)H\Big(\widehat{Q_n}(q_{k-1}), \widehat{Q_n}(q_k)\Big)(1-q_k)\Big)\widehat{Q_n}(q_k)$$
$$\text{if } \widehat{Q_n}(q_k) \geq x_n \cap \widehat{Q_n}(q_{k-1}) < x_n \cap \lambda > H\Big(\widehat{Q_n}(q_{k-1}), \widehat{Q_n}(q_k)\Big) \tag{12}$$

for $k = 2, \ldots, K - 1$. The special cases for $k = 1$ and $k = K$ are shown below. Equation (7) shows the case when x_n takes a value above $\widehat{Q_n}(q_{k+1})$ and therefore is no risk of violation of the monotone property. The update therefore is as in (1). Equation (8) shows the case when x_n takes a value between $\widehat{Q_n}(q_{k-1})$ and $\widehat{Q_n}(q_k)$ and we may potentially get a monotone violation. But since $\lambda < H\Big(\widehat{Q_n}(q_k), \widehat{Q_n}(q_{k+1})\Big)$ we are able to maintain the monotone property using λ. Thus, this update is also as in (1). Equation (9) shows the case when x_n takes a value between $\widehat{Q_n}(q_{k-1})$ and $\widehat{Q_n}(q_k)$ and $\lambda > H\Big(\widehat{Q_n}(q_k), \widehat{Q_n}(q_{k+1})\Big)$ and therefore we get a monotone violation using λ and we need to use $\tilde{\lambda}$ from (6) instead of λ in this update. Equations (10) to (12) show the similar updates when x_n takes a value below $\widehat{Q_n}(q_{k+1})$.

For the smallest and largest quantile estimates, we only get potential monotone violations upwards and downwards, respectively, resulting in the following updates

$$\widehat{Q_{n+1}}(q_1) \leftarrow (1 + \lambda q_1)\widehat{Q_n}(q_1) \quad \text{if } \widehat{Q_n}(q_1) < x_n \cap \widehat{Q_n}(q_2) < x_n \tag{13}$$

$$\widehat{Q_{n+1}}(q_1) \leftarrow (1 + \lambda q_1)\widehat{Q_n}(q_1)$$
$$\text{if } \widehat{Q_n}(q_1) < x_n \cap \widehat{Q_n}(q_2) \geq x_n \cap \lambda < H\Big(\widehat{Q_n}(q_1), \widehat{Q_n}(q_2)\Big) \tag{14}$$

$$\widehat{Q_{n+1}}(q_1) \leftarrow \Big(1 + (1-\alpha)H\Big(\widehat{Q_n}(q_1), \widehat{Q_n}(q_2)\Big) q_1\Big)\widehat{Q_n}(q_1)$$
$$\text{if } \widehat{Q_n}(q_1) < x_n \cap \widehat{Q_n}(q_2) \geq x_n \cap \lambda > H\Big(\widehat{Q_n}(q_1), \widehat{Q_n}(q_2)\Big) \tag{15}$$

$$\widehat{Q_{n+1}}(q_1) \leftarrow (1 - \lambda(1-q_1))\widehat{Q_n}(q_1) \quad \text{if } \widehat{Q_n}(q_1) \geq x_n \tag{16}$$

and

$$\widehat{Q_{n+1}}(q_K) \leftarrow (1 + \lambda q_K)\widehat{Q_n}(q_K) \quad \text{if } \widehat{Q_n}(q_K) < x_n \tag{17}$$

$$\widehat{Q_{n+1}}(q_K) \leftarrow (1 - \lambda(1 - q_K))\widehat{Q_n}(q_K) \quad \text{if } \widehat{Q_n}(q_K) \geq x_n \cap \widehat{Q_n}(q_{K-1}) \geq x_n \tag{18}$$

$$\widehat{Q_{n+1}}(q_K) \leftarrow (1 - \lambda(1 - q_K))\widehat{Q_n}(q_K)$$
$$\text{if } \widehat{Q_n}(q_K) \geq x_n \cap \widehat{Q_n}(q_{K-1}) < x_n \cap \lambda < H\left(\widehat{Q_n}(q_{K-1}), \widehat{Q_n}(q_K)\right) \tag{19}$$

$$\widehat{Q_{n+1}}(q_K) \leftarrow \left(1 - (1 - \alpha)H\left(\widehat{Q_n}(q_{K-1}), \widehat{Q_n}(q_K)\right)(1 - q_K)\right)\widehat{Q_n}(q_K)$$
$$\text{if } \widehat{Q_n}(q_K) \geq x_n \cap \widehat{Q_n}(q_{K-1}) < x_n \cap \lambda > H\left(\widehat{Q_n}(q_{K-1}), \widehat{Q_n}(q_K)\right) \tag{20}$$

By estimating all the quantiles using the rules in (7)–(12), we ensure that the monotone property in (2) is satisfied in every iteration $n = 1, 2, 3, \ldots$.

The most expensive part of this algorithm is to find the k in (3) that can be computed in $O(\log(K))$ operations which is less expensive than updating every quantile ,i.e, $O(K)$. The overall computational complexity of this approach thus is $O(K)$ in every iteration.

3   Experiments

It is possible to prove that the DUMIQE approach in (1) converges to the true quantiles [5]. Unfortunately, it is hard (or impossible) to prove convergence for the methods described above. As described above the running estimation process is then simply the DUMIQE in (1). Since the theoretical proofs of the methods above are intrinsically hard, we instead resort to simulations to document the effectiveness of the approaches.

The experiments focus on the methods ability to track quantile estimates when the distribution of the data stream changes with time. We consider the two different cases were we assume that the data correspond to outcomes from a normal distribution. Furthermore, we assume that the expectation of the distribution varies with time

$$\mu_n = a \sin\left(\frac{2\pi}{T}n\right), \quad n = 1, 2, 3, \ldots$$

which is the sinus function with period T. Moreover, we assume that the standard deviation of the distribution do not vary with time but is equal to one.

Now, we turn to conducting a thorough analysis of how well the proposed methods in Sect. 2 estimate quantiles of data streams. We estimated quantiles of both the normally and χ^2 distributed data streams above using two different periods, namely $T = 800$ (rapid variation) and $T = 8000$ (slow variation), i.e. in total four different data streams. In addition, for each of the four data streams we estimated quantiles that were centered around the median or in the tail of the distribution, i.e. eight different cases. We chose the quantiles close enough to get a fair amount of monotone property violations. Naturally, if we choose the quantiles far from each other we will rarely or never get any violations. In greater details, we estimated to following quantiles for the different cases.

- For the normal distribution and the quantiles around the median, we estimated the quantiles related to the following probabilities $q_k = \Phi(-0.8 + 0.2(k - 1))$, $k = 1, 2, \ldots, 9$ where $\Phi(\cdot)$ refers to the cumulative distribution function of the standard normal distribution. Recall that in dynamical systems, as in these experiments, the value of a quantile related to a specific probability varies with time.
- For the normal distribution and the quantiles in the tail of the distribution, we use $q_k = \Phi(0.8 + 0.2(k - 1))$, $k = 1, 2, \ldots, 9$.

The probabilities related to quantiles in the median and around the tail of the distribution are centered around the probabilities 0.5 and 0.95, respectively. The choices above resulted in a monotone property violation in about every third iteration using a typical value $\lambda = 0.05$ in (1).

To measure estimation error, we use the average of the root mean squares error (RMSE) for each quantile

$$RMSE = \frac{1}{K} \sum_{k=1}^{K} \sqrt{\frac{1}{N} \sum_{n=1}^{N} \left(Q_n(q_k) - \widehat{Q}_n(q_k) \right)^2}$$

where N is the total number of samples in the data stream. We investigate the estimation error for a large set of different values of the parameter λ. In the experiments we used $N = 10^7$ which efficiently removed any Monte Carlo errors in the experimental results.

The results for the normal are shown in Fig. 1. In the figure the abbreviations SORT, PREV refer to the estimation approaches presented in Sects. 2.1 and 2.2. For the sorting based approach in Sect. 2.1, bring = TRUE means that we fed the sorted quantiles back into the estimation procedure were fed back in to the estimation procedure. DUMIQE refers to updating the quantiles using (1) and ignoring that the monotone property may get violated.

For all the estimation methods, we observe that the estimation error increases when the period decreases or when estimating further into the tail of the distribution. It seems also that feeding the updated estimates $\widetilde{Q}_n(q_k)$ back into the estimation process further improves the estimation compared to not feeding them in. For the approach based on adjusting the size of λ in Sect. 2.2, it seems like using $\alpha = 0.5$ (making small updates) performs poor in all the experiments. Using $\alpha = 0$ we update as much as possible without violating the monotone property and performs about equally well to sorting the quantiles (Sect. 2.1). For the sorting approach, whether feeding the sorted estimates back in the estimation process or not has minimal effect on the estimation. An interesting observation is that almost all the approaches perform better than updating DUMIQE in isolation, i.e., without enforcing the monotone property. In other words, we are able to both satisfy the monotone property and improve estimation precision with a minimal extra computational costs.

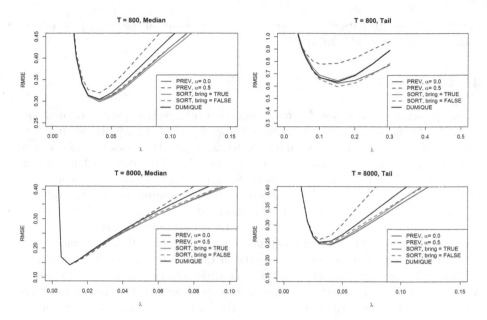

Fig. 1. Estimation error for data from the normal distribution.

Table 1. Estimation error using the method in Cao et al. (2009) [3].

	$T = 800$, Median	$T = 800$, Tail	$T = 8000$, Median	$T = 8000$, Tail
Normal distribution	0.312	0.630	0.259	0.370
	$T = 800$, Median	$T = 800$, Tail	$T = 8000$, Median	$T = 8000$, Tail
χ^2 distribution	0.79	2.40	0.445	1.611

For comparison we also tested the method in [3] for the eight estimation tasks described above. The latter method is the only method we have found in the literature that attempts to estimate multiple quantiles in a dynamical system. The method have two tuning parameters, a weight parameter similar to λ in the methods in this paper, and a parameter that controls the width of intervals to estimate the distribution of the data stream around a quantile. To achieve as good results as possible we ran the method for a large set of values for the two parameters. The best estimation results are shown in Table 1. We remark that for the normal distribution and $T = 800$ Cao et al. performs well. For the normal distribution and $T = 8000$, the methods in this paper outperforms Cao et al. (2009) [3]. For all the cases related to the χ^2 distribution, the methods in this paper outperforms Cao et al. (2009) [3] with a clear margin. Not only does the methods in this paper outperform Cao et al. (2009) [3], they are also far simpler to implement and only contain only one tuning parameters which makes it easier to tune the method to perform well. The experiments also showed that the methods in this paper are less sensitive to the choice of the tuning parameter compared to Cao et al. (2009) [3].

4   Closing Remarks

In this paper, we have devised two methods that incrementally estimate multiple quantiles from a dynamic data stream while enjoying the ability to maintain the monotone property of the quantiles. Surprisingly, the work on this type of incremental quantile estimators is very sparse. The first proposed method is simple and is based on sorting the quantiles whenever the monotone property is violated. The second method suggests to adjust in a online manner the value of the parameter λ to ensure that the monotone property is never violated.

The results show that the suggested methods perform very well in estimating multiple quantiles. Most of the methods outperform the DUMIQE and at the same time satisfy the monotone property of quantiles. The method of adjusting the value of λ (Sect. 2.2) is of the same order of computational complexity as DUMIQE. In other words, we are able to both satisfy the monotone property and improve estimation precision at the cost of a minimal increase of the computational cost.

A research avenue worth investigating in the future is to deploy multiple parallel quantile estimators in order to improve the accuracy of tracking a single quantile estimate.

References

1. Bu, T., Cao, J., Chen, A., Li, L.: Method and apparatus for incremental tracking of multiple quantiles. US Patent 8,589,329, 19 November 2013
2. Cao, J., Li, L., Chen, A., Bu, T.: Tracking quantiles of network data streams with dynamic operations. In: 2010 Proceedings IEEE on INFOCOM, pp. 1–5. IEEE (2010)
3. Cao, J., Li, L.E., Chen, A., Bu, T.: Incremental tracking of multiple quantiles for network monitoring in cellular networks. In: Proceedings of the 1st ACM Workshop on Mobile Internet Through Cellular Networks, pp. 7–12. ACM (2009)
4. Chen, F., Lambert, D., Pinheiro, J.C.: Incremental quantile estimation for massive tracking. In: Proceedings of the Sixth ACM SIGKDD International Conference on Knowledge Discovery and Data Mining, pp. 516–522. ACM (2000)
5. Yazidi, A., Hammer, H.L.: Multiplicative update methods for incremental quantile estimation. Journal Article, Under Review (2016)
6. Yazidi, A., Hammer, H.: Quantile estimation using the theory of stochastic learning. In: Proceedings of the 2015 Conference on Research in Adaptive and Convergent Systems, RACS, New York, NY, USA, pp. 7–14. ACM (2015)

Forecasting Passenger Flows Using Data Analytics

Nang Laik Ma[✉]

School of Business, SIM University, 461 Clementi Road, Singapore, 599491, Singapore
nlma@unisim.edu.sg

Abstract. In this paper, we focus on the forecasting of monthly departure passenger movements for one of the busiest airport in Asia. Firstly, we forecast the monthly airport departure passenger flows for the next 12 months for macro level planning. Next, we used SAS Forecast Studio for detailed-level planning based on airline and per airline-city combinations using hierarchical forecasting. We have also used the actual data to validate the accuracy of the forecast error. We have shown that in most cases, the mean absolute percentage error is less than 3%, which indicates the usefulness of our model for better decision making.

Keywords: Forecasting · Data analytics · Hierarchical forecasting · Seasonality · Trend · Airline · Passenger flow

1 Introduction

Being one of the busiest airports, with more than ten of million passenger movements annually, the airport operator needs to plan its resources and capacity effectively and efficiently so as to remain competitive. The airport operator needs to work closely with its partners, such as the airlines, ground handlers, tenants and the government agencies to continuously improving its services, as well as increasing its revenue. Based on the passenger traffic flow, the airport operator has to analyse if there is a need to raise the number of service staff, to expand the airport's capacity and to increase the airport amenities to satisfy the future growth in passenger traffic. Studying past passenger movement will aid it to recognise trends and patterns, hence enabling better forecasting of air passenger movements to be made.

Many airports in the world have benefited from the planned increase in their passenger volume by increasing their profitability through the use of shopping malls, duty free shopping and improve their operational efficiency with limited resources. Airlines are the major customers to the airport operators and the main objectives are to ensure the on-time departure of the aircraft and improve the passengers experience and convenience at the airport. One of the criteria for judging the efficiency of an airport is the availability of operational facilities such as runways, check-in counters, people movers, baggage handling system, aerobridges, and gate-hold rooms and so on. The arrival and departure processes of aircraft at the airport are two major operations which trigger various subsequent activities at the airport. After the aircraft arrives at the airport, it will move from the runway to taxi way, and later park at the designated gate. The passengers will walk to the terminals and the ground handlers will unload the baggage

© Springer International Publishing AG 2017
S. Benferhat et al. (Eds.): IEA/AIE 2017, Part I, LNAI 10350, pp. 211–220, 2017.
DOI: 10.1007/978-3-319-60042-0_24

and cargo to the baggage claim area in the shortest possible time. As for the passengers, they will go through the immigration before they collect their luggage and custom will inspect them before they depart the terminal building. For the departing flight, the passengers will arrive at the airport approximately 2.5 h before the departure time where most of the counters will be opened for check-in. The check-in counter will be opened for 2 h and it will be closed 30 min before the scheduled departure time to ensure that the passengers have enough time to board the plane and load the baggage on board.

Due to the annual increase in passenger movement (8% growth) and limited resources available at the airport, our client who is one of the busiest airports in Asia has decided to harness the power of decision and data analytics to predict passenger movements for better resource planning. In this paper, we focus on the tactical planning of the airport's resources. Hence the forecasts would be used to determine the operational needs, such as to assess if there was a need to increase the number resources such as service staff, check-in counters and airport amenities. The departing passenger spends the most amount of time at the airport, from check-in, shopping and sightseeing, hence it is important to enhance their experience at the airport. With more departure passengers, it will translate to more revenue for the operator as it can collect the passenger service charges and airport taxes from them.

Currently, most airlines do not submit the passenger load information to the terminal operator until the last minute as they continue to sell tickets through the last minute deals on empty seats. From the airport planning perspective, the number of passengers arriving and departing through the airport is one of the crucial factors to do the necessary planning for resources and man-power allocation. Since most of this information is only made available a few hours before the flight departures and arrival, hence for base planning, the terminal planning managers use a fixed rate heuristic of $Y\%$ passenger load to do the daily planning.

If there is an increase in the departure passenger movements, it is a hint to the airport operator to increase the number of check-in counters and service staff at various touch points, such as passenger service counters, retail shops, proportionately. It may also mean to increase or improve the airport amenities, such as trolleys, toilets, gardens etc.

In the next few sections, we discussed the literature review, current situation at one of the busiest airports in Asia, we proposed various forecasting model to get a better estimate of the departure passenger load for macro (i.e. monthly departure flow) and micro-level planning (i.e. per airline, per airline-city) to enhance the customer experience at the airport.

2   Literature Review

[1] studied UK airports' monthly air passenger figures from January 1949 to December 2004. It stated that the Holt-Winters method, a type of Exponential Smoothing methods, was surprisingly accurate in forecasting. However, the results were not acceptable for predicting intervals. The authors thus proposed the additive Holt-Winters method and introduced the elements of additive and homoscedastic, uncorrelated errors. Authors has transformed Holt-Winters method into a multivariate linear model. This would enable

the smoothing parameters to be optimized, as well as improved the consistency of the prediction intervals.

[3] analyzed the impact on demand for air travel after the terrorist attack in the USA. The first step was the estimation of the demand for air travel using the "Seasonal Autoregressive Integrated Moving Average (SARIMA) model". The second step was to conduct an intervention analysis to provide an estimated effect of the terrorist attack. Thirdly, a comparative study was performed to account for the effectiveness of the intervention analysis, benchmark against the SARIMA model. It was concluded that before the incident, there was already a decreasing trend due to the price wars and fierce competition from new airline competitors. The terrorist attack only aggravated the situation. Although it had a severe impact on the growth of domestic and international air traffic, the effect was not long-lasting. In paper [8], the authors used the "Seasonal ARIMA (SARIMA) model and ARIMAX model" built upon the ARIMA (AutoRegressive, Integrated and Moving Average combined) methodology to forecast Hong Kong International Airport (HKIA) passenger movements. The authors highlighted that the estimated values of the above input variables would affect the accuracy of the ARIMAX model, thus they need to be estimated with care. [7] used "the gravity model, a causal method to estimate an airport's demand or to explain a city-pair's air traffic density." They studied the factors affecting Hong Kong's passenger growth over the years 2001 to 2012 and identified the factors affecting it. To further illustrate the effect of the factors above, it was observed that HKIA's top 45 city routes accounted for about 85% of the airport's total passenger movements, although there was a dipping trend during the period of observation.

The number of air passenger movements was related to economic activity in a country and have a cause-and-effect relationship as mentioned in [5]. They studied the degree of correlation of the number of air passenger movements and the Gross Domestic Product (GDP) per capita for the different geographical areas. It is reported that "the number of air trips per 1000 inhabitants at world level increased from 145 in 1980 to 424 in 2013 and it could be expected to further increase to 560 in 2020 and to 812 in 2030." It was observed that the more affluent the geographical area was, the greater the degree of correlation between the number of flight trips and the gross domestic product per capita. In the case of Latin America, when plotted on a correlation curve, the number of flight trips and the gross domestic product per capita moved further away from the curve for 1980, 1990 and 2000 but it became closer for 2010 and 2013, as the air travel market matured in the later years. [2] pointed out that estimation of price elasticity for air travel was difficult due to unavailability of data such as prices, passenger numbers etc. Instead, they proposed the use of research synthesis which could be obtained from past studies or studies from other existing sources. Thus, they were able to find and study some common factors of the demand for air travel which could help explain the estimates of price elasticity. Finally, [6] described the process for econometric forecasting, which used additional data, besides the past values of the data series, to discover relationships between the data elements. The author mentioned that forecasting should be non-stop and one must obtain the forecasting errors upon the availability of the actual data regularly, and should modify his forecasting models accordingly from time to obtain better result.

Reference [4], the airport terminal operator has turned to data and decision analytics in an attempt to improve the customer satisfaction as well as profitability of the business. They would like to know what insights can analytics provide them and whether any interesting findings which could potentially assist them in making their business more sustainable. In this paper, the author have focused on strategic level planning in terminal operation to assign the airlines to three different terminals which belong to the same airport. The objective is to maintain the balanced workload across different terminals at different days of the week and achieving improved customer satisfaction level.

In the literature, a lot of researchers have worked on how to accurately predict the passenger loads using various forecasting method such as ARIMA, ARIMAX, SARIMA. But most researchers acknowledge that these forecasting methods have some limitation. They assume that historical data will present the future but we are all aware that there are other external conditions such as long weekends or marketing or promotions activities offered by the airline also affect the traffic passenger load drastically. But very few researchers have used special events like holidays to predict the passenger loads. In this paper, we are going to incorporate these special events in our forecasting methods.

3   Forecasting Monthly Departure Passenger

In this paper, we would like to forecast the monthly departure traffic using four forecasting methods namely: weighted moving average (WMA), exponential smoothing with trend (EST) and centered moving average with trend and seasonality (CMA-TS) and finally regression (REG) methods. The aggregated monthly number is useful for macro-level planning to estimate the resources required for the whole month, as it is unlikely for the airport to get the forecast of the passenger for each airline at the point of planning. In the meantime, the check-in counter resources are assigned to each airline, the demand forecast is necessary for daily operation. For detailed level planning per airline, per airline-city combination, we used the generated models in SAS Forecast Studio for the forecasting. The data used was monthly departure passenger movements from August 2013 to December 2015, with the inclusion of some variables, such as the airline code, translated city code (e.g. SFO, HKG, BKK) and day of the week (e.g. Mon, Tue, Wed). These allowed us to build a data hierarchy of 3 levels or more. Hierarchical Forecasting helped to improve the forecasting performance and to ease the burden of the overall forecast process. We also included some event variables, such as mid-year and end-of-year holiday seasons, to try to improve the accuracy of the forecasts.

First, we would like to forecast the passenger flow for the next twelve months using the monthly departure passenger flow from 2009 to 2015. It is important to get the forecast at the macro level for capacity planning. Based on the historical data, refer to the Fig. 1, it is noted that the departure passengers flow is greatly affected seasonality and there exist a trend in the time-series data.

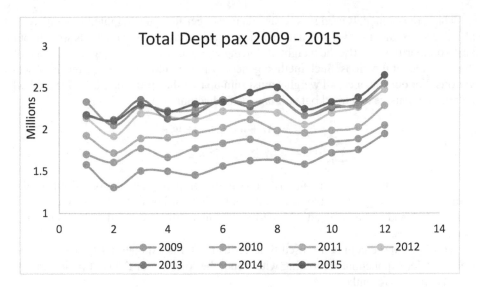

Fig. 1. Total departure passenger flow from 2009 to 2015

We use various forecasting methods to get the forecast for the next twelve months. We use mean absolute percentage error (MAPE) as an indicator to choose the best forecasting method. MAPE is a measure of prediction accuracy of a forecasting method, as the value show the magnitude of the error variation between the actual and predicted value.

$$\text{Mean absolute deviation (MAD)} = \frac{\sum\limits_{t=1}^{n} |A_t - F_t|}{n}$$

$$\text{Mean absolute percentage error (MAPE)} = \frac{MAD}{average - demand}$$

Quantitative approach is the use of numerical figures to project or forecast for the future. The approach allows adjustment to the numbers by giving more weightage to the more recent data which will allow better forecast figures to be generated. It also shows the trend and the seasonal pattern through the figures. Seasonality analysis uses the past data to retrieve useful information which the data can be used to do forecasting. The data provide comparison to the different years which can reveal the seasonal fluctuation patterns which can be better use as a basis for future forecast.

On the other hand, quantitative methods are based on historical numeric value and forecasts are generated via mathematical modelling. The advantages of quantitative methods are that it is more consistent and objective and able to consider much information and data at one time [5]. However, the downside of such methods are that quantifiable data may not be readily available.

The forecast models used to forecast the passenger flow are weighted moving averages, centered moving averages and exponential smoothing. These methods smooth out any irregularities. Firstly, the weighted moving average is of computing the average of the most recent n periods. Such method generally placed more weight on recent observations. For convenience, all weights must sum up to either 100% or 1.00. This method is more responsive to a trend but still lags behind actual data.

$$F_t = w_1 A_1 + w_2 A_2 + .. + w_n A_n$$
$$\sum\nolimits_{t=1}^{n} w_t = 1, w_n \geq w_{n-1} \geq .. \geq w_2 \geq w_1$$

Secondly, the centered moving averages is of computing an average of n periods' data and associating it with the midpoint of the periods. For instance, the average for periods 1, 2 and 3 is associated with period 2. This method is useful when computing season indexes.

Thirdly, a more commonly used time series model is exponential smoothing with trend. Under exponential smoothing with trend, the forecast for the next period can be found using the formula.

$$F_t = FIT_{t-1} + \alpha(A_{t-1} - FIT_{t-1})$$
$$T_t = T_{t-1} + \delta(F_t - FIT_{t-1})$$
$$FIT_t = F_t + T_t$$

where F_t is exponential smoothing forecast with trend for time t, T_t is exponential smoothed trend for time t, FIT_t is forecast inclusive of trend for time t, A_{t-1} is actual demand for prior period t − 1 and α, δ, are smooth constant between 0 and 1. For this forecast, we use the model to find the best α, δ which gives us the lowest MAPE.

Lastly, causal methods explore cause-and-effect relationship between the forecasted variable and another variable in the environment. When there exists random fluctuations around a long-term trend line in the time series, a linear regression Y = a + b*t is used to estimate the trend. In the event when only seasonal effects are present, seasonal indexes are computed and used to deseasonalize the data and to develop forecasts. In the scenario when both seasonal and long-term trend effects are present, a trend line is fitted to the deseasonalized data and the seasonal indexes are then used to adjust the trend projection. In conclusion, when determining which model makes a better forecast, we will need to consider the amount and type of available data, degree of accuracy required, length of forecast horizon and the presence of data patterns [5].

Table 1 shows the comparison of MAPE using four different forecasting methods. It is noted that CMA-TS gave us the lowest MAPE of 4.08% followed by EST 4.37%. In order for us to choose one method to implement, we have chosen the two best forecasting methods from above and compare it with the actual data collected from Jan 2016 to Dec 2016. In Table 2, we use the actual operational data from Jan 2016 to March 2016 and compare it with our forecast using the two methods CMA-TS and EST. It is noted that exponential smoothing with trend performs better than CMA. Exponential smoothing is the most commonly used forecasting model in most organization today. The reasons are it is quite robust, surprisingly accurate, formulating it is relative easy, user can understand how the model works and computation is very fast. Thus, the airport has decided to implement EST for their operational use according to our suggestion.

Table 1. MAPE for overall departure flow

	CMA-TS	EST	WMA	REG
MAPE	4.08%	4.37%	4.85%	4.90%

Table 2. MAPE for Jan–Mar 2016

	EST	CMA-TS
MAPE for Jan 16	2.55%	5.26%
MAPE for Feb 16	4.47%	1.08%
MAPE for Mar 16	2.62%	9.08%

4 Hierarchical Forecasting

The macro level planning only give us indication of the total passenger flow in the next year and airport operator needs to make judgement based on the forecasting result if there are enough resources to support the demand. If there are not enough counters, then they need to expand the airport facilities. However, for daily operation, we need to further our analysis for detailed (micro-level) planning. We need the demand forecast based on individual airline and airline-city code as check-in counters are assigned per airline and we can see larger variation by destination city based on earlier study [4]. For this purpose, we used the daily flight scheduled and daily departure passenger movements from August 2013 to December 2015. The total number of rows was 427,525 and the total departure passenger movements were 67 million with 16 variables. There were 96 different airlines, 2590 different flight numbers, 130 different aircraft types, 270 different translated city codes across 78 countries. We have done some data analysis and identify that airline, destination city, month and day of the weeks are some important variables to predict the departure passenger load. We use SAS Forecast Studio, which is a commercial software to predict time-series data, as a tool to do the forecasting. It could perform large-scale forecasting with good quality automatically and could also forecast a number of time series data at one time. The software could allow selection of events or holidays, and explanatory variables which could impact the forecasting process. It also has data creation tools which could create a hierarchical structure of the data to be forecasted. According to groups "BY" assigned by the forecaster, data accumulation could be applied at the bottom level, and data aggregation at the middle and top levels to form the forecasted series. We also partitioned the dataset into fitting (training) 60% and selecting (validation/testing) sets 40%, a process known as holdout sample validation or honest assessment.

4.1 Departure Passenger Movements by Airline

We have chosen "Airline_Operator_Code" and "City_Code" as the second and third level to get the forecast for departure passenger move based on given data from Aug 2013 to Dec 2015. The reconciliation method chosen was "Top-Down", meaning there would be no adjustment for the forecast series at the top. Only those in the middle and bottom levels would change.

Next, we would look at the forecasts generated for the airlines. However, it was not practical to examine all airlines for this report, hence we only assessed the forecasts for the top 10 airlines which have contributed to more than 70% of the departure passenger flows. To check for seasonality and trend that could be present in the respective series, we had created 2 filters, Seasonality_By_Airline and Trend_By _Airline which helped to identify the data with seasonal variation and trend variation respectively. The outcome for one of the largest airline A is followed. The model selected was Exponential Smoothing, Winters Method (Multiplicative). The generated MAPE for this model was 0.78, which was the lowest among all the models generated. The reconciled MAPE was 1.34. There was seasonality and trend. It was observed that Smoothing Method was chosen for all the top 10 airlines. For the top 10 airlines, seasonality and trend were present in the chosen models. The generated MAPE and reconciled MAPE for the following airlines were low; less than 3%.

4.2 Departure Passenger Movements by Airline-City Pairs

In this session, we continue to focus on the top ten airline but we would like to add another level of detail which is the destination city. To check for seasonality and trend that could be present in the respective series, we had created 2 filters, Seasonality_By_Airline_City and Trend_By_Airline _City which helped to identify those series with seasonal variation and trend variation respectively. The model selected was Exponential Smoothing, Winters Method (Additive). The generated MAPE for this model was 3.10%, which was the lower among the two models generated. The reconciled MAPE was 3.59.

4.3 Improving Forecasting Accuracy

There are some holidays which recur regularly, usually yearly. By creating special event as the event variables into the model would aid in accommodating the variation associated. A reasonable hypothesis for departure passenger movements was that there were recurring effects associated with the June school holidays and December school holidays. The effects could be described as follows:

a. **June school holidays:** Departure passenger movements were affected in June, as there was a tendency for family to travel overseas during the mid-year school holidays with children.
b. **December school holidays:** Departure passenger movements were affected in December, which is a festive season and families would travel overseas during the end-of-year school holidays.

c. **Chinese New Year:** Departure passenger movements were affected during the Chinese New Year period, as there was a tendency for passengers to travel overseas during this period.

The three event variables were created and included in the system-generated models if they were significant. We would use the actual data for January 2015 to March 2016 to test the accuracy of the forecast errors. Based on result, the actual MAPE for all months was less than 3%. The threshold set by the airport operators who can accept forecast error of less than 10%. Hence, the forecast for the overall departure passenger movements is good.

There are a few ways to improve the forecast accuracy for some of the airlines and airline – city series. An outlier is an event that had happened which the analyst might not be aware of. It could be promotions not documented and/or other demand drivers not incorporated into the models. It could also be random noise in the data generation process. By incorporating the appropriate event variables into the model for each series, we would be able to improve the models to provide better forecasts.

We could include an input variable, such as promotion plan with binary values flag in the dataset. We could then perform a scenario analysis to find out how changes in the promotion plan of a particular airline or airline – city pair could affect the future values of its forecast. We might need collaborate closely with the respective airline account managers for the future promotion plans of the airlines. If the scenarios analysis results are good and approved by the management, then we could incorporate it into the models by setting the scenario forecast values as overrides. In this way, the models could give better forecasts for the future months. Finally, manual adjustments to forecast results are common in the business world. If the stakeholders, for e.g. the airport operator foresees that some of the destinations are becoming more popular due to the recent economic development in the country, for example, Myanmar, then they can manually adjusting the forecasts to incorporate those events. The increase in frequency of flights or high load factors could actually help to improve the accuracy of the forecasts. Last but not least, it is important for business to constantly update the forecasting model and fine-tune it to capture various business scenario, so that the results are valuable for future decision making.

5 Conclusion

We use the data analytics techniques and various forecasting methods to get the forecast for the departure passenger flows in the airport at the macro level for capacity planning. Four forecasting methods were used and exponential smoothing method with trend is robust and produced consistent results for the forecast. The MAPEs (comparing the actual figures and the forecast figures) were low, less than 3% for January to March 2016. We have also acknowledged that we have not evaluated all the methods available today but we have set a threshold of 5% thus any forecasting methods which is able to produce within the threshold is valuable for the airport's decision making.

We have also use SAS forecast studio to do the demand forecasting for airline and airline-city pair. For most case, the forecast error are quite low. However, for some airlines, the MAPEs were more than 10. After looking at the plot of prediction errors, there were some months identified which might have outliers or undocumented events. To find out those events, we would need the assistance and inputs of the airline account managers. However, due to lack of time and resources, we was not able to carry out this step to check for historical and future events, as well as promotion plans of the airlines with our airline account managers. Furthermore, there may be a need to check with airlines directly especially if such information is not accessible or known to the account managers. Thus, it may even take a longer time for airlines to reply. There is also the possibility that airlines may not be willing to share due to confidential business issues.

Acknowledgement. This paper is a combination of work done by the faculty members and one of the analytics projects done the student in SIM University.

References

1. Bermúdez, J.D., Segura, J.V., Vercher, E.: Holt-winters forecasting: an alternative formulation applied to UK air passenger data. J. Appl. Stat. **34**(9), 1075–1090 (2007)
2. Brons, M., Pels, E., Nijkamp, P., Rietveld, P.: Price elasticities of demand for passenger air travel: a meta-analysis. J. Air Transp. Manage. **8**(3), 165–175 (2002)
3. Lai, S.L., Lu, W.L.: Impact analysis of September 11 on air travel demand in the USA. J. Air Transp. Manage. **11**(6), 455–458 (2005)
4. Ma, N.L., Choy, M., Cheong, M.: Uncovering interesting business insights through the use of data analytics in airport operation: an empirical study. In: Annual SRII Global Conference 2012, San Jose, USA (2012)
5. Profillidis, V., Botzoris, G.: Air passenger transport and economic activity. J. Air Transp. Manage. **49**, 23–27 (2015)
6. Tan, R.: Econometric forecasting. ANL302e Selected Topics in Regression Study Guide – Study Unit 4. SIM University, Singapore (2014)
7. Tsui, W.H.K., Fung, M.K.Y.: Analysing passenger network changes: the case of Hong Kong. J. Air Transp. Manage. **50**, 1–11 (2016)
8. Tsui, W.H.K., Balli, H.O., Gilbey, A., Gow, H.: Forecasting of Hong Kong airport's passenger throughput. Tour. Manag. **42**, 62–76 (2014)

Co-location Rules Discovery Process Focused on Reference Spatial Features Using Decision Tree Learning

Giovanni Daián Rottoli[1,2,3], Hernán Merlino[3],
and Ramón García-Martinez[3,4(✉)]

[1] Computer Sciences, National University of La Plata, La Plata, Argentina
gd.rottoli@gmail.com
[2] National Technological University, Buenos Aires, Argentina
[3] Information Systems Research Group,
National University of Lanús, Remedios de Escalada, Argentina
hmerlino@gmail.com, rgml960@yahoo.com
[4] Scientific Research Commission - CIC, Buenos Aires, Argentina

Abstract. The co-location discovery process serves to find subsets of spatial features frequently located together. Many algorithms and methods have been designed in recent years; however, finding this kind of patterns around specific spatial features is a task in which the existing solutions provide incorrect results. Throughout this paper we propose a knowledge discovery process to find co-location patterns focused on reference features using decision tree learning algorithms on transactional data generated using maximal cliques. A validation test of this process is provided.

Keywords: Co-location patterns · Spatial data mining · Decision trees algorithms · Maximal cliques · Knowledge discovery process

1 Introduction

Given a collection of boolean spatial features (also known as spatial events), the co-location pattern discovery process finds the subset of features frequently located together [1]. Some examples of this kind of relationships are symbiotic species, and public service buildings frequently built together, like hospitals and pharmacies [2]. Many algorithms and methods have been proposed for co-location pattern discovery based on association analysis. These algorithms generate transactional data from spatial objects neighborhoods and, based on that, they can be categorized into two classes: (i) transaction-free algorithms, which exploit the association analysis algorithm internally, e.g., the Aprori-like algorithms [3], but none of them generates or uses a transaction-type dataset externally; and (ii), transaction-based algorithms, which exploit association analysis methods after explicitly generating a transaction-type dataset. [1, 4, 5] In both options, it is necessary to choose a model to generate the transactional data. There are three different approaches: [1, 5, 6]

© Springer International Publishing AG 2017
S. Benferhat et al. (Eds.): IEA/AIE 2017, Part I, LNAI 10350, pp. 221–226, 2017.
DOI: 10.1007/978-3-319-60042-0_25

- **Window-Centric Model**: in a space discretized by a uniform grid, windows of size W can be enumerated. Each window corresponds to a transaction that contains a subset of spatial features related to the spatial instances found on the window.
- **Event-Centric Model**: used to find subsets of spatial features likely to occur in a neighborhood around instances of given subsets of event types.
- **Reference Feature-Centric Model**: the transactions are created by "materializing" the neighborhood of the instances of the reference spatial feature.

Nowadays, the spatial datasets are collected for a particular problem domain and, because of that, there is a spatial feature more relevant than the others. In this case, it is appropriate to select a Reference Feature-Centric Model for the generation of transactional data. However, two problems arise: all the applications and algorithms listed in previous works use an Event-Centric Model. Some examples of these publications are [1–14]. On the other hand, the transactional data generated using a Reference Feature-Centric Model may be incorrect and incomplete [5].

This paper is organized as follows: In Sect. 2, a problem derived from the analysis of the state-of-the-art is presented. In Sect. 3, we present a Knowledge Discovery Process to solve that problem. In Sect. 4, experimental results are presented. Finally, conclusions derived from the research are outlined in Sect. 5.

2 Problem Definition

When facing a co-location discovery problem, if there are many boolean spatial features to be considered for co-location pattern discovery, the Event-Centric Model may be expensive in terms of time and resources. With the presence of a spatial feature that is interesting in a particular problem domain, using a Reference Feature-Centric Model is a more suitable alternative. This model determines the neighborhoods in a special manner: first, a reference feature is selected and then, for each instance object of that feature, all spatial objects located within a pre-specified distance are selected, and transaction-type data generated [1, 5, 6]. This approach, however, cannot be used to generate correct or complete transactions, as it does not ensure that all objects in the transaction are neighbors; moreover, some neighborhoods may be lost [2, 5, 12]. For this reason, it is necessary to develop a solution that serves to discover correct and complete spatial co-location patterns around reference features. In this work, we develop a Knowledge Discovery Process [15, 16] to give a solution to this problem using an Event-Centric Model to generate transaction-based data, and induction of decision trees to generate co-location rules.

3 Proposed Solution

As mentioned before, this paper proposes a knowledge discovery process to find co-location relations between spatial features. This process serves to find correct relations around reference features without using a reference feature-centric model to generate transactional data. This work is based on the work of Kim et al. [5], proposing a transactional framework that uses an event-centric model to find co-location patterns using maximal cliques as a way to generate complete and correct transactions. In this context, Spatial Maximal Clique (SMC) is defined as follows [5]: Given a spatial dataset consisting of spatial objects, a spatial clique is a subset of the dataset whose elements have neighbor relationships with each other. A Spatial Maximal Clique is a Spatial Clique that is not part of the others. Using an SMC as a transaction generates two properties: all the elements in the SMC are neighbors with each other, ensuring the correctness of the method, and there is no neighbor relation that is excluded, ensuring the completeness in the transactional data. SMC seems to be a proper solution to solve the aforementioned problems, but finding a way of discovering co-location patterns around features relevant to the problem domain is necessary, because the classical association rules discovery algorithms used in the transactional-based approaches cannot be used to select a target feature. For this reason, a knowledge discovery process for co-location pattern discovery is proposed, focused on reference features, that uses an event-centric model for transaction-based data generation through spatial maximal cliques and using a Process of Discovery of Behavior Rules using Decision Tree Learning algorithms [15, 16]. Figure 1 shows the proposed process using BPMN [17].

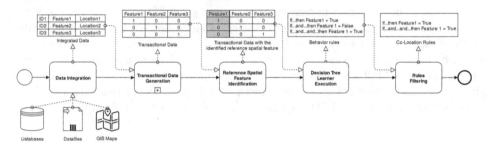

Fig. 1. Proposed co-location rules discovery process

The process takes a set of spatially referenced data as input, represented in different formats such as *inter alia*, plain text, databases, tables and geographic information system maps. These data are integrated to a table comprised of the object identifier, the spatial feature and the object location. Then, the integrated data are used to generate the transactional dataset. In this sub-process, as shown in Fig. 2, all the neighbor relationships are calculated by evaluating the distance between the spatial objects.

The distance function and the threshold will depend on the problem domain. Afterwards, finding all the maximal spatial cliques inside then neighboring graph is required to generate a transaction for each, in which the spatial features of each spatial object from that clique are presented. Once the transactional data are obtained, the reference spatial feature must be specified to find the co-location relations around it. That spatial feature will be used as the target attribute of a Decision Tree Learning algorithm, such as C4.5 [18] or Random Forest [19], using the rest of the attributes as input. A set of rules will be obtained from the generated decision tree in the last step as output. Due to the fact that the transactions have boolean values that show the presence or absence of the spatial features in the neighborhoods, it is necessary to filter the rules that show the presence of the reference spatial feature in the consequent.

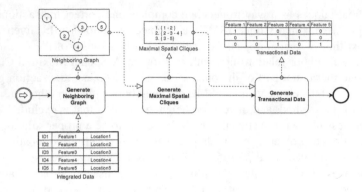

Fig. 2. Sub-process to generate transactional data

4 Concept Proof

To proof the concept, we create 10 synthetic sets of 500 points automatically generated and classified in 7 types, with random location in a small 2D space, and then used as input for our proposed process and for the selected algorithm: Co-Location Miner with a Reference Feature-Centric Model [1]. On the other hand, the euclidean distance function has been used to calculate the neighbouring graph using a constant threesome. The algorithm CLIQUES has been used for the generation of maximal spatial cliques because of its superior efficiency over other methods [20]. The software Tanagra [21] was used to run the selected TDIDT Learning Algorithm C4.5 [18]. After the execution

Table 1. Null hypothesis and alternative hypothesis considered in the Wilcoxon signed-rank test

H_0:	The number of correct co-location relationships discovered using the Co-Location Miner Algorithm is greater than or equal to the number of correct co-location relationships discovered using the proposed process
H_A:	The number of correct co-location relationships discovered using the proposed process is greater than the number of correct co-location relationships discovered using the Co-location Miner Algorithm

Table 2. Wilcoxon signed-rank test execution, sorted by the absolute value of the differences.

Set	Proposed process	Co-location miner algorithm.	Absolute value of the differences	Rank
7	3	3	0	-
8	2	1	1	2
9	2	1	1	2
10	5	4	1	2
1	3	1	2	5
2	3	1	2	5
5	4	2	2	5
4	4	1	3	7
3	6	2	4	8.5
6	7	3	4	8.5
Sum				45

of both methods, the co-location relationships obtained were evaluated to corroborate their correctness in order to determine how many correct relationships were found with each method.

To show that the proposed process can find a greater number of co-location relationships, the statistical Wilcoxon signed-rank test was used [22] considering the hypotheses shown in Table 1, obtaining a W-Value equals to 0 (see Table 2) that allows to reject the null hypothesis, confirming that the knowledge discovery process proposed in this paper serves to find a greater number of correct co-location relationships that the method using a reference feature-centric model.

5   Conclusion

This paper has described a knowledge discovery process that can be used to find correct and complete co-location patterns around reference spatial features. This process uses an event-centric model through maximal spatial cliques in order to generate transactional data from neighboring relationship between spatial data, and a decision tree learning algorithm, to obtain behavior rules that describe the neighborhoods that contain the spatial reference feature, an innovative method to achieve this goal. The proof of concept, by means of a non-parametrical statistical test, shows that the proposed process finds a greater number of correct co-location patterns than the methods that use a reference feature-centric model to generate transactional data.

The next planned step is to conduct validation proofs in the fields of accident prevention, civil defense and environmental determinants of diseases.

Acknowledgements. The research presented in this paper was partially funded by the PhD Scholarship Program to reinforce R+D+I areas (2016–2020) of the Technological National University, Research Project 80020160400001LA of National University of Lanús, and PIO CONICET-UNLa 22420160100032CO of National Research Council of Science and Technology (CONICET), Argentina. The authors also want to extend their gratitude to Kevin-Mark Bozell Poudereux for proofreading the translation.

References

1. Shekhar, S., Huang, Y.: Discovering spatial co-location patterns: a summary of results. In: Jensen, C.S., Schneider, M., Seeger, B., Tsotras, V.J. (eds.) SSTD 2001. LNCS, vol. 2121, pp. 236–256. Springer, Heidelberg (2001). doi:10.1007/3-540-47724-1_13
2. Yu, W.: Spatial co-location pattern mining for location-based services in road networks. Expert Syst. Appl. **46**, 324–335 (2016)
3. Agrawal, R., Srikant, R.: Fast algorithms for mining association rules. In: Proceedings of the 20th International Conference on Very Large Data Bases, VLDB, vol. 1215, pp. 487–499 (1994)
4. Shekhar, S., Evans, M.R., Kang, J.M., Mohan, P.: Identifying patterns in spatial information: a survey of methods. Wiley Interdisc. Rev. Data Min. Knowl. Discov. **1**(3), 193–214 (2011)

5. Kim, S.K., Lee, J.H., Ryu, K.H., Kim, U.: A framework of spatial co-location pattern mining for ubiquitous GIS. Multimedia Tools Appl. **71**(1), 199–218 (2014)
6. Xiong, H., Shekhar, S., Huang, Y., Kumar, V., Ma, X., Yoo, J.S.: A framework for discovering co-location patterns in data sets with extended spatial objects. In: SDM, pp. 78–89 (2004)
7. Huang, Y., Xiong, H., Shekhar, S., Pei, J.: Mining confident co-location rules without a support threshold. In: Proceedings of the 2003 ACM Symposium on Applied Computing, pp. 497–501. ACM (2003)
8. Huang, Y., Pei, J., Xiong, H.: Mining co-location patterns with rare events from spatial data sets. Geoinformatica **10**(3), 239–260 (2006)
9. Yoo, J.S., Shekhar, S.: A joinless approach for mining spatial colocation patterns. IEEE Trans. Knowl. Data Eng. **18**(10), 1323–1337 (2006)
10. Celik, M., Kang, J.M., Shekhar, S.: Zonal co-location pattern discovery with dynamic parameters. In: Seventh IEEE International Conference on Data Mining 2007, ICDM 2007, pp. 433–438. IEEE (2007)
11. Eick, C.F., Parmar, R., Ding, W., Stepinski, T.F., Nicot, J.P.: Finding regional co-location patterns for sets of continuous variables in spatial datasets. In: Proceedings of the 16th ACM SIGSPATIAL International Conference on Advances in Geographic Information Systems, p. 30. ACM (2008)
12. Adilmagambetov, A., Zaiane, O.R., Osornio-Vargas, A.: Discovering co-location patterns in datasets with extended spatial objects. In: Data Warehousing and Knowledge Discovery, pp. 84–96. Springer, Heidelberg (2013)
13. Venkatesan, M., Thangavelu, A., Prabhavathy, P.: Event centric modeling approach in colocation pattern analysis from spatial data. arXiv preprint arXiv:1109.1144 (2011)
14. Yoo, J.S., Shekhar, S., Celik, M.: A join-less approach for co-location pattern mining: a summary of results. In: Fifth IEEE International Conference on Data Mining, pp. 813–816. IEEE (2005)
15. García-Martínez, R., Britos, P., Rodríguez, D.: Information mining processes based on intelligent systems. In: Ali, M., Bosse, T., Hindriks, K.V., Hoogendoorn, M., Jonker, C.M., Treur, J. (eds.) IEA/AIE 2013. LNCS, vol. 7906, pp. 402–410. Springer, Heidelberg (2013). doi:10.1007/978-3-642-38577-3_41
16. Martins, S., Pesado, P., García-Martínez, R.: Intelligent systems in modeling phase of information mining development process. In: Fujita, H., Ali, M., Selamat, A., Sasaki, J., Kurematsu, M. (eds.) IEA/AIE 2016. LNCS, vol. 9799, pp. 3–15. Springer, Cham (2016)
17. Silver, B.: BPMN Method and Style, with BPMN Implementer's Guide: A Structured Approach for Business Process Modeling and Implementation Using BPMN 2.0, p. 450. Cody-Cassidy Press, Aptos (2011)
18. Quinlan, J.R.: C4.5: programs for machine learning (1993)
19. Ho, T.K.: The random subspace method for constructing decision forests. IEEE Trans. Pattern Anal. Mach. Intell. **20**(8), 832–844 (1998)
20. Tomita, E., Tanaka, A., Takahashi, H.: The worst-case time complexity for generating all maximal cliques and computational experiments. Theoret. Comput. Sci. **363**(1), 28–42 (2006)
21. Rakotomalala, R.: TANAGRA: a free software for research and academic purposes. In: Proceedings of EGC, vol. 2, pp. 697–702 (2005)
22. Wilcoxon, F.: Individual comparisons by ranking methods. Biometrics Bull. **1**(6), 80–83 (1945)

Virtual Career Advisor System with an Artificial Neural Network

Tracey John and Dwaine Clarke[✉]

University of the West Indies, Bridgetown, Barbados
tracey.john@mycavehill.uwi.edu, declarke@declarke.net

Abstract. We introduce the Dolphin system, a novel virtual career advisor system that implements artificial neural networks trained on student data to provide students with career advice. The Dolphin system's Experiences-to-Careers advisor uses an artificial neural network and takes as input a student's course experience ratings and returns as output a career ranking. We present our methods to train, validate and test the Experiences-to-Careers advisor's artificial neural network. We have implemented and deployed the Experiences-to-Careers advisor. We surveyed 39 students who used the Experiences-to-Careers advisor to receive career advice. Of these students, 5 students (12.8%) indicated that they prefer the Experiences-to-Careers advisor over a human advisor, 9 students (23.1%) indicated that they prefer a human advisor over the Experiences-to-Careers advisor and 25 students (64.1%) indicated that they prefer the Experiences-to-Careers advisor along with a human advisor. Of the 76.9% of the students who prefer the Experiences-to-Careers advisor over or along with a human advisor, a common reason for the students' choice is that the Experiences-to-Careers advisor provides a perspective different from that of a human advisor.

Keywords: Artificial intelligence · Artificial neural networks · Back-propagation learning algorithm · Machine learning · Virtual career advisor system

1 Introduction

A student at a university is typically assigned an advisor who is a faculty member that the student can contact to receive advice on which careers would be the best fit for the set of courses the student has taken or may be interested in taking. Unfortunately, in a department where the student to faculty ratio is very high, an advisor may not be able to devote as much time to each of his advisees as the advisor would like.

We introduce the Dolphin system, a novel virtual career advisor system that implements artificial neural networks (ANNs) trained on student data to provide students with career advice. We use ANNs for the Dolphin system as an ANN uses the regularity (patterns) in the data that the ANN has learned in training to predict the output for new input. The Dolphin system's Experiences-to-Careers

© Springer International Publishing AG 2017
S. Benferhat et al. (Eds.): IEA/AIE 2017, Part I, LNAI 10350, pp. 227–234, 2017.
DOI: 10.1007/978-3-319-60042-0_26

advisor uses an artificial neural network and takes as input a student's course experience ratings and returns as output a career ranking. The main objectives of the Dolphin system are to introduce a system that allows a student to receive satisfactory career advice and to introduce a system with which a student can interact any time the need arises on any device the student uses.

Importantly, the student data that the Dolphin system uses, a student's course experience ratings and career ranking, is different from the student's grades. For example, a student may earn an A in a course but not enjoy the course. At a university, student grades are under the authority of the university's registrar office. The university may not give access to student grades or allow student grades to be used to develop a virtual advisor system because of security and privacy concerns. The Dolphin system uses student data that a university does not typically collect to provide students with career advice.

The main contributions of this paper include:

- a novel virtual career advisor system, the Dolphin system, that implements artificial neural networks (ANNs) trained on student data to provide students with career advice.
- the data that we use for the Dolphin system's Experiences-to-Careers advisor.
- the design of the Dolphin system's Experiences-to-Careers advisor.
- the methods that we use to validate and test the Dolphin system's Experiences-to-Careers advisor's artificial neural network.
- results showing that the majority of students who used the Experiences-to-Careers advisor indicated that they would use the Experiences-to-Careers advisor over or along with a human advisor. Of these students, a common reason for the students' choice is that the Experiences-to-Careers advisor provides a perspective different from that of a human advisor.

2   Design

2.1   Data

We conducted this research among Computer Science students. The Computer Science program at the university at which we conducted this research is a three-year program with first year students generally at Level I, second year students generally at Level II and final year students generally at Level III.

We use an anonymous, paper survey to survey students for data to train, validate and test the Dolphin system's Experiences-to-Careers advisor's artificial neural network. We survey a set of students to indicate the courses the student has taken or is taking and rate each of the courses the student has taken/is taking with the student's course experience rating according to the student's level of enjoyment of the course with (5) as the highest rating and (1) as the lowest rating. These ratings form the student's course experience ratings.

We identify a list of popular Computer Science careers based on the courses the university offers and the employment opportunities available to students:

Computer Programmer/Software Engineer, Network Engineer, System Administrator, University Faculty Member and Web Developer. We also survey the set of students to each rank these careers in the order in which the student is most interested with (5) for the career in which the student is most interested and (1) for the career in which the student is least interested (careers are listed in alphabetical order). This ranking forms the student's career ranking.

We randomly separate the set of students into three subsets: a training set, a validation set and a test set. The training set is used to train configurations of the Experiences-to-Careers advisor's ANN, the validation set is used to select a configuration of the advisor's ANN and the test set is used to evaluate the performance of the selected ANN configuration.

The students on which we conducted this survey are typically at Level III. Thus, the Dolphin system uses data typically from final year students to provide students at all stages in the degree program with career advice.

2.2   Experiences-to-Careers Advisor Artificial Neural Network

ANN Input. Figure 1 presents an example of the representation of a student's course experience ratings that is used as input to the Experiences-to-Careers advisor's ANN during training, validation, testing and deployment. If the student did not take a course, zero is used as the course experience rating for this course. In the example in Fig. 1, the student highly enjoyed/enjoys the course COMP1115 and did not take the course COMP1125.

ANN Output. Figure 2 presents an example of the representation of a career ranking that is used as the Experiences-to-Careers advisor's ANN's output during training. In the example in Fig. 2, Network Engineer is ranked highest and University Faculty Member is ranked lowest.

Course	COMP1105	COMP1115	COMP1125	COMP1130	COMP2105
Course Experience Rating	4	5	0	0	5

Fig. 1. Example of the representation of a student's course experience ratings that is used as input to the Experiences-to-Careers advisor's ANN during training, validation, testing and deployment.

Career	Computer Programmer/ Software Engineer	Network Engineer	System Administrator	University Faculty Member	Web Developer
Rank	4	5	2	1	3

Fig. 2. Example of the representation of a career ranking that is used as the Experiences-to-Careers advisor's ANN's output during training.

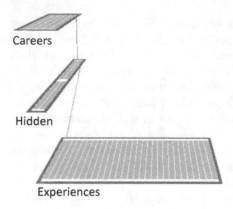

Fig. 3. Experiences-to-Careers advisor's Artificial Neural Network (ANN).

ANN Training and Validation. Figure 3 illustrates the ANN that we config-
ure for the Experiences-to-Careers advisor in the Dolphin system. Let numCourses
be the number of courses. The ANN's input layer, Experiences, is a numCourses
by 1 layer. We use an ANN with one hidden layer. Let numCareers be the number
of careers. The ANN's output layer, Careers, is a numCareers by 1 layer. The ANN
is a feed-forward artificial neural network using the back-propagation learning
algorithm. We use configurations with different settings for learning rate, number of nodes in the hidden layer, and number of epochs used during training for
the ANN. During training, the learning rate determines the rate at which the
ANN's weights are changed and an epoch is an iteration of the ANN through all
of the students in the training set.

For each configuration of learning rate, number of nodes in the hidden layer,
and number of epochs used during training, we train the ANN using the training
set with the input as the training set's students' course experience ratings and
the output as the corresponding career rankings. For each configuration, after
training the ANN with the configuration, we then run a validation program on
the trained ANN using the validation set. For each student in the validation set,
the validation program determines the ANN's values for each of the careers using
the student's course experience ratings as input to the ANN. For each career, the
ANN returns a value between 0 and 1. The validation program determines the
ANN's ranking of the careers by ranking the careers according to the ANN values.
For each career, the validation program then calculates the Squared Validation
Error (SVE) = (ANN's career rank - student's career rank)^2. For each student
in the validation set, the validation program then calculates the student's Mean
Squared Validation Error (MSVE) Per Career = sum of the Squared Validation
Errors of the careers/numCareers. After determining the MSVE Per Career of
each of the students in the validation set, the validation program then calculates
the ANN's configuration's Mean Squared Validation Error (MSVE) = sum of the
MSVE Per Careers of the students in the validation set/number of students in
the validation set. We note that, also, MSVE = sum of all of the SVEs of the

careers of the students in the validation set/(numCareers x number of students in the validation set).

After determining the MSVE for each configuration of the ANN, we select the configuration with the best validation result which is the configuration with the lowest MSVE. We denote the ANN with this configuration as ANN_α.

ANN Testing. After ANN training and validation, we then run a test program on ANN_α using the test set to evaluate the performance of the ANN. The test program calculates the Mean Squared Validation Error (MSVE) using the test set.

ANN Deployment. When deployed, the Dolphin system's Experiences-to-Careers advisor uses its ANN_α to take as input a student's course experience ratings and return as output the ANN values for each of the careers. For each career, the ANN returns a value between 0 and 1. The Experiences-to-Careers advisor determines the ANN's ranking of careers by ranking the careers according to the ANN values.

2.3   Web Interface

The Dolphin system's user interface is a web interface. A student registers an account with the Dolphin system with a username and password and logs into the student's account with the student's username and password. Other methods of access control [1,2] and other methods of authentication, such as multi-factor authentication, can also be used in the Dolphin system.

When the student logs in to the Dolphin system, the student is presented with the homepage and a navigation bar that includes the Experiences-to-Careers advisor page. The Dolphin system's Experiences-to-Careers advisor page allows a student to rate each of the courses the student has taken/is taking with the student's course experience rating with (5) as the highest rating and (1) as the lowest rating using a dropdown select menu. If the student did not take a course, the student leaves the course's dropdown menu option as the default, N/A. When the student submits the student's course experience ratings, the Experiences-to-Careers advisor page returns the career ranking at the top of the page. The Experiences-to-Careers advisor page presents the careers to the student in the order of the Experiences-to-Careers advisor's ANN's ranking of careers with the highest ranked career at the top, as well as the ANN's rank and the ANN's activations for each of the careers. The student can update the student's course experience ratings below the career ranking and resubmit the student's new course experience ratings to examine possible changes in the career ranking.

3   Implementation

We surveyed a set of 65 students for data to train, validate and test the Experiences-to-Careers advisor's ANN (cf. Sect. 2.1). We then randomly separated this set of students into three subsets: a training set, a validation set and a test set. The validation set and test set are each approximately 15% of the students. Thus, the training set consists of 45 students, the validation set consists of 10 students and the test set consists of 10 students.

In the Dolphin system, numCourses = 29 and numCareers = 5. Thus, the Experiences-to-Careers advisor's ANN's input layer is a 29 by 1 layer and its output layer is a 5 by 1 layer.

We use the emergent neural network simulator [3] to implement the ANN in the Experiences-to-Careers advisor. When the ANN is configured with learning rate = 0.01, hidden layer = 2 by 2, epochs = 1, the ANN has the best (lowest) validation result with MSVE = 2.32. Thus, we use this configuration as ANN_α's configuration. We note that Fig. 3 presents an image of the ANN with this configuration. When we ran the test program on ANN_α using the test set to evaluate the performance of the ANN, the result was MSVE = 2.12.

4   Results

We use an anonymous, paper survey to survey a set of 39 students to gather their feedback on the Dolphin system after they used the Dolphin system to receive career advice. We conducted this survey on students at Level II and Level III. None of the students on which we conducted this survey are among the students whose data we use to train, validate and test the Dolphin system's Experiences-to-Careers advisor's artificial neural network.

We asked students to circle the number that corresponds to the student's level of agreement with a statement on System Advice. Students were presented with the following options for which they were to circle the associated number:

- Strongly Disagree: 1
- Disagree: 2
- Neutral: 3
- Agree: 4
- Strongly Agree: 5

We received responses from 38 students. Table 1 presents the statement on System Advice and the statistics for the statement. Based on these results, students are typically satisfied with the career ranking the Experiences-to-Careers advisor gives to the student. We believe that the results presented in Table 1 validate our design of the Experiences-to-Careers advisor, presented in Sect. 2.

To compare the Experiences-to-Careers advisor with a human advisor, we asked students to circle one option from the following statements:

Table 1. Statistics for the results on system advice.

	Number of responses	Mode	Average	Std. Dev.
I am satisfied with the career ranking the Experiences-to-Careers Advisor gives me.	38	4	3.8	0.9

Table 2. Statistics for the results on the Experiences-to-Careers Advisor vs. a human advisor.

	Number of students	Percentage of students
a. I prefer the Experiences-to-Careers Advisor over a human advisor.	5	12.8%
b. I prefer a human advisor over the Experiences-to-Careers Advisor.	9	23.1%
c. I prefer the Experiences-to-Careers Advisor along with a human advisor.	25	64.1%
	Total = 39 students	

- a. I prefer the Experiences-to-Careers Advisor over a human advisor.
- b. I prefer a human advisor over the Experiences-to-Careers Advisor.
- c. I prefer the Experiences-to-Careers Advisor along with a human advisor.

We received responses from 39 students. Table 2 presents the statistics for each statement.

We also asked students to briefly explain the reason for the student's choice.

- Of the 5 students (12.8%) who circled statement a, common reasons for the students' choice were that:
  - the Experiences-to-Careers advisor gives satisfactory results.
  - the Experiences-to-Careers advisor is able to give a career ranking based on a student's course experience ratings.
  - the Experiences-to-Careers advisor is convenient/accessible anytime.
- Of the 9 students (23.1%) who circled statement b, common reasons for the students' choice were that:
  - a human advisor would be able to give more insight about the career advice that the human advisor recommends.
  - a human advisor would be able to listen to and respond to a student's queries.
- Of the 25 students (64.1%) who circled statement c, common reasons for the students' choice were that:
  - the Experiences-to-Careers advisor gives a perspective different from that of a human advisor.
  - using both the Experiences-to-Careers advisor and the human advisor can be beneficial as each advisor has its advantages.
  - students prefer to receive advice from both advisors.

In Table 2, 76.9% of the students prefer the Experiences-to-Careers advisor over or along with a human advisor. We believe that the results presented in Table 2 also validate our design of the Experiences-to-Careers advisor, presented in Sect. 2.

5   Related Work

MASACAD (Multi-Agent System for ACademic ADvising) [4] incorporates an ANN to offer university Computer Science students academic advice using a representation of students' grades as part of the input to the ANN. Whereas the MASACAD system used an ANN to determine academic advice for a student, the Dolphin system's Experiences-to-Careers advisor uses an ANN to determine career advice for a student. Importantly, the Dolphin system does not use student grades because a university may not give access to student grades or allow student grades to be used to develop a virtual advisor system because of security and privacy concerns. The Dolphin system uses student data that a university does not typically collect to provide students with career advice. We believe that the design of the Dolphin system's Experiences-to-Careers advisor and the methods that we use to validate and test the Dolphin system's Experiences-to-Careers advisor's artificial neural network are also novel.

6   Conclusion

We have introduced the Dolphin system, a novel virtual career advisor system that implements artificial neural networks (ANNs) trained on student data to provide students with career advice. After the Dolphin system was deployed, feedback from students who used the system to receive career advice was typically positive with the majority of students indicating that they would use the Experiences-to-Careers advisor over or along with a human advisor.

References

1. Clarke, D.: Design and implementation of a public key-based group collaboration system. Comput. Commun. **34**(3), 407–422 (2011)
2. Clarke, D.: Hybrid certificate closure-chain discovery public key system. Int. J. Comput. Sci. Eng. **9**(4), 312–324 (2014)
3. Emergent Neural Network Simulator. https://grey.colorado.edu/emergent/index.php
4. Hamdi, M.S.: MASACAD: a multi-agent approach to information customization for the purpose of academic advising of students. Appl. Soft Comput. **7**(3), 746–771 (2007)

Implicit Knowledge Extraction
and Structuration from Electrical Diagrams

Ikram Chraibi Kaadoud[1,2,3,4]([✉]), Nicolas Rougier[2,3,4]([✉]),
and Frederic Alexandre[2,3,4]([✉])

[1] Algo'Tech Informatique, Technopole Izarbel, Bidart, France
[2] INRIA Bordeaux Sud-Ouest, Talence, France
{ikram.chraibi-kaadoud,nicolas.rougier,frederic.alexandre}@inria.fr
[3] LaBRI, UMR 5800, CNRS, Talence, France
[4] IMN, UMR 5293, CNRS, U Bordeaux, Bordeaux, France

Abstract. The electrical domain, either domestic or industrial, benefits
from a huge set of well-defined norms at both the national and international levels. However and surprisingly enough, there is no such norm
regarding the actual conception and structuration of electrical diagrams,
even though the basic symbols and notations remain the same. Each
company is actually free to design such diagram relative to its own experience, expertise and know-how. The difficulty is that such diagrams,
which are most of the time materialized as a PDF booklet, do not reflect
this implicit knowledge. In this paper, we introduce our work on the
extraction and the structuration of such knowledge using ad-hoc graph
and text analysis as well as clustering techniques. Starting from a set of
raw documents, we propose an end-to-end solution that offers a company
dependent structured view, of any electrical diagram.

Keywords: Knowledge extraction · Knowledge representation · Hierarchical clustering · Knowledge structuration · Electrical diagrams

1 Introduction

The electrical domain, either domestic or industrial, benefits from a huge set of
well defined norms at both the national and international levels. These norms
have to be enforced when designing a new electrical diagram and during the
actual physical construction of the circuit. In that regards, electrical workers
have generally to deal with a booklet describing the overall circuit splitted into
several subparts, each one fitting on a regular A4 sheet paper. This arbitrary
and constrained segmentation of the whole diagram implies a graph structure
that does not follow the logical structure of the underlying object. It is indeed
quite similar to the decomposition of an image into pixels sharing no similarities with the inner structure of the image. The problem we are interested in
this paper is to find original methods for discovering the implicit structure of
electrical diagrams using the PDF description. In this context, we are working

© Springer International Publishing AG 2017
S. Benferhat et al. (Eds.): IEA/AIE 2017, Part I, LNAI 10350, pp. 235–241, 2017.
DOI: 10.1007/978-3-319-60042-0_27

with a software company, Algo'Tech Informatique, that provides a set of specialized tools for the design of electrical diagrams. These tools are able to provide a synthetic view of any electrical diagram and to produce the corresponding booklet. To do so, whenever Algo'Tech Informatique has a new customer, it gets its existing electrical diagrams to analyse them and then adapt the database and the softwares according them. Hence, Algo'Tech informatique experts face two challenges: the first one is to understand the reasoning and planning process of electrical diagrams by their customers in order to formalize it. The second challenge is to make the customer's experts explain their work by supporting them during the exploration of their own habits and knowledge. Besides, since each customer designs freely diagrams according its own experience, expertise and know-how, diagrams do not reflect the implicit knowledge. And yet this knowledge is important, since it holds the footprint of the customers. These ones are indeed attached to their way of drawing and disposing electrical components inside a circuit (they are able to recognize the work of their company whenever they see it) and they are attached to continue to have it once they used Algo'Tech Informatique softwares. So, to extract the "footprints", Algo'Tech Informatique has to review the internal arrangement of electrical components into each page of each electrical diagram and to compare the arrangements between them to find similarities. This work results from an extensive and non-automated collaboration between the software company and the customer. It is also time-consuming, informal (and not strictly replicable) and complex (documents mix texts and diagrams) in the sense that it results from non constrained interviews between humans. Consequently, we aim for an automatic knowledge extraction process specific to a customer and based on its past projects (generally materialized as a restricted set of scanned PDF booklets).

2   Review of Existing Work

2.1   Technical Documents Analysis

The capitalization of the knowledge of technical documents is a real problem in the industry. From one hand, the field of analysis of technical documents, which has been investigated for several years in many kinds of domains is mostly focused on image analysis and recognition [1]. On the other hand, there is a great deal of work in the field of document analysis, including PDFs, in order to retrieve the text content, but again, that leaves aside the graphical content [2]. However in the domain of technical diagrams, both of these elements, text content and image content, are important for the understanding and the interpretation of documents. Another neglected field is the diagram interpretation one. The identification of the structure in a diagram, the semantics of its constituents and their relationship, is almost always domain-specific which make global approach difficult. But, recently, [3] focuses on the problem of diagram interpretation and reasoning by exploiting a deep learning algorithm that learns on a basis of 5,000 diagrams, one order of magnitude bigger than our 160 PDF booklets that we are currently analysing (plus the 500 ones that we would like to test). These reasons makes us to look for an innovative solution to analyse small volume of electrical diagrams, without using standard methods.

2.2 Expertise Extraction

Another problem that industry faces is the expertise capitalization. Defined as an intellectual capital resulting from the knowledge and the experience from the collaborators and/or the experts, the expertise is represented implicitly through several documents. Using many different methods, companies try to collect and disseminate such expertise to all the employees, so that they can take advantage from it. But even then, the challenge is still complex because of the experts mental representation of their work. Indeed [4] confirmed the existence of difference between senior experts and beginner experts mental representation. The first ones have a conceptualization rather of gist-type, more fuzzy, conceptual, intuitive, using prototypes and high level concepts. In the opposite, beginner experts have a rather verbatim-type conceptualization, which means detailed, analytical, controlled, using low-level concepts.

There is thus different ways to describe diagrams: through the explicit structured data and through the implicit structure or mental representation of the experts. In the following section, we describe the knowledge extraction of raw data using the titles and text into electrical diagrams (Fig. 1, label A, B, C). From this point, we will refer to Algo'Tech Informatique experts as experts, and we will precise in other cases.

3 Raw Data: Electrical Diagrams in PDFs and DXFs Files

Companies that draw electrical diagrams have to deal mostly with two type of files: the PDF ones, the most commonly used type, and the Autodesk's Drawing Exchange Format (DXF). PDFs mix texts and diagrams and possess their own local structure: Usually the PDF document has a title, a list of pages, and thus, the circuit that goes through many pages, as in Fig. 1. In each folio, there are four important elements: its title, its number (different from the page number), the electrical components (and voltage indications) and its indication to other folios. These last ones are the link that make the rebuild of the whole diagram possible. A DXF file, in the other hand, is a Computer-aided design (CAD) data file that enables data interoperability between many CAD softwares. It is considered an open access format because it is basically an ASCII file that can be read by text editors. Considered as an ASCII translation of a drawing file, a DXF file, allow, by analysing the blocks and their attributes, to extract data and meta-data related to electrical components symbols, in particular coordinates, attributes and block name. It permits thus to avoid computer vision or image recognition on the PDF files. Hence, since PDF booklets give a graphical view of

electrical diagrams using symbols and texts, and DXF files contain more technical data about the layout of the diagram into pages, the alliance of their analysis
enables a quasi-complete analysis of electrical diagram and a more exhaustive
interpretation.

4   1st Approach: From Raw Data to Concepts

We present in this subsection a first approach that allow us to confirm hypothe-
sise regarding our data before to go further: for a given customer, just by studying
his electrical diagrams (PDF mainly), it is possible to put in light a structure
and dominant concepts that has a business meaning for him. We wanted to get
a global view of each electrical diagram to get a global idea about the structure.
For that, we transformed each diagram into graphs by mimicking the expert's
reasoning. We used the following process: for each folio of each diagram, we use
the folio's number (Fig. 1, label B) as the id of a node and the related folio's title
(Fig. 1, label A) as the label of that node. Then, we use the folio's indication
(Fig. 1, label C) to establish links between nodes. We thus manage to transform a
linear booklet of many pages, into one single representation holding in one sheet.
This first step make us realize redundancy in folios names, so we extracted all
the titles all booklets combined, to analyze them and compute an intersection
between them. We obtain thus a set of common words to all booklets that we
will refer to as the concepts of the customer from this point. These words were
used as a replacement for the nodes labels, which results in an homogenized set
of graphs. Finally, all the simplified graphs were merged into one global graph
of concepts by aggregating links and nodes gradually. We thus, obtain a single

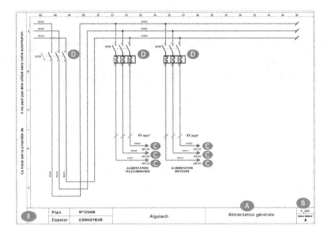

Fig. 1. The organisation and content of a folio: A - the folio's title, B - the folio's
number, C - the folio's indications, D - the electrical components, E - the caption
block, a frame surrounding the diagram. Sequences of electrical components according
the wiring cables in this folio are: Q100, Q101 and Q100, Q102.

view of the customer business logic grouping all the concepts that the customer have already used in his previous electrical diagrams, and all the possible relations between these concepts. The final graph is, hence, a representation of the knowledge of the customer. Through this preliminary work, we manage to do 2 things: First, we managed to group folios according their content. Indeed, by doing the reverse path (from the abstract view to the raw data), it is possible to group and analyse folios according to the concept they belong to. This capacity to group folios according to the concept will be used for the next section. Second, we structured raw data into a view of the customer's knowledge that put in light concepts and relations between them. By doing this, we confirm the existence of redundancy in the work or electrical diagrams designers for a given designer, at least at the global level. In the next section, we chose to focus on the layout of electrical components (Fig. 1, label D) into folios, in order to confirm the existence of redundancy, and by extend a footprint in the drawing.

5 2nd Approach: Footprint Extraction Using Datamining

This second approach is based on a second hypothesis: each electrical diagram is an instanciation of the customer knowledge and by studying it, it is possible to extract it. We thus based our work on the work of [5] and more recently [6], that both defined the KDD process as 3 steps: a pre-processing step, a data mining step and a post-processing step.

Preprocessing. Two treatments are done: the creation of data sets and their transformation. Considered data are sequences: a set of electrical components extracted from each folio and ordered according their growing x, y coordinates. We created two data sets: the first one group sequences according the concept they belong to, whereas the second gather together all sequences independently of the concepts they belong to. Finally, each sequence is translated into a binary vector of 25 units (since 25 families of electrical components exists according experts), each indicating the presence or absence of a family into a folio.

Data mining. Once the data prepared, we applied a Hierarchical clustering (HC) method on the two sets in order, from one hand, to study and compare the clusters that appear, and from the other hand, to put in light the footprint into the sequences. We get inspired by the work of [7], who use the HC analysis to rebuild the grammar (set of rules and patterns) from sequences. For further technical details on this method, please refer to [8]. On each set of data, the algorithm uses the Jaccard distance and average linkage method as parameters, since it was the combination that shows the better Cophenetic correlation coefficient. For every sets and subsets, it results in a dendogram (the standard representation in HC) and a cluster-tree (a graph).

Post-processing. For every sets of vectors, each cluster obtained is described as a binary vector corresponding to the union of the binary vectors of the previous clusters. This work of identification of clusters makes possible the comparison between the clusters obtained with both data sets: Exception apart (folios which weren't plot at the expected location), all the cluster-trees of the first data set were found in the cluster-tree of the second data set. Thus, besides this approach allows to put in light particular cases or mistakes in an electrical diagram, it also shows that there is indeed recurrence and regularities into a customer's working way: it then confirms the existence of a footprint.

6   Discussion

In this paper, we exposed two approaches we developed for knowledge extraction and representation in the field of electrical diagrams: the first one creates a global view of the customer business logic using graphs, on the basis of extracted text. The second approach spells implicit knowledge out from the internal arrangements of all the folios electrical components, using clustering analysis. It detects and extracts patterns, that represent customers footprints, from data sets. These two approaches complement each other in order to give a view of the electrical diagrams that assist, improve and accelerate experts analysis. In a more global dimension, this work shows that each electrical diagram is an instantiation of the customer knowledge from which it is possible to reconstruct the expertise knowledge as well as habits of work. The study of such habits is still an ongoing work. In order to have the full picture, and to provide more assistance to the experts, we are currently studying the electrical components sequences according the wiring cables with the hypothesis that such sequences held more information about the working rules and habits for a given customer. To explore this, we propose a neural network approach in order to discover the "grammar" rules governing the sequence arrangement: the Elman model [7]. Our preliminary results indicate that it is possible to learn and to predict as long as the sequence length is not too large. Tests and analysis are still on going and alternatives, like other recurrent neural networks, are also considered. On the medium term, by improving the expertise analysis and by extending the tools that assist the designer in her or his work, we aim at showing that there is an implicit dimension in the planning of every electrical diagrams as it was shown in [9].

References

1. Antoine, D., Collin, S., Tombre, K.: Analysis of technical documents: the REDRAW system. In: Baird, H.S., Bunke, H., Yamamoto, K. (eds.) Structured Document Image Analysis, pp. 385–402. Springer, Heidelberg (1992). doi:10.1007/978-3-642-77281-8_18
2. Futrelle, R.P., Shao, M., Cieslik, C., Grimes, A.E.: Extraction, layout analysis and classification of diagrams in PDF documents. In: ICDAR, vol. 3 (2003)
3. Kembhavi, A., Salvato, M., Kolve, E., Seo, M., Hajishirzi, H., Farhadi, A.: A diagram is worth a dozen images (2016). arXiv preprint: arXiv:1603.07396
4. Aimé, X., Charlet, J.: IC: Ingénierie des Connaissances ou Ingénierie du Conformisme? In: 24émes Journées francophones d'Ingénierie des Connaissances (2013)
5. Fayyad, U., Piatetsky-Shapiro, G., Smyth, P.: From data mining to knowledge discovery in databases. AI Mag. **17**(3), 37 (1996)

6. Ramos, S., Figueiredo, V., Rodrigues, F., Pinheiro, R., Vale, Z.: Knowledge extraction from medium voltage load diagrams to support the definition of electrical tariffs. Eng. Intell. Syst. Electr. Eng. Commun. **15**(3), 143–149 (2007)
7. Servan-Schreiber, D., Cleeremans, A., McClelland, J.L.: Encoding sequential structure in simple recurrent networks. Technical report, DTIC Document (1989)
8. Hees, J.: SciPy Hierarchical Clustering and Dendrogram Tutorial, August 2015
9. Cleeremans, A., McClelland, J.L.: Learning the structure of event sequences. J. Exp. Psychol. Gen. **120**(3), 235 (1991)

An Energy-Aware Learning Agent for Power Management in Mobile Devices

Ismat Chaib Draa[✉], Emmanuelle Grislin-Le Strugeon, and Smail Niar

LAMIH-UMR CNRS 8201, University of Valenciennes,
59313 Valenciennes Cedex 9, France
{ismat.chaibdraa,emmanuelle.grislin,smail.niar}@univ-valenciennes.fr

Abstract. The optimization of the energy consumption in mobile devices can be performed on hardware and software components. For example, reducing the screen brightness or switching off GPS. The energy control must take into account both the current context and user habits, on the base of usage knowledge acquired from sensors and OS data records. The whole process of energy management then includes data collection, usage learning and analysis, decision-making and control of device components. To integrate these activities, we propose to use a software agent whose goal is to save the energy of the mobile device with the lowest effect on QoS.

Keywords: Energy consumption · Mobile device · Context-awareness · Embedded agent

1 Introduction

While awaiting new solutions to increase battery life, the automatic management of energy consumption is still crucial for mobile devices (see the survey in [7]). In previous studies we have showed the relevance of controlling the components of a device to save battery and the feasibility of a context classification to balance energy saving and user satisfaction (refer to [1]). We define the context both by the current state of the mobile device, including its active components, applications and parameters, and by its predicted state, especially regarding the user's short-term activity. This paper presents an agent approach to encapsulate these different works in a context-aware and learning software component. Our previous works are initially presented, followed by the agent-based proposition, some related works on the use of agents for energy saving in mobile devices and a conclusion.

2 Context-Aware Modeling for Energy Optimization

Our previous works [1] proposed techniques based on learning mechanisms to adjust the resource consumption according to the context of use, the predicted

© Springer International Publishing AG 2017
S. Benferhat et al. (Eds.): IEA/AIE 2017, Part I, LNAI 10350, pp. 242–245, 2017.
DOI: 10.1007/978-3-319-60042-0_28

running applications and the user's preferences. All of them are based on data collection from probes dedicated to the user's actions, the environmental context and the system state. The actions on the device are performed to control components, such as screen brightness, Wi-Fi, CPU, Bluetooth or GPS states. At first, we have studied the energy optimization effect of predicting short-term running applications. The applications are classified by a naive Bayesian classifier to predict CPU and Wi-Fi needs. The application launching sequences are predicted using a sequential pattern discovery algorithm. Simulation results show a potential gain of 30% in comparison to the advanced energy management provided by the Windows 8.1 OS. Then we focused on the screen brightness, one of the most power consuming components in a mobile device. Experimental results show a gain between 1 and 20%. However, the evaluation of the solution costs (CPU, RAM and power consumption) shows also the necessity to perform this learning activity off-line.

3   Proposition: Resource Management by a Software Agent

We propose to group these different energy optimizing techniques to be used by an overall software component. This component must be able: to collect data about the current context of the device; to create models of context and usage from the collected data and potential other information; to decide in run-time upon the adjustment actions about energy consumption; to perform actions on hardware and software components. These abilities can be designed as parts of an embedded software agent. Indeed, the agent-based approach offers a relevant paradigm to the modeling and the development of applications that show proactive, learning and interactive behaviors.

The agent's activity is composed of two parts depending on what can be embedded and what should be done remotely to avoid memory and processing

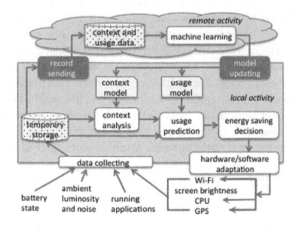

Fig. 1. The remote and local parts of the agent activity.

costs and overheads. The agent's local activity is a process that runs continuously. The agent collects data from its environment, analyzes the context and decides what resource optimization actions to perform on the basis of contexts and usage models (Fig. 1). Data are recorded in a temporary storage, awaiting to be sent to the remote learning unit. When the mobile device is connected to a power supply and the Wi-Fi is activated, the data can be sent to the learning unit to improve the existing models. The remote part of the agent's activity consists of learning behavior from the collected data to model both the applications needs (CPU, WiFi, etc.) and the user needs. Our aim is now to experiment and evaluate the relevance of the agent-based proposal, and especially the interaction between the local and remote parts of the agent.

4   Related Works

Much work is currently being done on energy management for mobile handsets, see the classification in [9] and the recent survey in [7]. Our work includes different strategies from the hardware-software category and from the pure software category. The approach is context-aware regarding the user's environment, the OS, sensors and wireless components states.

Agents are mainly used for energy saving in smart grids [10], wireless sensor networks or mobile ad-hoc networks [6], and building energy controls [4]. In these application fields, the agent-based solutions match the distributed nature of the encountered problems and the necessary interaction between autonomous entities. There are fewer studies about agents used for energy saving in mobile devices. In [3], agents perform computation off-loading: the applications that can migrate are implemented as mobile agents, which migrate to use the power of the cloud rather than the energy of the phone. Energy can also be negotiated by mobile agents representing seller or buyer devices in mobile grid. More generally collaborative mechanisms can enable sharing resources between co-located nodes [5]. An agent is used in [11] as a central unit to manage the power of non-CPU devices (accelerators, I/O controllers, etc.) at the OS level, instead of usual device drivers. The agent makes decisions based on information such as the device wakeup latency or power consumption, and whether a device has pending tasks. In these works, agents are used for their distribution, collaboration and decision-making characteristics. Our proposal is mainly based on the decision-making and learning abilities. An agent that can learn, can update its knowledge to adapt its behavior, e.g. to user's preferences [8]. This ability can be developed using data mining techniques, as in [2] where the authors propose to apply co-clustering to situation-awareness in the aim to improve task recommendation. Our proposal includes such techniques in a global approach of decision-making for energy saving.

5   Conclusion

In previous studies about energy saving on mobile devices [1], we have proposed technics based on learning mechanisms to adjust the resource consumption according to the context of use, the predicted running applications and the user's preferences. The agent-based approach aims at encapsulating the energy saving behaviour in a software able to adapt the software and/or hardware components configuration. The agent's decision to trigger saving actions is based on the mobile state, the environmental context and the user's current activity. To avoid inadequate actions, the agent takes into account some of the user's habits to be able to add the user's predicted activity in the decision parameters. Our aim is now to experiment and evaluate the relevance of the proposal according to different users in different contexts. The learning part of the agent is based on the assumption that the users' behaviours are recurrent when using mobile devices. This must be supported by experimental results, made over long time periods.

Acknowledgment. The authors would like to thank Intel Corporation and especially the Intel Research Council for the support given to this project.

References

1. Chaib-Draa, I., Niar, S., Tayeb, J., Grislin, E., Desertot, M.: Sensing user context and habits for run-time energy optimization. EURASIP J. Embed. Syst. **2017**, 4 (2017)
2. Cho, H., Mandava, D., Liu, Q., Chen, L., Jeong, S., Cheng, D.: Situation-aware on mobile phone using co-clustering: algorithms and extensions. In: Jiang, H., Ding, W., Ali, M., Wu, X. (eds.) IEA/AIE 2012. LNCS, vol. 7345, pp. 272–282. Springer, Heidelberg (2012). doi:10.1007/978-3-642-31087-4_29
3. Hao, W., Fu, J., Delaney, T., Trenkamp, C.: Cloud-based power management for mobile phones. In: SEDE Proceedings, pp. 149–154 (2012)
4. Klein, L., Kwak, J., Kavulya, G., Jazizadeh, F., Becerik-Gerber, B., Varakantham, P., Tambe, M.: Coordinating occupant behavior for building energy and comfort management using multi-agent systems. Autom. Construct. **22**, 525–536 (2012)
5. Li, C., Li, L.: Collaboration among mobile agents for efficient energy allocation in mobile grid. Inf. Syst. Front. **14**(3), 711–723 (2012)
6. Palaniappan, S., Chellan, K.: Energy-efficient stable routing using QOS monitoring agents in manet. EURASIP J. Wirel. Com. Netw. **1**, 1–11 (2015)
7. Pérez-Torres, R., Torres-Huitzil, C., Galeana-Zapién, H.: Power management techniques in smartphone-based mobility sensing systems: a survey. Pervasive Mob. Comput. **31**, 1–21 (2016)
8. Petit-Rozé, C., Grislin-Le Strugeon, E.: MAPIS, a multi-agent system for information personalization. Inf. Softw. Technol. **48**, 107–120 (2006)
9. Vallina-Rodriguez, N., Crowcroft, J.: Energy management techniques in modern mobile handsets. IEEE Commun. Surv. Tutorials **15**(1), 179–198 (2013)
10. Vrba, P., Marik, V., Siano, P., Leitao, P., Zhabelova, G., Vyatkin, V., Strasser, T.: A review of agent and service-oriented concepts applied to intelligent energy systems. IEEE Trans. Ind. Informatics **10**(3), 1890–1903 (2014)
11. Xu, C., Lin, F., Wang, Y., Zhong, L.: Automated OS-level device runtime power management. ACM SIGPLAN Notices **50**(4), 239–252 (2015)

Sensors, Signal Processing and Data Fusion

An Empirical Study on Verifier Order Selection in Serial Fusion Based Multi-biometric Verification System

Md Shafaeat Hossain[1]($\boxtimes$) and Khandaker Abir Rahman[2]

[1] Southern Connecticut State University, New Haven, CT, USA
HossainM3@SouthernCT.edu
[2] Saginaw Valley State University, Saginaw, MI, USA
krahman@svsu.edu

Abstract. Selecting the order of verifier in a serial fusion based multi-biometric system is a crucial parameter to fix because of its high impact on verification errors. A wrong choice of verifier order might lead to tremendous user inconvenience by denying a large number of genuine users and might cause severe security breach by accepting impostors frequently. Unfortunately, this design issue has been poorly investigated in multi-biometric literature. In this paper, we address this design issue by performing experiments using three different serial fusion based multi-biometric verification schemes, in particular (1) symmetric scheme, (2) SPRT-based scheme, and (3) Marcialis *et al.*'s scheme. We experimented on publicly available NIST-BSSR1 multi-modal database. We tested 24 orders—all possible orders originated from four individual verifiers—on a four-stage biometric verification system. Our experimental results show that the verifier order "best-to-worst", where the best performing individual verifier is placed in the first stage, the next best performing individual verifier is placed in the second stage, and so on, is the top performing order for all three serial fusion schemes mentioned above.

Keywords: Multi-biometric verification · Serial fusion · Verifier order selection

1 Introduction

Multi-biometric verification systems can be broadly categorized into two groups: (1) parallel fusion based verification systems (*e.g.*, [4,5,9,10,12,15,17]) and (2) serial fusion based verification systems (*e.g.*, [2,3,6,13,14,18,19]). In parallel fusion, to verify a user U, an n-biometric verification system collects n biometric traits from U, processes each trait individually, combines the information, and gives a genuine or impostor decision on the combined information. In contrast, in serial fusion, to verify a user U, an n-biometric verification system collects the first biometric trait in the processing chain from U, processes it, and gives verification decision on the processed information if it has enough evidence to

© Springer International Publishing AG 2017
S. Benferhat et al. (Eds.): IEA/AIE 2017, Part I, LNAI 10350, pp. 249–258, 2017.
DOI: 10.1007/978-3-319-60042-0_29

classify U as genuine or an impostor. If the verification system is not confident enough to ascertain whether U is genuine or an impostor, it *rejects* the sample and collects the sample of the next biometric trait to get more evidence for classification. The verification system collects the nth biometric trait only when it fails to give the verification decision using biometric traits 1 through $n-1$. A serial fusion based biometric system is also referred to as a multi-stage biometric system.

Parallel fusion based biometric verification systems have received more attention from the researchers because of its high accuracy [10]. However, several recent studies such as [3,13,14,19] have questioned the applicability of parallel fusion based systems in many real world applications because parallel fusion may cause a higher cost, longer verification time, and lower user convenience. A serial fusion based system can alleviate these problems by allowing the user to submit a subset of the available biometric traits. For example, when a serial fusion based system gets enough evidence for classification after processing the first biometric trait, the user does not need to submit other biometric traits. In contrast, in a parallel fusion based system, the user needs to submit all of the n biometric traits (in case of an n-biometric system).

Design of a serial fusion based multi-biometric verification system requires fixing several parameters, in particular (1) the reject thresholds at each stage of the architecture and (2) the order in which each individual verifier is placed within the multi-stage system. The verifier order is also called 'processing chain' in some literature such as [13,14]. Several recent studies (for example, [2,3, 13,14,18,19]) have deeply focused on choosing reject thresholds. Unfortunately, choosing the appropriate verifier order has been poorly investigated.

Selecting the verifier order is a crucial parameter to fix because of its high impact on verification errors [3]. A wrong choice of verifier order might lead to tremendous user inconvenience by denying a large number of genuine users and might cause severe security breach by accepting impostors frequently [19]. Also, a free choice of verifier order is not possible in high security applications because a clever impostor could be accepted by selecting the "weakest" biometric [13]. Though several studies mentioned the effectiveness of selecting a right verifier order, very few studies have attempted to resolve this issue. [3] implemented an eight-stage verification system, however, it did not follow any specific rule to select the verifier order. The best performing individual verifier was placed in the first stage and other verifiers were placed following "intuition". [13] devised an algorithm to select the appropriate verifier order and empirically evaluated its effectiveness. However, the algorithm was designed only for a two-stage verification system. There is no direction in [13] on how to select the verifier order in case of verification systems with more than two stages.

In this paper, we address this crucial design issue. We performed a rigorous experiment to determine the most appropriate verifier order. We tested 24 orders—all possible orders originated from four individual verifiers—on a four-stage biometric verification system. We evaluated the performance of the verifier orders by applying three serial fusion schemes: (1) symmetric scheme [7],

(2) SPRT-based scheme [3], and (3) Marcialis *et al.*'s scheme [13]. Our experimental results show that the verifier order "best-to-worst", where the best performing individual verifier is placed in the first stage, the next best performing individual verifier is placed in the second stage, and so on, is the top performing order for all three serial fusion schemes mentioned above.

Rest of the paper is organized as follows. In Sect. 2, we described the three serial fusion schemes we experimented on. In Sect. 3, we give our experimental details. In Sect. 4, we present our results and analysis. Finally, we conclude in Sect. 5.

2 Serial Fusion Based Multi-biometric Verification Schemes

In this section, we describe three serial fusion based multi-biometric verification schemes, in particular (1) symmetric scheme [7], (2) SPRT-based scheme [3], and (3) Marcialis *et al.*'s scheme [13], used in our experiments. The main difference among these schemes lie on how they select the reject thresholds (also called 'reject region' in some biometric literature). Below, we briefly describe these schemes.

2.1 Symmetric Scheme

Symmetric scheme rejects equal proportion of genuine scores and impostor scores to calculate the reject thresholds. More specifically, assuming dissimilarity scores, symmetric scheme takes the EER-threshold (the threshold where equal error rate occurs before exercising reject option) as the center, and rejects a certain proportion of genuine scores from the right side of the EER-threshold, and at the same time, rejects the same proportion of impostor scores from the left side of the EER-threshold (and vice versa for similarity scores). Symmetric scheme estimates the reject thresholds on the basis of user specified α_G [7]. Symmetric scheme does not fuse the verification score of ith stage with the verification scores of the previous stages.

2.2 SPRT-based Scheme

The SPRT (sequential probability ratio test) based scheme uses likelihood ratio of verification score and fuses the score of ith stage with the scores of the previous stages. Assuming real valued similarity scores, reject thresholds L and R, in SPRT-based scheme, are set as follows: $L = \frac{\alpha}{1-\beta}$, $R = \frac{1-\alpha}{\beta}$, where α and β are desired false reject rate and false accept rate, respectively [20].

2.3 Marcialis *et al.*'s Scheme

Marcialis *et al.*'s scheme does not fuse the verification score of ith stage with the verification scores of the previous stages. This scheme selects the whole confusion region (the region where genuine score distribution and impostor score distribution overlaps) as a reject region.

3 Experiments

3.1 Data

We experimented on NIST Biometric Scores Set Release 1 (BSSR 1) [1]. The NIST-BSSR1 database consists of three score sets–(1) fingerprint-face, (2) fingerprint, and (3) face. We experimented with score set fingerprint-face. The fingerprint-face set consists of face and fingerprint scores from the same set of 517 individuals. For each individual, the set contains one score from the comparison of two right index fingerprints, one score from the comparison of two left index fingerprints, and two scores (from two separate face systems, namely, C and G) from the comparison of two frontal faces. The scores of right and left index fingerprints were generated using the same fingerprint system. The fingerprint images and the face images used to compute the scores were collected from the same person and at the same time.

3.2 Experiment Setup

We divided the fingerprint-face score set into four disjoint subsets–(1) LI: set of scores of left index fingerprints, (2) RI: set of scores of right index fingerprints, (3) C: set of scores from face system C, and (4) G: set of scores from face system G. We used the scores of first 259 individuals from each of these sets (LI, RI, C, and G) for training (to find the reject regions) and the scores of the rest 258 individuals in testing (to evaluate the verification schemes). The number of genuine and impostor scores in training and testing sets are presented in Table 1. We present the genuine and impostor score distributions of the training sets of C, G, LI, and RI in Fig. 1. These scores are real valued **similarity** scores.

Table 1. The number of genuine and impostor scores in training and testing sets of LI, RI, C, and G.

	Score sets (LI/RI/C/G)	
	Training sets	Testing sets
Genuine scores	259*1	258*1
Impostor scores	259*516	258*516

We modeled a four-stage biometric verification system based on the score sets LI, RI, C, and G. Figure 2 presents this verification system, where Stage 1 uses score set C, Stage 2 uses score set RI, Stage 3 uses score set G, and Stage 4 uses score set LI. In stages 1, 2, and 3, the score s_i is compared with two reject thresholds L_i and R_i. If s_i lies in the interval $[L_i, R_i]$, the system proceeds to the next stage. In the fourth stage, the subject is classified into genuine or impostor using a single threshold T.

We tested all the verifier orders (24 in total) that are possible when LI, RI, C, and G are arranged into four stages. We tested the 24 verifier orders using three serial fusion schemes: symmetric, SPRT-based, and Marcialis *et al.*'s.

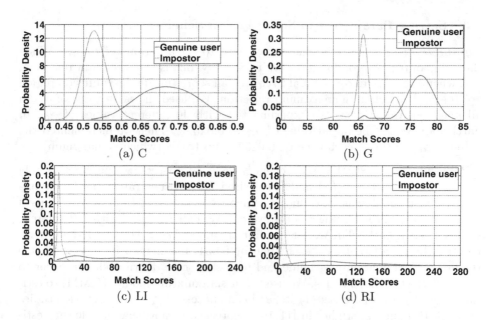

Fig. 1. Distributions of genuine and impostor scores for (a) face verifier C, (b) face verifier G, (c) left index (LI) fingerprint verifier, and (d) right index (RI) fingerprint verifier. The scores are real valued **similarity** scores.

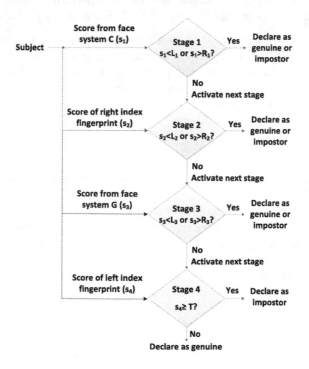

Fig. 2. A four-stage verification system based on the score sets LI, RI, C, and G.

3.3   Setting Parameters in Serial Fusion Schemes

Symmetric: In symmetric scheme, we need to set a parameter α_G [7]. When the value of α_G is zero, no scores are rejected, which is the minimum rejection, and when the value of α_G is equal to λ_G [7], all scores inside the confusion region are rejected, which is the maximum rejection. We used the same value of α_G in all stages of the system. We experimented with 40 different values of α_G. In particular, we set the initial value of α_G to $0.025\lambda_G$. Then we incremented the value of α_G 40 times, each time by $0.025\lambda_G$, up to λ_G (which is maximum).

SPRT-based: In SPRT-based scheme, we need to set two parameters: (1) desired false reject rate (α) and (2) desired false accept rate (β). We experimented with equal value of α and β, which we denote as ϵ ($= \alpha = \beta$). We used the same value of ϵ in all stages of the system. We experimented with 500 different values of ϵ. In particular, we set the initial value of ϵ to 0.001 and then incremented the value 500 times, each time by 0.001. Further, SPRT-based scheme requires the estimation of genuine and impostor score distributions in order to compute the likelihood ratios. We used Gaussian mixture models (GMM) to estimate the densities because: (1) it has been successfully used in several studies (*e.g.,* [3,15]) and (2) studies in [11,16] theoretically show that the density estimates produced by finite mixture models converge to the true densities if there are a sufficient number of training samples. In GMM-based density estimation, we need to set the number of components, k. After performing some preliminary experiments, we set the values of k to 2 for LI, RI, and C and 3 for G.

Marcialis et al.'s: Marcialis *et al.*'s scheme chooses the whole confusion region as the reject region. Note that Marcialis *et al.*'s scheme is an extreme case of the symmetric scheme. In particular, the reject region selected by Marcialis *et al.*'s scheme is same as the reject region selected by the symmetric scheme when α_G is maximum (*i.e.,* when $\alpha_G = \lambda_G$).

4   Results and Analysis

We measure the performance of the four-stage verification system, presented in Fig. 2, using the trade-off between area under receiver operating characteristic (ROC) curve [8] and average number of stages required. The area under the ROC curve (AUC) quantifies the overall ability of a verifier to discriminate between genuine users and impostors. The value of AUC for a perfect verifier, which yields zero false reject rate and zero false accept rate, is 1. The value of AUC for a verifier that performs like a random guess is 0.5. Minimally, a verifier should perform better than a random guess. The higher the value of AUC, the better the verifier. Average number of stages (ANS) indicates how user-convenient the system is. A small value of ANS indicates high user-convenience and vice versa.

Figure 3 shows AUC vs. ANS trade-off curves obtained by 24 (all possible) verifier orders when symmetric scheme is applied on the four-stage biometric verification system presented in Fig. 2. Because it will be difficult to distinguish 24

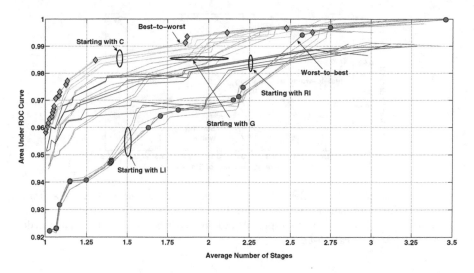

Fig. 3. Performance of 24 verifier orders evaluated on *symmetric scheme*. We group the trade-off curves into four sets based on how the corresponding verifier orders start with: (1) starting with LI, (2) starting with RI, (3) starting with C, and (4) starting with G. Also, we mark two special trade-off curves obtained by verifier orders *best-to-worst* and *worst-to-best*.

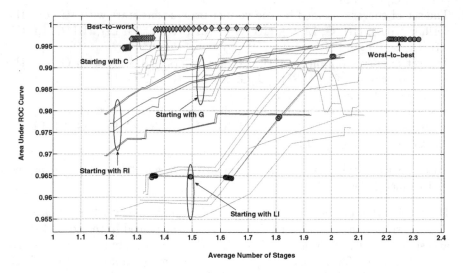

Fig. 4. Performance of 24 verifier orders evaluated on *SPRT-based scheme*. We group the trade-off curves into four sets based on how the corresponding verifier orders start with: (1) starting with LI, (2) starting with RI, (3) starting with C, and (4) starting with G. Also, we mark two special trade-off curves obtained by verifier orders *best-to-worst* and *worst-to-best*.

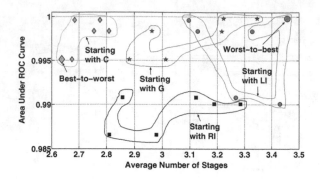

Fig. 5. Performance of 24 verifier orders evaluated on *Marcialis et al.'s scheme*. We group 24 trade-off *points* into four sets based on how the corresponding verifier orders start with. Also, we mark two special trade-off *points* obtained by verifier orders *best-to-worst* and *worst-to-best*.

different curves on the same figure, we did not show the legend of each individual curve. Rather, we grouped them into four sets:

1. The set of curves obtained by the verifier orders that start with LI (*i.e.*, the verifier orders: (LI, G, RI, C), (LI, G, C, RI), (LI, C, G, RI), (LI, C, RI, G), (LI, RI, G, C), and (LI, RI, C, G)).
2. The set of curves obtained by the verifier orders that start with RI (*i.e.*, the verifier orders: (RI, G, LI, C), (RI, G, C, LI), (RI, C, G, LI), (RI, C, LI, G), (RI, LI, G, C), and (RI, LI, C, G)).
3. The set of curves obtained by the verifier orders that start with C (*i.e.*, the verifier orders: (C, G, LI, RI), (C, G, RI, LI), (C, RI, G, LI), (C, RI, LI, G), (C, LI, G, RI), and (C, LI, RI, G)).
4. The set of curves obtained by the verifier orders that start with G (*i.e.*, the verifier orders: (G, C, LI, RI), (G, C, RI, LI), (G, RI, C, LI), (G, RI, LI, C), (G, LI, C, RI), and (G, LI, RI, C)).

Also, we separately marked two curves in Fig. 3, which are obtained by two special verifier orders:

1. **Best-to-worst order:** The best performing individual verifier is placed in the first stage, the next best performing verifier is placed in the second stage, and so on. Finally, the worst performing verifier is placed in the last stage. We evaluated the performance of the individual verifiers by equal error rate (EER) on training data. Table 2 shows the EER obtained by the four individual verifiers used in our experiments. According to the performance presented in Table 2, the best-to-worst verifier order is (C, RI, G, LI).
2. **Worst-to-best order:** This order is the opposite of the order best-to-worst. According to the Table 2, the worst-to-best verifier order is (LI, G, RI, C).

Table 2. Individual performance of the four verifiers (that generate the scores of LI, RI, C, and G) in terms of equal error rate (EER) on the training set.

	Fingerprint systems		Face systems	
	LI	RI	C	G
EER	0.0930	0.0581	0.0426	0.0594

Our observations from Fig. 3 are listed below:

1. Verifier orders starting with the best individual verifier (C) perform better than the verifier orders starting with individual verifiers G, LI, and RI.
2. Verifier orders starting with the worst individual verifier (LI) show extremely poor performance.
3. The verifier order "best-to-worst" is the best performing order.
4. The verifier order "worst-to-best" is one of the worst performing orders.

Figure 4 shows AUC vs. ANS trade-off curves obtained by 24 (all possible) verifier orders for SPRT-based scheme. To avoid cluttering in the figure, we only presented the AUCs and ANSs obtained by $\epsilon = 0.01$ to 0.05 (with the step size of 0.001). Figure 5 shows AUC vs. ANS trade-off *points* obtained by 24 (all possible) verifier orders for Marcialis *et al.*'s scheme. We observe that Figs. 4 and 5 give almost the same message as Fig. 3.

5   Discussion and Conclusion

The empirical study performed in this paper sheds some light on the problem of selecting the order of verifier in a serial fusion based multi-biometric system. We conducted extensive experiments on a four-stage biometric verification system using three different serial fusion based verification schemes: (1) symmetric scheme, (2) SPRT-based scheme, and (3) Marcialis *et al.*'s scheme. We tested 24 orders—all possible orders originated from four individual verifiers—on a four-stage biometric verification system. Results show that the "best-to-worst" verifier order achieves the best performance in all three verification schemes. This is not surprising because the best verifier in the first stage is expected to give the least verification error, the next best verifier in the second stage is expected to give less error than the third best verifier, and so on. If the worst individual verifier is placed in the first stage, it may generate a large number of wrong decision at the beginning which may drastically effect the whole performance of the system. Hence, based on our empirical study, we suggest to use the "best-to-worst" verifier order in multi-stage verification systems.

Our study has the following limitation. We used the same value of α_G in symmetric scheme and same value of ϵ in SPRT-based scheme in all stages of the four-stage system. Investigation of different values of α_G and ϵ in different stages may provide further insights on the effectiveness of the "best-to-worst" order, which is left as future work. Also, in future, we will analyze the complexity of implementing the "best-to-worst" order from the perspective of time consuming and usability.

Acknowledgments. This research is partly supported by Southern Connecticut State University Minority Recruitment and Retention Committee Grant.

References

1. http://www.nist.gov/itl/iad/ig/biometricscores.cfm
2. Akhtar, Z., Fumera, G., Marcialis, G., Roli, F.: Evaluation of serial and parallel multibiometric systems under spoofing attacks. In: IEEE International Conference on Biometrics: Theory, Applications and Systems, pp. 283–288, September 2012
3. Allano, L., Dorizzi, B., Garcia-Salicetti, S.: Tuning cost and performance in multi-biometric systems: A novel and consistent view of fusion strategies based on the sequential probability ratio test. Pattern Recogn. Lett. **31**(9), 884–890 (2010)
4. Brown, D., Bradshaw, K.: A multi-biometric feature-fusion framework for improved uni-modal and multi-modal human identification. In: 2016 IEEE Symposium on Technologies for Homeland Security (HST), pp. 1–6, May 2016
5. Hong, L., Jain, A.: Integrating faces and fingerprints for personal identification. IEEE Trans. Patt. Anal. Mach. Intel. **20**(12), 1295–1307 (1998)
6. Hossain, M.S.: On finding appropriate reject region in serial fusion based biometric verification. In: IEEE International Multi-Disciplinary Conference on Cognitive Methods in Situation Awareness and Decision Support, pp. 102–108, March 2016
7. Hossain, M., Balagani, K., Phoha, V.: On controlling genuine reject rate in multi-stage biometric verification. In: IEEE Computer Vision and Pattern Recognition Workshops (CVPRW), pp. 194–199 (2013)
8. Huang, J., Ling, C.: Using AUC and accuracy in evaluating learning algorithms. IEEE Trans. Knowl. Data Eng. **17**(3), 299–310 (2005)
9. Jain, A., Nandakumar, K., Ross, A.: Score normalization in multimodal biometric systems. Pattern Recogn. **38**(12), 2270–2285 (2005)
10. Jain, A.K., Flynn, P., Ross, A.A.: Handbook of Biometrics. Springer-Verlag New York Inc., Secaucus (2007)
11. Li, J.Q., Barron, A.R.: Mixture density estimation. Adv. Neural Inf. Process. Syst. **12**, 279–285 (1999)
12. Lumini, A., Nanni, L.: Overview of the combination of biometric matchers. Inf. Fusion **33**(C), 71–85 (2017)
13. Marcialis, G.L., Roli, F., Didaci, L.: Personal identity verification by serial fusion of fingerprint and face matchers. Pattern Recogn. **42**(11), 2807–2817 (2009)
14. Marcialis, G., Mastinu, P., Roli, F.: Serial fusion of multi-modal biometric systems. In: 2010 IEEE Workshop on Biometric Measurements and Systems for Security and Medical Applications (BIOMS), pp. 1–7, September 2010
15. Nandakumar, K., Chen, Y., Dass, S.C., Jain, A.: Likelihood ratio-based biometric score fusion. IEEE Trans. Patt. Anal. Mach. Intel. **30**, 342–347 (2008)
16. Rakhlin, A., Panchenko, D., Mukherjee, S.: Risk bounds for mixture density estimation. ESAIM: Probab. Stat. **9**, 220–229 (2005)
17. Ross, A., Jain, A.K.: Multimodal biometrics: an overview. In: Proceedings of the 12th European Signal Processing Conference, pp. 1221–1224 (2004)
18. Sansone, C., Vento, M.: Signature verification: Increasing performance by a multi-stage system. Pattern Anal. Appl. **3**, 169–181 (2000)
19. Takahashi, K., Mimura, M., Isobe, Y., Seto, Y.: A secure and user-friendly multi-modal biometric system. Proc. SPIE **5404**, 12–19 (2004)
20. Wald, A.: Sequential tests of statistical hypotheses. Ann. Math. Stat. **16**(2), 117–186 (1945)

Characterization of Cardiovascular Diseases Using Wavelet Packet Decomposition and Nonlinear Measures of Electrocardiogram Signal

Hamido Fujita[1(✉)], Vidya K. Sudarshan[2], Muhammad Adam[2], Shu Lih Oh[2],
Jen Hong Tan[2], Yuki Hagiwara[2], Kuang Chua Chua[2], Kok Poo Chua[2],
and U. Rajendra Acharya[2,3,4]

[1] Faculty of Software and Information Science, Iwate Prefectural University (IPU),
Takizawa, Iwate 020-0693, Japan
HFujita-799@acm.org
[2] Department of Electronics and Computer Engineering, Ngee Ann Polytechnic, Singapore,
Singapore
[3] Department of Biomedical Engineering, School of Science and Technology, SIM University,
Singapore, Singapore
[4] Department of Biomedical Engineering, Faculty of Engineering, University of Malaya,
Kuala Lumpur, Malaysia

Abstract. Cardiovascular diseases (CVDs) remain as the primary causes of disability and mortality worldwide and are predicted to continue rise in the future due to inadequate preventive actions. Electrocardiogram (ECG) signal contains vital clinical information that assists significantly in the diagnosis of CVDs. Assessment of subtle ECG parameters that indicate the presence of CVDs are extremely difficult and requires long hours of manual examination for accurate diagnosis. Hence, automated computer-aided diagnosis systems might help in overcoming these limitations. In this study, a novel algorithm is proposed based on the combination of wavelet packet decomposition (WPD) and nonlinear features. The proposed method achieved classification results of 97.98% accuracy, 99.61% sensitivity and 94.84% specificity with 8 reliefF ranked features. The proposed methodology is highly efficient in helping clinical staff to detect cardiac abnormalities using a single algorithm.

Keywords: Coronary artery disease · Myocardial infarction · Congestive heart failure · Electrocardiogram · Entropies · Wavelet packet decomposition

1 Introduction

Cardiovascular diseases (CVDs) are the primary cause of cardiac deaths worldwide. In 2012, an approximated 17.5 million CVD-related deaths are reported and it represents 31% of the overall global deaths [34]. CVDs are the leading cause of disability, particularly among myocardial infarction (MI) and stroke survivors. Moreover, the burden of CVDs is commonly measured by the disability-adjusted life years (DALY), whereby one DALY is similar to losing one year of healthy life. Evidently, the CVD burden for

© Springer International Publishing AG 2017
S. Benferhat et al. (Eds.): IEA/AIE 2017, Part I, LNAI 10350, pp. 259–266, 2017.
DOI: 10.1007/978-3-319-60042-0_30

developing countries are comparably greater (DALY > 5100 per 100 000) than for the developed countries (DALY < 3000 per 100 000) [48].

Coronary artery disease (CAD) is caused due to coronary arteriosclerosis, an inflammatory of the arterial wall. Atherosclerotic plaques start to build up on the wall of the coronary arteries [12, 13, 47] and this progressive buildup of plaques eventually obstruct and reduce the blood flow to a region of the myocardium [14]. Thus, oxygen deprived myocardium due to CAD leads to a fatal myocardial infarction (MI) [46].

MI is an irreversible death of the heart tissue which further expands in sizes and damages the left ventricular (LV) function causing LV dysfunction. Improper management and treatment of LV dysfunction together with other cardiac abnormalities leads to a catastrophic stage called Congestive Heart Failure (CHF) [14, 19].

Thus, CHF is characterized by impaired ventricles and also, changes to the neuro-hormonal regulation. Moreover, CHF is a terminal stage of CVD whereby the heart fails to sufficiently circulate the blood throughout the body. This complex clinical syndrome causes hypoxia, congestion, and even death [11, 15].

The electrocardiogram (ECG) is a commonly preferred clinical diagnostic tool for most of the cardiac conditions such as CAD, MI, and CHF. ECG is comparably cheaper and noninvasive and it contains vital information relating to the functioning of the heart. The morphology of the ECG signals is diagnostically important during an episode of CAD, MI, and CHF. T-waves are abnormally tall, the QT intervals are longer and ST segment is elevated or depressed during CAD and MI [5]. However, visually examining these morphological changes of features in voluminous ECG signals is tedious and highly prone to errors. Hence, an automated computer-aided technique is necessary to overcome the drawbacks of manual analysis of ECG signals.

Several improved methodologies have been developed for automated detection of CAD, MI and CHF using ECG signals or heart rate (HR) signals by researchers. Analysis of ST segment variation using various methods such as Radial Basis Function (RBF) neural networks [25], Principal component analysis (PCA) [7], Binary Particle Swarm Optimization (BPSO), Genetic algorithm [8], Discrete Wavelet Transform [23] have shown good results for classification of CAD affected ECG signals from normal ones.

For classification of normal and MI affected ECG signals, researchers have employed various DWT [21], linear [6, 26, 42] and nonlinear [1, 20, 43, 45] methods to evaluate the signal characteristics such as QRS complex [7], ST segment [6, 44], and T wave amplitude [6]. Even the evaluation of ECG signal variation using detrended fluctuation analysis (DFA) [22], entropies [22], and autoregressive burg [26, 28] have shown to be useful for differentiation of normal and CHF classes.

In the study of normal and CAD ECG signals, Acharya et al. [4] proposed the application of Higher Order Spectra (HOS). In addition, they developed a Coronary Artery Disease Index (CADI) that could automatically characterize normal and CAD ECG signals using a single number.

Furthermore, Acharya et al. [2] studied the classification of normal, CAD, and MI. They compared three different techniques namely Discrete Wavelet Transform (DWT), Empirical mode decomposition (EMD), and Discrete cosine transform (DCT) to differentiate among the three classes (normal, CAD, and MI). It is reported that utilizing DCT technique yielded the highest accuracy of 98.50% is obtained with only seven features.

It is evident from the literature review that, the majority of the studies proposed are on automated classification of two classes (normal and either CAD, MI or CHF). To date, no study has been published an algorithm for characterization of four classes (normal, CAD, MI and CHF) using ECG beats. Thus, in comparison to the literature review, this work proposes a novel algorithm for automated classification of normal, CAD, MI and CHF using ECG beats. The flowchart of the proposed method is illustrated in Fig. 1.

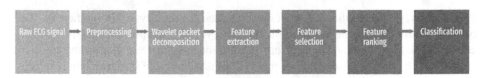

Fig. 1. Block diagram of the proposed methodology.

2 Methodology

2.1 Materials

In this study, the ECG signals of normal, CAD, MI, and CHF are acquired from various Physionet databases, namely PTB Diagnostic ECG Database (for normal and MI), St.-Petersburg Institute of Cardiology Technics 12-lead Arrhythmia Database (for CAD) and BIDMC Congestive Heart Failure Database (for CHF) [18].

2.2 Pre-processing

The ECG signals from the BIDMC Congestive Heart Failure and St.-Petersburg Institute of Cardiology Technics 12-lead Arrhythmia databases are sampled at 250 Hz and 257 Hz respectively whereas PTB Diagnostic ECG database is sampled at 1000 Hz. Thus, to maintain the uniformity for all the databases, a standard sample frequency of 1000 Hz is selected. In addition, the baseline wander and noise from ECG signals are eliminated by using Daubechies 6 (db6) wavelet [33].

2.3 Beats Segmentation

The pre-processed ECG signals are segmented into ECG beats by first detecting the R-peak using Pan Tompkins algorithm [33, 37]. The visibly tall amplitude of the R peaks is chosen as the distinctive point for this study. Each ECG beat is segmented by taking 250 and 400 samples before and after the R peak respectively.

2.4 Wavelet Packet Decomposition (WPD)

The wavelet packet decomposition (WPD) is a wavelet transform technique that utilizes wavelets to transform the ECG signals. Wavelets are the result of the translated and scaled shapes of the basic mother wavelet. Moreover, mother wavelets are localized in the time-frequency domain and have fluctuating amplitudes within a finite time [30]. As compared to DWT method, WPD decomposes the signal into both the low frequency components (approximations) and the high frequency components (details) at every level [30]. Hence, WPD provides more information as compared to DWT.

2.5   Features Extraction

In this study, twelve nonlinear features are obtained from thirty WPD coefficients. The twelve features are namely approximate entropy [38], sample entropy [40], fuzzy entropy [24], Kolmogorov-Sinai entropy [17], Renyi entropy [39], Tsallis entropy [10], fractal dimension [27], wavelet entropy [41], Signal energy [35], permutation entropy [9], recurrence quantification analysis [16], and bispectrum [36].

2.6   Features Selection – Sequential Forward Feature Selection (SFS)

Feature selection is a technique used to select a subset of significant features that yield minimal classification error [29]. Therefore, this step significantly enhances the performance of the classifier with the elimination of those redundant and insignificant features. In this study, sequential forward feature selection (SFS) is implemented for the feature selection process.

2.7   Features Ranking

In this study, ReliefF ranking technique is implemented. ReliefF estimates the significance of features by randomly sampling an instance and then consider the weighted value of features for the nearest instance of classes [32].

2.8   Classification – K-Nearest Neighbor (KNN)

KNN is an instance-based classification technique in which the unknown sample is classified according to either similarity or distance criteria [19]. In this work, the k value of the nearest neighbors is varied ranging from 5 to 10. We have experimented with different values of k and obtained maximum accuracy with k = 5.

3   Results

In total, 181,510 ECG beats of four classes are segmented from three separate ECG databases of 222 subjects. For each ECG beat, WPD of four level is implemented and resulted in 30 coefficients. Twelve different nonlinear features are obtained from the 30 coefficients, therefore, 1050 features are obtained from one beat. Further, out of the 1050 features extracted from each beat, 10 features are selected by SFS. The features have a p-value of $p < 0.0001$ which also means that these features are statistically significant.

The confusion matrix of the four classes is shown in Table 1.

Table 1. Confusion matrix of the 4 classes.

Original/ Predicted	N	MI	CAD	CHF	Acc (%)	PPV (%)	Sen (%)	Spec (%)
N	10002	440	103	1	99.34	93.81	94.84	99.61
MI	521	38826	835	0	98.15	95.12	96.63	98.59
CAD	139	1553	39845	8	98.51	97.56	95.91	99.29
CHF	0	0	59	89178	99.96	99.99	99.93	99.99

*Acc: Accuracy, Sen: Sensitivity, Spec: Specificity.

4 Discussion

In this study, a novel technique for automated characterization of various CVDs is proposed using WPD and nonlinear analysis of the ECG beats. A total of 181,510 ECG beats having normal, CAD, MI and CHF conditions are individually decomposed into 30 WPD coefficients. Twelve types of nonlinear features are then extracted from the coefficients. On the whole, the proposed methodology achieved maximum classification results of 97.98% accuracy, 99.61% sensitivity and 94.84% specificity with 8 ReliefF ranked features using KNN classifier.

The implementation of the various nonlinear analysis techniques is to measure the degree of complexity in the healthy and CVDs ECG signals. This relates to the presence of inherent patterns in the dynamics of nonlinear ECG signals [44]. Indeed, nonlinear techniques are highly sensitive towards the presence of subtle sudden changes in the ECG signals [3].

The main novelty of this work is the integration of WPD and nonlinear techniques into a computer-aided diagnosis (CAD) system which enhances the efficiency of the decision-making and diagnosis process. Thus, clinicians can expeditiously prescribe the relevant treatments to prevent the conditions from deteriorating further.

5 Conclusion

In this study, a novel technique is proposed for the identification and diagnosis of CAD, MI, and CHF by using nonlinear features that are obtained from the segmented ECG beats. The proposed automated diagnostic support system can reliably and efficiently assist clinical staff to detect and diagnose cardiac abnormalities. Thus, reducing the workload and the possibilities of manual errors in interpreting vital information during ECG data assessment. The integration of the proposed methodology with ECG system is cost effective and yield instantaneous results as compared to other conventional cardiac diagnostic modalities. Hence, the proposed cardiac diagnostic support system offers an alternative cheap cardiac screening especially for the developing countries whereby the majority of the CVDs deaths occur. For future work, authors aim to explore on different types of nonlinear feature extraction technique and a bigger database that can produce better accuracy with the lesser number of features. Subsequently, the work can be extended in the various stages of CAD, MI, and CHF. This helps in identifying early indicators of the cardiac diseases from the ECG signals and thus, promptly suppressing the conditions from deteriorating further with the necessary clinical medications and treatments.

Acknowledgment. First author appreciates the support given by Japan Society for Promotion of Science (JSPS) KAKENHI Grant Number: 15K00439.

References

1. Acharya, U.R., Fujita, H., Sudarshan, V.K., Oh, S.L., Adam, M., Koh, J.E.W., Tan, J.H., Ghista, D.N., Martis, R.J., Chua, C.K., Poo, C.K., Tan, R.S.: Automated detection and localization of myocardial infarction using electrocardiogram: a comparative study of different leads. Knowl.-Based Syst. **99**, 146–156 (2016a)
2. Acharya, U.R., Fujita, H., Adam, M., Lih, O.S., Sudarshan, V.K., Hong, T.J., Koh, E.W., Hagiwara, Y., Chua, C.K., Poo, C.K., San, T.R.: Automated characterization and classification of coronary artery disease and myocardial infarction by decomposition of ECG signals: a comparative study. Inf. Sci. **377**, 17–29 (2016b)
3. Acharya, U.R., Kannathal, N., Krishnan, S.M.: Comprehensive analysis of cardiac health using heart rate signals. Physiol. Meas. J. **25**, 1130–1151 (2004)
4. Acharya, U.R., Sudarshan, V.K., Koh, E.W., Martis, R.J., Tan, J.H., Oh, S.L., Adam, M., Hagiwara, Y., Mookiah, M.R.K., Chua, K.P., Chua, K.C., Tan, R.S.: Application of higher-order spectra for the characterization of coronary artery disease using electrocardiogram signals. Biomed. Sig. Process. Control **31**, 31–43 (2017)
5. Arafat, S., Dohrmann, M., Skubic, M.: Classification of coronary artery disease stress ECGs using uncertainty modeling, 1-4244-0020-1. IEEE (2005)
6. Arif, M., Malagore, I.A., Afsar, F.A.: Detection and localization of myocardial infarction using k-nearest neighbor classifier. J. Med. Syst. **36**, 279–289 (2012)
7. Babaoglu, I., Findik, O., Bayrak, M.: Effects of principle component analysis on assessment of coronary artery diseases using support vector machine. Expert Syst. Appl. **37**, 2182–2185 (2010a). Elsevier
8. Babaoglu, I., Findik, O., Ulker, E.: A comparison of feature selection models utilizing binary particle swarm optimization and genetic algorithm in determining coronary artery disease using support vector machine. Expert Syst. Appl. **37**, 3177–3183 (2010b). Elsevier
9. Bandt, C., Pompe, B.: Permutation entropy: a natural complexity measure for time series. Rev. Lett. **88**, 174102 (2002)
10. Bezerianos, A., Tong, S., Thankor, N.: Time dependent entropy of the EEG rhythm changes following brain ischemia. Ann. Biomed. Eng. **31**, 221–232 (2003)
11. Bui, A.L., Horwich, T.B., Fonarow, G.C.: Epidemiology and risk profile of heart failure. Nat. Rev. Cardiol. **8**, 3041 (2011)
12. Buja, L.M., Willerson, J.T.: The role of coronary artery lesions in ischemic heart disease: insights from recent clinicopathologic, coronary arteriographic, and experimental studies. Hum. Pathol. **18**, 451–461 (1987)
13. Buja, L.M., McAllister Jr., H.A.: Coronary artery disease: pathological anatomy and pathogenesis. In: Willerson, J.T., Cohn, J.N., Wellens, H.J.J., Holmes Jr., D.R. (eds.) Cardiovascular medicine, 3rd edn, pp. 593–610. Springer, London (2007)
14. Chee, J., Seow, S.C.: The electrocardiogram. In: Acharya, U.R., Suri, J.S., Spaan, J.A.E., Krishnan, S.M. (eds.) Advances in Cardiac Signal Processing, pp. 1–53. Springer, Heidelberg (2007)

15. Deedwania, P.C., Carbajal, E.V.: Congestive heart failure. In: Shanahan, J., Lebowitz, H. (eds.) Current diagnosis & treatment, Cardiology, pp. 203–232. McGraw-Hill Companies, USA (2009)
16. Eckmann, J.P., Kamphorst, S.O., Ruelle, D.: Recurrence plots of dynamical systems. Europhys. Lett. **5**, 973–977 (1987)
17. Farmer, J.D.: Information dimension and the probabilistic structure of chaos. Naturforsch. Z. **37**, 1304–1325 (1982)
18. Goldberger, A.L., Amaral, L.A.N., Glass, L., Hausdorff, J.M., Ivanov, PCh., Mark, R.G., Mietus, J.E., Moody, G.B., Peng, C.-K., Stanley, H.E.: PhysioBank, PhysioToolkit, and PhysioNet: components of a new research resource for complex physiologic signals. Circulation **101**(23), e215–e220 (2000)
19. Guyton, A.C., Hall, J.E.: Text Book of Medical Physiology, 11th edn. Elsevier, New York (2006)
20. Han, J., Kamber, M., Pei, J.: Data Mining: Concepts and Techniques. Morgan Kaufmann, San Francisco (2005)
21. Jayachandran, E.S., Joseph, K.P., Acharya, U.R.: Analysis of myocardial infarction using discrete wavelet transform. J. Med. Syst. **34**, 985–992 (2010)
22. Kamath, C.: A new approach to detect congestive heart failure using detrended fluctuation analysis of electrocardiogram signals. J. Eng. Sci. Technol. **10**(2), 145–159 (2015)
23. Kaveh, A., Chung, W.: Automated classification of coronary atherosclerosis using single lead ECG. In: IEEE Conference on Wireless Sensors, Kuching, Sarawak (2013)
24. Kosko, B.: Fuzzy entropy and conditioning. Inf. Sci. **40**, 165–174 (1986)
25. Lewenstein, K.: Radial basis function neural network approach for the diagnosis of coronary artery disease based on the standard electrocardiogram exercise test. Med. Biol. Eng. Comput. **39**, 1–6 (2001)
26. Liu, B., Liu, J., Wang, G., Huang, K., Li, F., Zheng, Y., Luo, Y., Zhou, F.: A novel electrocardiogram parameterization algorithm and its application in myocardial infarction detection. Comput. Biol. Med. **61**, 178–184 (2015)
27. Mandelbrot, B.B.: The Fractal Geometry of Nature. W.H. Freeman and Company (1982)
28. Masetic, Z., Subasi, A.: Detection of congestive heart failures using C4.5 decision tree. Southeast Eur. J. Soft Comput. **2**, 74–77 (2013). ISSN 2233-1859
29. Masetic, Z., Subasi, A.: Congestive heart failure detection using random forest classifier. Comput. Methods Programs Biomed. **130**, 54–64 (2016)
30. Masiti, M., Masiti, Y., Oppenheim, G., Poggi, J.M.: Wavelet toolbox for use with Matlab, User's Guide, Ver. 3. The MathWorks, Inc. (2004)
31. Marcano-Cedeno, A., Quintanilla-Dominguez, J., Cortina-Januchs, M.G., Andina, D.: Feature selection using sequential forward selection and classification applying artificial metaplasticity neural network. In: IEEE, IECON 2010, 36th Annual Conference on IEEE Industrial Electronics Society (2010)
32. Marko, R.S., Igor, K.: Theoretical and Empirical Analysis of ReliefF and RReliefF. Mach. Learn. J. **53**, 23–69 (2003). doi:10.1023/A:1025667309714
33. Martis, R.J., Acharya, U.R., Lim, C.M.: ECG beat classification using PCA, LDA, ICA and discrete wavelet transform. Biomed. Sig. Process. Control **8**(5), 437–448 (2013a)
34. Mendis, S., et al.: Global Status Report on Non-communicable Diseases 2014. World Health Organization (2014)
35. Mookiah, M.R.K., Acharya, U.R., Lim, C.M., Petznick, A., Suri, J.S.: Data mining technique for automated diagnosis of glaucoma using higher order spectra and wavelet energy features. Knowl. Based Syst. **33**, 73–82 (2012)

36. NIkias, C.I., Raghuveer, M.R.: Bispectrum estimation: a digital signal processing framework. Proc. IEEE **75**, 869–891 (1987)
37. Pan, J., Tompkins, W.J.: A Real Time QRS Detection Algorithm, 11th edn. WB Saunders Co, Philadelphia (2006)
38. Pincus, S.M.: Approximate entropy as a measure of system complexity. Proc. Natl. Acad. Sci. **88**, 2297–2301 (1991)
39. Renyi, A.: On measures of entropy and information. In: Proceedings of the Fourth Berkeley Symposium on Mathematical Statistics and Probability, pp. 547–561 (1961)
40. Richman, J.S., Mooran, J.R.: Physiological time-series analysis using approximate entropy and sample entropy. Am. J. Physiol. Heart Circ. Physiol. **278**, 2039–2049 (2000)
41. Rosso, O.A., Blanco, S., Yordanova, J., Kolev, V., Figliola, A., Schurmann, M., Basar, E.: Wavelet entropy: a new tool for analysis of short duration electrical signals. J. Neurosci. Methods **105**, 65–67 (2001)
42. Safdarian, N., Dabanloo, N.J., Attarodi, G.: A new pattern recognition method for detection and localization of myocardial infarction using T-wave integral and total integral as extracted features from one cycle of ECG signal. J. Biomed. Sci. Eng. **7**, 818–824 (2014)
43. Sharma, L.N., Tripathy, R.K., Dandapat, S.: Multiscale energy and eigenspace approach to detection and localization of myocardial infarction. IEEE Trans. Biomed. Eng. **62**(7), 1827–1837 (2015)
44. Sun, L., Lu, Y., Yang, K., Li, S.: ECG analysis using multiple instance learning for myocardial infarction detection. IEEE Trans. Biomed. Eng. **59**(12), 3348–3356 (2012)
45. Thuraisingham, R.A.: A classification to detect congestive heart failure using second-order difference plot of RR intervals. SAGE-Hindawi access to research Cardiology Research and Practice, article id 807379 (2009)
46. Townsend, N., Wickramasinghe, K., Bhatnagar, P., Smolina, K., Nichols, M., Leal, J., Luengo-Fernandez, R., Rayner, M.: Coronary Heart Disease Statistics, a Compendium of Health Statistics, 2012th edn. British Heart Foundation, London (2012)
47. Willerson, J.T., Hillis, L.D., Buja, L.M.: Ischemic Heart Disease Clinical and Pathophysiological Aspects. Raven, New York (1982)
48. World Health Organization (WHO). Disease and injury country estimates, Geneva, Switzerland (2009)

Biometric Keystroke Signal Preprocessing Part I: Signalization, Digitization and Alteration

Orcan Alpar and Ondrej Krejcar[✉]

Faculty of Informatics and Management, Center for Basic and Applied Research,
University of Hradec Kralove, Rokitanskeho 62,
500 03 Hradec Kralove, Czech Republic
orcan.alpar@uhk.cz, ondrej@krejcar.org

Abstract. Biometric keystroke term basically represents the classification of the users based on password entering style. The characteristic feature to be extracted in most keystroke authentication systems mainly is the inter-key times so the waiting time between key-press moments is supposed to be unique and hard to mimic. Therefore, the majority of the proposed systems start from computing the times in time-domain and the differences for each key in the password, without any pre-process. The performance of the systems as well as the accuracy of classification methodology merely depend on non-processed data. Given this fact, we present preparation methods starting form data acquisition for better post-processing of biometric keystroke signals.

Keywords: Biometrics · Keystroke · Authentication · Signal processing · Digitization

1   Introduction

Biometrics is a discipline that deals with the characteristics of the individuals by extracting and validating the unique features. Not as drastically as differences in physical or genetic traits that the individuals unintentionally have, habitual and behavioral traits may vary. If some significant features could be extracted from these traits, validation, classification and differentiation of the individuals could be possible.

However, the main argument in this point is questionable consistency of the uniqueness considering the type of the features. For instance, the signature samples which is a concern of habitual biometrics, of an individual, cannot be identical despite some characteristics exhibiting same pattern in each sample. These characteristics could be revealed successfully by offline signature analysis methods, comparing the distinctive features.

On the contrary, keystrokes can be totally indistinguishable since the classifiers react rapidly and online, just subsequent to login attempts. Therefore, keystroke authentication protocols are always subsidiary of the main authentication, not a substitute. An additional security level by comparing the keystroke signals are beneficial, when the passwords are publicized. The primary concept behind keystroke recognition is the unique password entering style of individuals on a keyboard. Placed in

© Springer International Publishing AG 2017
S. Benferhat et al. (Eds.): IEA/AIE 2017, Part I, LNAI 10350, pp. 267–276, 2017.
DOI: 10.1007/978-3-319-60042-0_31

behavioral biometrics including the habits or actions of the individuals, keystroke authentication systems enable password owners uniquely distinguished from others [1].

Regardless of the password control, most of the papers on keystroke recognition prove that the implementation of very basic algorithms in conventional login protocols, in password entering phase as stealth extraction of keystrokes and in validation phase as classification of the individual as real or fraud, give promising results. Unless some special devices exist for applying very rarely extracted features like pressure data [2, 3] or fingerprints [4], the mainstream of data acquisition phase in keystroke authentication is more or less similar: collecting the key-press times.

Any kind of data collector working stealthily, starts with a waiting time, no matter any data generation is triggered or not. If no data is generated in this phase, the time of pressing the very first key k_1 should be placed in $t_1 = 0$. Assuming that a password is consisting of m keys and the process is terminated by an "enter" key, t_m values will be extracted. It however is possible to consider the key-press time of the "enter" key, no matter it is actualized manually on keyboard or by a mouse, as the last data on the string, so that the password will have k_{m+1} t_{m+1} data couple.

Although the preferences always depend on the algorithms and on specific requirements, inter-key times are computed by $\Delta t_n = t_{n+1} - t_n$. Despite various representations, the keystroke collection algorithm, following the inter-key time pattern, could be visualized as follows, in Fig. 1.

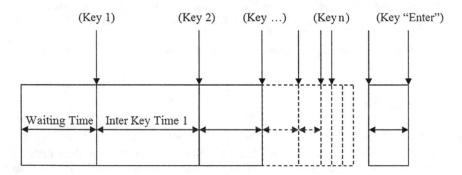

Fig. 1. Keystroke sequence

If the features of the keystroke are collected in a common manner, the results of data acquisition stage will be formed as a matrix, k_n t_n and Δt_n. After several repetitions, the intervals could be narrowed down or expanded, yet they still are very strictly based on these data couples or triples. At this point of the process, some common algorithms might be handy, like neural networks [5], k-nearest neighbors [6], support vector machines [7] or statistical methods [8].

On the other hand, the keystroke features could be extracted and treated as signals, again totally depending on the data acquisition algorithms. When the key-code string of the password is as crucial as the key-press or inter-key times, the signal could be generated as a discrete finite signal. Additionally, extraction of the keystrokes as a binary train signal is still possible when the exact key-codes are out of scope.

Moreover, the keystroke signal is sampled with a desired resolution, the points could be interpolated for achieving a pseudo-continuity and for dealing with a continuous signal. Depending on the level of the timer resolution, the signal could automatically be formed as a close-to-continuous, though.

Considering these possibilities, the signals could easily be processed for differentiating the unique features hidden in the keystroke dynamics of the individual. Therefore, the main concern of this paper is preprocessing the keystroke data to signify the uniqueness of the featured moments while an individual is entering the password. The outcomes of this research will shed light on the future keystroke authentication protocols, with the detailed suggestion on the signalization and digitization of the biometric keystroke signals.

In our previous papers, we, in fact, focused on adjusting the keystroke signals for our purposes. As the primary preparation for the training the Levenberg-Marquadt optimized neural network classifier in [9], we routinely focused on the inter-key times however we turned each inter-key time into a unique feature by colorizing the time intervals. The signal we dealt with was pseudo-continuous, forming the rectangles by key-code and inter-key time couples. Each rectangle is incrementally colorized to indicate the area versus the time so that higher area in a color channel would represent the length of the corresponding inter-key time.

In our very recent research [10], we presented a very innovative approach by changing the paradigm of keystroke recognition from the time-domain into frequency-domain to identify the high-frequency regions of an individual while entering the password. Despite the common transformation procedures, we proposed a short-time Fourier transformation methodology since the keystroke signal we dealt with was time variant and unsteady, as usual. If the regular Fourier was applied, the resulting data uncovered by the transformations would be only consisting of frequency information. In this paper, we totally neglected the key-codes and turned the whole sequence into binary train signal. We have many more papers published in recent years on keystroke and touchstroke recognition including signal preprocessing [11–13].

The major assumption of this paper is keeping the processed information of the signal exactly identical with the unprocessed string. The signal we create in each method would be reversible to achieve the original keystrokes produced by our main keystroke recognition kernel. Therefore this paper starts with introduction of data acquisition protocols for subsequent signalization and digitization. Each section will include corresponding results with suggestions and subsequently all results will be evaluated before conclusion section.

2 Data Acquisition

Every single bits and pieces of information is crucial in keystroke authentication, therefore we suggest to use a very high resolution timer, recording the passwords stealthily from the beginning of the waiting time. To overcome the ambiguity of "very high", we have to state that we usually use 500 tick/s timer while we are collecting all data from the beginning of the process until the enter key is pressed.

The kernel of the software is written on Matlab, using the Simulink infrastructure and collecting all data produced by a regular keyboard. The key-codes are extracted in every 0.002 s, so the results are so sensitive compared to the regular keystroke algorithms. Right after the main interface is initialized, the keystroke recognition program starts to collect the data including the key code "0" as waiting time where $k_0 = 0$ and $t_0 = 0$. Subsequently, when the first key K_1 is pressed, the hidden interface catches the key-code and it is assigned to $k_1 = K_1$ until the key-code 13 is generated by the user, which actually is the key-code of "enter". The system keeps recording the last key pressed for continuity and differentiating waiting time and inter-key times.

As a results of this process the key-press and inter-key times with corresponding key-codes could easily be extracted. Let's assume that the main password is selected as "orcan7890*" which is supposed to be strong for most of the websites since it includes alphanumeric, numeric and symbolic digits. Let's assume that length of the password is r, the digit of the password is K_r, the key-code of K_r is k_r, the key-press time of K_r is t_r and the inter-key time between t_r and t_{r+1} is Δt_r. The following table therefore would be an example of the outputs of this keystroke recognition algorithm, given that the corresponding times are in seconds while the system starts to count as the interface is brought into the working state.

Although this seems to be a very basic and implausible example, likes of this table are used in various keystroke recognition systems and succeeding classification algorithms. The main drawback of this approach is being stuck in the data provided by the algorithm since the table surely is a final output, not an input of any inference system. Therefore we suggest to treat the keystroke data as a signal which will enable the usage of signal processing algorithms afterwards without changing the content of the data.

3   Signalization

We presented the strings consisting of the triples for each key in the previous section, for the password of "orcan7890*". The data in the Table 1 is crucial indeed for many researches, nonetheless, it is not close to be a signal for processing. The alternatives of the succeeding protocols once the data is converted to signals could be helpful for better discrimination of the attempts.

Table 1. Example of a keystroke data consisting of data triples.

r	1	2	3	4	5	6	7	8	9	10	11
K_r	o	r	c	a	n	7	8	9	0	*	Enter
K_r	111	114	99	97	110	55	56	57	48	42	13
t_r	1.4	1.6	1.7	1.8	2	2.8	2.9	3.0	3.1	3.5	4
Δt_r	0.2	0.1	0.1	0.2	0.8	0.1	0.1	0.1	0.4	0.5	

Therefore, what we actually extracted and recommend for preprocessing is the signalized data instead of triples in Table 1. It still has the key-press and inter-key times with the key-codes however every tick in the times is represented by a key-code value.

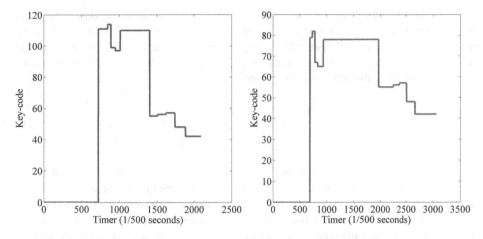

Fig. 2. Raw keystroke signal examples: orcan7890* on the left, ORCAN7890* on the right.

The signal of the keystroke exhibits pseudo-continuous dynamics, looks like continuous due to excessive number of data in very short time, yet not differentiable. Therefore it is necessary to be interpolated when the area under the curve is important to extract. Even though the password itself isn't validated by this hidden interface, the small letters have different key-codes than capital letters. The examples of the raw keystroke data are presented in Fig. 2.

As the brief comprehension of the first results presented above, it is obvious that the data acquisition phase enables the extraction of each possible feature from the log-in process. On the other hand, it is advised to discriminate the numpad entries from the regular numbers by assigning different key-codes. The algorithms presented is written and implemented by Dell Inspiron 15R laptop with an embedded keyboard therefore the key-codes of the numbers placed in numpad and under the function buttons are definitely identical, while it is applicable in touchscreen and some external keyboards. This approach is better than traditional keystroke recognition algorithms through automatic rectangle generation which has an area of $A_n = k_n \Delta t_n$ where all area of the graph could be calculated by $A = \sum_{n=1}^{m} k_n \Delta t_n$ starting from $k_1 t_1$ couple where the last rectangle is calculated by $k_n(t_{n+1} - t_n)$ where t_{n+1} is the moment that the enter key is pressed.

4   Digitization

The raw keystroke strings and related discrete signals generated by the interface represent the pseudo-interpolated continuous diagram of keystrokes, however it is still possible to analyze or to apply discrete signal processing on them. Considering that the main password still is "orcan7890*", if there is a hidden and unique feature sequence in the password which is more important and discriminative than the others, this sequence should be treated as the key feature. However resampling will change the original signal, if the resample rate is too low depending of the length of the signal.

First, let's assume $f_n(t)$ represents the whole string of the keystroke data, where t is the tick which is 1/500 s for our experiments and n is the length of the array; then we suggest to delete the irrelevant cells from the array. Since the waiting time in the beginning or the key-code of the enter button don't give any biometric information, we initially reconstruct the new array $g_m(t)$ by:

$$[g_m(z)] = \begin{cases} [\,] \mid f_n(t) = 0 \\ [\,] \mid f_n(t) = 13, \ t = 1, 2, 3, \ldots, n \\ [f_n(t)] \mid o/w \end{cases} \tag{1}$$

where m is the new length of the reconstructed array and z is the reconstructed timer. This conversion doesn't change any information of the original string at all while the new array $g_m(t)$ starts from the first key-press. Strictly depending on the resampling rate, it is still possible to lose some crucial keystroke data from the array. It is still possible to interpolate the signal yet it will create a new imaginary signal with an error rate. The new signals could be reproduced by following discretization using 10 and 100 Hz resampling, consecutively.

$$[g_k^{10}(z)] = [g_{10k+1}(z)], k = 0, 1, 2, \ldots, K_1 \tag{2}$$

$$[g_k^{100}(z)] = [g_{100k+1}(z)], k = 0, 1, 2, \ldots, K_2 \tag{3}$$

where K_1 and K_2 represent the maximum possible array size. Two examples of the discretization process is presented in Fig. 3, where all data is represented by discrete signal on the left while some data is lost on the right.

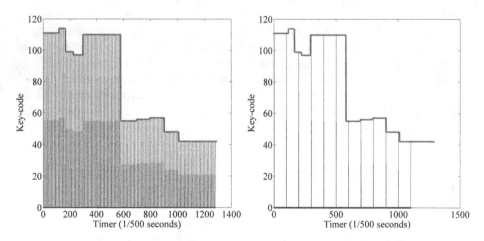

Fig. 3. Resampled discretized keystroke signals (10 Hz on the left, 100 Hz on the right)

Since the key-codes are always originated as integers, the digitization and discretization are totally the same in these cases. When the key-codes don't have any importance and only the key-press and inter-key times matter, the signal could be converted to binary or binary-train, yet this is not a concern of this paper since it will change the signal itself. The signal revealed by discretization could easily be used in discrete and short-time discrete Fourier transformation.

5 Alteration

After discretization, the signal is ready for alteration without changing the original content by reversible operations. The main concern is get rid of lucky fraud attempts and lower the false accept rate. Therefore first alteration we propose is the $k_n \rightarrow \Delta t_n$ transformation in 2D plane using the 10 Hz discretized signal by:

$$\left[\bar{g}_k^{10}(z)\right] = [\Delta t_k], k = 0, 1, 2, \ldots, K_1 \tag{4}$$

Like all operations presented in this paper, this transformation is an array operation as well, which means that the sting of key-codes are replaced with calculated inter-key times. The result of this transformation is presented in Fig. 4.

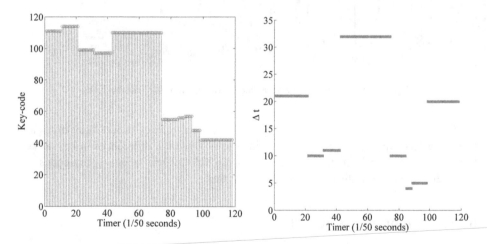

Fig. 4. 10 Hz Sampled discrete keystroke signal on the left, inter-key time transformation on the right.

This alteration will provide a new kind of information for the keystrokes yet it is totally symmetric with the x axis so that with the perfect scaling these lines would create exact squares. However it is possible for analyze these squares since in every keystroke; the patterns would be so unique. On the other hand, it is easier to highlight the hidden or least important features by applying known methods.

The final alterations we introduce for the $\left[\bar{g}_k^{10}(z)\right]$ signal is about the average of $t_a = \sum_{i=1}^{K_1} [\Delta t_i]/K_1$. Depending on the requirements, it sometimes is so important to find the diversity of the signal. While the diversity could be computed for partial or whole signal, the differences between neighbors of Δt_i could be calculated. We firstly find the average of the inter-key times $[\hat{t}] = [t - t_a]$ and applied the sigmoid function $[\phi(\hat{t})] = \left[1/\left(1 + e^{-\hat{t}}\right)\right]$ and secondly we applied a thresholding function $[\psi(\hat{t})] = \left([\Delta t_z]/[(1 + \hat{t}^2)]^{\frac{1}{2}} + 1\right)/2$. The main point of searching diversity is finding the closeness of each tick value t to the average t_a. The resulting keystroke signals are as follows in Fig. 5.

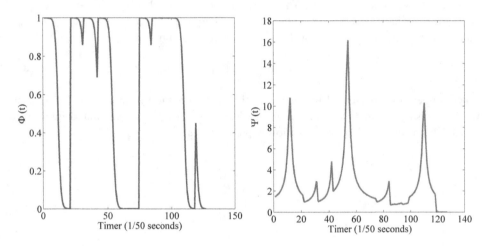

Fig. 5. Altered keystroke signals. $\phi(\hat{t})$ on the left $\psi(\hat{t})$ on the right

It is seen from the figures that, based on the characteristics of inter-key times and their averages, the signal could be diversified to analyze the differences in keystrokes. Many more alteration methods could be applicable, when ticks vs key-codes are extracted instead of finding only the inter-key times.

6   Evaluation of the Results

The methodology provided by this article is based on a sequence of signalization discretization and alteration of keystroke data. Instead of using the triples in Table 1, we suggest the methods mentioned above for better discrimination of real attempts and fraud attacks. Briefly we started with turning the data into discrete signals by our keystroke recognition algorithm and additional resampling. Afterwards, the inter-key times are presented by discrete finite signals and imaginary squares which are so unique based on the password entering style of individuals. By the help of these formations, we proposed two alteration methods, sigmoid and sigmoid-like thresholding, which both created significantly different diagrams.

7   Conclusion and Discussion

This paper proposes some new and crucial methodologies to provide an insight on preprocessing of keystroke signals without changing the original string. This work is a prerequisite of the part II, where we present some new methods for manipulating the signal and changing the original content for highlighting the biometric features. The main necessity as well as the importance of the outcomes of this research is absence of preprocessing in keystroke recognition algorithms.

Most of the papers deal with the novel classification algorithms disregarding any enhancement after data acquisition phase. Therefore the idea we put forward could be very beneficial when the raw keystroke couples or triples are not enough to discriminate the attempt. The second benefit is keeping the signal identical with the original by reversible operations. Part II includes the manipulation techniques for the keystrokes by changing the original signal irreversibly.

The main difference between Part I and Part II is the characteristics of the signals achieved by processing of the keystroke data. All signals would be used as the inputs of the classifiers while the signals are totally different in type and representation rate. In Part I, the altered signals maintain original features while in Part II, the newly created signals are somewhat relevant with the original yet have different characteristics.

Acknowledgement. This work and the contribution were supported by project "SP/2017 – 2102 - Smart Solutions for Ubiquitous Computing Environments" from University of Hradec Kralove.

References

1. Crawford, H.: Keystroke dynamics: characteristics and opportunities. In: 2010 Eighth Annual International Conference on Privacy Security and Trust (2010)
2. Saevanee, H., Bhattarakosol, P.: Authenticating user using keystroke dynamics and finger pressure. In: Proceedings of the 6th IEEE Consumer Communications and Networking Conference, CCNC 2009 (2009)
3. Zhong, Y., Deng, Y., Jain, A.: Keystroke dynamics for user authentication. In: 2012 IEEE Computer Society Conference on Computer Vision and Pattern Recognition Workshops (2012)
4. Ahmed, A.A.E., Traore, I., Almulhem, A.: Digital fingerprinting based on keystroke dynamics. In: Second International Symposium on Human Aspects of Information Security & Assurance (2008)
5. Ahmed, A.A., Traore, I.: Biometric recognition based on free-text keystroke dynamics. IEEE Trans. Cybern. **44**(4), 458–472 (2014)
6. Kambourakis, G., Damopoulos, D., Papamartzivanos, D., Pavlidakis, E.: Introducing touchstroke: keystroke-based authentication system for smartphones. Secur. Commun. Netw. **9**(6), 542–554 (2014). doi:10.1002/sec.1061
7. Buschek, D., De Luca, A., Alt, F.: Improving accuracy, applicability and usability of keystroke biometrics on mobile touchscreen devices. In: Proceedings of the 33rd Annual ACM Conference on Human Factors in Computing Systems. ACM (2015)

8. Kang, P., Cho, S.: Keystroke dynamics-based user authentication using long and free text strings from various input devices. Inf. Sci. **308**, 72–93 (2014). doi:10.1016/j.ins.2014.08. 070

9. Alpar, O.: Keystroke recognition in user authentication using ANN based RGB histogram technique. Eng. Appl. Artif. Intell. **32**, 213–217 (2014)

10. Alpar, O.: Frequency spectrograms for biometric keystroke authentication using neural network based classifier. Knowl. Based Syst. **116**, 163–171 (2017)

11. Alpar, O.: Intelligent biometric pattern password authentication systems for touchscreens. Expert Syst. Appl. **42**(17), 6286–6294 (2015)

12. Alpar, O., Krejcar, O.: Biometric swiping on touchscreens. In: Saeed, K., Homenda, W. (eds.) CISIM 2015. LNCS, vol. 9339, pp. 193–203. Springer, Cham (2015). doi:10.1007/ 978-3-319-24369-6_16

13. Alpar, O., Krejcar, O.: Pattern password authentication based on touching location. In: Jackowski, K., Burduk, R., Walkowiak, K., Woźniak, M., Yin, H. (eds.) IDEAL 2015. LNCS, vol. 9375, pp. 395–403. Springer, Cham (2015). doi:10.1007/978-3-319-24834-9_46

Robust Sensor Data Fusion Through Adaptive Threshold Learning

Bing Zhou[⊠], Hyuk Cho, and Adam Mansfield

Department of Computer Science, Sam Houston State University,
Huntsville, TX 77341, USA
zhou@shsu.edu

Abstract. Sensor fusion is the process of combining sensor readings from disparate resources so that the resulting information is more accurate and complete. The key challenge in sensor fusion arises from the inherent imperfection of data, commonly caused by sampling error, network respond time, imprecise measurement, and unreliable resources. Therefore, data fusion methods need to be advanced to address various aspects of data imperfections. In this paper, we first propose a novel unified data fusion framework based on rough set theory to systematically represent data granularity and imprecision. Then, we develop a cost-driven adaptive learning algorithm that can infer the optimal threshold values from data to obtain minimum cost. Our experimental study demonstrates the framework's effectiveness and validity.

Keywords: Sensor fusion · Rough sets · Cost-sensitive

1 Introduction

A sensor is a device that detects events or changes from physical environment and then provides sensed measurements. Multiple sensors are often used to monitor wider aspects of a system over a large geographical area. As different sensor data (e.g., sound, light, pressure, presence, heat, and temperature, to name a few) are collected overtime, sophisticated statistical techniques need to be applied to obtain a common representational format for further analysis. Sensor fusion is the process of combining sensor readings from a number of different resources in order to provide unified accurate, and complete information.

The inherent imperfection of data is the key challenge in sensor fusion as data from sensors is always affected by some levels of impreciseness and uncertainty in the measurements. Various data fusion methods can be employed to address different aspects of data-related problems. For example, a probabilistic distribution [1] can express data uncertainty; fuzzy set theory [2] can address vagueness of data; evidential belief theory [3] can represent uncertain as well as ambiguous data; and rough set theory [4] provides a systematic representation to data granularity and imprecision. The first three approaches have been applied individually to the context of data fusion; however, no single existing

© Springer International Publishing AG 2017
S. Benferhat et al. (Eds.): IEA/AIE 2017, Part I, LNAI 10350, pp. 277–282, 2017.
DOI: 10.1007/978-3-319-60042-0_32

data fusion method is capable of simultaneously addressing multiple aspects of imperfect data. Compared with other fusion methods like fuzzy set theory and Bayesian inference, rough set theory does not require any prior knowledge; it represents imprecise data based only on its internal structure; thus, it can effectively represent different aspects of data.

In this paper, we propose a novel decision-level sensor fusion system that performs the following two main tasks. First task is to build a rough set-based fusion model so as to systematically represent data imperfections. The proposed model is particularly suited to reasoning about imprecise data and discovering relationships latent in data, since it relies on robustness of rough set theory. Second task is to develop an adaptive threshold learning algorithm so as to minimize decision cost. It is often difficult to choose the best fixed cut-off threshold value at the final decision fusion stage. While a high fixed threshold usually leads to high precision, but resulting in low recall, a low fixed threshold produces the opposite results. Therefore, instead of directly using a fixed threshold, in this study, we identify cost controlling factors that are related to threshold values to be optimized.

The rest of the paper is organized as follows. Section 2 introduces a rough set-based sensor fusion model. A cost-driven learning algorithm that can adaptively infer the optimal threshold value is proposed in Sect. 3. The experimental results and conclusion are presented in Sects. 4 and 5, respectively.

2   Rough Set-Based Sensor Fusion Model

2.1   Decision-Level Sensor Fusion

The decision-level sensor fusion consists of the four main steps: (1) data collection from different sensors, (2) feature extraction to reduce both dimension and time complexity, (3) processing of each sensor to achieve a preliminary determination, and (4) integration of individual sensors decisions to obtain a joint identity declaration or decision.

The most commonly-used decision-level fusion is based on Bayesian inference for combining prior and observation information [5,6]. However, the prior probability and conditional probability must be known in advance. Other decision-level fusion methods include evidential belief theory [7], fuzzy probability approach [13], [14], rule-based method, and voting [8,9]. These existing sensor fusion methods target to optimize functions that give better estimations of sensor outputs, by fixing function thresholds either based on a hypothesis or given by domain experts. As threshold values play a critical role in estimating function values, it is desirable to adaptively infer proper threshold values that may result in better fusion accuracy.

2.2   The Rough Set Approach to Sensor Fusion

Traditional sensor fusion approaches use a discriminate function to differentiate positive and negative detection results based on the outputs of different sensors.

The output of each sensor is a measure of confidence in the presence of a positive result. The discriminant function $f(\boldsymbol{a})$ is defined as $f(\boldsymbol{a}) \geq \gamma$ to indicate the positive detection result, and $f(\boldsymbol{a}) < \gamma$ to indicate negative result, where $\boldsymbol{a} = \{a_1, ..., a_n\}$ with $a_i \in [0, 1]$, is a sensor output vector of n sensors, and γ is the threshold.

In the context of rough set theory, the discriminate function is defined as: $f(\boldsymbol{a}) = Pr(X|[x]) = \frac{|X \cap [x]|}{|[x]|}$, where X denotes a given set, $[x]$ denotes the equivalence class, and $|\cdot|$ denotes the cardinality of a set. Therefore, $f(\boldsymbol{a})$ can be interpreted as the conditional probability that considers the degrees of overlap between equivalence class $[x]$ and a set X to be approximated. The definitions of positive, negative, and boundary regions in rough sets lead to a three-way data fusion.

Within the sensor fusion problems, set X can be considered as representing the imprecise set of (target) states/classes of a system. Therefore, possible states of the system can be approximated based on the granularity of input data. After then, the states can be fused using simple conjunctive or disjunctive operators.

3   Computing Thresholds Through Cost-Driven Adaptive Learning Algorithm

Traditional data fusion methods use a fixed threshold $\gamma \in [0, 1]$ to control the final discrimination results. However, it is difficult to choose in advance the proper constant γ value that may lead to an optimal decision. In rough set based decision-level sensor fusion, we make a three-way decision based on each sensor output, although the true class is only binary. A pair of thresholds (α, β) with $0 \leq \beta < \alpha \leq 1$ is used to distinguish different value ranges of the discriminate function. The threshold α determines the probability necessary for a re-examination, and the threshold β determines the probability necessary for determining a negative results.

3.1   Decision-Theoretic Rough Set Model

Traditional data fusion tasks use minimizing error rate as the guideline. The error rate assigns a binary decision (no loss to a correct decision and a unit loss to any error); thus, all errors are equally costly. In sensor fusion problems, many errors have different cost. Therefore, we adopt the loss function from the Decision-Theoretic Rough Set (DTRS) model [10], in which the expected losses associated with making different decisions for objects with description $[x]$ can be expressed as: $R(a_P|[x]) = \lambda_{PP} Pr(X|[x]) + \lambda_{PN} Pr(X^c|[x])$, $R(a_B|[x]) = \lambda_{BP} Pr(X|[x]) + \lambda_{BN} Pr(X^c|[x])$, and $R(a_N|[x]) = \lambda_{NP} Pr(X|[x]) + \lambda_{NN} Pr(X^c|[x])$, where λ_{PP}, λ_{BP} and λ_{NP} denote the losses incurred for making three decisions for an object $x \in X$, and λ_{PN}, λ_{BN} and λ_{NN} denote the losses incurred for making these decisions for $x \notin X$.

Based on the derivation results from DTRS [10], three parameters can be obtained using different loss function values: $\alpha = \frac{(\lambda_{PN}-\lambda_{BN})}{(\lambda_{PN}-\lambda_{BN})+(\lambda_{BP}-\lambda_{PP})}$, $\beta = \frac{(\lambda_{BN}-\lambda_{NN})}{(\lambda_{BN}-\lambda_{NN})+(\lambda_{NP}-\lambda_{BP})}$, and $\gamma = \frac{(\lambda_{PN}-\lambda_{NN})}{(\lambda_{PN}-\lambda_{NN})+(\lambda_{NP}-\lambda_{PP})}$.

3.2   A Cost-Driven Adaptive Learning Algorithm

We propose an adaptive learning algorithm that can provide a sequence of cost modifications to find proper threshold values for an optimal data fusion. The core idea is to learn optimal thresholds based upon the minimization of the total decision cost, which can be formulated by the conditional probabilities of given data and loss functions.

To be more specific, assume the loss functions $\lambda_{PP} = \lambda_{NN} = 0$. Since $Pr(X|[x]) + Pr(X^c|[x]) = 1$, the expected cost can be rewritten as: $cost_P = \lambda_{PN}(1 - Pr(X|[x]))$, $cost_B = \lambda_{BP}Pr(X|[x]) + \lambda_{BN}(1 - Pr(X|[x]))$, $cost_N = \lambda_{NP}Pr(X|[x])$. Each represents the cost of making a positive decision, a deferment decision, and a negative decision, respectively. These three costs form the total decision cost:

$$
\begin{aligned}
cost_{total} &= cost_P + cost_B + cost_N \\
&= \sum_{Pr(X|[x]) \geq \alpha} \lambda_{PN}(1 - Pr(X|[x])) \\
&+ \sum_{\beta < Pr(X|[x]) < \alpha} (\lambda_{BP}Pr(X|[x]) + \lambda_{BN}(1 - Pr(X|[x]))) \\
&+ \sum_{Pr(X|[x]) \leq \beta} \lambda_{NP}Pr(X|[x]).
\end{aligned} \tag{1}
$$

Input: the pre-processed training dataset T, two classes X (positive) and X^c (negative), and a given 3×2 cost matrix.
Output: three threshold values (α, β, γ).
begin
  compute initial threshold (α, β, γ) based on the given cost matrix;
  $cost_{min} = DBL_{MAX}$;
  for each $x \in T$ do
    $p = Pr(X \mid [x])$;
    if $\alpha < p < 1$
      $cost_x = computeCost(x, T, p, \beta, \gamma)$;
      if $cost_x < cost_{min}$
        $cost_{min} = cost_x$;
        $\alpha = p$;
    if $\beta < p < \alpha$
      $cost_x = computeCost(x, T, \alpha, \beta, p)$;
      if $cost_x < cost_{min}$
        $cost_{min} = cost_x$;
        $\gamma = p$;
    if $0 < p < \beta$
      $cost_x = computeCost(x, T, \alpha, p, \gamma)$;
      if $cost_x < cost_{min}$
        $cost_{min} = cost_x$;
        $\beta = p$;
  end
  return (α, β, γ);
end

Fig. 1. The cost-driven adaptive learning algorithm.

The proposed cost-driven adaptive learning algorithm is described in Fig. 1, where the computeCost() function refers to Eq. (1). The optimal threshold values are systematically learned from data by adaptively searching for the minimal total decision cost.

4   Experimental Study

In this section, we compare the proposed rough set approach with existing fusion methods. Our experiments were performed on the well-known smartphone sensor dataset: Human Activity Recognition Using Smartphones from UCI repository [13]. It contains 561 continuous features from gyroscope and accelerometer sensors. There are six classes of activities, and 10,299 instances. We used the ReliefF algorithm [12] to rank the importance of each feature and the top 12 ranked features were selected. To reduce the number of equivalence classes, we used equal-frequency discretization method.

The fusion steps discussed in Sect. 2.1 were applied. The six classes were converted to 15 binary classification problems by pairing two class at a time. Figure 2 shows fusion performance comparison between Support Vector Machine (SVM) and the rough set (RS) approach. The RS approach provides better or similar precision performance on 13 out of 15 classes. Figure 3 shows the performance comparison between SVM, MetaCost (i.e., SVM cost sensitive) from WEKA, and the RS approach, under a different cost setting. The RS approach consistently performs better than SVM and MetaCost. In terms of cost-sensitive learning, the RS approach has more consistent results than the MetaCost method that results in very low precisions for five classes. In summary, the RS approach provides a consistent cost-sensitive sensor fusion while improving the fusion accuracy.

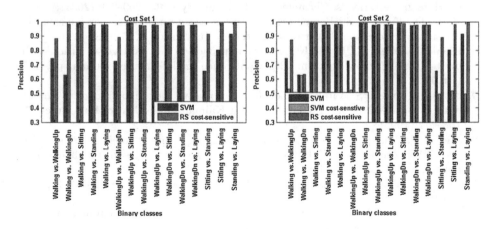

Fig. 2. Precision of SVM and RS.   **Fig. 3.** Precision of SVM, MetaCost, and RS.

5   Conclusions

In this paper, we propose a robust sensor fusion model based on rough set theory. The proposed system is unique in terms of the following aspects: (1) the rough set operations realize robust sensor fusion system that can collect and process heterogeneous sensor data so as to systematically represent data imperfections, and (2) the adaptive calculation of threshold values (based on loss function) will realize a cost-sensitive fusion model. Therefore, the proposed approach promotes the awareness of the necessity and importance of sensor fusion through a unified framework, makes significant research progress in heterogeneous sensor fusion, and obtains a better fusion accuracy.

Acknowledgements. The work was supported by the Enhancement Research Grant (ERG) from Office of Research Administration (SHSU).

References

1. Duda, R.O., Hart, P.E.: Pattern Classification and Scene Analysis. Wiley, New York (1973)
2. Zadeh, L.A.: Fuzzy sets. Inf. Control **8**(3), 338–353 (1965)
3. Shafer, G.: A Mathematical Theory of Evidence. Princeton University Press, Princeton (1976)
4. Pawlak, Z.: Rough Sets, Theoretical Aspects of Reasoning about Data. Kluwer Academic Publishers, Dordrecht (1991)
5. Williams, M., Wilson, R., Hancock, E.: Multi-sensor fusion with Bayesian inference. Comput. Anal. Images Patterns **1296**, 25–32 (2005)
6. Roussel, S., Bellon-Maurel, V., Roger, J., Grenier, P.: Fusion of aroma, FT-IR and UV sensor data based on the Bayesian inference. Application to the discrimination of white grape varieties. Chemometr. Intell. Lab. Syst. **65**, 209–219 (2003)
7. Basir, O., Yuan, X.H.: Engine fault diagnosis based on multi-sensor information fusion using Dempster-Shafer evidence theory. Inf. Fusion **8**, 379–386 (2007)
8. Blank, S., Fohst, T., Berns, K.: A fuzzy approach to low level sensor fusion with limited system knowledge. In: 13th Conference on Information Fusion, pp. 1–7 (2010)
9. Jetto, L., Longhi, S., Vitali, D.: Localization of a wheeled mobile robot by sensor data fusion based on a fuzzy logic adapted Kalman filter. Control Eng. Pract. **7**, 763–771 (1999)
10. Yao, Y.Y., Wong, S.K.M., Lingras, P.: A decision-theoretic rough set model. In: Ras, Z.W., Zemankova, M., Emrich, M.L. (eds.) Methodologies for Intelligent Systems 5, pp. 17–24. North-Holland, New York (1990)
11. Yao, Y.Y.: Three-way decisions with probabilistic rough sets. Inf. Sci. **180**, 341–353 (2010)
12. Robnik-ikonja, M., Kononenko, I.: Theoretical and empirical analysis of ReliefF and RReliefF. Mach. Learn. **53**(1–2), 23–69 (2003)
13. https://archive.ics.uci.edu/ml/datasets/Human+Activity+Recognition+Using+Smartphones

An Application of Fuzzy Signal-to-Noise Ratio to the Assessment of Manufacturing Processes

Shiang-Tai Liu[✉]

Graduate School of Business and Management, Vanung University, Chung-Li,
Tao-Yuan 320, Taiwan, ROC
stliu@vnu.edu.tw

Abstract. Taguchi method is an important tool used for robust design to produce high quality products efficiently. In Taguchi method, the signal-to-noise (SN) ratio serves as the objective function for optimization. This ratio is a useful measurement indicator for manufacturing processes. Conventionally, one calculates the SN ratio with the crisp observations. However, there are cases that observations are difficult to measure precisely, or observations need to be estimated. This paper develops a fuzzy nonlinear programming model, based on the SN ratio, to assess the manufacturing processes with fuzzy observations. A pair of nonlinear fractional programs is formulated to calculate the lower and upper bounds of the fuzzy SN ratio. By model reduction and variable substitutions, the nonlinear fractional programs are transformed into quadratic programs. Solving the transformed quadratic programs, we obtain the global optimum solutions of the lower bound and upper bound fuzzy SN ratio. By deriving the ranking index of the fuzzy SN ratios of the manufacturing process alternatives, the ranking result of the assessment is determined.

Keywords: Signal-to-noise ratio · Fuzzy sets · Manufacturing process

1 Introduction

Taguchi methodology is a powerful optimization tool, which is employed to improve the process performance. The signal-to-noise (SN) ratio, designed for optimizing the robustness of a product or process, is useful to measure the relative quality. This ratio is the quality indicator that indicates the scattering around a target value. Most studies concern the deterministic cases that the observations in the models are precisely known. However, in real world applications, there are cases that the observations might be inexact and have to be estimated. For examples, real observations of continuous quantities are not accurate numbers and the output measurements are judged with humans' partial knowledge. A way for dealing with uncertainty in observations is to represent uncertain observations by fuzzy numbers.

There are some studies in the literature discussing fuzzy product development and process performance evaluation. [7, 11, 12]. Conventionally, one calculates the SN ratio with the crisp observations. When the observations are fuzzy numbers, intuitively, the calculated SN ratio is fuzzy as well. A pair of nonlinear fractional programs is formulated

© Springer International Publishing AG 2017
S. Benferhat et al. (Eds.): IEA/AIE 2017, Part I, LNAI 10350, pp. 283–288, 2017.
DOI: 10.1007/978-3-319-60042-0_33

to calculate the lower bound and upper bound of the fuzzy SN ratio. By model reduction and variable substitutions, the nonlinear fractional programs, are transformed into quadratic programs. Solving the transformed quadratic programs at specified α-levels, we obtain the global optimum solutions of the lower bound and upper bound of the fuzzy SN ratio. By applying the associated fuzzy number ranking method, the ranking result of the assessment of manufacturing processes is obtained.

In the sections that follow, we first introduce the concept of SN ratio, and a pair of nonlinear fractional programs is formulated to find the lower bound and upper bound of the fuzzy SN ratio with fuzzy observations. Next, we utilize the model reduction and variable substitutions to transform the pair of nonlinear fractional programs into a pair of quadratic programs to solve. Finally, some conclusions of this work are presented.

2   SN Ratio

Taguchi method is an important tool used for robust design to produce high quality products efficiently. In Taguchi method, log functions of desired outputs, known as the signal-to-noise (SN) ratio, serve as the objective functions for optimization. There are three forms of SN ratio, namely, smaller-the-better, larger-the-better, and nominal-the-best that are of common interest for optimization of static problems. Denote y_i be the ith observation of an experiment. The nominal-the-best-type problem is narrated in (1).

$$r = 10 \times \log_{10} \left(\frac{\bar{y}^2}{s^2} \right),$$ (1)

where $\bar{y} = \sum_{i=1}^{n} y_i/n$ and $s^2 = \sum_{i=1}^{n} (y_i - \bar{y})^2/(n-1)$.

A nominal-the-best-type problem is the one where the minimization of the mean square error around a specific target value is desired. There are two important features of the nominal-the-best type problem. One is that the target value is finite and nonzero, and the other is that when the mean is zero, the standard deviation is also zero [8]. Since the nominal-the-best-type SN ratio is an effective tool that considers the mean and variance of observations, it is suitable to adopt this SN ratio as an index for evaluation of manufacturing-process alternatives.

3   SN Ratio with Fuzzy Observations

Without loss of generality and for convenience of notation, assume that all observations in manufacturing process are fuzzy numbers, as crisp values can be considered as degenerated fuzzy numbers with only one point in the domain. Let $\tilde{Y}_i$ denote the fuzzy counterpart of Y_i, and denote $\mu_{\tilde{Y}_i}$ as the membership functions of $\tilde{Y}_i$. Conceptually, Eq. (1) for fuzzy observations in manufacturing process can be formulated as:

$$\tilde{R} = 10\log_{10} \left(\frac{1}{n} \sum_{i=1}^{n} \tilde{Y}_i \right)^2 \Big/ \frac{1}{n-1} \sum_{i=1}^{n} \left(\tilde{Y}_i - \frac{1}{n} \sum_{i=1}^{n} \tilde{Y}_i \right)^2$$ (2)

When observations are fuzzy numbers, the measured SN ratio, $\tilde{R}$, is a fuzzy number as well. Let $(Y_i)_\alpha = \left[(Y_i)_\alpha^L, (Y_i)_\alpha^U\right]$ be the α-cuts of $\tilde{Y}_i$. To find $R_\alpha = \left[R_\alpha^L, R_\alpha^U\right]$, we need to find the lower and upper bounds of the α-cut of $\tilde{R}$. The upper bound R_α^U is equal to $\max\{r|\mu_{\tilde{R}}(r) \geq \alpha\}$, and the lower bound R_α^L is equal to $\min\{r|\mu_{\tilde{R}}(r) \geq \alpha\}$, where r is defined in (1). Thus, R_α^L and R_α^U can be calculated via the following mathematical programs:

$$R_\alpha^U = \max_{\substack{(Y_i)_\alpha^L \leq y_i \leq (Y_i)_\alpha^U \\ \forall i}} 10\log_{10} \frac{1}{n^2}\left(\sum_{i=1}^{n} \tilde{Y}_i\right)^2 \Big/ \frac{1}{n-1}\sum_{i=1}^{n}\left(\tilde{Y}_i - \frac{1}{n}\sum_{i=1}^{n}\tilde{Y}_i\right)^2 \tag{3}$$

$$R_\alpha^L = \min_{\substack{(Y_i)_\alpha^L \leq y_i \leq (Y_i)_\alpha^U \\ \forall i}} 10\log_{10} \frac{1}{n^2}\left(\sum_{i=1}^{n} \tilde{Y}_i\right)^2 \Big/ \frac{1}{n-1}\sum_{i=1}^{n}\left(\tilde{Y}_i - \frac{1}{n}\sum_{i=1}^{n}\tilde{Y}_i\right)^2 \tag{4}$$

The set of y_i values, which produces the smallest and largest SN ratios, is lying in ranges. Since the feasible region for variable y_i is a hyper-rectangle, which is a convex and compact set, the bounds R_α^U and R_α^L are continuous with respect to y_i. Based on this concept, a numerical method can be devised to solve this pair of mathematical programs. Clearly, Models (3) and (4) are nonlinear fractional programs, which do not guarantee to have stationary points. There are several studies discussing the solution methodologies of fractional programming [2, 5, 10]. However, they cannot be applied directly to solve (3) and (4). Therefore, we need to develop solution procedures for (3) and (4), respectively, to derive the optimum solutions. Both the objective functions of Models (3) and (4) can be reduced to:

$$-R_\alpha^U = \min 10\log_{10}\left[\frac{n^2}{n-1}\sum_{i=1}^{n}\left(\frac{y_i}{\sum_{i=1}^{n}y_i}\right)^2 - \frac{n}{n-1}\right], \text{ s.t. } (Y_i)_\alpha^L \leq y_i \leq (Y_i)_\alpha^U, \forall i. \tag{5}$$

$$-R_\alpha^L = \max 10\log_{10}\left[\frac{n^2}{n-1}\sum_{i=1}^{n}\left(\frac{y_i}{\sum_{i=1}^{n}y_i}\right)^2 - \frac{n}{n-1}\right], \text{ s.t. } (Y_i)_\alpha^L \leq y_i \leq (Y_i)_\alpha^U, \forall i. \tag{6}$$

Let $-R_\alpha = 10 \times \log_{10}\left[\frac{n^2}{n-1}Z_\alpha - \frac{n}{n-1}\right]$, where $Z_\alpha = [Z_\alpha^L, Z_\alpha^U] = \sum_{i=1}^{n}\left(y_i / \sum_{i=1}^{n}y_i\right)^2$,

s.t. $(Y_i)_\alpha^L \leq y_i \leq (Y_i)_\alpha^U, i = 1, \ldots, n$. Clearly, both $\frac{n^2}{n-1}$ and $\frac{n}{n-1}$ are known constants, and the larger the value of Z_α, the smaller the value of R_α is. Therefore, we can obtain the max/min value of R_α by finding the min/max value of Z_α. In other words, if Z_α^* is the optimal solution, then

$$-R_\alpha^* = 10 \times \log_{10}\left[\frac{n^2}{n-1}Z_\alpha^* - \frac{n}{n-1}\right] \tag{7}$$

which is equivalent to (8)

$$R_\alpha^* = -10 \times \log_{10}\left[\frac{n^2}{n-1}Z_\alpha^* - \frac{n}{n-1}\right] \tag{8}$$

Model (5) is to find $-R_\alpha^U$ with a set of fuzzy observations at a specified α-level. We first need to find the smallest value of $Z_\alpha^L = \sum_{i=1}^n \left(y_i / \sum_{i=1}^n y_i\right)^2$, s.t. $(Y_i)_\alpha^L \le y_i \le (Y_i)_\alpha^U, i = 1, \ldots, n$, so that we can obtain the largest value of R_α^U. The value of Z_α^L can be reached via the following mathematical form:

$$Z_\alpha^L = \min \sum_{i=1}^n \left(y_i / \sum_{i=1}^n y_i\right)^2, \text{ s.t. } (Y_i)_\alpha^L \le y_i \le (Y_i)_\alpha^U, i = 1, \ldots, n. \tag{9}$$

Following the variable substitution of Charnes and Cooper [3], we let $t = 1/\sum_{i=1}^n y_i$ and $w_i = ty_i$. Since $t > 0$, one can multiply the constraint of (13) by t and transform (9) into the following mathematical program:

$$Z_\alpha^L = \min \sum_{i=1}^n w_i^2, \text{ s.t. } \sum_{i=1}^n w_i = 1, (Y_i)_\alpha^L t \le w_i \le (Y_i)_\alpha^U t, \forall i, t > 0. \tag{10}$$

Clearly, Model (10) is a quadratic program with linear constraints. Since the quadratic function is concave upward and the feasible region is a convex set, the objective value Z_α^{L*} derived from (10) is the global optimum solution. Putting Z_α^{L*} into (8), we obtain the $R_\alpha^{U*} = -10 \times \log_{10}\left[n^2 Z_\alpha^{L*}/(n-1) - n/(n-1)\right]$.

On the other hand, Model (6) is to find $-R_\alpha^L$ with a set of fuzzy observations. Before finding the smallest value of R_α^L, we have to search the largest value of $Z_\alpha^U = \sum_{i=1}^n \left(y_i / \sum_{i=1}^n y_i\right)^2$, s.t. $(Y_i)_\alpha^L \le y_i \le (Y_i)_\alpha^U, i = 1, \ldots, n$, first, and its associated formulation is as follows:

$$Z_\alpha^U = \max \sum_{i=1}^n \left(y_i / \sum_{i=1}^n y_i\right)^2, \text{ s.t. } (Y_i)_\alpha^L \le y_i \le (Y_i)_\alpha^U, i = 1, \ldots, n. \tag{11}$$

Similar to (9), we can transform (11) into the following mathematical program:

$$Z_\alpha^U = \max \sum_{i=1}^n w_i^2, \text{ s.t. } \sum_{i=1}^n w_i = 1, (Y_i)_\alpha^L t \le w_i \le (Y_i)_\alpha^U t, \forall i, t > 0. \tag{12}$$

The only difference between (10) and (12) is the direction for optimization. Computing the upper bound of the objective value with the quadratic function is a NP-hard problem [9]. However, since the objective function is concave upward and the constraints are linear and boxed in (12), the optimal solution of (12) should occur at extreme points [1]. The algorithm for ranking the extreme points proposed by [6] can be applied to find the optimal solution. Moreover, $t = w_i/y_i > 0$ and $\sum_{i=1}^n w_i = 1$, it implies that the variables t and w_i, $\forall i$, are the basic variables and always stay at the basis in the solution processes. This property helps reduce the search times for the optimal solution. After solving (12), one can obtain the optimal solution Z_α^{U*} by verifying the solutions derived from the extreme points of (12). The corresponding value of R_α^L is calculated as $R_\alpha^{L*} = -10 \times \log_{10}\left[n^2 Z_\alpha^{U*}/(n-1) - n/(n-1)\right]$ via substituting Z_α^{U*} into (8). Together with R_α^{U*} solved from (10), $R_\alpha = \left[R_\alpha^{L*}, R_\alpha^{U*}\right]$ constitutes the fuzzy SN ratio at a specific α-level. The numerical solutions for R_α^{L*} and R_α^{U*} at different α-levels can be collected to depict the shape of the membership function $\mu_{\tilde{R}}$.

Since the derived values of the SN ratios are fuzzy numbers, a ranking method is needed to compare the fuzzy SN ratios. The method of Chen and Klein [4], which does not need the exact membership functions of the fuzzy numbers to be ranked, is a proper method for this study. Chen and Klein [4] devise the following index for ranking fuzzy numbers:

$$I(\tilde{R}_j) = \sum_{i=0}^{\infty}\left((R_j)_{\alpha_i}^U - p\right) \Big/ \left[\sum_{i=0}^{\infty}\left((R_j)_{\alpha_i}^U - p\right) - \sum_{i=0}^{\infty}\left((R_j)_{\alpha_i}^L - q\right)\right] \qquad (13)$$

where $p = \min\limits_{i,j}\{(R_j)_{\alpha_i}^L\}$ and $q = \max\limits_{i,j}\{(R_j)_{\alpha_i}^U\}$. The larger the value of the ranking index $I(\tilde{R}_j)$, the larger the number is. Now we utilize the ranking method proposed by [4] to distinguish the manufacturing processes. Since we have the fuzzy SN ratios of manufacturing processes, the number of α-cuts is set to 10 in (13).

4 Conclusion

This paper extends the calculation of the deterministic SN ratio to uncertain cases, where the observations are represented by fuzzy numbers, for the evaluation of manufacturing processes. A pair of two-level mathematical programs is developed to calculate the fuzzy SN ratio of the manufacturing process alternatives. Originally, the pair of mathematical programs is a pair of nonlinear fractional programming problems, which do not guarantee to have global optimum solutions. By model reduction and variable substitutions, the pair of nonlinear fractional programming problems is transformed into a pair of quadratic programs for the derivation of the global optimum solutions. At a specific α-cut, solving the pair of quadratic programs produces the lower bound and upper bound interval of the fuzzy SN ratio. The membership function of fuzzy SN ratio can be approximated numerically via enumerating various values of α. By deriving the ranking index of the fuzzy SN ratios of the manufacturing process alternatives, the rank of the assessment is determined.

Acknowledgment. Research was supported by the Ministry of Science and Technology of Taiwan under Grant No. NSC102-2410-H-238-005.

References

1. Bazaraa, M.S., Sherali, H.D., Shetty, C.M.: Nonlinear Programming-Theory and Algorithm, 2nd edn. Wiley, New York (1993)
2. Benson, H.P.: Fractional programming with convex quadratic forms and functions. Eur. J. Oper. Res. **173**, 351–369 (2006)
3. Charnes, A., Cooper, W.W.: Programming with linear fractional functional. Naval Res. Logistics Q. **9**, 181–186 (1962)
4. Chen, C.B., Klein, C.M.: A simple approach to ranking a group of aggregated utilities. IEEE Trans. Syst. Man Cybern. Part B **27**, 26–35 (1997)
5. Liu, S.T.: Fractional transportation problem with fuzzy parameters. Soft. Comput. **20**, 3629–3636 (2016)
6. Pardalos, P.M.: An algorithm for a class of nonlinear fractional problems using ranking of the vertices. BIT **26**, 392–395 (1986)
7. Shu, M.H., Wu, H.C.: Manufacturing process performance evaluation for fuzzy data based on loss-based capability index. Soft. Comput. **16**, 89–99 (2012)
8. Su, C.T.: Quality Engineering: Off-Line Methods and Applications. CRC Press, London (2013)
9. Vasant, P., Barsoum, N.N.: Fuzzy optimization of units products in mix-product selection problem using fuzzy linear programming approach. Soft. Comput. **10**, 144–151 (2006)
10. Wang, C.F., Shen, P.P.: A global optimization algorithm for linear fractional programming. Appl. Math. Comput. **204**, 281–287 (2008)
11. Wu, C.W., Liao, M.Y.: Fuzzy nonlinear programming approach for evaluating and ranking process yields with imprecise data. Fuzzy Sets Syst. **246**, 142–155 (2014)
12. Xu, Y.: Model for evaluating the mechanical product design quality with dual hesitant fuzzy information. J. Intell. Fuzzy Syst. **30**, 1–6 (2016)

Biometric Keystroke Signal Preprocessing
Part II: Manipulation

Orcan Alpar and Ondrej Krejcar[✉]

Faculty of Informatics and Management, Center for Basic and Applied Research,
University of Hradec Kralove, Rokitanskeho 62, 500 03 Hradec Kralove, Czech Republic
orcan.alpar@uhk.cz, ondrej@krejcar.org

Abstract. Biometric keystroke authentication methods deal with extracting the key-press times to validate the users considering the uniqueness of password entering style. When the proposed algorithms have no sub-system to check the password itself, the keystroke signal should include the key-codes for better discrimination. On the contrary, if the key-codes are already validated, the signal could be irreversibly manipulated to form a new and unique signal. In general, the key-press and inter-key times are directly used as array, subsequent to extraction without any process. Therefore in this paper we propose several techniques for preprocessing the keystroke signal. The main methods we dealt with are binarization, over-quantization and spectrogram conversion. As a result of these conversions, the new signals somehow exhibit same property and tendency of the original signal, while revealing the hidden features.

Keywords: Biometrics · Keystroke · Authentication · Signal processing · Manipulation

1 Introduction

Biometric keystroke authentication is a prominent approach to enhance the regular passwords typed on a keyboard. The systems mostly collect the key-press times to calculate the inter-key times of a password, therefore the majority of the algorithms proposed previously extract the similar features, the key-press and inter-key times, as presented in Part I. Many papers start from this point by utilizing what they have extracted without any kind of preprocessing. Therefore, the novelty is proposed regardless of data acquisition methodologies and thus the results presented are strictly dependent on the classification algorithms. These algorithms actually have a great variety in the literature, yet most of the prominent papers deal with statistical aspects for classification using inter-key times or related, while some researchers managed to extract some uncommon features like pressure [1, 2] or fingerprints [3]. On the other hand, it is possible to see some promising kernels for differentiating the keystrokes such as: neural networks [4] k-nearest neighbors [5], support vector machines [6]. We also presented some novel methodologies for classification the keystroke signals: such as adaptive-neurofuzzy inference [7] and Levenberg-Marquadt [8, 9], Gauss-Newton [10],

© Springer International Publishing AG 2017
S. Benferhat et al. (Eds.): IEA/AIE 2017, Part I, LNAI 10350, pp. 289–294, 2017.
DOI: 10.1007/978-3-319-60042-0_34

nonetheless the major novelty in our papers start with data manipulation and alteration, which will be presented in Sect. 2.

Regarding total and irreversible manipulation of the signals; we proposed a RGB methodology in [11] by coloring the intervals starting from red and gradiently approaching to blue. Afterwards, we omitted the original signal and applied neural network classification to the newly formed image. Moreover, in our latest published research [10], while applying a Gauss-Newton optimized neural classifier to the signal which had already been transformed into frequency-domain, we computed the spectrograms that will reveal the key-press time vs high-frequency regions. Therefore, we present several manipulation techniques for changing the signal of keystrokes irreversibly, in use throughout keyboard-based authentication protocols.

2   Keystroke Signal Acquisition

We firstly extract the whole signal $[f_n(t)]$ presented in Part I, as a matrix and manipulated by:

$$[g_m(z)] = \begin{cases} [\ ] \mid [f_n(t)] = 0 \\ [\ ] \mid f_n(t) = 13, \ t = 1, 2, 3, \ldots, n \\ [f_n(t)] \mid o/w \end{cases} \tag{1}$$

where m is the new length of the signal and z is the new timer value. As all operations mentioned in this paper, this shortening process is a matrix operation, therefore any function or variable in brackets [] represent a matrix. The signals $[f_n(t)]$ and $[g_m(z)]$ produced by our interface for the password "orcan7890*" are presented in Fig. 1.

We propose several methods by manipulating the original keystroke signal, subsequently to deal with a newly created, unique and irreversible signal in following sections.

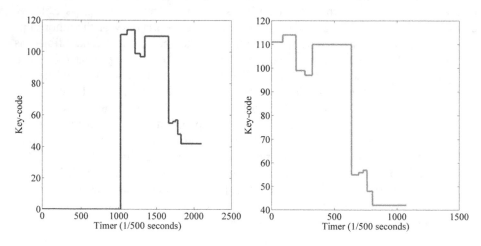

Fig. 1.   Keystroke signal examples $f_n(t)$ on the left, $g_m(z)$ on the right

3   Binarization

The very first method we investigate is the binarization to create a binary-finite or a binary-train signal. To form a binary signal for key-press times is simple that the algorithm searched for the key-code differences cell by cell to find the exact key-press times, namely:

$$[b_n(t)] = \begin{cases} 0 \mid f_n(t) = f_n(t+1) \\ 1 \mid f_n(t) \neq f_n(t+1) \end{cases}, t = 1, 2, 3, \ldots, n \tag{2}$$

$$[r_n(t+1)] = \begin{cases} r_n(t) \mid f_n(t+1) = f_n(t+2) \\ 1 \mid f_n(t+1) \neq f_n(t+2) \wedge r_n(t) = 0 \\ 0 \mid f_n(t+1) \neq f_n(t+2) \wedge r_n(t) = 1 \end{cases} \quad t = 1, ..n-1 \tag{3}$$

where the initial value of $r_n(t)$ is $r_n(1) = 0$. The results of these transformation could be found in Fig. 2.

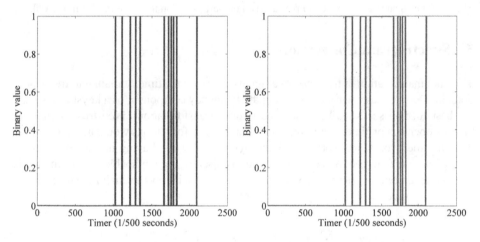

Fig. 2. Binary signal examples $b_n(t)$ on the left, $r_n(t)$ on the right

4   Over-Digitization

If the signal is over-digitized by an interval, the new digital signal somehow represents the original data, however if a decimalization and rounding protocol are simultaneously applied, the signal is converted into the new one, by $[d_n^q(t)] = q.fix[f_n(t)/q]$, $t = 0, 1, 2, \ldots, n$, where q is the quantization interval, fix is rounding operator. Strictly dependent on q, the following signals in Fig. 3 are achieved. The violet lines represent the over quantized signal, while the red dots are the original signal. The newly created signals are unique and still associated with the habitual biometric traits of the users, despite the new forms they have. While the quantization interval is increasing, the detail level decrease, nevertheless the signal created by this conversion could be used instead of the data triples.

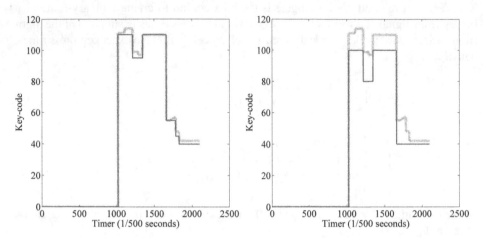

Fig. 3. Over-quantized signal examples $d_n^5(t)$ on the left, $d_n^{15}(t)$ on the right (Color figure online)

5   Spectrogram Conversion

The final manipulation of the keystroke signals is turning the time-domain into frequency-domain. Despite many ways of revealing the frequency component of a keystroke signal, the best method seems to be short-time Fourier transformations. Keystroke signal are highly dependent on time, therefore regular Fourier transformations would neglect the time data. In other words, we would know the frequencies while having no idea when these frequencies are emerged. Since the signal still is discrete, the applicable transformation is short-time discrete Fourier that divides the signals into windows to analyze. The common method to prosecco the signal $f_n(t)$ is as follows:

$$STDFT_f^u(t',u) = \sum_{x=0}^{N-1} \left[f_n(t)W(t-t') \right] e^{-j2\pi ut}, u = 0,1,\dots,N-1 \tag{4}$$

where W is the windowing function centered at $t = t'$, u is the frequency and t is the time parameter. If $W(t - t')$ is excessively large, the transformation will only reveal the frequency component, if is its too narrow, only the key-press times will be found. Among the various windowing function, we will use the Blackman window to calculate the spectrogram by $\left| STDFT_f^u(t',u) \right|^2$. It is still possible to process the spectrogram as an RGB image by mapping each pixel $p_{i,j,k}$ on the spectrogram by: and the

$$p_{i,j,k} \in \left| STDFT_f^u(t',u) \right|^2_{i,j,k} (i = [1{:}w], j = [1{:}h], k = [1{:}3]) \tag{5}$$

high-frequency regions are calculated by: $v_{i,j} = 0 \mid p_{i,j,1} < 128$, $v_{i,j} = 1 \mid o/w$, where $p_{i,j,1}$ represents the pixel on red-channel that can have a value of $0 \le p_{i,j,1} \le 255$. By vertical summation the histogram could be calculated by $H_i = \sum_{z=1}^{h} v_{i,h}$. The results of this process are presented in Fig. 4.

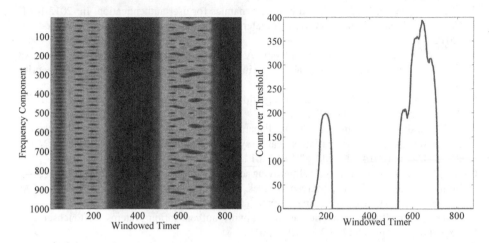

Fig. 4. Spectrogram $\left|STDFT_f^u(t', u)\right|^2$ on the left, High frequency histogram H_i (Color figure online)

6   Evaluation of the Results

The first results presented in this paper are the binarization protocol which can be used to omit the key-code data. The second method was over-quantitation of the signal for creating a new one yet still unique and depending on the traits of the users. The last methodology was Fourier transformation to reveal the frequency component versus time. These conversions should be so beneficial for researchers that deal with the keystrokes as a preliminary data acquisition or for fusion of the data when necessary.

7   Conclusion and Discussion

This paper proposes several techniques to prepare or alter the keystroke signal for classification. The main necessity for this research is lack of preprocessing of keystroke data since most of the papers start with acquisition of key-press times as the primary biometric trait, without any processing. This idea seems plausible indeed however turning the data into a signal or more precisely recording the keystrokes as a signal enables numerous transformations that can increase the validation accuracy afterwards.

Acknowledgement.   This work and the contribution were supported by project "SP/2017 – 2102 Smart Solutions for Ubiquitous Computing Environments" from University of Hradec Kralove.

References

1. Saevanee, H., Bhattarakosol, P.: Authenticating user using keystroke dynamics and finger pressure. In: Proceedings of the 6th IEEE Conference on Consumer Communications and Networking Conference, CCNC 2009 (2009)
2. Zhong, Y., Deng, Y., Jain, A.: Keystroke dynamics for user authentication. In: 2012 IEEE Computer Society Conference on Computer Vision and Pattern Recognition Workshops (2012)
3. Ahmed, A.A.E., Traore, I., Almulhem, A.: Digital fingerprinting based on keystroke dynamics. In: Second International Symposium on Human Aspects of Information Security & Assurance (2008)
4. Ahmed, A.A., Traore, I.: Biometric recognition based on free-text keystroke dynamics. IEEE Trans. Cybern. **44**(4), 458–472 (2014)
5. Kambourakis, G., Damopoulos, D., Papamartzivanos, D., Pavlidakis, E.: Introducing touchstroke: keystroke-based authentication system for smartphones. Secur. Commun. Netw. **9**(6), 542–554 (2014). doi:10.1002/sec.1061
6. Buschek, D., De Luca, D., Alt, F.: Improving accuracy, applicability and usability of keystroke biometrics on mobile touchscreen devices. In: Proceedings of the 33rd Annual ACM Conference on Human Factors in Computing Systems. ACM (2015)
7. Alpar, O.: Intelligent biometric pattern password authentication systems for touchscreens. Expert Syst. Appl. **42**(17), 6286–6294 (2015)
8. Alpar, O., Krejcar, O.: Pattern password authentication based on touching location. In: Jackowski, K., Burduk, R., Walkowiak, K., Woźniak, M., Yin, H. (eds.) IDEAL 2015. LNCS, vol. 9375, pp. 395–403. Springer, Cham (2015). doi:10.1007/978-3-319-24834-9_46
9. Alpar, O., Krejcar, O.: Biometric swiping on touchscreens. In: Saeed, K., Homenda, W. (eds.) CISIM 2015. LNCS, vol. 9339, pp. 193–203. Springer, Cham (2015). doi: 10.1007/978-3-319-24369-6_16
10. Alpar, O.: Frequency spectrograms for biometric keystroke authentication using neural network based classifier. Knowl. Based Syst. **116**, 163–171 (2017)
11. Alpar, O.: Keystroke recognition in user authentication using ANN based RGB histogram technique. Eng. Appl. Artif. Intell. **32**, 213–217 (2014)

Computational Intelligence Techniques for Modelling the Critical Flashover Voltage of Insulators: From Accuracy to Comprehensibility

Evangelos Karampotsis[1]([✉]), Konstantinos Boulas[1], Alexandros Tzanetos[1],
Vasilios P. Androvitsaneas[2], Ioannis F. Gonos[2], Georgios Dounias[1],
and Ioannis A. Stathopulos[2]

[1] Management and Decision Engineering Laboratory (MDE-Lab),
Department of Financial and Management Engineering, University of the Aegean,
41 Kountouriotou Street, 82100 Chios, Greece
karabotsis-evangelos@hotmail.com, g.dounias@aegean.gr
[2] High Voltage Laboratory, School of Electrical and Computer Engineering,
National Technical University of Athens, 9 Iroon Politechniou Street, Zografou Campus,
15780 Athens, Greece
v.andro@mail.ntua.gr

Abstract. This paper copes with the problem of flashover voltage on polluted insulators, being one of the most important components of electric power systems. A number of appropriately selected computational intelligence techniques are developed and applied for the modelling of the problem. Some of the applied techniques work as black-box models, but they are capable of achieving highly accurate results (artificial neural networks and gravitational search algorithms). Other techniques, on the contrary, obtain results somewhat less accurate, but highly comprehensible (genetic programming and inductive decision trees). However, all the applied techniques outperform standard data analysis approaches, such as regression models. The variables used in the analyses are the insulator's maximum diameter, height, creepage distance, insulator's manufacturing constant, and also the insulator's pollution. In this research work the critical flashover voltage on a polluted insulator is expressed as a function of the aforementioned variables. The used database consists of 168 different cases of polluted insulators, created through both actual and simulated values. Results are encouraging, with room for further study, aiming towards the development of models for the proper inspection and maintenance of insulators.

Keywords: Insulators · Critical flashover voltage · Computational intelligence · Artificial neural networks · Inductive decision trees · Genetic programming · Gravitational search algorithm

© Springer International Publishing AG 2017
S. Benferhat et al. (Eds.): IEA/AIE 2017, Part I, LNAI 10350, pp. 295–301, 2017.
DOI: 10.1007/978-3-319-60042-0_35

1   Introduction

One big problem, appearing on cap & pin insulators (Fig. 1) with surface pollution, is the flashover phenomenon. Briefly, the flashover phenomenon, has different occurrence process (depending on the material of the insulator), is presented at a particular operating voltage, called critical flashover voltage and can cause the partial or total evacuation of an insulator until the collapse of a power line [1].

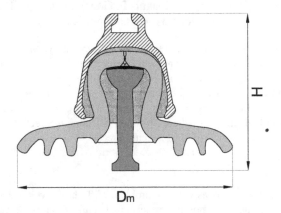

Fig. 1. Basic design parameters of Cap & Pin Insulator

This paper tries to balance between accurate and comprehensible results, through the modelling effort of the flashover phenomenon using Artificial Neural Networks (ANNs), Genetic Programming (GP) and Inductive Decision Trees (IDT) with reference point, a standard data analysis approach (Multiple Linear Regression-MLR). Finally, using an evolutionary algorithm (Gravitational Search Algorithm-GSA) we try to optimize the proposed model given from genetic programming.

The database was common to all four techniques applied to the problem and consists of 168 cases (i.e. series of related measurements) represented by six (6) numeric variables, namely the insulator's maximum diameter (D_m), height (H), creepage distance (L), insulator's manufacturing constant (F), and the insulator's pollution (C) and the critical flashover voltage (U_c). The critical flashover voltage of a polluted insulator is expressed in relation to these variables. A part of these application data (140 cases) are simulated data derived from a specialized model corresponding to incidents of flashover voltage on polluted Cap & Pin insulators, while the rest of the data (28 cases) consist of real experimental observations [1].

The main database was divided into two parts. The first part, which is called Training-Validation Set (130 cases of simulated data and 20 cases of actual data), was used for the development of the predictive models and the second part, which is called Test Set (10 cases of actual data and 8 cases of simulated data), was used to test the final predictive models.

2   Modelling Approaches

The **MLR model (MLR)** for the estimation of flashover voltage is described by Eq. 1 and its performance through different measures is given in Table 1.

$$U_C = 1.0368 \cdot D_m + 0.468 \cdot H + 1.8342 \cdot L + 0.4292 \cdot F - 6.8969 \cdot C + 13.0605 \qquad (1)$$

Table 1. Aggregation and comparative scoreboard of MLR, ANN-2 GP-1, GP-2 and GSA-1

	r	MAE (kV)	RMSE (kV)	RAE (%)	RRSE (%)
Model: MLR					
Training	0.8878	2.2314	2.6763	43.659	45.9127
Test	0.7942	2.5908	2.8413	–	–
Model: ANN-2					
Training	0.9991	0.146	0.2522	2.8568	4.3264
Test	0.9904	0.731	0.8256	–	–
Model: GP-1					
Training	0.9979685	0.169555	0.2499	1.2901	–
Validation	0.999247	0.171671	0.2177	1.2332	–
Test	0.993614	0.276758	0.4538	3.5585	–
Model: GP-2					
Training	0.99506	0.32137	0.41889	2.5808	–
Test	0.99564	0.26586	0.29275	2.2182	–
Validation	0.98985	0.50008	0.62641	3.4887	–
Model: GSA-1					
Training	0.99728	0.33031	0.19303	–	–
Test	0.99958	0.03388	0.01541	–	–
Validation	0.99027	0.46951	0.38056	–	–

Its performance is clearly lower than all other intelligent approaches applied, as it can also be seen in Table 1.

The **ANN model (ANN-2)**, presented in Fig. 2, is a Multilayer Perceptron (MLP) with 1 hidden layer (20 nodes) and activation function of hidden nodes was the logistic function. ANN-2 training was supervised, into batch mode and was performed using the back propagation algorithm (BP). Moreover, the validation was held together with the process of training using the 10-fold cross validation method based on the same dataset (Training-Validation Set). The performances are depicted in Table 1 [2, 3].

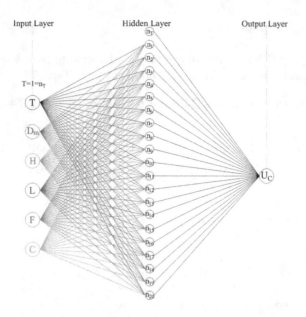

Fig. 2. The ANN-2 model

The **GP models (donate as GP-1 and GP-2)**, emerged using the Training-validation Set and following the procedure of 10-fold cross validation. Specifically, for each fold, 30 independent runs were made within the same modulation. All runs trained their solution with k-1 subsets and all were compared in the rest testing data. So, ten (10) candidate models resulted, which were compared in the second set of 18 cases, and the best model in terms of correlation coefficient was chosen. The GP-1 and GP-2 are presented, respectively in Eqs. 2 and 7. Their performances are depicted in Table 1 [4, 5].

$$U_C = A \cdot (B \cdot K + J) + 3.254 \tag{2}$$

where:

$$A = 2.159 \cdot \frac{10^{-6}}{0.998 \cdot F + \log(1.908 \cdot C) + 7.182} \cdot (\log(0.531 \cdot L) - 13.224) \cdot (-0.741 \cdot F - \log(0.106 \cdot L) + 11.943) \tag{3}$$

$$B = (-0.604 \cdot D_m \cdot F + 0.016 \cdot H \cdot (2.267 \cdot L + 277.2) - 24.76 \cdot L \cdot (-\log(0.106 \cdot L) + \frac{\log(1.022 \cdot C)}{-0.741 \cdot F - \log(0.352 \cdot F) + 11.943}) \tag{4}$$

$$K = 0.604 \cdot D_m \cdot F - 21.253 \cdot \log(1.908 \cdot C) - 21.253 \tag{5}$$

$$J = -151.67 \cdot L \cdot \left(0.604 \cdot D_m \cdot F - 21.253 \cdot \log\left(1.908 \cdot C\right) + 15.311\right)$$
$$+ \log\left(1.908 \cdot C\right) + \frac{\log\left(1.908 \cdot C\right)}{0.741 \cdot F - 24.76 \cdot L - 4.761} - \frac{6.813 \cdot 10^{-5}}{1.145 \cdot D_m + \dfrac{\log\left(1.908 \cdot C\right)}{0.083 \cdot C + 3020702}} \tag{6}$$

$$U_c = \left(\log\left(0.054012 \cdot C\right)\right)^2 \cdot \left(1.298 \cdot L + 1.4616 \cdot D_m\right) \cdot 0.0053419 + 1.9647 \tag{7}$$

The **GSA model (GSA-1)** arose during the optimization effort of the performances of GP models. The GSA-1 (Eq. 8) uses Harmony Search for initialization, is based on GP-2 and its performance are depicted in Table 1 [6, 7].

$$U_c = E \cdot Z + G \tag{8}$$

where:

$$E = \log^2\left(0.0544783402089791 \cdot C\right) \tag{9}$$

$$Z = 0.0053419 \cdot \left(1.29462312655721 \cdot L + 1.46957461951861 \cdot D_m\right) \tag{10}$$

$$G = 1.95794336098125 \tag{11}$$

Finally, the **IDT model (IDT-1)** presented in this work, emerged after of several tests, which were related to the number of the data cases, the classification of used data cases (according to the values of U_c and with the modify of key operating parameters, such as the training-validation process. Specifically, for comparison reasons with the other AI approaches used in this paper, a 10-fold cross validation and no pruning was selected for the entire data set (i.e. 150 cases for training and 18 cases for testing the produced model in new, unseen cases) according of the classification of 5 kV of U_c (i.e. six classes ranging within [5,10) kV, [10,15) kV, [15,20) kV, [20,25) kV, [25,30) kV, [30,35] kV) [8–11].

The resulting decision tree contains 32 internal nodes and is translated into 30 different rules (the detailed outcome is not given in the paper due to space limitations). Seven of the rules produced, are handy and accurate as they cover a considerable number of cases from the entire data set and no negative classifications and the probability of correct classification of new unseen cases in the future is higher than 95%, i.e. statistical tests can take place for the verification of the acquired rule-based knowledge. In total, 13 rules are interesting ("cover" means how many cases from the dataset verify the produced rule and the number in brackets following each rule corresponds to the probability of correct classification of new cases in the future using the specific rule):

- Rule 1: (cover 41) IF L ≤ 40.6 AND C > 0.28 THEN class U_c =5–10 kV   [0.977]
- Rule 2: (cover 32) IF F ≤ 0.9 AND C > 0.34 THEN class U_c =5–10 kV   [0.971]
- Rule 3: (cover 30) IF H ≤ 17 AND C > 0.37 THEN class U_c =5–10 kV   [0.969]
- Rule 4: (cover 25) IF L ≤ 33 AND C > 0.23 THEN class Uc =5–10 kV   [0.963]
- Rule 5: (cover 23) IF D_m ≤ 25.4 AND L ≤ 33 AND C > 0.1 THEN class U_c = 5–10 kV   [0.960]
- Rule 6: (cover 23) IF L > 33 AND L≤ 43.2 AND C > 0.1 AND C ≤ 0.28 THEN class U_c = 10–15 kV   [0.960]
- Rule 7: (cover 21) IF H ≤ 17 AND L > 33 AND C > 0.13 AND C ≤ 0.28 THEN class U_c =10–15 kV   [0.957]
- Rule 8: (cover 16) IF L> 33 AND C > 0.16 AND C ≤ 0.28 THEN class Uc =10–15 kV   [0.944]
- Rule 9: (cover 10) IF L≤ 33 AND C > 0.06 AND C ≤ 0.16 THEN class Uc =10–15 kV   [0.917]
- Rule 14: (cover 10) IF H≤17 AND C > 0.05 AND C ≤ 0.06 THEN class Uc =15–20 kV   [0.917]
- Rule 15: (cover 10) IF H≤ 14.6 AND C > 0.02 AND C ≤ 0.06 THEN class Uc =15–20 kV   [0.917]
- Rule 16: (cover 29) IF Dm≤ 28 AND C > 0.03 AND C ≤ 0.06 THEN class Uc =15–20 kV   [0.903]
- Rule 20: (cover 8) IF H> 14.6 AND L<= 40 AND C ≤ 0.03 THEN class Uc =20–25 kV   [0.900]

3   Comparative Results and Conclusions

In this paper four different intelligent techniques were employed to estimate the value of critical flashover voltage for polluted insulators. Results obtained cannot be compared always to exactly the same datasets and experimental conditions, but can be comparable in a somewhat fair manner, in order to draw general conclusions.

The results show that methods like ANNs and GP, which have inner procedures, not fully understandable by humans, produce accurate models. ANNs prove the strongest approach in terms of accuracy. Furthermore, GP may be programmed in such a way that can aim to shorter equations without any discount on accuracy. Its comprehensibility sometimes can be considered higher than that of the ANNs' structured, as standard mathematical formulas are some times more common to people. In addition, under proper encoding, grammar guided GP approaches can also produce fully comprehensible rule-based systems (IF-THEN rules or even Fuzzy Rule Based Systems). Models derived by GP-approaches can be optimized further by Nature Inspired Evolutionary Algorithms to give more accurate results, as it has been shown in this work. Inductive machine learning techniques presuppose the formation of reasonable decision classes when the target variable is of numerical nature (selecting a proper discretization). Its performance in terms of accuracy is lower, while there is need for larger collections of experimental data in order to be able to draw firm conclusions on the value of the technique. Nevertheless, experts find the acquired rules comprehensible and easy to use in the inspection process, while, as observed in the indicative results given in this paper, their comprehensibility is indeed high, in terms of measuring the number of resulting rules acquired and the conditions contained within these rules.

Further work includes experimentation to other competitive hybrid intelligent schemes based on nature inspired optimization approaches. The enrichment of the dataset is also a priority for the research team, as results seem encouraging.

References

1. Topalis, F.V., Gonos, I.F., Stathopulos, I.A.: Dielectric behaviour of polluted porcelain insulators. IEE Proc.-Gener. Transm. Distrib. **148**(4), 269–274 (2001)
2. Witten, I.H., Frank, E., Hall, M.A.: Data Mining: Practical Machine Learning Tools and Techniques, 3rd edn., pp. 233–244. Elsevier Inc. (2001)
3. Refaeilzadeh, P., Tang, L., Liu, H.: Cross-Validation. Arizona State University (2008)
4. Crane, E.F., McPhee, N.F.: The effects of size and depth limits on tree based genetic programming. In: Yu, T., Riolo, R., Worzel, B. (eds.) Genetic Programming Theory and Practice III. Genetic Programming, vol. 9, pp. 223–240. Springer, Boston (2006). doi: 10.1007/0-387-28111-8_15
5. Koza, J.R.: Genetic Programming: On the Programming of Computers by Means of Natural Selection. MIT Press, Cambridge (1992)
6. Rashedi, E., Nezamabadi-Pour, H., Saryazdi, S.: GSA: a gravitational search algorithm. Inf. Sci. **179**(13), 2232–2248 (2009)
7. Geem, Z.W., Kim, J.H., Loganathan, G.V.: A new heuristic optimization algorithm: harmony search. Simulation **76**(2), 60–68 (2001)
8. Quinlan, J.R.: C4.5: Programs for Machine Learning. Morgan Kaufmann, San Francisco (1994)
9. Quinlan, J.R.: Induction of decision trees. Mach. Learn. **1**(1), 81–106 (1986)
10. Quinlan, J.R.: Learning logical definitions from relations. Mach. Learn. **5**, 239–266 (1990)
11. Mitchell, T.M.: Machine Learning, pp. 55–58. McGraw-Hill (1997)

Recommender Systems

Replication and Reproduction in Recommender Systems Research - Evidence from a Case-Study with the rrecsys Library

Ludovik Çoba$^{(\boxtimes)}$ and Markus Zanker

Free University of Bozen-Bolzano, 39100 Bozen-Bolzano, Italy
Ludovik.Coba@inf.unibz.it, Markus.Zanker@unibz.it

Abstract. Recommender systems (RS) are a real-world application domain for Artificial Intelligence standing at the core of massively used e-commerce and social-media platforms like Amazon, Netflix, Spotify and many more. The research field of recommendation systems now has already a more than 20 years long tradition and issues like replication of results and reproducibility of algorithms become more important. Therefore this work is oriented towards better understanding the underlying challenges of reproducibility of offline measurements of recommendation techniques. We therefore introduce *rrecsys*, an open-source package in R, that implements many popular RS algorithms, expansion capabilities and has an integrated offline evaluation mechanism following an accepted methodology. In addition, we present a case study on the usability of the library along with results of benchmarking the provided algorithms with other open-source implementations.

1 Introduction

Recommender systems (RS) are an application of Artificial Intelligence techniques where past behavior of users is exploited to make predictions about their interests and to support them in identifying items they presumably like [10]. Thus recommender systems research combines efforts from multiple disciplines, such as Artificial Intelligence, Human Computer Interactions, Data Mining and Machine Learning and Statistics as well as Marketing or Psychology [12].

These systems come not only with the promise to help users in identifying useful information and making serendipitous discoveries but they also proved to be game-changing tools for the Web in an age of information overload. While RS are continuously applied in novel and diverse domains such as recommending people, food and lifestyle aspects, supporting software development or recommending business process flows the methodological basis of the field is still evolving when it comes to deciding which RS variant is *better* or more *useful* to its users than another one. Obviously, one cannot decide on *better* without fully specifying how the quality of recommendations is measured. However, Said and Bellogin [14] recently identified that even when implementations of the same algorithms in different recommender system libraries were tested against the

© Springer International Publishing AG 2017
S. Benferhat et al. (Eds.): IEA/AIE 2017, Part I, LNAI 10350, pp. 305–314, 2017.
DOI: 10.1007/978-3-319-60042-0_36

same measures and according to the same methodology they still did not show the same results due to different data management and slight deviations in the interpretation of the evaluation methodology and the algorithmic steps. Ensuring reproducibility in recommender systems is therefore a key issue which is currently not receiving the necessary attention in the community [1]. With our ongoing work we therefore want to contribute towards a better understanding of the challenges in achieving reproducible results and benchmarking algorithms against each other.

This paper presents *rrecsys* [2], an open-source extension package for R, as an infrastructure for the rapid prototyping and reproduction of algorithms. The package also includes an implementation of the well-accepted evaluation practice to support the immediate assessment of developed algorithms according to the most common measures. In addition, this paper contributes a case of studying the reproduction of recommendation algorithms on top of this library in R.

The paper is structured as follows. First, we discuss related work on the replication and reproduction of recommender systems results. Next, we provide a short survey on the *rrecsys* package that is the basis for our study. In Sect. 4 the design of our case study is explained and, finally, in Sect. 5 results are presented and discussed.

2   Related Work

A *recommender system* is defined as a functional software system that employs a predictive algorithm in order to recommend a piece of *useful*, *good* and *personalized* information that may satisfy the need of a client [14].

The *evaluation* is a process of assessment that measures the quality of a given recommendation algorithm [1]. As mentioned in Shani et al. [16] there are three categories of empirical studies to evaluate a recommender system: offline, user studies and online experiments.

In an offline evaluation scenario existing datasets are exploited to determine the prediction accuracy of a recommendation technique.

In contrast, online experimental studies measure the effectiveness of real systems by randomly assigning users to one system variant. These variants are subsequently compared according to outcome measures such as revenues, profit or user churn representing the dependent variable.

User studies lack the commercial real-world context of the previously mentioned online A/B testing. However, they provide the opportunity to more intensely observe users when they interact with systems in order to perform their tasks as well as to explicitly ask them about their perceptions and experience.

According to Jannach et al. [6] over two thirds of all published RS research is based on comparative evaluations with baselines following the offline methodology. Therefore, the findings of Said and Bellogin [14] are very discomforting, when they discovered that reported results according to the offline methodology might lack internal validity and constitute a neglect of the aspects of replicability and reproducibility. Replicability refers to the fact that the exact copy of an experiment should lead to the same outcome, meaning that the same algorithm under the same circumstance should determine identical results. Instead reproducibility refers to the case that a re-implementation of algorithm and evaluation setup in a comparable setting produces similar results. Thus, reproducibility stresses the importance of generalization of results and the ability to apply them in similar but different contexts [1].

The study performed by Said et al. [14] stresses the point of discrepancies of results for offline evaluation on three common recommender frameworks implementing the same recommendation approaches. The reported evaluation quality differs even when measured with the internal means of the framework and even when computed externally through Rival, the Java open source toolkit[1]. Indeed it is difficult to reproduce research results and to compare with prior results. This relates in many cases to a lack of open code, specific guidelines and reuse [1,4].

In this context it is worth mentioning that industry's possessive and secretive behavior towards data and resources is another factor that negatively impacts reproducibility issues [7].

In Beel et al. [1] a couple of notions are suggested to make recommender systems research more reproducible: thorough review of research literature in other disciplines dealing with the same issue; raise of awareness by invoking the help of key researchers in the recommender systems community and by imposing stricter algorithm publishing requirements; identify and define the source of discrepancies; conduct comprehensive experiments; ready to run and open source implementation of recommender systems frameworks; better guidelines for the entire process of development of a recommender framework.

Even though predominantly used in research, offline metrics are often criticized and are deemed questionable since they might not be based on a domain-specific optimization goal [7]. Moreover, as noticed by Rossetti et al. [13], online and offline evaluation showed to produce dissimilar rankings while comparing different algorithms.

3 rrecsys Package

R is a popular choice in the Machine Learning community and there is actually a vast number of available packages implementing all sorts of algorithms and support functions making R an amazing development environment. The structure of *rrecsys* permits the easy extension of the library in a few steps[2], permitting the user to use the entire structure of the library, including the evaluation functions implementing the best-practice methodology for offline data.

rrecsys is an open-source software package for researching, assessing and learning recommender systems. It has a modular structure as well as includes expansion capabilities. The core of the package includes the implementation of several popular algorithms, an evaluation component and a couple of auxiliary

---

[1] http://rival.recommenders.net/.
[2] https://cran.r-project.org/web/packages/rrecsys/vignettes/d1_extend.html.

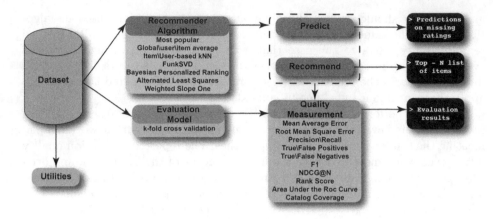

Fig. 1. The structure of *rrecsys* package.

parts for data analysis and convergence detection. In Fig. 1 its structure is depicted.

The package includes unpersonalized baseline algorithms such as *Most Popular*, *Item Average* or *User Average* as well as state of the art implementations of collaborative algorithms such as Item Based k-Nearest Neighbors (adjusted cosine similarity) [15], Simon Funk's SVD [8] or Weighted Slope One [9]. In addition, also algorithms for the one-class Collaborative Filtering problem like Weighted Alternated Least Squares and the Bayesian Personalized Ranking [11] are available.

Three of the above described algorithms (SVD, BPR and wALS) require to iterate a sequence of code until a convergence criterion is met. In analogy to [4], we implemented two loop controllers for iterative updates. The first stops once an iteration count reaches the specified value. The second stops when the error drops under a specified threshold for a preset number of consecutive iterations.

The evaluation module is based on the *k-fold cross-validation* method. A *stratified* random selection procedure is applied when dividing the set of rated items of each user into k folds such that each user is uniformly represented in each fold, i.e. the amount of ratings of each user in any fold differs at most by one. For k-fold cross validation each of the k disjunct fractions of the ratings are used $k - 1$ times for training (i.e. $\subset R_{train}$) and once for testing (i.e. $\subset R_{test}$). Practically, ratings in R_{test} are denoted as missing in the original dataset and predictions/recommendations are compared to R_{test} to compute the performance measures.

We included the most popular performance metrics according to the survey in [6]. These are mean absolute error (MAE), root mean squared error (RMSE), Precision, Recall, F1, True and False Positives, True and False Negatives, normalized discounted cumulative gain (NDCG), rank score, area under the ROC curve (AUC) and catalog coverage measuring the aggregated diversity of recommendation lists [16]. RMSE and MAE metrics are computed according to their two variants, user-based vs. global. The user-based variant weights each user uniformly by computing the metric for each user separately and averaging over all users while in the global variant users with larger test sets have relatively more weight since metrics are macro-averaged over all testset items.

4   Methodology

The goal of this empirical setup was to assess how usable the *rrecsys* environment is perceived in comparison to *LensKit* [4] and what practical problems students observe when it comes to implementing algorithms within the *rrecsys* framework. A course on Recommender Systems attended by master students and PhD candidates was subject to hand-on sessions and a homework assignment with *rrecsys* and *LensKit* libraries. The tasks were intended to be an exercise on reproducibility of algorithms and evaluation procedures to mitigate such issues in future research. The study was accompanied with a post-survey to collect qualitative feedback on the exercises.

4.1   Hands-on Sessions

The hands on sessions were divided into two tasks: re-implementation of a baseline CF algorithm and evaluation exercises. For this experiment we used the Movielens Latest dataset [5][3] which is a large and very sparse dataset. In order to become familiar with the system, participants were required to perform some general data transformation and analysis tasks. For instance, students had to observe dataset characteristics such as its sparsity before and after pruning less popular items or users with few ratings. Furthermore, they were asked to use *rrecsys* to perform non-personalized recommendations and personalized recommendations with the available implementations in the library and compare results. With this procedure participants acquired practical skills in using *rrecsys* and deepened their understanding of the functioning of recommender systems.

Consequently, we proceeded with performing the same evaluation task on a given dataset using the *LensKit* as well as the *rrecsys* environment. Students had to compare results between algorithms and platforms to get a practical overview of the task-specific metrics for quality assessment. Further understanding of algorithms and evaluation methodology was fostered by providing insight on how slight changes of procedures and algorithmic parameters impact the observed measures.

4.2   Implementation Assignment

The homework assignment required participants to perform a data analysis task with both libraries and an algorithm implementation task. Each participant was assigned with a unique subset of the Movielens Latest dataset that would lead to

---

[3] http://grouplens.org/datasets/movielens/latest/.

slightly distinct evaluation results in order to assure that students carried out the assigned tasks independently of each other. Students could decide autonomously which platform to use for their experiments. The second part of the homework assignment required an implementation of a popular recommendation algorithm and its integration into *rrecsys* called *Weighted Slope One* [9].

The Weighted Slope One performs prediction for a missing rating $\hat{r}_{ui}$ for user u on item i as the following average:

$$\hat{r}_{ui} = \frac{\sum_{\forall r_{uj}} (dev_{ij} + r_{uj}) c_{ij}}{\sum_{\forall r_{uj}} c_{ij}}.$$

The average deviation rating dev_{ij} between co-rated items is defined by:

$$dev_{ij} = \sum_{\forall u \in users} \frac{r_{ui} - r_{uj}}{c_{ij}}.$$

Where c_{ij} is the number of co-ratings between items i and j and r_{ui} is an existing rating for user u on item i. The Weighted Slope One takes into account both, information from users who rated the same item and the number of observed ratings. This approach was selected since it has shown to be a strong baseline with a not extremely complicated implementation scheme [9].

4.3 Survey

Before submitting the homework assignment a pre-survey was required to control for demographics and work experience. The post-survey focused on the perceived experience on using the libraries and required participants to submit feedback on both recommendation libraries. Furthermore, qualitative feedback on the exercise task was requested.

5 Results

The outcome of this research work targets several dimensions. First, we assessed the perceived usability and utility of *rrecsys* by asking participants for open-ended feedback. We discovered that users appreciated the transparency and availability of sourcecode and documentation as commented by one of the student on the survey:

> "...rrecsys library was intuitive to use, especially because all the implementations were easily accessible."

We noticed that the entire group was able to train models with *rrecsys* and could quickly start to evaluate them. *LensKit* seemed appealing as Java is a common programming language but the API requires a deeper knowledge to properly use the library, as another testimony mentioned:

"...I assume that anybody who ever programmed has encountered Java at some point, so with respect to this argument, LensKit should be easy to use but if we were not instructed on how to use LensKit library I would probably have problems on understanding how to use it..."

When it came to the implementation task we noticed that users had "warm-up" issues with the functional nature of the R programming language but after someone realizes the vectorization nature of functions in R this characteristic is perceived as pleasant:

"...R programming language is a bit different compared to other programming languages that I used before...What I especially liked is functions like lapply and that R supported vectors of list data structure, which made the task much easier for me at the end..."

The implementation task was successfully completed and delivered in all cases correct results, thus the goal of replicating evaluation results was achieved. The students' lack of experience in R development led them to use "day-to-day" programming skills in their task, where an experienced R programmer would have aimed at vectorizing the code as much as possible in order to avoid cycles. Vectorized code usually performs better in terms of computation time while delivering the same result.

In order to offer improved execution times *rrecsys* is growing and uses mixed implementations of code in R as well as C++ using the Rcpp library [3]. Both R/C++ and the Java implementations had similar runtimes. At this stage, the Funk's SVD implementation has already been re-implemented in C++ code in order to have a decent runtime efficiency.

In Table 1 results are given on evaluating the Funk SVD with 5-fold cross validation on *LensKit* version 2.2.1 and *rrecsys* version 0.9.6 (implemented in C++) platforms on the MovieLens 1M Dataset (ML1ML)[4] [5]. It can be noticed that both frameworks have nearly identical results for a sensitivity analysis on different model parameters which demonstrates the successful reproduction of algorithm and evaluation methodology in R. Both implementations are based on Simon Funk's original gradient descent optimization approach[5]. We are benchmarking it with *LensKit* since it is a very popular open source library among researchers that is well documented and continuously updated.

In addition we run the *recommenderlab*[6] version 0.2-1 implementation of SVD based on the the *irlba*[7] library. However we evaluate this implementation using *rrecsys* evaluation methodology for consistency of reported results. Note that the evaluation method implemented in *recommenderlab* cannot be configured to apply the standard stratified k-fold cross validation mechanism as it is used in most research papers reporting the prediction error measurements.

---

[4] http://grouplens.org/datasets/movielens/1m/.
[5] http://sifter.org/~simon/journal/20061211.html.
[6] https://CRAN.R-project.org/package=recommenderlab.
[7] https://CRAN.R-project.org/package=irlba.

Table 1. Benchmark *rrecsys* ver. 0.9.6 and *LensKit* ver. 2.2.1 on the dataset MovieLens 1 Million ratings. *Iter.* is the number of times the a feature is updated, γ the learning rate, λ the regularization term and *feat.* the number of features.

FunkSVD		MAE		RMSE		Global MAE		Global RMSE	
Config	feat.	LensKit	rrecsys	LensKit	rrecsys	LensKit	rrecsys	LensKit	rrecsys
$iter = 10$, $\lambda = 0.015$, $\gamma = 0.001$.	10	0.7320	0.7314	0.8950	0.8957	0.7155	0.7153	0.9095	0.9090
	20	0.7323	0.7317	0.8959	0.8966	0.7155	0.7154	0.9101	0.9097
	50	0.7361	0.7356	0.9003	0.9013	0.7175	0.7174	0.9122	0.9120
	100	0.7417	0.7418	0.9173	0.9166	0.7277	0.7263	0.9257	0.9242
$iter = 50$, $\lambda = 0.015$, $\gamma = 0.001$.	10	0.7321	0.7316	0.8916	0.8923	0.7128	0.7127	0.9031	0.9027
	20	0.7306	0.7299	0.8910	0.8916	0.7126	0.7121	0.9025	0.9018
	50	0.7287	0.7284	0.8897	0.8914	0.7103	0.7107	0.8998	0.9004
	100	0.7303	0.7303	0.8909	0.8932	0.7119	0.7128	0.9018	0.9030
$iter = 10$, $\lambda = 0.03$, $\gamma = 0.002$.	10	0.7320	0.7328	0.8950	0.8950	0.7155	0.7158	0.9095	0.9074
	20	0.7342	0.7335	0.8944	0.8951	0.7155	0.7153	0.9068	0.9064
	50	0.7328	0.7322	0.8962	0.8973	0.7177	0.7176	0.9088	0.9086
	100	0.7374	0.7378	0.9059	0.9108	0.7233	0.7236	0.9161	0.9176
$iter = 50$, $\lambda = 0.03$, $\gamma = 0.002$.	10	0.7168	0.7170	0.8737	0.8754	0.6914	0.6913	0.8786	0.8783
	20	0.7166	0.7156	0.8730	0.8735	0.6901	0.6897	0.8749	0.8746
	50	0.7148	0.7148	0.8702	0.8721	0.6878	0.6878	0.8714	0.8719
	100	0.7160	0.7153	0.8714	0.8723	0.6890	0.6879	0.8730	0.8719
$iter = 100$, $\lambda = 0.015$, $\gamma = 0.001$.	10	0.7091	0.7089	0.8662	0.8677	0.6825	0.6821	0.8695	0.8693
	20	0.7062	0.7058	0.8628	0.8640	0.6783	0.6781	0.8635	0.8633
	50	0.7041	0.7037	0.8595	0.8613	0.6754	0.6747	0.8591	0.8591
	100	0.7051	0.7043	0.8607	0.8617	0.6769	0.6747	0.8612	0.8592

Table 2. Evaluation of *recommenderlab*'s, ver. 0.2-1, implementation of *SVD approximation* with *stratified 5-fold cross validation* on the dataset MovieLens 1 Million ratings.

SVD Approximation		MAE	RMSE	Global MAE	Global RMSE
Maxiter	feat.		Recommenderlab		
10	10	1.27808	1.61039	1.35856	1.73125
	20	1.27122	1.60319	1.34465	1.71495
	50	1.26799	1.59980	1.33983	1.70918
	100	1.26933	1.60115	1.34544	1.71520
50	10	1.27808	1.61039	1.35856	1.73125
	20	1.27122	1.60319	1.34465	1.71495
	50	1.26799	1.59980	1.33983	1.70918
	100	1.26933	1.60115	1.34544	1.71520
100	10	1.27808	1.61039	1.35856	1.73125
	20	1.27122	1.60319	1.34465	1.71495
	50	1.26696	1.59885	1.33773	1.70700
	100	1.26842	1.60018	1.34445	1.71392

In contrast *recommenderlab* implements the *All but n* and *Given n* splitting criterion that ensures either the training set or the test set has exactly the same size for each individual user as has been used for instance in [17]. Since this SVD approximation algorithm in *recommenderlab* does not have the configuration parameter, like regularization term and learning rate, we report results in Table 2. Obviously the FunkSVD implementations in *LensKit* and *rrecsys* clearly outperform the SVD approximation in *recommenderlab*. In Table 3 we present accuracy results using the integrated implementation of Weighted Slope One on both *LensKit* and *rrecsys*, and we evaluated it on MovieLens 100K[8] and ML1ML datasets with a 5-fold cross validation. Small changes on results are related to random generations of the train\test set. We distribute the code[9] for replicating the examples discussed in this paper.

Table 3. Weighted Slope One evaluation on *LensKit* ver. 2.2.1 and *rrecsys* ver 0.9.6 on the Movielens 100 K datast and Movielens 1 Million dataset.

WSlopeOne	MAE		RMSE		Global MAE		Global RMSE	
Dataset.	LensKit	rrecsys	LensKit	rrecsys	LensKit	rrecsys	LensKit	rrecsys
ML100K	0.7622	0.7624	0.9221	0.9264	0.7391	0.7389	0.9387	0.9394
ML1ML	0.7307	0.7306	0.8906	0.8923	0.7108	0.7109	0.9011	0.9014

In the future even more mixed code implementations in *rrecsys* will be available such that this framework offers even more prototyping capabilities for an academic and industrial audience.

6   Conclusions

Reproducibility is a complex task and will remain an ardent issue in the next years. This work contributed to this topic by enhancing and developing *rrecsys*, a library for building and evaluating recommendation algorithms in R, as well as by reporting qualitative evidence from the class-room use of this library and by benchmarking it against *LensKit* to provide evidence of exact reproduction of standard recommendation techniques in R.

Many times the original code setup and proprietary data cannot be shared due to intellectual property rights and business interests. However, experience and practices in other communities might foster novel services like *Validation*[10] by *Science Exchange*, a platform for the validation of studies and methods via replication of experimental results.

Rising the awareness on this topic among researchers and students is for sure an avenue towards this direction and we believe that free Open Source environments fostering replication and reproduction of recommender systems research, like *rrecsys* and *LensKit*, play a crucial role in this regard.

---

[8] http://grouplens.org/datasets/movielens/100k/.
[9] https://github.com/ludovikcoba/iea2017.
[10] http://validation.scienceexchange.com/.

References

1. Beel, J., Breitinger, C., Langer, S., Lommatzsch, A., Gipp, B.: Towards reproducibility in recommender-systems research. User Model. User Adap. Inter. **26**(1), 69–101 (2016)
2. Çoba, L., Zanker, M.: rrecsys: an r-package for prototyping recommendation algorithms. In: Guy, I., Sharma, A. (eds.) Poster Track of the 10th ACM Conference on Recommender Systems (RecSys 2016) (RecSysPosters). No. 1688 in CEUR Workshop Proceedings, Aachen (2016). http://ceur-ws.org/Vol-1688/#paper-12
3. Eddelbuettel, D., François, R., Allaire, J., Chambers, J., Bates, D., Ushey, K.: Rcpp: Seamless r and C++ integration. J. Stat. Softw. **40**(8), 1–18 (2011)
4. Ekstrand, M.D., Ludwig, M., Konstan, J.A., Riedl, J.T.: Rethinking the recommender research ecosystem: reproducibility, openness, and lenskit. In: Proceedings of the Fifth ACM Conference on Recommender Systems, pp. 133–140. ACM (2011)
5. Harper, F.M., Konstan, J.A.: The movielens datasets: History and context. ACM Trans. Interact. Intell. Syst. (TiiS) **5**(4), 19 (2016)
6. Jannach, D., Lerche, L., Gedikli, F., Bonnin, G.: What recommenders recommend – an analysis of accuracy, popularity, and sales diversity effects. In: Carberry, S., Weibelzahl, S., Micarelli, A., Semeraro, G. (eds.) UMAP 2013. LNCS, vol. 7899, pp. 25–37. Springer, Heidelberg (2013). doi:10.1007/978-3-642-38844-6_3
7. Jannach, D., Resnick, P., Tuzhilin, A., Zanker, M.: Recommender systems—: beyond matrix completion. Commun. ACM **59**(11), 94–102 (2016)
8. Koren, Y., Bell, R., Volinsky, C., et al.: Matrix factorization techniques for recommender systems. Computer **42**(8), 30–37 (2009)
9. Lemire, D., Maclachlan, A.: Slope one predictors for online rating-based collaborative filtering. In: SDM, vol. 5, pp. 1–5. SIAM (2005)
10. Lops, P., De Gemmis, M., Semeraro, G.: Content-based recommender systems: state of the art and trends. In: Ricci, F., Rokach, L., Shapira, B., Kantor, P.B. (eds.) Recommender Systems Handbook, pp. 73–105. Springer, New York (2011)
11. Pan, R., Zhou, Y., Cao, B., Liu, N.N., Lukose, R., Scholz, M., Yang, Q.: One-class collaborative filtering. In: 2008 Eighth IEEE International Conference on Data Mining, pp. 502–511. IEEE (2008)
12. Ricci, F., Rokach, L., Shapira, B.: Introduction to recommender systems handbook. Springer, New York (2011)
13. Rossetti, M., Stella, F., Zanker, M.: Contrasting offline and online results when evaluating recommendation algorithms. In: Proceedings of the 10th ACM Conference on Recommender Systems, pp. 31–34. ACM (2016)
14. Said, A., Bellogín, A.: Comparative recommender system evaluation: benchmarking recommendation frameworks. In: Proceedings of the 8th ACM Conference on Recommender systems, pp. 129–136. ACM (2014)
15. Sarwar, B., Karypis, G., Konstan, J., Riedl, J.: Item-based collaborative filtering recommendation algorithms. In: Proceedings of the 10th International Conference on World Wide Web, pp. 285–295. ACM (2001)
16. Shani, G., Gunawardana, A.: Evaluating recommendation systems. In: Ricci, F., Rokach, L., Shapira, B., Kantor, P.B. (eds.) Recommender Systems Handbook, pp. 257–297. Springer, New York (2011)
17. Zanker, M., Jessenitschnig, M., Jannach, D., Gordea, S.: Comparing recommendation strategies in a commercial context. IEEE Intell. Syst. **22**(3), 69–73 (2007)

A New User-Based Collaborative Filtering Under the Belief Function Theory

Raoua Abdelkhalek[(⊠)], Imen Boukhris, and Zied Elouedi

LARODEC, Institut Supérieur de Gestion de Tunis,
Université de Tunis, Tunis, Tunisia
abdelkhalek_raoua@live.fr, imen.boukhris@hotmail.com, zied.elouedi@gmx.fr

Abstract. The collaborative filtering (CF) is considered as the most widely used approach in the field of Recommender Systems (RSs). It tends to predict the users' preferences based on the users sharing similar interests. However, ignoring the uncertainty involved in the provided predictions is among the limitations related to this approach. To deal with this issue, we propose in this paper a new user-based collaborative filtering within the belief function theory. In our approach, the evidence of each similar user is taken into account and Dempster's rule of combination is used for combining these pieces of evidence. A comparative evaluation on a real world data set shows that the proposed method outperforms traditional user-based collaborative filtering recommenders.

Keywords: User-based collaborative filtering · Uncertain reasoning · Belief function theory · Dempster's rule of combination

1 Introduction

In everyday life, people are generally overwhelmed with a large variety of options. That is why, they look forward to getting valuable advice that really fit their needs and preferences. In this context, Recommender Systems (RSs) [1] have emerged to predict the users' future preferences and suggest items accordingly [2]. Commonly, the collaborative filtering (CF) is considered as the most popular and the widely used approach in the field of RSs [3,4]. By making use of a user-item matrix, this type of RS is able to predict the users' future ratings towards items not yet rated. For instance, in a movie recommender, the prediction provided to the user would be a numerical value reflecting his degree of likeliness towards movies not yet watched. However, the predicted rating will not certainly fit users' preferences. The user might prefer a reliable prediction that gives him a complete overview about his preferences rather than a risky one that may not fit his interests and goals. Thus, it is obvious that providing certain predictions makes the RS less efficient, less reliable and easily dismissed [5]. Handling uncertainty has become an important challenge in real-world problems. However, the existing recommendation approaches are hardly able to deal with this challenge [6]. Indeed, few recommendation approaches have been recently

© Springer International Publishing AG 2017
S. Benferhat et al. (Eds.): IEA/AIE 2017, Part I, LNAI 10350, pp. 315–324, 2017.
DOI: 10.1007/978-3-319-60042-0_37

proposed to deal with uncertainty in Recommender Systems. These approaches have been based on different theories such as fuzzy set theory [5,7], belief function theory [6,8], probability theory [9,10] and possibility theory [11]. Among these theories, the belief function theory represents the general framework for dealing with different kinds of imperfection and combining pieces of evidence [12–14]. The belief function theory has been used in several disciplines such as the pattern classification field. In fact, an evidential version of the K-Nearest Neighbors, denoted by EKNN [15] has been developed under the belief function framework. Such classifier is characterized by its ability to allow a credal classification of the objects and hence a better classification performance. Based on the belief function theory, in particular the EKNN, we propose in this paper a new user-based collaborative filtering approach under this formalism. Through our proposed approach, we shed light on the advantage of covering uncertainty and using the EKNN in the user-based collaborative filtering.

The remainder of this paper is organized as follows: Sect. 2 represents a brief overview of the belief function theory. Section 3 recalls the standard version of user-based CF. In Sect. 4, we describe our proposed evidential user-based CF. Then, Sect. 5 provides the experimentation conducted on a real world data set as well as a comparative evaluation. Finally, the paper is concluded and some potential future works are depicted in Sect. 6.

2   Belief Function Theory

The belief function theory [13,14] is one of the most used theories for reasoning under uncertainty. In this section, we recall its basic concepts as interpreted in the Transferable Belief Model (TBM) [12] as well as the Evidential K-Nearest Neighbors classifier.

2.1   Basic Concepts

In the context of this theory, a problem domain is represented by a finite set of elementary events called the frame of discernment and denoted by Θ. The belief committed to the elements of Θ is expressed by a basic belief assignment (*bba*) which is a mapping function $m : 2^{\Theta} \rightarrow [0, 1]$ such that:

$$\sum_{A \subseteq \Theta} m(A) = 1 \tag{1}$$

where $m(A)$ is a basic belief mass (*bbm*) which quantifies the degree of belief exactly assigned to the event A of Θ.

To combine two *bba*'s m_1 and m_2 induced from two reliable and independent information sources, Dempster's rule of combination can be used. It is defined as:

$$(m_1 \oplus m_2)(A) = k. \sum_{B,C \subseteq \Theta : B \cap C = A} m_1(B) \cdot m_2(C) \tag{2}$$

$$where \quad (m_1 \oplus m_2)(\varnothing) = 0 \tag{3}$$

$$and \quad k^{-1} = 1 - \sum_{B,C \subseteq \Theta : B \cap C = \varnothing} m_1(B) \cdot m_2(C) \tag{4}$$

While beliefs can be represented and combined at the credal level, decisions are made at the pignistic level through the pignistic probabilities defined as:

$$BetP(A) = \sum_{B \subseteq \Theta} \frac{|A \cap B|}{|B|} \frac{m(B)}{(1 - m(\varnothing))} \text{ for all } A \in \Theta \tag{5}$$

2.2 Evidential K-Nearest Neighbors

The Evidential K-Nearest Neighbors (EKNN) [15] allows an improvement of the classification performance over the crisp K-Nearest Neighbors classifier. It is based on membership values serving as a confidence measure in the classification. Given a new object X to be classified, this method starts by finding the K-Nearest Neighbors of X according to a distance measure. Unlike the classical KNN, this approach is able to represent more faithfully the uncertainty that spreads through the predictions made by the classifier. Let $\Theta = \{L_1, L_2, \cdots, L_M\}$ be the frame of discernment containing the M possible class labels in the system and $N_K(X)$ the set of the K-Nearest Neighbors of X. A new object X can be assigned to one class of the $N_K(X)$ based on the selected neighbors. However, each object X from the $N_K(X)$ does not by itself provide 100% certainty. In the EKNN method, the K-Nearest Neighbors are assumed to provide pieces of evidence raising the belief that the object X to be classified belongs to the class L_q. Using the terminology of the belief function theory, the belief committed to each neighbor is then represented through a *bba*. Finally, the *bba*'s provided by the K-Nearest Neighbors can be aggregated using Dempster's rule of combination leading to a more valuable evidence denoted by m_X such that:

$$m_X = m_{X_1} \oplus ... \oplus m_{X_K} \tag{6}$$

3 Collaborative Filtering

Though our preferences and tastes vary, we generally follow patterns. This is the main idea behind the collaborative filtering approach (CF). It assumes that if two users rated some items similarly or had similar behaviors in the past then, they would rate or act on other items similarly [16]. The similarity in taste of two users is calculated based on the similarity in their rating history. That is why, CF is referred to as "people to people correlation" [17] or user-based CF [16]. One of the preferred approaches to CF is to use the KNN classifier [18]. The CF is basically user-based, on the other hand, this approach can be item-based [19] where the system looks into the items the active user has rated and computes similarity between items rather than users in order to perform the predictions.

In fact, an evidential version of the item-based CF approach has been proposed in [8]. However, uncertainty reigns also in the second category of the CF approach namely the user-based CF which we explore in the following example.

Example 1. *Let us consider the user-item matrix presented in Table 1.*

Table 1. User-item matrix

	Item$_1$	Item$_2$	Item$_3$	Item$_4$	Item$_5$
User$_1$	2	2	3	4	4
User$_2$	5	4	2	2	1
User$_3$	2	2	1	4	1
User$_4$	5	1	3	2	1
User$_5$	2	5	1	4	4
Active user	?	5	4	1	?

In this example, six users have rated a set of items. The ratings are in the range 1 to 5 which reflects the degrees of satisfaction of each user. These ratings represent the classes of the given objects (i.e. users) to be considered in the prediction process. Suppose that we aim to predict the rating of the active user for Item$_1$. The user-based CF process starts by computing the distances between the active user and each user in Table 1. In this example, we opt for the euclidean distance. Table 2 shows the obtained results:

Table 2. Computed distances between users

	User$_1$	User$_2$	User$_3$	User$_4$	User$_5$
Active user	1.4530	**0.816**	1.7321	**1.4142**	**1.4142**

Once the distances are computed, the K-nearest users are then selected to make the predictions. Assuming that K = 3, then the 3-Nearest-Neighbors of the active user are {User$_2$ (rating = 5), User$_4$ (rating = 5) and User$_5$ (rating = 2)}. According to the majority vote of the K-Nearest Neighbors, a rating of 5 would be assigned to the Item$_1$. Thereupon, the prediction indicates for the active user that he would be very satisfied with Item$_1$. This prediction does not reflect the reality which is by nature related to uncertainty. The user might prefer a reliable prediction that gives him a complete overview about his preferences rather than a risky one that may not fit his interests. Aiming to overcome such limitation and to get more significant and accurate predictions, we propose a new evidential user-based CF which is the topic of the next section.

4 Proposed Evidential User-Based CF

We propose a new recommendation approach which extends the standard user-based CF by the belief function theory using the Evidential K-Nearest Neighbors.

We define Θ defined as follows: $\Theta = \{r_1, r_2, \cdots, r_n\}$ where n denotes the number of the ratings r provided in the system.

By exploring the user-item matrix, we have to spot to the K-similar users by picking out only the K users having the lowest distances. We mention that the distance between two users u and v is defined as follows:

$$d(u, v) = \frac{\sum_{i \in I_u \cap I_v} (r_{u,i} - r_{v,i})^2}{|I_u \cap I_v|} \tag{7}$$

where $r_{u,i}$ and $r_{v,i}$ correspond to the rating of the user u and v for the item i. I_u and I_v are the items rated by both the user u and v.

Picking the K-most similar users is a crucial step in our method since they are the pieces of evidence on which we will rely in the prediction phase. Each different piece of evidence involves a particular hypothesis about the predicted rating. Hence, we generate bba's over the rating of each similar user as well as the frame of discernment Θ. Based on the principle invoked in [15], we can represent this bba as following:

$$m_{u,v}(\{r_i\}) = \alpha_0 \exp^{-(\gamma_{r_i}^2 \cdot dist(u,v)^2)} \tag{8}$$

$$m_{u,v}(\Theta) = 1 - \alpha_0 \exp^{-(\gamma_{r_i}^2 \cdot dist(u,v)^2)}$$

- u is the active user and v is its similar user such that: $v \in \{1, .., K\}$
- α_0 is fixed to the value 0.95 as invoked in [15].
- γ_{r_i} is the inverse of the mean distance between each pair of users sharing the same interest towards a given item corresponding to the rating r_i.

Once the bba's are generated for each similar user, we aggregate these bba's based on Dempster's rule of combination using the following expression:

$$m(\{r_i\}) = \frac{1}{R}(1 - \prod_{u \in u_K}(1 - \alpha_{r_i})) \cdot \prod_{r_j \neq r_i} \prod_{u \in u_K}(1 - \alpha_{r_j}) \qquad \forall r_i \in \{r_1, .., r_n\} \tag{9}$$

$$m(\Theta) = \frac{1}{R} \prod_{u=1}^{n}(1 - \prod_{u \in u_K}(1 - \alpha_{r_i}))$$

- R is a normalized factor defined by:

$$R = \sum_{u=1}^{n}(1 - \prod_{u \in u_K}(1 - \alpha_{r_i}) \prod_{r_j \neq r_i} \prod_{u \in u_K}(1 - \alpha_{r_j}) + \prod_{u=1}^{n}(\prod_{u \in u_K}(1 - \alpha_{r_j})) \tag{10}$$

- $u_K = \{u_1, u_2..., u_K\}$ is the set containing the indexes of the K-Nearest Neighbors of the active user over the user-item matrix.
- n is the number of the ratings provided by the similar users.
- α_{r_i} is the belief committed to the rating r_i such that: $\alpha_{r_i} = \alpha_0$ $\exp^{-(\gamma_{r_i}^2 \times dist(u,v)^2)}$
- α_{r_j} is the belief committed to the rating $r_j \neq r_i$ such that: $\alpha_{r_j} = \alpha_0$ $\exp^{-(\gamma_{r_j}^2 \times dist(u,v)^2)}$

To sum up, the resulting *bba* encodes the final belief of the K-Nearest Neighbors regarding the rating that should be provided to the active user as illustrated in Fig. 1.

$$m_{Active\ user} = m_{User\ 1} \oplus ... \oplus m_{User\ K}$$

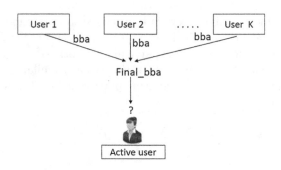

Fig. 1. Final prediction

Example 2. *Let continue with the same user-item matrix used in Example 1. The active user would receive the following bba's: $m(\{2\}) = 0.2588$, $m(\{5\}) = 0.3975$ and $m(\Theta) = 0.5728$. In other words, the prediction indicates for the active user that a bbm of 0.3957 supports that he will extremely like Item$_1$. On the other hand, a moderate satisfaction towards the suggested item is around 0.2588 while the rest of the committed belief is allocated to the frame of discernment Θ.*

5   Experiments and Discussions

We use the MovieLens[1] data set which is one of the widely used real word data sets in the field of CF. It contains in total 100.000 ratings collected from 943 users on 1682 movies. In our experiments, we perform a comparative evaluation over our proposed method as well as the traditional user-based CF using three different similarity measures commonly used in the CF category namely Euclidean distance [20], Pearson and Cosine similarities [21]. We adopted the method suggested in [22] for conducting our experiments. Firstly, we rank the movies

---

[1] http://movielens.org.

available in the data set according to the number of the provided ratings. Then, we extract 5 subsets each of which contains the ratings provided by the users for 20 movies. The selection of the subsets is performed by progressively increasing the number of the missing rates. Hence, each subset will contain a specific number of ratings leading to different degrees of sparsity. Note that the less the provided ratings are, the sparser the data set is. For all our experiments, we keep the same size of the extracted subsets for all the training and the testing sets by varying the number of ratings. For each subset, we randomly extract 20% of the available ratings as a testing data and the remaining 80% were considered as a training data.

5.1 Evaluation Metrics

To evaluate our approach, we carry out experiments over three evaluation metrics namely the *Mean Absolute Error* (MAE) [23], the *Root Mean Squared Error* (RMSE) [24] and the *Distance criteron* (dist_crit) [25] defined by:

$$MAE = \frac{\sum_{u,i} |p_{u,i} - r_{u,i}|}{N},$$ (11)

$$RMSE = \sqrt{\frac{\sum_{u,i} (p_{u,i} - r_{u,i})^2}{N}}$$ (12)

$$dist\_crit = \frac{\sum_{u,i} dist\_crit(i)}{N}$$ (13)

$$where \qquad dist\_crit(i) = \sum_{i=1}^{n} (BetP(\{r_{u,i}\}) - \delta_i)^2$$ (14)

- $r_{u,i}$ is the real rating for the user u on the item i.
- $p_{u,i}$ is the predicted value of the rating.
- N is the total number of the predicted ratings over all the users.
- n is the number of the possible ratings in the system.
- δ_i is equal to 1 if $r_{u,i}$ is equal to $p_{u,i}$ and 0 otherwise.

Note that the lower these measures are, the more accurate and efficient the user-based CF approach is. Hence, the small values of MAE, RMSE and dist_crit imply a better prediction accuracy and a higher performance.

5.2 Results

We carry on experiments over the different subsets corresponding to different sparsity levels. Besides, we switch each time the value of the neighborhood size K. The MAE, the RMSE and the dist_crit are then computed for each subset.

1. **Performance for Different Sparsity Degrees**

   Considering different sparsity degrees, the experimental results are summarize in Table 3. The performance of our evidential user-based CF is compared to that of the traditional ones working under a certain framework. For each subset, the obtained result corresponding to the evaluation measures is the average of the results obtained by the different values of the neighborhood size K. It can be seen that the evidential user-based approach provides better performance than the other user-based methods. In fact, we acquire the lowest values in terms of MAE, RMSE and dist_crit in all the sparsity degrees' levels. For instance, if we consider the second subset corresponding to a degree of 65%, our approach achieves better results in term of MAE with a value of 0.766 compared to 0.874 for Pearson user-based, 0.84 for Cosine user-based and 0.855 for the Euclidean user-based. Similarly, if we consider the dist_crit criterion for a sparsity of 75%, the value of the proposed approach (equal to 0.703) widely outperforms Pearson user-based (equal to 1.18), Cosine user-based (equal to 1.184) and Euclidean user-based (equal to 1.236). These results show that handling uncertainty pervaded in the prediction task is an important challenge in RSs.

2. **Performance for Different Neighborhood Sizes**

   We can observe through Figs. 2, 3, and 4 that the curve of the evidential user-based CF remains always under those of the three traditional methods under a certain framework. These results show the greatest performance of the evidential approach over all the neighborhood size values ranging from 20 to 60 in term of MAE, RMSE and dist_crit.

Table 3. The comparison results

Measure	Sparsity	Certain context			Uncertain context
		Pearson	Cosine	Euclidean	Evidential
MAE	60.95%	0.748	0.744	0.833	**0.74**
RMSE		1.178	1.231	1.158	**1.089**
dist_crit		1.195	1.27	1.205	**0.859**
MAE	65%	0.874	0.84	0.855	**0.766**
RMSE		1.186	1.14	1.172	**0.965**
dist_crit		1.237	1.263	1.249	**0.676**
MAE	70%	0.805	0.781	0.798	**0.737**
RMSE		1.089	1.083	1.025	**0.821**
dist_crit		1.128	1.227	1.27	**0.674**
MAE	75%	0.753	0.769	0.837	**0.685**
RMSE		1.071	1.093	1.171	**0.85**
dist_crit		1.18	1.184	1.236	**0.703**
MAE	80.8%	0.801	0.823	0.781	**0.65**
RMSE		1.15	1.198	1.115	**0.854**
dist_crit		1.144	1.174	1.134	**0.82**

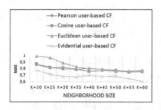 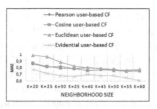 

Fig. 2. The MAE results   **Fig. 3.** The RMSE results   **Fig. 4.** The dist_crit results

6   Conclusion

In this paper, we have proposed a new user-based collaborative filtering approach under uncertainty within the Evidential K-Nearest Neighbors (EKNN). When predicting users' preferences, our approach takes the advantage of the belief function theory tools in order to combine the users' evidence and to represent the uncertainty of the predicted ratings. Hence, improving the user's confidence towards the system as well as the accuracy of the provided predictions present two challenges that the proposed approach deals with. As future works, we intend to unify both user-based and item-based approaches based on the belief function framework. Besides, we propose to define other distance criteria during the neighborhood selection as well as the alteration of the parameter α_0 used in the *bba*'s generation.

References

1. Bobadilla, J., Ortega, F., Hernando, A., Gutierrez, A.: Recommender systems survey. Knowl.-Based Syst. **46**, 109–132 (2013)
2. Ricci, F., Rokach, L., Shapira, B.: Recommender systems: introduction and challenges. In: Ricci, F., Rokach, L., Shapira, B. (eds.) Recommender Systems Handbook, pp. 1–34. Springer, US (2015)
3. Koren, Y., Sill, J.: Collaborative filtering on ordinal user feedback. In: International Joint Conference on Artificial Intelligence, pp. 3022–3026 (2013)
4. Zheng, Y., Ouyang, Y., Rong, W., Xiong, Z.: Multi-faceted distrust aware recommendation. In: Zhang, S., Wirsing, M., Zhang, Z. (eds.) KSEM 2015. LNCS, vol. 9403, pp. 435–446. Springer, Cham (2015). doi:10.1007/978-3-319-25159-2_39
5. Boulkrinat, S., Hadjali, A., Aissani Mokhtari, A.: Handling preferences under uncertainty in recommender systems. In: IEEE International Conference on Fuzzy Systems, pp. 2262–2269 (2014)
6. Nguyen, V.-D., Huynh, V.-N.: A reliably weighted collaborative filtering system. In: Destercke, S., Denoeux, T. (eds.) ECSQARU 2015. LNCS, vol. 9161, pp. 429–439. Springer, Cham (2015). doi:10.1007/978-3-319-20807-7_39
7. Zenebe, A., Norcio, A.F.: Representation, similarity measures and aggregation methods using fuzzy sets for content-based recommender systems. Fuzzy Sets Syst. **160**(1), 76–94 (2009)

8. Abdelkhalek, R., Boukhris, I., Elouedi, Z.: Evidential item-based collaborative filtering. In: Lehner, F., Fteimi, N. (eds.) KSEM 2016. LNCS, vol. 9983, pp. 628–639. Springer, Cham (2016). doi:10.1007/978-3-319-47650-6_49

9. Yu, K., Schwaighofer, A., Tresp, V., Xu, X., Kriegel, H.-P.: Probabilistic memory-based collaborative filtering. IEEE Trans. Knowl. Data Eng. **16**(1), 56–69 (2004)

10. Mehdi, M., Bouguila, N., Bentahar, J.: Probabilistic approach for QoS-aware recommender system for trustworthy web service selection. Appl. Intell. **41**(2), 503–524 (2014)

11. Slokom, M., Ayachi, R.: Towards a new possibilistic collaborative filtering approach. In: Second international conference on computer science, Computer Engineering, and Social Media, pp. 209–216 (2015)

12. Smets, P.: The transferable belief model for quantified belief representation. In: Smets, P. (ed.) Quantified Representation of Uncertainty and Imprecision, pp. 267–301. Springer, Dordrecht (1998)

13. Dempster, A.P.: A generalization of bayesian inference. J. R. Stat. Soc. Ser. B (Methodological) **30**, 205–247 (1968)

14. Shafer, G.: A Mathematical Theory of Evidence, vol. 1. Princeton University Press, Princeton (1976)

15. Denoeux, T.: A K-nearest neighbor classification rule based on Dempster-Shafer theory. IEEE Trans. Syst. Man Cybern. **25**(5), 804–813 (1995)

16. Zhao, Z.D., Shang, M.S.: User-based collaborative-filtering recommendation algorithms on hadoop. In: Third International Conference on Knowledge Discovery and Data Mining, pp. 478–481 (2010)

17. Schafer, J.B., Konstan, J.A., Riedl, J.: E-commerce recommendation applications. In: Kohavi, R., Provost, F. (eds.) Applications of Data Mining to Electronic Commerce, pp. 115–153. Springer, New York (2001)

18. Amatriain, X., Pujol, J.M.: Data mining methods for recommender systems. In: Ricci, F., Rokach, L., Shapira, B., Kantor, P.B. (eds.) Recommender Systems Handbook, pp. 227–262. Springer, US (2015)

19. Sarwar, B., Karypis, G., Konstan, J., Riedl, J.: Item-based collaborative filtering recommendation algorithms. In: International Conference on World Wide Web, pp. 285–295 (2001)

20. Sanchez, J., Serradilla, F., Martinez, E., Bobadilla, J.: Choice of metrics used in collaborative filtering and their impact on recommender systems. In: IEEE International Conference on Digital Ecosystems and Technologies, pp. 432–436 (2008)

21. Bobadilla, J., Hernando, A., Ortega, F., Bernal, J.: A framework for collaborative filtering recommender systems. Expert Syst. Appl. **38**(12), 14609–14623 (2011)

22. Su, X., Khoshgoftaar, T.M.: Collaborative filtering for multi-class data using bayesian networks. Int. J. Artif. Intell. Tools **17**(01), 71–85 (2008)

23. Pennock, D.M., Horvitz, E., Lawrence, S., Giles, C.L.: Collaborative filtering by personality diagnosis: a hybrid memory-and model-based approach. In: The Conference on Uncertainty in Artificial Intelligence, pp. 473–480 (2000)

24. Bennett, J., Lanning, S.: The Netflix prize. In: KDD Cup and Workshop, p. 35 (2007)

25. Elouedi, Z., Mellouli, K., Smets, P.: Assessing sensor reliability for multisensor data fusion within the transferable belief model. IEEE Trans. Syst. Man Cybern. Part B: Cybern. **34**(1), 782–787 (2004)

Aggregating Top-K Lists in Group Recommendation Using Borda Rule

Sabrine Ben Abdrabbah$^{(\boxtimes)}$, Manel Ayadi, Raouia Ayachi,
and Nahla Ben Amor

LARODEC, Université de Tunis, ISG Tunis, 2000 Bardo, Tunisia
abidrabbah.sabrine@gmail.com, manel.ayadi@hotmail.com,
raouia.ayachi@gmail.com, nahla.benamor@gmx.fr

Abstract. With the democratization of the web, recent works aimed at making recommendations for groups of people to consider the circumstances where the item is selected to be consumed collectively. This paper proposes a group recommender system which is able to support partial rankings of items from different users in the form of top-k lists. In fact, the proposed group recommender system is based on generating recommendation lists for the group members using user-based collaborative filtering, then applying approximation Borda rule to generate group recommendations. Experiments show that the proposed group recommender system using approximate voting rules produced more accurate and interesting recommendations than using the standard voting rules.

Keywords: Group recommender systems · Collaborative filtering · Partial rankings · Voting rules

1 Introduction

Group recommendation is designed to find a trade-off among all the group members' tastes and then, derive the group preference for each item. The popularity of group recommender systems has increased in the last years. In literature, there are two main group recommendation strategies [1] including (i) *preferences aggregation* which consists in combining the group members' prior ratings into virtual user's profile and then generating recommendations and (ii) *recommendations aggregation* which consists in generating the members' individual recommendations using an individual recommendation method, then combining them to return a single recommendation list for the group. In this paper, we are interested in the second category since it typically offers better flexibility [2].

Different aggregation functions have been used to aggregate the individual recommendation lists of group members, we can for instance cite *average* [5], *least misery* [4], *voting rules* [3], etc. These functions usually work with full list of items (i.e. complete linear orders over all possible candidates) and they cannot be able to consider the situations when the orderings may not be total.

© Springer International Publishing AG 2017
S. Benferhat et al. (Eds.): IEA/AIE 2017, Part I, LNAI 10350, pp. 325–334, 2017.
DOI: 10.1007/978-3-319-60042-0_38

For instance, recommendation lists are generally presented in the form of partial rankings/orders of the top-k relevant items of each user out of the set of all the unseen items.

In order to handle partial recommendation lists, we propose to use approximate voting rules adapting standard voting rules to the case of partial rankings (i.e. when the positions of some items are unknown). More precisely, we develop a new group recommender system based on partial voting rules. We start by generating top-k recommendation list for each group member based on *collaborative filtering* approach. Then, we propose to use approximate aggregation methods to combine the individual recommendation lists of group members into a single ranked list that captures the collective preference. Contrary to classical group recommender systems that are based on complete recommendation lists, the proposed recommender system can recommend items which are already seen and appreciated by some group members since it takes into account even the items appearing in at least one recommendation list.

The remaining of this paper is organized as follows. Section 2 gives basic concepts on group recommender systems and voting rules. Section 3 is dedicated to the new proposed group recommendation framework based on partial recommendation lists. Finally, Sect. 4 discusses experimental results.

2   Basic Concepts

This section presents relevant background on group recommender systems and voting rules.

2.1   Group Recommender Systems

Group recommender systems (GRS) have been proposed as an efficient tool to discover group preferences and provide recommendations of items that can better match the group interest and taste [1,3,4]. The main idea of GRS consists in aggregating information from individual user models in order to capture the group model. In literature, there are two main group recommendation strategies:

- *Preference aggregation strategy* consisting in aggregating all users' individual preferences into a single profile representing preferences of all group members on each item. Then, recommendations are generated using a traditional recommender system.
- *Recommendation aggregation strategy* consisting in generating recommendations for each group member using an individual recommender algorithm, then, the recommendation lists are aggregated to produce a single group recommendation list.

In this paper, we are concerned with group recommendations generation using the second strategy i.e. aggregating individual recommendation lists since it is efficient and flexible [2]. Within the most common aggregation methods we can mention: (i) the *Average* function that considers the group preference as the average of all ratings given by group's members per item, (ii) the *Least misery* that considers the group preference as the minimum of the ratings given by the group members per item, (iii) the *average without misery* that eliminates the items having at least one individual rating which is below a certain predefined threshold and it considers the group preference as the average of all group members' ratings.

Recently, few works focused on aggregating the individual recommendation lists using voting rules. These latter have been proved as an effective solution to address the problem of finding "consensus" ranking between items given the individual preference orders of several decision makers [9]. We cite, Baltrunas et al. [3] investigated to produce group recommendations based on rank aggregation. The authors started by generating the recommendation list of each group member using collaborative filtering, then, the individual recommendations are aggregated into a ranked list of recommendations using *spearman rule* and *Borda count* aggregation method. This method is only restricted to the items in the group members' test set (i.e. the items which are not yet seen by the group members) and it does no consider the group members' interactions when generating group recommendations. Furthermore, Boratto et al. [6] proposed a group recommender system which is able to detect groups based on K-Means clustering algorithm. The group preference of the clustered users is modeled using different aggregation strategies including the voting rules (e.g. Borda count, plurality voting method, etc.). It has been pinpointed that Borda count and the average strategy are the best strategies that model group preference.

All these methods used the standard voting rules which are limited to full lists of items (i.e. contain the same items) and consider the totally ordered sets (i.e. all the items are ranked in each recommendation list). Nevertheless, actual recommendation lists cannot contain the same 'K' items and consequently, the ranking (i.e. preference) of an item for some group members may be unknown. So, we consider that the partial information presented in these lists should be delved further when aggregating the individual orderings.

2.2 Approximate Voting Rules

Voting rules consist in aggregating users preferences over a set of items in order to determine a consensus decision or recommendation using a specific voting rule.

Definition 1. *A voting model is defined by three components including: $U = \{u_1, u_2, ..., u_n\}$ is the group of users, $A = \{a, b, ...\}$ is the set of candidate items, such that $|A| = m$; and $P = (RL_1, ..., RL_n)$ is the preference profile of users in U which corresponds to a collection of complete rankings on A. $RL_u \in P$ represents the complete preference order of user u over A. For any $a, b \in A$, $a \succ_i b$ means that user u prefers a to b. For example, if $A = \{a, b, c\}$, a user who prefers a to b and b to c (and, thus, has complete preferences) would have preference order $a \succ b \succ c$.*

Given a complete preference profile, we consider the problem of selecting a consensus alternative, requiring the design of a *voting rule* f which selects a winner or a set of winners from A given a preference profile P and a set of available candidates. Scoring rules are a broad class of voting rules defined by a non-negative vector $s = (s_1, ..., s_m)$ over a set of candidates of size m such that $s_1 \geq ... \geq s_m$. Each candidate receives s_j points from each voter who ranks her in the jth position, and the score of a candidate is the total number of points she receives from all voters. The winner is the candidate with highest total score over all the votes. The well known scoring rule is Borda [8], for which the scoring vector is $s = (m - 1, m - 2, ..., 0)$.

Example 1. *Let us consider a setting of 3 users with the following complete preferences over four films $m = \{a, b, c, d\}$: user 1   : $a \succ b \succ c \succ d$, user 2   : $b \succ c \succ d \succ a$, user 3   : $c \succ d \succ b \succ a$. Under Borda voting rule, the score of item a (resp. b, c and d) is equal to 3 (resp. 6, 6 and 3). In this setting, items b and c are the winners.*

Voting with top-k lists. Partial voting consists in allowing the users to provide incomplete preferences over the set of items. One natural form of partial voting is top-k voting where recommendation lists contain the k most preferred items out of m and they are indifferent among the remaining ones.

Definition 2. *Partial voting is defined by three components where: $U = \{u_1, u_2, ..., u_n\}$ is the group of users, $A = \{a, b, ...\}$ is the set of items, such that $|A| = m$; and $R = (RL_1^k, ..., RL_n^k)$ is the partial preference profile of users in U which corresponds to a collection of partial rankings on A. $RL_u^k \in R$ represents the partial preference order of user u who ranks only a k out of m items where $k \in \{1, ..., m - 1\}$.*

Standard definitions of many voting rules assume that the users have complete preferences. However, requiring the users to provide a complete ranking over the whole set of candidate items can be difficult and too costly. The necessity to adapt these methods to the case of partial voting is of great importance. This adaptation consists in combining the partial preference orders into a consensus ranking. In fact, in order to handle partial preferences under Borda, one possible way is to transform the scoring vector and score unranked items appropriately. In this way, the voting rule will take as input top-k partial preference orders from users and outputs a non-empty subset of approximated winners. We refer to the voting rule that supports partial preference information by *approximate voting rule*. Two possible schemes can be found in the literature for treating partially ordered preferences in the form of k out of the m items:

- **Zero score:** The number of points given for the users' first and subsequent preferences is determined by the total number of items they have actually ranked, rather than the total number standing. Given top-k partial preference profile, scores are awarded to the ranked items as follows: $(m - 1, ..., m - k)$ depending on their position in the vote; and unranked items get 0 points.

This method is known as *Modified Borda Count* [7]. We denote this method by $Borda_0$.

– **Average score:** The items not submitted by the users get an average share of the scores which the users have not exercised. Given top-k partial preference profile, scores are awarded to the ranked items as follows: $(m - 1, ..., m - k)$ depending on their position in the vote; and unranked items get the average of the remaining scores $\frac{\sum_{j=k}^{m} s_j}{m-k}$. We denote this method by $Borda_{av}$.

Example 2. *Let us consider the above example with only top-2 recommendation list of each user i.e. each user ranks her 2 most preferred items out of the 4 available* $m = \{a, b, c, d\}$*: user 1 : $a \succ b$, user 2 : $b \succ c$, user 3 : $c \succ d$.*

Under $Borda_0$, the score of item a (resp. b, c and d) is equal to 3 (resp. 5, 5 and 2). The winners are items b and c. Using $Borda_{av}$, each unranked item receives an average score equal to $\frac{1}{2}$ i.e. $\frac{1+0}{2}$. Then, the score of item a (resp. b, c and d) is equal to 4 (resp. 5.5, 5.5 and 3). The winners are also items b and c since they correspond to the highest score.

3   Group Preference Modeling Based on Partial Recommendation Lists

Our focus in this paper is to generate the top-k items which can capture the group preference even when the preferences of some group members on some candidate items are unknown. The main idea consists in generating the top-k recommendation list for each group member RL_u^k using user-based collaborative filtering as a first step, then, aggregating the group members' recommendation lists into a relevance or consensus top-k recommendation list RL_G^k using $Borda_{av}$ and $Borda_0$. The whole framework of the proposed group recommendations generation is presented in Fig. 1.

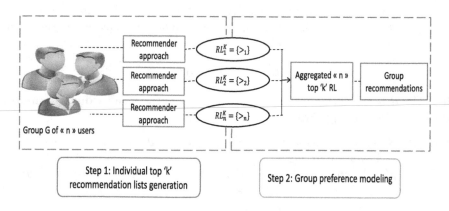

Fig. 1. Group recommendations generation

3.1   Step 1: The Individual Recommendation Lists Generation

In order to capture the group recommendations, we opt to generate the individual top-k recommendation lists of the group members by computing the members-items preferences using user-based collaborative filtering [10] since it is the most commonly used. Formally, let us consider a group G composed of n users $U = \{u_1, u_2, ..., u_n\}$ and a finite set of p items $I = \{i_1, i_2, ..., i_p\}$, the preference prediction of each user u on an item i is then computed as the weighted sum of the ratings given by the users similar to the active user:

$$P_{u,i} = \frac{\sum_{v \in S} r_{v,i} * s(u,v)}{\sum_{v \in S} |s(u,v)|} \tag{1}$$

where S is the set of the most similar users to u, $r_{u,i}$ is the rating given by the user u to the item i and $s(u,v)$ is the similarity degree between users u and v computed based on the *Pearson correlation measure* [11].

$$s(u_1, u_2) = \frac{\sum_{i \in I_{u_1} \cap I_{u_2}} (r_{u_1,i} - \bar{r}_{u_1})(r_{u_2,i} - \bar{r}_{u_2})}{\sqrt{\sum_{i \in I_{u_1} \cap I_{u_2}} (r_{u_1,i} - \bar{r}_{u_1})^2} \sqrt{\sum_{i \in I_{u_1} \cap I_{u_2}} (r_{u_2,i} - \bar{r}_{u_2})^2}} \tag{2}$$

where $I_{u_1} \cap I_{u_2}$ is the set of the co-rated items of users u_1 and u_2, $r_{u_1,i}$ is the rating of user u_1 on item i and $\bar{r}_{u_1}$ is the average rating of user u_1.

Clearly, the items having the highest preference prediction values are selected as the top-k recommendation list. The individual recommendation list RL_u^k represents the preference order of the group member over the top-k items.

3.2   Step 2: The Group Preference Modeling

In this step, the n individual recommendation lists of the group members generated from the previous step will be combined using the approximate voting rule to find out the group ranking RL_G over the m candidate items such that $m = \bigcup_{u=1}^{n} RL_u^k$. The top-k items appearing in RL_G are selected as the group recommendation list RL_G^k as follows:

$$RL_G^k = AVR_{j=1}^N RL_j^k \tag{3}$$

where AVR is the voting rule operator to combine the n individual recommendation list into a unique group recommendation list.

Example 3. *Let us consider a group G composed of four members $U = \{u_1, u_2, u_3, u_4\}$ and 50 items $I = \{a, b, c, ...etc.\}$. The following partial preference profile R contains the top '5' individual recommendation lists of the group members: $RL_1^5 : a \succ b \succ c \succ d \succ e$, $RL_2^5 : c \succ f \succ g \succ a \succ d$, $RL_3^5 : h \succ i \succ j \succ f \succ k$, $RL_4^5 : l \succ a \succ d \succ m \succ g$.*

Given the above individual recommendation lists, the candidate items is fixed to 12 (i.e. $m = \{a, b, c, d, e\} \bigcup \{c, f, g, a, d\} \bigcup \{h, i, j, f, k\} \bigcup \{l, a, d, m, g\} = \{a, b, c, d, e, f, g, h, i, j, l, m\}$).

Under $Borda_0$, the group ranking $RL_G = \{a, d, c, f, g, h, l, b, i, j, m, e, k\}$. Then, the group recommendation list RL_G^5 contains the top 5 items such as $RL_G^5 = \{a, d, c, f, g\}$.

Typically, the classical voting rules only work with complete recommendation lists which contain the same items. Indeed, recommendations are restricted to the items which are not yet seen by any group member since the items appearing in individual recommendation lists are often novel for active users. However, the recommendation list produced by the proposed group recommender system may contain items which are already seen and appreciated by some group members since it takes into account even the items appearing in at least one recommendation list.

4 Experimental Study

This section depicts the experimental study including the data set, the evaluation metrics, the experimental protocol and results.

4.1 Experimental Protocol

To evaluate the performance of the proposed group recommendation generation, we conduct our experiment on MovieLens[1] dataset. Movielens contains $100,000$ ratings collected from 942 users on 1681 movies. Movielens contains quantitative preferences which are scaled from 1 (low liking degree) to 5 (high liking degree).

To evaluate the effectiveness of the group recommendations, we focus on performing an *offline evaluation* which consists at first in dividing the data set chronologically in a training set (80%) and a test set (20%) (i.e. the testing data are selected in such a way that they occur after the training data over time). Then, we randomly organize users into groups of a specific size. For each group of 'n' members, we generate n top-k recommendation lists using user-based collaborative filtering. The individual recommendation lists will be combined into a single consensus ordering using different aggregation rules (i.e. the standard Borda count, $Borda_{av}$ and $Borda_0$). The k items which are classified in the top position of the group ordering are selected as group recommendations. Finally, the recommendations are evaluated individually as in the classical individual recommendation case, by comparing the generated recommendations to the existing data of the test set of each group member. In this experiment, we set 'k' to '5' as it is the most common recommendation list size in this context.

We choose the *Normalized Discounted Cumulative Gain* (nDCG) evaluation metric to compute the effectiveness of the group recommendations as it is one of the most popular IR metric measuring the quality of the ranking produced by a system [12]. The $nDCG$ measures the discounted cumulative gain of items positions in a given ranking list (DCG) according to the discounted cumulative gain of items positions in the optimal ordering of the recommendation list (IDCG).

---

[1] http://movieLens.umn.edu.

Formally, the discounted cumulative gain (DCG) accumulated at a particular rank position p is:

$$DCG_p = rel_1 + \sum_{i=2}^{p} \frac{rel_i}{log_2(i)} \tag{4}$$

where rel_i is the relevance value given by the user to the item at the position i.

Moreover, we choose the precision to evaluate the accuracy of the group recommendation list. The precision is defined in such a way that it detects the average of the true recommended alternatives relative to the total number of the alternative in the group recommendation list.

4.2   Experimental Results

The first experiment consists in computing the mean nDCG by varying the group size and the aggregation method used to combine the individual recommendation lists of group members.

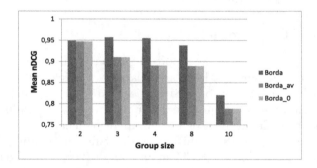

Fig. 2. Mean nDCG of Group recommendations under Borda, $Borda_{av}$ and $Borda_0$

As expected, Fig. 2 shows that the accuracy of the group recommendation list decreases when the group size increases. In fact, finding a consensus order for a large size of a random group is more difficult since the variation of recommendation lists is more significant. Results depicted in Fig. 2 show that the effectiveness of group recommendations when using $Borda_{av}$ and $Borda_0$ with a small group size (i.e. equal to '2') is almost the same as the standard Borda rule. However, with a large group size (i.e. ≥ 2), the effectiveness of the group recommendations in term of ranking quality is less good when using the approximate voting rules ($Borda_{av}$ and $Borda_0$) than the standard Borda rule. This is due to the lack of candidate items that can be considered when generating the group ranking and which consequently affects the mean nDCG.

The second experience is conducted to evaluate the validity of the generated group recommendation using the mean *precision* of the group members.

Figure 3 shows that the effectiveness of the group recommendation list is more significant using both $Borda_{av}$ and $Borda_0$ than the standard Borda rule. In fact,

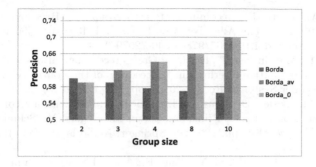

Fig. 3. Precision of Group recommendations under Borda, $Borda_{av}$ and $Borda_0$

by using approximate voting rules, group recommendations may contain more interesting items since it considers even the items with some unknown preferences and which are already seen by some group members. In fact, the group members will probably prefer to retain an item which has been appreciated by at least one user rather than an undiscovered item. However, with the standard Borda, the recommendation process is restricted to the items which are not yet seen by all the group members and with complete preference information. We note also that the precision of recommendations provided by the approximate Borda rules increases when the group size increases. This is due to the fact that the number of candidate items becomes more important with large groups and consequently, there are more chance to select relevant items in top-k recommendation list.

5   Conclusion

This paper proposes a new group recommendation method that offers to groups an efficient tool to support partial rankings contrarily to typical group recommender systems which handle only the total orders. It consists at first in generating top-k recommendation list for each group member. Then, the 'n' individual recommendation lists are aggregated together to produce top-k group recommendation list based on approximate voting rules ($Borda_{av}$ and $Borda_0$). Our experiments show that the group recommendation list generated using the approximate Borda rule is more accurate and interesting compared to group ranking created using the standard Borda. As a future work, one possible way is to consider *fuzzy* preference modeling to deal with incomplete recommendation lists. Additionally, we propose to consider the equally preferable items when aggregating the individual recommendation lists as it is a significant attribute in recommendations context.

References

1. De Pessemier, T., Dooms, S., Martens, L.: An improved data aggregation strategy for group recommendations. In: Proceedings of the 7th ACM Conference on Recommender Systems (RecSys 2013), pp. 36–39 (2013)

2. Jameson, A., Smyth, B.: Recommendation to groups. In: Brusilovsky, P., Kobsa, A., Nejdl, W. (eds.) The Adaptive Web. LNCS, vol. 4321, pp. 596–627. Springer, Heidelberg (2007). doi:10.1007/978-3-540-72079-9_20

3. Baltrunas, L., Makcinskas, T., Ricci, F.: Group recommendations with rank aggregation and collaborative filtering. In: Proceedings of the Fourth ACM Conference on Recommender Systems (RecSys 2010), pp. 119–126 (2010)

4. O'Connor, M., Cosley, D., Konstan, J.A., Riedl, J.: PolyLens: a recommender system for groups of users. In: Prinz, W., Jarke, M., Rogers, Y., Schmidt, K., Wulf, V. (eds.) ECSCW 2001, pp. 199–218. Springer, Netherlands (2001). doi:10.1007/0-306-48019-0_11

5. Song, Y., Hu, Z., Liu, H., Shi, Y., Tian, H.: A novel group recommendation algorithm with collaborative filtering. In: International Conference on Social Computing (SocialCom), pp. 901–904 (2013)

6. Boratto, L., Carta, S.: Modeling the preferences of a group of users detected by clustering: a group recommendation case-study. In: Proceedings of the 4th International Conference on Web Intelligence, Mining and Semantics (WIMS 2014), pp. 1–7 (2014)

7. Emerson, P.J.: The politics of consensus: for the resolution of conflict and reform of majority rule. Peter Emerson Belfast (1994)

8. Saari, D.G.: The Borda dictionary. Soc. Choice Welfare **7**, 279–319 (1990)

9. Dwork, C., Kumar, R., Naor, M., Sivakumar, D.: Rank aggregation methods for the web. In: Proceedings of the 10th International Conference on World Wide Web, New York, USA, pp. 613–622 (2001)

10. Zhao, Z.D., Shang, M.S.: User-based collaborative-filtering recommendation algorithms on Hadoop. In: Proceedings of Third International Conference on the Knowledge Discovery and Data Mining (WKDD 2010), pp. 478–481 (2010)

11. Sarwar, B.M., Karypis, G., Konstan, J.A., Riedl, J.: Analysis of recommendation algorithms for E-commerce. In: Proceedings of the ACM E-Commerce, Minneapolis, Minn, USA, pp. 158–167 (2000)

12. Luberg, A., Tammet, T., Järv, P.: Smart city: a rule-based tourist recommendation system. In: Law, R., Fuchs, M., Ricci, F. (eds.) Information and Communication Technologies in Tourism, pp. 51–62. Springer, Vienna (2011)

An Analysis of Group Recommendation Heuristics for High- and Low-Involvement Items

Alexander Felfernig[1], Muesluem Atas[1(✉)], Thi Ngoc Trang Tran[1],
Martin Stettinger[1], Seda Polat Erdeniz[1], and Gerhard Leitner[2]

[1] Institute of Software Technology, Graz University of Technology,
Inffeldgasse 16b/II, 8010 Graz, Austria
{alexander.felfernig,muesluem.atas,ttrang,martin.stettinger,
spolater}@ist.tugraz.at
[2] Institute for Informatics Systems, Alpen-Adria-Universität Klagenfurt,
Universitätsstraße 65-67, 9020 Klagenfurt, Austria
gerhard.leitner@aau.at
http://ase.ist.tugraz.at/
http://www.aau.at/

Abstract. Group recommender systems are based on aggregation heuristics that help to determine a recommendation for a group. These heuristics aggregate the preferences of individual users in order to reflect the preferences of the whole group. There exist a couple of different aggregation heuristics (e.g., most pleasure, least misery, and average voting) that are applied in group recommendation scenarios. However, to some extent it is still unclear which heuristics should be applied in which context. In this paper, we analyze the impact of the item domain (low involvement vs. high involvement) on the appropriateness of aggregation heuristics (we use *restaurants* as an example of low-involvement items and *shared apartments* as an example of high-involvement ones). The results of our study show that aggregation heuristics in group recommendation should be tailored to the underlying item domain.

Keywords: Recommender systems · Group decision making · Group recommendation · Decision heuristics

1 Introduction

In contrast to single user recommender systems [4,5], group recommenders focus on the recommendation of items to groups [2,8]. For example, Masthoff [6] presents concepts for television item sequencing for groups, O'Connor et al. [11] present a collaborative filtering based approach to movie recommendation for groups, McCarthy et al. [9] present a critiquing-based recommendation approach for groups of users (skiing holiday package selection), Ninaus et al. [10] demonstrate the application of group recommendation techniques in software requirements engineering, Jameson [3] presents user interface concepts that help to elicit and aggregate user preferences in the tourism domain (and beyond),

© Springer International Publishing AG 2017
S. Benferhat et al. (Eds.): IEA/AIE 2017, Part I, LNAI 10350, pp. 335–344, 2017.
DOI: 10.1007/978-3-319-60042-0_39

and Stettinger et al. [15,16] introduce a domain-independent recommendation-enhanced decision support environment for groups named CHOICLA[1].

There exist different approaches to determine recommendations for groups [2]. In most scenarios, preferences of individual group members are aggregated on the basis of aggregation functions (heuristics) [8]. The outcome of such an aggregation reflects the preferences of the whole group with regard to a given set of items. In the study presented in this paper, we simulate a situation where users have explicitly specified their preferences with regard to a set of items (restaurants and shared apartments) and aggregation heuristics are then used to infer the corresponding group preferences. In this context, the task of each study participant was to analyze a given set of user preferences with regard to an item set and then to provide a recommendation for the whole group.

Group recommender systems can be regarded as tools that support groups in decision making processes. Depending on the type of item, users tend to invest more or less time until a final decision is taken. For example, a car purchase comes along with a long-term decision process where different alternatives are compared in-depth against each other. In contrast, when choosing a restaurant, the corresponding decision is typically taken rather fast. An important question to be answered in this context is whether the underlying decision heuristics differ since this has a major impact on the development of group recommender systems.

Depending on the decision scenario, humans tend to achieve an acceptable trade-off between effort and accuracy related to a decision making process and the corresponding outcome [12]. *Satisficing* [14] is a related term that describes a human decision behavior where the first alternative is chosen that satisfies the wishes and needs of a user. Finally, items with high related decision efforts are often denoted as *high-involvement items* whereas items with low related decision efforts are denoted as *low-involvement items* [13]. The impact of suboptimal decisions regarding high-involvement items is much higher compared to low-involvement items. For instance, a suboptimal decision in the shared apartment domain manifests, e.g., in search efforts for a new apartment, unnecessary payments for the old apartment, relocation costs, and additional time efforts. In the restaurant domain, the effects of a suboptimal decision are typically negligible.

To the best of our knowledge, in-depth analyses of the selection of preference aggregation heuristics depending on the item domain do not exist. Related work is presented in [8] where individual aggregation heuristics are compared in the movie domain without further comparing the heuristics in other item domains. We present the results of a study that investigates the impact of item type (high-involvement vs. low-involvement) on the chosen decision strategy.

The remainder of this paper is organized as follows. In Sect. 2 we shortly introduce the aggregation heuristics that are often used in group recommendation scenarios. In Sect. 3 we analyze to which extent the item type has an impact

[1] The work presented in this paper has been partially conducted within the scope of the research projects WeWant (basic research project funded by the Austrian Research Promotion Agency) and OpenReq (Horizon 2020 project funded by the European Union).

on chosen decision heuristics and which heuristics have the highest prediction quality in specific item domains. With the final section we discuss research issues and conclude the paper.

2   Group Recommendation Heuristics

The scenario in our study is based on the assumption that each (hypothetical) member of a group explicitly specifies her preferences w.r.t. a given set of items. On the basis of this preference specification, corresponding aggregation functions (heuristics) aggregate preferences to a group model that represents the inferred preferences of the whole group. An example of a setting where each group member has already specified his/her preferences is depicted in Table 1.

Table 1. Example setting: four group members evaluated restaurants. Study participants had to recommend one "winner" item per setting. The individual decision heuristics *AVG (average)*, *LMIS (least misery)*, *MPLS (most pleasure)*, *MGD (minimal group distance)*, *ENS (ensemble voting)*, and *MUL (multiplicative)* will recommend "restaurant 1" to the group.

	Restaurant 1	Restaurant 2	Restaurant 3
1st user	5	1	3
2nd user	4	2	3
3rd user	5	1	3
4th user	4	2	3
AVG	**5**	2	3
LMIS	**4**	1	3
MPLS	**5**	2	3
MGD	**4 or 5**	1 or 2	3
ENS	**5**	2	3
MUL	**400**	4	81

The following set of aggregation functions was used within the scope of our study (corresponding examples of the application of these functions are depicted in Table 1).

Average (Formula 1) returns the average (in our example rounded to the nearest whole number) voting for item s as recommendation for the whole group. For example, the AVG value for *restaurant 1* is 5.

$$AVG(s) = \frac{\Sigma_{u \in Users} eval(u, s)}{|Users|} \tag{1}$$

Least Misery (Formula 2) returns the lowest voting for item s as group recommendation. For example, the LMIS value for *restaurant 1* is 4.

$$LMIS(s) = min(\bigcup_{u \in Users} eval(u, s)) \tag{2}$$

Most Pleasure (Formula 3) returns the highest voting for item s as group recommendation. For example, the MPLS value for *restaurant 1* is 5.

$$MPLS(s) = max(\bigcup_{u \in Users} eval(u, s)) \tag{3}$$

Minimal group distance (Formula 4) returns a rating d which has the minimum distance to the ratings of group members. For example, the MGD value for *restaurant 1* is 4 or 5.

$$MGD(s) = arg \min_{d \in \{1..5\}} (\Sigma_{u \in Users}|eval(u, s) - d|) \tag{4}$$

Ensemble voting (Formula 5) returns the majority value of the individual decision strategies. The majority of the following individual voting strategy results would be used to calculate the ensemble voting value: H = {AVG, LMIS, MPLS, MGD}. For example, the ENS value for *restaurant 1* is 5 because the value 5 occurs 3 times (result of AVG, MPLS, MGD) and the value 4 occurs only 2 times (result of LMIS, MGD).

$$ENS(s) = maxarg_{(d \in \{1..5\})}(\#(\bigcup_{u \in Users} eval(u, s) = d)) \tag{5}$$

Multiplicative heuristic (Formula 6) multiplies the rating values of all users for item s. For example, the MUL value for *restaurant 1* is 400 (5*4*5*4 = 400).

$$MUL(s) = \prod_{u \in Users} eval(u, s) \tag{6}$$

In the example depicted in Table 1, each of the used heuristics would recommend *restaurant 1* which is the dominating alternative in this scenario.

3   User Study

Overview. The overall goal of the user study was to figure out in which way decision heuristics of users change depending on the corresponding item domain. As an example of a high-involvement item we chose *shared apartments*, as an example of low-involvement items we chose *restaurants*.

We conducted a user study with students from two Austrian universities.[2] In the data collection phase, N = 420 subjects participated in the study where each participant had to perform two tasks: (1) *select* a restaurant for the given preferences of a synthesized group (each group had four group members – an example of such a synthesized setting is depicted in Table 1) with regard to a set of three restaurants and (2) *explain* the selection (recommendation). Overall, each of 20 different tasks (see Table 3) received about 20 evaluations from different study

---

[2] Graz University of Technology (http://www.tugraz.at) and Alpen-Adria Universität Klagenfurt (http://www.aau.at).

participants. The overall idea was that study participants were confronted with synthesized group settings (see, e.g., Table 1) and had to provide feedback on which item they would recommend to the group. This approach to analyze the decision making of groups is referred to as user as wizard evaluation method [7].

Evaluations of group members were simulated on the basis of six evaluation patterns (see Table 2) which follow a symmetric distribution of user preferences as follows.

– *average support (AV)*: there is an average support by each group member and none of the group members has a strong preference regarding acceptance or rejection.
– *disagreement (DIS)*: there is no clear opinion about the item, i.e., evaluations range from positive to negative.
– *majority positive (MAP)*: the majority has evaluated the item positively, only one user does not support the item.
– *majority negative (MAN)*: the majority has evaluated the item negatively, only one user likes the item.
– *no support (NO)*: none of the group members prefers the item, i.e., the group as a whole refuses the item.
– *full support (FULL)*: the item is a preferred one for each group member, i.e., fully supported by all group members.

Table 2 depicts the six different patterns used within the scope of our study. For example, in the task depicted in Table 1, pattern *FULL* was used for *restaurant 1*, pattern *NO* was used for *restaurant 2*, and pattern *AV* was used for *restaurant 3*.

Table 2. Patterns of user preferences (evaluations) used in the study, for example, pattern 6 (FULL) reflects a situation where all group members evaluate the alternative very positively.

Pattern	1st user	2nd user	3rd user	4th user
1 (AV)	3	3	3	3
2 (DIS)	1	2	3	4
3 (MAP)	1	4	5	4
4 (MAN)	5	2	1	2
5 (NO)	1	2	1	2
6 (FULL)	5	4	5	4

The complete set of tasks that were generated on the basis of the patterns depicted in Table 2 is depicted in Table 3. This table is the result of generating all possible combinations of three different patterns out from 6 patterns. The sequence in which the three patterns have been displayed to study participants was randomized. Each study participant had to solve two tasks, i.e., to select

Table 3. Tasks used in the user study. $N = 20$ tasks represent all possible combinations of three out of six patterns (see Table 2). *Dominance* denotes the fact that the item set used in the task includes a *dominant item*, i.e., an item that is not outperformed by another item in terms of a user evaluation. For example, *restaurant 1* in Table 1 is a dominating item.

Task	1st Pattern	2nd Pattern	3rd Pattern	Dominance
1	1	2	3	n
2	1	2	4	n
3	1	2	5	n
4	1	2	6	y
5	1	3	4	n
6	1	3	5	n
7	1	3	6	y
8	1	4	5	n
9	1	4	6	y
10	1	5	6	y
11	2	3	4	n
12	2	3	5	y
13	2	3	6	y
14	2	4	5	n
15	2	4	6	y
16	2	5	6	y
17	3	4	5	n
18	3	4	6	y
19	3	5	6	y
20	4	5	6	y

two items in two different settings (one in a restaurant and the other one in a shared apartment group decision context).

On the basis of the collected dataset, we evaluated the prediction quality of the group decision heuristics *AVG, LMIS, MPLS, MGD, ENS*, and *MUL* where *precision* [1] was measured in terms of the ratio between the number of correctly predicted group decisions (recommendations of study participants were interpreted as corresponding group decisions) and the overall number of predictions. Our hypothesis (*H1*) in this context was that for *the same overall combinations of patterns, study participants apply different decision heuristics depending on the item domain*, i.e., depending on the item domain (and related basic involvement type), different decision strategies are applied.

Within the scope of the study, participants had to provide *explanations* as to why they recommended (selected) a specific item for a defined group setting. This information is the basis for our second hypothesis (*H2*): *depending on the item type, different types of explanations are used for the selected item.* The explanation type was determined on the basis of sentiments which have been manually extracted from textual explanations provided by the study participants.

Results. Our goal was to figure out whether study participants used different decision strategies depending on the item domain (restaurants and shared apartments). First, we analyzed tasks in the dataset which included a *dominating item*, i.e., *an item that outperforms alternative items in at least one user evaluation and is not outperformed by other items.* For example, *restaurant 1* in Table 1 outperforms the other restaurants in all corresponding user evaluations.

Table 4 summarizes the results of this analysis for the tasks which include dominating items: in both item domains (*restaurants* and *shared apartments*), the *MPLS* heuristics had the highest precision compared to *AVG, LMIS, MGD, ENS* and *MUL* (chi-square test, p < 0.05). In all of our evaluations, the rather high precision rates can be explained by the low number of alternatives used in the individual task settings (the study participants had to compare only three items).

Table 4. Precision of decision heuristics in the domains of *restaurants* and *shared apartments* for tasks only *including* dominating items.

Domain	AVG	LMIS	MPLS	MGD	ENS	MUL
restaurants	90.7%	91.2%	**94.3%**	90.7%	92.0%	90.7%
Apartments	92.9%	93.4%	**93.7%**	92.9%	93.6%	92.9%

Second, we analyzed task settings which did not include dominating items. Table 5 summarizes the corresponding results: in the restaurant domain, the *AVG* heuristic had the highest precision (p < 0.05). In the shared apartment domain, *LMIS* significantly outperformed the other heuristics (p < 0.05). Consequently, in settings with no clear winner (settings where no dominating alternative is included), the choice of a decision heuristic depends on the item domain.

Table 5. Precision of decision heuristics in the domains of *restaurants* and *shared apartments* for tasks *not including* dominating items.

Domain	AVG	LMIS	MPLS	MGD	ENS	MUL
Restaurants	**81.2%**	75.0%	48.3%	79.1%	37.2%	70.9%
Apartments	74.1%	**83.3%**	35.7%	73.0%	22.1%	69.0%

Table 6 summarizes the precision of decision heuristics including dominating and non-dominating items in the domains restaurant and shared apartments. In restaurant domain, the AVG heuristic outperforms best and in the shared

Table 6. Precision of decision heuristics in the domains of *restaurants* and *shared apartments* for tasks including *dominating* and *non-dominating* items.

Domain	AVG	LMIS	MPLS	MGD	ENS	MUL
Restaurants	**86.5%**	83.9%	73.6%	85.5%	67.4%	81.8%
Apartments	84.5%	**88.9%**	67.6%	84.0	61.5%	85.7%

Table 7. Explanation focus depending on the item domain. The sentiment dimensions used in our analysis were *dominance* of an item, *fairness* with regard to every group member, and *consensus* within the group. Dominating alternatives in the item set (columns dom:restaurants and dom:apartments) trigger more explanations regarding item dominance. In scenarios that do not include dominating alternatives, other dimensions play a more important role. In apartment decisions, fairness plays a more important role. Finally, consensus plays a role in both, apartment and restaurant decisions.

Dimensions	dom:restaurants	dom:apartments	non-dom:restaurants	non-dom:apartments
Dominance	93.1%	93.3%	62.6%	54.1%
Fairness	2.3%	3.3%	13.9%	23.5%
Consensus	4.6%	3.3%	23.5%	22.4%

apartment domain, the LMIS heuristic significantly outperforms all the other heuristics.

In order to understand the reasons why study participants selected certain alternatives, we applied a manual sentiment analysis to analyze the *explanations* provided by the study participants (see Table 7). All explanations were analyzed with regard to the dimensions *dominance*, *fairness*, and *consensus*. In both item domains (restaurants and shared apartments), item *dominance* was the preferred way of explaining item recommendations. This can be explained by the fact that group recommendations identified by a study participant are in many cases considered as the best ones for the group (i.e., are considered as dominating the alternative ones).

If the task setting did not include dominating items, the share of consensus- and fairness-related explanations increased. In the restaurant domain, explanations more referred to the aspect of *consensus* whereas in the shared apartment domain, the aspect of *fairness* plays a more important role. Typically, restaurants are related to low-involvement decisions where the misery of a minority seems to be more acceptable compared to high-involvement decisions. The results of our sentiment analysis are summarized in Table 7.

In tasks that included dominating items, the explanations of users predominantly referred to the *dominance* of a specific item, for example, *I recommend item x since it dominates the other alternatives and thus is clearly the best recommendation in the given setting*. In situations with no clear winner, i.e., no dominating items were included in the task setting, the share of explanations related to the dimensions of *consensus* and *fairness* increases. From the three analyzed aggregation heuristics, *AVG* reflects the idea of *consensus*, i.e., items are recommended that represent a kind of trade-off for all group members. In this context, for example, completely negative evaluations of a single user do not necessarily prevent the recommendation of the corresponding item. *Fairness* is reflected by the *LMIS* heuristic since low evaluations of even single users have a much stronger impact on the recommendation and in most of the cases avoid the recommendation of items that are not preferred by a minority of group members.

4   Conclusions and Future Work

In this paper we have presented the results of a user study that focused on the analysis of the existing differences in used decision strategies depending on the item type. For the two domains of restaurants and shared apartments, we could show the existence of different aggregation heuristics especially in situations where there is no clearly dominating item. We consider our work as a first step towards a more in-depth analysis of the usage of aggregation heuristics in different item domains. Within the scope of our future work we will focus on the analysis of further group decision heuristics and compare their item domain-specific sensitivity. For example, we will analyze the impact of integrating different aspects of risk-awareness into the design of group recommendation heuristics. In this context we will also analyze variations in the number of items and group members. Furthermore, we will analyze the impact of factors such as gender, cultural background, and histories of decisions already taken by the same group on the decision making approach applied by the group. Finally, we will focus on the analysis of different possible ways to visualize and explain the current status of a decision process with the overall objective to increase consensus in the group and make high-quality decisions more efficiently.

References

1. Herlocker, J., Terveen, L., Konstan, J., Riedl, J.: Evaluating collaborative filtering recommender systems. ACM Trans. Inf. Syst. **22**(1), 5–53 (2004)
2. Jameson, A., Smyth, B.: Recommendation to groups. In: Brusilovsky, P., Kobsa, A., Nejdl, W. (eds.) The Adaptive Web. LNCS, vol. 4321, pp. 596–627. Springer, Heidelberg (2007). doi:10.1007/978-3-540-72079-9_20
3. Jameson, A.: More than the sum of its members: challenges for group recommender systems. In: Working Conference on Advanced Visual Interfaces, AVI 2004, pp. 48–54. ACM (2004)
4. Jameson, A., Willemsen, M.C., Felfernig, A., Gemmis, M., Lops, P., Semeraro, G., Chen, L.: Human decision making and recommender systems. In: Ricci, F., Rokach, L., Shapira, B. (eds.) Recommender Systems Handbook, pp. 611–648. Springer, Boston, MA (2015). doi:10.1007/978-1-4899-7637-6_18
5. Jannach, D., Zanker, M., Felfernig, A., Friedrich, G.: Recommender Systems: An Introduction. Cambridge University Press, Cambridge (2010)
6. Masthoff, J.: Group modeling: selecting a sequence of television items to suit a group of viewers. UMUAI **14**(1), 37–85 (2004)

7. Masthoff, J.: The user as wizard: A method for early involvement in the design and evaluation of adaptive systems. In: 5th Workshop on User-Centered Design and Evaluation of Adaptive Systems (2006)
8. Masthoff, J.: Group recommender systems: combining individual models. In: Ricci, F., Rokach, L., Shapira, B., Kantor, P.B. (eds.) Recommender Systems Handbook, pp. 677–702. Springer, Heidelberg (2011)
9. McCarthy, K., Salamo, M., Coyle, L., McGinty, L., Smyth, B., Nixon, P.: Group recommender systems: a critiquing based approach. In: IUI 2006. ACM, pp. 267–269 (2006)
10. Ninaus, G., Felfernig, A., Stettinger, M., Reiterer, S., Leitner, G., Weninger, L., Schanil, W.: Intelligent techniques for software requirements engineering. In: In European Conference on AI, Prestigious Applications of Intelligent Systems (PAIS), pp. 1161–1166 (2014)
11. O'Connor, M., Cosley, D., Konstan, J., Riedl, J.: PolyLens: A recommmender system for groups of users. In: European Conference on Computer-Supported Cooperative Work, pp. 199–218. ACM (2001)
12. Payne, J., Bettman, J., Johnson, E.: The Adaptive Decision Maker. Campridge University Press, New York (1993)
13. Petty, R., Cacioppo, J., Schumann, D.: Central and peripheral routes to advertising effectiveness: the moderating role of involvement. J. Consum. Res. **10**, 135–146 (1983)
14. Simon, H.: A behavioral model of rational choice. Q. J. Economics **69**, 99–118 (1955)
15. Stettinger, M., Felfernig, A., Leitner, G., Reiterer, S.: Counteracting anchoring effects in group decision making. In: Ricci, F., Bontcheva, K., Conlan, O., Lawless, S. (eds.) UMAP 2015. LNCS, vol. 9146, pp. 118–130. Springer, Cham (2015). doi:10.1007/978-3-319-20267-9_10
16. Stettinger, M., Felfernig, A., Leitner, G., Reiterer, S., Jeran, M.: Counteracting serial position effects in the CHOICLA group decision support environment. In: 20th ACM Conference on Intelligent User Interfaces (IUI 2015), Atlanta, Georgia, USA, pp. 148–157. ACM (2015)

SemCoTrip: A Variety-Seeking Model for Recommending Travel Activities in a Composite Trip

Montassar Ben Messaoud[1($\boxtimes$)], Ilyes Jenhani[2], Eya Garci[3],
and Toon De Pessemier[4]

[1] LARODEC, Institut Supérieur de Gestion de Tunis,
41, Avenue de la Liberté, 2000 Le Bardo, Tunisia
montassar.benmessaoud@gmail.com
[2] Prince Mohammad Bin Fahd University, Al Khobar, Kingdom of Saudi Arabia
ijenhani@pmu.edu.sa
[3] Institut Supérieur de Gestion de Sousse,
Rue Abdelaziz Il Behi, 4000 Sousse, Tunisia
garci.eya@gmail.com
[4] iMinds - Ghent University, G. Crommenlaan 8/201, 9050 Ghent, Belgium
toon.depessemier@ugent.be

Abstract. Selecting appropriate activities, especially in multi-destinations trips, is a hard task that many travellers face each time they want to plan for a trip. With the budget and time limitations, travellers will try to select activities that best fit their personal interests. Most of existing travel recommender systems don't focus on activities that a traveller might be interested in. In this paper, we go beyond the specific problem of combining regions in a composite trip to propose a variety-seeking model which is capable of providing travelllers with recommendations on what activities they can engage in when visiting different regions. A semantical hierarchical clustering-based model is proposed to guarantee diversity within the set of recommended activities. Experimental results on a real dataset have shown that the proposed approach helps the traveller to avoid doing the same or similar activities in a composite trip, thus, promoting less popular activities to be selected.

Keywords: Multi-destination trips · Leisure activities · Diversity · Hierarchical clustering · Ontology

1 Introduction

Recommendation systems have made a significant difference in people's lives. Being one of the early adoption areas, the tourism industry has taken advantage of the recent advances in recommender systems (RS) to enhance the quality of services offered to travellers and to enrich their travel experiences [12]. One of the potential applications of RS in tourism that has not yet been explored in details is

© Springer International Publishing AG 2017
S. Benferhat et al. (Eds.): IEA/AIE 2017, Part I, LNAI 10350, pp. 345–355, 2017.
DOI: 10.1007/978-3-319-60042-0_40

the recommendation of composite trips. Most of the existing approaches dealing with multi-destination trips focus on developing ways to combine single travel items like regions and routes in order to maximize the benefit for the traveller. Nevertheless, none of these works has directly tackled the issue of managing activities during the stay at each destination.

This paper provides a substantially extended version of a previous work [8], in which authors proposed an efficient algorithm for the recommendation of composite trips. Further attempts in this direction will be initiated in order to design complementary strategies to utilize semantic prior knowledge, to improve the diversity of the recommended activities and, most importantly, to enrich visitors' travel experience. The remainder of this paper is organized as follows: Sect. 2 discusses some related works where the diversity level is considered as a trip constraint. Section 3 gives the necessary background for both hierarchical clustering and ontologies. We then describe in details the SemCoTrip strategy in Sect. 4. In Sect. 5, we report experimental results that show the effectiveness of the proposed algorithm. Concluding remarks and future works will be given in Sect. 6.

2   State of the Art

In recent years, there has been a continuous line of research focusing on diversifying the recommended lists of activities and destinations to meet tourists' satisfaction. Diversity is commonly defined as the average pairwise distance between recommendations to users [4]. Authors in [14] proposed to use the K-means algorithm to assign users to clusters that have similar characteristics. When executing their clustering procedure, activities were weighted to ensure that their SigTur recommender system provides diverse recommendations. In [19], the diversity level was considered as a trip constraint. To ensure diversity, the authors used a measure of balance between the attractions' categories and the acceptable rating threshold. The work in [17] presents a search result clustering algorithm based on semantic data representation which chooses a set of objects from each cluster to increase the diversity of the proposal made to the visitor of a museum. [18] came up with a surprising result stating that the global error of k-Nearest Neighbours-based recommender systems decreases when a higher diversity is associated to the recommendations.

3   Background

In this section, we provide basic concepts related to semantic knowledge-based systems and hierarchical clustering which are essential in understanding the rest of the paper.

3.1 Knowledge-Based Systems

Knowledge-based systems (KBs) provide domain reasoning frameworks combined with inference engines that usually reason over logical languages. Ontology, which is one of those popular semantic driven knowledge based systems, has received numerous definitions in the literature. The most commonly cited definition was given in [6]. It defines the ontology as an explicit specification of a conceptualization. The "conceptualization", refers to a simplified view of the world by identifying its relevant concepts. The word "explicit" means that all concepts (resp. their specific properties and constraints) must be explicitly defined.

Definition 1. *An ontology can be formally expressed as:*

- *A set of concepts $\mathcal{C} = \{C_1, \ldots, C_n\}$, which are mainly interrelated by means of taxonomic (is-a) relations in the form of a hierarchy $\mathcal{H}$,*
- *A set of properties for each concept,*
- *Semantic (i.e. non-taxonomic) relations between concepts,*
- *A set of instances $\mathcal{I}$ (i.e. occurrences of concepts and semantic relations), and*
- *A set of assertions and formal axioms (i.e. constraint-relationships like should, should not, must, must not, etc.).*

3.2 Hierarchical Clustering

Clustering is a typical unsupervised learning task which aims at grouping together similar objects (with respect to their attribute values) into subsets called *clusters*. A cluster is therefore a collection of objects which are similar to each others and dissimilar to objects belonging to other clusters.

We can distinguish four main categories of clustering methods: (1) *Centroid-based clustering* such as K-means [13], (2) *Hierarchical clustering* [9] such as single-linkage and complete-linkage clustering methods, (3) *Distribution-based clustering* such as Expectation-Maximization (EM) algorithm [5] and (4) *Density-based clustering* such as DBSCAN algorithm [11].

Among these categories, we are interested in the hierarchical clustering one which could be either agglomerative or divisive. *Agglomerative methods* are "bottom up" approaches which start by assigning each element to a separate cluster then a merging of the two least distant (most similar) clusters is successively performed leading to larger clusters. However, *Divisive methods* are "top down" approaches in which all objects start in one cluster, and splits are performed recursively as one moves down. In practice, agglomerative techniques were more commonly used.

Distance (or similarity) between two clusters is determined by a *linkage criterion*, which is a function of the pairwise distances between instances one from each cluster. Most popular linkage criteria are: (1) *Single-linkage*: the distance between two clusters is the *minimum* pairwise distance between elements, one from each cluster (i.e. the shortest link between clusters). (2) *Complete-linkage*: the distance between two clusters is the *maximum* pairwise distance between elements, one from each cluster (i.e. the longest link between clusters). (3) *Average-linkage*: the distance between two clusters is the *average* pairwise distance between elements, one from each cluster. Other linkage criteria exist such as the Average group linkage (the sum of all intra-cluster variance), Ward's linkage (the increase in variance for the cluster being merged), V-linkage (the probability that candidate clusters spawn from the same distribution function). A good survey on hierarchical clustering algorithms could be found in [15].

The agglomerative clustering continues until a stopping criterion is met. We can apply a *distance-based stopping criterion* to stop clustering when the clusters are too far apart to be merged (i.e., distance between the closest clusters to be merged is greater to a user-predefined or computed threshold). A *number of clusters-based criterion* can also be used to stop clustering when there is a sufficiently predefined small number of clusters.

Hierarchical clustering has been mainly used in conjunction with recommender systems to deal with the problem of scalability. In fact, incremental hierarchical agglomerative clustering has been used in [7] to handle the large number of user profiles in e-commerce recommender systems. Moreover, in order to better personalize navigational recommendations in social tagging systems, authors in [20] applied hierarchical clustering to cluster the wide variety of tags. In [22], an ensemble hierarchical clustering approach has been applied to group users with similar reading profiles and get news hierarchies which are then used in recommending news articles. More recently, hierarchical clustering has been used in [21] to enhance the relevance of papers to recommend for researchers among a huge number of published papers.

4   SemCoTrip: A Semantical Algorithm for the Recommendation of Composite Trips

The general overview of the SemCoTrip (Semantical Composite Trip) algorithm is depicted in Fig. 1. SemCoTrip inputs are: a travel region dataset and a tourism-activity ontology. We follow approximately the same methodology proposed by authors in [8] to reproduce the same performance when combining regions and determining the optimal duration of stay per region. A blue shaded area was added in Fig. 1 to highlight the differences between the two algorithms and to visualize the recommendation process proposed by [8].

4.1   Search-Space Reduction

First, we start by reducing the search space by excluding irrelevant regions to the user query. Using the region tree hierarchy, if a region is removed, all its sub-regions and related activities will be removed as well.

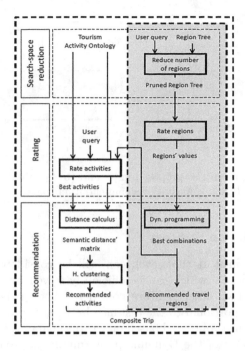

Fig. 1. SemCoTrip: Extending the composite trips' RS of [8] to consider a variety of leisure activities.

4.2   Rating

The remaining travel activities of the pruned region tree will be then rated. At this level, [8] used a 5-point Likert scale to rate regions' features depending on the month (season), which could potentially exclude many relevant destinations from the recommendations returned to users. Alternatively, we will simply assume that activities offered in each region are subject to change from season to season. Concepts' attributes in the input ontology will indicate how well the tourism activities match each traveling type group. By doing so, travel region ratings in our scenario will thus depend on their corresponding activities ratings.

Here, the standard rating schema of [8] that involves user and region dimensions is extended to three-dimensional schema involving activities (Refer to Fig. 2). Such multidimensional approach is usually used to deal with context in RSs [1]. For this case, we will further define a rating function R on the recommendation space User × Region × Activity specifying how much user u ∈ User liked activity a ∈ Activity in (sub-)region s ∈ Region, R(u, a, s).

At the end of this step, regions with low ratings will be removed and the remaining ones will be combined in a way to maximize their values for the user while still respecting the budget and the duration constraints.

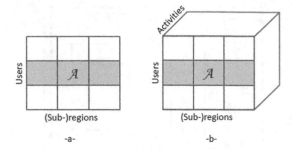

Fig. 2. (a) 2-D rating matrix as proposed in [8] and (b) SemCoTrip multidimensional model for the User × Region × Activity recommendation space.

4.3 Recommendation Strategy

The problem, as defined at that level, can still be considered as a variant of the knapsack problem [3] which can be efficiently solved by means of dynamic programming [10]. Two objectives are considered here: (1) The value of the composite trip is proportional to the distance between regions and (2) the best combination of regions is obtained based on the optimal duration of the stay per region. The application of the Dynamic programming approach to our dataset provided a candidate solution which consists of a subset of regions along with the duration time to spend in each of these regions.

The complementary component that we propose in our approach is to select the set of activities to recommend based on the recommended regions. An important criterion that we introduce in selecting the activities is diversity: we want our system to recommend activities which are as dissimilar as possible. To ensure that diversity, we will first use a semantic hierarchical clustering approach which will try to select heterogeneous clusters of activities. Then, a selection algorithm will be applied to find the optimal combination of clusters of activities found in the previous step. Throughout the hierarchical clustering step, we will consider Rada's distance [16] as the specific distance for calculating the semantic gain intra-(resp. inter) clusters.

Definition 2. *Let C_i and C_j be two concepts in an ontology restricted to taxonomic hierarchy. A measure of the conceptual Rada's distance is expressed as the minimum number of links separating the two concepts.*

We choose this distance because of its simplicity and its broad adoption. Note that Rada's distance can be replaced by any other semantic distance (refer to [2] for a comparative analysis between semantic distances).

As a first step of our approach, the clustering is performed on the total set of activities of each (sub-)region separately. As shown in Fig. 3, for each recommended (sub-)region, the hierarchical clustering will result in a set of one or more clusters. Activities within each cluster are selected based on the maximization of the semantic distance between the activities.

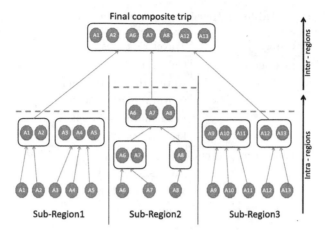

Fig. 3. Two-levels hierarchical clustering to optimize the diversity of the activities lists.

The second step of the approach is based on an inter-regions selection algorithm that be used to find out the optimal combination of clusters of activities (no more than one cluster will be selected from each (sub-)region). Clusters that maximize an average semantic distance between clusters of all remaining (sub-)regions will be selected and merged to form the final group of activities.

5   Experimental Study

5.1   Data Description

Dataset. Our variety-seeking model was tested on an extended version of the dataset used in [8]. The dataset (a region tree-like structure) is composed of a total of 152 regions with 124 leaves. The main difference with the original dataset is that we have assigned a range of seasonal activities to each (sub-)region. These activities are then mapped to their corresponding concepts in the used ontology and a 5-point Likert scale was used to indicate how well the proposed activity matches travellers types that we have categorized in four families according to the Canadian Tourism Commission[1] (See Table 1). All other input data (e.g. duration, budget, routing, crime level, etc.) is kept the same.

Ontology. The approach that we are proposing builds up on the use of a tourism activities ontology, which is presented as a hierarchy composed of a set of more than 200 concepts taxonomically related by subsumptions. The concepts are formalized into three related (sub-)ontologies, referred to as sport attractions, natural attractions and cultural attractions. Figure 4 shows a small excerpt of our tourism ontology.

---

[1] http://en.destinationcanada.com/resources-industry/explorer-quotient.

Table 1. Traveler's types classification.

Category	Traveler's types
Learners	Cultural explorer
	Authentic experiencers
	Cultural history buffs
	Personal history explorers
Indulgers	Free spirits
Familiarity seekers	Gentle explorers
	No Hassle travellers
	Virtual travellers
Escapists	Rejuvenators

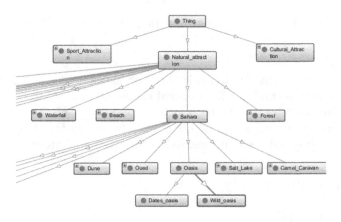

Fig. 4. Excerpt of the tourism activities ontology.

5.2 Experimental Design

A Java-based prototype was implemented in order to evaluate our approach. We used the prototype to handle a sample of 100 users queries. For each query, we changed input parameters (e.g. traveller's type, budget, total duration, etc.). The prototype executes each query separately and provides the top-rated recommendations; based on the recommendation procedures described in Sect. 4.

5.3 Results and Interpretations

The main objective of our approach is to ensure diversity when recommending a set of activities. The diversity degree of a set $A = \{A_1, ..., A_n\}$ of n recommended activities is measured by:

$$Diversity = \frac{\sum_{i=1}^{n} \sum_{j=i+1}^{n} Rada(A_i, A_j)}{\frac{n*(n-1)}{2}} \quad (1)$$

where $Rada(A_i, A_j)$ is the normalized Rada's distance between two activities A_i and A_j which lies on the unit interval.

Figure 5 shows, for the top-10 recommendations, the diversity level within the set of activities recommended by SemCoTrip as well as three other concurrent algorithms. The grey line refers to a variant of SemCoTrip which is only using the Intra-regions activities clustering algorithm. The red (resp. blue) curve shows the diversity relative to the baseline method that recommends random (resp. most popular) activities. We stress the fact that all four algorithms are based on the same basic regions recommendation idea proposed in [8]. Only activities' recommendation strategies have been changed.

For all four algorithms, a list of top-k recommendations is kept and sorted in descending order of the diversity within the activities. As we can observe from the Fig. 5, the popularity-based strategy gave the worst results, as it drastically reduces the activities' search space for each sub-region.

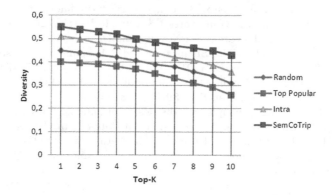

Fig. 5. Diversity for the top-K recommendations. (Color figure online)

Surprisingly, the random approach produced competitive results when compared to the variant "Intra". This could be explained by the fact that many sub-regions offer seasonal activities for several periods in the year. Those activities that depend on the weather are, usually, susceptible to be joined together on the corresponding ontology. This is the particular case where the random strategy provides nearly identical results to those provided by SemCoTrip.

The difference in performance between SemCoTrip and its variant "Intra" justifies that the whole clustering process is required to illustrate diversity in recommendations.

6   Conclusion

In this paper, we have proposed the SemCoTrip recommender system which seeks to recommend a set of diverse activities for a composite trip. A semantic-based hierarchical clustering approach has been used along with a tourism ontology to ensure diversity. Experimental results on a real dataset have shown that activities recommended by SemCoTrip are better, in terms of diversity, than activities recommended by a variant of SemCoTrip and two baseline approaches.

For future works, we intend to manage the sequence in which the activities need to occur and propose a complementary approach to improve novelty and serendipity whilst maintaining high accuracy of recommendations.

References

1. Adomavicius, G., Sankaranarayanan, R., Sen, S., Tuzhilin, A.: Incorporating contextual information in recommender systems using a multidimensional approach. ACM Trans. Inf. Syst. **23**(1), 103–145 (2005)
2. Blanchard, E., Harzallah, M., Briand, H., Kuntz, P.: A typology of ontology-based semantic measures. In: Missikoff, M. Nicola, A.D. (eds.) EMOI-INTEROP. CEUR Workshop Proceedings, vol. 160 (2005). CEUR-WS.org
3. Burg, J.J., Ainsworth, J., Casto, B., Lang, S.-D.: Experiments with the Oregon trail knapsack problem. Electron. Notes Discrete Math. **1**(B), 26–35 (1999)
4. Castells, P., Hurley, N.J., Vargas, S.: Novelty and Diversity in Recommender Systems. In: Ricci, F., Rokach, L., Shapira, B. (eds.) Recommender Systems Handbook, pp. 881–918. Springer, US (2015). doi:10.1007/978-1-4899-7637-6_26
5. Dempster, A., Laird, N., Rubin, D.: Maximum likelihood from incomplete data via the EM algorithm. J. Roy. Stat. Soc. **39**(B), 1–38 (1977)
6. Gruber, T.R.: Towards principles for the design of ontologies used for knowledge sharing. In: Guarino, N., Poli, R. (eds.) Formal Ontology in Conceptual Analysis and Knowledge Representation, Deventer, The Netherlands (1993)
7. Haruechaiyasak, C., Tipnoe, C., Kongyoung, S., Damrongrat, C., Angkawattanawit, N.: A dynamic framework for maintaining customer profiles in e-commerce recommender systems. In: EEE, pp. 768–771. IEEE Computer Society (2005)
8. Herzog, D., Wörndl, W.: A travel recommender system for combining multiple travel regions to a composite trip. In: Bogers, T., Koolen, M., Cantador, I. (eds.) CBRecSys@RecSys. CEUR Workshop Proceedings, vol. 1245, pp. 42–48 (2014). CEUR-WS.org
9. Jain, A.K., Dubes, R.: Algorithms for Clustering Data. Prentice Hall, Englewood Cliffs (1988)
10. Kellerer, H., Pferschy, U., Pisinger, D.: Knapsack Problems. Springer, Berlin (2004)
11. Kriegel, H.-P., Kröger, P., Sander, J., Zimek, A.: Density-based clustering. Wiley Interdisc. Rev.: Data Min. Knowl. Disc. **1**(3), 231–240 (2011)
12. Lu, C., Laublet, P., Stankovic, M.: Travel attractions recommendation with knowledge graphs. In: Blomqvist, E., Ciancarini, P., Poggi, F., Vitali, F. (eds.) EKAW 2016. LNCS (LNAI), vol. 10024, pp. 416–431. Springer, Cham (2016). doi:10.1007/978-3-319-49004-5_27
13. MacQueen, J.: Some methods for classification and analysis of multivariate observations. In: Berkeley Symposium on Mathematical Statistics and Probability (1966)
14. Moreno, A., Valls, A., Isern, D., Marin, L., Borràs, J.: Sigtur/e-destination: ontology-based personalized recommendation of tourism and leisure activities. Eng. Appl. AI **26**(1), 633–651 (2013)
15. Murtagh, F., Contreras, P.: Algorithms for hierarchical clustering: an overview. Wiley Interdisc. Rev.: Data Min. Knowl. Disc. **2**(1), 86–97 (2012)

16. Rada, R., Mili, H., Bicknell, E., Blettner, M.: Development and application of a metric on semantic nets. IEEE Trans. Syst. Man Cybern. **19**, 17–30 (1989)
17. Ruotsalo, T., Haav, K., Stoyanov, A., Roche, S., Fani, E., Deliai, R., Mäkelä, E., Kauppinen, T., Hyvönen, E.: Smartmuseum: a mobile recommender system for the web of data. J. Web Sem. **20**, 50–67 (2013)
18. Sanchez-Vilas, F., Ismailov, J., Sanchez, E.: The importance of diversity in profile-based recommendations: a case study in tourism. In: TouRS, Workshop on Tourism Recommender Systems, 9th ACM Conference on Recommender Systems, pp. 43–50. Austria, Vienna (2015)
19. Savir, A., Brafman, R.I., Shani, G.: Recommending improved configurations for complex objects with an application in travel planning. In: Yang, Q., King, I., Li, Q., Pu, P., Karypis, G. (eds.) RecSys, pp. 391–394. ACM (2013)
20. Shepitsen, A., Gemmell, J., Mobasher, B., Burke, R.: Personalized recommendation in social tagging systems using hierarchical clustering. In: Pu, P., Bridge, D.G., Mobasher, B., Ricci, F. (eds.) RecSys, pp. 259–266. ACM (2008)
21. West, J.D., Wesley-Smith, I., Bergstrom, C.T.: A recommendation system based on hierarchical clustering of an article-level citation network. IEEE Trans. Big Data **2**(2), 113–123 (2016)
22. Zheng, L., Li, L., Hong, W., Li, T.: Penetrate: personalized news recommendation using ensemble hierarchical clustering. Expert Syst. Appl. **40**(6), 2127–2136 (2013)

Decision Support Systems

A New Dynamic Model for Anticipatory Adaptive Control of Airline Seat Reservation via Order Statistics of Cumulative Customer Demand

Nicholas Nechval[✉], Gundars Berzins, and Vadims Danovics

BVEF Research Institute, University of Latvia, Raina Blvd 19, Riga 1050, Latvia
nechval@junik.lv

Abstract. This paper deals with dynamic anticipatory adaptive control of airline seat reservation for the stochastic customer demand that occurs over time T before the flight is scheduled to depart. It is assumed that time T is divided into m periods, namely a full fare period and $m-1$ discounted fare periods. The fare structure is given. An airplane has a seat capacity of U. For the sake of simplicity, but without loss of generality, we consider (for illustration) the case of nonstop flight with two fare classes (business and economy). The proposed policies of the airline seat inventory control are based on the use of order statistics of cumulative customer demand, which have such properties as bivariate dependence and conditional predictability. Dynamic adaptation of the airline seat reservation system to airline customer demand is carried out via the bivariate dependence of order statistics of cumulative customer demand. Dynamic anticipatory adaptive optimization of the airline seat allocation includes total dynamic anticipatory adaptive non-nested optimization of booking limits and local dynamic anticipatory adaptive nested optimization of protection levels over time T. It is carried out via the conditional predictability of order statistics. The airline seat reservation system makes on-line decisions as to whether to accept or reject any customer request using established decision rules based on order statistics of the current cumulative customer demand. The computer simulation results are promising.

Keywords: Stochastic demand · Airline seat reservation · Dynamic anticipatory adaptive control

1 Introduction

Assigning seats in the same compartment to different fare classes of customers in order to improve revenues is a major problem of airline seat reservation control. This problem has been considered in numerous papers. See for instance the articles by McGill and Van Ryzin [1], Park and Piersma [2] and Boyd and Bilegan [3] for excellent reviews, as well as the book by Talluri and van Ryzin [4]. For details, the reader is also referred to a review of yield management, as well as perishable asset revenue management, by Weatherford *et al.* [5], and a review by Belobaba [6].

© Springer International Publishing AG 2017
S. Benferhat et al. (Eds.): IEA/AIE 2017, Part I, LNAI 10350, pp. 359–370, 2017.
DOI: 10.1007/978-3-319-60042-0_41

Littlewood [7] was the first to propose a solution method of the airline seat allocation problem for a single-leg flight with two fare classes. The idea of his scheme is to equate the marginal revenues in each of the two fare classes. He suggests closing down the low fare class when the certain revenue from selling low fare seat is exceeded by the expected revenue of selling the same seat at the higher fare. That is, low fare booking requests should be accepted as long as

$$c_2 \geq c_1 \Pr\{Y_1 > u_1\}, \tag{1}$$

where c_1 and c_2 are the high and low fare levels respectively, Y_1 denotes the demand for the high fare (or business) class, u_1 is the number of seats to protect for the high fare class and $\Pr\{Y_1 > u_1\}$ is the probability of selling more than u_1 protected seats to high fare class customers. The smallest value of u_1 that satisfies the above condition is the number of seats to protect for the high fare class, and is known as the protection level of the high fare class customers.

It should be remarked that there is no protection level for the low fare (or economy) class; u_2 is the booking limit, or number of seats available, for the low fare class; the low fare class is open as long as the number of bookings in this class remains less than this limit. Thus, $(u_1 + u_2)$ is the booking limit or number of seats available for the high fare class at time. The high fare class is open as long as the number of bookings in this and low classes remain less than this limit.

Richter [8] gave a marginal analysis, which proved that (1) gives an optimal allocation (assuming certain continuity conditions). Optimal policies for more than two classes have been presented independently by Curry [9], Wollmer [10], Brumelle & McGill [11], and Nechval *et al.* [12–15].

The first purpose of this paper is to present the innovative information technologies for constructing the dynamic anticipatory adaptive policy of the airline seat reservation.

The second purpose of this paper is to introduce the idea of prediction of a future cumulative customer demand for the seats on a flight via the order statistics from the underlying distribution, where only the functional form of the distribution is specified, but some or all of its parameters are unspecified. This idea allows one to use a pivotal quantity averaging technique to eliminate the unknown parameters from the problem. The technique represents a simple and computationally attractive statistical method based on the constructive use of the invariance principle in mathematical statistics [15]. Unlike the Bayesian approach, the pivotal quantity averaging technique is independent of the choice of priors, i.e., subjectivity of investigator is eliminated from the problem. It allows one to find the improved invariant statistical decision rules, which have smaller risk than any of the well-known traditional statistical decision rules, and to use the previous and current sample data as completely as possible.

2 Static Models of Optimization of Airline Seat Reservation

Basically, there have been two static models of airline seat reservation: nested and non-nested. In non-nested model, distinct numbers of seats called buckets are exclusively assigned to each fare class. The sum of these buckets adds up to the total airplane seat capacity. In nested model, each fare class is assigned a booking limit, which is the total number of seats assigned to that fare class (protection level) plus the sum of all seat allocations to its lower fare classes.

Earlier revenue management models considered non-nested seat allocations. However, a major difficulty with non-nested seat allocation is that if the limit for a fare class is reached, a booking request to that class is denied, while a lower fare bucket remains open. In a nested seat allocation, this booking denial does not happen as the inventories are shared among each fare class and its lower classes.

For the sake of simplicity but without loss of generality, consider the problem of optimal allocation of seats between two independent (i.e., non-nested) fare classes, subject to the total airplane seat capacity constraint, which is given as follows.

Maximize the total expected revenue for a single-leg flight with two non-nested fare classes (business and economy),

$$R_2(u_1, u_2) = \sum_{j=1}^{2} R_j(u_j) \text{ subject to } u_1 + u_2 = U, \quad u_j \geq 0 \quad \text{for } j = 1, 2, \qquad (2)$$

where

$$
R_j(u_j) = E_{\theta_j}\{c_j \min(u_j, X_j)\} = c_j \left(\int_0^{u_j} x_j f_{\theta_j}(x_j) dx_j + \int_{u_j}^{\infty} u_j f_{\theta_j}(x_j) dx_j \right)
$$

$$
= c_j \left(u_j F_{\theta_j}(u_j) + u_j[1 - F_{\theta_j}(u_j)] - \int_0^{u_j} F_{\theta_j}(x_j) dx_j \right) = c_j \left(u_j - \int_0^{u_j} F_{\theta_j}(x_j) dx_j \right)
\qquad (3)
$$

represents the expected revenue from the jth fare class, c_1 and c_2 are the high and low fare levels respectively ($c_1 > c_2$), u_j denotes the booking limit for the jth fare class, X_j denotes the customer demand for the jth fare class, $f_{\theta_j}(x_j)$ is the probability density function of X_j with the parameter θ_j (in general, vector), U is the total capacity of the cabin to be shared among the two fare classes. A simple application of the Lagrange multipliers technique leads to the optimal solution satisfying (2) and

$$c_1 \bar{F}_{\theta_1}(u_1^*) = c_2 \bar{F}_{\theta_2}(u_2^*), \qquad (4)$$

where $\bar{F}_\theta(x) = 1 - F_\theta(x)$. Let us assume that

$$c_1 = 2, c_2 = 1; X_j \sim f_{\theta_j}(x_j) = (1/\theta_j) \exp(-x_j/\theta_j), j = 1, 2; \theta_1 = 10.4, \theta_2 = 20; U = 30. \quad (5)$$

Then the optimal solution (for two non-nested fare classes) is given by

$$u_1^* = 15, u_2^* = 15, \quad R_2(u_1^*, u_2^*) = 26.43593. \qquad (6)$$

Now we describe how booking limits can be determined when we deal with nested seat allocations. The performance index which can be used to determine the optimal allocation of seats between two dependent (i.e., nested) fare classes, subject to the total airplane seat capacity constraint, is given as follows.

Maximize the total expected revenue for a single-leg flight with two nested fare classes (business and economy),

$$\tilde{R}_2(\tilde{u}_1, \tilde{u}_2) = \tilde{R}_2(\tilde{u}_2) + E_{\theta_2}\{\tilde{R}_1(\tilde{u}_1 + \tilde{u}_2 - \min(\tilde{u}_2, X_2))\}, \tag{7}$$

where

$$\tilde{R}_2(\tilde{u}_2) = E_{\theta_2}\{c_2 \min(\tilde{u}_2, X_2)\} = c_2\left(\tilde{u}_2 - \int_0^{\tilde{u}_2} F_{\theta_2}(x_2)dx_2\right), \tag{8}$$

$$E_{\theta_2}\{\tilde{R}_1(\tilde{u}_1 + \tilde{u}_2 - \min(\tilde{u}_2, X_2))\} = c_1\int_0^{\tilde{u}_2}\left(\tilde{u}_1 + \tilde{u}_2 - x_2 - \int_0^{\tilde{u}_1 + \tilde{u}_2 - x_2} F_{\theta_1}(x_1)dx_1\right)f_{\theta_2}(x_2)dx_2$$
$$+ c_1\left(\tilde{u}_1 - \int_0^{\tilde{u}_1} F_{\theta_1}(x_1)dx_1\right)\int_{\tilde{u}_2}^{\infty} f_{\theta_2}(x_2)dx_2. \tag{9}$$

subject to

$$\tilde{u}_1 + \tilde{u}_2 = U, \quad \tilde{u}_j \geq 0 \text{ for } j = 1, 2. \tag{10}$$

A simple application of the technique of Lagrange multipliers leads to the optimal solution satisfying

$$c_2/c_1 = P_{\theta_1}\{X_1 > \tilde{u}_1^*\} = 1 - F_{\theta_1}(\tilde{u}_1^*), \quad \tilde{u}_2^* = \min(0, U - \tilde{u}_1^*), \tag{11}$$

where $\tilde{u}_1^*$ denotes the optimal protection level for the high fare class, $\tilde{u}_2^*$ denotes the optimal booking limit for the low fare class. The optimal solution (for two nested fare classes) is given by

$$\tilde{u}_1^* = 7, \quad \tilde{u}_2^* = U - \tilde{u}_1^* = 23, \quad \tilde{R}_2(\tilde{u}_1^*, \tilde{u}_2^*) = 28.7268. \tag{12}$$

Comparing (6) and (12) learns that the solution (6) always protects more seats for the high-fare class than the optimal protection level from (12). In order to carry larger numbers of high-fare passengers, it is not necessary to reserve an accordingly large number of seats. Nesting can often accommodate the remaining part of high-fare demand. Lower protection levels lead to higher load factors.

The index of relative efficiency of non-nested seat allocation as compared with nested seat allocation is given by

$$I_{\text{rel.eff.}}(R_2(u_1^*, u_2^*), \tilde{R}_2(\tilde{u}_1^*, \tilde{u}_2^*)) = \frac{R_2(u_1^*, u_2^*)}{\tilde{R}_2(\tilde{u}_1^*, \tilde{u}_2^*)} = \frac{26.43593}{28.7268} = 0.92. \tag{13}$$

The index of improvement percentage in the expected revenue for nested seat allocation as compared with non-nested seat allocation is given by

$$I_{\text{imp.per.}}(\tilde{R}_2(\tilde{u}_1^*, \tilde{u}_2^*), R_2(u_1^*, u_2^*)) = \frac{\tilde{R}_2(\tilde{u}_1^*, \tilde{u}_2^*) - R_2(u_1^*, u_2^*)}{R_2(u_1^*, u_2^*)} 100\% = 8.67\%. \qquad (14)$$

3 Some Results on Order Statistics

Theorem 1. Let $X_1 \leq \ldots \leq X_k$ be the first k ordered observations (order statistics) in a sample of size m from a continuous distribution with some probability density function $f_\theta(x)$ and distribution function $F_\theta(x)$, where θ is a parameter (in general, vector). Then the conditional probability density function of the lth order statistic X_l ($1 \leq k < l \leq m$), given $X_i = x_i$ for all $i = 1, \ldots, k$, is given by

$$g_\theta(x_l | x_1, \ldots, x_k) = g_\theta(x_l | x_k), \qquad (15)$$

where

$$g_\theta(x_l | x_k) = \frac{(m-k)!}{(l-k-1)!(m-l)!} \left[\frac{F_\theta(x_l) - F_\theta(x_k)}{1 - F_\theta(x_k)} \right]^{l-k-1} \left[1 - \frac{F_\theta(x_l) - F_\theta(x_k)}{1 - F_\theta(x_k)} \right]^{m-l} \frac{f_\theta(x_l)}{1 - F_\theta(x_k)}$$

$$= \frac{(m-k)!}{(l-k-1)!(m-l)!} \sum_{j=0}^{m-l} \binom{m-l}{j} (-1)^j \left[\frac{F_\theta(x_l) - F_\theta(x_k)}{1 - F_\theta(x_k)} \right]^{l-k-1+j} \frac{f_\theta(x_l)}{1 - F_\theta(x_k)}, x_k \leq x_l < \infty, \qquad (16)$$

i.e., the conditional distribution of X_l, given $X_i = x_i$ for all $i = 1, \ldots, k$, is the same as the conditional distribution of X_l, given only $X_k = x_k$, which is given by (16).

Proof. The joint density of $X_1 \leq \ldots \leq X_k$ and X_l is given by

$$g_\theta(x_1, \ldots, x_k, x_l) = \frac{m!}{(l-k-1)!(m-l)!} \prod_{i=1}^{k} f_\theta(x_i) [F_\theta(x_l) - F_\theta(x_k)]^{l-k-1} f_\theta(x_l) [1 - F_\theta(x_l)]^{m-l} \qquad (17)$$

$$= g_\theta(x_1, \ldots, x_k) g_\theta(x_l | x_k),$$

where

$$g_\theta(x_1, \ldots, x_k) = \frac{m!}{(m-k)!} \prod_{i=1}^{k} f_\theta(x_i) [1 - F_\theta(x_k)]^{m-k}. \qquad (18)$$

Using (17) and (18) we have that

$$g_\theta(x_l | x_1, \ldots, x_k) = \frac{g_\theta(x_1, \ldots, x_k, x_l)}{g_\theta(x_1, \ldots, x_k)} = g_\theta(x_l | x_k). \qquad (19)$$

This ends the proof.

Corollary 1.1. If $l = k + 1$, then it follows from (16) that

$$g_\theta(x_{k+1}|x_k) = (m - k)\left[\frac{1 - F_\theta(x_{k+1})}{1 - F_\theta(x_k)}\right]^{m-k-1}\frac{f_\theta(x_{k+1})}{1 - F_\theta(x_k)}, x_k \le x_{k+1} < \infty, \qquad (20)$$

and

$$P_\theta\{X_{k+1} \le x_{k+1}|X_k = x_k\} = G_\theta(x_{k+1}|x_k) = 1 - \left[\frac{1 - F_\theta(x_{k+1})}{1 - F_\theta(x_k)}\right]^{m-k} \qquad (21)$$

$$x_k \le x_{k+1} < \infty,$$

Corollary 1.2. It follows from (20) and (21) that

$$g_\theta(x_1) = m[1 - F_\theta(x_1)]^{m-1}f_\theta(x_1), \quad 0 \le x_1 < \infty, \qquad (22)$$

and

$$P_\theta\{X_1 \le x_1\} = G_\theta(x_1) = 1 - [1 - F_\theta(x_1)]^m, \quad 0 \le x_1 < \infty, \qquad (23)$$

Corollary 1.3. Let $X_1 \le \ldots \le X_m$ be the m ordered observations (order statistics) in a sample of size m from a continuous distribution with some probability density function $f_\theta(x)$ and distribution function $F_\theta(x)$, where θ is a parameter (in general, vector). Then the joint probability density function of all the m order statistics is given by

$$g_\theta(x_1, \ldots, x_m) = g_\theta(x_1)g_\theta(x_2|x_1)g_\theta(x_3|x_2) \cdots g_\theta(x_m|x_{m-1}) = m! \prod_{k=1}^{m} f_\theta(x_k), \qquad (24)$$

$$-\infty < x_1 < \cdots < x_m < \infty.$$

4   Dynamic Model of Adaptive Airline Seat Reservation Control

In this section, we consider a single-leg flight with two fare classes (business and economy) for a single departure date with m predefined reading dates at which the dynamic policy is to be updated, i.e., the booking period before departure is divided into m reading periods: $(\tau_0 = 0, \tau_1], (\tau_1, \tau_2], \ldots, (\tau_{m-1}, \tau_m]$ determined by the m reading dates: $\tau_1, \tau_2, \ldots, \tau_m$. These reading dates are indexed in increasing order: $0 < \tau_1 < _2 < \cdots < \tau_m$, where $(\tau_{m-1}, \tau_m]$ denotes the reading period immediately preceding departure, and τ_m is at departure. Typically, the reading periods that are closer to departure cover much shorter periods of time than those further from departure. For example, the reading period immediately preceding departure may cover 1 day whereas the reading period (1 month) from departure may cover 1 week.

Let us suppose that the cumulative customer demand for the high (business) fare class at the kth reading date (time τ_k, $1 \leq k \leq m$) is Y_k representing the kth order statistic from the underlying distribution with the probability density function $f_\theta(y)$ and cumulative distribution function $F_\theta(y)$, where θ is a parameter (in general, vector). This parameter is assumed to be unknown, but there is a sample of past observations (order statistics) $X_1 \leq \ldots \leq X_m$ from the underling distribution $f_\theta(y)$ to find an initial maximum likelihood estimate $\widehat{\theta}$ of the unknown parameter θ,

$$\widehat{\theta} = \arg \max_\theta \left(m! \prod_{k=1}^m f_\theta(x_k) \right). \tag{25}$$

The cumulative customer demand for the low (economy) fare class at the kth reading date (time τ_k, $1 \leq k \leq m$) is $\underline{Y}_k$ representing the kth order statistic from the underlying distribution with the probability density function $f_{\underline{\theta}}(\underline{y})$ and cumulative distribution function $F_{\underline{\theta}}(\underline{y})$, where $\underline{\theta}$ is a parameter (in general, vector). This parameter is also assumed to be unknown, but there is a sample of past observations (order statistics) $\underline{X}_1 \leq \ldots \leq \underline{X}_m$ from the underling distribution $f_{\underline{\theta}}(\underline{y})$ to find an initial maximum likelihood estimate $\widehat{\underline{\theta}}$ of the unknown parameter $\underline{\theta}$,

$$\widehat{\underline{\theta}} = \arg \max_{\underline{\theta}} \left(m! \prod_{k=1}^m f_{\underline{\theta}}(\underline{x}_k) \right). \tag{26}$$

We suppose that the cumulative customer demands for the high and low fare classes are stochastically independent. Each booking of a seat of the high fare class in the reading period $(\tau_{k-1}, \tau_k]$ generates revenue of c_k. Each booking of a seat of the low fare class in the reading period $(\tau_{k-1}, \tau_k]$ generates revenue of $\underline{c}_k$, where $\underline{c}_k < c_k$ for all $k \in \{1, \ldots, m\}$. It is assumed that

$$c_1 < c_2 < \ldots < c_m, \quad \underline{c}_1 < \underline{c}_2 < \ldots < \underline{c}_m, \quad \underline{c}_k / c_k < 1 \quad \forall k \in \{1, \ldots, m\}. \tag{27}$$

For the sake of simplicity, but without loss of generality, we consider (for illustration) the case of single-leg flight with two fare classes (business and economy) and $m = 3$ reading periods. Then the airline seat reservation process includes the following steps.

Step 1 (time $\tau = \tau_0 = 0$; available seat inventory: U seats; past data samples: $(\underline{X}_1 \leq \underline{X}_2 \leq \underline{X}_3)$, $(\underline{X}_1 \leq \underline{X}_2 \leq \underline{X}_3)$). At this step of the airline seat reservation control (before the reading period $(\tau_0, \tau_1]$), the following optimization problems are solved.

Total anticipatory non-nested optimization of booking limits. In the next at time τ_0 prior to flight departure, maximize the total expected revenue for the single-leg flight with two non-nested fare classes (business and economy) and with $m = 3$ fare levels each,

$$R(u_1, u_2, u_3; \underline{u}_1, \underline{u}_2, \underline{u}_3) = \sum_{k=1}^{3} R_1(u_k | u_{k-1}) + \sum_{k=1}^{3} R_1(\underline{u}_k | \underline{u}_{k-1}), \tag{28}$$

subject to

$$\sum_{k=1}^{3} (u_k - u_{k-1}) + \sum_{k=1}^{3} (\underline{u}_k - \underline{u}_{k-1}) = U, \quad 0 \le u_1 \le u_2 \le u_3, \quad 0 \le \underline{u}_1 \le \underline{u}_2 \le \underline{u}_3, \tag{29}$$

where $u_0 = \underline{u}_0 = 0$,

$$R_1(u_k | u_{k-1}) = c_k \left(u_k - u_{k-1} - \int_{u_{k-1}}^{u_k} G_{\hat{\theta}}(y_k | u_{k-1}) dy_k \right) \tag{30}$$

represents the expected revenue from the kth fare level of the high fare class, u_k denotes the cumulative booking limit for the high fare class in the kth reading period $(\tau_{k-1}, \tau_k]$, $k \in \{1, 2, 3\}$, Y_k denotes the cumulative customer demand for the high (business) fare class at the kth reading date, $G_{\hat{\theta}}(y_k | u_{k-1})$ is the conditional probability distribution function of the kth order statistic Y_k, U is the total capacity of the airplane cabin to be shared among the 6 fare levels,

$$\hat{\theta} = \arg\max_{\theta} \left(3! \prod_{k=1}^{3} f_{\theta}(x_j) \right), \quad \hat{\underline{\theta}} = \arg\max_{\theta} \left(3! \prod_{k=1}^{3} f_{\theta}(\underline{x}_j) \right), \tag{31}$$

$$R_1(\underline{u}_k | \underline{u}_{k-1}) = \underline{c}_k \left(\underline{u}_k - \underline{u}_{k-1} - \int_{\underline{u}_{k-1}}^{\underline{u}_k} G_{\hat{\underline{\theta}}}(\underline{y}_k | \underline{u}_{k-1}) d\underline{y}_k \right), \tag{32}$$

represents the expected revenue from the kth fare level of a low fare class, $\underline{u}_k$ denotes the cumulative booking limit for the low fare class in the kth reading period $(\tau_{k-1}, \tau_k]$, $k \in \{1, 2, 3\}$, $\underline{Y}_k$ denotes the cumulative customer demand for the low (economy) fare class at the kth reading date, $G_{\hat{\underline{\theta}}}(\underline{y}_k | \underline{u}_{k-1})$ is the conditional probability distribution function of the kth order statistic $\underline{Y}_k$.

Thus, in this case we obtain the following booking limits from optimization of (28), (29):

$$\Delta_1^{\circ}, \Delta_2^{\circ}, \Delta_3^{\circ}; \quad \underline{\Delta}_1^{\circ}, \underline{\Delta}_2^{\circ}, \underline{\Delta}_3^{\circ}, \tag{33}$$

where

$$\Delta_k^{\circ} = u_k^{\circ} - u_{k-1}^{\circ}, \quad k \in \{1, 2, 3\}, \tag{34}$$

represents the booking limit for customers of the high fare class with fare level c_k in the reading period $(\tau_{k-1}, \tau_k]$,

$$\overline{\Delta}_k^\circ = \overline{u}_k^\circ - \overline{u}_{k-1}^\circ, k \in \{1,2,3\}, \tag{35}$$

represents the booking limit for customers of the low fare class with fare level $\underline{c}_k$ in the reading period $(\tau_{k-1}, \tau_k]$,

$$\Delta_k = \overline{\Delta}_k^\circ + \underline{\Delta}_k^\circ, k \in \{1,2,3\}, \tag{36}$$

represents the booking limit for customers of the single-leg flight in the reading period $(\tau_{k-1}, \tau_k]$,

Further, in order to improve the results of non-nested optimization, the following problem of nested optimization based on (36) is solved.

Local anticipatory nested optimization of protection levels based on booking limits (33). In the next at time τ_0 prior to flight departure, maximize the expected revenue in each future reading period $(\tau_{k-1}, \tau_k]$, $k \in \{1, 2, 3\}$, with two nested fare classes (business and economy) and fares c_k and $\underline{c}_k$, respectively,

$$\widetilde{R}(\tilde{u}_k, \underline{\tilde{u}}_k) = \underline{\widetilde{R}}_1(\underline{\tilde{u}}_k | \underline{u}_{k-1}^\circ) + E_{\hat\theta}\{R_1(\tilde{u}_k + \underline{\tilde{u}}_k - \min(\underline{\tilde{u}}_k, \underline{Y}_k) | u_{k-1}^\circ)\}, \tag{37}$$

where $u_0^\circ = \underline{u}_0^\circ = 0$,

$$\underline{R}_1(\underline{\tilde{u}}_k | \underline{u}_{k-1}^\circ) = E_{\hat\theta}\{\underline{c}_k[\min(\underline{\tilde{u}}_k, \underline{Y}_k) - \underline{u}_{k-1}^\circ])\}$$

$$= \underline{c}_k\left(\underline{\tilde{u}}_k - \underline{u}_{k-1}^\circ - \int_{\underline{u}_{k-1}^\circ}^{\underline{\tilde{u}}_k} G_{\hat\theta}(\underline{y}_k | \underline{u}_{k-1}^\circ) d\underline{y}_k\right), \tag{38}$$

$$E_{\hat\theta}\{\widetilde{R}_1(\tilde{u}_k + \underline{\tilde{u}}_k - \min(\underline{\tilde{u}}_k, \underline{Y}_k) | u_{k-1}^\circ)\}$$

$$= c_k \int_{\underline{u}_{k-1}^\circ}^{\underline{\tilde{u}}_k}\left(\tilde{u}_k + \underline{\tilde{u}}_k - \underline{y}_k - u_{k-1}^\circ - \int_{u_{k-1}^\circ}^{\tilde{u}_k + \underline{\tilde{u}}_k - \underline{y}_k} G_{\hat\theta}(y_k | u_{k-1}^\circ) dy_k\right) g_{\hat\theta}(\underline{y}_k | \underline{u}_{k-1}^\circ) d\underline{y}_k$$

$$+ c_k\left(\tilde{u}_k - u_{k-1}^\circ - \int_{u_{k-1}^\circ}^{\tilde{u}_k} G_{\hat\theta}(y_k | u_{k-1}^\circ) dy_k\right) \int_{\underline{\tilde{u}}_k}^{\infty} g_{\hat\theta}(\underline{y}_k | \underline{u}_{k-1}^\circ) d\underline{y}_k. \tag{39}$$

subject to

$$\widetilde{u}_k - u_{k-1}^\circ + \underline{\widetilde{u}}_k - \underline{u}_{k-1}^\circ = \Delta_k. \tag{40}$$

A simple application of the technique of Lagrange multipliers leads to the optimal solution satisfying (40) and

$$\underline{c}_k / c_k = 1 - G_{\widehat{\theta}}(\widetilde{u}_k | u_{k-1}^\circ), \quad \underline{\widetilde{u}}_k = \max(0, \Delta_k - \widetilde{u}_k), \tag{41}$$

where

$$\widetilde{u}_k^* = \widetilde{u}_k - u_{k-1}^\circ \tag{42}$$

denotes the optimal protection level for customers of the high fare class with discount fare level c_k in the reading period $(\tau_{k-1}, \tau_k]$.

$$\underline{\widetilde{u}}_k^* = \underline{\widetilde{u}}_k - \underline{u}_{k-1}^\circ \tag{43}$$

denotes the optimal booking limit for customers of the low fare class with fare level $\underline{c}_k$ in the reading period $(\tau_{k-1}, \tau_k]$.

Step 2 (time $\tau = \tau_1$; remaining seat inventory: U_1 seats; observed cumulative customer demand: Y_1, $\underline{Y}_1$). At this step of the airline seat reservation control (before the reading period $(\tau_1, \tau_2]$), in the same way as above, *total anticipatory non-nested optimization problem of booking limits* and *local anticipatory nested optimization problem of protection levels* are solved.

Step 3 (time $\tau = \tau_2$; remaining seat inventory: U_2 seats; observed cumulative customer demand: Y_2, $\underline{Y}_2$). At this step of the airline seat reservation control (before the reading period $(\tau_2, \tau_3]$), in the same way as above, *total anticipatory non-nested optimization problem of booking limits* and *local anticipatory nested optimization problem of protection levels* are solved.

Departure (time $\tau = \tau_3$; remaining seat inventory: U_3 seats; observed cumulative customer demand: Y_3, $\underline{Y}_3$).

5   Conclusion

In this paper, we develop a new dynamic discrete-time model to improve anticipatory predictive statistical decisions for airline seat allocation problems via order statistics of the cumulative customer demand under parametric uncertainty of the underlying distributions. The model allows one to find an optimal airline seat reservation policy, which can be reduced to a set of critical values. Unlike many existing models, this model does not require any assumptions about the arrival pattern for customers of the various fare levels. Furthermore, multiple seat bookings, which are a practical issue in airline seat reservation control, can be also incorporated into the model. Frequentist probability interpretations of the methods considered here are clear. Bayesian methods are not considered here. We note, however, that, although subjective Bayesian prediction has a clear personal probability interpretation, it is not generally clear how this should be applied to non-personal prediction or decisions. Objective Bayesian methods, on the other hand, do not have clear probability interpretations in finite samples.

The control policy of airline booking is optimal as long as no change in the probability distributions of the customer demand is foreseen. However, information on the actual customer demand process can reduce the uncertainty associated with the estimates of demand. Hence, repetitive use of a control policy over the booking period, based on the most recent demand and capacity information, is the general way to proceed.

The control policy, which is developed in this paper for the use in the airline industry under parametric uncertainty of airline customer demand models, may be found to be useful in other industries such as hotels, car rental companies, shipping companies, etc. While the details of problems considered in the paper can change significantly from one industry to the next, the focus is always on making better demand decisions - and not manually with guess work and intuition - but rather scientifically with models and technology, all implemented with disciplined processes and systems.

The methodology described here can be extended in several different directions to handle various problems that arise in practice.

Acknowledgments. This research was supported in part by Grant No. 06.1936 and Grant No. 07.2036 from the Latvian Council of Science and the National Institute of Mathematics and Informatics of Latvia.

References

1. McGill, J.I., Van Ryzin, G.J.: Revenue management: research overview and prospects. Transp. Sci. **33**, 233–256 (1999)
2. Park, K., Piersma, N.: Overview of OR techniques for airline revenue management. Stat. Neerl. **56**, 479–495 (2002)
3. Boyd, E.A., Bilegan, I.: Revenue management and e-commerce. Manage. Sci. **49**, 1363–1386 (2003)
4. Talluri, K.T., van Ryzin, G.J.: The Theory and Practice of Revenue Management. Springer, New York (2005)
5. Weatherford, L.R., Bodily, S.E., Pfeifer, P.E.: Modeling the customer arrival process and comparing decision rules in perishable asset revenue management situations. Transp. Sci. **27**, 239–251 (1993)
6. Belobaba, P.P.: Airline yield management: an overview of seat inventory control. Transp. Sci. **21**, 66–73 (1987)
7. Littlewood, K.: Forecasting and control of passenger bookings. In: Proceedings of the 12th AGIFORS Symposium, pp. 95–117. American Airlines, New York (1972)
8. Richter, H.: The differential revenue method to determine optimal seat allotments by fare type. In: Proceedings of the XXII AGIFORS Symposium, pp. 339–362. American Airlines, New York (1982)

9. Curry, R.E.: Optimal airline seat allocation with fare classes nested by origins and destinations. Transp. Sci. **24**, 193–203 (1990)
10. Wollmer, R.D.: An airline seat management model for a single leg route when lower fare classes book first. Oper. Res. **40**, 26–37 (1992)
11. Brumelle, S.L., McGill, J.I.: Airline seat allocation with multiple nested fare classes. Oper. Res. **41**, 127–137 (1993)
12. Nechval, N.A, Nechval, K.N., Vasermanis, E.K.: Optimal control of airline booking process. In: Proceedings of the 15th IFAC World Congress: Barcelona, Spain, 21–26 July 2002 (in 21 volumes), vol. D: Optimal Control, Paper 1692, pp. 1–6. IFAC, TIBKAT (2003)
13. Nechval, K.N., Nechval, N.A., Rozite, K., Vasermanis, E.K.: Optimal airline seat inventory control for multi-leg flights. In: Proceedings of the 16th IFAC World Congress, Prague, Czech Republic, vol. 38, no. 1, pp. 31–36 (2005)
14. Nechval, N.A., Rozite, K., Strelchonok, V.F.: Optimal airline multi-leg flight seat inventory control. In: Dubois, D.M. (ed.) Computing Anticipatory Systems. AIP (American Institute of Physics) Proceedings, Melville, New York, vol. 839, pp. 591–600 (2006)
15. Nechval, N.A., Berzins, G., Nechval, K.N.: Improved airline seat inventory control under incomplete information. In: Ao, S., Hoi-Shou Chan, A., Katagiri, H., Xu, L. (eds.) IAENG Transactions on Engineering Sciences, London, UK, pp. 269–277. Taylor & Francis Group (2014)

A Multi-Criteria Decision Support Framework
for Interactive Adaptive Systems Evaluation

Amira Dhouib[1(✉)], Abdelwaheb Trabelsi[2], Christophe Kolski[3], and Mahmoud Neji[1]

[1] Miracl Laboratory, Faculty of Economics and Management Sciences,
University of Sfax, B.P. 1088, 3000 Sfax, Tunisia
{amira.dhouib,mahmoud.neji}@fsegs.rnu.tn
[2] College of Computation and Informatics, Saudi Electronic University, Dammam, Saudi Arabia
atrabelsi@seu.edu.sa
[3] University of Valenciennes and Hainaut-Cambrésis, LAMIH-UMR CNRS
8201, Valenciennes, France
Christophe.Kolski@univ-valenciennes.fr

Abstract. Many usability evaluation methods for interactive adaptive systems exist in the literature. There is not yet an agreement in the adaptive system community about which method is more useful than another in specific evaluation situations. This raises the question, "What is (are) the best evaluation method(s) that need(s) to be used in specific evaluation constraints?" This paper presents possible directions to address this issue by proposing a multi-criteria decision support framework for selecting the appropriate evaluation methods for interactive adaptive systems. The proposed decision support framework is applied to determine the suitable usability evaluation methods for a specific adaptation layer of a given adaptive hypermedia system.

Keywords: Interactive adaptive system · Adaptation layer · Evaluation method · Multi-criteria decision support framework

1 Introduction

Interactive Adaptive Systems (IAS) can be defined as "interactive systems that adapt their behavior to users on the basis of processes of user model acquisition and application that involve some form of learning, inference, or decision making" [1]. The evaluation of interactive adaptive systems is an important part of their development process and it should be as comprehensive as possible. The layered evaluation is considered as one of the peculiarities that distinguish between the evaluation of interactive adaptive systems and the non-adaptive ones [2, 3]. The aim of this evaluation is to decompose the adaptation process into different components (layers) and to evaluate them separately [4, 5]. A variety of Usability Evaluation Methods (UEMs) exist in literature [3, 6, 8]. In each layer, different evaluation methods can be used. The diversity of UEMs engenders a difficulty of choosing the most suitable ones in particular evaluation constraints. In fact, a major problem which evaluators are confronted with is the choice of suitable methods in a particular context [9]. The choice problem concerning UEMs is a challenging issue

© Springer International Publishing AG 2017
S. Benferhat et al. (Eds.): IEA/AIE 2017, Part I, LNAI 10350, pp. 371–382, 2017.
DOI: 10.1007/978-3-319-60042-0_42

and it depends on different factors [9, 10]. For instance, huge efforts are needed in order to understand the suitability of each usability evaluation method in particular contexts [11]. The suitable evaluation methods to be used for specific situations dependent essentially on the characteristics of the layer under consideration and the available evaluation resources [2]. The aim of this work is to propose a multi-criteria decision support framework that guides evaluators in the choice of appropriate usability evaluation methods for the layered evaluation. In order to address the goal of this research, a multi-criteria decision-making method, namely Analytic Hierarchy Process (AHP) is used to assist the decision-making process. The present paper expands on [12] by developing a decision support framework (it extends the state of the art, it enhances the proposed approach in order to guide the layered evaluation of interactive adaptive systems, and it details the case study).

The outline of this paper is organized as follows. We introduce first a background of the evaluation of interactive adaptive systems. We also provide an overview of some existing works for IAS evaluation and their limitations, and we provide subsequently the motivation for our proposal (Sect. 2). In the following, we introduce the proposed decision support framework. We present AHP decision aid method and the steps of the process of choosing the suitable evaluation methods (Sect. 3). Next, we present a case study related to an adaptive hypermedia system and we discuss the obtained results (Sect. 4). Finally, we conclude the paper with a summary and a look at perspective future works (Sect. 5).

2   State of the Art and Related Literature

2.1   The Evaluation of Interactive Adaptive Systems

One of the peculiarities that differentiate the evaluation of interactive adaptive systems and regular non-adaptive ones is the layered evaluation. The aim of this approach is to assess the success of adaptation by decomposing it into different layers and evaluating them separately [3, 13]. The different layers reflect the various stages of adaptation. Layered evaluation helps evaluators to identify the exact cause of the adaptation failure. Many studies identified several adaptation components in IAS literature [2, 13, 14]. In each layer, different evaluations have to be taken into account. The layered evaluation approach suggested by Karagiannidis and Sampson [13] discerns two layers that refer to the information processing steps within the adaptation process which should be investigated separately in IAS evaluation: the interaction assessment layer where the assessment process is being evaluated, and the adaptation decision making layer where the adaptation decision is evaluated. Similar layered evaluations but with a greater level of granularity have been proposed by Paramythis et al. [2]; the authors identify five layers, including collection of input data which refers to the collection of user interaction data, interpretation of the collected data which refers to the parts of the system that interpret the information, modelling the current state of the world which reflects the explicit or implicit representations of the users, deciding upon adaptation which refers to the parts of the system that are responsible for deciding upon adaptations, and applying adaptation which refers to the actual introduction of adaptations in the user-system interaction, on the basis of the related decisions. Recently, Manouselis *et al.* [14] proposed a layered evaluation for adaptive recommender systems, in which two layers are identified, namely evaluation of user modelling, and evaluation of adaptation decision making.

2.2 The Existing Works for the Evaluation of Interactive Adaptive Systems

From 2000 onwards, some frameworks that can assist the evaluation of interactive adaptive systems have been proposed [2, 15, 17]. Gupta and Grover [15] suggested a framework that treats evaluation as an integral part of the development process of adaptive hypermedia systems. It takes into consideration the environment in which adaptive hypermedia systems are used and the type of adaptation while evaluating individual modules in these systems. Another framework was presented by Tarpin-Bernard *et al.* [16], called AnAmeter. It provides the first steps towards the evaluation of the quality of a system's adaptation and it quantifies the adaptation degree of IAS. AnAmeter guides evaluators in the determination of the adaptation components in adaptive systems in a tabular form. In 2013, Mulwa and Wade [17] proposed a framework called EFEx. EFEx proposes the appropriate methods to be applied for the evaluation of adaptive e-learning systems considering different factors. Examples of these factors are the type of publications in which the evaluation methods have been proposed, the number of adaptive e-learning systems belonging to the same category that has been evaluated using the considered methods, etc.

The evaluation of interactive adaptive systems is an important task. However, important as it is, the research area is still open. This is due to some limitations in the existing evaluation works, including: (1) the difficulty of assisting automatically the choice of suitable evaluation methods to be applied for different layers, (2) the limited application domain of most of the existing works; the majority of them support only the evaluation of a unique type of interactive adaptive systems, (3) some of the existing works such as [15, 16] do not provide results in the form of reports or recommendations to evaluators. To address these limitations, this paper aims at proposing a decision support framework which helps evaluators in the selection of appropriate methods to be applied for the layered evaluation of IAS.

3   The Proposed Decision Support Framework

3.1   Concept of Analytical Hierarchy Process

The Analytic Hierarchy Process (AHP), proposed by Saaty [18], is a Multi-Criteria Decision Making (MCDM) method. It is applied to uncertain decision problems with multiple criteria in order to choose the best alternatives via a pair comparison process. One advantage of AHP is that it is simple to use since there is no need to build a complex expert system with the decision maker's knowledge embedded in it [19]. It allows us to make qualitative and quantitative analyses in the same decision-making methodology. The AHP method is based on five essential steps [20]:

1. Decomposing the problem into a hierarchy tree of different decision elements (i.e. goals, criteria, sub-criteria, and alternatives).
2. Creating a pair-wise comparison matrix, at each level of the hierarchical structure; the elements are compared using a Saaty's nine-point scale [20], as displayed in Table 1. The pair-wise comparison matrix A is shown in Eq. (1). In the comparison matrix A, a_{ij} refers to the degree of preference of i (row) criteria over j (column) criteria.

$$A = \begin{bmatrix} 1 & a_{12} & \dots & a_{1n} \\ a_{21} & 1 & \dots & a_{2n} \\ \dots & \dots & 1 & \dots \\ a_{n1} & a_{n2} & \dots & 1 \end{bmatrix} = \begin{bmatrix} 1 & 1/a_{21} & \dots & 1/a_{n1} \\ 1/a_{12} & 1 & \dots & 1/a_{n2} \\ \dots & \dots & 1 & \dots \\ 1/a_{1n} & 1/a_{2n} & \dots & 1 \end{bmatrix} \tag{1}$$

Table 1. Fundamental scale for making judgments adapted from [20]

Definition	Description
1	Equal importance
3	Moderate importance
5	Strong importance
7	Very strong importance
9	Extreme importance
2, 4, 6, 8	Intermediate values between two adjacent judgments

3. Determining the normalized weights, in which the eigenvector is derived from the matrix created in the last step measures of relative importance among the criteria and is used to determine the normalized priority weights for each criterion.
4. Determining the priority weights of alternatives with respect to decision criteria.
5. Analyzing the Consistency Ratio (CR) in order to validate and determine the acceptance of the weights. More details can be found in [20]. Based on Saaty's empirical suggestion [20] that a CR ≤ 0.1 is acceptable, it is concluded that the foregoing pairwise comparisons to obtain attribute weights are reasonably consistent. In contrast, if CR > 0.1, the matrix results are inconsistent and are exempted for the further analysis.

3.2 Choice Process of Evaluation Methods for the Layered Evaluation

The choice of appropriate evaluation methods for a particular evaluation situation is an essential step in the evaluation process of any interactive system. In this paper, we present a decision support framework for choosing the suitable UEMs to be used for the layered evaluation. As shown in Fig. 1, it consists of two main phases, namely: the preparation of data phase, and the selection of usability evaluation methods phase.

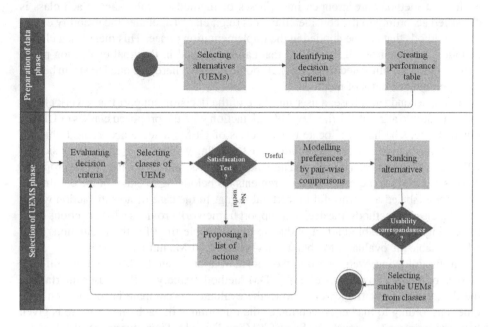

Fig. 1. The proposed decision support framework functioning flowchart

The process starts with the identification of the alternative usability evaluation methods, and the decision criteria influencing the choice of appropriate UEMs for the layered evaluation. From an overview of IAS literature, it is clear that there are different criteria that can affect UEMs choice. In this paper, the considered criteria are those related to the specificities of layered evaluation. They include: (1) the adaptation layer's input data that reflect the input data of the adaptive system's functionalities to be assessed by a layer. The input can be either given to the participants or decided by them [2]; (2) the layer's output data which reflect the data produced by the layers. Similarly to the input data, it can be either given or decided by the participants [2]; (3) the type of inter-active adaptive system on which the evaluation methods may be applied [15]; (4) the system development phase that highlights the moment at which the evaluation can be used. According to [2], an adaptation layer may be evaluated in: the analysis, design, and implementation phases; (5) the human resources which refer to the group of persons involved in the evaluation process [9]; (6) the temporal resources that underline the available time for conducting the evaluation of IAS [9]; and (7) the financial resources which reflect the available budget for conducting the evaluation of interactive adaptive systems [9].

Then, an evaluation of the performance of alternative UEMs is provided in terms of the different decision criteria under consideration. A performance table is created then which consists of UEMs versus an array of decision criteria. This classification is based on previous works such as those of [2, 3, 8]. In the next step, the evaluator has to evaluate the decision criteria through questionnaires. The decision support framework retrieves then all the evaluation methods related to each factor. For instance, all the usability evaluation methods are grouped into classes of methods at this stage. Each class is classified according to the considered factors (e.g., class 1 includes the usability evaluation methods that can be applied in the implementation phase. This means that class 1 includes, for instance, all the UEMs that can be applied in the final evaluation phase such as user test, simulated users, etc.). It should be noted here that one UEM can belong to more than one class of methods.

In the second sub-phase, a user interface of the decision support framework allows the evaluator to attribute his/her level of satisfaction with the proposed classes of UEMs. For instance, s/he has to allocate to each class of UEMs a score according to his/her level of satisfaction. This score can adopt the following values: (1) useful: the considered UEMs are useful and can be grouped into the same class, and (2) not useful: the proposed classes of UEMs do not meet the requirements for belonging to either of the constraints have been labeled as not useful in the total rating. In the case of no satisfaction with a specific class of methods, the decision support framework provides a list of actions (e.g., increasing the available budget, reducing the available time for the evaluation, etc.), which enable the evaluator to obtain a new class of UEMs until satisfaction.

In the following, we proceed to the choice of appropriate UEMs from the different classes of methods by means of an MCDM method, namely AHP. A user interface in the decision support framework allows the evaluator to compare each criterion with others according to his/her perception of the importance of each one. A score is given to a nine-point scale proposed by Saaty [20] (See Table 1). Then, our proposal calculates automatically the scores of the pair-wise comparison matrix once the scores are entered and the 'Calculate' button is clicked. All the entries along the diagonals are 1. After exposing the comparison matrixes of each criterion with the AHP method, appropriate UEMs from different classes of methods are determined. The last step corresponds to the validation of the obtained results. In this step, we propose to compare the usability criteria covered in the identified UEMs and the usability criteria of the adaptation layer under consideration. If the usability criteria to be assessed in each layer match the ones covered by the identified UEMs, then the process of choice is stopped and the identified usability evaluation methods are displayed as the most appropriate ones. Otherwise, the evaluator has to go back to the step called "evaluating decision criteria" in order to modify the input data. Depending on the available evaluation constraints, a number of criteria must be evaluated at every layer. Finally, the most appropriate usability evaluation methods will be displayed in a list that represents their suitability for the considered adaptation layer in given evaluation constraints. Further information is provided about the final results of the appropriate methods to be used, including links to recommendations on how to use them.

4   Application

To demonstrate the applicability of our proposal, a problem of selection of the most appropriate UEMs for an adaptive hypermedia system is presented. The considered system is intended to assist users in their information-seeking tasks by offering personalized access to news through a Web interface. In this study, we determine the appropriate UEMs for a layer-specific of the considered system, namely the deciding upon adaptation layer. According to [2], this layer reflects the decision taken in order to apply the suitable adaptation strategy on the adaptive system.

4.1 Procedure

Before proceeding to the different steps of the proposed decision support framework, the evaluator has to identify the different usability evaluation methods and the factors that have an impact on the UEMs' selection. In this study, thirteen methods commonly used for the evaluation of usability in interactive adaptive systems are considered; some of these methods are focus group [21], heuristic evaluation [22], cognitive walkthrough [23], user-as-wizard [24], etc. Next, the evaluator has to define the different decision criteria that have an impact when deciding the suitable UEMs. As already mentioned in Sect. 3.2, seven criteria are considered in this study (i.e., layer's input data, layer's output data, type of interactive adaptive system, system development phase, stakeholders, temporal resources, and financial resources). These criteria are meant to assist in the decision of choice of suitable methods for the layered evaluation. A performance table is created, in which the different UEMs are classified according to the criteria. The evaluator has to identify the available constraints of the considered layer of the given system which is to be evaluated through a questionnaire. These questionnaires ensure the capture of the characteristics of the layer under evaluation. Once the different criteria are evaluated, the proposed framework retrieves all the evaluation methods related to each decision criterion.

The evaluation methods are classified in the next step into seven classes corresponding to the different decision criteria. Class 5, for example, includes all the methods that can be applied in design evaluation phase. A score of satisfaction will be allocated to every class of methods according to the level of satisfaction of the evaluator. If so, s/he has to move on to the next step and no further analysis is required. In order to select the most appropriate usability evaluation methods from the identified classes, an MCDM method, namely AHP is applied. In this study, six UEMs are selected from the proposed classes of methods. The considered methods correspond to simulated users, user-as-wizard, heuristic evaluation, focus group, user test, and cognitive walkthrough. The priority weights of each criterion and alternative in every level are determined by using the AHP method. The decision matrixes which are created by the developed decision support framework are shown below. The evaluator has to fill the matrix according to his/her evaluation by using Saaty's scale method [20].

For instance, the criterion "human resources" is moderately stronger than the "financial resources", so we give the value 1/4 to the "financial resources" criterion compared to the "human resources" one and the evaluator has to click below the scale (shown by the value of 1/4). A screen shot of the proposed decision support framework at this stage is shown in Fig. 2.

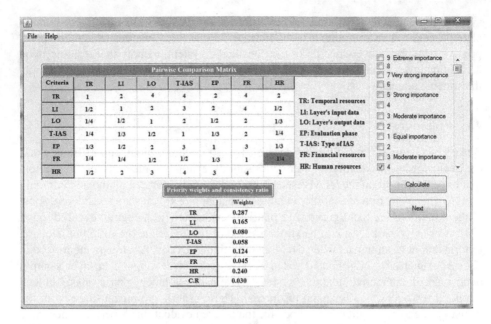

Fig. 2. The evaluation matrix of decision criteria

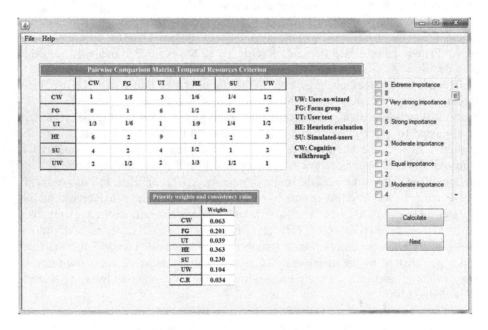

Fig. 3. Evaluation of alternatives with respect to temporal resources criterion

The consistency ratio for the comparison below is calculated to determine the acceptance of the priority weighting. The consistency test is one of the essential features of the AHP aid method. It aims to eliminate the possible inconsistency in the weights revealed through the computation of the consistency level of each matrix.

At this stage, the consistency ratio for the criteria is 0.034, which means that the pair-wise comparisons are consistent because the results are valid if this ratio is smaller than 0.1. Then, the evaluator has to fill the comparison matrix of each alternative in order to evaluate all the alternatives with respect to the different decision criteria. Figure 3 shows an example of evaluation of alternatives with respect to the temporal resource criterion. According to the temporal resource criterion, the most appropriate usability evaluation methods found are heuristic evaluation, and respectively, simulated users, focus group, user-as-wizard, cognitive walkthrough, and user test. After evaluating the alternatives with respect to the temporal resources criterion, the evaluator has to enter the judgments for the rest of the decision criteria. For each criterion, every possible combination of two alternatives is judged in this way (Table 2).

Table 2. Priority weights of decision criteria

	Temporal resources	Layers' input data	Layers' output data	Type of IAS	Evaluation phases	Financial resources	Human resources
Cognitive walkthrough	0.063	0.143	0.044	0.037	0.069	0.071	0.391
Focus group	0.201	0.036	0.039	0.379	0.414	0.251	0.145
User test	0.039	0.478	0.248	0.059	0.038	0.043	0.263
Heuristic evaluation	0.363	0.047	0.085	0.275	0.251	0.160	0,059
Simulated users	0.230	0.212	0.131	0.099	0.131	0.375	0.04
User-as-wizard	0.104	0.084	0.057	0.151	0.098	0.100	0.102
C.R	0.034	0.088	0.039	0.052	0.026	0.035	0.035

4.2   Results and Discussion

Figure 4 gives a summary of the proposed appropriate evaluation methods using the AHP aid method. In this study, the heuristic evaluation method (19.2) was the most appropriate usability evaluation method for the deciding upon adaptation layer in the given evaluation constraints. Followed respectively by focus group (18.6), cognitive walkthrough (18.4), user test (18.2), simulated users (15.9), and user-as-wizard (9.7). Further information is provided about each usability evaluation method, including links to recommendations on how to use them.

When the evaluators are confronted with the difficulty of choosing the suitable UEMs for interactive systems in general and adaptive systems in particular, the decision can often be very complex. In this paper, we have proposed a multi-criteria decision support framework based on the AHP method in order to select the appropriate usability evaluation methods for a layered evaluation. We presented a case study in which we applied AHP in order to determine the suitable UEMs for a specific layer. It should be noted that the choice of evaluation methods for different layers depends primarily on the

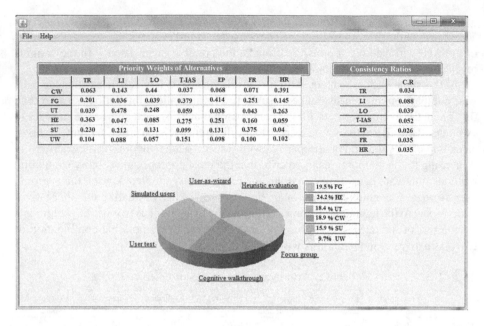

Fig. 4. Obtained final results of the proposed decision support framework

system's development lifecycle and the characteristics of the layer under consideration. The proposed decision support framework offers a flexible guide for prioritizing the usability evaluation methods to be applied for the layered evaluation and for supporting the decision making in a coherent and transparent way.

5 Conclusion and Future Work

The choice of the best evaluation methods is a key part of the process of evaluation of interactive adaptive systems. Different evaluation methods exist which differ along many dimensions such as the resource requirements, the system's development lifecycle, etc. The diversity of these methods engenders a difficulty in choosing the most suitable ones in particular constraints. This paper addresses these challenges by proposing a multi-criteria decision support framework that aims to help evaluators in the selection of best usability evaluation methods for the layered evaluation. A case study concerning an adaptive hypermedia system was presented, in which we determined the suitable methods to be applied to a specific adaptation layer.

As a perspective for future research, we intend to conduct a usability evaluation of the overall decision support framework. We intend also to test the proposed decision support framework in other fields of adaptive systems.

References

1. Jameson, A.: Adaptive interfaces and agents. In: Jacko, J.A., Sears, A. (eds.) The Human-Computer Interaction Handbook: Fundamentals, Evolving Technologies and Emerging Applications, pp. 305–330. Erlbaum, Mahwah (2003)
2. Paramythis, A., Weibelzahl, S., Masthoff, J.: Layered evaluation of interactive adaptive systems: framework and formative methods. User Model. User-Adap. Inter. **20**, 383–453 (2010)
3. Gena, C., Weibelzahl, S.: Usability engineering for the adaptive web. In: Brusilovsky, P., Kobsa, A., Nejdl, W. (eds.) The Adaptive Web: Methods and Strategies of Web Personalization, pp. 720–762 (2007)
4. Brusilovsky, P., Karagiannidis, C., Sampson, D.: The benefits of layered evaluation of adaptive applications and services. In: Weibelzahl, S., Chin, D.N., Weber, G. (eds.) Empirical Evaluation of Adaptive Systems, Proceedings of Workshop at the Eighth International Conference on User Modeling, UM2001, pp. 1–8 (2001)
5. Totterdell, P., Boyle, E.: The evaluation of adaptive systems. In: Browne, D., Totterdell, P., Norman, M. (eds.) Adaptive User Interfaces, pp. 161–194. Academic Press, London (1990)
6. Van Velsen, L., Van der Geest, T., Klaassen, R., Steehouder, M.: User-centered evaluation of adaptive and adaptable systems: a literature review. Knowl. Eng. Rev. **23**, 261–281 (2008)
7. Mulwa, C., Lawless, S., Sharp, M., Wade, V.: The evaluation of adaptive and user-adaptive systems: a review. Int. J. Knowl. Web Intell. **2**, 138–156 (2011)
8. Gena, C.: Methods and techniques for the evaluation of user-adaptive systems. Knowl. Eng. Rev. **20**, 1–37 (2005)
9. Dhouib, A., Trabelsi, A., Kolski, C., Neji, M.: A classification and comparison of usability evaluation methods for interactive adaptive systems. In: 9th International Conference on Human System Interactions, Portsmouth, UK, pp. 246–251 (2016)
10. Ferré, X., Bevan, N., Escobar, T.A.: UCD method selection with usability planner. In: Proceedings of the 6th Nordic Conference on Human-Computer Interaction: Extending Boundaries (2010)
11. Ferre, X., Bevan, N.: Usability planner: a tool to support the process of selecting usability methods. In: Campos, P., Graham, N., Jorge, J., Nunes, N., Palanque, P., Winckler, M. (eds.) INTERACT 2011. LNCS, vol. 6949, pp. 652–655. Springer, Heidelberg (2011). doi:10.1007/978-3-642-23768-3_105
12. Dhouib, A., Trablesi, A., Kolski, C., Neji, M.: An approach for the selection of evaluation methods for interactive adaptive systems using analytic hierarchy process. In: IEEE Tenth International Conference on Research Challenges in Information Science, 1–3 June, Grenoble, France, pp. 1–10 (2016)
13. Karagiannidis, C., Sampson, D.G.: Layered evaluation of adaptive applications and services. In: Brusilovsky, P., Stock, O., Strapparava, C. (eds.) AH 2000. LNCS, vol. 1892, pp. 343–346. Springer, Heidelberg (2000). doi:10.1007/3-540-44595-1_43
14. Manouselis, N., Karagiannidis, C., Sampson, D.G.: Layered evaluation for data discovery and recommendation systems an initial set of principles. In: IEEE 14th International Conference on Advanced Learning Technologies, pp. 518–519 (2014)
15. Gupta. A., Grover, P.: Proposed evaluation framework for adaptive hypermedia systems. In: 3rd Workshop on Empirical Evaluation of Adaptive Systems, Eindhoven University of Technology, The Netherlands, pp. 161–171 (2004)
16. Tarpin-Bernard, F., Marfisi-Schottman, I., Habieb-Mammar, H.: AnAmeter: the first steps to evaluating adaptation. In: 6th Workshop on User-Centred Design and Evaluation of Adaptive Systems at UMAP2009, Trento, Italy, pp. 11–20 (2009)

17. Mulwa, C., Wade, V.: A web-based evaluation framework for supporting novice and expert evaluators of adaptive e-Learning systems. In: International Conference on e-Technologies and Business on the Web (EBW201z3), Thailand, pp. 62–67 (2003)
18. Saaty, T.L.: The Analytic Hierarchy Process. McGraw-Hill International, New York (1980)
19. Omkarprasad, S.V., Kumar, S.: Analytic hierarchy process: an overview of applications. Eur. J. Oper. Res. **169**, 1–29 (2006)
20. Saaty, T.L.: Decision making with the analytic hierarchy process. Int. J. Serv. Sci. **1**, 83–98 (2008)
21. Krueger, R., Casey, M.: Focus Groups: A Practical Guide for Applied Research, 4th edn. Sage Publications, Los Angeles (2009)
22. Nielsen, J.: Heuristic evaluation. In: Nielsen, J., Mack, R.L. (eds.) Usability Inspection Methods, pp. 25–64. Wiley, New York (1994)
23. Mahatody, T., Sagar, M., Kolski, C.: State of the art on the cognitive walkthrough method, its variants and evolutions. Int. J. Hum. Comput. Interact. **26**(8), 741–785 (2010)
24. Masthoff, J.: The user as wizard: a method for early involvement in the design and evaluation of adaptive systems. In: 5th Workshop on User- Centred Design and Evaluation of Adaptive Systems at AH 2006, Dublin, Ireland, pp. 460–469 (2006)

Application of Multi-Criteria Decision Making Method for Developing a Control Plan

Fadwa Oukhay$^{(\boxtimes)}$, Hajer Ben Mahmoud, and Taieb Ben Romdhane

LISI Lab, INSAT Institute, Carthage University, Tunis, Tunisia
oukhayfadwa@gmail.com, hajerbenmahmoud@hotmail.com, benromdhane.t@planet.tn

Abstract. The control plan optimization is an important issue for manufacturing companies in order to produce high quality products at lower costs. This paper presents a Multi-Criteria Decision Making framework to establish an efficient control plan. The proposed approach models the problem of selecting the best control scenario based on the decision maker preferences, and takes into account conflicting criteria such as reducing the Risk Priority Number and minimizing the control cost and time. At the first stage, Analytic Hierarchy Process (AHP) is used to provide priorities ratings for the available control alternatives. In the second step, the Choquet integral operator is employed for the aggregation of the partial scores obtained for the different alternatives according to each criterion in order to deal with the existing interactions between the criteria. An industrial case study from a manufacturing enterprise is provided to illustrate the application of the suggested approach.

Keywords: Control plan · Failure mode and effect analysis · Multi-criteria decision making · Analytic hierarchy process · Choquet integral

1 Introduction

In a competitive economic environment, manufacturing companies are constantly encountering the challenge of designing and producing high-quality products on time and within the required quantities. To be able to attend their objectives and to meet customers' expectations, mastering the production process variability presents a key element. To reduce this variability, various control techniques are used to detect abnormal process and product variations. Control operations include: (i) Conformity control, which aims to check the product compliance with the specifications (to be accepted or rejected), and (ii) Monitoring control whose purpose is to check the process features (e.g. force, temperature...) for not deviating from their set values. All controls used are specified in a designed quality Control Plan (CP) which is a requirement of ISO/TS 16949 [8]. Although control activities are essential for assuring quality and preventing defective products to be delivered to customers, they present the disadvantages of being costly in terms of time delays as they enhance time cycles losses and in terms of direct costs (expensive equipments, operator salary...). Therefore, the optimization of

© Springer International Publishing AG 2017
S. Benferhat et al. (Eds.): IEA/AIE 2017, Part I, LNAI 10350, pp. 383–393, 2017.
DOI: 10.1007/978-3-319-60042-0_43

control plans is considered an important issue for manufacturers in order to increase productivity and to offer high quality products at lower costs.

The classical approach for generating the CP is based on risk assessment using the famous Failure Mode and Effect Analysis (FMEA) method [2]. The main objective of the FMEA method is to prioritize potential failures within their Risk Priority Numbers (RPNs), so that the critical characteristics are identified then included in the CP. This approach is included within the Advanced Product Quality Planning (APQP) which is required for automotive suppliers in accordance with QS 9000 standards. After determining the RPN risk sequence, the Decision Maker (DM) needs to specify, in the CP, what type of control to perform and with which frequency in order to reduce potential failure RPNs. Nevertheless, the traditional RPN approach lacks control activities selection method that takes into account factors related to the control costs in addition to the risk values. In this context, several researches have been developed to support the control planning in an efficient way.

Considerable works focus on cost optimization approaches. A mathematical model has been developed to optimize inspection plans in a multi-stage manufacturing system. The proposed model minimizes the total inspection related costs while assuring a required output quality. For each stage, the model is able to determine the type of inspection (0%, 100% or sampling) and the inspection parameters for the stations where sampling should be performed [17]. A new optimization framework based on a Mixed-Integer Linear Programming (MILP) model has been proposed for the process inspection planning of a manufacturing system with multiple quality characteristics. This model minimizes the total manufacturing cost and provides decision on which quality characteristic needs what kind of inspection and the time when the inspection should be performed [11]. The work in [15] presents a methodology based on Cost-benefit analysis for the evaluation of the economic impact of metrology in manufacturing.

Further approaches are proposed to minimize the risk while taking into account the limited control resources. A heuristic algorithm for quality control planning is presented in [4] aiming at minimizing the number of products with doubtful quality. The proposed algorithm consists of two stages: The first stage allocates the controls to keep the exposure to risk below a threshold. The second stage is an iterative greedy heuristic, which adjusts the CP defined in the first stage. The time delay is also considered as a criterion in the optimization process. The author in [14] employs a multi-objective Genetic Algorithm (GA) to define the optimized CP. The proposed algorithm aims to find a near-optimal sampling plan while reducing the risk level of processing machines, the metrology capacity used and the metrology time delay. In fact, the mentioned models consider different relevant criteria to optimize efficiently the control plans such as the cost, the risk and the time. However, the majority of these models are based on complex mathematical techniques which are subject to rather restrictive assumptions. Another perspective based on Multi-criteria Decision Making (MCDM) methods is suggested in the literature to model the control planning problem. A multi-criteria quality control model for acceptance sampling is developed in [9].

The criteria considered in this model are the minimization of the inspection cost as well as the minimization of the number of defects. In order to identify the most desirable sample sizes, an interactive paired comparison method is used based on the DM preferences. A multi-attribute decision model is proposed to establish inspection intervals of condition monitoring considering the DM preferences in cost and downtime [6]. In the proposed model, mutual preferential independence among criteria is assumed. Yet, such assumption is rarely verified in real world applications.

In this paper, an MCDM approach based on AHP method and Choquet Integral (CI) operator is proposed to establish an efficient CP. This approach models the DM preferences in minimizing the risk (RPN), the control cost and the control time as well as modeling the existing interactions among the criteria. The framework of this approach is described in Sect. 2. The proposed MCDM approach is presented in Sect. 3. In order to illustrate the application of the suggested approach, an industrial case study and experimental results are exposed in Sect. 4. The last section is devoted to the discussions and to the conclusion.

2   Motivations and Problem Framework

Within the APQP, the CP is generated based on the process FMEA and the Process Flow Diagram (PFD). The PFD provides information about the process functions which are transferred to the process FMEA. The latter is used to evaluate the risk by: (1) Identifying potential Failure Modes (FMs) for each process function, (2) Identifying the causes and effects of each FM, (3) Rating the probability of FM occurrence (O), the effect severity (S) and the probability of detecting the failure (D) on a scale ranging from 1 to 10, (3) Determining the RPN of each FM by multiplying the ranking values of O, S and D. Once RPNs are determined, the information about the characteristics that need to be controlled is determined and transferred to the CP. At this stage, our approach is applied to help the DM in selecting the best control scenario for each critical FM, which is considered an MCDM problem. The approach framework is represented by Fig. 1.

3   Multi-Criteria Decision Making Approach to Develop a Control Plan

3.1   Model Description

The proposed MCDM model is developed within six phases and is described by the flowchart shown in Fig. 2.

- **Phase 1:** The goal defined in this study is to evaluate and prioritize the different control scenarios available for each critical FM, according to a finite set of criteria in order to select the most efficient one.

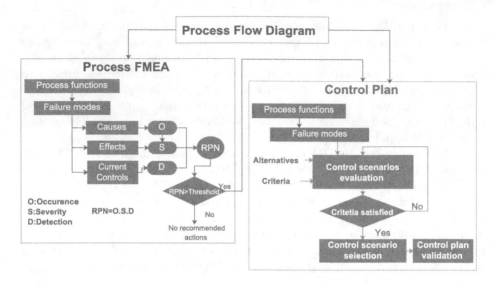

Fig. 1. The framework of the proposed MCDM approach

- **Phase 2:** Let C be a finite set of criteria denoted by $C = \{c_1, c_2, \ldots, c_p\}$. Three criteria are considered in this work: (i) the RPN esteemed which is the new value of the RPN if the considered scenario is applied. It reflects the efficiency of the scenario in reducing the RPN calculated in the FMEA. (ii) the control cost (instrument cost, operator cost, ...) which should be minimized, and (iii) the control Time.
- **Phase 3:** For each critical FM, the DM provides a set $S = \{S_1, S_2, \ldots, S_n\}$ of control scenarios that may be applied in order to choose the best one.
- **Phases 4 and 5:** These phases are explained in details in Subsects. 3.2 and 3.3, respectively.
- **Phase 6:** For each FM, an efficient control scenario is selected. Therefore the CP can be validated and applied in the process operations.

3.2   Analytic Hierarchy Process (AHP)

Introduced by Thomas Saaty [13], AHP is one of the most widely used MCDM tools. The use of AHP in this paper is motivated by the ability of this method to organize the problem of selecting the best control scenario into a hierarchical structure of objective, criteria, and alternatives. Moreover, by using a set of pairwise comparisons, the AHP enables obtaining the importance weights of the criteria and the relative performance scores of the alternatives related to each individual criterion. Furthermore, it provides a mechanism for checking and improving the evaluations consistency, which set AHP apart from other multi-criteria methods [1]. The application of this method for selecting the best control scenario is performed within four steps:

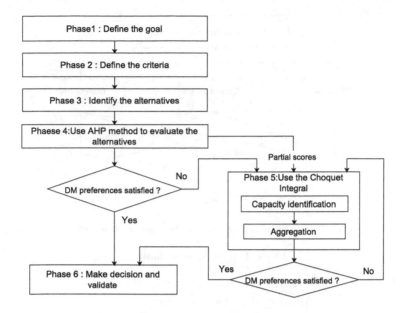

Fig. 2. The flowchart of the proposed MCDM approach

1. Define the problem and determine the overall goal: Select the best control scenario.
2. Structure the problem in a hierarchy of different levels constituting the goal, the criteria, the sub-criteria and the alternatives as shown in Fig. 3.
3. Weigh the criteria, the sub-criteria and the alternatives as a function of their importance for the corresponding element of the higher level by developing pairwise comparison matrices for each element using Saaty 9-point scale.
4. Calculate the Weighted Arithmetic Mean (WAM) for each decision alternative. Choose the one with the highest score. The obtained decision matrix is represented in Table 1, where w_j is the weight of criterion j with $w_j >= 0$, $sum(w_j) = 1$ and X_i is defined as follows:

$$X_i = \sum_{j=1}^{p}(x_{ij}.w_j) \qquad (1)$$

3.3   Representing Preferences Using the Choquet Integral

Using the AHP method, each alternative S_i belonging to the alternatives set S is given a profile of performance scores $(x_{i1}...x_{ip}) \in E^p$ where E is an interval of R and x_{ij} represents the partial score of S_i related to the criterion j. The aggregation of these partial scores that calculates the global scores X_i, is performed using the WAM (see Eq. (1)). However, this operator is unable to model the existing interaction between the criteria as it assumes their independence. In order to be able to take the interaction phenomena among criteria into account,

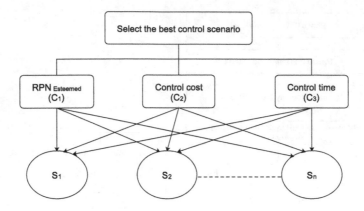

Fig. 3. Hierarchy scheme for control scenario selection

Table 1. The decision matrix

Criteria	c_1	c_2	$\cdots$	c_p	WAM
Weights	(w_1)	(w_2)	$\cdots$	(w_p)	
Alternatives					
S_1	x_{11}	x_{12}	$\cdots$	x_{1p}	X_1
S_2	x_{21}	x_{22}	$\cdots$	x_{2p}	X_2
$\vdots$	$\vdots$	$\vdots$	$\vdots$	$\vdots$	$\vdots$
S_n	x_{n1}	x_{n2}	$\cdots$	x_{np}	X_n

we propose to deal with the problem of aggregation using the CI. Extending the aggregation scheme of the AHP from the standard WAM to the general Choquet integration is proposed in [5]. Based on a monotone set function called Choquet capacity or fuzzy measure, the CI operator enables modeling not only the importance of each criterion but also the importance of each subset of criteria [10]. The application of this approach in the CP optimization context presents the main contribution of this paper.

Concept of Choquet Capacity. Let $C = \{1, \ldots, p\}$ a set of criteria. A capacity on C is a set function $\mu : 2^P \to [0, 1]$, satisfying the following conditions: (i) $\mu(\phi) = 0, \mu(C) = 1$ (ii) For any $A, B \subseteq C, A \subseteq B \Rightarrow \mu(A) \leq \mu(B)$.

Aggregation with CI. Let S the set of scenarios and $S_i \in S$, the global score X_i given by the CI according to a fuzzy measure μ and a set C of criteria, is defined by:

$$Ch_\mu(x_{i1}, \cdots, x_{ip}) = \sum_{j=1}^{p} (x_{i(j)}[\mu(A_{(j)}) - \mu(A_{(j-1)})]) \qquad (2)$$

Where the notation $_{(.)}$ indicates a permutation on C such that $x_{i(1)} \leq \cdots \leq x_{i(p)}$. Also, $A_{(j)} = \{(1) \cdots (p)\}$, for all $j \in \{1, \ldots, p\}$ and $A_{(p-1)} = \phi$.

Criteria Interactions. There are three types of interactions among criteria that can be modeled by fuzzy measurement [7]: (1) Negative interaction or negative synergy: Two criteria i and j interact in a negative way when they are considered by the DM as redundant i.e. the importance of the pair $\{i, j\}$ is almost the same as the importance of the single criteria i and j. (2) Positive interaction or positive synergy: this type of interaction exists between criteria that are considered as complementary i.e. although the importance of a single criterion is almost zero, the importance of the pair is high. (3) Independence: two criteria i and j are said independent when there is no interaction among them. In this case, the fuzzy measure is additive: $\mu(i, j) = \mu(i) + \mu(j)$. In this paper, the DM considers the time and the cost as redundant criteria. Moreover, the RPN and the cost as well as the RPN and the time are considered complementary criteria. In order to explain better the interaction phenomena, some numerical indices can be computed such as the Shapley value [16] and the interaction index [12]. The Shapley value measures the overall importance of a criterion i while the interaction index measures the average interaction between two criteria i and j.

Capacity Identification. When dealing with multidimensional aggregation with the CI on the basis of fuzzy measurements, the major challenge is the identification of capacities. To meet this challenge, a well known method in the literature which is the least squares method is used for the capacity determination. It requires the additional knowledge of the desired overall evaluations Y_i of the available objects $S_i \in S$. The objective of the least square method is to minimize the total quadratic error E^2 between the desired scores Y_i given on each scenario and the global scores calculated by the CI [7]. The formula for calculating the quadratic error is given by:

$$E^2 = \sum_{i=1}^{n}(Ch_\mu(x_{i1}, x_{i2}, \cdots, x_{ip}) - Y_i)^2 \tag{3}$$

4   Case Study

4.1   Presentation

In order to illustrate the proposed contribution, we present an industrial case study. The latter is a small and medium sized enterprise of automobile components located in Tunisia, which manufactures different wires to command airbags for vehicles [3]. The process FMEA method is used to evaluate the risk. The synoptic process is presented in Fig. 4. The process FMEA is shown in Table 2. For simplicity, the approach is applied to one critical FM considered ("Long. Cutting N.C"). The available control scenarios alternatives for this FM are the followings: S_1: Control by attribute (100%); S_2: Sampling control by attribute(simple

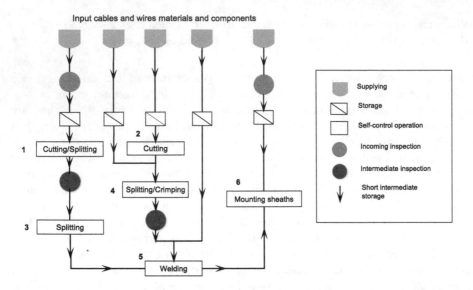

Fig. 4. Manufacturing bloc of Airbag wires

Table 2. Process FMEA

Num	Phase	FM	O	S	D	RPN
1	Cutting/Splitting	Long. Cutting (N.C)	2	4	2	16
		Long. Splitting (N.C)	1	2	3	6
		Driver missing	1	4	2	8
		Bonded insulator	1	2	2	4

plan); S_3: Sampling control by attribute (double plan); S_4: Sampling control by attribute (multiple plan); S_5: Sampling control by measure (100%); S_6: Sampling control by measure (simple plan); S_7: Sampling control by measure (double plan); S_8: Sampling control by measure (multiple plan).

4.2 Experimental Results

The results obtained for the control scenarios evaluation using the AHP method are shown in Table 3. Using the WAM, the scenario S_5 presents the highest priority rating. However, the DM prefers a scenario that satisfy all the criteria rather then a scenario presenting remarkable weakness on one of the criteria even if it presents the highest partial score on the most important criterion. Therefore, the aggregation of partial scores is performed using the CI instead of the WAM. At a first step, the DM is asked for presenting a preference order for a relevant subset of scenarios i.e. a subset which is considered particularly useful to represent his preferences: $S_7 \succ S_6 \succ S_3 \succ S_5$ as well as the correspondent desired overall scores $Y_i = [0.95 \quad 0.8 \quad 0.7 \quad 0.65]$. Then, the Choquet capacity

Table 3. The priority ratings obtained with the AHP method

Criteria	$RPN_{Esteemed}$	Cost	Time	WAM
Weights	$(w_1 = 0.7)$	$(w_2 = 0.2)$	$(w_3 = 0.1)$	
Control scenarios				
S_1	0.85	0.35	0.3	0.695
S_2	0.5	0.72	0.65	0.559
S_3	0.58	0.7	0.6	0.606
S_4	0.65	0.59	0.61	0.634
S_5	0.95	0.25	0.2	0.735
S_6	0.65	0.62	0.6	0.639
S_7	0.7	0.6	0.55	0.665
S_8	0.75	0.5	0.39	0.664

Table 4. The priority ratings obtained with AHP method and CI

Control scenarios	S_1	S_2	S_3	S_4	S_5	S_6	S_7	S_8
WAM	0.695	0.559	0.606	0.634	0.735	0.639	0.665	0.664
CI	0.549	0.599	0.625	0.624	0.529	0.631	0.639	0.597

is determined by using the least squares method. The capacities obtained are the following: $\mu(\{c_1\}) = 0.4$; $\mu(\{c_2\}) = 0.35$; $\mu(\{c_3\}) = 0.32$; $\mu(\{c_1, c_2\}) = 0.98$; $\mu(\{c_1, c_3\}) = 0.94$; $\mu(\{c_2, c_3\}) = 0.5$; $\mu(\{c_1, c_2, c_3\}) = 1$. The Table 4 represents the comparison between the results obtained using the WAM and the CI. By applying the CI, the preference order of the DM is satisfied as the scenario S_7 presents the highest priority rating. Therefore, S_7 is the one selected to be applied for the corresponding FM. Furthermore, the Shapley values ϕ_μ and the interactions indices I_μ of the obtained capacity are computed: $\phi_\mu(c_1) = 0.5$; $\phi_\mu(c_2) = 0.26$; $\phi_\mu(c_3) = 0.22$; $I_\mu(c_1, c_2) = 0.055$; $I_\mu(c_1, c_3) = 0.045$; $I_\mu(c_2, c_3) = -0.34$. These results show that the DM preferences on the criteria importance are satisfied. In fact, the criterion c_1 presents the highest overall importance. The criteria c_1 and c_2 as well as c_1 and c_3 present positive interactions while the criteria c_2 and c_3 present negative interaction.

5 Discussions and Conclusion

The paper presents an MCDM approach based on AHP method and CI operator. The AHP method provides the criteria weights, the partial scores and the overall scores for the control scenarios alternatives. However, the priority ratings obtained by AHP does not meet the DM preferences in terms of selecting a control scenario with a balanced profile of performance scores. Therefore, the CI based on Choquet capacity is used in order to model the interactions between the criteria and the DM preferences. The application of the proposed MCDM approach in a real case study enables performing an efficient CP by helping the DM to select control scenarios that provide the best compromise between the different criteria (RPN reduction, control cost and the control time). In future work, we are interested in developing a dynamic CP which takes into account real-time parameters that support the decision making.

References

1. Alexander, M.: Decision-making using the analytic hierarchy process (AHP) and SAS/IML® (2012). Last checked 28 July 2014
2. Bahrami, M., Bazzaz, D.H., Sajjadi, S.M.: Innovation and improvements in project implementation and management; using fmea technique. Procedia-Soc. Behav. Sci. **41**, 418–425 (2012)
3. Ben Romdhane, T., Badreddine, A., Sansa, M.: A new model to implement six sigma in small-and medium-sized enterprises. Int. J. Prod. Res. **55**, 1–22 (2016)
4. Bettayeb, B., Bassetto, S., Vialletelle, P., Tollenaere, M.: Quality and exposure control in semiconductor manufacturing. Part I: modelling. Int. J. Prod. Res. **50**(23), 6835–6851 (2012)
5. Bortot, S., Marques Pereira, R.A.: Choquet integration and the AHP: inconsistency and non-additivity. In: Greco, S., Bouchon-Meunier, B., Coletti, G., Fedrizzi, M., Matarazzo, B., Yager, R.R. (eds.) IPMU 2012. CCIS, vol. 300, pp. 188–197. Springer, Heidelberg (2012). doi:10.1007/978-3-642-31724-8_20
6. Ferreira, R.J., de Almeida, A.T., Cavalcante, C.A.: A multi-criteria decision model to determine inspection intervals of condition monitoring based on delay time analysis. Reliab. Eng. Syst. Saf. **94**(5), 905–912 (2009)
7. Grabisch, M., Kojadinovic, I., Meyer, P.: A review of methods for capacity identification in choquet integral based multi-attribute utility theory: applications of the kappalab r package. Eur. J. Oper. Res. **186**(2), 766–785 (2008)
8. ISO, T.: ISO 16949 (2009). Quality Management Systems-Particular requirements for the application of ISO 9001 (2008)
9. Malakooti, B., Balhorn, W.H.: Selection of acceptance sampling plans with multi-attribute defects in computer-aided quality control. Int. J. Prod. Res. **25**(6), 869–887 (1987)
10. Marichal, J.L.: An axiomatic approach of the discrete choquet integral as a tool to aggregate interacting criteria. IEEE Trans. Fuzzy Syst. **8**(6), 800–807 (2000)
11. Mohammadi, M., Siadat, A., Dantan, J.Y., Tavakkoli-Moghaddam, R.: Mathematical modelling of a robust inspection process plan: Taguchi and Monte Carlo methods. Int. J. Prod. Res. **53**(7), 2202–2224 (2015)
12. Murofushi, T., Soneda, S.: Techniques for reading fuzzy measures (iii): interaction index. In: 9th Fuzzy System Symposium, Sapporo, Japan, pp. 693–696 (1993)
13. Saaty, T.L.: How to make a decision: the analytic hierarchy process. Eur. J. Oper. Res. **48**(1), 9–26 (1990)
14. Sahnoun, M., Bettayeb, B., Bassetto, S.J., Tollenaere, M.: Simulation-based optimization of sampling plans to reduce inspections while mastering the risk exposure in semiconductor manufacturing. J. Intell. Manufact. **27**, 1–15 (2014)

15. Savio, E.: A methodology for the quantification of value-adding by manufacturing metrology. CIRP Ann. Manufact. Technol. **61**(1), 503–506 (2012)
16. Shapley, L.S.: A value for n-person games. Contrib. Theory Games **2**(28), 307–317 (1953)
17. Vaghefi, A., Sarhangian, V.: Contribution of simulation to the optimization of inspection plans for multi-stage manufacturing systems. Comput. Ind. Eng. **57**(4), 1226–1234 (2009)

Efficient Matching in Heterogeneous Rule Engines

Kennedy Kambona[✉], Thierry Renaux, and Wolfgang De Meuter

Vrije Universiteit Brussel, Pleinlaan 2, Brussels, Belgium
{kkambona,trenaux,wdmeuter}@vub.ac.be

Abstract. Modern institutions seeking more complex software solutions to represent knowledge in the Cloud are using rule-based systems that serve several applications or clients. Rule-based systems hosted in the Cloud are thus required to support its heterogeneous nature. However, current systems only focus on techniques that isolate instances of rule engines. This paper builds upon earlier work on scoped rule engines that provide mechanisms for supporting shared heterogeneous contexts. We present the scope-based hashing algorithm (SBH) that enables efficient matching in scoped rule engines based on the Rete algorithm. SBH introduces scoped hash tables in alpha memories that help in avoiding unnecessary join tests that hamper performance. Our experimental results show that SBH offers significant improvements in efficiency during the matching process of a heterogeneous rule engine. Consequently, SBH significantly decreases the response time of rule engines in heterogeneous environments having entities sharing the same knowledge base.

Keywords: Heterogeneity · Rule engines · Rete algorithm · Scoping

1 Introduction

As the Internet matures, modern institutions are seeking more complex software solutions for their operations in cloud service providers. One area that is gaining momentum is in the provision of complex services for knowledge representation using rule-based definitions, e.g., IBM ODM Decision Server [6] and Amazon IoT Rules [2]. Such rule-based systems (or RBS) are known to use complex event processing for reasoning about events of interest to business applications. A rule-based language is often used for programming definitions of event patterns because rules are intuitively appealing to express [3].

Rule engines were fundamentally designed in the era where isolated computing was prevalent: at the time, rule engines were programmed to encode a localised set of rules and to work on homogeneous data [13]. Rule engines were therefore characterised by a *flat design space* where activations could be observed from all data without discriminating their sources. When deployed to hybrid or

T. Renaux—Supported by a doctoral scholarship of the Agency for Innovation by Science and Technology in Flanders (IWT), Belgium.

S. Benferhat et al. (Eds.): IEA/AIE 2017, Part I, LNAI 10350, pp. 394–406, 2017.
DOI: 10.1007/978-3-319-60042-0_44

heterogeneous environments, RBS need manual interventions to enforce rule and data isolation [13]. Previously, the concept of isolation in modern rule engines was manually enforced through the use of separate rule engines using rulebooks or rule modules to separate instances of rulesets from different clients or event sources. Recent work has provided a solution by introducing scoping in the rule engine through the use of scoped rules [12]. Scoped rules support heterogeneous RBS by exposing formalised mechanisms in which applications can perform data isolation in rule definitions for different clients. Scoped rules keep isolation logic cleanly separated from the application logic: the basic purpose of the rule is not mixed with the logic required for distinguishing client data. The result is that the logical intent of a rule becomes easier to understand by rule creators.

In this work we propose a novel improvement in rule engines that improves matching efficiency in scope-aware RBS. Our technique involves an inventive optimisation to the popular Rete algorithm during the matching process, identified as the most computationally-intensive execution phase of any Rete-based rule engine [7]. The *scope-based hashing* (SBH) approach utilises the scoped hash tables and fact metadata to exclusively and efficiently compute compatible data that is relevant for computing joins in heterogenous environments.

The contributions of this work are as follows. We extend the work on scoped inference engines with a novel algorithm that provides an optimisation to the underlying Rete algorithm. In particular, our approach extends the Rete network within an inference engine with scoped hash tables in the alpha memories that are used to efficiently determine compatible data in heterogeneous contexts. We further justify our scheme by performing an evaluation using a representative heterogeneous application backed by a rule engine utilising our approach, comparing the results with the state-of-the-art.

2   Motivating Example

To motivate the concepts that this work proposes we present a practical scenario of a security monitoring system deployed to serve a number of departments across universities. A sample computer labs policy is defined below:

> "*All main campus master's thesis students in the science faculty are allowed extended access to computer labs in their own departments until 10pm weekdays while in the final stages of their theses (in the months between March and August). Students in the department of computer science are additionally allowed on the weekends between 10–16 h.*"

A typical structure of a university is depicted in Fig. 1a. The structure shows various entities as groups and users are connected to one or more groups in the hierarchy. Staff and students are issued readable ID cards and are required to scan their IDs on devices strategically placed at access points to gain entry. Every access request on a device is relayed to a central server that logs and processes the request according to the defined policies. Any granted accesses according to the defined security policies should be promptly shown on the dashboard of

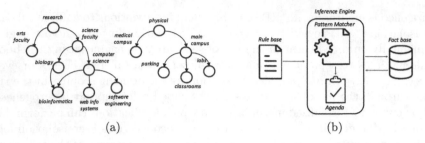

Fig. 1. (a) Typical university group hierarchy – Represented as acyclic graphs of hierarchies of departments for students and physical locations for scanning devices (b) Rule engine architecture – Rules from clients are added to the global rule base and event data as facts in the global fact base.

the security team's interface. In this scenario, we have articulated around 40 such policies across different faculty and departments of universities. A service provider can support several of such universities with their own policies.

3   Reactive Rule Engine Architecture

The motivating example represents a typical reactive application that exposes services to clients contributing data intermittently. It quickly becomes apparent that the policies can be suitably captured in traditional rule-based syntax, and the intermittent access requests from different student entities can be easily captured and processed by a rule engine.

In this work we focus on the most computationally expensive phase in an RBS, the matching process. Because the system *reacts* when the data is sent, the approach should provide a data-driven mechanism for reasoning through forward-chaining. In this work we therefore employ the most efficient algorithm used in forward-chaining RBS, the Rete algorithm [9]. In a typical Rete-based system (Fig. 1b), rules are added into the rule base and event data from other client devices such as sensors are constructed as facts and added into the fact base. The inference engine contains the pattern matcher and the agenda which employ Rete to determine which rule to fire given the current state of the engine. A Rete inference engine converts rules into an acyclic graph with intermediate memories that cache intermediate results. This eliminates extra work that would otherwise need to be performed during each matching cycle.

4   Heterogeneity in Rule-Based Systems

This work proposes efficient matching in heterogeneous rule engines. Using the motivating example we illustrate how current rule-based systems deal with heterogeneity and contrast it with recent work involving scoped engines.

4.1   Classic vs. Scoped Rule-Based Systems

The lab access rule definition. The policy for science faculty students can be represented in classic rules syntax as shown in Listing 1.1 and using scoped rules in Listing 1.2.

They show a customised JSON Rules [10] syntax sent by a client (which can be built intuitively using a graphical interface). The conditions capture the access request, the student making the request and the device scanned. The test expressions confirm the time constraints of the policy. A separate rule can be similarly designed to determine the second part of the policy specifically for computer science students.

In **classic rules** there is need to determine if the student and device originate from the same department, to ensure the rule will not cause unintended activations. This will avoid students from other faculties having access to the labs they are not a member of (e.g., a student from the arts faculty gaining access to a bioinformatics lab). Because the student can belong to any of the sub-departments, the check needs to confirm if the student or device's group is a descendant of a faculty group. Classical approaches use compatibility checks such as those in Line 6 and 7 of Listing 1.1 through *relation facts* that show a group is related to a particular parent group.

Listing 1.1: Classic rule for lab access

```
 1  {rulename: "MastersStudentsLabAccess",
 2   conditions:[
 3    {type:"accessreq", id: "?reqid", badge: "?badgid", time: "?t", device: "?devid"},
 4    {$s: {type:"student", name: "?nam", badge: "?badgid", level: "master", group:"?stugrp"}},
 5    {$d: {type:"accessdevice", id: "?devid", group:"?devgrp"}},
 6    {type:"belongsTo" grp:"?devgrp", parent:"?pgrp"},
 7    {type:"belongsTo" grp:"?stugrp", parent:"pgrp"},
 8    {type:"$test", expr:"( month(?t) > 1 && month(?t) < 9 && hour(?t) > 18 && hour(?t) < 16  && isWeekend(?t)"}
 9   ],
10   actions:[
11    {assert: {type: "accessrep", reqid:"?reqid", allowed: true}}
12   ]
13  }
```

Listing 1.2: Scoped rule for lab access

```
 1  {rulename: "MastersStudentsLabAccess-Scoped",
 2   conditions:[
 3    {type:"accessreq", id: "?reqid", badge: "?badgid", time: "?t", device: "?devid"},
 4    {$s: {type:"student", name: "?nam", badge: "?badgid", level: "master"}},
 5    {$d: {type:"accessdevice", id: "?devid"}},
 6    {type:"$test", expr:"( month(?t) > 1 && month(?t) < 9 && hour(?t) > 18 && hour(?t) < 16  && isWeekend(?t)"},
 7   ],
 8   actions:[
 9    {assert: {type: "accessrep", reqid:"?reqid", allowed: true}}
10   ],
11   scopes: ["($s & $d) subgroupof science", "$d private labs"]
12  }
```

In contrast, **scoped rules** [12] extend rule syntax to support the definition of flexible constructs that ensure data compatibility between instances of data from different entities during matching. Listing 1.2 shows the same rule as Listing 1.1, but with s special `scopes` construct in line 11 instead of conditions with relation facts. The first scope definition specifies that the data for the rule to be matched should be captured from the `science` group and any of its children or subgroups. The second scope definition specifies that only device data from the group `labs` should privately be matched.

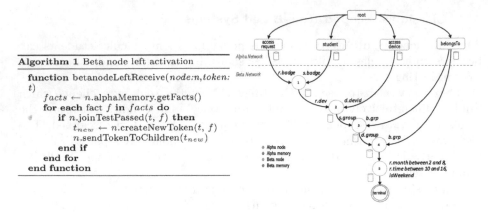

Algorithm 1 Beta node left activation
_____

    function betanodeLeftReceive($node$:n, $token$:
t)
        $facts \leftarrow n$.alphaMemory.getFacts()
        for each fact f in $facts$ do
           if n.joinTestPassed(t, f) then
             $t_{new} \leftarrow n$.createNewToken(t, f)
             n.sendTokenToChildren(t_{new})
           end if
        end for
    end function
_____

Fig. 2. Left activation and classic Rete graph for lab rule – Relation facts can distinguish between entities in heterogeneous RBS.

Rete graph for lab access rule. The *MasterStudentsLabAccess* rule is designed by a security staff member and sent to the server. The server builds a Rete graph [9] from the rule, which we show in Figs. 2 and 3. The graph performs both intra-condition checks such as student, device etc. It also performs inter-condition tests, e.g., in node 1 that makes sure that an access request is matched with the student that made the request, propagating compatible data as tokens to its children. Node 2 checks the same for the device.

Matching in the Rete graph. When a token is received at the left input of any join node, a *left activation* is triggered that issues a request for all the items in its right alpha memory to perform its inter-condition tests – this process is also known as matching and the test is called a *join*. A similar process happens on a right activation. The *beta test* nodes before the terminal node perform processing to check for the time constraints of the policy on the accessrequest fact. If a token passes the tests it reaches the terminal node and is added to the agenda for activation of the policy rule, granting access to the student.

For a **classic RBS** (Fig. 2), left-activating beta node 3 results in a need to access all the items in the belongsTo alpha memory to find relation facts with groups same as its student's group. A similar process happens in beta node 4 for devices. This method and other similar approaches for finding compatible data with heterogeneous users sharing the same knowledge base is inefficient and quickly becomes cumbersome: the rule logic becomes difficult to follow and processing is dominated by expensive join computations that are necessary to distinguish incompatible facts from different users or user groups – like during matching in nodes 3 and 4.

In a **scoped RBS** an internal representation of physical or logical organisations of clients is first precomputed, stored and maintained efficiently as an encoding that will be used to expeditiously process constraints used to enforce reentrancy within the inference engine. This is done by constructing a *bit-*

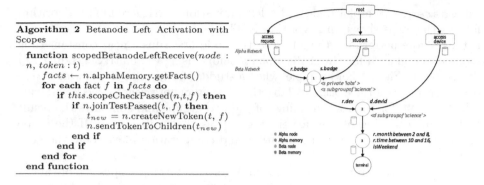

Algorithm 2 Betanode Left Activation with Scopes

function scopedBetanodeLeftReceive(*node* : *n, token* : *t*)
    facts ← *n*.alphaMemory.getFacts()
    for each fact *f* **in** *facts* **do**
        if *this*.scopeCheckPassed(*n,t,f*) **then**
            if *n*.joinTestPassed(*t, f*) **then**
                t_{new} = *n*.createNewToken(*t, f*)
                n.sendTokenToChildren(t_{new})
            end if
        end if
    end for
end function

Fig. 3. Scoped left activation and scoped Rete graph – Scoped approach adds scope checks to beta nodes at opportune node locations.

vector encoding that allows for near-constant time scope checks during matching, thereby reducing the processing overhead when isolating compatible data matches in heterogeneous contexts. The university group hierarchy in Fig. 1a is converted into the matrix encoding M_ϑ shown in Fig. 4a through a process that is based on Ait Kaci's method in [1]. In the encoding, there is an entry at $M_{\vartheta(a,b)}$ iff b is an ancestor of a. The engine also automatically adds metadata to all facts added to a client. For instance, if a device sends an access request, the fact is automatically tagged with the device's group when inserted to the rule engine.

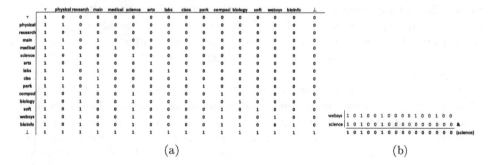

(a)   (b)

Fig. 4. (a) Matrix encoding M_ϑ – The rows and columns refer to groups in a hierarchy. (b) Example of a bitwise scope check operation – The operation confirms that websys is a part of the science faculty.

Figure 3 shows the Rete graph built from the scoped rule. In the graph of a scoped engine, *scope checks or guards* are added to beta nodes 1 and 2. The <s subgroupof science> guard can be interpreted as check for any bound fact for a student (in the alpha node for the condition in line 4 of rule Listing 1.2) that is a member of any subgroup of the science faculty in the university. When an access request is made its token is received in beta node 1 through the `accessrequest` alpha node and a left activation is triggered. The algorithm follows the steps shown in Algorithm 2. The main difference with Algorithm 1 is that before performing the join test, the node first runs a near constant-time scope check in each fact from the alpha memory using the matrix encoding M_ϑ illustrated in Fig. 4a. For example, when a student from `websys` requests access on the entrance of the `compsci` labs, the `<s subgroupof science>` check performs a bitwise AND for the row encodings of the two groups and compares the result to the row encoding of the `science` group as shown in Fig. 4b. If the scope check fails then the data is incompatible and computation moves onto the next fact.

In essence, the processing outlined in Algorithm 2 using scopes is more adept compared to the relation fact technique or other current approaches due to the fast encoded binary tests. However, it is clear that with each left activation, of a beta node scope checks **are still performed on every fact** in the alpha memory, regardless. This makes the approach inefficient. To this end, we present an approach that makes join computations in Rete networks more efficient using the scope-based hashing algorithm (SBH).

5   The Scope-Based Hashing Algorithm

Alpha Memory Hashing via Groups. Alpha memories in Rete can be simply viewed as nodes that store facts of a particular type, e.g., the memories of `student` and `device` nodes in Fig. 3. The purpose of alpha memories is to supply beta nodes with fact items. As event data is added to the engine the cached dataset increases especially in heterogeneous rule engines since multiple users and their devices all contribute data. The result is that although scope-based rule engines offer a reasonable improvement when computing joins, the rule engines still suffer when performing scope checks for **every** data item added in the alpha memory.

We propose an approach that improves this scope-checking process. Our technique constructs a hash table that dynamically assigns buckets based on user groups in the group hierarchy (e.g. the groups in Fig. 1a). Each bucket points to a list that holds a set of facts of that group. As facts are added to the system SBH assigns each fact to the correct bucket dynamically. For instance, for a device located at the entry point of the science department the fact will be added to the `science` bucket of the `student` SBH hash table.

Matching with Scope-based Hashing. The matching process stage is where any rule engine performs most of its computation. Matching in scopeful engines involves updating the beta network with scope guards that check compatibility of left and right inputs. SBH introduces a way to efficiently determine which fact items are compatible with an incoming token at a beta node to be subsequently used in the join test of the node.

Take an example of an access request made by a student in `web info systems` on a device located at the `computer science` labs. This is a valid access request that should be granted (assuming it is made in the correct time-line). Using the Rete graph of the same policy (Fig. 5), the fact will trickle down to beta node 1 causing a left activation. A left activation with the SBH technique is shown in Algorithm 3, where this refers to the SBH instance.

We describe the algorithm using the scope guard <$s subgroupof science> in beta node 1. In this case, s is bound to the fact representing the websys student. Instead of performing the check with every student fact in the alpha memory, SBH retrieves the matrix codes for all the subgroups of science via calculateCodeFromScopeGuards.

Let n be the total number of elements of a row in the encoding matrix M_ϑ (Fig. 4a). calculateCodeFromScopeGuards constructs a bit vector V_n with all elements having a 0. Conceptually, the V_n represents all groups in the hierarchy. At this point, no groups have passed the scope check (all have 0s as entries in V_n). SBH then performs operations that assign a group element 1 iff it satisfies the scope guard <s subgroupof science>. In this case, the method retrieves the column vector $M_{\vartheta(*,science)} = $ [0000010000111111] which represents all the subgroups of science.

The next step in Algorithm 3 is to retrieve the corresponding groups in method getGroupsFromCode which will then be used to retrieve the items per group in the alpha memory. The method getGroupsFromCode retrieves the group names or labels which have a 1 in V_n excluding $\perp$, which in this case $V_g = $ [science, compsci, biology, soft, websys, bioinfo]. Retrieving V_g should be relatively easy since the groups have direct mappings to the labels in the matrix.

Next, the getFacts method of the alpha memory now accepts V_g as an argument. The method uses the student alpha memory's internal SBH table (introduced in Sect. 5) to efficiently access the fact items that are pertinent to the child beta node, node 1. The alpha memory will thus retrieve the facts residing each of the named groups in V_g from its buckets. Essentially, the facts retrieved are a local subset of all the items in the alpha memory and as such the join computation of node 1 will be performed on a these rather than all the fact items residing in the student alpha memory. The rest of the code in Algorithm 3 iterates through all the retrieved items and performs the normal join tests for the node.

Additionally, in reality a number of nodes will have multiple scope expressions in one node: a good example is node 1 which not only has <s subgroupof science> but also <s private labs>. Furthermore, scope tests can contain complex expressions – to specify "an access device that is in the classrooms of the computer science and biology department or the arts faculty," the expression becomes <$d subgroupof (science & biology) | $d private arts>.

One option to compute such expressions is to repeatedly call calculateCode FromScopeGuards on each scope test, store multiple vectors of V_g and send these to the alpha memory to retrieve the items needed for a beta node's join computations. A more efficient way that SBH uses is that it performs reductions using bitwise operations given every V_{ni}

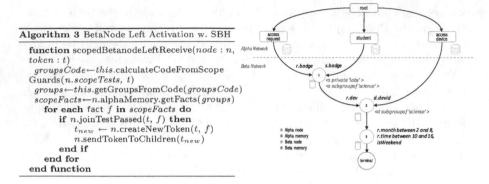

Algorithm 3 BetaNode Left Activation w. SBH

```
function scopedBetanodeLeftReceive(node : n,
token : t)
    groupsCode←this.calculateCodeFromScope
    Guards(n.scopeTests, t)
    groups←this.getGroupsFromCode(groupsCode)
    scopeFacts←n.alphaMemory.getFacts(groups)
    for each fact f in scopeFacts do
        if n.joinTestPassed(t, f) then
            t_new ← n.createNewToken(t, f)
            n.sendTokenToChildren(t_new)
        end if
    end for
end function
```

Fig. 5. SBH algorithm and scoped Rete graph with SBH – The alpha memories are replaced with SBH alpha memories that make scope-based computations more efficient

bit vector result of each scope test i of a beta node. This is used by method `calculateCodeFromScopeGuards` to construct V_n for the scope test,

```
    <d subgroupof (science & biology) | d private arts>
  = <(d subgroupof science & d subgroupof biology)
       | d private arts >
  = [(0000010000111111 & 0000000000010011) | 0000001000000000]
  = 0000000000010011 | 0000001000000000
  = 0000001000010011
```

Note that the vector V_{ni} of a scope <private u> is the unit vector of u. The result V_n is returned from the method `calculateCodeFromScopeGuards`. Next V_g is computed which in this case evaluates to [arts,bio,bioinfo]. The SBH algorithm proceeds normally as outlined in Algorithm 3, retrieving the scope facts of groups in V_g and preforming the join tests if the scope check succeeds.

6   Experimental Evaluation

For the evaluation we focus on investigating whether a rule engine with SBH experiences significant improvements in efficiency compared to the current alternative techniques available in contemporary rule engines. The evaluation was based on the complete university security monitoring application staged in an experimental setup as introduced in Sect. 2.

Setup and Methodology. We performed our evaluation in an experimental setup consisting of a web server running a rule engine based on the Rete algorithm. The server hardware was configured with a AMD Opteron Processor 6272 at 2.1 Ghz. The server processes were assigned a maximum of 20 GB RAM. To model a practical real-world scenario we designed a user hierarchy of 60 groups in total and 40 typical access policies modelled as rules serving 70 clients concurrently. To simulate practical delays in access requests clients were configured to generate access requests intermittently at intervals of 1–5 s and devices received reactive feedback, with a security console receiving push-based updates of accesses to entry points. Each access request was randomised, with a random client belonging to any group(s) making an access request at a device from a random location in the university hierarchy.

We split the experiment into three categories. The first category was running a traditional rule engine without scopes, the second was running a scoped rule engine and the third had a rule engine running the scope-based hashing algorithm. For each category a total of 62 sessions were performed with one session running for a duration of 12 h. The total experiment therefore spanned 186 sessions and 2332 h runtime.

Results and Discussion. During the experiment the activation times (comparable to response time) and the memory used were logged and compared. We graphically chart the results using bean charts that show the quartiles as well as the density estimates.

Figure 6a shows the results of the activation times of the unscoped, scoped and SBH rule engines. Rule activation time is the time it takes the engine to perform a matching process, between assertion and rule activation. The chart shows that, on average, the scoped rule engine showed slightly less activation times than the unscoped engine. Comparing the first two with the SBH approach, it is clear that SBH exhibits an advantage with reduced activation times of up to 80% in

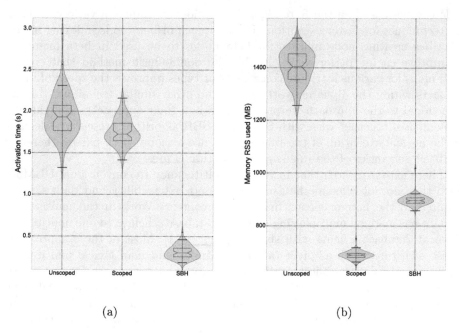

(a)   (b)

Fig. 6. Bean plots of the results – Results of over 60 runs of random 12-hour sessions show that the SBH approach offers faster activation times than both the scoped and typical unscoped engines. SBH still exhibits less memory usage than traditional unscoped engines, but consumes more memory than a plain scoped approach.

some cases. Figure 6b shows the results of the recorded memory consumption (measured by resident set size) averages of each category. The classical approach of managing heterogeneity in rule engines leads to a much higher memory consumption, due to redundant information and inefficiencies brought about by the complexity of enforcing reentrancy. The scoped engine showed a lesser amount of memory consumed by reducing and optimising redundant information used for computing scopes. When we compared the memory usage of the three, the SBH approach is seen to consume up to 30% more than using a pure scoped engine on average, but uses 35% less than a classic unscoped engine. The alpha memory hashing of SBH leads to a more complex node memory structure that needs more space than the conventional structures of node memories.

From the results we observe that for a rule engine in a heterogeneous environment, adopting the SBH algorithm leads to faster execution of the engine's matching process resulting in less activation times. This improves the responsiveness of the RBS as a whole while still having lower space requirements than in unscoped RBS. We therefore find that SBH offers significant efficiency benefits for heterogeneous rule engines over both traditional and purely scoped approaches.

7   Related Work

Rule engines based on the Rete algorithm optionally employ a variety of hashing techniques for faster execution. The approach of beta node indexing in [16] describes creating node indexes for beta nodes to be used in beta memories to improve engine performance. In [15] the double-hash method that creates hash maps for various attribute constraints or types improves the speed of filtering facts within the alpha network. These and other similar techniques [14] are orthogonal to the approach we present here and their approaches can thus be implemented together with with SBH. The SBH algorithm presented delegates to the normal execution of the rule engine once a scope check passes, therefore the basic semantics of the rule engine execution is preserved.

There exists research that introduce multitenancy to conventional DBMSes since they do not offer mechanisms to support extensibility and data sharing required in the heterogeneous multitenant context. Work in the multitenacy domain has mapped multiple single logical database schemas to one multitenant physical database schema with shared tables [8,11]. Most of these approaches utilise structures such as pivot tables that index and map logical multitenant schemas onto physical ones. Additionally, advanced techniques for the multitenant setup such as Chunk Folding [4] and XOR Delta [5] also exist. All these approaches only focus on statically optimising data schemas of largely persistent or static data sets of multiple tenants and do not employ advanced techniques for efficient reactive incremental processing at runtime.

8   Conclusions and Future Work

Modern rule engines are increasingly deployed to support heterogeneous multitenant setups and other similar multiuser environments. We have described
the scope-based hashing algorithm SBH, which is a novel optimisation to the
popular Rete algorithm in forward-chaining rule engines. SBH extends the Rete
network within a scoped engine with scoped hash tables in the alpha memories
that are used to efficiently optimise the expressions that compute the compatibility of inputs of a join node in a heterogeneous RBS. From the evaluation
we conclude that SBH offers a significant improvement in efficiency during the
matching process for heterogeneous data in the rule engine. The cost that comes
with this is a relatively higher memory consumption compared to scoped engines
without SBH. As future work we would like to extend the SBH algorithm to right
activations of beta nodes during the matching process. This intrinsically implies
that the beta memories should be hashed and brings about research questions
about the semantics of hashing token compositions.

References

1. Aït-Kaci, H., Boyer, R., Lincoln, P., Nasr, R.: Efficient implementation of
   lattice operations. ACM Trans. Program. Lang. Syst. **11**(1), 115–146 (1989).
   http://doi.acm.org/10.1145/59287.59293
2. Amazon Web Services Inc: Rules for AWS IoT. http://docs.aws.amazon.com/iot/
   latest/developerguide/iot-rules.html. Accessed 12 Oct 2016
3. Anderson, J.R.: The Architecture of Cognition. Psychology Press, Hove (2013)
4. Aulbach, S., Grust, T., Jacobs, D., Kemper, A., Rittinger, J.: Multi-tenant databases for software as a service: schema-mapping techniques. In: Proceedings of
   the 2008 ACM SIGMOD International Conference on Management of Data, pp.
   1195–1206. ACM (2008)
5. Aulbach, S., Seibold, M., Jacobs, D., Kemper, A.: Extensibility and data sharing
   in evolving multi-tenant databases. In: 2011 IEEE 27th International Conference
   on Data Engineering, pp. 99–110. IEEE (2011)
6. Dettori, P., Frank, D., Seelam, S.R., Feillet, P.: Blueprint for business middleware
   as a managed cloud service. In: 2014 IEEE International Conference on Cloud
   Engineering (IC2E), pp. 261–270. IEEE (2014)
7. Doorenbos, R.B.: Production matching for large learning systems. Ph.D. thesis,
   University of Southern California (1995)
8. Fiaidhi, J., Bojanova, I., Zhang, J., Zhang, L.J.: Enforcing multitenancy for cloud
   computing environments. IT Prof. **14**(1), 16–18 (2012)
9. Forgy, C.L.: Rete: a fast algorithm for the many pattern/many object pattern
   match problem. Artif. Intell. **19**(1), 17–37 (1982)
10. Giurca, A., Pascalau, E.: JSON rules. In: Proceedings of 4th Knowledge Engineering and Software Engineering, KESE, vol. 425, pp. 7–18 (2008)
11. Grund, M., Schapranow, M., Krueger, J., Schaffner, J., Bog, A.: Shared table access
   pattern analysis for multi-tenant applications. In: IEEE Symposium on Advanced
   Management of Information for Globalized Enterprises, AMIGE 2008, pp. 1–5,
   September 2008

12. Kambona, K., Thierry, R., De Meuter, W.: Reentrancy and scoping in multitenant inference engines. In: 13th International Conference on Web Information Systems and Technologies (WEBIST) (2017)
13. Nalepa, G.J.: Architecture of the HeaRT hybrid rule engine. In: Rutkowski, L., Scherer, R., Tadeusiewicz, R., Zadeh, L.A., Zurada, J.M. (eds.) ICAISC 2010. LNCS, vol. 6114, pp. 598–605. Springer, Heidelberg (2010). doi:10.1007/978-3-642-13232-2_73
14. Scales, D.J.: Efficient matching algorithms for the SOAR/OPS5 production system. Technical report, DTIC Document (1986)
15. Tianyang, D., Jing, F., Zhang, L.: An improved Rete algorithm based on double hash filter and node indexing for distributed rule engine. Trans. Inf. Syst. **96**(12), 2635–2644 (2013)
16. Xiao, D., Zhong, X.: Improving rete algorithm to enhance performance of rule engine systems. In: 2010 International Conference on Computer Design and Applications (ICCDA), vol. 3, p. V3–572. IEEE (2010)

Towards Extending Business Process Modeling Formalisms with Information and Knowledge Dimensions

Mariam Ben Hassen[✉], Mohamed Turki, and Faïez Gargouri

ISIMS, MIRACL Laboratory, University of Sfax,
P.O. Box 242, 3021 Sfax, Tunisia
mariem.benhassen@isims.usf.tn,
mohamed.turki@isetsf.rnu.tn,
faiez.gargouri@isims.usf.tn

Abstract. Sensitive Business Processes (SBPs) modeling has become an effective way of managing and developing organization's knowledge which needs to be capitalized. These processes are characterized by a high complexity and dynamism in their execution, high number of critical activities with intensive acquisition, sharing, storage and (re)use of very specific crucial knowledge, diversity of knowledge sources, and high degree of collaboration among experts. Hence, we propose a semantically rich conceptualization for describing an SBP organized in a generic Business Process Meta-model for Knowledge Identification (BPM4KI), in order to develop a rich and expressive representation of SBPs to identify and localize the crucial knowledge. BPM4KI covers all aspects of business process modeling: the functional, organizational, behavioral, informational, intentional and knowledge perspectives. This paper aims to introduce a more explicit border between information and knowledge concepts and dimensions which are relevant in SBP models, based on «core» domain ontologies.

Keywords: Knowledge management · Knowledge identification · Sensitive business process · Business process modeling · «core» domain ontologies · DOLCE

1 Introduction

The necessity to formalize and manage knowledge produced and used in organizations has rapidly increased in the last few years. Organizations have become aware of the importance of the intellectual capital owned by their members which corresponds to their experience and accumulated knowledge about the firm activities.

Considering the large amount of knowledge to be preserved, the organizations must first identify and model the Sensitive Business Processes (SBPs) which are likely to mobilize crucial knowledge, i.e., knowledge on which it is necessary to focus and capitalize. In fact, the more organization's BPs are sensitive, the more they can mobilize crucial knowledge. Few existing research on Knowledge Management (KM)-BPM focusing on the analysis, identification and modeling of SBPs in order to localize and identify the crucial knowledge. We quote, the identifying crucial knowledge

© Springer International Publishing AG 2017
S. Benferhat et al. (Eds.): IEA/AIE 2017, Part I, LNAI 10350, pp. 407–425, 2017.
DOI: 10.1007/978-3-319-60042-0_45

methodology [1] and the Sensitive Organization's Process Identification Methodology [2]. However, the critical phase of «SBPs modeling» has not been studied in depth [3, 4]. In particular, the knowledge dimension needed for performing SBP is not explicitly represented, integrated and implemented in BP models and BPM approaches.

In this paper, we aim to address the gap between BPM and KM and enrich the operation of «modeling and representation of SBPs» in order to increase the probability of identifying the crucial knowledge and reduce the cost of the operation of capitalizing on knowledge. Precisely, this research work presents a conceptual specification of SBP organized in new multi-perspective meta-model, entitled «BPM4KI: Business Process Meta-Model for Knowledge Identification». BPM4KI intends to explicit and organize the key concepts and relationships that characterize an SBP. It integrates all relevant perspectives/dimensions relating to BPM-KM, i.e. the functional, the organizational, the behavioral, the informational, the intentional and the knowledge perspectives. In this research work, we focus more on the «Informational Dimension» and the «Knowledge Dimension» which are not yet explicited, fully supported and integrated within BPs models and BPM approaches and formalisms. Indeed, the three different phenomena: data, information, and knowledge are very relevant in BPM. However, there is no clear theoretical background and successful practical experiments of inclusion and clear distinction between them in BP models. This leads to ambiguity and misunderstanding of the developed models, especially in SBP modeling. Therefore, we propose, in the current research, to provide a more explicit border between information and knowledge concepts and dimensions in SBP models. We aim at obtaining new knowledge helpful for developing BPM formalisms that could handle all relevant aspects related to knowledge dimension (including data and information).

The «Informational Perspective» and the «Knowledge Dimension», modeled as *Ontological Design Patterns* (ODP) [5], are semantically rich and well-based on «core» domain ontologies (which are based on top of the DOLCE foundational ontology [6]. These ontologies offer repositories of generic concepts and relationships semantically rich and consensual which we reused, firstly, to broaden and deepen the elements of definition of information and knowledge dimensions, and on the other hand, to characterize the useful concepts for a rigorous specification and an enriched modeling of the SBPs.

The remainder of this paper is organized as follows: Sect. 2 presents the specification of SBP. Section 3 presents the central concepts that describe the information and knowledge dimensions relevant for SBP modeling. Section 4 concludes the paper and underlines some future research topics.

2   Sensitive Business Process Specification

An SBP represents the core BP of organization which constitutes the heart of the organization's activities. It has its own characteristics that distinguish it from classical BP [4, 7].

2.1 Describing Sensitive Business Process

According to Ben Hassen et al. [3, 4, 7], an SBP comprises a high number of critical organizational activities (individual/collective) mobilizing very specific knowledge «crucial knowledge» (tacit and explicit/individual and collective). It mobilizes a large diversity of information and knowledge sources, consigning a great amount of heterogeneous knowledge. Moreover, an SBP requires a high degree of collaboration and interaction (intra/inter-organizational) among participants. Its execution involves many external agents and the assistance of many experts, who apply, create and share a great amount of very important tacit organizational knowledge, in order to achieve collective objectives and create value. In addition, SBP are typically an unstructured or semi-structured organizational actions, requires substantial flexibility, encompassing a highly dynamic complexity.

Due to those characteristics, modeling and organizing the knowledge involved in SBP is relatively critical. In this context, several BPM formalisms have been proposed in BP and engineering as likely to represent SBP [7]. Thus, some conventional graphical BPM formalisms, include, amongst others, Event Driven Process Chain (EPC), Business Process Modeling Notation (BPMN 2.0) and Unified Modeling Language (UML 2.0) activity diagram, have been adapted to allow the representation of the intrinsic elements of knowledge within BPs. In addition, the literature shows a set of approaches and notations dedicated for the representation of processes with high knowledge intensity [8], originate from the knowledge modeling context, including the Business Process Knowledge Method (BPKM), PROMOTE, Knowledge Modeling and Description Language (KMDL 2.2), Oliveira's methodology, the Notation for Knowledge-Intensive Processes (NKIP), etc. Tables 1 and 2 present a summary of the Strengths and Weakness of the above-mentioned BPM formalisms with respect to characteristics/issues relevant to the SBP modeling. These formalisms were mainly analyzed from the following two points of view (1) possibilities to represent data, information and knowledge, and (2) possibilities to represent process logics. Both views are important for representation of static and dynamic aspects of SBP.

Tables 1 and 2 show that none of these proposals can adequately include all or at least most of the relevant SBP elements. This leads to ambiguity and misunderstanding of the developed SBPs models [3, 7]. In order to address existing limitations, the differents types of BPM formalisms will be adapted and extended to address conveniently the SBP particularities. So, we develop a BP independent generic meta-model common to these BPM formalisms which ensures the best suitability to model SBP, entitled «BPM4KI».

2.2 BPM4KI: A Multi Perspective Meta-model of BPs for Knowledge Identification Based on Core Ontologies

In order to enrich and improve the SBP modeling, we propose a semantically rich conceptualization for specifying an SBP organized in a new generic meta-model of BP representation, the Business Process Meta-model for Knowledge Identification (BPM4KI). The enriched meta-model serves two purposes: (i) to deepen the elements

Table 1. Analysis of conventional BPM formalisms for SBP modeling

Conventional workflow/BPM approaches	Strengths
• Process Specification Language (PSL) [9] • Role Activity Diagram (RAD) [10] • Petri net [11] • (extended)Event-driven Process Chains (eEPC) [12] • UML 2.0 Activity Diagrams (UML AD) [13] • Business Process Modeling Notation (BPMN 2.0) [14]	• Largely used in current research and practice scenarios in organizations • Suitable for process perspective representation (that display a defined, well structured, highly stable and (low) complex sequence of activities) • Support data and information inclusion into BP models • Identify (implicitly) certain issues related to knowledge flows, such as the information sources that are required, generated, or modified by an activity
	Weakness
	• Focus on the representation of "deterministic" BP, composed by a well-structured control flow among its activities, low uncertainty and complexity (that is the existence of few and pre-defined exceptions) • Not suited to deal with the flexibility, frequent exceptions, and common changes in SBP activities • Shortcomings concerning the inclusion and modeling of knowledge dimension (knowledge types, individual and collective dimension of knowledge/actions, knowledge conversion types, etc.) • Limited capabilities to explicitly and strictly separate data from information during BPM (they are modeled using the same modeling constructs) • The owner of data, information, and knowledge is not indicated • Less appropriate for BPM that involve the cooperation of multiple agents

and dimensions defining an SBP, by offering a coherent conceptual specification for this BP type, and (ii) to develop a rich and expressive graphical representation of SBPs to improve the localization and identification of crucial knowledge mobilized and created by these processes. The new extended BPM4KI, which is a continuation of previous works [3], is well founded meta-model whose concepts (and the relationships between them) are semantically enriched by the «core» domain ontologies [5, 22]. Concretely, our approach for building the new extended version of BPM4KI meta-model is jointly supported, on the one hand, by the specialization of the *DOLCE* foundational ontology [6], to specify and define the invariant generic BP concepts, including SBPs, and on the other hand, by the conception of Ontology Design Patterns (ODP) [5] which are based on the reuse of ontological modules relating to the «core» domain ontologies (which were based on top of DOLCE) [22–24]. More precisely, our proposal is based on the reuse and the specification of central generic concepts defined in different ontological modules of the global and consistent ontology OntoSpec[1] [30]:

---

[1] http://home.mis.u-picardie.fr/~ site-ic/site/spip.php?article53.

Table 2. Analysis of process-oriented knowledge modeling formalisms for SBP modeling

Process-oriented knowledge modeling approaches and formalisms	Strengths
• DECOR [15] • GPO-WM [16] • DCR Graphs [17] • PROMOTE [18] • Oliveira's methodology [19] • Knowledge Modeling and Description Language (KMDL 2.2) [8, 20] • Notation for Knowledge Intensive Processes (NKIP) [21]	• Support knowledge modeling and focus on storing and sharing knowledge • Support information inclusion into BP models
	Weakness
	• Poor capabilities to adequately model the BP sequence/control flow and the process perspective as a whole • Knowledge dimension modeling support is incomplete (as differentiation between tacit knowledge from explicit knowledge, dynamic aspects of knowledge, different sources of knowledge, etc.) • Limited capabilities to separately represent knowledge used to perform BPs knowledge created as a result of BP activities • Shortcomings concerning the modeling of individual and collective dimension of knowledge/actions • Limited capabilities to clearly distinguish between data, information and knowledge • Limited capabilities to represent dynamics and collaboration BP aspects

Action-OS, Action of Organization-OS, Partcipation-role-OS, Agentive Entity-OS, Organization-OS, Function & Artefact-OS, Capacity-OS, Artefact-OS, Resource-OS, Communication-OS, Discourse_Message_Discoure_act-OS, I&DA-OS (Information and Discourse Acts) and *Action Model-OS.* These ontological modules are available online (See Footnote 1), which are sufficient to characterize the useful concepts for a rigorous specification and an enriched modeling of SBPs.

The current version of BPM4KI offers a referential of generic concepts and semantic relationships relevant to the BPM-KM domain, exploring the dynamic, the collaboration and the knowledge aspects of the SBP in greater detail. It is categorized in six perspectives (or dimensions), namely, the functional perspective, the organizational perspective, the behavioral perspective, the informational perspective, the intentional perspective and the knowledge perspective. The different dimensions are crucial for a complete understanding, characterization and representation of an SBP (see [4]).

Particularly, in SBP modeling, it is necessary to separately and accurately represent knowledge concept from data and information concepts that form a basis for knowledge creation and sharing. Or, this distinction is very essential in KM domain and it is useful to characterize the SBPs. Therefore, in this paper, we focus on the analysis of the informational and knowledge dimensions which are the most relevant aspects in SBP modeling. These dimensions are not yet, however, explicited and integrated into the BPs models and they are not yet fully supported in any of the above-mentioned BPM and knowledge modeling formalisms/approaches.

3 Information and Knowledge Representation in Sensitive Business Process Models

While importance of knowledge dimension is well recognized, there is no clear theoretical background and successful practical experiments of inclusion and integration of this dimension in BP meta-models and BPM formalisms. In this section, we propose to introduce a more explicit border between information and knowledge dimensions in SBPs models based on core domain ontologies [5, 22–24]. We aim at obtaining new knowledge helpful for developing BPM formalisms that could handle all relevant aspects related to knowledge dimension (including data and information). For this purpose, we will give at first brief overview of data, information, and knowledge concepts interpretation.

3.1 Data, Information and Knowledge

Data, information, and knowledge are concepts that are widely used in various fields of human activities. Their meaning is discussed in various fields of research since ancient times. Despite of numerous research works and scientific theories on interpretation of data, information, and knowledge in psychology, epistemology, social science, philosophy, cognitive science, information theory and knowledge creation theory. These terms are still used intuitively and often lack explicit unified definition within the areas of research. Uncertainty exists not only in definitions, but also in the practical use of the concepts in BP models.

(I) *Data.* Information theory considers *data* as a functional value of information used for the actions of an interpretation device [25]. D*ata* participate in processes within an object and play the role as a «thing for itself». This is a set of facts which do not have concrete interpretation (such as data in system repositories and data bases or facts inside the human brain), which gives it the character of objectivity. According to Gray [26], a *data* is a discrete element, a result like numbers, symbols, figures, schemas, without context neither interpretation. It is a recording having a certain stability over time (e.g., recording of a numerical value in a database table) and is exploitable by treatments (e.g., comparing two numbers), especially their interpretation into information [27]. The authors [27] also consider that the result of an observation is a data (e.g., a technical report may be a data for further action such as writing another report or thesis).

(II) *Information.* Scientific literature proposes different definitions of information that are relevant in certain application domains. In the context of human information, proceeding information is an instrument of a knowledge transfer. The information is a data (or series of data) having a meaning, i.e., which is placed in a precise context [28] in order to convey a message [29].

According to [30], information is a set of unstructured and organized data to give form to a message resulting from a given context and then perfectly subjective. It is, therefore, an interpreted data by an individual in a well-defined context with a particular meaning (for example, «the outside temperature is 4°», the interpretation of this data by individual shows that it is cold outside). So, it is often linked to its holder who interprets it. Information can be shared in different ways, e.g., via verbal communication, sharing information stored in a data base, externalizing information in paper format, using information as an electronic document.

(III)   ***Knowledge.*** A wide variety of knowledge definitions are used in different domains and environments. The knowledge concept is associated to such terms as skill, capability, competence, and experience. It is owned by a person and it has subjective characteristics. Knowledge is a fluid mix of framed experiences, values, contextual information, and expert insights that provides a framework for evaluating and incorporating new experiences and information. The knowledge is derived and is applied in people's minds [31]. According to Nonaka et al. [32], information is a message flow while knowledge is created by the flow of information and is rooted in the beliefs and adhesion of the person who holds it. This understanding emphasizes that knowledge is essentially related to human action. In fact, when a member of an organization is trying to pass his/her knowledge to another member, for the receiver this is just a set of information. The receiver needs to execute a set of internal activities to transform the received information into knowledge. Thus, BP participants interact with information during process execution and everyone can use the received information to create his own knowledge.

We point out that both BPM and knowledge modeling approaches and formalisms concern the linkage between the business processes and knowledge. However, they do not explicitly and fully consider the knowledge dimension (including data and information) into BP models. Usually, in representation of flows between BP activities, available BPM notations do not provide an opportunity to clearly distinguish between data, information and knowledge. In fact, in such languages as IDEF0, IDEF3, GRAPES BM in GRADE tool, EPC diagrams in ARIS tool [12], UML 2.0 activity diagram [13] and BPMN 2.0 [14], data, information and material flows are often represented in BP models by the same symbols/artifacts, and without any unambiguous definitions of the concepts. At the same time knowledge has poor or no modeling capabilities in these formalisms. On the other hand, knowledge modeling languages (KMDL [8, 20], GPO-WM [16], PROMOTE [18], DCR Graphs [17] and NKIP [21]) have shortcomings concerning their ability to explicitly and fully incorporate the knowledge dimension within BPs models as well as relevant issues at the intersection of KM and BPM. They have limited process perspective representation, i.e. they do not address process logic to full extent and thus there is no possibility to represent data [7]. Currently, from the point of view of various ways how data, information, and knowledge are used in organizations, the following issues are not yet fully supported in any of the above-mentioned BPM and knowledge modeling formalisms:

- Possibility to strictly separate information and data during BPM, that form a basis for knowledge creation and sharing.
- Possibility to separate data, information, and knowledge used to perform BPs and those created as a result of BP activities.
- Opportunity to identify the owner of data, information, and knowledge and location where they can be obtained and can be clearly stated.
- Opportunity to illustrate the knowledge sources involved (used, generated and/or modified) in the BP and activities.
- Opportunity to integrate and separate the different types/kinds of knowledge (tacit/explicit dimension, factual/procedural dimension, individual/collective dimension, etc.).
- Possibility to illustrate the way in which specific knowledge flows among the activities, or how a specific source is used and modified through the activities.
- Possibility to illustrate transfers (sharing and dissemination) of knowledge between sources and among activities.
- Possibility to represent the different types of knowledge conversion in BP activities (the dynamic generation and use of existing knowledge embedded into a BP).
- Opportunity to improve understanding about the knowledge usefulness, validity, and relevance for particular activities in a BP.

The goal of this research work is to provide a rigorous representation of the knowledge dimension that would give an opportunity to support above-mentioned issues in BP/SBP modeling. The results will be expressed as new and specific graphical notations (symbols) for knowledge, information, and data flows/objects.

3.2 Informational Dimension in SBP Modeling

Coordination of BP activities within an organization is achieved with information exchange between organization members. This is the basis for knowledge generation and distribution. The proposed informational perspective describes the informational entities that are involved in a BP (i.e. which are generated, consumed, or exchanged within a BP/activity and between different agentive entities). At the same time, this dimension represents inputs and outputs of a BP as data/data objects, information/ information objects, artifacts, material resources, as well as messages or communications, discourses/conversations exchanged between different agentive entities involved in the BP.

Our proposal, presented in the form of an Informational ODP (see Fig. 1), is based on the reuse and the specification of central generic concepts (and the relationships between them) defined in different ontological modules of the global and consistent ontology OntoSpec [22]: *Action-OS*, *Action of Organization-OS*, *Partcipation-role-OS*, *Organization-OS*, *Function & Artefact-OS*, *Artefact-OS*, *Resource-OS*, *Communication-OS*, *Action Model-OS*, *I&DA-OS* (Information and Discourse Acts) [33] and *IE&C-OS* (Inscription, Expression and Conceptualization). Figure 1 organizes and explicit the main concepts of the informational perspective (marked in gray), in addition to inter-aspects relationships (the various concepts are recognizable by their thicker borders), giving a view of all relevant aspects of the BPM4KI meta-model as a whole.

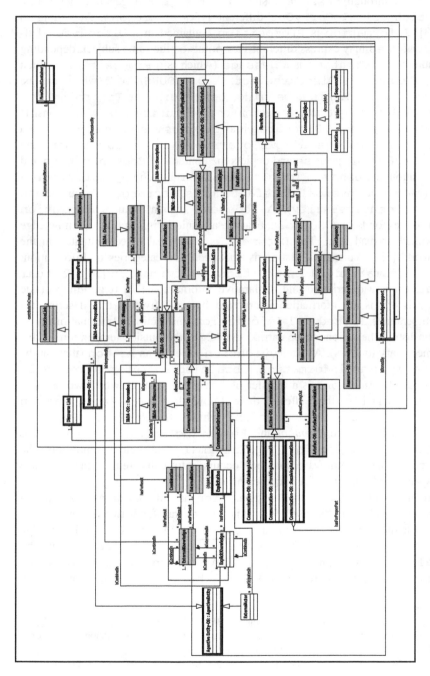

Fig. 1. BPM4KI Meta-model: Conceptual Ontology design Pattern relating to the Informational Perspective/Dimension of SBP (with inter-aspects relationships).

In order to achieve an intentionally defined objective, different Agentive Entities[2] (playing the role of Senders and Receivers) interact and exchange Information through Messages, share Knowledge and generate new ones. Information allowToCarryOut different types of Actions. According to I&DA [33], Information is Proposition contained in a Discourse[3]. Different Discourses may express different viewpoints on the same subject, depending on their author. Information is a Message (which is a Proposition) which allowsToCarryOut a Discourse Act. A DISCOURSE ACT (which can be either Authorizing, Asking, Defining, Describing or Informing) is a Deliberate Action (premeditated action) or a Communication which consists in creating a Discourse. A Discourse is an Expression which expresses a Message. Every Message allowsToCarryOut a Discourse Act and isExpressedBy a Discourse and depicts the contents of Communication and transmitted through Message Flow. Information isBornBy Information Medium (which is a Physical Artefact and isInterpretedBy an Human (which is an AgentiveEntity). A Document (which is an Information Medium) corresponds to a Support bearing a semiotic inscription of knowledge (e.g., a printed or read text). The Document is a physical objects situated in the physical world [33]. We mainly distinguish between two categories of Information: Factual Information and Instructional Information [34]. Factual Information is a descriptive and declarative information [34] (e.g., «the outside temperature is 4°» is an information interpreted by an individual that describe the outside temperature). Procedural Information (Instructional Information) is an information listing the actions to be carried out (e.g., «the outside temperature is 4°» then it is necessary to dress). A Communication which is an Action (that can be either Receiving an information, Obtaining an information, Providing an information) is a transfer of Information between two or more Agentive Entities that affects their knowledge state. Receiving an Information is a Communication which hasForProperPart an Informing such that the *agent of* the Receiving an Information is the addresseeOf the Informing. An Informal Exchange represents the Information and/or Knowledge that occurs informally (either face- to-face between agents, or by means of a documentation).

In our modeling context, an Information is interpreted as externalized knowledge or meaningful data used for a knowledge transfer between subjects and activities. Note that, Information and Data constitute the basis for the knowledge dissemination and generation. The creation of new Knowledge is done by Externalization or combination [32]. An Externalization is a Communicative Interaction which is a Deliberate Action, during which

---

[2] With respect to our notation, the informal labels on BPM4KI concepts appear in the text in the Courrier new font with First Capital Letters for the concepts and a javaLikeNotation for relations.

[3] According to I&DA [33], Knowledge - for an Agent - corresponds to Propositions to which the Agent confers a truth value: this then allows him/her to use these Propositions in reasoning (whatever their truth value) in order to derive new knowledge.

several Explicit Knowledge areExternalizedTo to divers External Knowledge or Information and leads to detached knowledge as seen from the perspective of the human being, which areBorneBy (i.e. which can be kept in) organizational memory systems (which are Physical Knowledge Supports). A Combination is a Communicative Interaction which is a Deliberate Action which combines existing External or Explicit Knowledge in new forms (more complex). Combination hasForAgent one or more Humans, which hasForResult either new Explicit Knowledge External Knowledge or Information. The new knowledge, i.e. External Knowledge and/or Explicit Knowledge areBornedBy and stored in Physical Knowledge Supports (e.g. electronic media, organizational memories, etc.). A Document is a subtype of Physical Knowledge Supports.

Besides, for its accomplishment, an Action uses (hasForInput) Inputs (such as materials, data or/and information Objects), mobilizes Resources to produce (hasForOutput) Outputs (like data or/and information Objects, services, results, etc.). An Information (Output) is an Artefact, which is an entity intentionally made or produced to allow carrying out at least one Action [35]. It can be either a Physical Artifact (decision of medical care which may be contained in documents), or Non Phycial Artifact. A Resource is an entity which has a capacity to enable an Action (mobilizable for action [23]. A Resource can be either a Material Resource or Immaterial Resource. A Material Resource (or Tangible resource) is anything of material value or usefulness that is owned by a person or company [23]. It has actual physical existence (such as documentary, informational, material and software resources, etc.).While Immaterial Resource (or intangible resources) are things like corporate images, brands and patents that are present but cannot be grasped or contained in physical support (Wikipedia). Besides, an Organizational Action can be triggered by Events (which may take various forms), which can in turn produce Events. A Contingency is an external and unpredictable event that influences the process execution (the elements produced or handled and decisions made). This type of events is responsible for determining the execution of unforeseen activities. It should be emphasized that the output or the result of an activity may be an input, an event, a resource for the successor activity or another activity. It can also be a terminal output standing for the achievement of a product awaited by an internal or external client to the organization.

3.3 Knowledge Dimension Representation in SBP Models

At the root of the success of modeling, design, reengineering, and running BPs is effective use and support of organizational knowledge. It is worth to remember that BP engineering has to be a holistic approach and take into consideration various aspects or dimensions of the business system, including organizational and individual knowledge. Therefore, the relationships between a BP and organizational knowledge should be clearly documented. Knowledge might be considered as one of the BP dimensions, because knowledge is related to action, it is implemented in the action, and is essential to its development [3]. Knowledge is used to perform a process, it is created as a result of process execution, and it is distributed among process participants. In this context, several methods have already been elaborated to integrate the domain of KM and BPM that introduce the process dimension into KM [8, 11, 16] or the knowledge concept/dimension into BP models [10, 18, 21, 36–38]. However, while importance of knowledge dimension is well recognized, there is no successful practical experiments of inclusion and implementation of this dimension in BP models. In fact, approaches that focus on KM within the BP level have limited capabilities. Usually knowledge is modeled using specific knowledge modeling notations (e.g., KMDL 2.2 [8] [20], GPO-WM [16], Oliveira's methodology [19], and only few of them partially include process perspective (e.g., PROMOTE [18], RAD [10]). At the same time, none of those proposals adequately and fully support the knowledge dimension (e.g., differentiation between tacit and explicit knowledge, the different types of knowledge conversion which are relevant in SBPs due to, for instance, the high degree of tacit knowledge developed and exchanged among agents through inter-organizational collaboration, etc.).

To address this research gap, this section describes our proposal of modeling of the «Knowledge Perspective» that we have extended, in order to explicitly incorporate all relevant aspects related to KM within BPs models, and on the other hand, to enrich the graphical representation of SBPs and improve the localization and identification of crucial knowledge mobilized and created by these processes. The extended BPM dimension focuses on the knowledge flow and the dynamics of acquisition, preservation, conversion, transfer, sharing, development, and (re) use of individual and organizational knowledge within and between organizations. Moreover, the knowledge perspective considers the different types of knowledge (tacit/explicit dimension, declarative/procedural dimension, etc.) mobilized and created by each type of activity related to the organization's BPs, the different sources of knowledge, their localization and where they are usable or used, their nature, their organizational coverage (individual/collective dimension), the different opportunity of knowledge conversion, etc.

Our proposal, presented in the form of an ODP of knowledge [4][4] is based on the reuse and the specification of central generic concepts (and the relationships between them) defined in different ontological modules of the global and consistent ontology OntoSpec [22]: *Capacity-OS, Action-OS, Action of Organization-OS, Agentive Entity-OS, Partcipation-role-OS, Organization-OS, Function & Artefact-OS, Resource-OS, Communication-OS, Discourse_Message_Discoure- act-OS, IE&C-OS* and COOP (Core Ontology of Organization's Processes [24]. Table 3 presents the core knowledge perspective concepts definitions.

Therefore, extending BP models with the knowledge dimension would provide the following benefits:

- Possibility to relate different forms of knowledge, information and data to the BP model.
- Possibility to identify data, information and knowledge inputs and outputs in organizational activities.

---

[4] https://www.dropbox.com/s/0ia9xrjwrtoqqkq/Ontological%20Conceptual%20Pattern%20relating%20to%20the%20Knowledge%20Perspective%20of%20SBP.pdf?dl=0. The figure explicit the core concepts of the knowledge perspective of BPM4KI meta-model (marked in gray), in addition to inter-aspects relationships [4].

Table 3. Definitions of core Knowledge dimension concepts

Concepts	Definition
Capacity	A state (that can be acquired or lost) which enables to fulfill at least one Action Role (i.e. play some role of participation in an Action) [35]. In other words, a `Capacity` is a `State` which `isBorneBy` an `Endurant` (i.e. an `Agentive Entities`) and which represents its capacity or disposition to play some role in an `Action`
Knowledge	Capacity (or disposition) to perform (and affects) a type of action aiming to achieve an objective [4]. It `isBorneBy` an `Agentive Entity` (which can be a `Human`, a `Collective`, an `Expert` or an `Organization`).- Knowledge is divided into `Internal Knowledge`, `Explicit Knowledge` and `External Knowledge` according to the *source of knowledge* dimension.- Knowledge is divided into `Propositional Knowledge` and `Procedural Knowledge` according to the *nature of knowledge* dimension. - Knowledge is divided into `Strategic Knowledge` and `Familiarity Knowledge` according to the *organizational value of knowledge* dimension - Knowledge is divided into `Individual Knowledge` and `Collective Knowledge` according to the *organizational coverage of knowledge* dimension
Individual knowledge	Combination of individual's own knowledge, experience and skills. It `isBorneBy` an `Individual` (a `Human`) and includes, besides the intellectual capacity, the vision that every individual holds of the organization to which he/she is affiliated, as well as the explicit knowledge in the form of personal notes
Collective knowledge	Knowledge which `isBorneBy` a `Collective`. It's a knowledge sharable by several `Agentive Entities`. Their coverage can be global, or partial which bound to a structure
Organizational knowledge	Collective knowledge which `isBorneBy` an `Organization`. A sum of individuals' knowledge which integrates a firm's experiences and firm-specific knowledge, and already existing in organizational systems, organizational routines, documents, decision-making procedures, practices, products, rules, and culture
Internal knowledge	An implicit knowledge which is borne by one or more Persons (related to the human being). It is all that, what a person has "in its brain" due to experience, history, activities, learning, and includes innate or acquired competences and skills, mental models, talents, abilities, trades secrets, beliefs and aspirations - An `Internal Knowledge` can be either divided into `Conscious Knowledge`, `Latent Knowledge` or `Tacit Knowledge` (where those subtypes do partly overlap with each other)

(*continued*)

Table 3. (*continued*)

Concepts	Definition
Conscious knowledge	It is conscious and intentional, is cognitively available and may be made explicit easily. It is often transmitted by implicit collective apprenticeship or by a master–apprentice relationship
Latent knowledge	It has been typically learning as a by-product and is not available consciously. It may be made explicit, for example in situations, which are similar to the original learning situation
Tacit knowledge	It is highly personal, developed and acquired through experiences and (cultural) socialization situations. It is specific in its context (rooted in action, procedures, commitment, values and emotions) and based on intuition and perception. It is a non explainable knowledge, difficult to be formalized, articulated, communicated, explained and shared by the persons who possess it
Explicit knowledge	It concerns knowledge that is «made explicit», which is often verbalized, communicated and transmitted to the outside world in an implicit manner (e.g., through spoken language), but is still bound to the human being. It isBorneBy a Human and may be shared and exchanged through direct interaction and communication with others, practice, observation, meetings, constructive discussions, collective thinking, learning, etc.)
External knowledge	It is a formalized knowledge detached from the human being and may be relatively easily codified, formalized, accessible and transferable in the form of reusable storage media (e.g. documents) as part of the organizational memory and independently of the subject which specified it
Individual external knowledge	An External Knowledge is borne by a Human. Its dissemination depends on the person who owns the document
Collective external knowledge	An External Knowledge which isBorneBy a Collective, easily shared, usable and reusable at the collective level of the organization. Its coverage can be global (e.g. the enterprise culture) or partial (i.e. related to structure). In organizations, it often becomes embedded and represented in documents or knowledge repositories (data and knowledge bases), in organizational routines, processes, practices, norms, etc.
Belief state	A propositional attitude, then, is the mental state of having some attitude, stance, take, or opinion about a proposition or about the potential state of affairs in which that proposition is true [39]
Propositional knowledge	Theoretical knowledge «Knowing-That/What» (also called declarative, factual or descriptive knowledge [40], which is about content, facts in a domain, events, rules, principles, semantic interrelationship and theories. They are usually made in a formal language. Formally, a Propositional Knowledge is a Belief State (which is a State) which has for theme a Description (which can be factual or prescriptive). Propositional Knowledge can be explicit/external in terms that can be represented on physical or numerical support, individual (which is borne by an Individual), collective (which is borne by a Collective) or Organizational (which is borne by an Organization)

(*continued*)

Table 3. (*continued*)

Concepts	Definition
Procedural knowledge	Practical knowledge «Knowing-How», capacity to perform an Action, which corresponds to the experience, the knowledge on «how-to-do». These are dynamic knowledge that may develop only in a context of action. Procedural Knowledge can be individual (which is borne by one Expert) or Collective (which isBorneBy at least two Experts)
Strategic knowledge	A meta-cognitive knowledge on optimal strategies for structuring a problem-solving approach or for carry out an Action. It is also a dynamic knowledge («Know-Why/When»), which corresponds to the why and how of the action and, also, allow to determine the time and context in which it is appropriate to use such a procedure or such knowledge. This type of knowledge is one of the characteristics of expertise
Familiarity knowledge	Familiarity is acquaintance with certain situations and environments; it also resembles aspects of situational knowledge, i.e., knowledge about situations, which typically appear in particular domains
Expert	An Experiencer (which is an Agentive Entity) who bears a Capacity To Perform a type of Action with high levels of experience, expertise, performance, creativity and innovation
Physical knowledge support	A Material Resource (informational resource), having "source of knowledge information" interpreted and mobilized by the agents (operating in the BP) during the execution of their activities (these supports transmit not only information, but also significance). Available Knowledge (either Explicit Knowledge or External Knowledge) isBorneBy one or more Physical Knowledge Supports (e.g. documents, computer system, etc.) enabling their capitalization, formalization, storage, dissemination and sharing among stakeholders of the organization
Communicative interaction	A Collective Action during which different types of Agentive Entities interact and exchange information and knowledge through messages. It has for proper part Communications
Socialization	A Deliberate Action which hasForAgent a Collective (which has for proper part at least two Humans), which is generated by Communication, and has for result new Tacit Knowledge (mental models). It may involve the participation of External Actors. During the execution of a Socialization, Individual Tacit Knowledge is transmitted in Collective Tacit Knowledge through practice, sharing of experiences, conscious or unconscious observation, constructive discussions or in a learning-by-doing situation (in the context of a Communicative Interaction)

(*continued*)

Table 3. (*continued*)

Concepts	Definition
Internalization	A Deliberate Action which converts either External or Explicit Knowledge isInternaliszedIn Internal Knowledge of the conscious or latent types. It leads to an integration of experiences and competences in your own mental model. Internalization hasForAgent one or more Humans, which isGeneratedBy Communication and hasForResult Internal Knowledge
Externalization	A Deliberate Action, during which several Explicit Knowledge isExternalizedTo to divers External Knowledge (or Information) and leads to detached knowledge as seen from the perspective of the human being, which can be kept in organizational memory systems. Externalization hasForAgent one or more Humans, which isGeneratedBy Communication and hasForResult External Knowledge
Explicitation	A Deliberate Action, that represents the internal process of a person, to make internal knowledge of the latent or conscious type explicit, e.g., by articulation and formulation (in the conscious case) or by using metaphors, analogies and models (in the latent case). Explicitation hasForAgent a Human, which isGeneratedBy Communication and hasForResult Explicit Knowledge
Combination	A Deliberate Action, which combines existing External or Explicit Knowledge in new forms. Combination hasForAgent one or more Humans, which isGeneratedBy Communication and hasForResult either new Explicit Knowledge or new External Knowledge. (Explicit Knowledge of several Humans are exchanged, combined to produce, by induction and deduction new Explicit Knowledge)
Knowledge flow	Represents the dynamics of Knowledge, i.e., all of organization, exchange, conversion, sharing, development and usage of knowledge among the different sources of knowledge and among BP activities

- Illustrating and separating the data, information and knowledge sources that are required to perform BP activities and knowledge that are generated, created and/or modified as a results of activities.
- Enhance the localization and identification of knowledge (where knowledge can be obtained and clearly stated) as well as experts who hold the (internal) knowledge.
- Integration and distinction of different knowledge types.
- Specifying the different opportunities of knowledge conversion between knowledge types (the dynamic sharing, dissemination, generation and use of existing knowledge).
- Possibility to represent knowledge flows between sources, and among activities which are about creation, organization, distribution and reuse of knowledge among BP participants.

- Giving an opportunity to improve understanding about the knowledge usefulness, validity, and relevance for particular activities (i.e. critical activities) in an SBP.
- Possibility to evaluate the amount of lost knowledge if a person-owner of knowledge-leaves the organization (to identify which tacit knowledge in which cases should be transformed into explicit knowledge).

However, it is important that an appropriate BPM formalism provides explicit representation of the different issues related to the information and knowledge dimensions in BPM. In this context, the SBPs can be graphically represented, using the well-known standard for BPM, BPMN 2.0 [14], in order to localize and identify the knowledge that is mobilized and created by these processes. BPMN was selected as the most suitable BPM notations for representing SBPs, because it incorporates requirements for SBP modeling better than other BPM formalisms [7]. Nevertheless, despite its expressiveness, BPMN 2.0 does not yet provide support for SBP modeling. In fact, this notation does not explicitly represent the key concepts of the Informational perspective and the Knowledge perspective of BPM (such as Information, Material Resource, Immaterial Resource, Knowledge, Explicit Knowledge, External Knowledge, Individual Internal Knowledge, Collective Tacit Knowledge, Expert, Externalization, Socialization, etc.). To overcoming the shortcomings of BPMN 2.0, some of its concepts should be adapted and extended to be convenient for a rich and expressive representation of SBPs.

4   Conclusion and Perspectives

In this paper, we focused on the description of the «Informational Perspective» and «Knowledge Perspective» of the proposed BPM4KI meta-model. These two dimensions are not yet explicited, fully supported and integrated within BPs models and BPM approaches. Our main objective consists in introducing more explicit border between information and knowledge concepts/dimensions which are relevant in SBP models, based on «core» domain ontologies.

Our current research activities focus on proposing rigorous approach to extend BPMN 2.0 for KM. This extension must incorporate all relevant aspects related to knowledge and information dimensions in order to generate a rich and expressive representation of SBPs and improve the identification of crucial knowledge.

As further work, we will validate the developed generic BPM4KI by instantiating it in depth (using extended BPMN) with a real case study in the medical domain in the context of the Association of Protection of the Motor-disabled of Sfax-Tunisia (ASHMS) [11], in order to verify the completeness and the relevance of the proposed concepts.

References

1. Saad, I., Grundstein, M., Sabroux, C.: Une méthode d'aide à l'identification des connaissances cruciales pour l'entreprise. Revue SIM **14**(3), 43–78 (2009)
2. Turki, M., Saad, I., Gargouri, F., Kassel, G.: A business process evaluation methodology for knowledge management based on multi-criteria decision making approach. In: Information Systems for Knowledge Management. Wiley-ISTE (2014). ISBN: 978-1-84821-664-8

3. Ben Hassen, M., Turki, M., Gargouri, F.: A business process meta-model for knowledge identification based on a core ontology. In: Shishkov, B. (ed.) BMSD 2015. LNBIP, vol. 257, pp. 37–61. Springer, Cham (2016). doi:10.1007/978-3-319-40512-4_3

4. Ben Hassen, M., Turki, M., Gargouri, F.: A proposal to model knowledge dimension in sensitive business processes. In: Madureira, A.M., Abraham, A., Gamboa, D., Novais, P. (eds.) ISDA 2016. AISC, vol. 557, pp. 1015–1030. Springer, Cham (2017). doi:10.1007/978-3-319-53480-0_100

5. Gangemi, A.: Ontology Design Patterns: A primer, with applications and perspectives. Tutorial on ODP, Laboratory for Applied Ontology Institute of Cognitive Sciences and Technology CNR, Rome, Italy (2006)

6. Masolo, C., Vieu, L., Bottazzi, E., Catenacci, C., Ferrario, R., Gangemi, A., Guarino, N.: Social roles and their descriptions. In: Dubois, D., Welty, C., Williams, M.-A. (eds.) Proceedings of the Ninth International Conference on the Principles of Knowledge Representation and Reasoning, pp. 267–277 (2004)

7. Ben Hassen, M., Turki, M., Gargouri, F.: Choosing a sensitive business process modeling formalism for knowledge identification. Procedia Comput. Sci. **100**, 1002–1015 (2016)

8. Gronau, N., Korf, R., Müller, C.: KMDL-capturing, analysing and improving knowledge-intensive business processes. J. Univ. Comput. Sci. **11**(4), 452–472 (2005)

9. Schlenoff, C., Gruninger, M., Tissot, F., Valois, J.: The process specification language (PSL) overview and version 1.0 specification (2000). http://www.mel.nist.gov/psl/

10. Weidong, Z., Weihui, D.: Integrated modeling of business processes and knowledge flow based on RAD. In: IEEE International Symposium on Knowledge Acquisition and Modeling, Wuhan, China, pp. 49–53 (2008)

11. Zhaoli, Z., Zongkai, Y., Qingtang, L.: Modeling knowledge flow using petri net. In: International Symposium on Knowledge Acquisition and Modeling, Wuhan, China, pp. 142–146 (2008)

12. ARIS Expert Paper: Business Process Design as the Basis for Compliance Management, Enterprise Architecture and Business Rules (2007)

13. Unified Modeling Language (UML). Version 2.0. OMG (2011). http://www.uml.org/

14. Business Process Modeling and Notation (BPMN). Version 2.0. OMG (2011). http://www.bpmn.org/

15. Abecker, A.: DECOR Consortium: DECOR-Delivery of Context-Sensitive Organizational Knowledge. E-Work and E-Commerce. IOS Press, Amsterdam (2008)

16. Heisig, P.: The GPO-WM® method for the integration of knowledge management into business processes. In: International Conference on Knowledge Management, Graz, Austria, pp. 331–337 (2006)

17. Hildebrandt, T.T., Mukkamala, R.R.: Declarative event-based workflow as distributed dynamic condition response graphs. In: Programming Languages Approaches to Concurrency and Communication-cEntric Software, Cyprus, pp. 59–73 (2010)

18. Woitsch, R., Karagiannis, D.: Process oriented knowledge management: a service based approach. J. Univ. Comput. Sci. **11**(4), 565–588 (2005)

19. Oliveira, F.F.: Ontology Collaboration and its Applications. MSc Dissertation. Programa de Pós-Graduação em Informática, Universidade Federal do Espírito Santo, Vitória, Brazil (2009)

20. Arbeitsbericht.: KMDL® v2.2 (2009). http://www.kmdl.de/

21. Netto, J.M, Franca, J.B.S., Baião, F.A., Santoro, F.M.: A notation for knowledge-intensive processes. In: IEEE 17th International Conference on Computer Supported Cooperative Work in Design, vol. 1, pp. 1–6 (2013)

22. Kassel, G.: Integration of the DOLCE top-level ontology into the OntoSpec methodology (2005)

23. Kassel, G., Turki, M., Saad, I., Gargouri, F.: From collective actions to actions of organizations: an ontological analysis. In: Symposium Understanding and Modelling Collective Phenomena (UMoCop). University of Birmingham, Birmingham, England (2012)
24. Turki, M., Kassel, G., Saad, I., Gargouri, F.: A core ontology of business processes based on DOLCE. J. Data Semant. **5**(3), 165–177 (2016)
25. Yankovsky, S.Ya.: Les concepts de la théorie de l'information générale (2001). http://n-t.ru/tp/ng/oti.htm
26. Gray, P.: Knowledge management Overview. Center for Research on Information Technology and Organizations, University of California (2000)
27. Gibaut, B., Kassel, G.: Sémantique des données de l'observation: une approche ontologique. Technical report, Boston, MA, USA (2013)
28. Fitchett, J.: Managing your organization's key asset: knowledge. Health Forum J. **9**(41), 50–60 (1998)
29. Ferrary, M., Pesqueux, Y.: Management de la connaissance: knowledge management, apprentissage organisationnel et société de la connaissance, Economica Edition. Eyrolles (2006)
30. CIFREG. Gérer les connaissances. Défi, enjeu et conduite de projet. (Report No. ATTJ8KE4, p. 15). CIGREF, Club Informatique des GRandes Entreprises Françaises, Paris (2000)
31. Davenport, T., Long, D.D., Beers, M.: Successful knowledge management projects. Sloan Manag. Rev. **39**(2), 43–57 (1998)
32. Nonaka, I., Takeuchi, H.: Knowledge-Creating Company: How Japanese Companies Create the Dynamics of Innovation. Oxford University Press, New York (1995)
33. Fortier, J.-Y., Kassel, G.: Managing knowledge at the information level: an ontological approach. In: Proceedings of the ECAI 2004 Workshop on Knowledge Management and Organizational Memories, Valencia, Spain, pp. 39–45 (2004)
34. Floridi, L.: Semantic conceptions of information. The Stanford Encyclopedia of Philosophy (2013)
35. Kassel, G.: A formal ontology of artefacts. Appl. Ontology **5**(3–4), 223–246 (2010)
36. Sultanow, E., Zhou, X., Gronau, N.: Modeling of processes, systems and knowledge: a multi-dimensional comparison of 13 chosen methods. Int. Rev. Comput. Softw. **7**(6), 3309–3319 (2012)
37. Liu, D.R., Lai, D.R., Liu, C.H., Chih-Wei, L.: Modeling the knowledge-flow view for collaborative knowledge support. J. Know. Based Syst. **31**, 41–54 (2012)
38. Ammann, E.: Modeling of knowledge-intensive business processes. Int. J. Soc. Behav. Educ. Bus. Ind. Eng. **6**(11), 3144–3150 (2012)
39. Schwitzgebel, E.: Belief. In: Zalta, E.N. (ed.) The Stanford Encyclopedia of Philosophy (2014). http://plato.stanford.edu/archives/spr2014/entries/belief/
40. Bonnet, C., Ghiglione, R., Richard, J.-F.: Traité de Psychologie Cognitive, Tome 1: Perception, action, langage. Dunod, vol. 3, Paris, 280 p. (2003). ISBN: 2100078445

Adaptive Planning in-Service Inspections of Fatigued Structures in Damage Tolerance Situations via Observations of Crack Growth Process

Nicholas Nechval[1($\boxtimes$)], Gundars Berzins[2], and Vadims Danovics[2]

[1] BVEF Research Institute, University of Latvia, Raina Blvd 19, Riga 1050, Latvia
nechval@junik.lv
[2] Management Department, University of Latvia, Raina Blvd 19, Riga 1050, Latvia
{gundars.berzins,vadims.danovics}@lu.lv

Abstract. From an engineering standpoint the fatigue life of a fatigued structure consists of two periods: (i) crack initiation period, which starts with the first load cycle and ends when a technically detectable crack is presented, and (ii) crack propagation period, which starts with a technically detectable crack and ends when the remaining cross section can no longer withstand the loads applied and fails statically. The main aim of this paper is to present more accurate innovative stochastic fatigue model for adaptive planning inspections of fatigued structures in damage tolerance situations via observations of crack growth process during a crack propagation period. A new crack growth equation is based on this model. It is attractively simple and easy to apply in practice for effective in-service inspection planning (with decreasing intervals between sequential inspections as alternative to constant intervals often used in practice for convenience in operation). During the period of crack propagation (when the damage tolerance situation is used), the proposed crack growth equation, based on the innovative model, allows one to construct more accurate and effective reliability-based inspection strategy in this case. For illustration, a numerical example is given.

Keywords: Fatigued structure · Damage tolerance situation · Crack propagation · In-service inspection planning

1 Introduction

Fatigue is one of the most important problems of aircraft arising from their nature as multiple-component structures, subjected to random dynamic loads. The analysis of fatigue crack growth is one of the most important tasks in the design and life prediction of aircraft fatigue-sensitive structures (for instance, wing, fuselage) and their components (for instance, aileron or balancing flap as part of the wing panel, stringer, etc.). An example of in-service cracking from B727 aircraft [1] (year of manufacture 1981; flight hours not available; flight cycles 39,523) is given on Fig. 1.

© Springer International Publishing AG 2017
S. Benferhat et al. (Eds.): IEA/AIE 2017, Part I, LNAI 10350, pp. 426–432, 2017.
DOI: 10.1007/978-3-319-60042-0_46

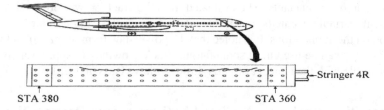

Fig. 1. Example of in-service cracking from B727 aircraft.

Certain fatigued structures must be inspected in order to detect fatigue damages that would otherwise not be apparent. For fatigued structures for which fatigue damages are only detected at the time of inspection, it is important to be able to determine the optimal times of inspections.

For guaranteeing safety, the structural life ceiling limits of the fleet aircraft are defined from three distinct situations: Safe-Life, Damage Tolerance, and Fail-Safe situations.

To keep structures reliable against fatigue damage by inspections, it is clearly important in engineering to examine the optimal inspection strategy. In particular, it should be noticed that periodical inspections with predetermined constant intervals are not always effective, since a fatigue crack growth rate is gradually accelerated as fatigue damage grows. Munford and Shahani [2] suggested a sub-optimal (or nearly optimal) but computationally easier inspection policy. Numerical comparisons among certain inspection policies are given by Munford [3] for the case of Weibull failure times. This case under parametric uncertainty was considered by Nechval *et al.* [4].

In this paper, the approach based on a novel crack growth equation to effective in-service inspection planning (with decreasing intervals between sequential inspections) is proposed to construct more accurate reliability-based inspection strategy during the period of crack propagation (when the damage tolerance situation is used).

2   Stochastic Models of Fatigue Crack Propagation (Growth)

To capture the statistical nature of fatigue crack growth, different stochastic models have been proposed in the literature. These models, however, have been criticized by other researchers, because less crack growth mechanisms have been included in them. To overcome this difficulty, many probabilistic models adopted the crack growth equations proposed by fatigue experimentalists, and randomized the equations by including random factors into them (Lin and Yang [5]; Yang and Manning [6]; Nechval *et al.* [7, 8]; Straub and Faber [9]).

Many probabilistic models of fatigue crack growth are based on the deterministic crack growth equations. The most well known equation is

$$\frac{da(t)}{dt} = q(a(t))^b \tag{1}$$

in which q and b are constants to be evaluated from the crack growth observations. The independent variable t can be interpreted as stress cycles, flight hours, or flights depending on the applications. It is noted that the power-law form of $q(a(t))^b$ at the right hand side of (1) can be used to fit some fatigue crack growth data appropriately and is also compatible with the concept of Paris–Erdogan law (Paris and Erdogan [10]).

3   Innovative Stochastic Model of Fatigue Crack Propagation

This model of fatigue crack propagation (growth) is based on the following deterministic crack growth equation,

$$\frac{dt(a)}{da} = \frac{q_1 q_0}{a^2} \exp\left(-\frac{q_0}{a}\right), \tag{2}$$

in which q_1 and q_0 are constants to be evaluated from the crack growth observations. The variable t can be interpreted as stress cycles, flight hours, or flights depending on the applications. The service time for a crack to grow from size a_0 to a (where $a > a_0$) can be found by performing the necessary integration

$$\int_{t(a_0)}^{t(a)} dt = q_1 \int_{a_0}^{a} \frac{q_0}{v^2} \exp\left(-\frac{q_0}{v}\right) dv \tag{3}$$

to obtain

$$t(a) - t(a_0) = q_1 \left[\exp\left(-\frac{q_0}{a}\right) - \exp\left(-\frac{q_0}{a_0}\right)\right]. \tag{4}$$

If $a_0 = 0$, then it follows from (4) that

$$t(a) = q_1 \exp\left(-\frac{q_0}{a}\right) \tag{5}$$

or

$$a \ln t(a) = \beta_0 + \beta_1 a, \tag{6}$$

where

$$\beta_1 = \ln q_1, \beta_0 = -q_0. \tag{7}$$

Including a stochastic factor ε (say, $\varepsilon \sim N(0,\sigma^2)$) into (7), we obtain the innovative stochastic model of fatigue crack propagation

$$a \ln t(a) = \beta_0 + \beta_1 a + \varepsilon. \tag{8}$$

4 New Equation for Adaptive Planning in-Service Inspections Under Fatigue Crack Growth

Let us assume that we have a sample of k data points consisting of pairs of observed values of a and τ, say $(\tau_1, a_1), (\tau_2, a_2), \ldots, (\tau_k, a_k)$, where $k > 2$, τ_j is the time of the jth inspection, a_j is the crack size detected by means of the jth inspection, $j = 1(1)k$. Then, taking into account (8), it can be shown that the time τ_{k+1} of the next inspection is determined as

$$\tau_{k+1} = \exp\left(\frac{h_{k+1}^{(1-\alpha)}}{\tilde{a}_{k+1}}\right), \tag{9}$$

where

$$\tilde{a}_{k+1} = a_k + \Delta_k \tag{10}$$

represents an assumed value of future crack size a_{k+1} (not yet observed), $\Delta_k = \tilde{a}_{k+1} - a_k$ represents an increment of a_k,

$$h_{k+1}^{(1-\alpha)} = \hat{\beta}_0 + \hat{\beta}_1 \tilde{a}_{k+1} - t_{k-2;1-\alpha}\hat{\sigma}\left[1 + \frac{1}{k} + \frac{\left(\tilde{a}_{k+1} - \frac{1}{k}\sum_{j=1}^{k} a_j\right)^2}{(k-1)\left[\sum_{j=1}^{k} a_j^2 - \frac{1}{k}\left(\sum_{j=1}^{k} a_j\right)^2\right]}\right]^{1/2} \tag{11}$$

represents the $100(1 - \alpha)\%$ lower prediction limit for a single future value of $a_{k+1} \ln \tau_{k+1}$, $t_{n-2;1-\alpha}$ denotes the $(1 - \alpha)$ quantile of the t-distribution with $(n - 2)$ degrees of freedom,

$$\hat{\beta}_0 = \frac{1}{k}\sum_{j=1}^{k} a_j \ln \tau_j - \hat{\beta}_1 \frac{1}{k}\sum_{j=1}^{k} a_j, \quad \hat{\beta}_1 = \frac{\sum_{j=1}^{k} a_j^2 \ln \tau_j - \frac{1}{k}\left(\sum_{j=1}^{k} a_j\right)\left(\sum_{j=1}^{k} a_j \ln \tau_j\right)}{\sum_{j=1}^{k} a_j^2 - \frac{1}{k}\left(\sum_{j=1}^{k} a_j\right)^2}, \tag{12}$$

$$\hat{\sigma} = \left[\frac{1}{k-2}\sum_{j=1}^{k}(a_j \ln \tau_j - \hat{\beta}_0 - \hat{\beta}_1 a_j)^2\right]^{1/2}. \tag{13}$$

5 Numerical Example

For illustration, the procedure of inspection planning based on the innovative model (8) was used for the upper longeron of RNLAF F-16 aircraft [11] (Fig. 2).

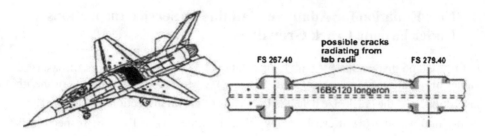

Fig. 2. Inspection points of the upper longeron of RNLAF F-16 aircraft.

Figure 3 shows the deterministic damage tolerance inspection requirements [11] for the RNLAF longerons.

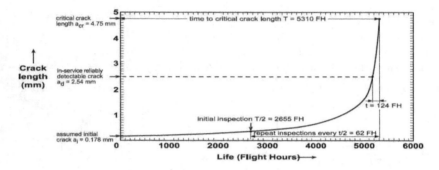

Fig. 3. Deterministic damage tolerance inspection requirements for the RNLAF longerons.

These requirements led to the following inspection scheme which includes $N_{\text{const.int.}}^{\text{inspections.}}$ = 42 inspections: (i) initial inspection after 2655 flights hours; (ii) repeat inspections every 62 flight hours. It will be noted that this inspection scheme has an unknown safety level.

Using the RNLAF longeron mean crack growth curve (Fig. 3) and the innovative stochastic model of fatigue crack propagation (8), we have obtained from (9), where the safety level was specified to be $1 - \alpha = 0.99$, $\Delta_k = 4$ mm for all k, the following in-service inspection time sequence with decreasing intervals (see Table 1).

Table 1. Inspection time sequence under fatigue crack propagation.

Inspection time (in terms of flight hours) $\tau_j, j = 1(1)12$											
τ_1	τ_2	τ_3	τ_4	τ_5	τ_6	τ_7	τ_8	τ_9	τ_{10}	τ_{11}	τ_{12}
2655	4200	4600	4800	4930	5030	5110	5170	5220	5260	5290	5310
Interval (in terms of flight hours) $\tau_{j+1} - \tau_j, j = 0(1)11, \tau_0 = 0$											
2655	1545	400	200	130	100	80	60	50	40	30	20

Graphical representation of decreasing in-service inspection intervals under crack propagation for the proposed inspection scheme (Table 1) is shown in Fig. 4. Thus, the proposed inspection scheme contains only $N_{\text{decr.int.}}^{\text{inspections}} = 12$ inspections.

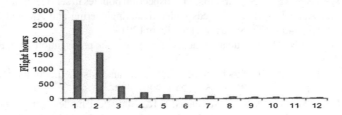

Fig. 4. Graphical representation of inspection intervals under fatigue crack propagation.

The index of relative efficiency of the inspection scheme with constant intervals as compared with the inspection scheme with decreasing intervals is given by

$$I_{\text{rel.eff.}}(N_{\text{const.int.}}^{\text{inspections}}, N_{\text{decr.int.}}^{\text{inspections}}) = N_{\text{decr.int.}}^{\text{inspections}}/N_{\text{const.int.}}^{\text{inspections}} = 12/42 = 0.29. \qquad (14)$$

The index of reduction percentage in the inspection costs for the inspection scheme with decreasing intervals as compared with the inspection scheme with constant intervals is given by

$$I_{\text{red.per.}}(N_{\text{decr.int.}}^{\text{inspections}}, N_{\text{const.int.}}^{\text{inspections}}) = [1 - I_{\text{rel.eff.}}(N_{\text{const.int.}}^{\text{inspections}}, N_{\text{decr.int.}}^{\text{inspections}})]100\% = 71\%. \qquad (15)$$

6   Conclusion

In this paper, under fatigue crack growth, the damage tolerance situation is considered. As a result of our investigations of the experimental data of fatigue crack growth, we have found that for adaptive planning in-service inspections of fatigued structures under crack propagation it can be used the approach based on a novel crack growth equation to construct more effective and accurate reliability-based inspection strategy in this case. The new technique proposed for adaptive planning in-service inspections of fatigued structures under crack propagation requires a quantile of the t-distribution and is conceptually simple and easy to use.

Acknowledgments. This research was supported in part by Grant No. 06.1936 and Grant No. 07.2036 from the Latvian Council of Science and the National Institute of Mathematics and Informatics of Latvia.

References

1. Jones, R., Molent, L., Pitt, S.: Studies in multi-site damage of fuselage lap joints. J. Theor. Appl. Fract. Mech. **32**, 18–100 (1999)

2. Munford, A.G., Shahani, A.K.: A nearly optimal inspection policy. Oper. Res. Q. **23**, 373–379 (1972)
3. Munford, A.G.: Comparison among certain inspection policies. Manage. Sci. **27**, 260–267 (1981)
4. Nechval, N.A., Nechval, K.N., Purgailis, M.: Inspection policies in service of fatigued aircraft structures. In: Ao, S.I., Gelman, L. (eds.) Electrical Engineering and Applied Computing. LNEE, vol. 90, pp. 459–472. Springer, Heidelberg (2011)
5. Lin, Y.K., Yang, J.N.: On statistical moments of fatigue crack propagation. Eng. Fract. Mech. **18**, 243–256 (1985)
6. Yang, J.N., Manning, S.D.: Stochastic crack growth analysis methodologies for metallic structures. Eng. Fract. Mech. **37**, 1105–1124 (1990)
7. Nechval, N.A., Nechval, K.N., Vasermanis, E.K.: Statistical models for prediction of the fatigue crack growth in aircraft service. In: Varvani-Farahani, A., Brebbia, C.A. (eds.) Fatigue Damage of Materials 2003, pp. 435–445. WIT Press, Southampton, Boston (2003)
8. Nechval, N.A., Nechval, K.N., Vasermanis, E.K.: Estimation of warranty period for structural components of aircraft. Aviation VIII **3**, 3–9 (2004)
9. Straub, D., Faber, M.H.: Risk based inspection planning for structural systems. Struct. Saf. **27**, 335–355 (2005)
10. Paris, R., Erdogan, F.: A critical analysis of crack propagation laws. J. Basic Eng. **85**, 528–534 (1963)
11. Military Specification, Airplane Damage Tolerance Requirements. MIL-A-83444 (USAF) (1974)

Introducing Causality in Business Rule-Based Decisions

Karim El Mernissi[1,2]($\boxtimes$), Pierre Feillet[1], Nicolas Maudet[2],
and Wassila Ouerdane[3]

[1] IBM France Lab, Gentilly, France
{kelmernissi,feillet}@fr.ibm.com
[2] Sorbonne Universités, UPMC Université Paris 6, CNRS,
LIP6 UMR 7606, Paris, France
nicolas.maudet@lip6.fr
[3] Université Paris-Saclay, CentraleSupélec, LGI, Chatenay Malabry, France
wassila.ouerdane@centralesupelec.fr

Abstract. Decision automation is expanding as many corporations capture and operate their business policies through business rules. Because laws and corporate regulations require transparency, decision automation must also provide some explanation capabilities. Most rule engines provide information about the rules that are executed, but rarely give an explanation about why those rules executed without degrading their performance. A need exists for a human readable decision trace that explains why decisions are made. This paper proposes a first approach to introduce causality to describe the existing (and sometimes hidden) relations in a decision trace of a Business Rule-Based System (BRBS). This involves a static analysis of the business rules and the construction of causal models.

Keywords: Business rules · Intelligent systems · Causal model · Automated decision · Symbolic decision-making system

1 Introduction

During the last thirty years, the development of artificial intelligence techniques and their accessibility sparked a rise in decision automation. Meanwhile, complexity of the decision logic automated by machines has increased and has been applied on large volume of data. More specifically, Business Rule Management Systems (aka. BRMS) have been widely adopted by financial services and public organizations to process, manage and record their decisions for later reference. A decision trace is composed of: (i) a request that contains the input data and potential states to take the decisions, (ii) a sequence of executed rules, with optionally details about the algorithm evaluation, (iii) an answer that contains the output data of the decision with the modified states.

Large organizations have to serialize and store billions of decisions in "decision warehouses" for legal or analytic purposes. Saving resources in the development, execution and storing phases makes a significant difference due to the

© Springer International Publishing AG 2017
S. Benferhat et al. (Eds.): IEA/AIE 2017, Part I, LNAI 10350, pp. 433–439, 2017.
DOI: 10.1007/978-3-319-60042-0_47

volume of decisions processed and recorded. The goal of such data warehouses is to keep an audit trail of all automated decisions taken by an organization. Moreover, each recorded trace is leveraged to justify how decision has been made. The ultimate objective of such tools is to present clear and precise explanations to business analysts, citizens and consumers. Delivering such explanation capabilities means that the necessary information about each decision are traced. Some challenges remain in production and exploitation of common rule engine traces to generate feedback explanations.

(1) *readability* - As simple logs of events occurred during decision processes, traces suffer from a lack of intelligibility and are not well suited for human readers.
(2) *sufficiency* - Traces may not be complete enough to answer "Why" questions. A sequence of executed rules is captured but not the information revealing the genuine causes of their eligibility.
(3) *minimality* - Traces may contain unnecessary information to justify a decision. Modification of data or rule agenda that have no impact on the outcome of a decision have no interest for the explanation. This point is important because the instrumentation of a rule engine to produce traces may significantly burden execution resources including CPU cycles and memory.
(4) *maintainability* - Common practices rely on adhoc messages added to the rules, or additional descriptions specific to the domain. This approach induces a significant cost in the development of the business rules and a recurrent maintenance cost to keep in sync the explanation material with the modified rules.

The decisions taken by BRBS are known to follow causal processes and business rules explicitly represent their reasoning logic. Because of this, causal relations can be extracted without any precise knowledge of the working of the inference engine provided that a "counterfactual aspect" is considered. Thus, identifying and capturing sufficient and minimal information to handle causation modeling is key for the adoption of a generic explanation feature. Indeed, because of the causal nature of business rules, considering the causality is a prerequisite to provide explanations that increase the transparency and the acceptance of business rule decisions. [6] claims that qualitative information increase the readability of decisions taken by rule-based systems. [2] and [5] also highlight that causal models have a strong role in the construction of explanations. These statements are illustrated by the survey of [8] where most of the expert system explanation capabilities consider causation. Like [9] the majority of research do not go deep in the definition and extraction of causal relations from BRBS and often focus on other aspects. Moreover, as defended by [1], the notion of causality is not consistent and there is a special care to have when defining what should be a causal relation.

We propose preliminary ideas of causal relations in such systems and provide a general approach of how to exploit such relations to construct causal models in BRBS. The remainder of this paper is as follows. In Sect. 2 we present some concepts on business rule-bases systems. In Sect. 3 we discuss the difficulties in defining causality in rule-based systems. Section 4 provides the first insights in building causal models in rule-based systems. Finally, we conclude in Sect. 5.

2   Concepts and Definitions

2.1   Business Rules

The most fundamental notion in Business Rule-based Systems (BRBS) is the one of *business rule*. A *business rule* is a statement of the form:

$$\text{IF } \langle c_1 \text{ AND } \cdots \text{ AND } c_m \rangle \text{ THEN } \langle a_1; \cdots; a_n \rangle$$

where the premisses is a conjunction of conditions and the consequent is a sequence of actions. Conditions are expressions that can be evaluated. Actions are typically variable assignments, and can involve various arithmetic operations. When a rule is *triggered*, the sequence of actions corresponding to its consequences is executed.

2.2   Execution and Orchestration of the Rules

Once the rules are defined, they can be executed (if their conditions are satisfied). This procedural aspect can vary, and may be controlled at different levels:

- *rulesets and ruleflow definition:* to allow high-level control of the ordering rule, business rules can be grouped in coherent sets. These "rulesets" can be attached to *tasks* that correspond to different reasoning steps of a decision process whose the organization depends on a *ruleflow*. A *ruleflow* is thus simply a directed graph that describes transitions between tasks.
- *priority among rules:* within the same ruleset, different priorities can be assigned to rules. In what follows we shall assume that the ordering is following their top to bottom ranking.
- *choice of the algorithm of execution:* there are mainly two classes of algorithms.
  - INFERENTIAL (EX. RETE): repeat the following (i) finds all eligible rules in the ruleset, rank them according to priority (ii) trigger highest priority rule, and make this rule ineligible until at least one of its conditions becomes false.
  - NON-INFERENTIAL (EX. SEQUENTIAL): trigger rules in priority order (only once), re-evaluate eligibility of rules lower in the order

Example 1. The decision is taken based on five business variables: "bankruptcy", "score", "bonus", "rate" and "eligibility". A first task called *compute* is defined for computing a rate, with the ruleset RS_1 attached to it. Another task called *evaluate* aims at evaluating a loan, with the ruleset RS_2 attached to it.

```
Business Variables:
variable bankruptcy : bankruptcy = {false,true} %input
variable score : score = [0,100] %input
variable bonus : bonus = [0,80] %input
variable eligibility : eligibility = {false,true} %output
variable rate : rate = [0,1] %output
Task compute: (RS₁)
Rule A: IF bankruptcy == false THEN score = score + 5 ;
Rule B: IF score >= 10 THEN rate = (score + bonus)/100 ;
Rule C: IF rate >= 0.2 AND score >= 12 THEN rate = rate * 2 ;
Task evaluate: (RS₂)
Rule D: IF rate < 0.6 THEN score = score - 5 ;
Rule E: IF bonus < 20 THEN rate=rate-0.1; score = score - 1 ;
Rule F: IF rate >= 0.5 THEN eligibility = TRUE ;
```

2.3   Tracing the Decision Process

Decision traces, as mentioned in the introduction, simply provide the complete list of rules triggered. Such traces may contain irrelevant information, and are not well suited to emphasize causal links (and, as a consequence, to serve as a basis for explanation). The traces we consider contain at least sufficient information about a decision to enable a "causal analysis" and has the following form:

Example 2 (Ex. 1 Cont.)

```
BEGIN DECISION
-> INPUTS (bankruptcy=false,score=8,bonus=15)
Inst.(Task compute;<bankruptcy=false,score=8,bonus=15>;...;step 1)
Inst.(Rule A;bankruptcy=false;score=13;step 2)
Inst.(Rule B;score=13;rate=0.28;step 3)
Inst.(Rule C;<rate=0.28,score=13>; rate=0.56;step 4)
Inst.(Task evaluate;rate=0.56;...;step 5)
Inst.(Rule D;rate=0.56; score=13;step 6)
Inst.(Rule E;bonus=15; <rate=0.55, score=7>;step 7)
Inst.(Rule F;rate=0.55; eligibility=true;step 8)
-> OUTPUTS (eligibility=true,rate=0.55)
END DECISION
```

Our ambition is to go beyond such traces by proposing a proper account of causality.

3   The Challenge of Causality in Rule-Based Systems

The contribution of [4] on the notion of causality has been influential in many domains, including databases [7] and specification [3]. It relies on three fundamental ideas: the first one is the *counterfactual* nature of causation: *A* causes

B if event A and event B occurred and if, had A not occurred, B would not have occurred either. The second one is the idea of *contingency*: an event is an *actual cause* if one can find a contingency (a context), where A could be a counter-factual cause for B. The third one is the idea of *minimality*: no subset of A is an actual cause of B. [4] makes this formal by introducing a setting where systems are affected by variables, either *exogeneous* (fixed by factors external to the systems) or *endogeneous* (which can serve as causes). Together, they define the signature S of the system. The behavior of the system is captured via structural equations. In our context, exogeneous variables would be variables that the decision-maker has no access to (and cannot be used as potential causes). Defining the structural equations of a rule-based system is very challenging though, because, as we have seen, there are many parameters that may affect the output: the rules themselves, the ruleflow, the ordering of rules within a rule set, and the algorithm used.

3.1   A Simplified View of Causality in Rule-Based Systems

We first approach this difficult problem by studying a notion of causality which will make a number of simplifying assumptions. One important question to ask is what events can occur in such a system, *i.e.* how the working memory can be affected:

- (v) "variable x is assigned value α",
- (c) "condition c is evaluated" (satisfied or not),
- (r) "rule R is triggered",
- (t) "task T is triggered".

The need to differentiate events (c) and (r) can be understood by recalling that some procedures do not directly trigger a rule upon evaluation of their premises (eg. FastPath). This would allow to provide causal relations mentioning this procedural level, for instance: "the fact that this procedure was used was a cause for triggering this rule". However, we shall abstract away from this level and assume that only events (v) and (c) are meaningful to the decision-maker. Thus we propose an analysis which remains independent from the ordering of the rules, and from the algorithm used. In our current contribution we distinguish three types of causal relations that may occur:

- *execution relation–* It describes the existing connection between the conditions and the actions of a business rule. This relates (c) and (v) events.
- *(in)eligibility relation–* It describes the existing connection between the modification of a parameter resulting from the action of a business rule and the (un)satisfaction of the condition of another business rule. This relates (v) and (c) events.
- *computation relation–* It describes the existing connection between an action of a business rule, and another action. This relates two (v) events.

All these notions can be interpreted under the definition of actual causes: finding a contingency such that the relation holds. For instance, for eligibility relations, it means there are circumstances under which an action makes a condition satisfied.

4   A First Approach for Modeling Causality in a BRBS

In this section we propose a first outline of the causal modeling in BRBS.

(1) A *causal model of the BRBS* is constructed thanks to the three identified causal relations: execution, (in)eligibility and computation (see Sect. 3).
After that, a *minimal causal model of the BRBS* can be obtained by removing all relationships that have no path leading to an output parameter. The
idea is to maintain only elements that have an impact on the outcomes.
Based on this, a list of decision artifacts having an influence on the output
parameters is established.

(2) A *minimal trace* of the decision can then be obtained by tracing only the
events allowed by the list of pertinent decision artifacts. Indeed, as it was
discussed in the introduction, rule engine traces may contain unnecessary
information that have no impact on the decision, thus no interest for the
explanation. For instance, the bold elements of the decision trace presented
in Sect. 2 can be removed from the trace without impacting the outcomes
variables (rate and eligibility).

(3) A *minimal causal model of a decision* is obtained by applying the *minimal
causal model of the BRBS* against a *minimal trace* of this decision. In this
paper, we will not discuss the method by which such a model is constructed.
This is an ongoing work. An example of the expected result is presented on
Fig. 1, where the nodes represent the rules (see Example 1 in Sect. 2) and the
arrows represents computation and eligibility links. We note that the nodes
related to the rule E and rule F are connected to the outcomes values of
$rate = 0.55$ and $eligibility = true$ which are not represented in the causal
network of Fig. 1.

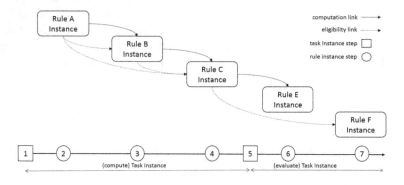

Fig. 1. An example of causal network for Example 2

5   Conclusion and Perspectives

We proposed in this work a first approach to integrate causality in BRBS. A causal representation of such systems can be used for various applications as maintenance and optimization. Here, we are interested in explaining decisions. Causal models offer an interesting framework to enhance BRBS explanation capabilities and may increase the transparency and acceptance of automated decisions. Despite the additional cost of such models, as minimal traces get only pertinent information, they can limit the extra-cost of the tracing tool at execution and save space in decision warehouses. Because of their causal nature they guarantee to keep all the information needed to provide a qualitative view of a decision process. To take a step in the direction of explanations, the ongoing works aim to (i) establish a formal representation of causal models for BRBS and (ii) provide strategies to exploit such models to answer "how" and "why" questions.

References

1. Benferhat, S., Bonnefon, J.-F., Chassy, P., Silva Neves, R., Dubois, D., Dupin de Saint-Cyr, F., Kayser, D., Nouioua, F., Nouioua-Boutouhami, S., Prade, H., Smaoui, S.: A comparative study of six formal models of causal ascription. In: Greco, S., Lukasiewicz, T. (eds.) SUM 2008. LNCS (LNAI), vol. 5291, pp. 47–62. Springer, Heidelberg (2008). doi:10.1007/978-3-540-87993-0_6
2. Besnard, P., Cordier, M.-O., Moinard, Y.: Arguments using ontological and causal knowledge. In: Beierle, C., Meghini, C. (eds.) FoIKS 2014. LNCS, vol. 8367, pp. 79–96. Springer, Cham (2014). doi:10.1007/978-3-319-04939-7_3
3. Chockler, H., Halpern, J.Y., Kupferman, O.: What causes a system to satisfy a specification? ACM Trans. Comput. Logic (TOCL) 9(3), 20 (2008)
4. Halpern, J.Y., Pearl, J.: Causes and explanations: a structural-model approach. part I: causes. Br. J. Philos. Sci. 56(4), 843–887 (2005)
5. Halpern, J.Y., Pearl, J.: Causes and explanations: a structural-model approach. part II: explanations. Br. J. Philos. Sci. 56(4), 889–911 (2005)
6. Korver, M., Lucas, P.J.: Converting a rule-based expert system into a belief network. Med. Inform. 18(3), 219–241 (1993)
7. Meliou, A., Gatterbauer, W., Halpern, J.Y., Koch, C., Moore, K.F., Suciu, D.: Causality in databases. IEEE Data Eng. Bull. 33, 59–67 (2010). (EPFL-ARTICLE-165841)
8. Moore, J.D., Swartout, W.R.: Explanation in expert systems: a survey. Technical report ISI-RR-88-228, University of Southern California (Marina del Rey, CA US) (1988)
9. Rai, V.K.: Systems approach to business rules. In: Proceedings of the 20th System Dynamics Conference (2002)

Model-Based Diagnosis in Practice: Interaction Design of an Integrated Diagnosis Application for Industrial Wind Turbines

Roxane Koitz[✉], Johannes Lüftenegger, and Franz Wotawa

Institute for Software Technology, Graz University of Technology, Graz, Austria
{rkoitz,jlueften,wotawa}@ist.tugraz.at

Abstract. Model-based diagnosis derives explanations for discrepancies between the expected and observed system behavior by relying on a formal representation of the artifact under consideration. Although its theoretical background has been established decades ago and various research prototypes have been implemented, industrial applications are sparse. This paper emphasizes the role of essential technology acceptance factors, i.e., usefulness and usability, within the context of model-based diagnosis. In particular, we develop a concept and interface design for an abductive model-based diagnosis application integrated into existing condition monitoring software for industrial wind turbines. This fault identification tool should enhance the performance of the maintenance personnel while respecting their current work processes, taking into account their particular needs, and being easy to use under the given work conditions. By employing an iterative design process, continuous feedback in regard to the users' work goals, tasks, and patterns can be included, while also considering other stakeholders' requirements. The result is a workflow and interface design proposal to be implemented in the final software product.

1 Introduction

For decades diagnostic reasoning has been investigated, with application areas ranging from the medical domain to the debugging of knowledge bases. Model-based diagnosis (MBD) has been proposed as a generally suitable method for fault identification. By exploiting a formalization of the artifact's behavior, root causes for a given set of observations can be computed. Two notions of MBD have been proposed: the traditional consistency-based variation [6] and a method utilizing abductive reasoning for deriving explanations [1]. Both forms have been explored in regard to their suitability for diverse domains, such as the automotive industry [7], space probes [8], or environmental decision support systems [9].

Authors are listed in alphabetical order.

The work presented in this paper has been supported by the SFG project EXPERT. We would further like to express our gratitude to our industrial partner, Uptime Engineering GmbH.

© Springer International Publishing AG 2017
S. Benferhat et al. (Eds.): IEA/AIE 2017, Part I, LNAI 10350, pp. 440–445, 2017.
DOI: 10.1007/978-3-319-60042-0_48

Even though various prototypes have been developed over the years, there is still a lack of MBD applications in industry. We argue that an essential aspect in successfully incorporating a new technology in practice is given little attention, namely, user acceptance. User acceptance is tightly linked to the usefulness of the product as well as its ease of use [2]. Yet, research on interface and interaction design or usability in general within the context of MBD is missing.

In this paper, we have applied iterative design to develop a concept for the user interaction and interface of an abductive MBD application within the domain of industrial wind turbines. This application field is of particular interest in regard to fault identification, as maintenance activities account for a predominant part of the overall operation cost due to system complexity and remote locations on- and offshore. In order to bridge the gap between theoretical research on MBD and its practical use, we are currently working with our industrial partner to integrate a diagnosis application into their existing condition monitoring software for wind turbines. Together with our partner and their customer, a large energy provider, we are iteratively working on a suitable workflow and graphical user interface (GUI) design for the incorporated diagnosis software.

2 Abductive Model-Based Diagnosis

In abductive MBD a representation of the faulty behavior of the system and a set of discovered anomalies is exploited to determine explanations, i.e., causes or faults, for the observed symptoms. These causes are derived by relying on the notion of logical entailment [1]. There are various approaches capable of computing abductive diagnoses such as the Assumption-based Truth Maintenance System (ATMS) [3] or SAT-based approaches [4].

Recently, we have developed a general process for abductive MBD in industrial settings based on automatically generated diagnosis models from failure assessments [5]. Once a symptom is detected, the diagnosis computation is triggered by supplying a diagnosis problem, i.e., the system description and the set of perceived observations, to the diagnosis engine. The result is a set of diagnoses, where each diagnosis consists of a set of faults. In practice a single solution is preferred; however, in the worst case an exponential number of explanations is possible. Thus, a refinement of the initial results is necessary. There are two ways to improve the diagnosis results: (1) by computing a prioritization of the solutions, e.g., based on the a priori fault probabilities or knowledge on load history and damage accumulation, and (2) by determining auxiliary information in form of measurement points, which can help discriminate diagnoses.

3 Diagnosis Application

In this section, we give an overview of the iterative user interface and interaction design process of the diagnosis software prototype. The resulting GUI proposal should later allow for a useful and usable implementation of a diagnosis application integrated into our industrial partner's condition monitoring software.

As a starting point to derive requirements and create a GUI, all stakeholders needed to be identified. The stakeholders involved in the design process were (1) the service technicians, (2) the management of the wind energy provider, and (3) our industrial partner Uptime Engineering GmbH. The technicians are the users and will operate the diagnosis software for troubleshooting from their service center and in the field. It is essential to them that the tool supports them in creating their required maintenance reports and further is intuitive and can be easily used inside a wind turbine. The energy provider plans on extending the self-maintenance activities for wind turbine plants in the future and is interested in supporting industry digitalization as well as an increase in productivity and safety. Uptime Engineering currently develops condition monitoring software for wind turbines and wants to extend their portfolio with a diagnosis software. It is essential for our partner that the abductive model can be augmented and updated. Thus, the users should be able to report new fault modes, which have not been previously contemplated. Further, the user interface should be extendable and adaptable to satisfy other customers as well as other domains for future projects.

After meetings with all stakeholders, we identified a suitable workflow (see Fig. 1). Not shown is the off-line portion, where we automatically generate an abductive diagnosis model from failure assessments provided by our partner. The diagnosis process starts once an anomaly has been detected. Wind turbines are supplied with sensors and a basic monitoring software, which produces alarms in case sensor values exceed or fall beneath certain thresholds. Uptime's condition monitoring software augments this feature by further processing this information to allow for a more accurate irregularity detection. Once a symptom has been identified, the software triggers the diagnosis computation by supplying the model as well as the observations from the wind turbine to an MBD diagnosis engine. After the initial diagnoses have been determined, they are available to the user at the *Operations Center (OC)*. Figure 2 illustrates the layout of the *OC*, where in the main panel the user can see the results of several turbine instances as well as the triggering symptoms, e.g., *Error Converter Bus*. The diagnoses are represented by a collapsible panel that contains for each diagnosis the list of possible faults. This gives the user a brief overview of the results while hiding unneeded information. The *OC* screen in Fig. 2 is designed for desktop computers, since the work assignments are distributed from the service technicians' service center. Regarding the environment within a wind turbine and the service technicians request not to carry laptops with them, we concluded that the software used in the field would be most usable on a mobile device. To guarantee a practicable interface, guidelines and best practices for mobile application design were taken into account. The prototype features a flat navigation, which ensures minimal user interaction and gives every screen a defined role in the work process of the users.

Once the service technician starts working on the problem-solving task at the turbine, he opens the *Diagnosis* screen of the mobile application, which contains the possible faults of the turbine with the calculated probabilities, providing

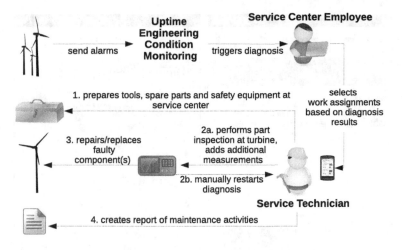

Fig. 1. Workflow of the diagnosis application

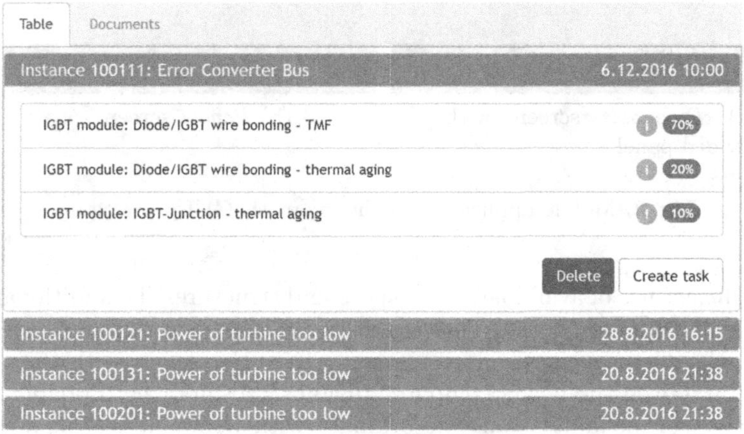

Fig. 2. *Operations Center* GUI design

a ranking of the solutions. Again the diagnoses are represented as collapsible panels. For each fault, the panel contains information about the root cause, repair/replacement tasks and a subset of the next best probing points to discriminate diagnoses. To retrieve these additional measurements, the application asks the users to answer a set of questions, which represent the computed ideal probing points (see Fig. 3a). Besides the textual description of the question, a picture is provided and additional details concerning the probe can be shown. Each question can either be confirmed (*Yes*), denied (*No*), or not answered (*?*) and the device camera can be used to separately documented each measurement; these pictures are later appended to the maintenance report. This layout

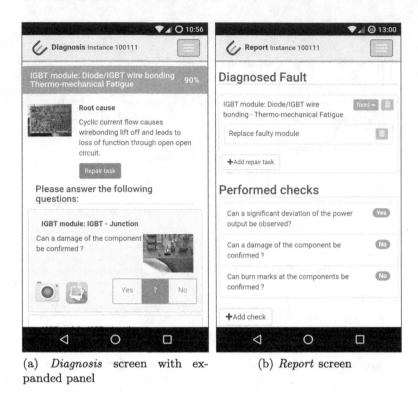

(a) *Diagnosis* screen with expanded panel

(b) *Report* screen

Fig. 3. Mobile application of the diagnosis GUI prototype

ensures efficient use of available screen space and structures the additional observation tasks to a handy batch. Once the discriminating observations have been a recorded, the diagnosis is restarted manually from the device with the updated information. Given the newly computed diagnosis results, the probabilities and arrangements of the faults change accordingly, with arrows indicating if the fault converges or not. This is depicted in Fig. 3a at the top right of the panel. The diagnoses can be refined several times until an acceptable certainty for a fault has been reached. Finally, a *Report* page gives the user the possibility to notify the system of the final confirmed diagnosis as well as additional information, e.g., consumed spare parts, performed repair or replacement, and made observations (see Fig. 3b). The maintenance task documentation is automatically generated out of the entered data and sent to the *OC*, where it is either stored or post processed.

4   Conclusion and Future Work

In this paper, we report on an iterative design process, in which we have created a GUI for an integrated MBD application for the industrial wind turbine domain. Based on a general diagnosis process and continuous evaluation and feedback from the stakeholders, we have created an interface and interaction design which should facilitate the service technicians' maintenance activities and is embedded within their existing work patterns, while being easy to use on their computing devices.

Yet, some open issues and future work remain. For instance, even after performing a repair, a failure might prevail. In this case the original fault report should be re-opened. Further, from repair actions and the knowledge on damage accumulation and load history the remaining life time of components can be used for deriving and updating fault likelihoods. To formally evaluate the design, we will perform summative usability studies on the deployed application involving the service personnel to ensure that the concept and design we have developed is in fact usable in practice.

References

1. Console, L., Dupre, D.T., Torasso, P.: On the relationship between abduction and deduction. J. Logic Comput. **1**(5), 661–690 (1991)
2. Davis, F.D.: Perceived usefulness, perceived ease of use, and user acceptance of information technology. MIS Q. **13**(3), 319–340 (1989)
3. de Kleer, J.: A general labeling algorithm for assumption-based truth maintenance. In: Proceedings of the AAAI, pp. 188–192. Morgan Kaufmann, Saint Paul, August 1988
4. Koitz, R., Wotawa, F.: Finding explanations: an empirical evaluation of abductive diagnosis algorithms. In: Proceedings of the International Conference on Defeasible and Ampliative Reasoning, pp. 36–42. CEUR-WS.org (2015)
5. Koitz, R., Wotawa, F.: Integration of failure assessments into the diagnostic process. In: Annual Conference of the Prognostics and Health Management Society (2016)
6. Reiter, R.: A theory of diagnosis from first principles. Artif. Intell. **32**(1), 57–95 (1987)
7. Struss, P., Sachenbacher, M., Carlén, C.: Insights from building a prototype for model-based on-board diagnosis of automotive systems. In: Proceedings of the International Workshop on Principles of Diagnosis (2000)
8. Williams, B.C., Nayak, P.P.: A model-based approach to reactive self-configuring systems. In: Proceedings of the Seventh International Workshop on Principles of Diagnosis, pp. 267–274 (1996)
9. Wotawa, F., Rodriguez-Roda, I., Comas, J.: Environmental decision support systems based on models and model-based reasoning. Environ. Eng. Manag. J. **9**(2), 189–195 (2010)

A New Model to Implement
a SWOT Fuzzy ANP

Mounira Souli[1(✉)], Ahmed Badreddine[2], and Taieb Ben Romdhane[1]

[1] LISI, Institut National des Sciences Appliquées et de Technologie,
Université de Carthage, Centre Urbain Nord BP 676, 1080 Tunis, Tunisia
souli.mounira1@gmail.com
[2] LARODEC, Institut Supérieur de Gestion de Tunis,
41 Avenue de la liberté, 2000 Le Bardo, Tunisia

Abstract. SWOT (i.e. Strengths, Weaknesses, Opportunities, Threats) analysis is considered as an important tool to conduct a strategic planning process by providing an internal and an external context analysis. However, these analyzes are based on the brainstorming of decision makers which may lead to subjectivity problems. Therefore, this paper aims to propose a new SWOT analysis model based on the fuzzy analytic network process (ANP) that deals with the subjectivity shortcoming.

Keywords: SWOT analysis · Fuzzy ANP · Group decision making

1 Introduction

The context analysis is performed by organization's internal and external analysis. It is the main key for a successful strategic planning process. Among the existing methods used to conduct such analysis, SWOT method is the most used one [1]. The decision makers carry out the SWOT analysis in order to: (i) build business strategies, (ii) better understand the environment and connect it to the available resources to optimize the performance and minimize the risks, (iii) map the position of the company [2]. SWOT was firstly dedicated to business and industry then the use has been extended to the community health, environment, education, tourism and even for personal growth.

Although its advantages, the researchers have neglected the subjectivity relative to the judgments of participant members, which may lead to improper strategic actions. To overcome these problems, we propose a new SWOT model based on the fuzzy ANP. This model considers the subjectivity of judgments.

The remainder of this paper is organized as follows: Sect. 2 presents the SWOT analysis method. Section 3 presents the proposed model. Section 4 provides an application of the proposed model on vehicles wires manufacturer to select the most adequate strategy.

© Springer International Publishing AG 2017
S. Benferhat et al. (Eds.): IEA/AIE 2017, Part I, LNAI 10350, pp. 446–452, 2017.
DOI: 10.1007/978-3-319-60042-0_49

2   Basics of SWOT Analysis

Through a brainstorming session, creating a SWOT analysis begins by defining the goal then identifying the sub-factors of strengths (S), weaknesses (W), opportunities (O) and threats (T) in the context of the goal. Once the sub-factors are analyzed and combined, four types of strategies are recognized: (i) SO: use the strengths to exploit the available opportunities, (ii) ST: use strengths to minimize the impact of threats, (iii) WO: improve weaknesses by taking advantage of opportunities, (iiii) WT: work on eliminating weaknesses to avoid threats [3,4].

Although its advantages and widespread use in multiple fields, the SWOT analysis has mainly three shortcomings namely: the incapability to rank the factors, sub-factors and strategies [5], the non consideration of the existing dependency, interdependency and feedback between the SWOT elements [3] and the ignorance of the imprecision aspect relative to human's judgment and the uncertainty of information [3]. To overcome these weaknesses, many researches were developed, we classified them into three categories as follows:

– To deal with the first shortcoming, researchers propose to use the Analytic Hierarchy Process (AHP) method [5]. The AHP SWOT is used in many sectors such as: the milk sector [6] and the watershed management [7].
– To treat the second shortcoming, the analytic network process (ANP) [8] was used. This technique has been utilized in the textile firm [4].
– To deal with the third shortcoming, the fuzzy set theory [9] has been integrated in various fields such as: the nuclear power plant site [2] and the aerospace industry [3].

We noticed that researches have ignored the subjectivity aspect due to the selection of a single dominant opinion. To overcome this problem, our idea is to propose a new fuzzy ANP method allowing us on one hand to deal with ranking, dependency and uncertainty problems, and on the other hand to treat the subjectivity aspect relative to SWOT analysis.

3   The Proposed SWOT Fuzzy ANP Model

As shown in Fig. 1, our model consists of four main phases detailed below.

3.1   Recognize the Decision Context

The expert team is charged to precisely define the needs and the problems in order to better understand the purpose of the decision.

3.2   Build the ANP Structure

The expert team conducts a SWOT analysis (see Sect. 2) to build the ANP structure [3,4] by according connections among the goal, the factors, the sub-factors and the strategies, in order to perform the influences of the dependency among them.

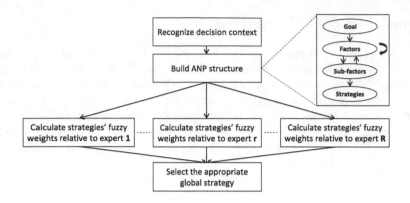

Fig. 1. SWOT fuzzy ANP proposed model

3.3   Calculate Strategies' Fuzzy Weights for Each Decision Maker

By considering the ANP structure and according to the fuzzy ANP method proposed in [3], each decision maker calculates individually the strategies' fuzzy weights.

3.4   Select the Appropriate Global Strategy

The main idea is to select the appropriate strategy based on all decision makers' individual preferences. To this end, the Group AHP technique [10] allows us to cope with subjectivity by integrating different opinions of the decision makers into one consensus result. This technique is based on computing two main compounds: the gap between the individual and the group overall alternatives' weights, and the gap between the individual and the group preferential ranks, to get the overall aggregated priority alternatives. The steps are as the following:

Step 1: Calculation of the overall strategies' weights with the consideration of the preferential differences w^{diff}.

Let W_r be the set of n strategies' weights by the rth decision maker, $W_r^t = [W_{r1}, ..W_{ri}, ..W_{rn}]$. Then, for each decision maker, determine the preferential differences between the ith and the jth strategies:

$$d_{rij} = |W_{ri} - W_{rj}| \tag{1}$$

For each decision maker r, let $W_{r.SF}$ be the vector that contains the weights of m sub-factors, where $W_{r.SF}^t = [W_{r.SF1}, ..W_{r.SFm}]$. Let a_{rij} be the vector of the pairwise comparison judgments comparing the ith and the jth strategies with respect to each mth sub-factor. The relative importance comparing the ith and the jth strategies is given by:

$$x_{rij} = W_{r.SF} \cdot a_{rij} \tag{2}$$

The aggregation matrix of the pairwise comparison for the R decision makers with the consideration of preferential differences is given by:

$$
X^{diff} = \begin{pmatrix} 1 & \cdots & \Sigma_{r=1}^{R} d_{r1n}\sqrt{\prod_{r=1}^{R} x_{r1n}^{d_{r1n}}} \\ \Sigma_{r=1}^{R} d_{r21}\sqrt{\prod_{r=1}^{R} x_{r21}^{d_{r21}}} & \cdots & \Sigma_{r=1}^{R} d_{r2n}\sqrt{\prod_{r=1}^{R} x_{r2n}^{d_{r2n}}} \\ \vdots & \ddots & \vdots \\ \Sigma_{r=1}^{R} d_{rn1}\sqrt{\prod_{r=1}^{R} x_{rn1}^{d_{rn1}}} & \cdots & 1 \end{pmatrix} \tag{3}
$$

The overall strategies' weights with the consideration of the preferential differences of the n strategies can be obtained by:

$$
W_i^{diff} = \frac{(\prod_{j=1}^{n} x_{ij}^{diff})^{1/n}}{\sum_{i=1}^{n}(\prod_{j=1}^{n} x_{ij}^{diff})^{1/n}} \tag{4}
$$

Step 2: Calculation of the overall strategies' weights with the consideration of the preferential ranks w^{rank}.

Let K_{ri} be the preferential rank of the the ith strategy assessed by the rth decision maker. Then the rank adjusting factors are calculated by: $K_{ri.adj} = \sum_{r=1}^{R} \frac{n}{K_{ri}}$. The adjusting weights with the consideration of the preferential ranks of the n strategies can be obtained by:

$$
W_i^{rank} = \frac{K_{ri.adj}}{\sum_{i=1}^{n} K_{ri.adj}} \tag{5}
$$

Step 3: Calculation of the global aggregated strategies' weights.

$$
W_{iAG} = \frac{W_i^{diff} \times W_i^{rank}}{\sum_{i=1}^{n} W_i^{diff} \times W_i^{rank}} \tag{6}
$$

Based on the global aggregated strategies' weights, the decision makers can select the best strategy.

4   Case Study

4.1   Recognize the Decision Context

The case study is a company that manufactures wires used to command airbags for vehicles [11]. To evaluate the changing environment and to take advantages of the current situation, the company decided to carry out a SWOT analysis in order to develop business strategies and to grow its market share. To this end, we set up an expert team of 5 persons representing the different departments of the company: maintenance, quality, production, logistic and an external expert in the field.

4.2 Build the ANP Structure

The expert team is charged to perform SWOT analysis. The goal is to choose the best strategy, then the sub-factors and the strategies are identified in the goal context. Table 1 represents the developed SWOT analysis results, 12 sub-factors and 4 strategies are revealed. The ANP structure was built as shown in Fig. 2.

Table 1. SWOT matrix

External factors	Internal factors	
	Strengths (S)	**Weaknesses** (W)
	- Staff experience	- Not calibrated control instruments
	- Strong leadership	- Limited machines' capability
	- Skill and versatility of staff	- frequent machinery breakdowns
Opportunities (O)	**Strategy 1 (SO)**	**Strategy 2 (WO)**
- Possibility of new markets in the automotive field	Development of the new product	Implementation of preventive and corrective maintenance system
- Encourage the investment of products for export		
- Machines' purchase free of value added tax		
Threats (O)	**Strategy 3 (ST)**	**Strategy 4 (WT)**
- Possible competition	Establishment of a system for obtaining the cost price of the products	Renewal of machines
- New regulatory requirements on products		
- Suppliers predict increases in raw material prices		

4.3 Calculate Strategies' Fuzzy Weights for Each Decision Maker

On the basis of the fuzzy ANP method [3], each decision maker conducts 18 comparison matrices and computes their relative weights. Due to lack of space, only the final results of the individual strategies' preferences are presented in Table 2.

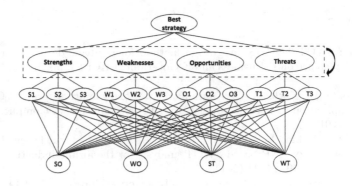

Fig. 2. The ANP structure

Table 2. Individual preferences

Strategy	DM1			DM2			DM3			DM4			DM5		
	W_{1i}^l	W_{1i}^m	W_{1i}^u	W_{2i}^l	W_{2i}^m	W_{2i}^u	W_{3i}^l	W_{3i}^m	W_{3i}^u	W_{4i}^l	W_{4i}^m	W_{4i}^u	W_{5i}^l	W_{5i}^m	W_{5i}^u
SO	0,439	0,489	0,500	0,360	0,417	0,423	0,251	0,268	0,267	0,250	0,292	0,290	0,419	0,475	0,490
WO	0,173	0,169	0,164	0,187	0,180	0,175	0,218	0,208	0,206	0,241	0,223	0,219	0,193	0,196	0,190
ST	0,228	0,207	0,204	0,269	0,253	0,256	0,344	0,368	0,374	0,236	0,217	0,219	0,208	0,195	0,190
WT	0,160	0,136	0,132	0,184	0,151	0,146	0,187	0,156	0,153	0,273	0,268	0,271	0,180	0,134	0,130

4.4 Select the Appropriate Global Strategy

The final results of each step are as follows: $(W_i^{diff})^t = [0,442; 0,147; 0,255; 0,156]$, $(W_i^{rank})^t = [0,416; 0,171; 0,253; 0,160]$, $(W_{iAG})^t = [0,615; 0,084; 0,216; 0,085]$. Based on the obtained W_{iAG}, we can conclude that strategy 1 (SO) is the best strategy, since it has the highest weight, $W_{1AG} = 0,615$.

Therefore, it can be reasonably concluded that the outcomes of the proposed model accurately reflect the general group perspective and not the subjective choices of some dominant members.

5   Conclusion

The SWOT analysis was criticized for generating only qualitative and subjective analyzes. To this end, we proposed an innovative SWOT fuzzy ANP model that attempts to treat the subjectivity problem in order to have more realistic and reliable results for more efficient decisions. In fact, this model helps to save time of long discussions and to avoid the influences and the disagreement related to the group judgments while comparing the SWOT elements.

As future works, we propose to identify and to evaluate the risks relative to the SWOT factors. This perspective can be extended to establish action plans and to manage the strategic processes of organizations. Moreover, we aim to use strategic axes in order to identify the objectives relative to organization's processes.

References

1. Ying, Y.: SWOT-TOPSIS integration method for strategic decision. In: International Conference on E-Business and E-Government (ICEE), pp. 1575–1578. IEEE (2010)
2. Ekmekioglu, M., Kutlu, A.-C., Kahraman, C.: A fuzzy multi-criteria SWOT analysis: an application to nuclear power plant site selection. Int. J. Comput. Intell. **4**, 583–595 (2011)
3. Sevkli, M., Oztekin, A., Uysal, O., Torlak, G., Turkyilmaz, A., Delen, D.: Development of a fuzzy ANP based SWOT analysis for the airline industry in Turkey. Exp. Syst. App. **39**, 14–24 (2011)
4. Yuksel, I., Dagdeviren, M.: Using the analytic network process (ANP) in a SWOT analysis-a case study for a textile firm. Inf. Sci. **177**, 3364–3382 (2007)
5. Saaty, T.L.: The Analytic Hierarchy Process. McGraw-Hill, New York (1980)
6. Erdil, A., Erbiyik, H.: Selection strategy via analytic hierarchy process: an application for a small enterprise in milk sector. Procedia Soc. Behav. Sci. **195**, 2618–2628 (2015)
7. Yavuz, F., Baycan, T.: Use of swot and analytic hierarchy process integration as a participatory decision making tool in watershed management. Procedia Technol. **8**, 134–143 (2013)
8. Saaty, T.L.: Decision Making with Dependence and Feedback: The Analytic Network Process. RWS Publications, Pittsburgh (1996)
9. Zadeh, L.A.: Fuzzy sets. Inf. Control **8**, 338–353 (1965)
10. Huang, Y.-S., Liao, J.-T., Lin, Z.-L.: A study on aggregation of group decisions. Syst. Res. Behav. Sci. **26**, 445–454 (2009)
11. Ben Romdhane, T., Badreddine, A., Sansa, M.: A new model to implement Six Sigma in small-and medium-sized enterprises. Int. J. Prod. Res. **55**, 1–22 (2016)

Knowledge Representation and Reasoning

Argumentative Approaches to Reasoning with Consistent Subsets of Premises

Ofer Arieli[1(✉)], AnneMarie Borg[2], and Christian Straßer[2]

[1] School of Computer Science,, The Academic College of Tel-Aviv, Tel-Aviv, Israel
oarieli@mta.ac.il
[2] Institute of Philosophy II, Ruhr University Bochum, Bochum, Germany

Abstract. It has been shown that entailments based on the maximally consistent subsets (MCS) of a given set of premises can be captured by Dung-style semantics for argumentation frameworks. This paper shows that these links are much tighter and go way beyond simplified forms of reasoning with MCS. Among others, we consider different types of entailments that these kinds of reasoning induce, extend the framework for arbitrary (not necessarily maximal) consistent subsets, and incorporate non-classical logics. The introduction of declarative methods for reasoning with MCS by means of (sequent-based) argumentation frameworks provides, in particular, a better understanding of logic-based argumentation and allows to reevaluate some negative results concerning the latter.

1 Introduction

Reasoning with maximally consistent subsets (MCS) is a common way of maintaining consistency when the set of premises is contradictory. This approach has gained a considerable interest since its introduction by Rescher and Manor [19]. As a result, a number of applications of this approach and its extensions (e.g., [6,9]) were considered for different AI-related areas, such as integration systems [5], belief revision consistency operators [15], and computational linguistics [16].

The relation between MCS-based reasoning and argumentation theory has been already identified in the literature (see, e.g., [1,10,22]). Recently (see [4]), it was shown that sequent-based argumentation frameworks provide a useful platform for representing and reasoning with MCS. In this work we extend the results of [4] to several related formalisms for reasoning with consistent subsets. More specifically, we show that declarative methods based on Dung's semantics for argumentation frameworks [12] can be generalized to more extended settings in which the entailment relations may be moderated, the consistent subsets may not be maximal, and the underlying logic may not be classical logic.

O. Arieli and A. Borg—Supported by the Israel Science Foundation (grant 817/15).
A. Borg and C. Straßer—Supported by the Alexander von Humboldt Foundation and the German Ministry for Education and Research.

S. Benferhat et al. (Eds.): IEA/AIE 2017, Part I, LNAI 10350, pp. 455–465, 2017.
DOI: 10.1007/978-3-319-60042-0_50

An important aspect of this work is that our generalizations allow to overcome some shortcoming of reasoning with maximal consistency by argumentation frameworks, reported in [1] (see Sect. 7). We believe that this helps to
better understand and evaluate the role of logic-based argumentation systems
in properly capturing deductive non-monotonic formalisms.

2   Sequent-Based Argumentation Frameworks

Below, we denote by $\mathcal{L}$ an arbitrary propositional language. Atomic formulas in
$\mathcal{L}$ are denoted by p, q, compound formulas are denoted by ψ, ϕ, sets of formulas
are denoted by S, T, and *finite* sets of formulas are denoted by Γ, Δ.[1]

Definition 1. A (propositional) *logic* for a language $\mathcal{L}$ is a pair $\mathfrak{L} = \langle \mathcal{L}, \vdash \rangle$,
where $\vdash$ is a (Tarskian) consequence relation for $\mathcal{L}$, that is, a binary relation
between sets of formulas and formulas in $\mathcal{L}$, which is reflexive (if $\psi \in \mathsf{S}$ then
$\mathsf{S} \vdash \psi$), monotonic (if $\mathsf{S} \vdash \psi$ and $\mathsf{S} \subseteq \mathsf{S}'$, then $\mathsf{S}' \vdash \psi$) and transitive (if $\mathsf{S} \vdash \psi$
and $\mathsf{S}', \psi \vdash \phi$, then $\mathsf{S}, \mathsf{S}' \vdash \phi$).

A logical *argument* is usually regarded as a pair $\langle \Gamma, \psi \rangle$, where Γ is the support
set of the argument and ψ is its conclusion (see, [1,7,8,14]). Since we are dealing
with arbitrary Tarskian logics, a natural representation of arguments is by the
proof theoretical notion of a *sequent* [13] (for a justification of this, see also [3]).

Definition 2. Let $\mathfrak{L} = \langle \mathcal{L}, \vdash \rangle$ be a propositional logic and S a set of $\mathcal{L}$-formulas.

- A *sequent* is an expression of the form $\Gamma \Rightarrow \Delta$, where Γ, Δ are finite sets of
  $\mathcal{L}$-formulas, and $\Rightarrow$ is a new symbol (not in $\mathcal{L}$).
- An $\mathfrak{L}$-*argument* (or just *argument*) is a sequent $\Gamma \Rightarrow \{\psi\}$, where $\Gamma \vdash \psi$.
- An *argument based on* S is a sequent $\Gamma \Rightarrow \{\psi\}$, for which $\Gamma \subseteq \mathsf{S}$. The set of
  all the $\mathfrak{L}$-arguments that are based on S is denoted $\mathsf{Arg}_{\mathfrak{L}}(\mathsf{S})$.

In what follows we shall omit the set signs around the premises and conclusions
of arguments. We denote: $\mathsf{Prem}(\Gamma \Rightarrow \psi) = \Gamma$ and $\mathsf{Con}(\Gamma \Rightarrow \psi) = \psi$. For a set $\mathcal{S}$
of arguments, $\mathsf{Prem}(\mathcal{S}) = \bigcup \{\mathsf{Prem}(s) \mid s \in \mathcal{S}\}$ and $\mathsf{Con}(\mathcal{S}) = \bigcup \{\mathsf{Con}(s) \mid s \in \mathcal{S}\}$.

We shall use standard *sequent calculi* [13] for constructing arguments from
simpler arguments. This is done by *inference rules* of the following form:

$$\frac{\Gamma_1 \Rightarrow \Delta_1 \ \ldots \ \Gamma_n \Rightarrow \Delta_n}{\Gamma \Rightarrow \Delta}. \tag{1}$$

We shall say that the sequents $\Gamma_i \Rightarrow \Delta_i$ $(i = 1, \ldots, n)$ are the *conditions* (or the
prerequisites) of the rule in (1) and that $\Gamma \Rightarrow \Delta$ is its *conclusion*.

Attack rules in our case allow for the elimination (discharging) of sequents.
We shall denote by $\Gamma \not\Rightarrow \psi$ the elimination of the sequent $\Gamma \Rightarrow \psi$. Alternatively, $\overline{s}$

---

[1] Thus, unlike Γ, Δ, when S, T are assumed to be finite, this will be indicated explicitly.

denotes the elimination of s. Now, a *sequent elimination rule* (or an *attack rule*) is a rule of the following form:

$$\frac{\Gamma_1 \Rightarrow \Delta_1 \ \ldots \ \Gamma_n \Rightarrow \Delta_n}{\Gamma_n \not\Rightarrow \Delta_n}. \tag{2}$$

The prerequisites of attack rules usually consist of three ingredients. The first sequent in the rule's prerequisites is the "attacking" sequent, the last sequent in the rule's prerequisites is the "attacked" sequent, and the other prerequisites are the conditions for the attack. Conclusions of elimination rules are the eliminations of the attacked arguments.

Example 1. The following rule is known as Undercut (abbreviation: Ucut):

$$\frac{\Gamma_1 \Rightarrow \psi_1 \quad \Rightarrow \psi_1 \leftrightarrow \neg \bigwedge \Gamma_2' \quad \Gamma_2, \Gamma_2' \Rightarrow \psi_2}{\Gamma_2, \Gamma_2' \not\Rightarrow \psi_2}.$$

This rule intuitively reflects the idea that an argument attacks another argument when the conclusion of the former contradicts some premises of the latter. We refer to [7,8,14,17] for other attack rules and to [3] for their representations by sequents. Further elimination rules for normative reasoning and deontic logics can be found in [20].

Given two arguments s_1 and s_2 in $\mathsf{Arg}_{\mathfrak{L}}(\mathsf{S})$ and an elimination rule $\mathcal{R}$, we say that s_1 $\mathcal{R}$-*attacks* s_2 if s_1 is in the form of the attacker of $\mathcal{R}$, s_2 is in the form of the attacked sequent of $\mathcal{R}$, and all the conditions in $\mathcal{R}$ hold (i.e., are provable by the underlying sequent calculus).

Example 2. Let $\mathsf{S} = \{p, \neg p, q\}$ and denote classical logic by CL. Then $p \Rightarrow p$ and $\neg p \Rightarrow \neg p$ are both in $\mathsf{Arg}_{\mathsf{CL}}(\mathsf{S})$ and each one Undercut-attacks the other one.

Our setting induces an argumentation framework in the sense of Dung [12]:

Definition 3. Given a set S of $\mathcal{L}$-formulas, a *sequent-based argumentation framework* for S (induced by a logic $\mathfrak{L} = \langle \mathcal{L}, \vdash \rangle$, a sequent calculus $\mathfrak{C}$ for $\mathfrak{L}$, and a set $\mathfrak{A}$ of attack rules) is the pair $\mathcal{AF}(\mathsf{S}) = \langle \mathsf{Arg}_{\mathfrak{L}}(\mathsf{S}), Attack \rangle$, where $(s_1, s_2) \in Attack$ iff s_1 $\mathcal{R}$-attacks s_2 for some $\mathcal{R} \in \mathfrak{A}$.[2]

Following Dung [12], to define the sets of arguments (called *extensions*), the elements of which can collectively be accepted from a given sequent-based framework $\mathcal{AF}(\mathsf{S}) = \langle \mathsf{Arg}_{\mathfrak{L}}(\mathsf{S}), Attack \rangle$, we first extend the notion of attack to sets of arguments. A set $\mathcal{S} \subseteq \mathsf{Arg}_{\mathfrak{L}}(\mathsf{S})$ *attacks* an argument t if there is an argument $s \in \mathcal{S}$ that attacks t (i.e., $(s, t) \in Attack$). The set of arguments that are attacked by $\mathcal{S}$ is denoted $\mathcal{S}^+$. We say that $\mathcal{S}$ *defends* s if $\mathcal{S}$ attacks every argument t that attacks s.

Now, $\mathcal{S}$ is called *conflict-free* (in $\mathcal{AF}(\mathsf{S})$) if it does not attack any of its elements (i.e., $\mathcal{S}^+ \cap \mathcal{S} = \emptyset$), $\mathcal{S}$ is an *admissible extension* of $\mathcal{AF}(\mathsf{S})$ if it is

---

[2] Somewhat abusing the notations, we shall sometimes identify *Attack* with $\mathfrak{A}$.

conflict-free and defends all of its elements, and $\mathcal{S}$ is a *complete extension* of $\mathcal{AF}(S)$ if it is admissible and contains all the arguments that it defends.

The minimal complete extension of $\mathcal{AF}(S)$ is called the *grounded extension* of $\mathcal{AF}(S)$, and a maximal complete extension $\mathcal{AF}(S)$ is called a *preferred extension* of $\mathcal{AF}(S)$. A complete extension $\mathcal{AF}(S)$ is called a *stable extension* of $\mathcal{AF}(S)$ if $\mathcal{S} \cup \mathcal{S}^+ = \mathsf{Arg}_{\mathfrak{L}}(S)$. We write $\mathsf{Adm}(\mathcal{AF}(S))$ [respectively: $\mathsf{Cmp}(\mathcal{AF}(S))$, $\mathsf{Prf}(\mathcal{AF}(S))$, $\mathsf{Stb}(\mathcal{AF}(S))$] for the set of all the admissible [respectively: complete, preferred, stable] extensions of $\mathcal{AF}(S)$. Similarly, $\mathsf{Grd}(\mathcal{AF}(S))$ denotes the unique grounded extension of $\mathcal{AF}(S)$.

Example 3. Figure 1 depicts part of an argumentation framework for the set $S = \{p, \neg p, q\}$, based on classical logic, where Undercut is the single attack rule.

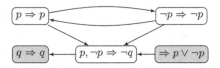

Fig. 1. (Part of the) argumentation framework for Example 3

Note that the gray-colored rightmost node is non-attacked since it has an empty support set. That node counter attacks any attacker of the other gray-colored node, whose sequent is $q \Rightarrow q$, because any argument in $\mathsf{Arg}_{\mathsf{CL}}(S)$ whose conclusion is logically equivalent to $\neg q$ must contain both p and $\neg p$ in its support set. It follows that the gray-colored nodes of the figure are in the grounded extension (and so in every complete extension) of $\mathsf{Arg}_{\mathsf{CL}}(S)$.

3   Reasoning with Maximally Consistent Subsets

As indicated previously, our primary goal in this work is to provide argumentative approaches for reasoning with inconsistent premises by their (maximally) consistent subsets. This may be represented as follows:

Definition 4. Let S be a set of formulas. We denote by $\mathsf{Cn}(S)$ the transitive closure of S with respect to classical logic and by $\mathsf{MCS}(S)$ the set of all the maximally consistent subsets of S (where maximality is taken with respect to the subset relation). We denote:

- $S \mid\!\sim_{\mathsf{mcs}} \psi$ iff $\psi \in \mathsf{Cn}(\bigcap \mathsf{MCS}(S))$.
- $S \mid\!\sim_{\cup\mathsf{mcs}} \psi$ iff $\psi \in \bigcup_{T \in \mathsf{MCS}(S)} \mathsf{Cn}(T)$.

Example 4. Consider the theory $S = \{p, \neg p, q\}$. Since $\mathsf{MCS}(S) = \{\{p, q\}, \{\neg p, q\}\}$, every formula in S follows according to $\mid\!\sim_{\cup\mathsf{mcs}}$ from S, but (unlike classical logic!) $S \not\mid\!\sim_{\cup\mathsf{mcs}} r$ and $S \not\mid\!\sim_{\cup\mathsf{mcs}} p \wedge \neg p$. Note that $\mid\!\sim_{\mathsf{mcs}}$ is more cautious than $\mid\!\sim_{\cup\mathsf{mcs}}$, and it does not allow to infer p nor $\neg p$ from S. Still, we have, e.g., that $S \mid\!\sim_{\mathsf{mcs}} q$, since $q \in \bigcap \mathsf{MCS}(S)$.

The entailments $\mathrel{\vdash\!\!\!\sim}_{\mathsf{mcs}}$ and $\mathrel{\vdash\!\!\!\sim}_{\cup\mathsf{mcs}}$ are sometimes called "free" and "existential", respectively. Next, we recall the two argumentation-based approaches, introduced in [4], for computing these entailments.

Definition 5. Let $\mathcal{AF}(\mathsf{S}) = \langle \mathsf{Arg}_{\mathfrak{L}}(\mathsf{S}), Attack \rangle$. We denote $\mathsf{S} \mathrel{\vdash\!\!\!\sim}_{\mathsf{gr}} \psi$ if there is an $s \in \mathsf{Grd}(\mathcal{AF}(\mathsf{S}))$ such that $\mathsf{Con}(s) = \psi$. The entailments $\mathrel{\vdash\!\!\!\sim}_{\cap\mathsf{prf}}, \mathrel{\vdash\!\!\!\sim}_{\cup\mathsf{prf}}, \mathrel{\vdash\!\!\!\sim}_{\cap\mathsf{stb}}$ and $\mathrel{\vdash\!\!\!\sim}_{\cup\mathsf{stb}}$ are defined similarly, where $\mathsf{Grd}(\mathcal{AF}(\mathsf{S}))$ is replaced, respectively, by $\bigcap \mathsf{Prf}(\mathcal{AF}(\mathsf{S})), \bigcup \mathsf{Prf}(\mathcal{AF}(\mathsf{S})), \bigcap \mathsf{Stb}(\mathcal{AF}(\mathsf{S}))$, and $\bigcup \mathsf{Stb}(\mathcal{AF}(\mathsf{S}))$.

Proposition 1. [4] *Let S be a set of formulas and ψ a formula. Consider the sequent-based argumentation framework $\mathcal{AF}(\mathsf{S})$ for S, induced by classical logic, Gentzen's sequent calculus LK for it [13], and Undercut (Example 1) as the sole attack rule. Then:*

1. *$\mathsf{S} \mathrel{\vdash\!\!\!\sim}_{\mathsf{gr}} \psi$ iff $\mathsf{S} \mathrel{\vdash\!\!\!\sim}_{\cap\mathsf{prf}} \psi$ iff $\mathsf{S} \mathrel{\vdash\!\!\!\sim}_{\cap\mathsf{stb}} \psi$ iff $\mathsf{S} \mathrel{\vdash\!\!\!\sim}_{\mathsf{mcs}} \psi$.*
2. *$\mathsf{S} \mathrel{\vdash\!\!\!\sim}_{\cup\mathsf{prf}} \psi$ iff $\mathsf{S} \mathrel{\vdash\!\!\!\sim}_{\cup\mathsf{stb}} \psi$ iff $\mathsf{S} \mathrel{\vdash\!\!\!\sim}_{\cup\mathsf{mcs}} \psi$.*

Example 5. Let $\mathsf{S} = \{p, \neg p, q\}$. By the discussion in Examples 3 and 4, $\mathsf{S} \mathrel{\vdash\!\!\!\sim}_{\mathsf{mcs}} q$, $\mathsf{S} \mathrel{\vdash\!\!\!\sim}_{\mathsf{gr}} q$, $\mathsf{S} \mathrel{\vdash\!\!\!\sim}_{\cap\mathsf{prf}} q$, and $\mathsf{S} \mathrel{\vdash\!\!\!\sim}_{\cap\mathsf{stb}} q$. By Proposition 1, this is not a coincidence.

4   Generalization I: More Moderated Entailments

Let $\mathsf{S}' = \{p \wedge q, \neg p \wedge q\}$. Here, $\bigcap \mathsf{MCS}(\mathsf{S}') = \emptyset$, and so only tautological formulas follow according to $\mathrel{\vdash\!\!\!\sim}_{\mathsf{mcs}}$ from S'. Yet, one may argue that in this case formulas in $\mathsf{Cn}(\{q\})$ should also follow from S', since they follow according to classical logic from every set in $\mathsf{MCS}(\mathsf{S}')$. This gives rise to the following variation of $\mathrel{\vdash\!\!\!\sim}_{\mathsf{mcs}}$.

Definition 6. Given a set S of formulas and a formula ψ, we denote by $\mathsf{S} \mathrel{\vdash\!\!\!\sim}_{\cap\mathsf{mcs}} \psi$ that $\psi \in \bigcap_{\mathsf{T} \in \mathsf{MCS}(\mathsf{S})} \mathsf{Cn}(\mathsf{T})$.

Note 1. Clearly, if $\mathsf{S} \mathrel{\vdash\!\!\!\sim}_{\mathsf{mcs}} \psi$ then $\mathsf{S} \mathrel{\vdash\!\!\!\sim}_{\cap\mathsf{mcs}} \psi$. However, as noted in the discussion before Definition 6, the converse does not hold. Indeed, $\mathsf{S}' \mathrel{\vdash\!\!\!\sim}_{\cap\mathsf{mcs}} q$ while $\mathsf{S}' \mathrel{\not\vdash\!\!\!\sim}_{\mathsf{mcs}} q$.

For characterizing $\mathrel{\vdash\!\!\!\sim}_{\cap\mathsf{mcs}}$ in terms of Dung-style semantics we need to revise the set of arguments as follows: Let $\mathfrak{L} = \langle \mathcal{L}, \vdash \rangle$ be a logic, then

$$\mathsf{Arg}_{\mathfrak{L}}^{\star}(\mathsf{S}) = \{\psi \Rightarrow \phi \mid \psi \vdash \phi \text{ and } \psi = \bigvee_{1 \le i \le n} \bigwedge \Gamma_i, \text{ where } \forall_i \Gamma_i \subseteq \mathsf{S}\}.$$

Note that the definition of $\mathsf{Arg}_{\mathfrak{L}}^{\star}(\mathsf{S})$ resembles that of $\mathsf{Arg}_{\mathfrak{L}}(\mathsf{S})$ using a different form of support sets. Intuitively, this is explained by the need to provide in the support set different alternatives for deriving the conclusion of the argument, according to the more moderated entailment $\mathrel{\vdash\!\!\!\sim}_{\cap\mathsf{mcs}}$.

Example 6. Consider again the set $\mathsf{S}' = \{p \wedge q, \neg p \wedge q\}$. Then, e.g., $p \wedge q \Rightarrow q$, $\neg p \wedge q \Rightarrow q$ and $(p \wedge q) \vee (\neg p \wedge q) \Rightarrow q$ are all in $\mathsf{Arg}_{\mathfrak{L}}^{\star}(\mathsf{S}')$. Note that while the first two sequents are also in $\mathsf{Arg}_{\mathfrak{L}}(\mathsf{S}')$, the last one is not.

Now, for sem $\in \{\mathsf{grd}, \cap\mathsf{prf}, \cap\mathsf{stb}\}$, we define $\vdash^*_{\mathsf{sem}}$ just as $\vdash_{\mathsf{sem}}$ (Definition 5), where $\mathcal{AF}(\mathsf{S}) = \langle \mathsf{Arg}_{\mathfrak{L}}(\mathsf{S}), Attack \rangle$ is substituted by $\mathcal{AF}^*(\mathsf{S}) = \langle \mathsf{Arg}^*_{\mathfrak{L}}(\mathsf{S}), Attack \rangle$. Like Proposition 1, these Dung-style semantics may be used for characterizing the MCS-based entailments under consideration.

Proposition 2. *Let* S *be a finite set of formulas and* ψ *a formula. Consider the sequent-based argumentation framework* $\mathcal{AF}^*(\mathsf{S})$ *for* S, *induced by classical logic, Gentzen's sequent calculus LK for it, and Undercut as the sole attack rule. Then:* $\mathsf{S} \vdash^*_{\mathsf{gr}} \psi$ *iff* $\mathsf{S} \vdash^*_{\cap\mathsf{prf}} \psi$ *iff* $\mathsf{S} \vdash^*_{\cap\mathsf{stb}} \psi$ *iff* $\mathsf{S} \vdash_{\cap\mathsf{mcs}} \psi$.

Outline of proof. Given a finite set S of formulas, we let: $\mathsf{S}^{\wedge} = \{\bigwedge \Gamma \mid \Gamma \subseteq \mathsf{S}\}$ and $\mathsf{S}^{\star} = \{\Psi_1 \vee \ldots \vee \Psi_n \mid \Psi_1, \ldots, \Psi_n \in \mathsf{S}^{\wedge}\}$. Then, for every sem $\in \{\mathsf{grd}, \cap\mathsf{prf}, \cap\mathsf{stb}\}$ it can be shown that $\mathsf{S} \vdash_{\cap\mathsf{mcs}} \phi$ iff $\mathsf{S}^{\star} \vdash_{\cap\mathsf{mcs}} \phi$ iff $\mathsf{S}^{\star} \vdash_{\mathsf{mcs}} \phi$ iff $\mathsf{S}^{\star} \vdash_{\mathsf{sem}} \phi$ iff $\mathsf{S} \vdash^*_{\mathsf{sem}} \phi$, and so the proposition is obtained.   □

5   Generalization II: Lifting Subset Maximality

Next, we consider the following strengthening, by Benferhat, Dubois and Prade [6], of the entailment relation from Definition 4.

Definition 7. Given a set S of propositions and a formula ϕ, we denote by $\mathsf{S} \Vdash_{\mathsf{mcs}} \phi$ that: (1) $\mathsf{T} \vdash_{\mathsf{CL}} \phi$ for some consistent subset T of S, and (2) There is no consistent subset T' of S such that $\mathsf{T}' \vdash_{\mathsf{CL}} \neg\phi$.

To see how the entailment relation of the last definition is represented in sequent-based argumentation frameworks, let us denote by $\Vdash_{\mathsf{gr}}$ the entailment that is defined like $\vdash_{\mathsf{gr}}$ (Definition 5), except that instead of Undercut the attack relations are the following[3]:

Consistency Undercut (ConUcut): $\dfrac{\Rightarrow \neg\bigwedge\Gamma'_2 \qquad \Gamma_2, \Gamma'_2 \Rightarrow \psi_2}{\Gamma_2, \Gamma'_2 \not\Rightarrow \psi_2}$

Defeating Rebuttal (DefReb): $\dfrac{\Gamma_1 \Rightarrow \psi_1 \qquad \Rightarrow \psi_1 \supset \neg\psi_2 \qquad \Gamma_2 \Rightarrow \psi_2}{\Gamma_2 \not\Rightarrow \psi_2}$

Again, $\Vdash_{\mathsf{mcs}}$-entailments are characterized by Dung's semantics as follows:

Proposition 3. *For a finite set* S *of formulas and a formula* ψ, *we have that* $\mathsf{S} \Vdash_{\mathsf{mcs}} \psi$ *iff* $\mathsf{S} \Vdash_{\mathsf{gr}} \psi$.

Proof. If $\mathsf{S} \Vdash_{\mathsf{mcs}} \psi$ then $\mathsf{T} \vdash_{\mathsf{CL}} \psi$ for some $\mathsf{T} \in \mathsf{MCS}(\mathsf{S})$ and there is no $\mathsf{T}' \in \mathsf{MCS}(\mathsf{S})$ such that $\mathsf{T}' \vdash_{\mathsf{CL}} \neg\psi$. Thus, $s = \Delta \Rightarrow \psi \in \mathsf{Arg}(\mathsf{S})$ for some finite $\Delta \subseteq \mathsf{T}$. Since Δ is consistent, s is not ConUcut-attacked. To see that s is defended from any DefReb-attack, suppose that $\Gamma' \Rightarrow \neg\psi \in \mathsf{Arg}(\mathsf{S})$. Then $\Gamma' \vdash_{\mathsf{CL}} \neg\psi$, thus Γ' is an inconsistent finite subset of S. It follows that $\Rightarrow \neg\bigwedge\Gamma' \in \mathsf{Arg}(\mathsf{S})$. Clearly,

---

[3] To prevent attacks on tautologies, in Defeating Rebuttal we assume that $\Gamma_2 \neq \emptyset$.

$\Rightarrow \neg \bigwedge \Gamma' \in \mathsf{Arg}(\mathsf{S}) \setminus \mathsf{Arg}(\mathsf{S})^+$, and so indeed any DefReb-attacker of s is counter-ConUcut-attacked by an argument in $\mathsf{Arg}(\mathsf{S})$ (which itself is not attacked), thus s is defended. It follows, then, that $s \in \mathsf{Grd}(\mathcal{AF}(\mathsf{S}))$.

Suppose now that $\mathsf{S} \not\Vdash_{\mathsf{mcs}} \psi$. This means that either there is no $\mathsf{T} \in \mathsf{MCS}(\mathsf{S})$ such that $\mathsf{T} \vdash_{\mathsf{CL}} \psi$, or otherwise there is a set $\mathsf{T} \in \mathsf{MCS}(\mathsf{S})$ such that $\mathsf{T} \vdash_{\mathsf{CL}} \neg\psi$. In the first case the only sequents s such that $\mathsf{Prem}(s) \subseteq \mathsf{S}$ and $\mathsf{Cons}(s) = \psi$ are those for which $\Rightarrow \neg \bigwedge \Gamma$ is provable in LK, where $\Gamma \subseteq \mathsf{Prem}(s)$. Hence, all of these sequents are not members of any admissible extension of $\mathcal{AF}(\mathsf{S})$. In the second case we can construct an admissible extension $\mathcal{E}$ such that $s \in \mathcal{E}^+$ for any $s = \Delta \Rightarrow \psi \in \mathsf{Arg}(\mathsf{S})$ by letting $\mathcal{E} = \mathsf{Arg}(\mathsf{T})$. It is easy to verify that $\mathcal{E} \in \mathsf{Adm}(\mathcal{AF}(\mathsf{S}))$, thus $s \notin \mathsf{Grd}(\mathcal{AF}(\mathsf{S}))$. $\square$

6 Generalization III: Beyond Classical Logic

In this section we consider base logics that may not be classical. In this context we also introduce generalized definitions for consistency.

Extending the setting to arbitrary propositional Tarskian logics (Definition 1) is straightforward, as the sequent-based frameworks described in the second section may be based on any such logic. The extended settings allow to introduce more expressive arguments (involving, for instance, modal operators) or exclude unwanted arguments (like $\neg\neg\psi \Rightarrow \psi$, which is unacceptable by intuitionists).

Example 7. Let $\mathsf{S} = \{p, q, \neg(p \wedge q)\}$. When classical logic is the base logic each pair of assertions in S initiates an Undercut-attack on the sequent corresponding to the third assertion. For instance, $p, \neg(p \wedge q) \Rightarrow \neg q$ Ucut-attacks $q \Rightarrow q$.

Suppose now that the base logic is Priest's 3-valued paraconsistent logic LP [18]. This time, while $\neg(p \wedge q) \Rightarrow \neg(p \wedge q)$ is still attacked (by $p, q \Rightarrow p \wedge q$), the sequents $p \Rightarrow p$ and $q \Rightarrow q$ are not attacked by Ucut, since in LP sequents of the form $p, \neg(p \wedge q) \Rightarrow \neg q$ are *not* derivable.

For extending the condition of consistency we introduce the following notion:

Definition 8. Let $\varrho(\mathcal{L})$ be the set of the finite sets of the formulas in $\mathcal{L}$. A function $g : \varrho(\mathcal{L}) \to \mathcal{L}$ is called *cautiously $\vdash$-reversing* if the following two properties are satisfied:

$\vdash$-monotonicity: If $\Gamma \vdash g(\Delta)$ then $\Gamma \vdash g(\Delta \cup \Delta')$.

$\vdash$-reversibility: If $\Gamma, \Sigma \vdash g(\Sigma \cup \Delta)$ then $\Gamma \vdash g(\Sigma \cup \Delta)$.

Example 8. Let $g(\Gamma) = \bigvee_{\psi \in \Gamma} \neg\psi$. It can be shown that g is cautiously reversing with respect to different many-valued logics, among which are Priest's LP (mentioned above), Post's many-valued systems with a single designated element, and Łukasiewicz m-valued logics L_m, where the truth values are linearly ordered and no more than the top $\frac{m}{2}$-ones are designated (see [21, pages 252 and 260]).

Frequently, the conditions of the attack rules considered e.g. in [7,8,14,17] are violated in logics that do not respect (at least one of) the standard negation rules of LK (i.e., if $\Gamma \Rightarrow \psi, \Delta$ then $\Gamma, \neg\psi \Rightarrow \Delta$ and if $\Gamma, \psi \Rightarrow \Delta$ then $\Gamma \Rightarrow \neg\psi, \Delta$), in which cases alternative negation rules often operate on one side of the sequents. One way to reflect this in our case is to consider confluence of premises in the attacking and the attacked sequents:

Definition 9. Let g be a cautiously $\vdash$-reversing function. For $\Gamma_1' \cup \Gamma_2' \neq \emptyset$ and $\gamma = g(\Gamma_1' \cup \Gamma_2')$, we define:

$$\text{Confluent } g\text{-Undercut: } \frac{\Gamma_1, \Gamma_1' \Rightarrow \psi_1 \quad \psi_1 \Rightarrow \gamma \quad \gamma \Rightarrow \psi_1 \quad \Gamma_2, \Gamma_2' \Rightarrow \psi_2}{\Gamma_2, \Gamma_2' \not\Rightarrow \psi_2}.$$

We denote by $\vdash^g_{gr}, \vdash^g_{\cap prf}, \vdash^g_{\cap stb}, \vdash^g_{\cup prf}$ and $\vdash^g_{\cup stb}$, the counterparts, for a logic $\mathfrak{L}$, of the entailments in Definition 5, where the attack relation of the underlying sequent-based argumentation framework is Confluent g-Undercut.

Next, we characterize the above entailments in terms of the following generalizations of maximally consistent subsets, based on $\vdash$-reversing functions.

Definition 10. Let $g : \varrho(\mathcal{L}) \to \mathcal{L}$, and $\Sigma_1, \Sigma_2 \in \varrho(\mathcal{L})$.

- Σ_1, Σ_2 are g-reversible, if $\Sigma_1 \vdash g(\Sigma_2)$ or $\Sigma_2 \vdash g(\Sigma_1)$.
- Σ_1, Σ_2 are g-coherent, if there are no subsets Σ_1' and Σ_2' of Σ_1 and Σ_2 that are g-reversible.
- $\Sigma \in \varrho(\mathcal{L})$ is g-coherent if so are every $\Sigma_1, \Sigma_2 \subseteq \Sigma$.
- A g-coherent set Σ is *maximal*, if none of its proper supersets is g-coherent. We denote by $\mathsf{MAX}_g(\mathsf{S})$ the set of the maximally g-coherent subsets of S.

Note 2. If $\Sigma_1, \Sigma_2 \in \varrho(\mathcal{L})$ are g-reversible, then (without loss of generality) $\Sigma_1 \vdash g(\Sigma_2)$. By monotonicity, $\Sigma_1 \vdash g(\Sigma_1 \cup \Sigma_2)$ and so by $\vdash$-reversibility, $\vdash g(\Sigma_1 \cup \Sigma_2)$. It follows that g-coherence makes sense only for logics that have tautologies (like CL and LP). In the rest of this section we thus restrict ourselves to such logics.

Example 9. Consider the logic LP and the cautiously reversing function $g(\Gamma) = \bigvee_{\psi \in \Gamma} \neg\psi$, considered in Example 8. For $\mathsf{S} = \{p, q, \neg(p \wedge q)\}$ (Example 7) we have that $\mathsf{MAX}_g(\mathsf{S}) = \{\{p, q\}, \{p, \neg(p \wedge q)\}, \{q, \neg(p \wedge q)\}\}$.

Note that while the elements in $\mathsf{MAX}_g(\mathsf{S})$ are the same as the maximally consistent subsets of S with respect to classical logic, the setting in Example 9 is different from the one that is based on classical logic and Undercut. Indeed,

1. Since LP is weaker than CL, the extensions of the current framework are $\subseteq$-smaller than those of the CL-based framework. For instance, we have that $p, \neg(p \wedge q) \Rightarrow \neg q \in \mathsf{Arg}_{\mathsf{CL}}(\mathsf{S})$ while $p, \neg(p \wedge q) \Rightarrow \neg q \notin \mathsf{Arg}_{\mathsf{LP}}(\mathsf{S})$.
2. The use of Undercut instead of Confluent g-Undercut is not appropriate for LP, since the extensions for the framework with Undercut (unlike those of the framework with Confluent g-Undercut) are not closed under LP-inferences.

Definition 11. Let g be a $\vdash$-reversing function and S a set of formulas, and let $\mathsf{Cn}_\vdash(\mathsf{S})$ be the transitive closure of S with respect to $\vdash$. We denote:

- $S \hspace{0.1em}\vdash\hspace{-0.5em}\sim_{\mathsf{MAX}g} \psi$ iff $\psi \in \mathsf{Cn}_\vdash(\bigcap \mathsf{MAX}_g(S))$.
- $S \hspace{0.1em}\vdash\hspace{-0.5em}\sim_{\cup\mathsf{MAX}g} \psi$ iff $\psi \in \bigcup_{T \in \mathsf{MAX}_g(S)} \mathsf{Cn}_\vdash(T)$.

Next we show that the correspondence between Dung's semantics and MCS-reasoning carries on to non-classical logics (proof is omitted due to lack of space).

Proposition 4. *Let g be a $\vdash$-reversing function and S a set of formulas. Then:*

1. $S \hspace{0.1em}\vdash\hspace{-0.5em}\sim^g_{\mathsf{gr}} \psi$ *iff* $S \hspace{0.1em}\vdash\hspace{-0.5em}\sim^g_{\cap\mathsf{prf}} \psi$ *iff* $S \hspace{0.1em}\vdash\hspace{-0.5em}\sim^g_{\cap\mathsf{stb}} \psi$ *iff* $S \hspace{0.1em}\vdash\hspace{-0.5em}\sim_{\mathsf{MAX}g} \psi$.
2. $S \hspace{0.1em}\vdash\hspace{-0.5em}\sim^g_{\cup\mathsf{prf}} \psi$ *iff* $S \hspace{0.1em}\vdash\hspace{-0.5em}\sim^g_{\cup\mathsf{stb}} \psi$ *iff* $S \hspace{0.1em}\vdash\hspace{-0.5em}\sim_{\cup\mathsf{MAX}g} \psi$.

7   Discussion, In View of Related Work

In this paper we have introduced a series of generalizations of the work in [4], concerning the relations between Dung-style semantics for argumentation frameworks. The relations between these two formalisms have already been investigated in [10] and then in [1,22]. Our approach extends these works in several ways, the most significant ones are the following:

1. In [10,22] the base logic is classical logic. Here (as well as in [1], which continues the work in [10]), *any* propositional language and Tarskian logic is supported. This allows, for instance, to include modal operators in arguments and use paraconsistent logics [11] as the underlying platform for reasoning.

2. According to [1,22] (following [7]), the support of an argument s must be a *consistent and $\subseteq$-minimal* set of formulas that entails the conclusion.
   In our setting the argument's support may be *any* finite set that logically implies the argument's conclusion (see [2,3] for a justification of this).

3. The intended semantics in [1] is captured by the entailment $\hspace{0.1em}\vdash\hspace{-0.5em}\sim_{\cap\mathsf{mcs}}$ in Definition 6, which is only one way of reasoning with MCS. In this paper we also provide argumentation inspired characterizations of other entailments, such as $\hspace{0.1em}\vdash\hspace{-0.5em}\sim_{\mathsf{mcs}}$ (Definition 4) and $\|\hspace{0.1em}\vdash\hspace{-0.5em}\sim_{\mathsf{mcs}}$ (Definition 7).

Interestingly, the study of reasoning with maximal consistency by deductive argumentation has led the authors of [1] to conclude that according to Dung's setting, maximal conflict-free sets of arguments (forming what is known as 'naive semantics') are sufficient in order to derive reasonable conclusions and so "the different acceptability semantics defined in the literature are not necessary, and the notion of defense is useless". In view of this statement we note that the removal of the restrictions on the notion of arguments, as well as the introduction of new types of consistency-based entailments, allow us to overcome the shortcoming identified in [1]. Indeed, as the next example shows, in our setting argumentation-based MCS-reasoning does not collapse to naive semantics.

Example 10. Let us consider a sequent-based argumentation framework for $S = \{p \land \neg p\}$, based on classical logic, in which Undercut is the single attack rule.

Let $\mathcal{E} = \{p \wedge \neg p \Rightarrow \psi \mid \psi$ is not a classical logic tautology$\}$. This set is maximal conflict-free. Indeed, the only way to undercut the arguments in $\mathcal{E}$ is by producing an argument of the form $\Gamma \Rightarrow \phi$ where ϕ is logically equivalent to $\neg(p \wedge \neg p)$, which means that ϕ is a classical logic tautology. However, these attacking arguments are excluded from $\mathcal{E}$ and so $\mathcal{E}$ is conflict-free. Moreover, the only arguments from $\mathsf{Arg}_{\mathsf{CL}}(\mathsf{S})$ that were excluded from $\mathcal{E}$ are those that have tautologies of classical logic as conclusions. This implies that $\mathcal{E}$ is maximal in the property of being conflict-free. Now, $\mathsf{S} \hspace{0.5mm}\vert\!\sim_{\mathsf{mcs}} \neg(p \wedge \neg p)$ while with naive semantics $\neg(p \wedge \neg p)$ doesn't follow from S, since $\mathcal{E}$ is a maximal conflict-free set that does not entail $\neg(p \wedge \neg p)$.

The more lenient view of arguments in our setting (Item 2 above) not only enables the last example, but also warrants a large variety of attack rules which can be applied to arguments in the form of sequents. This is demonstrated, for instance, by the results and the attack rules in [20], which somewhat challenge the observation in [1] that "the notion of inconsistency [...] should be captured by a symmetric attack relation". Furthermore, the results given in this paper stand against the conclusion in [1], that "Dung's framework seems problematic when applied over deductive logical formalisms". We thus believe that, beyond our primary goal of demonstrating the strong ties between reasoning with maximal consistency and argumentation theory, this paper calls for a reevaluation of some negative conclusions in the literature concerning logic-based argumentation.

References

1. Amgoud, L., Besnard, P.: Logical limits of abstract argumentation frameworks. J. Appl. Non-Classical Logics **23**(3), 229–267 (2013)
2. Arieli, O.: A sequent-based representation of logical argumentation. In: Leite, J., Son, T.C., Torroni, P., Torre, L., Woltran, S. (eds.) CLIMA 2013. LNCS (LNAI), vol. 8143, pp. 69–85. Springer, Heidelberg (2013). doi:10.1007/978-3-642-40624-9_5
3. Arieli, O., Straßer, C.: Sequent-based logical argumentation. J. Argument Comput. **6**(1), 73–99 (2015)
4. Arieli, O., Straßer, C.: Argumentative approaches to reasoning with maximal consistency. In: Proceedings of KR 2016, pp. 509–512. AAAI Press (2016)
5. Baral, C., Kraus, S., Minker, J.: Combining multiple knowledge bases. IEEE Trans. Knowl. Data Eng. **3**(2), 208–220 (1991)
6. Benferhat, S., Dubois, D., Prade, H.: Some syntactic approaches to the handling of inconsistent knowledge bases: a comparative study part 1: The flat case. Stud. Logica. **58**(1), 17–45 (1997)
7. Besnard, P., Hunter, A.: A logic-based theory of deductive arguments. Artif. Intell. **128**(1–2), 203–235 (2001)
8. Besnard, P., Hunter, A.: Argumentation based on classical logic. In: Rahwan, I., Simary, G.R. (eds.) Argumentation in Artificial Intelligence, pp. 133–152. Springer, New York (2009)
9. Brewka, G.: Preferred subtheories: an extended logical framework for default reasoning. In: Proceedings of IJCAI 1989, pp. 1043–1048. Morgan Kaufmann (1989)
10. Cayrol, C.: On the relation between argumentation and non-monotonic coherence-based entailment. In: Proceedings of IJCAI 1995, pp. 1443–1448. Morgan Kaufmann (1995)

11. da Costa, N.C.A.: On the theory of inconsistent formal systems. Notre Dame J. Formal Logic **15**, 497–510 (1974)
12. Dung, P.M.: On the acceptability of arguments and its fundamental role in nonmonotonic reasoning, logic programming and n-person games. Artif. Intell. **77**, 321–357 (1995)
13. Gentzen, G.: Untersuchungen über das logische Schliessen. Math. Z. **39**, 176–210 (1934)
14. Gorogiannis, N., Hunter, A.: Instantiating abstract argumentation with classical logic arguments: postulates and properties. Artif. Intell. **175**(9–10), 1479–1497 (2011)
15. Konieczny, S., Pino Pérez, R.: Merging information under constraints: a logical framework. Logic Comput. **12**(5), 773–808 (2002)
16. Malouf, R.: Maximal consistent subsets. Comput. Linguist. **33**(2), 153–160 (2007)
17. Pollock, J.: How to reason defeasibly. Artif. Intell. **57**(1), 1–42 (1992)
18. Priest, G.: Reasoning about truth. Artif. Intell. **39**, 231–244 (1989)
19. Rescher, N., Manor, R.: On inference from inconsistent premises. Theor. Decis. **1**, 179–217 (1970)
20. Straßer, C., Arieli, O.: Sequent-based argumentation for normative reasoning. In: Cariani, F., Grossi, D., Meheus, J., Parent, X. (eds.) DEON 2014. LNCS (LNAI), vol. 8554, pp. 224–240. Springer, Cham (2014). doi:10.1007/978-3-319-08615-6_17
21. Urquhart, A.: Basic many-valued logic. In: Gabbay, D., Guenthner, F. (eds.) Handbook of Philosophical Logic, vol. II, 2nd edn., pp. 249–295. Kluwer (2001)
22. Vesic, S.: Identifying the class of maxi-consistent operators in argumentation. J. Artif. Intell. Res. **47**, 71–93 (2013)

Volunteered Geographic Information Management Supported by Fuzzy Ontologies and Level-Based Approximate Reasoning

Gloria Bordogna[1]([✉]) and Simone Sterlacchini[2]

[1] IREA-CNR, via Bassini 15, 20133 Milan, Italy
bordogna.g@irea.cnr.it
[2] IDPA-CNR, piazza della Scienza 1, 20133 Milan, Italy
simone.sterlacchini@idpa.cnr.it

Abstract. The paper proposes level-based approximate reasoning on a fuzzy ontology as a modeling framework to support the creation and retrieval of Volunteered Geographic Information (VGI) affected by observation deficiencies causing both uncertainty and fuzziness. The paper recalls the inadequacy of classic ontologies to create VGI, the limitation of the use of fuzzy ontologies to model both fuzziness and uncertainty, and proposes level based reasoning to answer user queries on a VGI collection supported by a fuzzy ontology.

Keywords: Volunteered Geographic Information (VGI) · Geo-database · Fuzzy ontology · Approximate reasoning

1 Introduction

With the diffusion of both the Internet and smart devices a widely diffused practice to carry out collaborative scientific projects, also named "Citizen science" projects, exploits the contributions of volunteers for some specific tasks [10]. Volunteers are asked to provide information of various forms and nature such as textual notes, pictures, measurements of properties relative to target objects and categories, by associating a geographic reference with their observations, i.e., Volunteer Geographic Information (VGI) [9]. Nevertheless, one main issue of scientists when using VGI collections is to understand how reliable the single items are, that is, how the VGI items satisfy their needs expressed in queries to the database where VGI items are stored. In fact, VGI is recognized as invariably characterized by unknown defects, mainly uncertainty and imprecision/fuzziness, due to both variable expertise and commitment of the VGI authors and the unknown conditions in which VGI was created [2]. Uncertainty is relative to a doubt on the truth of an observation, imprecision and fuzziness are related to the meaning of VGI content, mainly due to the use of linguistic and imprecise values to tag the observations. To reduce as much as possible VGI defects citizen science projects have provided user interfaces, knowledge bases and training facilities [2, 6, 13]. Specifically, citizen science projects that ask volunteers to classify objects of interest according to predefined categories provide domain ontologies that describe the characteristics of the single categories. Nevertheless, even with the support of ontologies,

S. Benferhat et al. (Eds.): IEA/AIE 2017, Part I, LNAI 10350, pp. 466–476, 2017.
DOI: 10.1007/978-3-319-60042-0_51

many volunteers are doubtful about their classifications and many of them explicitly ask for the community review [17]. This uncertainty can depend on the ill-defined criteria in the ontologies which often are expressed by linguistic and vague terms. To cope with ill-defined knowledge, fuzzy ontologies have been proposed [1, 14, 15]. Nevertheless, within such framework the uncertainty derived by volunteer's low expertise, and the context of the observation, such as adverse weather conditions and low resolution of the means of observations, is not modeled [14].

The original contribution of this paper is twofold: first to propose an approach to create, represent and retrieve VGI by modeling both uncertainty of the observations and ill-defined domain knowledge; secondly the definition of level-based approximate reasoning on a fuzzy ontology to model both uncertainty and imprecision/fuzziness. On one side, we allow VGI authors to specify the overall defect of their observations and, on the other side we allow VGI users, i.e., the scientists who exploit VGI for their projects, to filter the VGI items satisfying maximum tolerable levels of defect. At present, as far as we know, there are no VGI applications that employ fuzzy ontologies. We first introduce the problem of uncertainty and imprecision/fuzziness of VGI. Then, we discuss the inadequacy of the approaches based on classic ontologies and recap the notion of fuzzy ontologies for representing ill-defined knowledge. Furthermore, we propose a fuzzy ontology approach with level based approximate reasoning to deal with volunteer's observation defects when creating VGI, and needs of users for when retrieving VGI.

2 Uncertainty and Fuzziness of Volunteered Geographic Information

VGI uncertainty and fuzziness are strictly related to the representation of both VGI semantics and conditions of VGI creation and use. The main causes are the following:

- On the volunteers' side:
  - incomplete or inadequate knowledge of the volunteer in performing the requested task: this may be particularly impacting in citizen science projects involving as volunteers the general public without providing sufficient training facilities and information on the scope of the project;
  - vagueness of the criteria provided to support volunteers in correctly classifying or tagging their observations. This may happen in domains where volunteers' task consists in tagging objects based on linguistic descriptions of category prototypes; an example is the following description of roses [17]: "*Roses are flowers which vary in size and shape and are usually large and showy, in colors ranging from white through yellows and reds*".
  - Limitations of the means of observation: this may depend on the context of the observation such as weather conditions, distance from the target object, or characteristics of observation and measurement tools.
- On the user (consumer) side:
  - missing information on the created VGI, such as the lack of appropriate metadata describing the VGI creation conditions;
  - lack of information on the imprecision of the geo-localization of VGI, etc.

Haklay in [10] suggests that VGI uncertainty should not be regarded as something that can be eliminated, but as an integral part of any VGI collection, and thus he advocates novel methods to represent and to deal with VGI uncertainty during both its creation and its analysis phases. We share this point of view and define level-based approximate reasoning in a fuzzy ontology to manage VGI affected by both uncertainty and imprecision/vagueness.

3 Fuzzy Ontology Limitation to Model Uncertainty on VGI

Many citizen science projects support volunteers in creating VGI by providing descriptions of the categories of interest by means of taxonomies or ontologies. A common way to define ontologies is by means of the Web Ontology Language (OWL) [5, 11, 12] supported by the reasoning power of Description Logic (DL). Since OWL-DL allows representing the world in terms of crisp concepts (sets) and relationships among entities (that are either true or false) it becomes unsuitable in domains in which concepts are ill-defined, i.e., vague by their nature. In order to support the representation of fuzzy concepts and relationships in a domain, fuzzy ontologies have been defined [15]. According to [15] a fuzzy ontology is defined by an extension of Description Logic (DL), specifically Fuzzy-DL (FDL). The difference with classic DL is that fuzzy predicates can be satisfied to a degree. The main notions of FDL that have a counterpart in classic DL are [14, 15] *fuzzy concepts* (*c*) (OWL classes), denoting unary fuzzy predicates, *fuzzy roles* (*r*) (OWL properties), denoting binary fuzzy predicates, *individuals* (*x*) (OWL instances), denoting instances of a fuzzy set, and *fuzzy datatypes* (*t*) (OWL concrete domains). In FDL, a concept *c*, rather than being interpreted as a classical set over the universe of elements $x \in X$, is interpreted as a fuzzy set, where the degree of membership $\mu_C(x) \in [0,1]$ is regarded as the degree of truth of the statement "x is *c*" [16]. *Axioms* are formal statements defined on the above notions and, differently than in classic DL, can hold to some degree of truth. In FDL the semantics of conjunction ⊓, disjunction ⊔, negation ¬ and subsumption ⊑ depend on the choice of the fuzzy operators defined to combine fuzzy sets, t-norm (ex. min) t-conorm (ex. max), not (ex. 1-) and implication function (ex. min., the Mandani's implication). By means of FDL one can represent ill-defined statement, for example the axiom (1) describing the fuzzy concept "*Rose*":

Rose ⊑ ∃*Flower* ⊓ ∃*hasSizeLarge* ⊓ ∃*hasAppearenceShowy* ⊓ ∃*hasColor.shaded WhiteYellowReddish*

$$(1)$$

where ∃*Flower*, ∃*hasSize.Large*, ∃*hasAppearance* ∃*Showvy*, ∃*hasColor.shades White Yellow Reddish* mean that in order for an instance x to a be a rose its membership degrees $\mu_{Flower}(x)$, $\mu_{Size\ Large}(x)$, $\mu_{AppearenceShowvy}(x)$, $\mu_{Color\ shades\ of\ White\ Yellow\ Reddish}(x)$ representing the satisfaction of the fuzzy predicates must be greater than 0.

FDL allows performing several reasoning tasks among which instance retrieval which is the one we apply for the retrieval of VGI items (instances stored into a geo-database that have been created by different volunteers) by a user who specifies as query a concept of interest selected from the TBox of a fuzzy ontology.

3.1 Example of Retrieval of VGI Items Supported by a Fuzzy Ontology and Fuzzy DL

Let us assume that a naturalistic project collecting voluntary observations of flowers and plants, provides a smart app that allows VGI authors specifying some character-istics of the observed instances. Let us assume that, when the volunteer specifies his/her observation of an *individual* x that he/she tags as a *"Flower"* the app asks him/her to specify the values of the discriminating characteristics used in the fuzzy ontology for the classification of the instances into a family and species of flower: *size, appearance, color, number of petals, etc.* Let us assume that the VGI author is able to provide precise measurements of the characteristic such as *size* in cm, *number of petals* on N^+, and can select linguistic values for characteristics such as *color*, and *appearance* taking values on categorical domains [5]. For example, *"x is Flower"*, *"x size is 10 cm"*, *"x Appearance is Showy"*, *"x Color is pink"*, *"number of petals 5"*. These ABox axioms are stored into the geo database together with the location of the individual x and the timestamp of its creation and are uniquely identified by an ID as a VGI item. Let us assume that a user is interested in retrieving from the geo-database all the VGI items that are observation of "Roses" because he/she is studying their geographic distribu-tion. He will select from the fuzzy ontology the concept *"Rose"* (definition (1)) as query to submit to the database. The query evaluation mechanism, computes the degree of truth of *"x is a Rose "*, $\mu_{Rose}(x)$, based on the evaluation of axiom (1) by the following formula (2), by each stored instance *x*, and then will retrieve only those instances that have a not null degree of truth. This can be done by combining the degrees of satis-faction of the fuzzy predicates for an individual x, described by the ABox axioms stored in the database in terms of precise values of the properties, based on the operators' definitions, and on the membership functions of the fuzzy predicates. [1]:

$$\mu_{Rose}(x) = \min(\mu_{Flower}(x \text{ is } Flower), \mu_{Size.Large}(x \text{ is } 10cm), \mu_{AppearenceShowvy}(x \text{ is } slowy)$$

$$\mu_{ColorshadesofWhiteYellowReddish.}(x \text{ is } pink))$$

$$(2)$$

Based on the degree of satisfaction of the query by each instance, one can rank the VGI items to the user, who is thus made aware of the fact that the instances may be *"Roses"* to a distinct degree.

3.2 Limitation of Fuzzy Ontology to Manage VGI

Nevertheless, Fuzzy-DL reasoning illustrated so far is suitable to deal with precise observations and ill-defined knowledge. A dual situation that may happen in the real world of observations is when the VGI author is not completely sure about his/her observation, either because he/she does not have adequate knowledge of the terms (e.g., what does showy means?), or because of deficiencies of the means of observation. This may happen both when the domain knowledge is encoded into a precise ontology and when it is ill-defined. Let us represent by the fuzzy ontology depicted in Fig. 1 the following description of the three main groups of roses:

- *"Wild roses are mainly reddish, 4–6 cm diameter, generally with 4–5 petals"*
- *"Old Garden roses are notably fragrant, double-flowered blooms primarily in shades of white, pink and crimson-red."*
- *"Modern roses are well-formed with large, high-centred buds, and their colors range from shades of deep yellow, apricot, copper, orange, true scarlet, yellow bi-colours, lavender, gray, and even brown were now possible."*

It can be noticed that some characteristics may be difficult to observe, for example the fragrance from a far observation point.

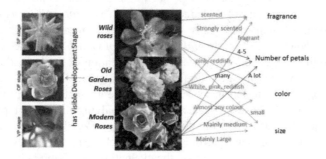

Fig. 1. Fuzzy ontology of the three main groups of roses.

4 Fuzzy Ontology and Level-Based Approximate Reasoning

Often there is a misunderstanding on the uncertainty and imprecision/fuzziness modeling [15]. Under uncertainty theory statements are either completely true or completely false but we do not know if they are true of false, so we define a probability or possibility distribution over the worlds. For example, the statement "x is a Flower" is a crisp one: x can be either a Flower or not, it cannot be partially a Flower, the degree that we can associate to this statement is relative to our knowledge on the truth about x being a Flower, which may depend on some deficiency of the observation. In fuzzy logic, statements are true and false to a degree since they contain vague concepts such as in a fuzzy ontology: for example the statement "x has a *many* petals", contains the fuzzy term *many* whose meaning is a matter of number, the more the petals the greater the degree by which the statement is satisfied. We can model observations affected by some deficiency of the conditions by two alternative statements [3]: for example, by observing a rose from a far point of view one could either specify the uncertainty on the truth of a precise statement such as "*I am 0.6 certain that the Petals are 5*" or one could express a certain fuzzy statement such as "*I am sure that x has a few Petals*" or both an uncertain and imprecise statement such as "*I am 0.8 certain that the Petals are 4 or 5*".

In these statements we can notice that the uncertainty degrees are inversely related with the amount of imprecision/fuzziness of the predicates. One can guess that the total amounts of uncertainty plus imprecision/fuzziness in all alternative statements describing the same observation are constant and depend on the degree of overall deficiency of the observation, and the greater the deficiency of the observation the greater is the total amount of uncertainty plus imprecision/fuzziness of the statement.

In fuzzy databases the occurrence of both uncertainty and imprecise/fuzzy values FV have been modeled by combining the uncertainty u with the membership function μ_{FV} of the fuzzy value so as to derive a modified membership function $\mu_{FV}'(x) = I(u, \mu_{FV}(x))$ where I is an implication function [8]. Specifically, two main definitions of the implication have been used, either Mamdani or the Kleene-Dienes' implications which correspond either to reduce or to expand the imprecision/fuzziness of the fuzzy value respectively, based on the uncertainty degree u. As pointed out in [8] although these proposals can be useful in many applications, unfortunately they are inappropriate when reasoning in fuzzy databases. Mamdani's implication obliges us to work with non- normalized fuzzy values while Kleene-Dienes' implication, obliges to assign the same possibility degree to all the basic values of the underlying domain independently of the distance to the support set of the fuzzy value. In fact, it is reasonable to think that a small uncertainty on a value v means that one cannot exclude as possible some values near to v, but still can exclude as possible the values far from v [3]. For this reason we define a novel approximate reasoning model when retrieving VGI affected by both uncertainty and imprecision/fuzziness.

In our proposal volunteers can create VGI with the support of a fuzzy ontology, from where they can select simple concepts, discriminating characteristic or properties such as fragrance, number of petals, color, size, etc.), possibly fuzzy, to tag their observations, and with each selected concept they can associate a degree d in [0,1] representing the overall deficiency of their observation, which may comprise both the limitations of the means of observation (far point of view) and/or the subjective inexperience of the volunteer who may find it difficult to understand the criteria he/she must apply for the classification. We take into account d when answering user queries for VGI items stored in the geo database, asking for the selection of concepts from the fuzzy ontology. Hereafter, we will make an example relative to the fuzzy ontology describing Roses and their observable development stages [7], *Visible Petals* (VP), *Open Flower* (OF), and *Senescing Flower* (SF) reported in Fig. 2. The fuzzy development stages F-VP, F-OF, and F-SF were defined by exploiting the fact that there is a gradual transition of the characteristics of each stage to the next one. The triangular membership functions were chosen for their simplicity and point-like core, nevertheless we could use other defi- nitions. We could even quantify the amount of imprecision/fuzziness of the fuzzy stages. $d = 1$ means maximally uncertain and imprecise/fuzzy description, then the specified characteristic, for example F-VP, must be interpreted with maximum fuzziness, i.e., more stages close to the selected one are possible to a distinct degree. See the case depicted in Fig. 2, where it is questionable to state if the rose in the middle is in the VP or SF stage. As far as categorical values, are considered, for example, colors, indeed, one can be inaccurate in selecting one value in a domain like {*white, pink, yellow, red, any color*} to tag the rose on the right of Fig. 2, so one can cope with the inaccuracy of the selection by associating a degree expressing the imprecision of the selection. $d = 0$

Fig. 2. Fuzzy development stages of Roses [7], and examples of questionable stage and color.

means the most certain and most precise description one can make as far as the possible choices are considered in the fuzzy ontology. For example, the specified development stage VP is the only possible; by increasing d towards 1 it means that the description becomes more uncertain/fuzzier, and thus the selected stage or the color is not exclusive.

To model this behavior, d defines a threshold on the membership function of the selected fuzzy concept so that only the values of the basic domain with degrees equal or greater than $(1 - d)$, are considered as the possible values of the observation. When the fuzzy concept has a point-like core, in the case of $d = 0$, only one precise value is possible. Nevertheless, when the fuzzy concept has a not punctual core (see the concepts *many, fragrant, scented* in Fig. 3), more values for the characteristics are still fully possible, all the values in the core set.

Formally, let us consider a faulty observation of an instance x defined by a pair $(FV, d)_x$ in which FV is a fuzzy concept with basic domain D defined in the fuzzy ontology O and $d \in [0,1]$ is the defect of the observation of instance x. $(FV, d)_x$ indicates that the author is doubtful to the degree d on the truth of "x is FV". In fact, in this specific case FV is selected from the fuzzy ontology by the user and thus d refers to the uncertainty of attributing value FV to the observation. Thus we consider d as a degree of uncertainty of the fuzzy proposition. We translate it into the fuzzy axiom:

"x is FV with a certainty at most equal to $(1 - d)$": $Certain(x$ is $FV) \leq 1 - d$.

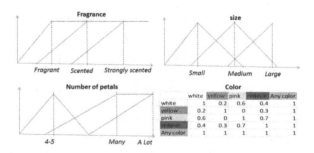

Fig. 3. Membership functions of the fuzzy values and co-occurrence matrix of colors

Based on this axiom and on the membership function of *FV* we can compute the degree of possibility that "*x* is *V*" is true, i.e., π (x is V), for each concept *V* defined on the basic domain D of *FV*, and belonging to the fuzzy ontology *O*:

If *Certainty*(x is FV) $\leq$ (1 − d) → $\forall V \in$ D $\wedge V \subseteq O$ π (x is V) = μ_V(x) where

$$\mu_V(x) = I(d, \mu_{FV}(V)) = \mu_{FV}(V) \text{ if } \mu_{FV}(V) \geq (1 - d) \text{ else } \mu_V(x) = 0 \qquad (3)$$

I is a generalized fuzzy implication function [4]. When *d* = 0, precise and certain description, $\mu_V(x) \in$ {0,1} and $\mu_V(x)$ = 1 only if $\mu_{FV}(V)$ = 1 with *V* defined in the fuzzy ontology *O*. When *d* = 1, maximally imprecise and uncertain description, $\mu_V(x) > 0$ $\forall V$ in *O* and *V* defined on the same domain D of *FV* so that $V \in$ *Support* (*FV*) $\subseteq$ D. For increasing *d* values the more the concepts of the fuzzy ontology that are possible.

$$\forall d_1 < d_2 \in [0, 1], \{V_1, \dots V_n | \mu_{FV}(V_i) \geq 1 - d_1\} \subseteq \{V_1, \dots V_m | \mu_{FV}(V_i) \geq 1 - d_2\} \quad (4)$$

Notice that when the membership function μ_{FV} defines a crisp set on the domain D, i.e., μ_{FV} (x) $\in$ {0,1}, formula (3) reduces to the Rescher-Gaines implication:

$$\pi \text{ (x is V)} = \mu_V(x) = 1 \text{ if } \mu_{FV}(V) \geq (1 - d) \text{ else } \mu_V(x) = 0$$

In this case, when all concepts have crisp membership functions the ontology is a classic one and the reasoning reduces to classic reasoning.

4.1 Example of Retrieval of Uncertain VGI Based on a Fuzzy Ontology

Assume the definition of the membership functions of the roses' fuzzy development stages in Fig. 2, and the membership functions of the fuzzy *fragrance, size, number of petals,* and *color* in Fig. 3. Specifically, an entry of the matrix of colors indicates the possibility of finding the two colors in a single rose by considering all varieties. Assume the following three fuzzy axioms in TBox in Table 1 where each axiom admits a degree of possibility in [0,1] to be true, defining the three groups of roses, and let us define the intersection and inclusion by the min.

Observing the rose *x* on the extreme right of Fig. 2 we can describe it as follows:

$x \sqsubseteq (\exists \text{rose}, d_1 = 0) \sqcap (\exists \text{Fragrant}, d_2 = 1) \sqcap (\exists \text{Many petals}, d_3 = 0.1) \sqcap (\exists \text{pink}$
$\text{color}, d_4 = 0.5) \sqcap (\exists \text{large size}, d_5 = 0.9)) \sqcap (\exists \text{F\_VP stage}, d_5 = 0.8)$

$$(5)$$

In the geodatabase we store (*Certainty*(rose)$_x$ = 1) (*Certainty*(fragrant)$_x$ = 0), (*Certainty*(many petals)$_x$ $\leq$ 0.9), (*Certainty*(pink color)$_x$ $\leq$ 0.5), (*Certainty* (size)$_x$ $\leq$ 0.1), (*Certainty*(VP stage)$_x$ $\leq$ 0.2) together with the date and time of the observation (25 May 2016, 12:00) as well as its geographic coordinates. Let us assume that a user wants to retrieve from the VGI collection all observations of

Table 1. TBox defining the three main types of Roses

1	Wild rose ⊑ rose ⊓ (∃Scented-Fragrance) ⊓ (∃4–5 petals) ⊓ (∃ pink reddish color) ⊓ (∃small size)
2	Old Garden rose ⊑ rose ⊓ (∃Strongly Scented-Fragrance) ⊓ (∃Many petals) ⊓ (∃ white pink reddish color) ⊓ (∃medium size)
3	Modern rose ⊑ rose ⊓ (∃Fragrant) ⊓ (∃A lot of petals) ⊓ (∃ Any) ⊓ (∃ large size)

modern roses that are blossomed, i.e. in Open Flower stage OF, observed before 30 May 2016. The query is translated into the following:

$$x \sqsubseteq (\exists\text{date} < 30 \text{ May } 2016) \sqcap (\exists\text{Modern rose}) \sqcap (\exists\text{OF stage}) \qquad (6)$$

We can compute the degrees of possibility that x satisfies the query as follows:

$min(\mu_{\text{date} < 30 \text{ MAY}}(x), \mu_{\text{Modern rose}}(x), \mu_{OF}(x))$ where $\mu_{\text{Modern rose}}(x)$ is computed by applying axiom 3 of the fuzzy TBox as follows: $\mu_{\text{Modern rose}}(x) = min(\mu_{\text{rose}}(x), \mu_{\text{Fragrant}}(x), \mu_{\text{A lot petals}}(x), \mu_{\text{Any color}}(x), \mu_{\text{large size}}(x)) = min(1, 1, 1, 1, 1) = 1$.

Furthermore $\mu_{OF}(x) = \mu_{F-VP}(OF) > 0$ since $\mu_{F-VP}(OF) = 0.5 \geq 1 - 0.8$. Thus we can rank instance x based on its possibility to satisfy the query: $Rank(x) = min(1, 1, \mu_{F-VP}(OF)) = min(1, 1, 0.5) = 0.5$

A linguistic summary of the observation could be expressed as follows: "it is *fully possible* that x is a Modern rose but it is only averagely possible that x is in the Open Flower stage".

Assuming the following query asking for Old garden roses in OF stage:

$$x \sqsubseteq (\exists\text{date} < 30 \text{ May } 2016) \sqcap (\exists\text{Old garden roses}) \sqcap (\exists\text{OF stage}) \qquad (7)$$

we should evaluate axiom 2 in Table 1 as follows: $\mu_{\text{Old Garden rose}}(x) = min(\mu_{\text{rose}}(x), \mu_{\text{Strongly Scented}}(x), \mu_{\text{Many petals}}(x), \mu_{\text{white pink reddish color}}(x), \mu_{\text{medium size}}(x)) = min(1, 1, 1, 1, 0.2) = 0.2$

In this case x would appear among the results of the query but with a lower rank with respect to the rank computed for Modern roses. Thus, we can conclude that "it is fully possible that x is a Modern rose but there is a low possibility that it is an old Garden rose too."

Let us assume that we observe a rose x without any defects:

$$x \sqsubseteq (\exists\text{rose}, d_1 = 0) \sqcap (\exists\text{Fragrant}, d_2 = 0) \sqcap (\exists\text{Many}, d_3 = 0) \sqcap (\exists\text{pinkcolor},$$
$$d_4 = 0) \sqcap (\exists\text{largesize}, d_5 = 0)) \sqcap (\exists\text{F\_VPstage}, d_5 = 0)$$

$$(8)$$

In this case, in the geodatabase we store $(Certainty(\text{rose})_x = 1)$ $(Certainty(\text{fragrant})_x = 1)$, $(Certainty(\text{many petals})_x = 1)$, $(Certainty(\text{pink color})_x = 1)$,

($Certainty(\texttt{size})_x = 1$), ($Certainty(\texttt{VP stage})_x = 1$) together with the date and time of the observation ($\texttt{25 May 2016, 12:00}$) as well as its geographic coordinates.

By asking the query defined in formula (6) we would not retrieve x. In fact, $\mu_{OF}(x) = \mu_{F-VP}(\texttt{OF}) = 0$ since $\mu_{F-VP}(\texttt{OF}) = 0.5 < 1$.

On the other side, when $d = 1$ (worst situation), the threshold in formula (4) is 0. Thus in this case we model the worst observation conditions in which there is no limit imposed by d to the fuzziness by which we interpret the concepts in the fuzzy ontology.

5 Conclusions

In this contribution we analyse the use and limitation of fuzzy ontologies to create and query VGI in citizen science projects for modelling both ill-defined knowledge and observation uncertainty, and define an original approach, named level-based reasoning. It allows ranking the VGI items based on the degree of possibility of satisfying a user query formulated by selecting a (fuzzy) concept from the fuzzy ontology. VGI items are tagged by either fuzzy or crisp concepts, each one associated with a degree quantifying the uncertainty of the observation. d is not merely a threshold on the degree of truth of the query fuzzy axiom, but is used to select the concepts of the ontology that possibly satisfy the query. To this end the fuzzy concepts are restricted by d through a generalized fuzzy implication that in the case of crisp concepts reduces to the Rescher-Gaines implication, i.e., to classic ontology reasoning.

Aknowledgements. The work presented in the paper has been partially supported by the projects *FHfFC*, jointly funded by CNR and Regione Lombardia, and *STRESS* funded by Cariplo.

References

1. Bobillo, F., Straccia, U.: The fuzzy ontology reasoner fuzzyDL. Knowl. Based Syst. **95**, 12–34 (2016)
2. Bordogna, G., Carrara, P., Criscuolo, L., Pepe, M., Rampini, A.: On predicting and improving the quality of volunteer geographic information projects. Int. J. Digital Earth **9**, 1–22 (2014). on-line edition
3. Bordogna, G., Pasi, G.: Modeling linguistic qualifiers of uncertainty in a Fuzzy database. Int. J. Intell. Syst. **15**, 995–1014 (2000)
4. Bordogna, G., Pasi, G.: Modeling preferences in fuzzy queries by tuning the evaluation function of selection conditions. In: Proceedings of IFSA 2003, pp. 296–299, 29 June–2 July 2003, Istanbul (2003)
5. Cho, W.C., Richards, D.: Ontology construction and concept reuse with formal concept analysis for improved web document retrieval. Web Intell. Agent Syst. Int. J. **5**, 109–126 (2007)
6. Crall, A.W., Newman, G.J., Stohlgren, T.J., Holfelder, K.A., Graham, J., Waller, D.M.: Assessing citizen science data quality: an invasive species case study. Conserv. Lett. **4**(6), 433–442 (2011). Blackwell Publishing Inc., 1755-263X

7. Dubois, A., Raymond, O., Remay, A., Bendahmane, L.M.: Genomic approach to study floral development genes in Rosa sp. PLoS One **6**(12), e28455 (2011). doi:10.1371/journal.pone.0028455

8. Gonzalez, A., Marın, N., Pons, O., Vila, M.A.: Fuzzy certainty on fuzzy values. Control Cybern. **38**(2), 311–339 (2009)

9. Goodchild, M.F.: Citizens as voluntary sensors: spatial data infrastructure in the world of web 2.0. Int. J. Spatial Data Infrastruct. Res. **2**, 24–32 (2007)

10. Haklay, M.: Citizen science and volunteered geographic information – overview and typology of participation. In: Sui, D.Z., Elwood, S., Goodchild, M.F. (eds.) Volunteered Geographic Information, Public Participation, and Crowdsourced Production of Geographic Knowledge. Springer, Berlin (2012)

11. Hitzler, P., Krötzsch, M., Parsia, B., Patel-Schneider, P.F., Rudolph, S.: OWL 2 web ontology language primer. W3C recommendation (2009a). http://www.w3.org/TR/owl2-primer/. Cited on page(s) 11

12. Hitzler, P., Krötzsch, M., Rudolph, S.: Foundations of Semantic Web Technologies. Chapman & Hall/CRC, New York (2009b). Cited on page(s) 11, 18

13. Schade, S., Tsinaraki, C.: Survey report: data management in Citizen Science projects. JRC Technical report for European Commission (2016)

14. Straccia, U.: Towards a fuzzy description logic for the semantic web. In: Gomez-Perez, A., Euzenat, J. (eds.) ESWC 2005. LNCS, vol. 3532, pp. 167–181. Springer, Berlin (2005)

15. Straccia, U.: All about fuzzy description logics and applications. In: Faber, W., Paschke, A. (eds.) Reasoning Web 2015. LNCS, pp. 1–31. Springer, Heidelberg (2015). doi:10.1007/978-3-319-21768-0

16. Zadeh, L.A.: Fuzzy sets. Inf. Control **8**(3), 338–353 (1965)

17. http://www.inaturalist.org/. Accessed 8 Aug 2016

Regular and Sufficient Bounds of Finite Domain Constraints for Skeptical C-Inference

Christoph Beierle$^{(\boxtimes)}$ and Steven Kutsch

Department of Computer Science, University of Hagen, 58084 Hagen, Germany
christoph.beierle@fernuni-hagen.de

Abstract. Skeptical c-inference based on a set of conditionals of the form *If A then usually B* is defined by taking the set of c-representations into account. C-representations are ranking functions induced by impact vectors encoding the conditional impact on each possible world. By setting a bound for the maximal impact value, c-inference can be approximated. We investigate the concepts of regular and sufficient upper bounds for conditional impacts and how they can be employed for implementing c-inference as a finite domain constraint solving problem.

1 Introduction

When working with a set of conditionals of the form *If A then usually B*, OCFs [8], also called ranking functions, are a popular way to encapsulate not only the stated rules, but also the beliefs consistent with the knowledge base. C-representations are a way to inductively complete a knowledge base to a ranking function that exibit excellent inference properties [6, 7]. In [1], the notion of c-inference is introduced as a skeptical inference relation taking all c-representations of a knowledge base $\mathcal{R}$ into account. For implementing c-inference, a constraint satisfaction problem is defined so that c-inference can be carried out using a CSP solver. In [3], the work presented in [1] is extended and the CSPs used for c-representations and c-inference in [1] are sharpened to CSPs over finite domains. For this modelling, several open problems arise. In this paper, we investigate questions about upper bounds and minimal upper bounds for both the CSP modelling c-representations and the CSP modelling c-inference.

2 Background

Conditional Logic and OCFs. Let $\Sigma = \{v_1, ..., v_m\}$ be a propositional alphabet. A *literal* is the positive (v_i) or negated ($\overline{v_i}$) form of a propositional variable, $\dot{v}_i$ stands for either v_i or $\overline{v_i}$. From these we obtain the propositional language $\mathcal{L}$ as the set of formulas of Σ closed under negation $\neg$, conjunction $\wedge$, and disjunction $\vee$. For shorter formulas, we abbreviate conjunction by juxtaposition (i.e., AB stands for $A \wedge B$), and negation by overlining (i.e., $\overline{A}$ is equivalent to $\neg A$). Let Ω_Σ denote the set of possible worlds over $\mathcal{L}$; Ω_Σ will be taken here simply as the set of all propositional interpretations over $\mathcal{L}$ and can be identified with

© Springer International Publishing AG 2017
S. Benferhat et al. (Eds.): IEA/AIE 2017, Part I, LNAI 10350, pp. 477–487, 2017.
DOI: 10.1007/978-3-319-60042-0_52

the set of all complete conjunctions over Σ; we will often just write Ω instead of Ω_Σ. For $\omega \in \Omega$, $\omega \models A$ means that the propositional formula $A \in \mathcal{L}$ holds in the possible world ω.

A *conditional* $(B|A)$ with $A, B \in \mathcal{L}$ encodes the defeasible rule "if A then normally B" and is a trivalent logical entity with the evaluation [4,6]

$$[\![(B|A)]\!]_\omega = \begin{cases} true & \text{iff} \quad \omega \models AB & \text{(verification)} \\ false & \text{iff} \quad \omega \models A\overline{B} & \text{(falsification)} \\ undefined & \text{iff} \quad \omega \models \overline{A} & \text{(not applicable)} \end{cases}$$

An *Ordinal Conditional Function* (OCF, ranking function) [8] is a function $\kappa : \Omega \to \mathbb{N}_0 \cup \{\infty\}$ that assigns to each world $\omega \in \Omega$ an implausibility rank $\kappa(\omega)$: the higher $\kappa(\omega)$, the more surprising ω is. OCFs have to satisfy the normalization condition that there has to be a world that is maximally plausible, i.e., $\kappa^{-1}(0) \neq \emptyset$. The rank of a formula A is defined by $\kappa(A) = \min\{\kappa(\omega) \mid \omega \models A\}$. An OCF κ *accepts* a conditional $(B|A)$, denoted by $\kappa \models (B|A)$, iff the verification of the conditional is less surprising than its falsification, i.e., iff $\kappa(AB) < \kappa(A\overline{B})$. This can also be understood as a nonmonotonic inference relation between the premise A and the conclusion B: We say that A κ-*entails* B, written $A \hspace{0.2em}\vdash\hspace{-0.4em}\sim^\kappa B$, iff κ accepts the conditional $(B|A)$: $\kappa \models (B|A)$ iff $\kappa(AB) < \kappa(A\overline{B})$ iff $A \hspace{0.2em}\vdash\hspace{-0.4em}\sim^\kappa B$.

The acceptance relation is extended as usual to a set $\mathcal{R}$ of conditionals, called a *knowledge base*, by defining $\kappa \models \mathcal{R}$ iff $\kappa \models (B|A)$ for all $(B|A) \in \mathcal{R}$. This is synonymous to saying that κ is *admissible* with respect to $\mathcal{R}$ [5], or that κ is a *ranking model* of $\mathcal{R}$. $\mathcal{R}$ is *consistent* iff it has a ranking model.

C-Representations and C-Inference. Among the models of $\mathcal{R}$, c-representations are special models obtained by assigning an individual impact to each conditional and generating the world ranks as the sum of impacts of falsified conditionals. C-inference is an inference relation taking all c-representations of $\mathcal{R}$ into account.

Definition 1 (c-representation [6,7]). *A c-representation of a knowledge base $\mathcal{R}$ is a ranking function κ constructed from integer impacts $\eta_i \in \mathbb{N}_0$ assigned to each conditional $(B_i|A_i)$ such that κ accepts $\mathcal{R}$ and is given by:*

$$\kappa(\omega) = \sum_{\substack{1 \leqslant i \leqslant n \\ \omega \models A_i\overline{B}_i}} \eta_i \tag{1}$$

Definition 2 (c-inference, $\hspace{0.2em}\vdash\hspace{-0.4em}\sim^c_\mathcal{R}$ [1]). *Let $\mathcal{R}$ be a knowledge base and let A, B be formulas. B is a (skeptical) c-inference from A in the context of $\mathcal{R}$, denoted by $A \hspace{0.2em}\vdash\hspace{-0.4em}\sim^c_\mathcal{R} B$, iff $A \hspace{0.2em}\vdash\hspace{-0.4em}\sim^\kappa B$ holds for all c-representations κ for $\mathcal{R}$.*

3   Finite Domains and Regular Upper Bounds

If a knowledge base $\mathcal{R}$ is consistent, there are in general infinitely many c-representations accepting $\mathcal{R}$, including inferentially equivalent ones.

Definition 3 ($\equiv_{\sim}$). *Two ranking functions* κ, κ' *are inferentially equivalent, denoted by* $\kappa \equiv_{\sim} \kappa'$ *iff for all* $(B|A)$ *it is the case that* $\kappa \models (B|A)$ *iff* $\kappa' \models (B|A)$.

For instance, if there is a $k \in \mathbb{N}$ such that $\kappa'(\omega) = k \cdot \kappa(\omega)$ for all worlds ω, then $\kappa \equiv_{\sim} \kappa'$; in general, two ranking functions are inferentially equivalent iff they induce the same total preorder on worlds.

Proposition 1. *For ranking functions* κ *and* κ', *we have* $\kappa \equiv_{\sim} \kappa'$ *iff for all* $\omega_1, \omega_2 \in \Omega$ *it is the case that* $\kappa(\omega_1) \leqslant \kappa(\omega_2)$ *iff* $\kappa'(\omega_1) \leqslant \kappa'(\omega_2)$.

For a set $\mathcal{O}$ of OCFs, $\mathcal{O}_{/\equiv_{\sim}}$ denotes the set of induced equivalence classes.

In [1], a modeling of c-representations as solutions of a constraint satisfaction problem $CR(\mathcal{R})$ is given and shown to be correct and complete with respect to the set of all c-representations of $\mathcal{R}$. Recently, it has been suggested to take inferential equivalence of c-representations into account and to sharpen $CR(\mathcal{R})$ by introducing an upper bound for the impact values η_i.

Definition 4 ($CR^u(\mathcal{R})$ [3]). *Let* $\mathcal{R} = \{(B_1|A_1), \dots, (B_n|A_n)\}$ *and* $u \in \mathbb{N}$. *The finite domain constraint satisfaction problem* $CR^u(\mathcal{R})$ *on the constraint variables* $\{\eta_1, \dots, \eta_n\}$ *ranging over* $\mathbb{N}$ *is given by the conjunction of the constraints, for all* $i \in \{1, \dots, n\}$:

$$\eta_i \geqslant 0 \tag{2}$$

$$\eta_i > \min_{\omega \models A_i B_i} \sum_{\substack{j \neq i \\ \omega \models A_j \overline{B_j}}} \eta_j - \min_{\omega \models A_i \overline{B_i}} \sum_{\substack{j \neq i \\ \omega \models A_j \overline{B_j}}} \eta_j \tag{3}$$

$$\eta_i \leqslant u \tag{4}$$

A solution of $CR^u(\mathcal{R})$ is an n-tuple $(\eta_1, \dots, \eta_n)$ of natural numbers, its set of solutions is denoted by $Sol(CR^u(\mathcal{R}))$. For $\overrightarrow{\eta} \in Sol(CR^u(\mathcal{R}))$ and κ as in Eq. (1), κ is the *OCF induced by* $\overrightarrow{\eta}$, denoted by $\kappa_{\overrightarrow{\eta}}$, and the set of all induced OCFs is denoted by $\mathcal{O}(CR^u(\mathcal{R})) = \{\kappa_{\overrightarrow{\eta}} \mid \overrightarrow{\eta} \in Sol(CR^u(\mathcal{R}))\}$.

Example 1 ($\mathcal{R}_{birds}$). Let $\Sigma = \{b, p, f, w\}$ representing birds, penguins, fliying things and winged things and let $\mathcal{R}_{birds} = \{r_1, r_2, r_3, r_4\}$ be the knowledge base with $r_1 = (f|b)$, $r_2 = (\overline{f}|p)$, $r_3 = (b|p)$, $r_4 = (w|b)$. Taking the verification and falsification of these conditionals by the worlds in Ω_Σ into account (cf. Table 1) the CSP $CR^u(\mathcal{R}_{birds})$ is then given as:

$\eta_i \geqslant 0 \quad \text{for } 1 \leqslant i \leqslant 4 \qquad\qquad \eta_3 > min\{\eta_1, \eta_2\} - \eta_2$

$\eta_1 > min\{\eta_2, \eta_4\} - \eta_1 \qquad\qquad \eta_4 > min\{\eta_1, \eta_2, 0\} - min\{\eta_1, \eta_2, 0\} = 0$

$\eta_2 > min\{\eta_1, \eta_3\} - min\{\eta_3, \eta_4\} \qquad \eta_i \leqslant u \quad \text{for } 1 \leqslant i \leqslant 4$

For illustration, some solutions to $CR(\mathcal{R}_{birds})$ and the induced ranking functions are given in Table 1. The solutions η_1 and η_2 are elements of $Sol(CR^u(\mathcal{R}_{birds}))$ for $u \geqslant 4$ while the solution η_3 is only an element of $Sol(CR^u(\mathcal{R}_{birds}))$ for $u \geqslant 7$.

C-inference defined with respect to a maximal impact value can be viewed as a kind of resource-bounded inference operation.

Table 1. Verification and falsification with induced impacts for $\mathcal{R}_{birds}$ in Example 1.

ω	r_1: $(f\|b)$	r_2: $(\overline{f}\|p)$	r_3: $(b\|p)$	r_4: $(w\|b)$	impact on ω	$\kappa_{\overrightarrow{\eta}_1}(\omega)$	$\kappa_{\overrightarrow{\eta}_2}(\omega)$	$\kappa_{\overrightarrow{\eta}_3}(\omega)$
$b\,p\,f\,w$	v	f	v	v	η_2	2	4	5
$b\,p\,f\,\overline{w}$	v	f	v	f	$\eta_2+\eta_4$	3	7	12
$b\,p\,\overline{f}\,w$	f	v	v	v	η_1	1	3	4
$b\,p\,\overline{f}\,\overline{w}$	f	v	v	f	$\eta_1+\eta_4$	2	6	11
$b\,\overline{p}\,f\,w$	v	$-$	$-$	v	0	0	0	0
$b\,\overline{p}\,f\,\overline{w}$	v	$-$	$-$	f	η_4	1	3	7
$b\,\overline{p}\,\overline{f}\,w$	f	$-$	$-$	v	η_1	1	3	4
$b\,\overline{p}\,\overline{f}\,\overline{w}$	f	$-$	$-$	f	$\eta_1+\eta_4$	2	6	11
$\overline{b}\,p\,f\,w$	$-$	f	f	$-$	$\eta_2+\eta_3$	4	8	11
$\overline{b}\,p\,f\,\overline{w}$	$-$	f	f	$-$	$\eta_2+\eta_3$	4	8	11
$\overline{b}\,p\,\overline{f}\,w$	$-$	v	f	$-$	η_3	2	4	6
$\overline{b}\,p\,\overline{f}\,\overline{w}$	$-$	v	f	$-$	η_3	2	4	6
$\overline{b}\,\overline{p}\,f\,w$	$-$	$-$	$-$	$-$	0	0	0	0
$\overline{b}\,\overline{p}\,f\,\overline{w}$	$-$	$-$	$-$	$-$	0	0	0	0
$\overline{b}\,\overline{p}\,\overline{f}\,w$	$-$	$-$	$-$	$-$	0	0	0	0
$\overline{b}\,\overline{p}\,\overline{f}\,\overline{w}$	$-$	$-$	$-$	$-$	0	0	0	0
impacts:	η_1	η_2	η_3	η_4				
$\overrightarrow{\eta}_1$	1	2	2	1				
$\overrightarrow{\eta}_2$	3	4	4	3				
$\overrightarrow{\eta}_3$	4	5	6	7				

Definition 5 (c-inference under maximal impact value, $\hspace{1pt}\vdash^{c,u}_{\mathcal{R}}$). *Let $\mathcal{R}$ be a knowledge base, $u \in \mathbb{N}$, and let A, B be formulas. B is a (skeptical) c-inference from A in the context of $\mathcal{R}$ under maximal impact value u, denoted by $A \hspace{1pt}\vdash^{c,u}_{\mathcal{R}} B$, iff $A \hspace{1pt}\vdash^{\kappa} B$ holds for all c-representations κ with $\kappa \in \mathcal{O}(CR^u(\mathcal{R}))$.*

The relationships $\mathcal{O}(CR^u(\mathcal{R})) \subseteq \mathcal{O}(CR^{u'}(\mathcal{R})) \subseteq \mathcal{O}(CR(\mathcal{R}))$ for $u' \geqslant u$ imply:

Proposition 2 ($\hspace{1pt}\vdash^{c,u}_{\mathcal{R}}$). *Let $\mathcal{R}$ be a knowledge base, $u, u' \in \mathbb{N}$, $u' \geqslant u$, and let A, B be formulas. Then $A \hspace{1pt}\vdash^{c}_{\mathcal{R}} B$ implies $A \hspace{1pt}\vdash^{c,u}_{\mathcal{R}} B$, and $A \hspace{1pt}\vdash^{c,u'}_{\mathcal{R}} B$ implies $A \hspace{1pt}\vdash^{c,u}_{\mathcal{R}} B$.*

Thus, Proposition 2 shows that $\hspace{1pt}\vdash^{c,u}_{\mathcal{R}}$ approximates c-inference $\hspace{1pt}\vdash^{c}_{\mathcal{R}}$. The following definition introduces a criterion for a maximal impact value ensuring that $\hspace{1pt}\vdash^{c,u}_{\mathcal{R}}$ fully realizes skeptical c-inference. For an OCF κ, the definition uses the total preorder $\preccurlyeq_{\kappa}$ on worlds given by $\omega_1 \preccurlyeq_{\kappa} \omega_2$ iff $\kappa(\omega_1) \leqslant \kappa(\omega_2)$.

Definition 6 (regular, minimally regular). *For $\mathcal{R}$ let $\hat{u} \in \mathbb{N}$ be the smallest number such that $|\{\preccurlyeq_{\kappa}| \; \kappa \in \mathcal{O}(CR^{\hat{u}}(\mathcal{R}))\}| = |\{\preccurlyeq_{\kappa}| \; \kappa \in \mathcal{O}(CR(\mathcal{R}))|$. Then $CR^u(\mathcal{R})$ is called regular iff $u \geqslant \hat{u}$, and $CR^{\hat{u}}(\mathcal{R})$ is minimally regular; we also say that u is regular for $\mathcal{R}$ and $\hat{u}$ is minimally regular for $\mathcal{R}$.*

While $CR(\mathcal{R})$ correctly and completely models the set of all c-representations for $\mathcal{R}$ [1], every regular $CR^u(\mathcal{R})$ is correct and complete when taking inferential equivalence into account [3]. Thus, for regular u, $\hspace{1pt}\vdash^{c}_{\mathcal{R}}$ and $\hspace{1pt}\vdash^{c,u}_{\mathcal{R}}$ coincide.

Proposition 3 ([3]). *Let $\mathcal{R}$ be a knowledge base, $CR^u(\mathcal{R})$ regular, and A, B be formulas. Then $A \mathrel{\vdash\!\!\!\!\sim}^c_{\mathcal{R}} B$ iff $A \mathrel{\vdash\!\!\!\!\sim}^{c,u}_{\mathcal{R}} B$.*

The modelling of c-inference by a CSP given in [1] and using $CR(\mathcal{R})$ directly transfers to the finite domain case when using a regular $CR^u(\mathcal{R})$.

Proposition 4 (c-inference as a FD CSP [3]). *Let $\mathcal{R}$ be a consistent knowledge base, $CR^u(\mathcal{R})$ regular, and A, B formulas. Then the following holds:*

$$A \mathrel{\vdash\!\!\!\!\sim}^c_{\mathcal{R}} B \quad iff \quad CR^u(\mathcal{R}) \cup \{\neg CR_{\mathcal{R}}(B|A)\} \ is \ not \ solvable. \tag{5}$$

where $\neg CR_{\mathcal{R}}(B|A)$ is the constraint:

$$\min_{\omega \models AB} \sum_{\substack{1 \leqslant i \leqslant n \\ \omega \models A_i \overline{B_i}}} \eta_i \quad \geqslant \quad \min_{\omega \models A\overline{B}} \sum_{\substack{1 \leqslant i \leqslant n \\ \omega \models A_i \overline{B_i}}} \eta_i \tag{6}$$

Note that since $\neg CR_{\mathcal{R}}(B|A)$ does not introduce any variables not already in the CSP $CR^u(\mathcal{R})$ over finite domains, also $CR^u(\mathcal{R}) \cup \{\neg CR_{\mathcal{R}}(B|A)\}$ is a CSP over finite domains. Thus, with a regular $CR^u(\mathcal{R})$ for a knowledge base $\mathcal{R}$, we can immediately exploit the techniques developed for finite domain constraint solvers, as they are available e.g. in constraint logic programming, for computing the inference relation $A \mathrel{\vdash\!\!\!\!\sim}^c_{\mathcal{R}} B$ induced by c-representations (cf. [2]).

4   Sufficient Upper Bounds for Skeptical C-Inference

When we are not interested in capturing all c-representations as done by a regular $CR^u(\mathcal{R})$, but aim at capturing c-inference instead, we can specify a maximal impact value from this perspective in order to obtain a finite domain CSP.

Definition 7 (sufficient, minimally sufficient). *Let $\mathcal{R}$ be a knowledge base and let $u \in \mathbb{N}$. Then $CR^u(\mathcal{R})$ is called sufficient iff for all formulas A, B we have*

$$A \mathrel{\vdash\!\!\!\!\sim}^c_{\mathcal{R}} B \quad iff \quad A \mathrel{\vdash\!\!\!\!\sim}^{c,u}_{\mathcal{R}} B.$$

If $CR^u(\mathcal{R})$ is sufficient, we will also call u sufficient for $\mathcal{R}$. If $\hat{u}$ is sufficient for $\mathcal{R}$ and $\hat{u} - 1$ is not sufficient for $\mathcal{R}$, then $\hat{u}$ is minimally sufficient for $\mathcal{R}$.

The next proposition states the relationship between a regular u and a sufficient u', and shows that the latter may be strictly smaller.

Proposition 5 (regular vs. sufficient). *Let $\mathcal{R}$ be consistent and $u \in \mathbb{N}$. If $CR^u(\mathcal{R})$ is regular, then it is also sufficient; the reverse is not true in general.*

Proof. If $CR^u(\mathcal{R})$ is regular, it is also sufficient according to Proposition 3. For the other direction, it suffices to give a $CR^u(\mathcal{R})$ that is sufficient, but not regular. Consider the alphabet $\Sigma = \{a_1, a_2\}$ and the knowledge base $\mathcal{R}_2 = \{(a_1|\top), (a_2|\top)\}$. The CSP $CR^2(\mathcal{R}_2)$ is regular and has four solutions:

$$\overrightarrow{\eta}^{(1)} = (1,1) \qquad \overrightarrow{\eta}^{(2)} = (1,2) \qquad \overrightarrow{\eta}^{(3)} = (2,1) \qquad \overrightarrow{\eta}^{(4)} = (2,2)$$

Since $\overrightarrow{\eta}^{(4)}$ is a multiple of $\overrightarrow{\eta}^{(1)}$, the inference relations associated with their induced ranking functions are inferentially equivalent. Obviously, $CR^1(\mathcal{R}_2)$ only has $\overrightarrow{\eta}^{(1)}$ as a solution. Every inference that requires a different ranking of the worlds $a_1\overline{a_2}$ and $\overline{a_1}a_2$ only holds when considering either $\kappa_{\overrightarrow{\eta}^{(2)}}$ or $\kappa_{\overrightarrow{\eta}^{(3)}}$, but not when taking $\kappa_{\overrightarrow{\eta}^{(1)}}$ into account. Hence, such inferences do not hold under skeptical inference. On the other hand, every inference that holds in $\kappa_{\overrightarrow{\eta}^{(1)}}$ also holds in $\kappa_{\overrightarrow{\eta}^{(2)}}$ and $\kappa_{\overrightarrow{\eta}^{(3)}}$. Therefore, $CR^1(\mathcal{R}_1)$ is sufficient but not regular. $\square$

The proof of Proposition 5 also shows that in general, a sufficient $CR^u(\mathcal{R})$ is incomplete in the sense that there may be c-representations κ for $\mathcal{R}$ that is not inferentially equivalent to any solution of $CR^u(\mathcal{R})$. For further investigating properties and the size of regular and sufficient bounds, we will use the following.

Definition 8 ($\Sigma_n, \mathcal{R}_n$). *For $n \geqslant 1$, $\mathcal{R}_n = \{(a_1|\top), \ldots, (a_n|\top)\}$ is called the* knowledge base of n conditional facts *over $\Sigma_n = \{a_1, \ldots, a_n\}$.*

Example 2 ($\mathcal{R}_2, \mathcal{R}_3, \mathcal{R}_4$). For $\mathcal{R}_2$, $CR^1(\mathcal{R}_2)$ is minimally sufficient and $CR^2(\mathcal{R}_2)$ is minimally regular (cf. Proposition 5).

For $\mathcal{R}_3 = \{(a_1|\top), (a_2|\top), (a_3|\top)\}$ over the signature $\Sigma_3 = \{a_1, a_2, a_3\}$, we observe that $CR^4(\mathcal{R}_3)$ is minimally regular, producing 31 inferentially different c-representations; furthermore, we observe that $CR^2(\mathcal{R}_3)$ is minimally sufficient. Computing the c-representations and minimally regular and sufficient bounds for this example as well as for the other examples presented in this paper has also been done by the software system InfOCF [2].

If we add just an additional atom a_4 to the signature and thus view $\mathcal{R}_3$ as a knowledge base over Σ_4, the number of possible worlds doubles. However, the number of inferentially different c-representations stays at 31, because there is no conditional causing a preference of a world $\dot{a}_1\dot{a}_2\dot{a}_3 a_4$ over $\dot{a}_1\dot{a}_2\dot{a}_3\overline{a_4}$ or vice versa. Hence, 2 is still minimally sufficient and 4 is still minimally regular for $\mathcal{R}_3$ when considered as a knowledge base over Σ_4.

On the other hand, moving to the knowledge base $\mathcal{R}_4 = \{(a_1|\top), (a_2|\top), (a_3|\top), (a_4|\top)\}$ over the signature $\Sigma_4 = \{a_1, a_2, a_3, a_4\}$, causes worlds ω with $\omega \models a_4$ to be preferred over worlds ω' with $\omega' \models \overline{a_4}$. The number of inferentially different c-representations accepting $\mathcal{R}_4$ increases to 1519, and $CR^{10}(\mathcal{R}_4)$ is now minimally regular. In order to illustrate that $CR^9(\mathcal{R}_4)$ is not regular, consider the impact vector $\overrightarrow{\eta}_2 = (9, 7, 2, 4)$ that is an element of $Sol(CR^9(\mathcal{R}_4))$, cf. Table 2. Then $\kappa_{\overrightarrow{\eta}_2}(a_1\overline{a_2}\overline{a_3}a_4) = 9 = \kappa_{\overrightarrow{\eta}_2}(\overline{a_1}a_2 a_3 a_4)$ and $\kappa_{\overrightarrow{\eta}_2}(a_1\overline{a_2}\overline{a_3}\overline{a_4}) = 13 = \kappa_{\overrightarrow{\eta}_2}(\overline{a_1}a_2 a_3 \overline{a_4})$. By increasing the impact of $(a_1|\top)$ from 9 to 10, we get $\kappa_{\overrightarrow{\eta}_3}(a_1\overline{a_2}\overline{a_3}a_4) = 9 < 10 = \kappa_{\overrightarrow{\eta}_3}(\overline{a_1}a_2 a_3 a_4)$ and $\kappa_{\overrightarrow{\eta}_3}(a_1\overline{a_2}\overline{a_3}\overline{a_4}) = 13 < 14 = \kappa_{\overrightarrow{\eta}_3}(\overline{a_1}a_2 a_3 \overline{a_4})$. These differences in ranking in this particular combination first emerge when considering the impact vector $\overrightarrow{\eta}_3$, meaning that the total preorder induced by $\kappa_{\overrightarrow{\eta}_3}$ is not induced by any ranking function in $\mathcal{O}(CR^9(\mathcal{R}_n))$.

Thus, while going from $\mathcal{R}_3$ to $\mathcal{R}_4$ increases the minimally regular bound from 4 to 10, the minimally sufficient bound only slightly increases from 2 to 3 since $CR^3(\mathcal{R}_4)$ is minimally sufficient. We will further investigate this effect, using:

Table 2. Verification and falsification with induced impacts for $\mathcal{R}_4$ in Example 2.

ω	r_1: $(a_1\|\top)$	r_2: $(a_2\|\top)$	r_3: $(a_3\|\top)$	r_4: $(a_4\|\top)$	impact on ω	$\kappa_{\overrightarrow{\eta}_1}(\omega)$	$\kappa_{\overrightarrow{\eta}_2}(\omega)$	$\kappa_{\overrightarrow{\eta}_3}(\omega)$
$a_1\,a_2\,a_3\,a_4$	v	v	v	v	0	0	0	0
$a_1\,a_2\,a_3\,\overline{a_4}$	v	v	v	f	η_4	1	4	4
$a_1\,a_2\,\overline{a_3}\,a_4$	v	v	f	v	η_3	1	2	2
$a_1\,a_2\,\overline{a_3}\,\overline{a_4}$	v	v	f	f	$\eta_3 + \eta_4$	2	6	6
$a_1\,\overline{a_2}\,a_3\,a_4$	v	f	v	v	η_2	1	7	7
$a_1\,\overline{a_2}\,a_3\,\overline{a_4}$	v	f	v	f	$\eta_2 + \eta_4$	2	11	11
$a_1\,\overline{a_2}\,\overline{a_3}\,a_4$	v	f	f	v	$\eta_2 + \eta_3$	2	9	9
$a_1\,\overline{a_2}\,\overline{a_3}\,\overline{a_4}$	v	f	f	f	$\eta_2 + \eta_3 + \eta_4$	3	13	13
$\overline{a_1}\,a_2\,a_3\,a_4$	f	v	v	v	η_1	3	9	10
$\overline{a_1}\,a_2\,a_3\,\overline{a_4}$	f	v	v	f	$\eta_1 + \eta_4$	4	13	11
$\overline{a_1}\,a_2\,\overline{a_3}\,a_4$	f	v	f	v	$\eta_1 + \eta_3$	4	11	12
$\overline{a_1}\,a_2\,\overline{a_3}\,\overline{a_4}$	f	v	f	f	$\eta_1 + \eta_3 + \eta_4$	5	15	16
$\overline{a_1}\,\overline{a_2}\,a_3\,a_4$	f	f	v	v	$\eta_1 + \eta_2$	4	16	17
$\overline{a_1}\,\overline{a_2}\,a_3\,\overline{a_4}$	f	f	v	f	$\eta_1 + \eta_2 + \eta_4$	5	20	21
$\overline{a_1}\,\overline{a_2}\,\overline{a_3}\,a_4$	f	f	f	v	$\eta_1 + \eta_2 + \eta_3$	5	18	19
$\overline{a_1}\,\overline{a_2}\,\overline{a_3}\,\overline{a_4}$	f	f	f	f	$\eta_1 + \eta_2 + \eta_3 + \eta_4$	6	22	23
impacts:	η_1	η_2	η_3	η_4				
$\overrightarrow{\eta}_1$	3	1	1	1				
$\overrightarrow{\eta}_2$	9	7	2	4				
$\overrightarrow{\eta}_3$	10	7	2	4				

Definition 9 $(fal(\omega))$**.** *For ω over Σ_n, $fal(\omega) = \{i | \omega \models \overline{a_i}, i \in \{1, \ldots, n\}\}$ is the set of indices of the negated literals in ω.*

The special structure of $\mathcal{R}_n$ yields the following properties about the correspondence between negated literals in a world and c-representations accepting $\mathcal{R}_n$.

Proposition 6. *For all $\kappa \in \mathcal{O}(CR(\mathcal{R}_n))$ and for all $\omega, \omega' \in \Omega_{\Sigma_n}$:*

$$\text{If } fal(\omega) \subseteq fal(\omega') \text{ then } \kappa(\omega) \leqslant \kappa(\omega'). \tag{7}$$

$$\text{If } fal(\omega) \subsetneq fal(\omega') \text{ then } \kappa(\omega) < \kappa(\omega') \tag{8}$$

$$\text{If } \omega \neq a_1 \ldots a_n \text{ then } 0 = \kappa(a_1 \ldots a_n) < \kappa(\omega) \tag{9}$$

$$\text{If } \omega \neq \overline{a_1} \ldots \overline{a_n} \text{ then } \kappa(\omega) < \kappa(\overline{a_1} \ldots \overline{a_n}) \tag{10}$$

Furthermore, for any n, the special structure of $\mathcal{R}_n$ ensures that $\overrightarrow{\eta} = (1, \ldots, 1)$ induces an OCF that accepts $\mathcal{R}_n$ and that orders worlds according to their number of negated literals.

Proposition 7. *For all $\mathcal{R}_n$, $\overrightarrow{\eta} = (1, \ldots, 1) \in Sol(\mathcal{R}_n)$, and for all $\omega, \omega' \in \Omega_{\Sigma_n}$ $\kappa_{\overrightarrow{\eta}}(\omega) = |fal(\omega)|$ and therefore $\kappa_{\overrightarrow{\eta}}(\omega) = \kappa_{\overrightarrow{\eta}}(\omega')$ iff $|fal(\omega)| = |fal(\omega')|$.*

The following example illustrates how, in the case of pairs $(\Sigma_n, \mathcal{R}_n)$ the ranking of worlds ω and ω' with $fal(\omega) \not\subseteq fal(\omega')$ and $fal(\omega') \not\subseteq fal(\omega)$ by c-representations may be in any order.

Example 3 ($\mathcal{R}_3$). For $\mathcal{R}_3$ over the alphabet Σ_3, there are c-representations κ, κ' and κ'' such that for the two worlds $\omega = \overline{a_1}\,a_2\,a_3$ and $\omega' = a_1\,\overline{a_2}\,\overline{a_3}$ we have

$\kappa(\omega) < \kappa(\omega')$, $\kappa'(\omega) = \kappa'(\omega')$, and $\kappa''(\omega) > \kappa''(\omega')$ as demonstrated by the following. For $\overrightarrow{\eta}_1 = (1,1,1)$, from Proposition 7 we get $\kappa_{\overrightarrow{\eta}_1}(\omega) = 1 < 2 = \kappa_{\overrightarrow{\eta}_1}(\omega')$. By increasing the impact of the conditional $(a_1|\top)$ from 1 to 2, we get the impact vector $\overrightarrow{\eta}_2 = (2,1,1)$. In the induced ranking function $\kappa_{\overrightarrow{\eta}_2}$ we now have $\kappa_{\overrightarrow{\eta}_2}(\omega) = 2 = \kappa_{\overrightarrow{\eta}_2}(\omega')$. Finally, the impact vector $\overrightarrow{\eta}_3 = (3,1,1)$ induces the ranking function $\kappa_{\overrightarrow{\eta}_3}$ in which $\kappa_{\overrightarrow{\eta}_3}(\omega) = 3 > 2 = \kappa_{\overrightarrow{\eta}_3}(\omega')$.

The next proposition generalizes the observation from Example 3 to arbitrary n.

Proposition 8 ($\mathcal{R}_n$). *For all $\mathcal{R}_n$ and for all $\omega, \omega' \in \Omega_{\Sigma_n}$: If $fal(\omega) \not\subseteq fal(\omega')$ and $fal(\omega') \not\subseteq fal(\omega)$ then there exist c-representations $\kappa, \kappa', \kappa''$ accepting $\mathcal{R}_n$ such that:*

$$\kappa(\omega) < \kappa(\omega') \tag{11}$$
$$\kappa'(\omega) = \kappa'(\omega') \tag{12}$$
$$\kappa''(\omega) > \kappa''(\omega') \tag{13}$$

Proof. For proving (11), let $j \in \{1, \ldots, n\}$ such that $j \in fal(\omega') \setminus fal(\omega)$; hence, $\omega \models a_j$ and $\omega' \models \overline{a_j}$. Let $\overrightarrow{\eta} = (\eta_1, \ldots, \eta_n)$ where for $i \in \{1, \ldots, n\}$:

$$\eta_i = \begin{cases} 1 & \text{if } i \neq j \\ 1 & \text{if } i = j \text{ and } |fal(\omega)| < |fal(\omega')| \\ |fal(\omega)| - |fal(\omega')| + 2 & \text{otherwise} \end{cases}$$

Then $\kappa_{\overrightarrow{\eta}} \in \mathcal{O}(CR(\mathcal{R}_n))$. If $|fal(\omega)| < |fal(\omega')|$ then $\kappa_{\overrightarrow{\eta}}(\omega) = |fal(\omega)| < |fal(\omega')| = \kappa_{\overrightarrow{\eta}}(\omega')$. Otherwise we have $\kappa_{\overrightarrow{\eta}}(\omega) = |fal(\omega)| < |fal(\omega)| + 1 = |fal(\omega)| + 1 + (|fal(\omega')| - |fal(\omega')|) + (1-1) = (|fal(\omega')| - 1) + (|fal(\omega)| - |fal(\omega')| + 2) = \kappa_{\overrightarrow{\eta}}(\omega')$ and therefore $\kappa(\omega) < \kappa(\omega')$ for $\kappa = \kappa_{\overrightarrow{\eta}}$.

For proving (12), we first observe that if $|fal(\omega)| = |fal(\omega')|$, then for $\overrightarrow{\eta} = (1, \ldots, 1)$ we get $\kappa_{\overrightarrow{\eta}}(\omega) = |fal(\omega)| = |fal(\omega')| = \kappa_{\overrightarrow{\eta}}(\omega')$, yielding (12) with $\kappa' = \kappa_{\overrightarrow{\eta}}$. Otherwise, if $|fal(\omega)| \neq |fal(\omega')|$, without loss of generality assume that $|fal(\omega)| > |fal(\omega')|$. Since $fal(\omega') \not\subseteq fal(\omega)$ there is $j \in \{1, \ldots, n\}$ such that $j \in fal(\omega') \setminus fal(\omega)$; hence, $\omega \models a_j$ and $\omega' \models \overline{a_j}$. Let $\overrightarrow{\eta} = (\eta_1, \ldots, \eta_n)$ where for $i \in \{1, \ldots, n\}$:

$$\eta_i = \begin{cases} 1 & \text{if } i \neq j \\ |fal(\omega)| - |fal(\omega')| + 1 & \text{otherwise} \end{cases}$$

Then $\kappa_{\overrightarrow{\eta}} \in \mathcal{O}(CR(\mathcal{R}_n))$ with $\kappa_{\overrightarrow{\eta}}(\omega) = |fal(\omega)| = |fal(\omega)| + |fal(\omega')| - |fal(\omega')| + (1-1) = (|fal(\omega')| - 1) + (|fal(\omega)| - |fal(\omega')| + 1) = \kappa_{\overrightarrow{\eta}}(\omega')$ and therefore $\kappa'(\omega) = \kappa'(\omega')$ for $\kappa' = \kappa_{\overrightarrow{\eta}}$.

The case (13) is completely dual to (11) and can be handled analogously. $\square$

Corollary 1 ($\mathcal{R}_n$). *Proposition 8 still holds when restricting $\kappa, \kappa', \kappa''$ to OCFs in $\mathcal{O}(CR^n(\mathcal{R}_n))$.*

Proof. Conditions $fal(\omega) \not\subseteq fal(\omega')$ and $fal(\omega') \not\subseteq fal(\omega)$ imply $\omega, \omega' \in \Sigma_n \setminus \{a_1 \dots a_n, \overline{a_1} \dots \overline{a_n}\}$; thus $0 < |fal(\omega)| < n$ and $0 < |fal(\omega')| < n$. Hence, the maximal value for an impact η_i obtained in the proof of Proposition 8 is obtained in the proof of (11) as $|fal(\omega)| - |fal(\omega')| + 2 \leqslant ((n-1) - 1) + 2 = n$. □

Proposition 8 and Corollary 1 are in accordance with the elaborations in Example 2. Since we only require the two minimal worlds in question for an inference to be equal in order to reject the inference, a maximal impact of $n-1$ is sufficient, since this is the maximal impact needed to construct an impact vector that induces a ranking function that ranks two worlds ω and ω' with $fal(\omega) \not\subseteq fal(\omega')$ and $fal(\omega') \not\subseteq fal(\omega)$ equally. In fact, while we can currently prove that $CR^1(\mathcal{R}_2)$ and $CR^2(\mathcal{R}_3)$ are minimally sufficient, also $CR^3(\mathcal{R}_4)$ and more generally $CR^{n-1}(\mathcal{R}_n)$ for every n seems to be minimally sufficient, while the bound for minimally regular increases much faster. Given these observations that are also supported by extensive empirical evaluations involving several hundred thousands of inferences drawn by InfOCF [2], the sequence $\mathcal{R}_2, \mathcal{R}_3, \mathcal{R}_4, \dots$ shows that the quotient of the minimally regular bound for a knowledge base and of the minimally sufficient bound for this knowledge base can get arbitrarily large. In general, there is a large gap between minimally sufficient and minimally regular.

5   Implementation and First Evaluation Results

We extended the implementation of InfOCF [2] by a maximal impact feature (cf. the screenshot in Fig. 1). Calculating the minimally regular n for $\mathcal{R}$ automatically is done by calculating all possible solutions to $CR^i(\mathcal{R})$ for increasing i until no

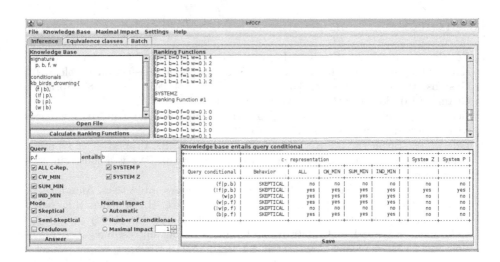

Fig. 1. User interface of InfOCF for nonmonotonic inference based on ranking functions with maximal impact selection in the lower left area of the UI

new total pre-orders are obtained. While this heuristic seems plausible, a formal proof is still needed. The other options use the maximal impact n with $n = |\mathcal{R}|$ which is currently our best approximation of a sufficient u. The third option allows for experimentation with a selected maximal impact.

For $\mathcal{R}_{birds}$ from Example 1, also shown in Fig. 1, we calculated a minimally regular maximal impact of 8 producing 91 inferentially different c-representations. All experiments indicate that there is no difference between inference using the maximal impact 8 or the maximal impact 4, i.e. the number of conditionals. For our experiments with $\mathcal{R}_3$ we generated the set of all 52.670 conditionals over the alphabet Σ_3, respecting propositional equivalences in antecedent and consequence, that can be both verified and falsified. Since 4 is regular for $\mathcal{R}_3$ and no difference in the inference behavior of $\vdash^{c,2}_{\mathcal{R}_3}$ and $\vdash^{c,4}_{\mathcal{R}_3}$ occurred for any of the conditionals, 2 is minimally sufficient for $\mathcal{R}_3$. In a similar process for $\mathcal{R}_4$, several hundred thousand conditionals where evaluated both with the assumed minimally sufficient maximal impact of 3 and with the impact of 10 determined to be minimally regular. Again no difference was found between $\vdash^{c,3}_{\mathcal{R}_4}$ and $\vdash^{c,10}_{\mathcal{R}_4}$.

6   Conclusions

Both c-representation as well as c-inference taking all c-representations of a conditional knowledge base $\mathcal{R}$ into account can be modeled by constraint satisfaction problems. We discussed regular and sufficient upper bounds when using finite domain CSPs for this and how they can be employed when approximating and implementing c-inference. Our current work includes developing further methods for determining such bounds for arbitry knowledge bases, and the investigation of complexity issues.

References

1. Beierle, C., Eichhorn, C., Kern-Isberner, G.: Skeptical inference based on C-representations and its characterization as a constraint satisfaction problem. In: Gyssens, M., Simari, G. (eds.) FoIKS 2016. LNCS, vol. 9616, pp. 65–82. Springer, Cham (2016). doi:10.1007/978-3-319-30024-5_4
2. Beierle, C., Eichhorn, C., Kutsch, S.: A practical comparison of qualitative inferences with preferred ranking models. KI **31**, 41–52 (2017)
3. Beierle, C., Eichhorn, C., Kern-Isberner, G., Kutsch, S.: Properties of skeptical C-inference for conditional knowledge bases and its realization as a constraint satisfaction problem (2016). (submitted)
4. de Finetti, B.: La prévision, ses lois logiques et ses sources subjectives. Ann. Inst. H. Poincaré **7**(1), 1–68 (1937). English translation: Kyburg, H., Smokler, H.E. (eds.) Studies in Subjective Probability. Wiley, New York, pp. 93–158 (1974)
5. Goldszmidt, M., Pearl, J.: Qualitative probabilities for default reasoning, belief revision, and causal modeling. Artif. Intell. **84**(1–2), 57–112 (1996)
6. Kern-Isberner, G.: Conditionals in Nonmonotonic Reasoning and Belief Revision. LNCS (LNAI), vol. 2087. Springer, Heidelberg (2001).

7. Kern-Isberner, G.: A thorough axiomatization of a principle of conditional preservation in belief revision. Ann. Math. Artif. Intell. **40**(1–2), 127–164 (2004)
8. Spohn, W.: Ordinal conditional functions: a dynamic theory of epistemic states. In: Harper, W., Skyrms, B. (eds.) Causation in Decision, Belief Change, and Statistics, vol. II, pp. 105–134. Kluwer Academic Publishers (1988)

On Transformations and Normal Forms
of Conditional Knowledge Bases

Christoph Beierle[1(✉)], Christian Eichhorn[2], and Gabriele Kern-Isberner[2]

[1] Department of Computer Science, University of Hagen, 58084 Hagen, Germany
christoph.beierle@fernuni-hagen.de
[2] Department of Computer Science, TU Dortmund, 44221 Dortmund, Germany

Abstract. Background knowledge is often represented by sets of conditionals of the form "if A then usually B". Such knowledge bases should not be circuitous, but compact and easy to compare in order to allow for efficient processing in approaches dealing with and inferring from background knowledge, such as nonmonotonic reasoning. In this paper we present transformation systems on conditional knowledge bases that allow to identify and remove unnecessary conditionals from the knowledge base while preserving the knowledge base's model set.

1   Introduction

Conditional knowledge bases formalize the background knowledge of a reasoning agent. They are often used as the base of the agent's inferences and hence play a major role in nonmonotonic reasoning. A short, compact normal form of this representations is desirable. Containing no unnecessary conditionals, the computational complexity of inductively generating an epistemic state based on a normalized knowledge base is reduced significantly, the number of conditionals being an important factor of this task's complexity. Additionally, normalized knowledge bases are easier to compare, which makes it easier to check whether two knowledge bases should license for the same inferences.

In this paper we devise transformation systems that allow to normalize conditional knowledge bases to such an extent that they reduce the number of conditionals while keeping the set of models constant.

2   Conditionals and OCFs

Let $\Sigma = \{V_1, ..., V_m\}$ be a propositional alphabet. A *literal* is the positive (v_i) or negated ($\overline{v}_i$) form of a propositional variable V_i. From these we obtain the propositional language $\mathfrak{L}$ as the set of formulas of Σ closed under negation $\neg$, conjunction $\wedge$, and disjunction $\vee$, as usual; for formulas $A, B \in \mathfrak{L}$, $A \Rightarrow B$ denotes the material implication and stands for $\neg A \vee B$. For shorter formulas, we abbreviate conjunction by juxtaposition (i.e., AB stands for $A \wedge B$), and negation by overlining (i.e., $\overline{A}$ is equivalent to $\neg A$). Let Ω denote the set of possible worlds over $\mathfrak{L}$; Ω will be taken here simply as the set of all propositional interpretations

© Springer International Publishing AG 2017
S. Benferhat et al. (Eds.): IEA/AIE 2017, Part I, LNAI 10350, pp. 488–494, 2017.
DOI: 10.1007/978-3-319-60042-0_53

over $\mathcal{L}$ and can be identified with the set of all complete conjunctions over Σ. For $\omega \in \Omega$, $\omega \models A$ means that the propositional formula $A \in \mathcal{L}$ holds in the possible world ω.

A *conditional* $(B|A)$ with $A, B \in \mathcal{L}$ encodes the defeasible rule "if A then normally B" and is a trivalent logical entity with the evaluation [1,3]

$$
[\![(B|A)]\!]_\omega = \begin{cases} true & \text{iff} \quad \omega \models AB & \text{(verification)} \\ false & \text{iff} \quad \omega \models A\overline{B} & \text{(falsification)} \\ undefined & \text{iff} \quad \omega \models \overline{A} & \text{(not applicable)} \end{cases}
$$

A *knowledge base* $\mathcal{R} = \{(B_1|A_1), ..., (B_n|A_n)\}$ is a finite set of conditionals.

An *Ordinal Conditional Function* (OCF, ranking function) [5] is a function $\kappa : \Omega \to \mathbb{N}_0 \cup \{\infty\}$ that assigns to each world $\omega \in \Omega$ an implausibility rank $\kappa(\omega)$, that is, the higher $\kappa(\omega)$, the more surprising ω is. OCFs have to satisfy the normalization condition that there has to be a world that is maximally plausible, i.e., the preimage of 0 cannot be empty, formally $\kappa^{-1}(0) \neq \emptyset$. The rank of a formula A is defined by $\kappa(A) = \min\{\kappa(\omega) \mid \omega \models A\}$.

An OCF κ *accepts* a conditional $(B|A)$ (denoted by $\kappa \models (B|A)$) iff the verification of the conditional is less surprising than its falsification, i.e., iff $\kappa(AB) < \kappa(A\overline{B})$. This can also be understood as a nonmonotonic inference relation between the premise A and the conclusion B: We say that A κ-*entails* B (written $A \models^\kappa B$) if and only if κ accepts the conditional $(B|A)$, formally

$$
\kappa \models (B|A) \quad \text{iff} \quad \kappa(AB) < \kappa(A\overline{B}) \quad \text{iff} \quad A \models^\kappa B. \tag{1}
$$

The acceptance relation in (1) is extended as usual to a set $\mathcal{R}$ of conditionals by defining $\kappa \models \mathcal{R}$ iff $\kappa \models (B|A)$ for all $(B|A) \in \mathcal{R}$. This is synonymous to saying that $\mathcal{R}$ is *admissible* with respect to $\mathcal{R}$ [2].

A knowledge base $\mathcal{R}$ is *consistent* iff there exists an OCF κ such that $\kappa \models \mathcal{R}$.

Example 1 ($\mathcal{R}_{bird}$). Let $\Sigma = \{P, B, F\}$ be an alphabet where P indicates whether something is a penguin (p), or not ($\overline{p}$), B indicates whether something is a bird (b), or not ($\overline{b}$), and F indicates whether something is capable of flying (f), or not ($\overline{f}$). From this language we compose the knowledge base

$$
\mathcal{R}_{bird} = \begin{cases} r_1 = (f|b), & r_2 = (\overline{f}|p), & r_3 = (b|p), & r_4 = (p|p\overline{f}), \\ r_5 = (p\overline{f}|p), & r_6 = (\overline{p}|\top), & r_7 = (bf \vee \overline{b}f | pb \vee \overline{p}b) \end{cases} \tag{2}
$$

to formalize the following rules:

r_1: Usually birds can fly. r_4: Non-flying penguins usually are penguins.
r_2: Usually penguins cannot fly. r_5: Penguins usually are non-flying penguins.
r_3: Penguins usually are birds. r_6: Usually, individuals are no penguins.
r_7: Individuals that are penguins and birds or are no penguins but birds
  usually are birds that can fly or birds that cannot fly.

This knowledge base is consistent: For instance, a ranking model κ for $\mathcal{R}_{bird}$ is

ω	$p\,b\,f$	$p\,b\,\overline{f}$	$p\,\overline{b}\,f$	$p\,\overline{b}\,\overline{f}$	$\overline{p}\,b\,f$	$\overline{p}\,b\,\overline{f}$	$\overline{p}\,\overline{b}\,f$	$\overline{p}\,\overline{b}\,\overline{f}$
$\kappa(\omega)$	2	1	4	2	0	1	0	0

with, e.g., $\kappa \models (\overline{f}|p)$ because $\kappa(p\overline{f}) = 1 < 2 = \kappa(pf)$ and $\kappa \models (\overline{p}|\top)$ because $\kappa(\overline{p}) = 0 < 1 = \kappa(\overline{p})$.

3   Model Based Equivalences and Normal Forms

With the acceptance relation between ranking functions and knowledge bases, we now can define the set of ranking models of a knowledge base.

Definition 1 (Ranking models). *Let $\mathcal{R} = \{(B_1|A_1), \ldots, (B_n|A_n)\}$ be a finite conditional knowledge base. The set of* ranking models *of $\mathcal{R}$ is the set of OCFs that are admissible with respect to $\mathcal{R}$, formally $Mod(\mathcal{R}) = \{\kappa | \kappa \models \mathcal{R}\}$.*

The notion of inconsistency gives us a possibility to determine whether every ranking model of a knowledge base accepts a given conditional:

Proposition 1 ([2]). *Let $\mathcal{R} = \{(B_1|A_1), \ldots, (B_n|A_n)\}$ be a finite conditional knowledge base. A conditional $(B|A)$ is accepted by every ranking model $\kappa \in Mod(\mathcal{R})$ if and only if $\mathcal{R} \cup \{(\overline{B}|A)\}$ is inconsistent.*

Definition 2 (Equivalence of knowledge bases). *Let $\mathcal{R}, \mathcal{R}'$ be knowledge bases over Σ. $\mathcal{R}$ and $\mathcal{R}'$ are equivalent, denoted $\mathcal{R} \equiv \mathcal{R}'$, iff $Mod(\mathcal{R}) = Mod(\mathcal{R}')$.*

By definition, the model set of an inconsistent knowledge base is empty, so all inconsistent knowledge bases are equivalent with respect to this definition. We introduce the special knowledge base $\diamond$ that is inconsistent by definition; thus $\diamond \equiv \mathcal{R}$ for every $\mathcal{R}$ with $Mod(\mathcal{R}) = \emptyset$; for instance, $\{(\bot|\top)\} \equiv \diamond$.

For propositional formulas over a propositional alphabet Σ, there are various ways of defining a normal form such that precisely semantically equivalent formulas are mapped to the same normal form, using e.g. disjunctions of worlds or selected shortest formulas. In order to abstract from a particular choice, for the rest of this paper we assume a function ν that maps a propositional formula A to a unique normal form $\nu(A)$ such that $A \equiv A'$ iff $\nu(A) = \nu(A')$. Using ν, the transformation system NF is given in Fig. 1:

(SF) removes a conditional $(B|A)$ if $A \models B$ since such a conditional is self-fulfilling because it can not be falsified by any world.

(DP) removes a conditional $(B'|A')$ which is a duplicate of a conditional $(B|A)$ under propositional equivalences of A and A' and of B and B'.

(CE) removes a conditional that is conditionally equivalent to another one.

(PN) propositionally normalizes antecedent and consequent of a conditional.

(SC) transforms a knowledge base containing a conditional that can not be verified by any world into the inconsistent knowledge base $\diamond$.

Example 2 ($NF(\mathcal{R}_{bird})$). Consider the knowledge base $\mathcal{R}_{bird}$ from Example 1.

(SF) *self-fulfilling* :
$$\frac{\mathcal{R} \cup \{(B|A)\}}{\mathcal{R}} \qquad A \models B, \ A \not\equiv \bot$$

(DP) *duplicate* :
$$\frac{\mathcal{R} \cup \{(B|A), (B'|A')\}}{\mathcal{R} \cup \{(B|A)\}} \qquad A \equiv A', \ B \equiv B'$$

(CE) *conditional equivalence* :
$$\frac{\mathcal{R} \cup \{(B|A), (B'|A')\}}{\mathcal{R} \cup \{(B|A)\}} \qquad AB \equiv A'B', \ A\overline{B} \equiv A'\overline{B'}$$

(PN) *propositional normal form* :
$$\frac{\mathcal{R} \cup \{(B|A)\}}{\mathcal{R} \cup \{(\nu(B)|\nu(A))\}} \qquad A \neq \nu(A) \text{ or } B \neq \nu(B)$$

(SC) *self-contradictory* :
$$\frac{\mathcal{R} \cup \{(B|A)\}}{\diamond} \qquad AB \equiv \bot$$

Fig. 1. Transformation rules NF for conditional knowledge bases

(SF) In $\mathcal{R}_{bird}$, r_4 is self fulfilling since $pf \models p$, hence the application of (SF) yields $\mathcal{R}_{bird}^{(SF)} = \mathcal{R}_{bird} \setminus \{r_4\}$.

(DP) The conditionals r_1 and r_7 are duplicates since $b \equiv pb \vee \overline{p}b$ and $f \equiv (bf \vee \overline{b}f)$. So applying (DP) to $\mathcal{R}_{bird}$ gives us $\mathcal{R}_{bird}^{(DP)} = \mathcal{R}_{bird} \setminus \{r_7\}$.

(CE) We have $p\overline{f} \equiv pp\overline{f}$ and $pf \equiv p \wedge (\overline{p} \vee f)$, therefore r_2 and r_5 are conditionally equivalent; applying (CE) to $\mathcal{R}_{bird}$ yields $\mathcal{R}_{bird}^{(CE)} = \mathcal{R}_{bird} \setminus \{r_5\}$.

(PN) The conditional r_1 is equivalent to r_7 but shorter, so let us assume the shorter formula as propositional normal form. With ν being a function that converts a propositional formula to this normal form, applying (PN) to $\mathcal{R}_{bird}$ gives us the same results as (DP), that is, $\mathcal{R}_{bird}^{(PN)} = \mathcal{R}_{bird} \setminus \{r_7\}$.

(SC) The knowledge base $\mathcal{R}_{bird}$ contains no self-contradictory conditional; hence, (SC) can not be applied to $\mathcal{R}_{bird}$.

Applying NF exhaustively and in arbitrary sequence to $\mathcal{R}_{bird}$ gives us the the knowledge base $\mathcal{R}_{bird}^{NF} = NF(\mathcal{R}_{bird}) = \{r_1, r_2, r_3, r_6\}$.

Note that NF is not a minimal set of transformation rules. For instance, (DP) is redundant since the effect of removing a conditional $(B'|A')$ as a duplicate of $(B|A)$ could also be achieved by applying (PN) to both conditionals, thereby mapping them both to the same normalized conditional in the resulting knowledge base. However, our objective here was not to present a minimal set of rules, but a set of more or less naturally arising transformation rules.

Proposition 2 (NF terminating). *NF is terminating.*

Proof. The transformation rules (SF), (DP), (CE), and (IC) all remove at least one conditional, and (PN) can be applied at most once to any conditional; hence, NF is terminating. $\square$

Proposition 3 (NF correct). *Let $NF(\mathcal{R})$ be the knowledge base obtained from $\mathcal{R}$ by exhaustively applying NF to $\mathcal{R}$. Then $\mathcal{R} \equiv NF(\mathcal{R})$.*

Proof. We prove the proposition by showing that each single rule is correct.

- (SF) is correct since $(B|A)$ with $A \models B$ is verified by every OCF.
- (DP) is correct since $A \equiv A'$, $B \equiv B'$ implies that $\kappa \models (B|A)$ iff $\kappa \models (B'|A')$ for every OCF κ.
- (CE) is correct since $AB \equiv A'B'$, $A\overline{B} \equiv A\overline{B'}$ implies that $\kappa \models (B|A)$ iff $\kappa \models (B'|A')$ for every OCF κ.
- (PN) is correct since for every OCF κ, we have $\kappa \models (B|A)$ iff $\kappa \models (\nu(B)|\nu(A))$.
- (SC) is correct since there is no OCF κ with $\kappa \models (B|A)$ if $AB \equiv \bot$. $\square$

While *NF* always terminates and yields a correct result, *NF* is not confluent as the choice of the transformation rule applications may influence the result as illustrated by the following example.

Example 3 (NF not confluent). Let $\mathcal{R} = \{(B|A), (AB|A)\}$. To this knowledge base, only (CE) is applicable, but this rule has no preference over the conditionally equivalent conditionals, and hence both $\mathcal{R}' = \{(B|A)\}$ and $\mathcal{R}'' = \{(AB|A)\}$ are results of exhaustively applying *NF* to $\mathcal{R}$.

4   Redundant Conditionals

Note that the properties stated about *NF* so far do not yet imply that *NF*-normalized knowledge bases are minimal under semantical equivalence.

Example 4 (NF not minimizing). We illustrate that *NF* is not minimizing using the running example with the knowledge bases $\mathcal{R}_{bird}$ and $\mathcal{R}_{bird}^{NF}$. We already illustrated that $\mathcal{R}_{bird}^{NF}$ can be obtained from $\mathcal{R}_{bird}$ by exhaustive application of the rules of *NF* in Example 2, i.e. $NF(\mathcal{R}_{bird}) = \mathcal{R}_{bird}^{NF}$. But $\mathcal{R}_{bird}^{NF}$ is not minimal with respect to set inclusion: Consider the knowledge base $\mathcal{R}'_{bird} = \{r_1, r_2, r_3\} \subsetneq \mathcal{R}_{bird}^{NF} = \{r_1, r_2, r_3, r_6\}$. We have $\mathcal{R}'_{bird} \cup \{(p|\top)\} \equiv \diamond$ and thus Proposition 1 gives us $\kappa \models (\overline{p}|\top)$ for all $\kappa \models \mathcal{R}'_{bird}$. Therefore, since $r_6 = (\overline{p}|\top)$, every ranking model of $\mathcal{R}'_{bird}$ is also a ranking model of $\mathcal{R}_{bird}^{NF}$, thus $\mathcal{R}'_{bird} \equiv \mathcal{R}_{bird}^{NF}$.

   NF is also not minimizing for inconsistency. The knowledge base $\mathcal{R}_1 = \{(B|A), (\overline{B}|A)\}$ is inconsistent and thus $\mathcal{R}_1 \equiv \diamond$, but $NF(\mathcal{R}_1) = \mathcal{R}_1 \neq \diamond$.

In the following, we will use a function Π that assigns to a knowledge base $\mathcal{R}$ an ordered partition $\Pi(\mathcal{R}) = (\mathcal{R}_0, \dots, \mathcal{R}_m)$ such that all conditionals in $\mathcal{R}_i$, $1 \le i \le m$, are tolerated by the set $\bigcup_{j=i}^{m} \mathcal{R}_j$ [4]; if no such partition exists, then $\Pi(\mathcal{R}) = \circ$. Thus, $\mathcal{R}$ is consistent iff $\Pi(\mathcal{R}) \neq \circ$ [4].

   Using Π, we define the transformation systems NF_2 as in Fig. 2, and NF_3 as the sequential composition of *NF* and NF_2, i.e., $NF_3(\mathcal{R}) = NF_2(NF(\mathcal{R}))$.

Proposition 4. NF_3 *is terminating and correct.*

Proof. NF_2 terminates since each rule reduces the size of the knowledge base. (RC) is correct since $\Pi(\mathcal{R} \cup \{(\overline{B}|A)\}) = \circ$ implies $\kappa \models (B|A)$ for all $\kappa \in Mod(\mathcal{R})$ (Proposition 1). (IC) is correct since $Mod(\mathcal{R}) = \emptyset$ for any inconsistent $\mathcal{R}$. Obviously, these properties of NF_2 also hold for NF_3. $\square$

(RC) *redundant conditional* : $\dfrac{\mathcal{R} \cup \{(B|A)\}}{\mathcal{R}}$ $\Pi(\mathcal{R} \cup \{(\overline{B}|A)\}) = \circ$

(IC) *inconsistency* : $\dfrac{\mathcal{R}}{\diamond}$ $\Pi(\mathcal{R}) = \circ$

Fig. 2. Transformation rules NF_2 for conditional knowledge bases

Just as NF, also NF_3 is not confluent (cf. Example 3), but it is minimizing.

Proposition 5 (NF_3 minimizing). *For all $\mathcal{R}, \mathcal{R}'$ we have*

$$\mathcal{R}' \subsetneqq NF_3(\mathcal{R}) \quad \text{implies} \quad \mathcal{R}' \not\equiv \mathcal{R} \tag{3}$$

$$NF_3(\mathcal{R}) = \diamond \quad \text{iff} \quad \mathcal{R} \equiv \diamond \tag{4}$$

Proof. (3) holds since any conditional $(B|A)$ in $NF_3(\mathcal{R})$ can not be a p-entailment of the set of the other conditionals in $NF_3(\mathcal{R})$ (Proposition 1). (4) holds since the existence of an ordered partion is a consistency test [4].

5 Conclusions and Future Work

We defined equivalence of conditional knowledge bases by means of identical sets of ranking models, and devised transformation systems for knowledge bases yielding compacter normal forms. While NF_3 is terminating, correct, and minimizing, it is not confluent. In future work, we will improve its confluence behaviour, e.g. by transforming $(B|A)$ into the conditional normal from $(AB|A)$. Since the transformation systems are model preserving, the obtained normal forms can be used for all inference relations taking all models into account; we are currently investigating to which extent this also applies to inference relations defined with respect to set of preferred models. Our future work also includes the study of practical consequences obtained by using normalized knowledge bases instead of their non-normalized versions.

Acknowledgment. This work was supported by DFG-Grant KI1413/5-1 to Gabriele Kern-Isberner as part of the priority program "New Frameworks of Rationality" (SPP 1516). Christian Eichhorn is supported by this Grant.

References

1. B. de Finetti. La prévision, ses lois logiques et ses sources subjectives. Ann. Inst. H. Poincaré, 7(1):1–68, 1937. Engl. transl. Theory of Probability, J. Wiley & Sons, 1974
2. Goldszmidt, M., Pearl, J.: Qualitative probabilities for default reasoning, belief revision, and causal modeling. Artificial Intelligence **84**(1–2), 57–112 (1996)
3. G. Kern-Isberner. Conditionals in Nonmonotonic Reasoning and Belief Revision - Considering Conditionals as Agents. Number 2087 in Lecture Notes in Computer Science. Springer Science+Business Media, Berlin, DE, 2001

4. Pearl, J.: System Z: A natural ordering of defaults with tractable applications to nonmonotonic reasoning. In: Parikh, R. (ed.) Proceedings of the 3rd conference on Theoretical aspects of reasoning about knowledge (TARK1990). pp, pp. 121–135. Morgan Kaufmann Publishers Inc, San Francisco, CA, USA (1990)
5. Spohn, W.: The Laws of Belief: Ranking Theory and Its Philosophical Applications. Oxford University Press, Oxford, UK (2012)

ADNOTO: A Self-adaptive System
for Automatic Ontology-Based Annotation
of Unstructured Documents

Laura Pandolfo[✉] and Luca Pulina

POLCOMING, Università di Sassari, Viale Mancini N. 5, 07100 Sassari, Italy
{laura.pandolfo,lpulina}@uniss.it

Abstract. In this paper we describe ADNOTO, a self-adaptive system for automatic ontology-based document annotation. The main goal of ADNOTO is the automatization of the document annotation process, particularly in the context of ontology-based digital libraries.

1 Introduction

It is a well-known fact that the amount of textual information available on the Web is growing exponentially, and annotation tasks represent a solution to the long-standing problem of finding relevant information from documents. The process of document annotation consists of detecting keywords, or simple expressions, and then adding metadata to these portions of document. Semantic Web technologies are known to provide support to give additional and semantic information about existing pieces of data in the documents, in terms of ontologies or vocabularies. In particular, Ontology-Based document annotation allows methods to combine annotated entities with their related ontology classes. Whilst manual document annotation requires specialized expertise and a great deal of time, automatic annotation techniques of the state-of-the-art do not seem mature enough since there are some unresolved open issues, e.g., the task of detecting accurately entities from unstructured texts is a challenging problem, and in general processing natural language.

The annotation task is particularly pronounced in the digital libraries field, in which metadata is often the first step towards the development of efficient query and retrieval mechanisms. Therefore, a large part of documents stored in these repositories are represented by unstructured and heterogeneous texts, making it tricky to apply effectively automatic Ontology-Based annotation tools. In this context, Ontology-Based Information Extraction (OBIE) systems and Natural Language Processing (NLP) techniques could be used for reducing the burden of automatic annotation process from texts in natural language.

In this paper we present ADNOTO, a self-adaptive system for automatic ontology-based annotation of unstructured documents. The main purpose of this system is the automatization of the annotation process from texts in natural language, especially in the context of ontology-based digital libraries.

© Springer International Publishing AG 2017
S. Benferhat et al. (Eds.): IEA/AIE 2017, Part I, LNAI 10350, pp. 495–501, 2017.
DOI: 10.1007/978-3-319-60042-0_54

The self-adaptivity feature of ADNOTO allows to improve the accuracy annotation performance when the usage scenario changes. In particular, ADNOTO implements a mechanism called *retraining*, that is close to the one used successfully in the context of QBF and ASP solving by the solver AQME [1] and ME-ASP [2], respectively. ADNOTO builds on and extend the methodology described in [3] and to the extent of our knowledge, it is the only self-adaptive system for automatic annotation. ADNOTO also provides a triplet extraction mechanism devoted to detect RDF triples, making it also suitable for ontology population task.

Several ontology-based annotation tools have been developed in the last years. The system presented in this paper differs from [4,5] since we take into account unstructured and heterogeneous documents instead of web pages. Moreover, unlike [6], our ontology-based annotation system it is not based for the most part on gazetteers, namely a predefined list of instances of ontology concepts. Also, the self-adaptivity feature remains the main peculiarity of ADNOTO, that differentiates it from others systems.

We test ADNOTO in the context of the ontology-based digital library STOLE [7]. This case study offers several challenges concerning automatic annotation and ontology population tasks. Our preliminary results show that self-adaptation in the context of automated annotation and ontology population can be a promising direction for further research. The rest of the paper is organized as follows. In Sect. 2 we describe the architecture and implementation details of ADNOTO, while in Sect. 3 we describe the case study mentioned above. In Sect. 4 we report the results of a preliminary experimental analysis and we conclude the paper with some final remarks.

2   Design and Implementation of ADNOTO

In this section we present both architecture and implementation details of ADNOTO. Looking at Fig. 1, we can see that ADNOTO is composed of the modules described in the following.

The **Text Converter** (TC) module is devoted to convert in plain text the content of the input document. In the current implementation, we use Apache Tika 1.13. The **Text Preprocessing** (TP) module aims to accomplish different Information Extraction (IE) and NLP tasks, namely Sentence Splitting, Named Entity Recognition, and Part-Of-Speech tagging. They have been implemented (on top of OpenNLP 1.6.0) in different submodules, namely – with reference to Fig. 1 – **Sentence Detector** (SD), **Named Entity Recognition** (NER), and **Part-Of-Speech Tagger** (POS). In addition, NER includes a pool of model files, one for each entity to recognize. In ADNOTO, entities have the same name of the ontology classes considered for the automatic annotation. The set of ontology classes to annotate is given as input by the user.

Entity Filter (EF) aims to refine the results returned by NER on the basis of the output obtained by POS – details are available in [3]. The **Triplet Extractor** (TE) module is devoted to extract relevant triples from the text and add

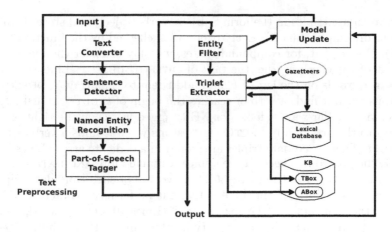

Fig. 1. Overview of the architecture of the ADnOTO.

them to the Knowledge Base. Our approach to TE exploits the fact that the verb is the dynamic element which allocates the meaning of a concept in the speaker's mind.

Figure 2 shows the pseudo-code of the triple extraction algorithm implemented in TE. Looking at the figure, we can see that TRIPLETEXTRACTOR takes as input an array T (containing text lines coming from the output of EF), the schema of the KB – denoted as TB, and an array G, in which every element is an array containing a gazetteer of verbs (**Gazetteers** in Fig. 1). Looking at the code in Fig. 2 (Lines 2–14), we can see that the procedure first looks for a

```
TRIPLETEXTRACTOR(T, TB, G)
 1  CANDIDATE ← NIL
 2  foreach t in T
 3      S ← NIL
 4      O ← NIL
 5      for i = 1 to SIZE(t)
 6          v ← t[i]
 7          if ISVERB(v) then
 8              DETECTSUBJECT(i, S)
 9              DETECTOBJECT(i, O)
10          if not EMPTY(S) and not EMPTY(O)
11              foreach s in S
12                  foreach o in O
13                      ADDCANDIDATE(CANDIDATE, s, v, o)
14          i ← i + 1
15  TRIPLE ← NIL
16  foreach c in CANDIDATE
17      v ← GETVERB(c)
18      op ← NIL
19      foreach g in G
20          for i = 1 to SIZE(g)
21              if v == g[i]
22                  op ← NAMEOF(g)
23                  break
24              GETSYNSET(SYN, g[i])
25              foreach syn in SYN
26                  if (syn == v)
27                      op ← NAMEOF(g)
28                      break
29              i ← i + 1
30      if op ≠ NIL
31          d ← GETDOMAINNAME(TB, op)
32          r ← GETRANGENAME(TB, op)
33          s ← GETSUBJECT(c)
34          o ← GETOBJECT(c)
35          if ENTITY(s) == d and ENTITY(o) == r
36              t ← MAKETRIPLE(TB, s, op, o)
37              PUSH(TRIPLE, t)
```

Fig. 2. Pseudo-code of triplet extraction basic routine.

pool of candidate triples in the form Subject-Verb-Object, and store them in an array initially empty (Line 1). Each token in t is checked by the function ISVERB (Line 7). Notice that, for compound tenses, we only consider the main verb. If the result of the check is true, the task of DETECTSUBJECT (Line 8) is to find NER tagged words on the left of v, and add them to the array S. DETECTSUBJECT stops when it finds a verb or reaches the begin of t. DETECTOBJECT (Line 9) works in a similar way; it looks for NER tagged words on the right of v, and add them to the array O. DETECTOBJECT stops when it finds a verb or reaches the end of t. Then, candidate triples are stored in a dedicate array (Lines 10–13).

Next, the procedure checks if the triples contained in CANDIDATE are consistent with respect to TB (Lines 16–36). The verb v of each candidate triple c is conjugate to its infinitive form (Line 17), and it performs a syntactic check with respect to the elements g of the gazetteers G (Lines 19–21). Notice that G contains a g related to each Object Property involved in the RDF triples detection. If the match is positive, the name of the Object Property related to g is stored in op, and the loop ends (Lines 21–23). If it is not the case, synonyms of the current element $g[i]$ of g are collected and stored in the array SYN (Line 24) – see also Lexical Database in Fig. 1. Then, v is syntactic checked against each element of SYN (Lines 25–28). Once detected op, TB is queried in order to obtain the name of domain and range – d and r, respectively – related to op (Lines 31–32). Both d and r are compared with the entity names of subject and object of c – s and o, respectively (Line 35). If the resulting triple t is consistent with respect to the ontology, it is collected in the array TRIPLE (Lines 35–37), else c is discarded. Finally, triples are added to the KB.

The self-adaptivity features of ADNOTO are contained in the Model Update (MU) module. Considering that manual annotation is a very time-consuming process, the main idea under MU is to leverage (correct) automatic annotation of ADNOTO to improve the accuracy of NER models. In order to do that, MU takes as input the output of EF – a set of processed sentences tagged by the NER module – and the set of triples detected by TE. Each sentence related to a triple is then appended to the training set(s) corresponding the entity occurring in the subject/object, and a new NER model is built.

Finally, we report that TE is implemented in JAVA language. The interaction with TBox is implemented on top of the OWL APIs (Version 3), while as triple store we use Stardog 4 Community. Lexical Database is implemented using MultiWordNet [8].

3   The STOLE Ontology-Based Digital Library

STOLE is an ontology-based digital library [7] that collects journal articles published in the 19th and 20th centuries concerning the history of public administration in Italy. The case study here presented offers several challenging issues related to automatic annotation and ontology population tasks. First, most part of the historical journal articles in STOLE are low-quality scanned PDFs of photocopies, so the converted file in text format contains several typos and errors.

Second, most part of the considered journal articles are written in an old technical Italian language, and even the manual annotation by experts required a great deal of effort. The complexity of the language represents a significant barrier since there are not available models for IE and NLP tasks, neither for old Italian language nor for the investigated domain. The STOLE ontology is the conceptual layer of the digital library[1]. In the following we briefly describe the classes of the STOLE ontology involved in the experiments presented in Sect. 4:

- Article is the class that represents the collection of journal articles.
- Event contains relevant events for this specific domain.
- Institution is the class that represents the different public institutions.
- LegalSystem includes the successive systems for interpreting and enforcing the laws.
- Person is the class representing people cited in the articles or involved in events. This class contains one subclass, Author, that includes the contributors of the articles.

The object properties of STOLE involved in our analysis are listed below:

- cites is the object property that connects individuals in Article to individuals in Person, highlighting the people that are mentioned in an article.
- hasInstitutionEventOf, hasLegalSystemEventOf, hasLifeEventOf are object properties connecting individuals from classes Institution, LegalSystem, and Person to the class Event.
- mentions highlights which historical event is mentioned in a given article. Its domain is Article, while its range is Event.
- reportsInstitution and reportsLegalSystem point out which institutions and legal systems, respectively, appear in an article.

4 Experimental Analysis

In this section, we present a preliminary experimental analysis aiming at show the effectiveness of the self-adaptive component of ADNOTO. In order to do that, we consider a pool of 20 articles and book chapters manually annotated by domain experts, and related to the case study presented in Sect. 3.

Our first experiment concerns the computation of the base performance of ADNOTO ($ADNOTO_b$ in the following), i.e., with the self-adaptive feature disabled. The results of this experiment will allow us to evaluate if there is an improvement on the performance using the self-adaptivity. Considering the pool of documents listed above, we report that $ADNOTO_b$ was able to detect 448 (out of 721) triples, with P and R equals to 0.78 and 0.48, respectively. Notice that the value of F is 0.59.

Table 1 shows the results of ADNOTO. Because the self-adaptive mechanism of ADNOTO can be sensitive to the input order of the document, in the table

---

[1] We refer the reader to [9] for a detailed description of the STOLE ontology.

Table 1. Performance of ADNOTO. The table is organized as follows. The first column ("Input Order") is followed by three columns reporting values of Precision, Recall, and F-Measure (columns "P", "R", and "F", respectively).

Input Order	P	R	F
Order 1	0.79	0.53	0.63
Order 2	0.80	0.51	0.63
Order 3	0.79	0.51	0.62

we report the results related to three different (random) input orders of the documents listed above. Looking at Table 1, "Order 1", we can see that P of ADNOTO is slightly increased with respect to the one related to $ADNOTO_b$, while values of R and F increase of 5% and 4%, respectively. Looking at the results related to Order 2 and 3, we can see that the picture is similar.

To conclude, the results shown before let us conclude that self-adaptation in this context is an interesting direction for further investigations. As part of future work, we are planning to improve the self-adaptive mechanism involving co-reference resolution analysis for resolving anaphoric references by pronouns and definite noun phrases. Finally, further experimental analysis of the case study proposed will be performed using the described system.

References

1. Pulina, L., Tacchella, A.: A self-adaptive multi-engine solver for quantified Boolean formulas. Constraints **14**(1), 80–116 (2009)
2. Maratea, M., Pulina, L., Ricca, F.: Multi-engine ASP solving with policy adaptation. J. Logic Comput. **25**(6), 1285–1306 (2015)
3. Pandolfo, L., Pulina, L., Adorni, G.: A framework for automatic population of ontology-based digital libraries. In: Adorni, G., Cagnoni, S., Gori, M., Maratea, M. (eds.) AI*IA 2016. LNCS, vol. 10037, pp. 406–417. Springer, Cham (2016). doi:10.1007/978-3-319-49130-1_30
4. Vargas-Vera, M., Motta, E., Domingue, J., Lanzoni, M., Stutt, A., Ciravegna, F.: MnM: ontology driven semi-automatic and automatic support for semantic markup. In: Gómez-Pérez, A., Benjamins, V.R. (eds.) EKAW 2002. LNCS, vol. 2473, pp. 379–391. Springer, Heidelberg (2002). doi:10.1007/3-540-45810-7_34
5. Fragkou, P., Petasis, G., Theodorakos, A., Karkaletsis, V., Spyropoulos, C.D.: BOEMIE ontology-based text annotation tool. In: Proceedings of the Language Resources and Evaluation Conference (LREC), pp. 28–30 (2008)
6. Cunningham, H., Maynard, D., Bontcheva, K., Tablan, V.: GATE: an architecture for development of robust HLT applications. In: Proceedings of the 40th Annual Meeting on Association for Computational Linguistics, pp. 168–175. Association for Computational Linguistics (2002)
7. Adorni, G., Maratea, M., Pandolfo, L., Pulina, L.: An ontology-based archive for historical research. In: Proceedings of the 28th International Workshop on Description Logics, Athens, Greece. CEUR Workshop Proceedings, vol. 1350. CEUR-WS.org, 7–10 June 2015

8. Pianta, E., Bentivogli, L., Girardi, C.: MultiWordNet: developing an aligned multilingual database. In: Proceedings of the 1st International Conference on Global WordNet, pp. 293–302 (2002)
9. Adorni, G., Maratea, M., Pandolfo, L., Pulina, L.: An ontology for historical research documents. In: Cate, B., Mileo, A. (eds.) RR 2015. LNCS, vol. 9209, pp. 11–18. Springer, Cham (2015). doi:10.1007/978-3-319-22002-4_2

Ontologies in System Engineering: A Field Report

Marco Menapace and Armando Tacchella$^{(\boxtimes)}$

DIBRIS - Università degli studi di Genova, Viale F. Causa 13, 16145 Genova, Italy
marco.menapace@edu.unige.it, armando.tacchella@unige.it

Abstract. In this paper, we consider four different contributions to system engineering wherein ontologies provide enhancements over traditional techniques.

Ontologies are witnessing an increasing popularity outside the AI community for their ability to cope with taxonomies and part-whole relationships, to handle heterogeneous attributes, and their provision for various automated reasoning services—see, e.g., [1]. These features have been recognized since long time in system engineering: for instance, in the operations and maintenance sub-community, the use of ontologies is explicitly advocated[1]. However, the adoption of ontologies faces some challenges, mostly due to speed and reliability constraints imposed by industrial settings. Here we consider four case studies wherein ontologies provide key capabilities. For each of them, we sketch the context, the underlying motivations and intended objectives. Details can be found in the full version of this paper available at:

https://arxiv.org/abs/1702.07193

Ontologies for condition analysis. We introduced an ontology-based condition analyzer (CA) [2] for the EU project Integrail[2]. Our CA focuses on fault detection on Trenitalia E414 locomotives, and its main task is to perform fault classification according to priority for maintenance, and impact on mission-related and safety-related aspects. The ontology for the E414 locomotive is written in OWL 2 language and it builds on the SP3A core ontology—see [2] for details. The CA collects signals from locomotives, and it leverages the ontology to correlate observed data, symptoms and faults. In doing this, two competing needs must be mated: (*i*) railway regulations require hardware which is highly reliable, and whose performances are thus necessarily modest; (*ii*) ontology-related tools, e.g., description logic reasoners, have relatively large memory, processor and storage footprints. In this experience, the main goal was thus to check whether reasoning with ontologies can provide useful diagnostic feedback in a resource-restricted scenario. In one of the three sets of experiments performed in [2], we ran several tests using different fault scenarios using the PELLET DL reasoner.

---

[1] See, e.g., the MIMOSA open standard architecture at www.mimosa.org.
[2] More details about Integrail at http://www.integrail.eu/.

© Springer International Publishing AG 2017
S. Benferhat et al. (Eds.): IEA/AIE 2017, Part I, LNAI 10350, pp. 502–506, 2017.
DOI: 10.1007/978-3-319-60042-0_55

Table 1. Results with (a) lazy and (b) eager implementations of the CA.

Scenario	Memory consumption [MB]	CPU time [ms]	Amortized CPU time [ms]
1a	38	90	ND
2a	74	25373	25373
3a	106	1053656	210731
4a	OUT OF MEMORY	3253637	191390
1b	37	90	ND
2b	72	21506	21506
3b	104	86938	17387
4b	105	279523	16442

Table 1 shows the results obtained by running the CA on four different scenarios—the first includes no fault, the second includes only one fault, the third includes five contemporary faults, and the last 17 contemporary faults—using two different configurations. Configuration (a) is "lazy", i.e., it keeps all the individuals, while configuration (b) is "eager", i.e., it deletes individuals as soon as possible. As we can see in Table 1, the eager version results in a great improvement over the lazy one, both in terms of memory consumption and in terms of computation time.

Ontologies for system monitoring. In [3] we provided strong evidence of practical uses for ontologies in complex systems engineering by implementing a monitor for *Intermodal Logistics Systems* (ILSs), i.e., systems supporting the movement of containerized goods. In particular, we considered combination of rail and road transport, where rail transport is provided by short-distance shuttle trains, and network coverage is achieved through connections at specialized terminals. In this experience, the main goal was to gather data about terminal operations and compute global performances indicators, where access to data is mediated by an ontology. Unlike the CA case study, the ability to handle large amount of data is crucial, but reasoning is limited. In Fig. 1 we present a graphical outline of the ontology at the heart of our OBDA solution to monitor the ILS. The ontology—ILS ontology in the following—is compliant with the OWL 2 QL profile described in the official W3C's recommendation as *"[the sub-language of OWL 2] aimed at applications that use very large volumes of instance data, and where query answering is the most important reasoning task."*. Given the ILS application domain, OWL 2 QL guarantees that conjunctive query answering and consistency checking can be implemented efficiently with respect to the size of data and ontology, respectively. The restrictions that OWL 2 QL implies did not hamper the modeling accuracy of our ILS ontology.

Ontologies for diagnostic support system generation. Diagnostic Decision Support Systems (DDSSs) help humans to infer the health status of physical systems. In [4] we introduced DiSeGnO—for "Diagnostic Server Generation through Ontology"—to generate DDSSs. As in ILS monitoring, since it is expected that

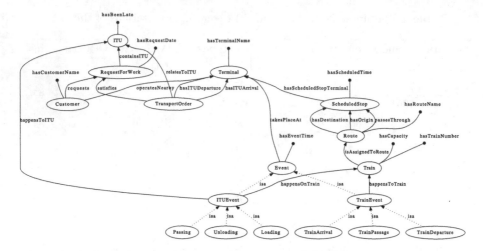

Fig. 1. ILS ontology describing the design of the OBDA solution. Ellipses denote concepts with datatype properties; directed edges are object properties; dotted edges are concept inclusions.

large quantities of data should be handled, the ontology language is restricted to those designed for tractable reasoning In this case, ontology-based reasoning is not leveraged, as DiSeGnO generates relational databases from the domain ontology and then computes diagnostic rules with PTOLEMY II, an open-source software simulating actor-based models. DiSeGnO, whose functional architecture and work-flow is sketched in Fig. 2, fulfills this task in three phases: in the USER phase, a domain ontology and diagnostic rules model are designed by the user; in the DiSeGnO phase, the system reads and analyzes the ontology and the rules to output the actual DDSS; in the DDSS phase, input web services receive data from the observed physical system and record them in the generated data store. According to the ISO 13374-1 standard a DDSS consists of six modules of which DiSeGnO implements three: *Data Manipulation* to perform signal analysis and compute meaningful descriptors, *State Detection* to check conformity to reference patterns, and *Health Assessment* to diagnose faults and rate the current health of the equipment or process. The ontology must be written using OWL 2 QL language. The diagnostic computation model must be a sound actor diagram generated by PTOLEMY II which describes the processing to be applied to incoming data in order to generated diagnostic events. The DiSeGnO phase contains the actual DDSS generation system which consists of the Data Store Generator, i.e., a piece of software that creates a relational database by mapping the domain ontology to suitable tables, and the Web Services Generator, i.e., a module that creates interface services for incoming and outgoing events.

Ontologies for computer-automated design. In mechanical design the term computer-automated design (CautoD) usually refers to techniques that mitigate the effort in exploring alternative solutions for structural implements. In our

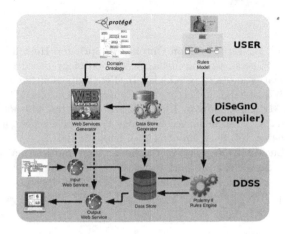

Fig. 2. Functional architecture and work-flow of DiSeGnO framework.

LIFTCREATE CautoD program for elevator systems[3], ontologies support intelligent design creation and optimization by managing detailed part-whole taxonomies, wherein different relations among components can be expressed. This case study provides thus yet another application of ontologies, mostly oriented to intelligent computation and data persistency. LIFTCREATE works in three steps. In the first step, the user is asked to enter relevant parameters characterizing the project, and an overall "design philosophy" to be implemented. For instance, if the size of the elevator's shaft is known and fixed in advance, LIFTCREATE can generate solutions which maximize payload, door size, or car size. A design philosophy is just a set of heuristics which, e.g., prioritize door size over other elements, still keeping into account hard constraints, e.g., payload and car size should not fall below some threshold. In the second phase, LIFTCREATE retrieves components from a database of parts and explores the (combinatorial) space of potential solutions, either using heuristic search techniques, or resorting to optimizations techniques. In the third phase, a set of feasible designs is proposed to the user, sorted according to decreasing relevance considering the initial design philosophy. For instance, if door size is to be maximized, the first alternatives shown to the user are those with the widest doors, perhaps at the expense of payload or car size.

To summarize, while ontologies provide an effective tool for conceptualizing diverse scenarios, some ontology-based tools are untenable unless small-to-medium scale systems are considered. In the case of E414 expressive ontologies required us to implement strategies to "forget" data to avoid cluttering the reasoner. In the ILS ontology, scaling requires discarding data using a recency approach. On the other hand, in DiSeGnO and LIFTCREATE, ontologies merely provide means for conceptualizing data and, as such, flexibility is gained without sacrificing performances.

---

[3] Part of the AILIFT software suite www.ailift.it.

References

1. Staab, S., Studer, R.: Handbook on Ontologies. Springer, Heidelberg (2013)
2. De Ambrosi, C., Ghersi, C., Tacchella, A.: An ontology-based condition analyzer for fault classification on railway vehicles. In: Proceedings of the 22nd International Conference on Industrial, Engineering and Other Applications of Applied Intelligent Systems, IEA/AIE 2009, Tainan, Taiwan, 24–27 June, pp. 449–458 (2009)
3. Casu, M., Cicala, G., Tacchella, A.: Ontology-based data access: an application to intermodal logistics. Inf. Syst. Front. **15**(5), 849–871 (2013)
4. Cicala, G., De Luca, M., Oreggia, M., Tacchella, A.: A multi-formalism framework to generate diagnostic decision support systems. In: Proceedings of the 30th European Conference on Modelling and Simulation, ECMS 2016, Regensburg, Germany, 31 May–3 June, pp. 628–634 (2016)

An Argumentative Agent-Based Model of Scientific Inquiry

AnneMarie Borg[1]([✉]), Daniel Frey[3], Dunja Šešelja[1,2], and Christian Straßer[1,2]

[1] Institute for Philosophy II, Ruhr-University Bochum, Bochum, Germany
{annemarie.borg,Christian.Strasser}@rub.de
[2] Center for Logic and Philosophy of Science, Ghent University, Ghent, Belgium
[3] Heidelberg University, Heidelberg, Germany

Abstract. In this paper we present an agent-based model (ABM) of scientific inquiry aimed at investigating how different social networks impact the efficiency of scientists in acquiring knowledge. As such, the ABM is a computational tool for tackling issues in the domain of scientific methodology and science policy. In contrast to existing ABMs of science, our model aims to represent the argumentative dynamics that underlies scientific practice. To this end we employ abstract argumentation theory as the core design feature of the model.

1 Introduction

In this paper we present an agent-based model (ABM) as a computational tool for tackling issues in the domain of scientific methodology and science policy, which concern social aspects of scientific inquiry.[1] In contrast to most other ABMs of science (e.g. [2,8–11]), our model is based on the idea that an essential component of scientific inquiry is an argumentative dynamics between scientists. To this end, we employ abstract argumentation frameworks as one of the design features of our ABM (previously shown fruitful for the modeling of scientific debates in [7] and employed in an ABM of social behavior in [4]). The model is designed to investigate how different social networks impact the efficiency of scientists in discovering the best of the pursued scientific theories.

2 The Model

The aim of our ABM is to represent scientists engaged in an inquiry with the goal of finding the best of the given rivaling theories, where they occasionally exchange arguments with other scientists, *pro* or *con* the given pursued theories. We tackle the question, which structure of the information flow leads scientists

A. Borg and C. Straßer—Supported by the Alexander von Humboldt Foundation and the German Ministry for Education and Research.

[1] For an extended version of our paper see: https://arxiv.org/abs/1612.04432..

© Springer International Publishing AG 2017
S. Benferhat et al. (Eds.): IEA/AIE 2017, Part I, LNAI 10350, pp. 507–510, 2017.
DOI: 10.1007/978-3-319-60042-0_56

to most efficiently discover the best theory, where efficiency is measured in terms of their success and the time they need to complete their exploration.[2]

Agents, representing scientists, move along an *argumentative landscape*. The argumentative landscape, which represents rivaling theories in a given scientific domain, is based on a dynamic abstract argumentation framework.

Similarly to Dung's abstract argumentation framework (AF) [3], the framework underlying our model consists of a set of *arguments* $\mathcal{A}$ and an *attack relation* $\rightsquigarrow$ over $\mathcal{A}$. In addition to attacking each other, arguments may also be connected by a *discovery relation* $\hookrightarrow$. The latter represents the path which scientists have to take in order to discover different parts of the given theory.

An argumentative landscape is given by a triple $\langle \mathcal{A}, \rightsquigarrow, \hookrightarrow \rangle$ where $\mathcal{A} = \langle \mathcal{A}_1, \ldots, \mathcal{A}_m \rangle$ is partitioned in m many theories $T_i = \langle \mathcal{A}_i, a_i, \hookrightarrow \rangle$ which are trees with $a_i \in \mathcal{A}_i$ as a root and

$$\rightsquigarrow \ \subseteq \bigcup_{\substack{1 \leq i,j \leq m \\ i \neq j}} (\mathcal{A}_i \times \mathcal{A}_j) \quad \text{and} \quad \hookrightarrow \ \subseteq \bigcup_{1 \leq i \leq m} (\mathcal{A}_i \times \mathcal{A}_i).$$

Given the abstract nature of arguments, we interpret them as hypotheses which scientists investigate, occasionally encountering defeating evidence, represented by attacks from other arguments, and then attempting to find defending arguments for the attacked hypothesis.

The model is round-based. Each round ($\approx$ a research day) agents perform one of the following actions: 1a. Explore a single argument a. This way they gradually discover possible attacks (on a and from a to an argument from another theory) as well as neighboring arguments via the discovery relation. 1b. Alternatively, if probabilistically triggered, move to a neighboring argument along the discovery relation. 2. Move to an argument of a rivaling theory. In order to decide whether to work on the current theory (1a, 1b) or to move to another one (2), every five rounds ($\approx$ a research week) agents assess the *degree of defensibility* of the theories. A theory has degree of defensibility n if it has n defended arguments where an argument a is defended in the theory if each attacker b from another theory is itself attacked by some argument c in the current theory. Agents always prefer the most defensible theory.

An agent discovers the argumentative landscape by investigating arguments or by means of exchanging information about the landscape with other agents, connected by so-called *social networks*. We distinguish between two types of social networks. First, our agents are divided into *collaborative networks* that consist of up to five individuals who start from the same theory root. While each agent gathers information on her own, every five steps this information is shared with all other agents forming the same collaborative network.

Second, besides sharing information with agents from the same network, every five steps each agent shares information with agents from other

---

[2] The source code is available at https://github.com/g4v4g4i/ArgABM/tree/AppArg2017.

collaborative networks with a given *probability of information sharing*.[3] This way the agents form ad-hoc and random *communal networks* with agents from other collaborations. A higher probability of information sharing leads to a higher degree of interaction among agents.

Finally, we represent *reliable* and *deceptive* scientists. Reliable agents share all the information they have gathered during their exploration of the current theory, while deceptive agents don't share the information regarding the discovered attacks on their current theory. Hence, deceptive agents only provide some information while they withhold other. In this way they lead the receiver to a wrong inference [1].

Agents share information in a unidirectional or a bidirectional way (with a 50/50 chance). Moreover, our model takes into account the fact that receiving information is time costly.

3   The Main Findings

We have run the simulation 100 times with 10, 20, 30, 40, 70 and 100 agents by varying: the *probability of information sharing* (namely: 0.3; 0.5; 1.0); *reliable* and *deceptive* agents. The landscape consists of 3 theories, only one of which has the maximum degree of defensibility, representing the objectively best theory.[4] The program runs until each agent is on a fully explored theory. In order to assess the efficiency of agents, we have defined their success similarly to other ABMs of science, e.g. in [10,11]: a run is considered successful if, at the end of the run, all agents have converged onto the objectively best theory.

In what follows we present the most significant results of our simulations.

Information sharing. For smaller groups of reliable agents (up to 20) the impact of information sharing is rather small (Fig. 1a). From 30 agents on, we observe a positive impact of an increase in information sharing on the successful convergence, with no negative effect on time steps needed (Fig. 1b). While for smaller groups of deceptive agents a higher degree of information sharing has a relatively small impact, we notice positive effects in cases of larger communities, without slowdowns.

Reliable vs. deceptive agents. If we compare groups with same degrees of information sharing, reliable agents tend to be more successful than the deceptive ones, while being equally fast (and only sometimes being slightly slower).

Size of the scientific community. Larger populations of 70 and 100 agents are outperformed by smaller populations (with an optimum around 20 and 30). A possible explanation is that with larger sized populations information circulates less among research groups, which may prevent them from converging.

---

[3] While agents share their full subjective knowledge within their collaborative networks, the information which they share with agents from other networks concerns recently obtained knowledge of the theory which they are currently exploring.

[4] Each theory is modeled as a (discovery-)tree of depth 3, where each argument (except for the final leaves) has 4 child-arguments (altogether 85 arguments).

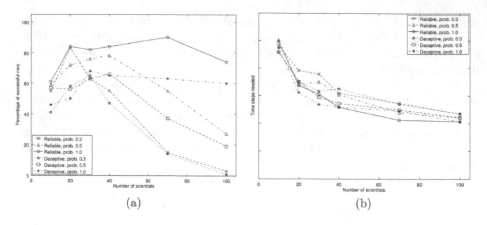

Fig. 1. (a) Success (b) Time needed

Our finding that increased communication tends to be epistemically beneficial (or at least, not epistemically harmful) undermines the robustness of conclusions drawn from ABMs in [5,6,10,11], under different modeling choices.

References

1. Caminada, M.: Truth, lies and bullshit: distinguishing classes of dishonesty. In: Social Simulation Workshop at the International Joint Conference on Artificial Intelligence (SS@ IJCAI). Citeseer (2009)
2. Douven, I.: Simulating peer disagreements. Stud. Hist. Philos. Sci. Part A **41**(2), 148–157 (2010)
3. Dung, P.M.: An argumentation-theoretic foundation for logic programming. J. Logic program. **22**(2), 151–171 (1995)
4. Gabbriellini, S., Torroni, P.: A new framework for ABMs based on argumentative reasoning. In: Kamiński, B., Koloch, G. (eds.) Advances in Social Simulation, pp. 25–36. Springer, Heidelberg (2014)
5. Grim, P.: Threshold phenomena in epistemic networks. In: AAAI Fall Symposium: Complex Adaptive Systems and the Threshold Effect, pp. 53–60 (2009)
6. Grim, P., Singer, D.J., Fisher, S., Bramson, A., Berger, W.J., Reade, C., Flocken, C., Sales, A.: Scientific networks on data landscapes: question difficulty, epistemic success, and convergence. Episteme **10**(04), 441–464 (2013)
7. Šešelja, D., Straßer, C.: Abstract argumentation and explanation applied to scientific debates. Synthese **190**, 2195–2217 (2013)
8. Thoma, J.: The epistemic division of labor revisited. Philos. Sci. **82**(3), 454–472 (2015)
9. Weisberg, M., Muldoon, R.: Epistemic landscapes and the division of cognitive labor. Philos. Sci. **76**(2), 225–252 (2009)
10. Zollman, K.J.S.: The communication structure of epistemic communities. Philos. Sci. **74**(5), 574–587 (2007)
11. Zollman, K.J.S.: The epistemic benefit of transient diversity. Erkenntnis **72**(1), 17–35 (2010)

Navigation, Control and Autonomous Agents

Development of a Novel Driver Model Offering Human like Longitudinal Vehicle Control in Order to Simulate Emission in Real Driving Conditions

Aymeric Rateau[1(✉)], Wim van der Borght[1], Marcello Mastroleo[2(✉)],
Alessandro Pietro Bardelli[2], Alessandro Bacchini[2], and Federico Sassi[2]

[1] Toyota Motor Europe Technical Centre, Hoge Wei 33, 1930 Zaventem, Belgium
aymeric.rateau@toyota-europe.com
[2] Camlin Italy s.r.l, Strada Budellungo 2, 43123 Parma, Italy
m.mastroleo@camlintechnologies.com

Abstract. Toyota would like to simulate emissions in real-world conditions and support future engine development newly regulated by Real Driving Emission from 2017. A realistic driver model is necessary to simulate representative vehicle emissions. This paper presents a new driver model trained using real-world data including GPS localization and recorded engine ECU parameters. From a geolocalisation webservice, the proposed approach extracts the road attributes that influence human driving behaviour such as traffic signs, road cross, etc. The novel BiMap innovative algorithm, is then used to learn and map the driver behaviour with respect to the road properties while a regression tree algorithm is used to learn a realistic gear selection model. Experimental tests, executed within Carmaker™ vehicle simulation platform, show that the resulting model can drive along arbitrary real-world routes, generated using a map service. Moreover, it exhibits a human-like driving behaviour while being robust to different car setups. Finally, the realism of the proposed driver's behaviour is supported by both a high similarity in Engine Operative Point usage and a less than 1.5% deviation in terms CO_2 emission versus measured data.

1 Introduction

A particular challenge in the light duty vehicle Engine and Powertrain field is the upcoming European 'Real Driving Emissions' (RDE) regulation [1]. Its compliance requires control of vehicle exhaust emissions over a wide area of operating conditions (city-urban-highway driving, altitude, cold-hot environmental air) and therefore requires an intensive workload on testing and calibration process.

In order to reduce this workload, the IPG Carmaker™ vehicle simulation platform [2] is one of the tools used to "virtualize" part of this calibration process. It allows the evaluation of vehicle and engine behaviour under various real-life driving conditions by running a vehicle model operated by a virtual Driver Model in a virtual driving environment.

However, the standard Driver Model provided with IPG Carmaker™ is mainly designed to explore vehicle limits (like max speed in curve, etc.) or follow a dedicated

© Springer International Publishing AG 2017
S. Benferhat et al. (Eds.): IEA/AIE 2017, Part I, LNAI 10350, pp. 513–522, 2017.
DOI: 10.1007/978-3-319-60042-0_57

speed trace. Therefore, simulations of real driving conditions may be not representative in terms of exhaust emission. In literature, several studies were found regarding driver modelling but most of them are related to Advanced Driving Assistance System [3], racing/gaming condition driving like for TORCS [4] or traffic modelling [5] and not directly targeting emission. On the other hand, a number of Proportional-Integral-Derivative (PID) driver models have been proposed, like in [6]. This kind of model has been extensively used to characterise vehicle performance and emission but they can reproduce only a predefined speed-time trace. Moreover, the transitions on pedals, which are essential for RDE, may be not statistically representative of generic human driver.

A first attempt to model both the generation and the execution of a speed profile has been made in [7] where distance-based stimuli and statistics extracted from the recorded data are used to generate a new speed trace. However, that model has been validated only for high speed cruising at constant speed which is way too limiting for a complete RDE simulation.

In this paper, a novel PowerTrain Artificial Intelligent Driver Model (PTAIDM) is presented.

The PTAIDM, thanks to a machine learning approach, learns directly from recorded data and replicates driver's behaviour over any arbitrary route, thus overcoming all the limitations of previously presented approaches and making it suitable for RDE simulation. Moreover, PTAIDM can be used as an external Driver Model for Carmaker™ that handles acceleration/brake, clutch and gearshift in a human-like way, while steering wheel remains controlled by standard Carmaker™'s IPG Driver, since lateral car dynamics have minimal influence on emission.

2   Driver Modelling Toolchain for RDE Simulation

The proposed architecture is composed by a chain of three main modules to fill the gap between recorded data from driving tests and the simulation environment (Fig. 1):

1. A Map Attribute Extractor, which can serve two purposes:
   (a) To process recorded Engine Control Unit (ECU) data along with the GPS position and prepare the inputs needed to learn a real driver's behaviour.
   (b) To produce the attributes used later as input to extrapolate the learned behaviour on a new route by starting from a GPS trace only.
2. An Offline Model, which learns the real driver behaviour on the driven route and generalizes this behaviour to replicate it over new routes.
3. An Online Module, which is an FMU (Functional Mock-up Unit) controller in closed loop with the simulation environment and that implements the driver longitudinal behaviour by acting, in a human feasible way, on the car controls (gear-shift and pedals).

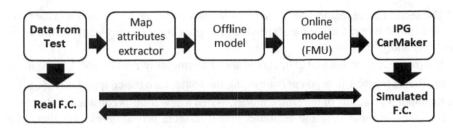

Fig. 1. Driver model tool chain

2.1 Map Attributes Extractor

The main purpose of the Map Attribute Extractor is to prepare the input data either to train a new Offline Model or to exploit an already trained one.

Recorded GPS positions are used to query a Geolocalisation WebService (GWS, like HERE [8] which was used in this research) to recover a synthetic representation of the driven route together with some boundary information which cannot be logged from the ECU like traffic signs, traffic lights and average traffic conditions. GWS can also be used to extract data of real-world arbitrary routes to be used in simulation environment along with a previously trained Driver Model.

After querying the GWS, there are two different sets of data:

1. The original ECU and GPS data which are sampled uniformly over time
2. The data extracted by the GWS which are sampled on a segmented base to reduce distortions on the roads representation.

The most sensitive task is to align the two datasets by obtaining Time On Points (TOPs), i.e. the time at which the real car passes through the points of the HERE's GWS road (denoted with H). TOPs are the keys to associate route properties to the driver behaviour recorded from the ECU.

Dynamical Spatial Warping, a novel spatial variation of the DTW [9, 10] algorithm, is used to connect GWS points with closest GPS points in order to determine the logger time at which GWS points are crossed by the real vehicle by considering WGS84 spatial information, bearing angle and the cumulative distance.

Once the two tracks have been aligned, the ECU data can be directly matched with the GWS representation of the route. In particular, denoting h_i the segment between $\left(x_i^H, y_i^H\right)$ and $\left(x_{i+1}^H, y_{i+1}^H\right)$, T_i^H the logged time interval the driver spent on h_i, the observed joint probability distribution of speed and gears $P_i(\text{s,g})$ can be extracted for each $h_i \in H$.

Observations $h_i \rightarrow P_i(\text{s,g})$ are used to link driver behaviour to the road but, in order to have a general model, a set of quantitative features need to be extracted to characterise raw GWS segments and to assess similarity among them. Two sets of features are considered in the system.

The first set codifies geometric attributes; for instance, length of segments, angles between current and previous segment, angles between current and following segment and vertical inclination of segment.

The second set of features codifies the most relevant visual inputs to which the driver reacts while driving; for instance, speed limits, proximity to stop signs, traffic lights, junctions and yield signs.

If $A(h)$ is the function that extracts the above segments attributes and $A_i = A(h_i)$ are the attributes for the i-th segment composing the route, then the couples $(A_i, P_i(s,g))_{i=1}^{n}$ are the input for training of the offline model. When a new route is considered, the offline model takes as input only the attributes and infers the probabilities over them. The representation H is often poorly discretised (e.g., lack of coverage of GWSs, over-simplified geometry, etc.) or presents very sharp turns that cannot be strictly followed by a car in a simulated environment. A new high resolution representation H_{HD}, aligned with H and driveable within Carmaker™, is therefore obtained by injecting points into H and then by processing the result with a smoothing filter such as Savitzky-Golay [11].

2.2   The Offline Model

The Offline model aims to learn the relation between driver behaviour (in terms of speed and gears distribution) and the driving context (e.g., route geometry, traffic signs) and to be then able to reproduce a realistic behaviour both on the same route as well as generalising it to a new route.

This process can be then decomposed in two phases:

- a training phase in which a model of the context is learnt from the route segmentation and mapped to the speed and gear distribution;
- an extrapolation phase in which the model is queried with a new context and new speed (and possibly gear) profile is built

Learning the context
In order to build the context model, a novel algorithm called Bi-Directional Map (BiMap) [12] has been developed. BiMap is an extension of the well-known dimensionality reduction algorithm t-SNE [13], which overcomes some of the limitations of the original algorithm.

The original t-SNE algorithm has state-of-the-art self-clustering capability, is robust to noisy data and is designed to discover hidden relations in high dimensional data by projecting them in a two or three-dimensional space ("maps"). This feature allows to identify similar context and enable the user to inspect and understand the resulting model. Unfortunately, t-SNE requires a new training phase for each newly included data point and therefore lacks of the extrapolation capabilities essential to generalise the model to new contexts.

BiMap algorithm, instead, is able to lookup for new points without re-training the whole map, preserves the self-clustering feature and produces a lower-dimensional representation of the training space of attributes on which a chosen distance function can be properly used as measure of closeness. BiMap training procedure is similar to t-SNE's.

BiMap training points (input) and their correspondence in the low dimensional space (output) are used as a transform function to map points of the first space X into points of the second space Y (and vice-versa). This is done by solving the following optimisation problems:

$$BiMap(m) = \text{argmin}_{t \, in \, Y} D(G(\mu_x(P,m)), T(\mu_y(Q,t))) \quad \text{(Compression)}$$

$$BiMap^{-1}(t) = \text{argmin}_{m \, in \, X} D(G(\mu_x(P,m)), T(\mu_y(Q,t))) \quad \text{(Decompression)}$$

Where m is the point to be projected, D is a symmetric distance function, (μ_x, P, G) and (μ_y, Q, T) are a closeness measure, the training points and an activation function in the X and Y spaces respectively. In particular, G and T belong to the family $f:\mathbb{R}^+ \rightarrow (0, 1]$ and satisfy the following conditions:

$$f(0) = 1 \quad \lim_{t \to \infty} f(t) = 0 \quad f(t_1) > f(t_2) \Leftrightarrow t_1 < t_2$$

For instance, in this research, D is the Kullback–Leibler divergence [14] (it is not symmetric but decompression is not needed), μ_x and μ_y are the usual Euclidean distance, G and T are Gaussian and t-Student activation functions respectively.

Speed and gear generation

Once the context model has been trained the recorded speed/gear distribution is associated to each BiMap point. Therefore, given a sequence H_{new} of road segments, the resulting BiMap can be used to extract speed information and build a new speed profile according to the following procedure.

1. Compute the projections: $\hat{h} = BiMap(A(h)) \forall h \in H_{new}$
2. Compute the distances with learned points:

$$\vec{d}_{\text{BiMap}}(\hat{h}) = \left(\left(d_{\text{BiMap}}(\hat{h}, h_1) \right), \left(d_{\text{BiMap}}(\hat{h}, h_2) \right), \ldots, \left(d_{\text{BiMap}}(\hat{h}, h_n) \right) \right)$$

3. Transform the distance vector into a normalised activation vector $\vec{w}(\hat{h})$, according to a t-Student function:

$$\vec{w}(\hat{h}) = \frac{\vec{t}(\hat{h})}{\vec{t}(\hat{h})_1} \quad \text{where} \quad \vec{t}(\hat{h}) = \frac{1}{1 + d_{\text{BiMap}}(\hat{h})^2}$$

4. Aggregate the learned probability distributions using activations $\vec{w}(\hat{h})$ as weights:

$$P(s|\hat{h}) = \sum \vec{w}_i(h) \cdot P_i(s)$$

5. Generate a probabilistic speed profile $S(H_{new})$, by sampling (4) $\forall h \in H_{new}$ and then create a deterministic speed profile with a maximum likelihood approach.

It is worth noting that the resulting speed profiles are compatible with both the road geometry and the visual information along the route since both are codified in the road attributes. Moreover, they also embed the speed variations the real driver faced along the recording (e.g., traffic jams, obstacles, traffic lights). As a consequence, we are able to model the effect of the interaction of the driver with its environment without modelling the environment itself.

Thanks to the BiMap representation, the PTAIDM can extrapolate realistic speed distributions also for road segments similar but not present in the training data.

Following a similar procedure, it is possible to extract the gear profile $G(H_{\text{new}})$ from $P\left(g\middle|S(H_{\text{new}})H_{\text{new}}\right)$ with a maximum likelihood approach.

Once the driver's intentions $\left(S(\text{GWS}_{\text{new}}), G(\text{GWS}_{\text{new}})\right)$ are computed for the route GWS_{new}, this route can be played in the simulation environment by the Online Model. An example of generated speed and gear intentions is in Fig. 2

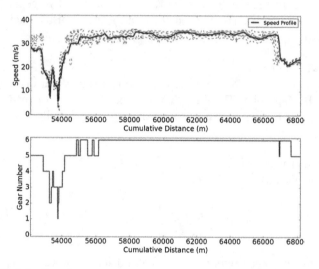

Fig. 2. A detail of the Speed (top) and Gear (bottom) intention generated for a recorded route. The dashed regions around the speed profiles are iso-probable areas.

Alternative Gear Prediction Model

The offline model generation of the gear profiles is a quite simple procedure and works very well for vehicles with characteristics (e.g., weight, gear ratio, road load) quite close to the training but may have problems to realistically handle previously unseen situations. This means that it would be necessary to have a dedicated recording and model training for each different vehicle setup. Therefore, a more complex and general online Gear Prediction Model (GPM) has been designed to overcome these limitations.

The GPM uses the road perception (BiMap projection), current and desired (2s ahead) speed and acceleration. A regression tree [15] is used to predict the desired transmission ratio (*speed/engine_speed*). This tree is generated by minimizing the Mean Square Error (MSE) of the prediction over the training data.

On the one hand, usage of transmission ratios enables to abstract the model from the specific gearboxes while focusing more on the driver behaviour. On the other hand, regression trees are very efficient from a computational point of view and provides a representation that can be easily inspected by humans. For instance, Fig. 3 shows a possible interpretation of a small portion of a learned tree: the driver does not use the 5th gear when driving through towns, while at high speed the 5th gear is preferred during accelerations over the 6th.

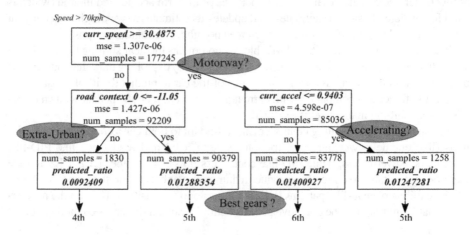

Fig. 3. Regression tree example: at each node a decision based on one or more constraint over the training features is made. Leaf nodes contains the predicted transmission ratio that can be then converted to the most appropriate gear for the car setup at hand.

2.3 Online Model

The Online Model is the actual longitudinal driver that acts within the simulation environment to realize the driver's intentions over the route H_{new} exploiting the information generated by the Offline Model.

The Online Model is implemented as a Functional Mock-up Unit (FMU) [16], thus it can be used in any simulation system implementing the Functional Mock-up Interface standard (i.e. Carmaker™, Simulink®/Matlab®, OpenModelica©).

The FMU is structured in sub-modules for each specific task (e.g. taking-off the car, shifting gear and following a speed profile) and it is designed to act on the vehicle pedals to be as close as possible to a human driver; in particular, we gathered the following evidence from the data:

E1 Pedals are almost constant over time or the time spent in transiting between different positions is negligible compared to the total time

E2 There are no feedback adjustments: transitions are monotonous from one level to the next one.

E1 can be explained by the hypothesis that a real driver plans next speeds according to the visual inputs in a predictive and non-linear way. While E2 is the evidence that the driver knows the right position of pedals needed to generate the planned speed variation.

The Speed Following Module (SFM) FMU block forecasts the near future vehicle speed, compares it with the target speed profile and acts on the brake or accelerator pedal when needed. This is possible because driver's intentions have been generated offline and the Online Model can foresee future target speed by simply reading the speed profile ahead of few meters. SFM behaves under the hypothesis of uniform accelerated motion (which is valid for sufficiently small timeframes) and updates its estimates at very high frequency (at least 100 Hz), thus providing forecasts accurate enough for simulation purposes.

The Gear Shift Module (GSM) FMU block implements the gear shifting logic and may acts either by following offline generated gear profiles or by exploiting the behaviour learned by the GPM. In the latter case, it uses the status of the car to predict the ideal transmission ratio. If the forecast is compatible with current gear, no action on the pedals is taken otherwise a gear shifting manoeuver is executed.

In conclusion, the resulting controller can self-adapt to both car's characteristics variations (like engine power, air drag, frictions, weight, etc.) and road slope like PID-like controllers. Nevertheless, while PID-like controllers do satisfy neither E1 nor E2 and are therefore not suitable to correctly reproduce a human driver behaviour, the proposed Online Model exhibits plateau-like patterns (E1) and monotonous transitions (E2) on the accelerator pedal by mimicking the cognitive process behind a human driver speed modulation.

3   Results and Discussion

PTAIDM was tested with RDE PEMS (Portable Emission Measurement System) records. Two kinds of routes, each longer than 110 km, were considered. One is called "Aggressive" and the other called "Soft" PEMS. Both share a portion of highway but differs in the rural route. The Aggressive route includes hills driving while the Soft route covers more city driving. The ability of PTAIDM to realistically simulate a human driver behaviour was tested by looking both at Engine Operative Points (EOP) usage in speed and load that are main parameters for emissions like NOx, CO, HC and PM/PN, and at the simulated Fuel Consumption (FC) or CO2 emission accuracy.

Different recordings of the same human driver on the same route were used to assess an objective driver self-similarity score on EOP usage. Table 1 reports the EOP similarity scores of both the proposed driver and the IPG Carmaker™ Driver Model against the reference human driver self-similarity, and shows the effectiveness of the proposed model.

Table 1. Engine Operative Points similarity between artificial and human drivers

Artificial driver	EOP similarity
PTAIDM - Online Module with recorded speed and gears	89.04%
PTAIDM - Full toolchain: Offline Model and Online Module	79.06%
IPG Carmaker™ DM - Recorded speed, data tuned gearshift thresholds	68.30%
IPG Carmaker™ DM - Data tuned gearshift thresholds	39.73%

Table 2 shows PTAIDM full toolchain accuracy simulating FC. The model can reproduce real emission with a margin less than 1.5%.

Table 2. Fuel consumption (L/100 km) simulation error

Route	Simulated FC	Real FC	Difference
Aggressive PEMS Day1	5.204	5.28	−1.44%
Aggressive PEMS Day2	5.311	5.30	+0.21%
Soft PEMS	4.874	4.88	−0.12%

PTAIDM learns to assess speed and gear by what it has seen in training data. Therefore, the model extrapolation capability is directly influenced by the richness of the training recordings and a trained model can fail to properly drive in conditions far away from the training ones. For example, if the simulated car is less powerful than the training one, then the new car may not be able to cope with the accelerations needed to follow the generated speed profile. Similarly, if the training dataset is almost on flat ground, then the driver can have problems in dealing with mountain-like slopes.

To overcome these limitations, tests have been done by merging different RDE PEMS recordings that have different distributions of highway, city, rural and rural on hill. These enriched datasets have been used to train wider PTAIDMs. The resulting PTAIDMs cover more various driving contexts than the ones trained only on single recording and they show an improved extrapolation quality. In fact, they are able to drive in conditions which are much farther from the training ones than the single-recording ones can do. This confirms two hypotheses:

1. The proposed PTAIDM can handle heterogeneous recordings in a consistent way.
2. The more several datasets with diverse driving contexts are merged, the more a global, robust and "universal" driver can be approached.

Future developments in this direction would be to merge bigger datasets to have a more robust and general driver. However, to train such unique driver, further improvements will

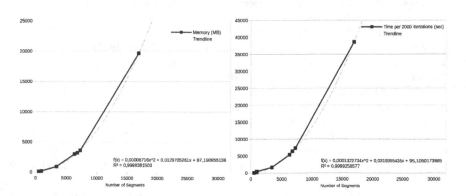

Fig. 4. Memory and computation time scaling with respect to the number of segments used to train the BiMap model.

be needed in term of memory consumption and computation time since, as highlighted in Fig. 4, the training algorithm scales quadratically.

4   Summary

We presented a novel approach to an artificial intelligence longitudinal driver, which learns real driver behaviour on recorded routes and reproduces it on arbitrary routes. The proposed driver model exhibits human-like driving behaviour on both vehicle pedals and gear selection and is suitable for simulating Real Driving Emissions. Using regression trees to assess the desired ratio between vehicle speed and engine speed allows to robustly select gears against variations of gear box ratios, vehicle weight or road load. The proposed model was tested and validated on RDE PEMS recordings and showed a good correlation in EOP usage and accuracy in simulating CO_2 emissions.

References

1. European Real Driving Emissions Regulation. https://ec.europa.eu/info/law/better-regulation/initiatives/ares-2016-6339064_en
2. IPG Carmaker™. https://ipg-automotive.com
3. Liebner, M., Baumann, M., Klanner, F., Stiller, C.: A probabilistic model for estimating driver behaviors and vehicle trajectories in traffic environments. In: Intelligent Vehicles Symposium (2012)
4. TORCS. http://torcs.sourceforge.net/
5. Liu, R.: The DRACULA dynamic network microsimulation model. In: Kitamura, R., Kuwahara, M. (eds.) Simulation Approaches in Transportation Analysis. Operations Research/Computer Science Interfaces Series, vol. 31, pp. 23–56. Springer, US (2005). doi:10.1007/0-387-24109-4_2
6. Allen, A.J., Beardmore, R., Nash, R.: Generic integrated systems modelling for low carbon, zero emission and concept whole vehicle simulation. In: Proceedings of Hybrid and Eco-Friendly Vehicle Conference (IET HEVC 2008), pp. 1–8 (2008)
7. McGordon, A., Poxon, J.E.W., Poxon, J.E.W., Cheng, C., Jones, R.P., Jennings, P.A.: Development of a driver model to study the effects of real-world driver behaviour on the fuel consumption. Proc. IMechE. Part D: J. Automobile Eng. **225**, 1518–1530 (1978)
8. HERE. https://www.here.com/
9. Sakoe, H., Chiba, S.: Dynamic programming algorithm optimization for spoken word recognition. IEEE Trans. Acoust. Speech Signal Process. **26**(1), 43–49 (1978)
10. Salvador, S., Chan, P.: FastDTW: toward accurate dynamic time warping in linear time and space. Intell. Data Anal. **11**(5), 561–580 (2007)
11. Savitzky, A., Golay, M.J.E.: Smoothing and differentiation of data by simplified least squares procedures. Anal. Chem. **36**(8), 1627–1639 (1964)
12. Patent publication number WO2017/012677
13. van der Maaten, L.J.P., Hinton, G.E.: Visualizing high-dimensional data using t-SNE. J. Mach. Learn. Res. **9**, 2579–2605 (2008)
14. Kullback, S., Leibler, R.A.: On information and sufficiency. Ann. Math. Stat. **22**(1), 79–86 (1951)
15. Breiman, L., Friedman, J., Olshen, R., Stone, C.: Classification and Regression Trees. Wadsworth, Belmont (1984)
16. FMI standard. https://www.fmi-standard.org/

Consistency Check in a Multiple Viewpoint System for Reasoning About Occlusion

Ana Paula Martin[1]([⊠]), Paulo E. Santos[1], and Marjan Safi-Samghabadi[2]

[1] Centro Universitário da FEI, São Bernardo do Campo, Brazil
{ana.martin,psantos}@fei.edu.br
[2] Alzahra University, Tehran, Iran

Abstract. This paper presents the implementation of a qualitative spatial reasoning formalism called Interval Occlusion Calculus based on Allen's Algebra, that considers multiple viewpoints in a scene and the interpretation of the observations made from each point from the perspective of other agents. Furthermore we present a mechanism to check consistency for the information provided by the agents using a constraint satisfaction process. This formalism was tested in a 3D domain with real and simulated robot's viewpoints.

Keywords: Qualitative Spatial Reasoning · Multiple viewpoints

1 Introduction

Recently, the use of robots has gradually increased to support human teams in performing various tasks, such as searching for and rescuing victims from disaster situations [3]. In scenarios of natural disasters, where there are victims and a large number of unknown and disordered scenes, robots are useful to reduce the human exposure to the risks that these situations offer, increase the speed of access to obstructed areas and to reach potentially inaccessible areas. An Artificial Intelligence subfield called Qualitative Spatial Reasoning (QSR) provides representations and inference systems for spatial entities, which approximate the way humans describe and reason about space, in contrast to numerical techniques for representing distances, sizes, orientation, among others [4].

In order to reason about space, the vision is a fundamental tool in the process of acquisition of spatial information [5]. One piece of visual information that could be enhanced by reasoning is occlusion. Most previous work about occlusion assume only the viewpoint from a single agent, leaving aside issues related to reasoning about multiple viewpoints in a scene. In order to cope with this issue, [6] presents a multiple-view spatial reasoning system called Interval Occlusion Calculus (IOC), based on Allen's Interval Algebra [1]. This formalism integrates several distinct points of view from which notions of object occlusion are shared by all agents present in the environment. This work assumes a 3D domain.

© Springer International Publishing AG 2017
S. Benferhat et al. (Eds.): IEA/AIE 2017, Part I, LNAI 10350, pp. 523–532, 2017.
DOI: 10.1007/978-3-319-60042-0_58

2   Related Work

The concept of visibility is fundamental for performing a series of tasks by both humans and robotic agents, so this concept is related to many fields of application such as robot navigation and computer graphics [5]. Many formalisms in Qualitative Space Reasoning (QSR) use vision to acquire information and to reason about occlusion. Occlusion occurs when one body interposes between another and a viewpoint.

One of the first qualitative formalisms about spatial occlusion was proposed in [7] where a set of axioms was designed to restrict occlusion relations using ternary relations. [8] proposed a calculus based on Lines of Sight, which represent the relative position between two bodies from the point of view of an observer, deriving 14 different relations. Based on this idea, [10] proposed the Region Occlusion Calculus (ROC) defining the occlusion as a mereotopological theory, deriving twenty occlusion relations known as ROC-20. The work described in [11] proposes a modal logic about binary relations representing visibility. With a different approach, [12] proposes a set of 14 occlusion relations making it explicit whether an observed object is fragmented or not, and whether it is being hidden by a moving object or the background of the scene. [14] develops a QSR approach within a 3D domain and [13] extends the calculation of region occlusion with the notion of depth.

The formalisms presented above, and most QSR work, address the issue from the point of view of a single observer. However, in general, researchers in the area of artificial intelligence agree that multi-agent systems behave more robustly and efficiently performing collaborative tasks [2,3]. This paper presents a QSR theory on occlusion and multiple viewpoints defined on a relation algebra: Allen's Interval Algebra.

3   Allen's Interval Algebra

Allen's interval algebra [1] is defined by a set of 13 jointly-exhaustive and pairwise-disjoint base relations representing the possible relations between pairs of intervals taking into account their upper and lower limits. Given two intervals, x and y, the Allen interval relations are shown in Fig. 1.

One of the QSR challenges is to verify whether the information provided by agents is consistent, i.e. to verify the existence of at least one scenario in which the configurations provided are possible. A scenario described by a set of Allen's relations may have its consistency verified from the algebraic closure in a constraint network. A constraint network consists of a pair (N, C), where N is a finite set of vertices composed of domain variables and C is the set of constraints that determine how the variables relate, in which case the vertices represent intervals and the constraints between nodes are Allen's relations [15]. Taking a constraint network with three vertices (i, j, k) the constraint $C(i, k)$ must be compatible with the composition of $C(i, j)$ and $C(j, k)$, so we have:

$$C(i, k) \cap (C(i, k) \circ C(k, j)) \neq 0.$$

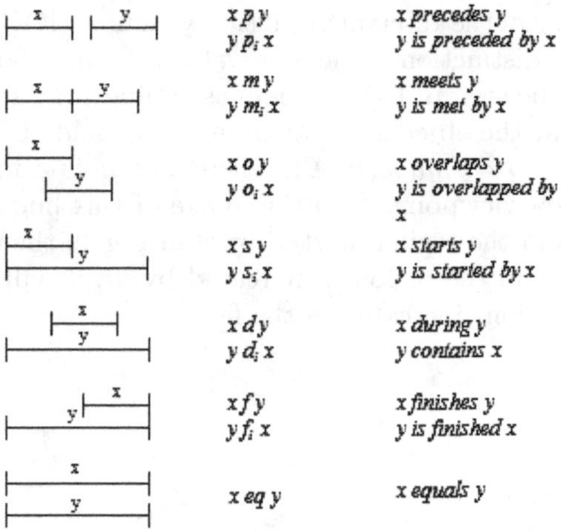

$x\,p\,y$	$x\ precedes\ y$	
$y\,p_i\,x$	$y\ is\ preceded\ by\ x$	
$x\,m\,y$	$x\ meets\ y$	
$y\,m_i\,x$	$y\ is\ met\ by\ x$	
$x\,o\,y$	$x\ overlaps\ y$	
$y\,o_i\,x$	$y\ is\ overlapped\ by$ x	
$x\,s\,y$	$x\ starts\ y$	
$y\,s_i\,x$	$y\ is\ started\ by\ x$	
$x\,d\,y$	$x\ during\ y$	
$y\,d_i\,x$	$y\ contains\ x$	
$x\,f\,y$	$x\ finishes\ y$	
$y\,f_i\,x$	$y\ is\ finished\ x$	
$x\,eq\,y$	$x\ equals\ y$	

Fig. 1. Allen's relations. (adapted from [15])

If the intersection above is empty, then the network is not consistent, since there is no scenario that represents the set of relations.

Allen's interval algebra is fundamental for the formalism presented in this work. This work also uses another formalism called Region Connection Calculus (RCC) [9] that is a QSR formalism that formalizes mereotopological relations between two regions. This formalism is based on a primitive relation $C(x, y)$ that means "x is connected to y". From this relation two objects x and y can be defined as being disconnected $DC(x, y)$, externally connected $EC(x, y)$, x partially overlaps y $PO(x, y)$, x is a tangential part of y $TPP(x, y)$, x is an interior part of y $NTPP(x, y)$ and x is equal y $EQ(x, y)$.

RCC is used in this paper to qualify the relations between objects from a global viewpoint and this is used in the extension to a calculus of occlusion (the Interval Occlusion Calculus) proposed in this work. This calculus is introduced in the next section.

4   Interval Occlusion Calculus

In the Interval Occlusion Calculus (IOC) [6] two entities are considered in the Euclidean plane: objects and observers. Objects can be identified by the 2D position of their centroids, while observers are represented by a pair $\Sigma = (x_i, v_i)$, where x_i represents the 2D position of the observer's centroid and v_i is a unit vector indicating its orientation. Objects are perceived by observers as a function $image(x, \Sigma)$ that maps the projection of the object x from the point of view Σ.

It is assumed that each observer is able to describe the relations between visible objects within their field of view and the observations made from one observer is available to the other agents by means of a message-passing procedure.

The basic relations of the Interval Occlusion Calculus (IOC) [6] can be understood as a qualitative distinction of the observation of pairs of objects, given their lines of sight, as can be seen in Fig. 2, where assuming that a point of view Σ is oriented in a way that the objects A and B are in its field of view, we have that $a = image(A, \Sigma)$ and $b = image(B, \Sigma)$, where $image$ is a function that maps a physical body and a viewpoint Σ to the image of this body as seem from Σ. For instance, if Σ is in the region marked by p in Fig. 2, then it will see that a precedes b, but if it is in the region demarcated by m, it will find that a meets b, and so on for all regions indicated in the figure.

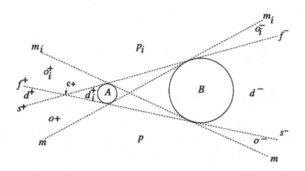

Fig. 2. The lines of sight between two objects A and B and the IOC base relations [6].

In addition to its relative position, an interval can be identified by its distance from the observer, and for this we consider intervals in layers. Let L be a linear ordering, a layered interval is defined by $I = (I_a, l)$, where I_a is an interval and l is the interval layer with $l \in L$. For layered intervals we assume two functions, $ext(I)$ that maps the extension of an interval and $\ell(I)$ that maps the interval layer, where ℓ represents the proximity of the object to the observer: the closer the object is to the observer the greater is the value of ℓ. So, if an observer is in the region marked by o^+ then it will see that a overlaps and is in front of b and if the observer is in the region marker by d^- it will see that a occurs during b and is behind it.

Given two intervals I and J $(I \neq J)$ and the Allen Relations (described in Sect. 3) we have the IOC relations as follows: $I\ p\ J : \Sigma$, read as "I precedes J from Σ if $ext(I)\ p\ ext(J)$"; $I\ m\ J : \Sigma$, read as "I meets J from Σ if $ext(I)\ m\ ext(J)$"; $I\ o^+\ J : \Sigma$, read as "I overlaps and is in front of J from Σ if $ext(I)\ o\ ext(J)$ and $\ell(I) > \ell(J)$"; $I\ o^-\ J : \Sigma$, read as "I overlaps and is behind J from Σ if $ext(I)\ o\ ext(J)$ and $\ell(I) < \ell(J)$"; $I\ s^+\ J : \Sigma$, read as "I starts and is in front of J from Σ if $ext(I)\ s\ ext(J)$ and $\ell(I) > \ell(J)$" (resp. for $I\ s^-\ J : \Sigma$); $I\ d^+\ J : \Sigma$, read as "I is during and is in front of J from Σ if $ext(I)\ d\ ext(J)$ and $\ell(I) > \ell(J)$" (resp. for $I\ d^-\ J : \Sigma$); $I\ f^+\ J : \Sigma$, read as "I finishes and is in front of J from Σ if $ext(I)\ f\ ext(J)$ and $\ell(I) > \ell(J)$" (resp. for $I\ f^-\ J : \Sigma$); $I\ c^+\ J : \Sigma$, read as "I coincides with and is in front of J from Σ if $ext(I)\ eq\ ext(J)$ and $\ell(I) > \ell(J)$"; $I\ c^-\ J : \Sigma$, read as "I coincides with and is behind of J from Σ

if *ext(I) eq ext(J)* and $\ell(I) > \ell(J)$"; *I eq J* : Σ, read as "*I* is equal *J* from Σ if *ext(I) eq ext(J)* and $\ell(I) = \ell(J)$".

From these relations and the diagram shown in Fig. 2 it is possible to define the translation from the observations of one agent to another agent's viewpoint. This translation can be encoded by a table called IOC translation table, as described in the next section.

4.1   IOC Translation Table

As mentioned previously, IOC allows the observations made by the agents in the same environment to be shared among them, with that comes the need of an agent to be able to understand or recognize the observations made by another agent.

Let Σ_1 and Σ_2 be two distinct viewpoints, and $a = image(A, \Sigma_1)$, $b = image(B, \Sigma_1)$, $\sigma_2 = image(\Sigma_2, \Sigma_1)$, $a' = image(A, \Sigma_2)$, $b' = image(B, \Sigma_2)$, $\sigma_1 = image(\Sigma_1, \Sigma_2)$. The translation table is a function with three arguments $R_i(a, b)$, $R_j(a, \sigma_2)$, $R_k(b, \sigma_2)$ and returns the set of possible relations observed from Σ_2, that is $a' R b'$, given a, b, and σ_2.

In order to build a translation table, we consider every location of an observer Σ_1 around a pair of objects A and B, given that Σ_1 also views the observer Σ_2. The table is built by considering exhaustively all the possible locations of Σ_2, excluding those that are inconsistent with Σ_1 observations.

Assuming that Σ_1 is located in the region where it can observe a p b, as shown in Fig. 3, considering the lines of sight between Σ_1, A and B we have five regions to consider: 1, 2, 3 and the two red-dashed regions.

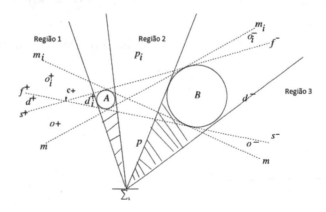

Fig. 3. Example of how to build a translation table [6].

So, for instance if Σ_2 is in region 1 in Fig. 3, then Σ_1 observes a p b, σ_2 $\{p, m, o^+\}$ a and σ_2 p b; therefore, Σ_2 can observe the set of relations a' $\{p, m, o^+, s^+, f^+, c^+, d_i^+, d^+, o_i^+, m_i, p_i\}$ b'. The information between brackets represent a disjunction of relations that could possibly hold between the pair of objects outside the brackets. In [6] a IOC table for two disconnected objects is introduced, in the present paper we propose a mechanism to generalize the IOC translation table, so that it can identify regions and build the translation table for any arrangements between two convex objects.

5   Extending the IOC Translation Table

From the RCC relations, this defines the lines-of-sights to build the IOC translation table for any arrangement between any pair of objects. For an arrangement where two objects (A and B) are externally connected $EC(A, B)$, we have the lines-of-sight represented in Fig. 4. In this figure we have the representation of two objects with distinct (Fig. 4(a)) and equal size (Fig. 4(b)).

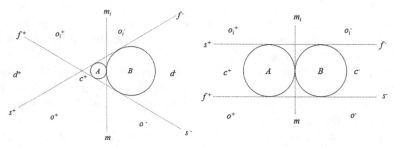

(a) Two objects with different size (b) Two objects with the same size

Fig. 4. Lines-of-sight between objects A and B and the IOC relations for $EC(A, B)$.

For the arrangement where an object A partially overlaps B, we have the lines-of-sight shown in Fig. 5.

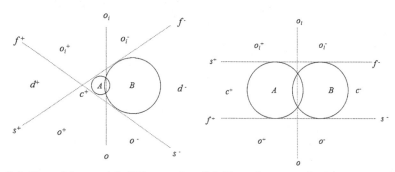

(a) Two objects with different size (b) Two objects with the same size

Fig. 5. Lines-of-sight between objects A and B and the IOC relations for $PO(A, B)$.

Finally, we have the arrangement where an object A is a proper part of B. For this situation we have qualitative regions defined with the possible observations made around these objects (Fig. 6).

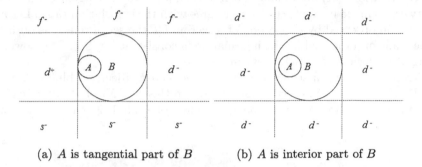

(a) A is tangential part of B (b) A is interior part of B

Fig. 6. Qualitative regions for object A and B and the IOC relations for $PP(A, B)$.

With these qualitative maps it is possible to build the IOC translation table for any arrangement between two convex objects. In this way, robotic agents can be able to perceive and share their spatial observations so that one agent is able to understand the information obtained by another agent, although they have different perspectives. The next section shows how the IOC was tested in simulated and real environments.

6   Tests and Results

With the definitions presented in the previous sections we developed a solution to implement IOC in simulated and real robots with the aim to verify if the theory presented in this work can be applied in a real situation. Figure 7 shows the functions that each agent must execute to use IOC for reasoning about spatial information.

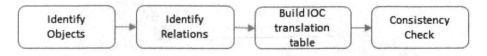

Fig. 7. Flowchart of the algorithms to apply the IOC.

The first step is to identify the objects and observers in a scene and to define the intervals for each object, for this a color code was adopted, so that each color represents an object, and no two objects have the same color. So, since the intervals are defined, the IOC relations between these intervals are identified.

Using this information we were able to build the IOC translation table for each of the scenes considered. With the IOC translation tables, and the observations made by the agents, the goal is to verify the consistency of the information provided. First, an agent checks the consistency of its own observations. Since the IOC relations (R) are binary, if $a\ R\ b$, then $b\ R^{-1}\ a$. The agent checks if the observations made by another observer agree with the translation table. Let r be the relation observed by the second observer and T the set of relations obtained in the transformation table, the information is consistent if $r \in T$. The flowchart in Fig. 7 is executed for each agent in a scene.

Figure 8(a) shows a scene with two disconnected objects, a blue (B) and a red (R) block, and two observers Σ_1 and Σ_2. In this case Σ_1 observes $\sigma_2\ p\ B$, $\sigma_2\ p\ R$ and $B\ p\ R$, as we can see in the first column of Table 1. From Fig. 3 we know

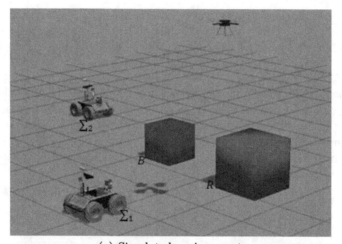

(a) Simulated environment

(b) Real environment

Fig. 8. Scenario for two objects B and R where $DC(B, R)$.

that Σ_2 is in the region 1, with that information we have that Σ_2 can observe B $\{p, m, o^+, s^+, c^+, d_i^+, d^+, f^+, o_i^+, m_i, p_i\}$ R which are the transformed relations (as shown in the second column of Table 1). By a message-passing procedure, we obtain that Σ_2 is observing B o_i^+ R, that is in the third column of Table 1, being $o_i^+ \cap \{p, m, o^+, s^+, c^+, d_i^+, d^+, f^+, o_i^+, m_i, p_i\} \neq 0$, so the information provided is consistent as we can see in the last column of Table 1. This test was applied in various situations by changing the positions of Σ_1 and Σ_2. In all the cases tested in the simulated scenarios we obtained that the observations made by the agents were consistent.

Table 1. Results of IOC for Fig. 8(a).

Vision from Σ_1	Transformed relations	Vision from Σ_2	Consistency
σ_2 p B, σ_2 p R, B p_i σ_2, B p R, R p_i σ_2, R p_i B	B $\{p, m, o^+, s^+, c^+, d_i^+, d^+, f^+, o_i^+, m_i, p_i\}$ R	R o^- B, B o_i^+ R	True

However, when applying the same idea to a real environment, due the difference of illumination and sensor noise, not always the agents provide the correct information. Figure 8(b) shows a scene where IOC was tested on a real environment. Σ_1 is in the bottom of the image, not visible. In this case, by Σ_1 we obtained the same relations as the simulated environment σ_2 p B, σ_2 p R, B p R, and in consequence we have the same transformed relations, but because of reflection Σ_2 provided an incorrect layer for the intervals, so we obtained from this point of view B o_i^- R, and as $o_i^+ \cap \{p, m, o^+, s^+, c^+, d_i^+, d^+, f^+, o_i^+, m_i, p_i\}$ is empty, an inconsistency was detected, as shown in Table 2.

Table 2. Result of IOC for the Fig. 8(b).

Vision from Σ_1	Transformed relations	Vision from Σ_2	Consistency
σ_2 p B, σ_2 p R, B p_i σ_2, B p R, R p_i σ_2, R p_i B	B $\{p, m, o^+, s^+, c^+, d_i^+, d^+, f^+, o_i^+, m_i, p_i\}$ R	R o^+ B, B o_i^- R	False

So the Interval Occlusion Calculus was successfully applied in situations where one of the agents provided noisy information, since the system could detect the inconsistency. In the experiments, the positions of the two agents Σ_1 and Σ_2 were varied over all regions around objects A and B, The same procedure was conducted in others configurations ($EC(A, B)$, $PO(A, B)$, $PP(A, B)$) and, in every case that some agent provided incorrect information, the algorithm identified the inconsistency.

7 Conclusion

This paper presented the first implementation of Interval Occlusion Calculus (IOC), a calculus based on occlusion and multiple viewpoints. In this work we extended the IOC to be applied for any configurations between two objects and implemented this calculus in an environment with multiple agents. In this environment, the agents were set to share their observations among themselves so that each agent was able to interpret the information provided by the other agents, and check the consistency of this information. Future work shall consider the development of a more robust algorithm to identify objects and the related intervals. It is also our interest to apply IOC in a dynamic scenario.

References

1. Allen, J.F.: Maintaining knowledge about temporal intervals. Commun. ACM **26**(11), 832–843 (1983)
2. Karacapidilis, N.I., Papadias, D., Egenhofer, M.J.: Collaborative spatial decision making with qualitative constraints. In: ACM-GIS, pp. 53–59 (1995)
3. Doherty, P., Heintz, F., Landén, D.: A delegation-based architecture for collaborative robotics. In: Weyns, D., Gleizes, M.-P. (eds.) AOSE 2010. LNCS, vol. 6788, pp. 205–247. Springer, Heidelberg (2011). doi:10.1007/978-3-642-22636-6_13
4. Cohn, A.G., Renz, J.: Chapter 13 qualitative spatial representation and reasoning. In: Handbook of Knowledge Representation, vol. 3, pp. 551–596 (2008)
5. Tarquini, F., Felice, G., Fogliaroni, P., Clementini, E.: A qualitative model for visibility relations. In: Hertzberg, J., Beetz, M., Englert, R. (eds.) KI 2007, LNAI, vol. 4667, pp. 510–513. Springer, Heidelberg (2007)
6. Santos, P.E., Ligozat, G., Safi-Samghabad, M.: An occlusion calculus based on an interval algebra. In: Proceedings-2015 Brazilian Conference on Intelligent Systems, BRACIS 2015, pp. 128–133 (2016)
7. Petrov, A., Kuzmin, L.: Visual space geometry derived from occlusion axioms. J. Math. Imaging Vis. **6**(2–3), 291–308 (1996). Springer
8. Galton, A.: Lines of sight. In: AISB Workshop on Spatial and Spatio-Temporal Reasoning (1994)
9. Randell, D.A., Cui, Z., Cohn, A.G.: A spatial logic based on regions and connection. In: Nebel, B., Swartout, W., Rich, C. (eds.) Proceedings of the 3rd International Conference on Knowledge Representation and Reasoning, pp. 165-176. Morgan Kaufmann, Los Altos, CA (1992)
10. Randell, D., Witkowski, M., Shanahan, M.: From images to bodies: modelling and exploiting spatial occlusion and motion parallax. In: IJCAI International Joint Conference on Artificial Intelligence, pp. 57–63 (2001). ISSN 10450823
11. Villemaire, R., Hallé, S.: Reasoning about visibility. J. Appl. Logic **10**(2), 163–178 (2012). Elsevier
12. Guha, P., Mukerjee, A., Venkatesh, K.S.: OCS-14: you can get occluded in fourteen ways. In: Proceedings of the Twenty-Second International Joint Conference on Artificial Intelligence, IJCAI 2011, vol. 2, pp. 1665–1670. AAAI Press (2011)
13. Sabharwal, C.L.: A complete classification of occlusion observer's point of view for 3D qualitative spatial reasoning. In: The proceedings of 21st International Conference on Distributed Multimedia Systems, and Journal of Visual Languages and Sentient Systems, vol. 1, pp. 94–100 (2015)
14. Tassoni, S., Fogliaroni, P., Bhatt, M., Felice, G.D.: Toward a qualitative 3D visibility model. In: 25th International Workshop on Qualitative Reasoning, Co-located with the IJCAI-11 Conference, Barcelona, Spain (2011)
15. Ligozat, G.: Qualitative Spatial and Temporal Reasoning. Wiley, New York (2013)

An Advanced Teleassistance System to Improve Life Quality in the Elderly

Fernando Ropero[✉], Daniel Vaquerizo, Pablo Muñoz, and María D. R-Moreno

Departamento de Automática, Universidad de Alcalá,
Alcalá de Henares, Madrid, Spain
fernando.ropero@uah.es

Abstract. Over the last decades the population in developed countries is becoming increasingly older, while the life expectancy is growing supported on medical advances. In despite of such progress, how to support older adults to continue living independently and retaining their current lifestyle is becoming a social problem. Through the careful placement of technological support, elders can continue living in their own homes longer and thus, maintaining and enhancing their quality of life. In this paper we present an AI-based system that integrates a (i) Wireless Sensor Network for receiving information of the environment and the dependent person, (ii) an autonomous robot able to take decisions based on the received information, and (iii) a Web-based system to provide telecare assistance.

1 Introduction

Nowadays, ageing is the most important factor driving the disability of the citizens in developed countries. According to *The 2015 Ageing Report* of the EU, the number of people aged 65 years or over in the total population in EU is projected to increase from 18% in nowadays to 28% in 2060. Similarly, the number of people aged 80 years or over is rising from 5% to 12% becoming as numerous as the young population in 2060.

Although medical advances have highly improved life expectancy in the last decades, it has tied to a huge risk of experiencing age-related limitations and, then, increasing care need. In this context, a growing social problem in developed countries is to support elderly people (and/or people with some disabilities) who would prefer to continue being self-dependent, keeping their current lifestyle instead of moving away to nursing homes. Through the careful placement of technological support, it is considered that elderly people can continue living in their own homes longer, and thus maintaining and enhancing their life quality.

An important technical advance for elder independence are *telecare* systems. It is a service designed to offer remote health-care, to facilitate dependent people to remain in his/her natural environment, and to break free caregivers as far as possible. These systems offer to individuals, families and caregivers the security and peace of mind, through services that allow dependent people to stay in their own home as long as possible.

© Springer International Publishing AG 2017
S. Benferhat et al. (Eds.): IEA/AIE 2017, Part I, LNAI 10350, pp. 533–542, 2017.
DOI: 10.1007/978-3-319-60042-0_59

The most extended telecare system in Spain is a connection to a telephone network device associated to a necklace with an emergency button. The dependent person can press the emergency button at any moment, and automatically the device will communicate with a teleoperator in a monitoring center. Despite of the success of this approach, some studies suggest negative effects of this solution both in economic and care terms [1].

However, professionals and users of those systems are more concerned about other important limitations referred to the daily live. For instance, dependent people often do not wear the necklace device because they may think they do not need it or they just forget to wear it. In other cases, dependent people may press the button accidentally, without being aware of it. In this sense, we can say that classic telecare systems need cooperation of the dependent people in order to give them full support.

In this direction, we present a non-invasive Artificial Intelligent (AI)-based system designed to operate without dependent people or caregivers interaction. It is based on three keystones: (i) a Wireless Sensor Network (WSN), i.e., a network of wireless interconnected sensor nodes, to receive both environment data (e.g., temperature, presence, noise) and dependent people health information (e.g., detect falls); (ii) an AI engine to detect emergency situations through collected data; and (iii) a robot located at the dependent person's home to autonomously analyze anomalous situations and to facilitate caregivers telepresence.

The paper is structured as follows. Next section presents some related works to the one presented here. Section 3 describes the architecture and its different components. Section 4 shows some experiments which have been done so far. Finally, conclusions and future work are outlined.

2   Related Works

Smart Environments and Ambient Intelligence (AmI) are perceived as two key enabling technologies for telecare systems. WSN are often used in these systems due to the flexibility of the wires lackness. As an example, we can mention Carelab [2], developed by Philips, is structured as a one bedroom apartment that incorporates a sensor infrastructure that is used to construct behavior patterns and identify activities.

Other approaches focus on handling the problem of assisting elder by exploiting techniques from the plan synthesis area and adapt it to perform plan recognition such as Autominder [3] that makes decisions about whether and when it is most appropriate to issue reminders. (The latest version of Autominder was deployed on a mobile robot.) The Independent Life Style Assistant [4] integrates sensors and situation assessment. Finally, the Aware Home Project [5] has addressed three key areas in the elder care: recognizing and adverting crisis, assisting daily routines, and providing awareness of daily life and long-term trends.

An important concern for elder living alone are the falls. A recent line of research which is being developed in the last decade is fall detection. The reason is that fall injuries are one of the most common problems in dependent people.

There are several techniques for detecting them. By one side, we have fall recognition based on artificial vision. In this direction we can mention the work by Fu et al. [6] that create an algorithm to be able to pick out different activities through the position, height and velocity of the person movement. Other approaches use dedicated devices, that is accelerometers [7], usually placed on the trunk [8], while others exploit the capabilities and popularity of smart-watches [9]. Also, Pan et al. [10] present a homecare service for fall discovery using a body-worn tri-axial accelerometer and reporting such a discovery to an emergency center. Finally, other projects have focused on using sound as a data source to detect falls or activities in general, like the work of Zigel et al. [11].

Inside telecare services, there are some approaches such as GrandCare[1] and WellAWARE[2] systems whose goal is monitoring the elderly people status through several automatic procedures. However, these are invasive systems which do not guarantee people's privacy. This kind of systems use a wide variety of closed methods, so it is too complex to do a direct comparative among them. But, it is worth noting that GiraffPlus project[3], funded by EU, seeks the elderly supervision using all kinds of sensors [12]. The greatest interest of this project lies on the Giraff robot. This robot allows virtual access to the dependent people [13], and thus can get in contact in case of an alert as fast as possible [14]. Nonetheless, it does not perform processing of sensor data to infer improper conduct and it does not performs any kind of inference on tasks or goals achieved.

However, those approaches are not taking into account the joint work of a web page service together with AI alarms detection and path planing movement system as well as the adaptability to any commercial product. In this terms, using the Robotic Operation Systems (ROS) into a commercial robotic platform like TurtleBot, path planing algorithms inclusion turn out to be quick and precise. Also, the adaptability to any commercial product results in a costs reduction. The aim of this paper is to show our implemented system and each module to be able to apply in elderly care sector.

3   The General Architecture

Our system is a passive telecare one with three main advantages respect to current solutions. First the dependent person is not an active component, i.e., the system works without the user interaction. Second, it provides caregivers a detailed vision of the patient's environment, monitoring variables such as the temperature, humidity or presence among others. Based on such variables the system, using AI technologies, is able to determine unexpected situations in the house (e.g., low temperature, fire), alerting the caregiver. And third, a robot in the dependent's house provides telepresence capabilities to the caregiver, enabling an audio/video channel to check the patient's status in order to attend him and mobilize the appropriate resources if required.

---

[1] http://www.grandcare.com.

[2] http://www.wellawaresystems.com.

[3] http://www.giraffplus.eu/.

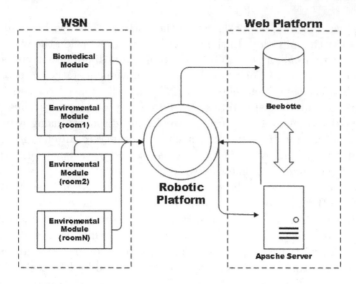

Fig. 1. The general architecture

The system is made up of three components, as shown in Fig. 1: a WSN, a robotic platform, and a web platform. The WSN monitors the environment variables, providing those data to the robotic platform. The robotic platform provides telepresence for all the house, plus the AI methods to analyze unexpected events and autonomous navigation. Finally, the web platform shows a log of the collected values of the variables and the reported alarms, while allows teleoperating the robot if needed.

The WSN consists of two types of modules: environmental and biomedical. The environmental modules are a set of sensors placed in every room and the biomedical module is a bracelet placed on the wrist of the dependent person. Both modules provide information about the state of the dependent person. All modules send the information collected to the robotic platform to process it.

The robotic platform integrates an autonomous control architecture supported on ROS [15]. The robot is in charge of analyzing the environment conditions using the data given by the WSN and in case of an anomalous situation notifying the caregiver via the web platform. In this situation the robot could autonomously move to reach the room in which the alarms is produced. Or the caregiver could take control of the robot. When no further actions are required, the robot autonomously returns to a charging station, remaining in standby until a new alarm is produced.

Finally, the web platform is an implementation of an IoT cloud solution (currently we are using Beebotte[4]) that gives caregivers a visualization of the historical values of the environment variables, as well as the alarms detected. Moreover, the web platform enables the telepresence, providing the control of

---

[4] www.beebotte.com.

the robot using a joystick, displaying the video in real-time and allowing the caregiver to talk to the patient anywhere in the house.

Next subsections explain in detail each component.

3.1 The Sensor Network

The WSN is a mesh network composed of a ZigBee protocol above a MAC layer and the IEEE 802.15.4-2003 standard on a 2.4 GHz band. The elements used are XBee Series 2. This allows that the network can consist of a maximum of 65535 distributed nodes in subnets of 255 nodes and 170 m of maximum distance of communication between two elements without obstacles.

Each room has an environmental module in a strategic place. The environmental modules measure the temperature, humidity, luminosity and presence of each room. Regardless of the room, the dependent person wears the biomedical module that collects techniques to detect possible user falls using Machine Learning techniques [9]. Depending on some particular house features (for instance, if the kitchen has a butane stove) other kind of sensors can be included (e.g., butane sensors).

The robotic platform, each environmental and biomedical module contain a Xbee Series 2 component. The XBee located in the robotic platform corresponds to the master of the network. The others XBee placed in the environment and in biomedical modules correspond to end-devices. Then, there is only one master device that gathers the data from all the other end-devices.

In this regard, the master device is waiting for retrieving information from the end-devices. Meanwhile, the end-devices are in sleeping mode until new data have to be sent to the master device. The environmental modules send information when there is a change in a value of a measured variable and the biomedical module forwards a notification when a fall is detected. Each device has a unique MAC address, so each device corresponds to an unique location in the house.

3.2 The Robotic Platform

The robotic platform is the *brain* of the system. It is in charge of analyzing the information gathered from the sensors and providing telepresence anywhere in the house. Since it hosts the master device, it coordinates the information flow between the WSN and the web platform.

In our approach, the robotic platform is able to infer what is happening in the environment thanks to an AI goal recognition system [16]. The system aims to infer actor's goal from some or all of the actor's observed (performed) actions. This is done by continuously analyzing the information given by the WSN to infer the user behavior. The objective is to predict when the user will be in a potentially hazardous situation for a faster response in case of contingency. A goal recognition problem with a planning domain and initial conditions is defined. Then, based on the sensors information, the system will infer unusual situations.

Once any dangerous/unusual situation has been detected, the robot determines where the situation happened and autonomously generate a route to reach the destination as a result of the autonomous mobility through a path planning algorithm [17]. For example, if the information received by the system is that the person is on the bathroom floor because of a fall, the robot will generate an alarm, move from its recharging position to the bathroom where the person is, activate the cameras and audio, and connect to the monitoring center (web platform), where the caregiver will analyze the situation from the images received and attend the dependent person to made the appropriate decisions.

Our current robotic platform is a modified TurtleBot II[5] endorsed with a Raspberry Pi 3 micro computer, a microphone, a speaker, three sonars and two cameras (a wide angle and a hd camera). The TurtleBot provides a differential driver locomotion system and it incorporates utilities to control it based on ROS. The Rasbperry PI 3 serves a medium to link the hardware to the web platform and thus, allowing the streaming and sending the information to the web platform. As well, this micro computer implements the path planning algorithm, the autonomous behaviors of the robot and the AI techniques to analyze the environment conditions.

To provide telepresence, the robotic platform exploits the User space Video4 Linux collection (UV4L)[6] project. The video and the audio data collected by the robot are sent to the web platform whereas that the audio from the caregiver is reproduced by the robot's speaker.

3.3   Web Platform

Our web platform is an Apache-PHP-JavaScript solution based on Beebotte. It is in charge of providing a readable visualization of the historic values of the environment modules and biomedical module as well the alarms. Also, it is charge of to assign a dependent people to one or more caregivers and to enable telepresence.

On the web, the caregivers can read the temperature, the humidity and the presence of each room over time as well the alarms of the falls of the dependent persons and the alarms of anomalous situations. Also, the video-audio streaming of the robotic platform can be seeing on-demand. Finally, the web platform provides utilities to telecontrol the robot in addition to the autonomous decisions explained previously.

4   Experiments

The current deployment of the telecare system consists of: (i) the robot shown in Fig. 2b; (ii) 4 sensor modules such as the depicted in Fig. 2a; (iii) a bracelet for one user and; (iv) the web platform for caregivers. For the testing, we have to consider the situations that trigger an alarm, based on the variables monitored by the enviromental/biomedical modules:

---

[5] www.turtlebot.com.

[6] www.linux-projects.org/uv4l.

(a) Sensor module spotlight, robot returning to charge station   (b) Robot

Fig. 2. LARES testing in our laboratory.

- For the temperature we have an admissible range between 15 °C and 25 °C. Values out of this range trigger an alarm.
- Similarly, the humidity must be between 15% and 30%.
- Moreover, an alarm is produced if there is an abrupt variation (higher than 20% between two consecutive values) of the temperature or humidity.
- The luminosity can also produce an alarm if a sensor detects more than 500 lux.
- As well, a night period is defined between 0 h to 8 h in which alarms are triggered due to: movement detection or light detection (values higher than 65 lux).
- Finally, if the biomedical module detects that the user falls over, an alarm is generated.

During the nominal operation, the system is in standby, i.e., the robot is at the charging station and the environmental modules are providing the information to the robot. When some of the above presented situations produce an alarm, it means that there is an anomalous situation to be analyzed and then the robot moves to where the alarm occurs. If required, the caregiver can mobilize the necessary resources to the user's house. Otherwise, the caregiver close the communication and the robot automatically goes back to the charging station.

The tests presented here follow such scheme but in a controlled laboratory instead of a house. The map shown in Fig. 3 is a binary grid that represents the laboratory place. On this grid, the orange items are free locations where the robot can move and the gray items are occupied locations that the robot cannot cross. The place where the robot is located corresponds to a circle, the place where the environmental modules is located corresponds to a square and the place where the biomedical module is placed corresponds to a triangle. Likewise, the grid size is 7.6 m × 6.8 m, being each square 0.4 m × 0.4 m.

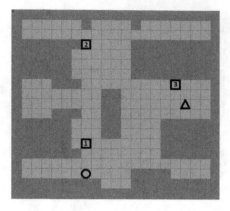

Fig. 3. Laboratory map

The laboratory has temperature control and the working hours are from 8 h to 20h period, so it is expected that there are no alarms during our tests. In this regard, after four days of tests only one alarm was detected by the system. Particularly, one sensor detects 90 lux at 7:58 due to an open window. When an alarm is detected, the robot goes to the location where it was detected and then it waits until the caregiver takes the control. If it has been longer than 5 min since the alarm was detected, the robot goes back to the charging station. In this terms, when the staff arrives to the laboratory, the robot is on the charging station because no caregiver takes control of the robot within five minutes after the robot achieves a sensor location. The robot employed 97 s for the movement and traveled 2.4 m from the initial position to where the environmental module 1 is placed to attend the alarm.

As there are no more anomalous situations, we have artificially produced different events on the sensors to check the system behaviors. For instance, we use a flashlight directly on the light detector, producing a saturation of the sensor that, in a house, may be produced due to a electric spark. In that case, the robot achieves the sensor position after traveling 5.16 m from the initial position to the environmental module 2 in 133 s. The caregiver takes the control, observing that there is nothing remarkable, finishing the communication so the robot returns to the charging station. We also perform a similar test using a lighter near to a sensor, being triggered an alarm due to an abrupt variation of the temperature, which could be due to a fire in a house.

For the last test, we drop the bracelet of the biomedical module where the grid map shows. In that case, the biomedical module triggers the fall alarm, being the robot in charge of determining the location. This is done by assessing the movement history of the environmental modules: before falling over, the user is detected by the environmental module 3, but, after falling over, the environmental module 3 indicates that there is no movement in the room. Then, the robot achieves the room in which the user falls, allowing the caregiver to see if the s/he has injuries in order to mobilize the medical care.

It is remarkable that in four weeks of testing, the robot battery did not fall 70% of its capacity during the operation and the sensors voltage decay was negligible. In this sense, it is expected that the sensors' battery life exceeds two months of continuous operation. As well, the robot is able to reach any position of the monitored environment in less than three minutes (currently we are using a low speed mode), enabling a fast response in case of emergency.

5   Conclusions and Future Work

Population aging in developed countries is becoming a growing social problem. Elders want to continue living independently and retaining their current lifestyle, instead of moving to nursing homes one. To try to help both patients and caregivers, technological solutions such as the presented in this paper can be deployed in order to allow activities monitoring without privacy violations.

Our system is an AI-based system that integrates WSN for environment and dependent person monitoring, an AI goal-recogniser and an autonomous robot able to made decisions based on the received information. These elements enables fast response from caregivers meanwhile the user's privacy is safeguarded at all times.

At the moment the system is deployed on three real homes and in the future we want to deploy it on elderly residences. For future work, fuzzy logic can be used using all the variables information registered with the aim to infer possible alarms.

Acknowledgments. The work is supported by the Universidad de Alcalá project 2016/00351/001 and MINECO project Epheme-CH TIN2014-56494-C4-4-P. Authors want to thanks Diego López and Antonio Escobar for their contributions.

References

1. Finkelstein, S.M., Speedie, S.M., Potthoff, S.: Home telehealth improves clinical outcomes at lower cost for home healthcare. Telemedicine J. e-health **12**(2), 128–136 (2006). The official journal of the American Telemedicine Association
2. Ruyter, B., Pelgrim, E.: Ambient assisted-living research in carelab. Interactions **14**(4), 30–33 (2007)
3. Pollack, M.E., Brownb, L., Colbryc, D., McCarthyd, C.E., Orosza, C., Peintnera, B., Ramakrishnane, S., Tsamardinos, I.: Autominder: an intelligent cognitive orthotic system for people with memory impairment. Robot. Auton. Syst. **44**(3), 273–282 (2003)
4. Haigh, K.Z., Phelps, J., Geib, C.W.: An open agent architecture for assisting elder independence. In: Proceedings of the First International Joint Conference on Autonomous Agents and Multiagent Systems: Part 2, Bologna, Italy, July 2002
5. Mynatt, E.D., Essa, I., Rogers, W.: Increasing the opportunities for aging in place. In: Proceedings of the 2000 Conference on Universal Usability, Virginia, USA, November 2000

6. Fu, Z., Culurciello, E., Lichtsteiner, P., Delbruck, T.: Fall detection using an address-event temporal contrast vision sensor. In: Proceedings of the IEEE International Symposium on Circuits and Systems (ISCAS 2008), Boston, MA, USA, pp. 424–427 (2008)

7. Noury, N., Fleury, A., Rumeau, P., Bourke, A.K., Laighin, G.O., Rialle, V., Lundy, J.E.: Fall detection - principles and methods. In: 2007 29th Annual International Conference of the IEEE Engineering in Medicine and Biology Society, pp. 1663–1666 (2007)

8. Gibson, R.M., Amira, A., Ramzan, N., Casaseca-de-la higuera, P., Pervez, Z.: Multiple comparator classifier framework for accelerometer-based fall detection and diagnostic. Appl. Soft Comput. J. **39**, 94–103 (2016)

9. Villaverde, A.C., R-Moreno, M.D., Rodriguez, D., Barrero, D.F.: Triaxial accelerometer located on the wrist for elderly people's fall detection. In: Proceedings of the 17th International Conference on Intelligent Data Engineering and Automated Learning, Yangzhou, China, October 2016

10. Pan, J.-I., Yung, C.-J., Liang, C.-C., Lai, L.-F.: An intelligent homecare emergency service system for elder falling. In: Magjarevic, R., Nagel, J.H. (eds.) World Congress on Medical Physics and Biomedical Engineering 2006, pp. 424–428. Springer, Heidelberg (2007)

11. Zigel, Y., Litvak, D., Gannot, I.: A method for automatic fall detection of elderly people using floor vibrations and soundProof of concept on human mimicking doll falls. IEEE Trans. Biomed. Eng. **56**(12), 2858–2867 (2009)

12. Coradeschi, S., Cesta, A., Cortellessa, G., Coraci, L., Gonzalez, J., Karlsson, L., Furfari, F., Loutfi, A., Orlandini, A., Palumbo, F., Pecora, F., von Rump, S., Stimec, A., Ullberg, J., Otslund, B.: GiraffPlus: combining social interaction and long term monitoring for promoting independent living. In: 2013 6th International Conference on Human System Interactions (HSI), pp. 578–585. IEEE, June 2013

13. Frennert, S., Östlund, B.: Domestication of a telehealthcare system. Gerontechnology **13**(2), 197 (2014)

14. Frennert, S.A., Forsberg, A., Östlund, B.: Elderly people's perceptions of a telehealthcare system: relative advantage, compatibility, complexity and observability. J. Technol. Hum. Serv. **31**(3), 218–237 (2013)

15. Quigley, M., Conley, K., Gerkey, B., Faust, J., Foote, T., Leibs, J., Wheeler, R., Ng, A.Y.: ROS: an open-source robot operating system. In: ICRA Workshop on Open Source Software, May 2009

16. E-Martín, Y., R-Moreno, M.D., Smith, D.: A fast goal recognition technique based on interaction estimates. In: Proceedings of 23rd International Joint Conference on Artificial Intelligence (IJCAI 2015), Buenos Aires, Argentina (2015)

17. Muñoz, P., R-Moreno, M.D.: S-Theta: low steering path-planning algorithm. In: Proceedings of the 32nd SGAI International Conference on Artificial Intelligence, Cambridge, UK, December 2012

Learning the Elasticity of a Series-Elastic Actuator for Accurate Torque Control

Bingbin Yu[(✉)], José de Gea Fernández, Yohannes Kassahun,
and Vinzenz Bargsten

DFKI, Robotics Innovation Center, 28359 Bremen, Germany
{bingbin.yu,jose.de_gea_fernandez,yohannes.kassahun,
vinzenz.bargsten}@dfki.de

Abstract. Series elastic actuators (SEAs) have been frequently used in torque control mode by using the elastic element as torque measuring device. In order to precisely control the torque, an ideal torque source is critical for higher level control strategies. The elastic elements are traditionally metal springs which are normally considered as linear elements in the control scheme. However, many elastic elements are not perfectly linear, especially for an elastic element built out of multiple springs or using special materials and thus their nonlinearities are very noticeable. This paper presents two data-driven methods for learning the spring model of a series-elastic actuator: (1) a Dynamic Gaussian Mixture Model (DGMM) is used to capture the relationship between actuator torque, velocity, spring deflection and its history. Once the DGMM is trained, the spring deflection can be estimated by using the conditional probability function which later is used for torque control. For comparison, (2) a deep-learning approach is also evaluated which uses the same variables as training data for learning the spring model. Results show that the data-driven methods improve the accuracy of the torque control as compared to traditional linear models.

Keywords: Series-elastic actuators · Nonlinear springs · DGMM · Deep learning · Torque control

1 Introduction

In recent years, robots are increasingly developed to assist humans on direct physical interaction, not only in the field of assistance and rehabilitation robotics [1], but also start to be used in industrial scenarios [2]. For these robots that work close to humans in shared workspaces, safety is of outmost concern (especially for industrial robots which normally are fast and powerful). To achieve a safe human-robot interaction, one possible solution is to use a compliant actuator that is able to immediately sense the torque and accommodate for external force disturbances. For a rigid actuator, the torque can be measured by torque sensors, e.g. a load cell, a strain gauge or a current sensor, and then be controlled by using a feedback loop [3]. Different from a rigid actuator, a serial elastic

© Springer International Publishing AG 2017
S. Benferhat et al. (Eds.): IEA/AIE 2017, Part I, LNAI 10350, pp. 543–552, 2017.
DOI: 10.1007/978-3-319-60042-0_60

actuator (SEA) can estimate the torque from the deflection of its elastic element. Due to the passive compliance between the actuator and its link, SEAs provide additional benefits including lower reflected inertia, greater shock tolerance and more accurate force control.

A large number of SEA designs has already been developed, for instance as surveyed in [1,4]. A typical design is a linear SEA, in which the spring system either uses a single spring [5] or a set of serial-connected springs [6], which connect to the motor through a ball screw. For a rotary series elastic actuator (RSEA) the design of the elastic coupling that restricts the size and reduces the weight of the device is usually challenging. For example, Kong and Jeon developed a compact RSEA with a coil spring and worm gears for knee joint assistance [7]; Stienen et al. developed a rotational hydroelastic actuator with a symmetric torsion spring for a powered exoskeleton [8]; or the elastic element of the CAPIO actuator [9] includes a set of small disc springs placed at both sides of a lever which connects to the link. In recent years, new elastic materials are also utilized: scientists at the Carnegie Mellon University used nonlinear rubber as the elastic element of the actuators for their snake robots [10]; Sudano et al. integrated a magnetic nonlinear torsion spring in a rotary elastic actuator for biorobotic applications [11]. However, due to mechanical effects caused by the construction itself, by the structure of the spring system (e.g. different initial pre-compression of coil springs), or the properties of the materials, many of these elastic couplings show very poor linearity, which is usually neglected. In this work, we propose two data-driven methods for modeling the torque profile of an SEA, which consider the nonlinearity of the elastic couplings for realizing better torque control approaches. The data-driven modeling methods are validated and compared using a newly designed RSEA.

Various torque control approaches have already been proposed for SEAs, e.g. velocity-source control [12], a cascade control by using velocity or current in inner loop and torque in outer loop; or feedforward force control with distur-bance observer [13]. The performances of these higher level control strategies are influenced by the torque sources, if the nonlinearity of the spring and resistive frictions are too large, a precise model of the elastic element and the frictions is needed. Therefore, Ford et al. [14] proposed an online calibration method to compensate the nonlinear effects of the spring and accurately estimate the mod-ules output torque by using motor current and spring deflection together. Lu [15] modelled the nonlinearity of the spring of a SEA by using a back propagation neural network and realized a stable velocity control. The paper is organized as follows. In Sect. 2, the hardware design of the RSEA and analysis of the spring coupling are presented. In Sect. 3, the two modeling methods of the elastic ele-ment are discussed. The experimental validation of the two models is performed in Sect. 4. In Sect. 5, based on the learned models, a torque control task is demon-strated. Finally, conclusions are given in Sect. 6.

2   SEA Design and Spring Analysis

The assembled serial elastic actuator (see Fig. 1 left) is designed within the project FourByThree [16]. The actuator is powered by a Robodrive brushless DC motor and provides a maximum 50 Nm torque and 15 rpm speed in the link side by using a 1:120 Harmonic Drive gear. An FPGA (Spartan6)-based control stack incorporates all the required sensors (three absolute encoders, two motor current sensors, temperature sensors, etc.) and perform the required actuator control with an in-house developed communication protocol. A new elastic element based on coil springs has been developed for the actuator (see Fig. 1 right) which consists two springs in each spring segment: a lower-stiff spring firstly compresses singly until its deflection reaches approx. 5°, then a smaller higher-stiff spring which is placed inside the other starts to work. By using this design, the elastic spring is relatively 'soft' in the lower torque range, so that it provides a higher torque to deflection resolution in this torque range. Since the elastic spring is 'stiff' for a higher torque input, it brings a larger working range and avoid that the spring completely compresses at the maximum torque.

Fig. 1. *left:* FourByThree 50 Nm-Actuator. *right:* Elastic element based on coil springs.

As shown in Fig. 1, coil springs are used and each single spring is a linear element. However due to the internal friction and different pre-compression during assembly, the torque-deflection curve of the overall spring module is nonlinear. Figure 2 shows the result of an experiment used to demonstrate the nonlinearity of the spring coupling. In this experiment, the elastic actuator is controlled to a fixed rotation angle in position control. An external force/torque sensor (Lorenz-DF30) is employed to provide a torque ground truth in a range of −50 Nm to +50 Nm with an accuracy class of 0.05%. The motor is fixed on a test bed, the external torque is externally applied to the spring through the link lever in both directions. As the plot shows, the torque-deflection model of the spring presents a hysteresis characteristic, where a simple linear regression line is a poor choice of representation.

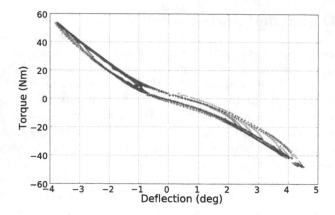

Fig. 2. Torque to deflection curve of the spring coupling. The output torque is measured with an external force/torque sensor and the deflection is measured by computing the difference of two absolute encoders at both sides of the spring.

3   Spring Modeling Methods

Since a spring is used as a torque sensor in a series-elastic actuator, an accurate spring model is the basis of a successful and accurate torque control. As discussed in Sect. 2, the torque-deflection curve of the coil spring component exhibits a nonlinear property. In order to account for the nonlinearity, two data-driven modeling approaches are used: (1) a dynamic Gaussian mixture model (DGMM) [17] and (2) a neural network (NN). Both methods will be described briefly in the following sections.

3.1   Spring Modeling by DGMM

As a probabilistic modeling method, Gaussian mixture models (GMM) are widely used in modeling complex and multi-variable data. To model the spring with more variables besides deflection, a dynamic Gaussian mixture model (DGMM) is studied, which represents a probability density function $P(x)$ as a variable-sized set of weighted Gaussian pairs (Eq. 1).

$$P(x) = \Sigma_{i=1}^{m} \hat{\omega}_i g_i(x),$$ (1)

where $g_i(x)$ is a multivariate Gaussian distribution

$$g_i(x) = p_i(x) \sim \mathcal{N}_i(\mu_i, \Sigma_i),$$ (2)

and $\hat{\omega}_i$ is the weight of the Gaussian $g_i(x)$

$$\hat{\omega}_i = \omega_i / \Sigma_{k=1}^{m}.$$ (3)

The quantity x is the observation vector. As Fig. 2 shows, the torque to deflection curve of the spring coupling is nonlinear, therefore more variables are required:

the rotation velocity v and the history of the spring deflection δ'. Consequently, the observation vector is

$$x = [\tau, \delta, \delta', v], \tag{4}$$

and the model of the system can be represented by

$$P[\tau, \delta, \delta', v]. \tag{5}$$

As a result, once a DGMM model $P[\tau, \delta, \delta', v]$ is learned with a training data set, the output torque can be estimated analytically as

$$\mathbb{E}[\tau | \delta, \delta', v]. \tag{6}$$

For control purposes one can also similarly estimate the deflection using

$$\mathbb{E}[\delta | \tau, \delta', v]. \tag{7}$$

3.2   Spring Modeling by Using Neural Network

An artificial neural network consists of an interconnected assembly of simple processing units [18]. In most of the cases, each processing unit calculates its output by taking a weighted sum of its inputs and transforming the sum by an activation function. In addition to the connection weights, the function represented by an artificial neural network is determined by the architecture of the neural network. Because of the possibility of optimizing a large number of parameters due to the advancement in computing, neural networks are used in various application areas such as computer vision, speech recognition and natural language processing resulting in progress beyond the state-of-the-art in terms of performance in most of the cases.

In this paper, five layered neural networks are used for modeling the spring component, which are realized using an open-source Deep Learning tool Keras [19]. Unlike DGMM, two separate networks are trained independently: once for $\mathbb{E}[\tau | \delta, \delta', v]$ and once for $\mathbb{E}[\delta | \tau, \delta', v]$. In both networks, three hidden layers are created with 50, 20 and 10 neurons with relu activation function in each layer. A relu is defined as $f(a) = \max(0, a)$, where a is a weighted sum of the inputs to a unit. To optimize the networks, "Adam" [20] is used which is an algorithm for the first-order gradient-based optimization of stochastic objective functions. After training, 771 parameters are learned for the networks of inverse model $\mathbb{E}[\delta | \tau, \delta', v]$.

4   Spring Models Validation

In order to validate the two modeling approaches, an experiment setup has been constructed as shown Fig. 3. The FourByThree 50 Nm SEA (for more details, see Sect. 2) is used and fixed on an adjustable base, so that the inclination of the actuator can be changed and the effects of gravity can be accounted for. An external force/torque sensor is mounted between the spring coupling and the

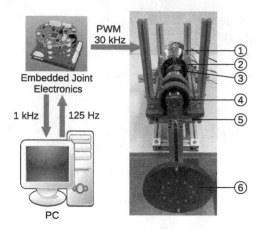

Fig. 3. Experimental setup used for spring modeling and torque control: (1) actuator; (2) spring coupling; (3) external force/torque sensor; (4) brake; (5) adjustable base; (6) load.

link lever, which measures the output torque with a 125 Hz sampling frequency in order to validate the results.

The models need to be trained first and then be used in the validation phase by estimating the output torque given measured variables. In the training procedure, the inclination angle of the actuator base is set to $0°$ and the training data is gathered by controlling the load to rotate in the range of approx. $\pm170°$ with position control smoothly in a very low speed. The position of the load at the link lever is changed in the 5 train tests and 5000 samples of the actuator torque τ, deflection δ, first derivative of deflection δ' and velocity v are measured in each test as the training inputs. The spring deflection is extracted from two absolute encoders, the first derivative of deflection δ' is calculated from the change of the deflection and the time used in a control cycle and the velocity v is acquired from the position sensor.

In the validation phase, the same load is fixed at random selected position on the lever arm and the inclination angle of the base is set to $37.8°$. Based on the trained DGMM and neural network models, the actuator torque τ can be estimated by both methods respectively with given measured data $[\delta, \delta', v]$ from the testing experiment. Figure 4 shows the comparison results between the trained DGMM model $P[\tau, \delta, \delta', v]$, the neural network model, and the linear regression model.

As can be seen from the upper left and upper right plots, both DGMM and neural network models are able to predict the output torque given the measured variables with high accuracy. In contrast, the fitted linear regression function has problems to represent the torque-deflection curve (see lower left plot). The RMSE between the estimated torque and measured torque is calculated for each model, as the lower right plot shows; the DGMM and neural network models present a comparable performances and have a large advantage compared to the linear model.

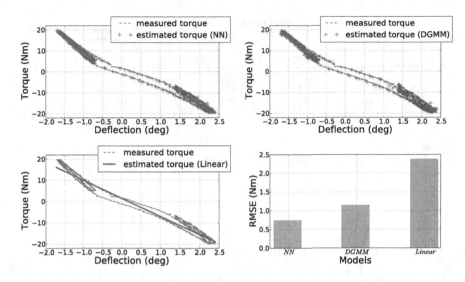

Fig. 4. *Upper left:* measured torque-deflection curve (dash line) and estimated torque with neural network model (crosses), *Upper right:* measured torque-deflection curves (dash line) and estimated torque with DGMM model (crosses), *lower left:* measured torque-deflection curve (dash line) and corresponding fitted linear line (line), *lower right:* root mean square errors (bars) of the three models in torque estimation.

5   Torque Control

Based on the learned spring models, a torque controller is proposed to control the spring torque to track the desired torque as precisely as possible. The complete torque control scheme of the SEA consists of three cascaded control loops for motor current, spring deflection and torque (see Fig. 5). Two absolute encoders are installed at both sides of the spring coupling for measuring the rotation angle and calculate the spring deflection. A deflection PID controller is implemented into the FPGA which closes the loop with the spring deflection and then cascades with an inner motor current controller. The first derivative of the deflection and the velocity are calculated to be used as the inputs of the spring model, together with the given desired torque, and the corresponding deflection value is estimated. This deflection will be then controlled by the inner deflection and current controllers. Due to an intrinsic property of the DGMM model, once the model $P[\tau, \delta, \delta', v]$ is learned from the training experiments, both forward $E[\tau|\delta, \delta', v]$ and inverse models $E[\delta|\tau, \delta', v]$ can be estimated, whereas the inverse model is then used in the torque control. In contrast, the forward and inverse models need to be trained individually when using a neural network model.

The proposed torque control is verified in two torque tracking experiments. A chirp signal and a random-walk are given as the desired torques in these two experiments respectively and the different controllers which are based on different spring models are evaluated in measured output torques (see plot a, b of Fig. 6). As can be seen from the comparison in tracking errors (see plot c, d),

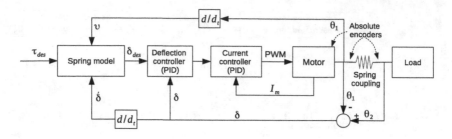

Fig. 5. Complete actuator torque control scheme.

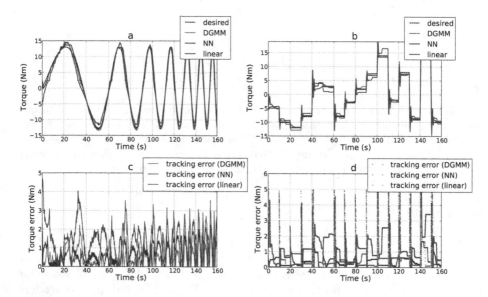

Fig. 6. *a:* Result of the torque tracking with a chirp reference signal, *b:* Result of the torque tracking with a random walk reference signal, *c:* Torque tracking error with given chirp reference, the root mean square errors are $RMSE_{DGMM} = 0.93$, $RMSE_{NN} = 1.07$ and $RMSE_{linear} = 1.77$, *d:* Torque tracking error with given random walk reference, the root mean square errors are $RMSE_{DGMM} = 0.90$, $RMSE_{NN} = 0.80$ and $RMSE_{linear} = 1.61$ respectively.

the torque control by using DGMM model and neural networks present better results than by using linear model in both experiments. Since the viscous friction of the system can not be compensated by the spring models completely, the performance of random-walk tracking is better than chirp tracking, and the error of the chirp tracking is also raised slightly when the reference frequency is increased.

6   Conclusion

In this paper, two data-driven modeling methods are proposed to account for the nonlinearities of the spring coupling of a rotary elastic actuator. The models are learned from the training experiments of the actuator and verified by estimating the output torque with given measured variables in the test experiments. The experiment result presents a comparable performances of the DGMM and the deep learning/NN methods, which show a significant advantage compared to a linear regression model. As compared to the DGMM model, the deep learning model shows a slight improvement in torque estimation. On the other side, the DGMM model captures multiple relationship among the observed variables, which is more flexible to be utilized once learned in multiple ways by choosing which variables are used as inputs and which ones as outputs of the model. The learned nonlinear spring model is then used as an torque estimation module for a torque controller, which cascades with an inner motor current and deflection control loops. The proposed torque controller is verified by a set of experiments which demonstrated a precise torque control.

Acknowledgment. The FourByThree project has received funding from the European Union's Horizon 2020 research and innovation programme, under Grant Agreement No. 637095.

References

1. Yu, H., Huang, S., Thakor, N.V., Chen, G., Toh, S.L.: A novel compact compliant actuator design for rehabilitation robots. In: 2013 IEEE International Conference on Rehabilitation Robotics (2013)
2. Rethink Robotics. www.rethinkrobotics.com
3. Bargsten, V., de Gea Fernández, J.: COMPI: development of a 6-DOF compliant robot arm for human-robot cooperation. In: Proceedings of the 8th International Workshop on Human-Friendly Robotics (2015)
4. Paine, N., Oh, S., Sentis, L.: Design and control considerations for high-performance series elastic actuators. IEEE/ASME Trans. Mechatron. **19**(3), 1080–1091 (2014)
5. Pratt, G.A., Williamson, M.M.: Series elastic actuators. IEEE Int. Conf. Intell. Rob. Syst. **1**, 399–406 (1995)
6. Arumugom, S., Muthuraman, S., Ponselvan, V.: Modeling and application of series elastic actuators for force control multi legged robots. J. Comput. **1**, 26–33 (2009)
7. Kong, K., Bae, J., Tomizuka, M.: A compact rotary series elastic actuator for human assistive systems. IEEE/ASME Trans. Mechatron. **17**(2), 288–297 (2012)
8. Stienen, A.H.A., Hekman, E.E.G., Braak, H., Aalsma, A.M.M., Van der Helm, F.C.T., van der Kooij, H.: Design of a rotational hydroelastic actuator for a powered exoskeleton for upper limb rehabilitation. IEEE Trans. Biomed. Eng. **57**(3), 728–735 (2010)
9. Mallwitz, M., Will, N., Teiwes, J., Kirchner, E.A.: The CAPIO active upper body exoskeleton and its application for teleoperation. In: Proceedings of the 13th Symposium on Advanced Space Technologies in Robotics and Automation, ESA/Estec Symposium on Advanced Space Technologies in Robotics and Automation (ASTRA) (2015)

10. Rollinson, D., Ford, S., Brown, B., Choset, H.: Design and modeling of a series elastic element for snake robots. In: Proceedings of the ASME 2013 Dynamic Systems and Control Conference (2013)
11. Sudano, A., Tagliamonte, N.L., Accoto, D., Guglielmelli, E.: A resonant parallel elastic actuator for biorobotic applications. In: 2014 IEEE/RSJ International Conference on Intelligent Robots and Systems (IROS) (2014)
12. Wyeth, G.: Demonstrating the safety and performance of a velocity sourced series elastic actuator. In: 2008 IEEE International Conference on Robotics and Automation (2008)
13. Li, Y., Feng, H.: Force control of series elastic acutator. In: 2015 Fifth International Conference on Instrumentation and Measurement, Computer, Communication and Control (2015)
14. Ford, S., Rollinson, D., Willig, A., Choset, H.: Online calibration of a compact series elastic actuator. In: 2014 American Control Conference (2014)
15. Lu, C., Mao, Y., Zhu, Q., Xiong, R.: Novel series elastic actuator design and velocity control. Electr. Mach. Control **19**, 83–88 (2015)
16. de Gea Fernández, J., Sprengel, H., Mallwitz, M., Zipper, M., Yu, B., Bargsten, V.: Designing modular series-elastic actuators for safe human-robot collaboration in industrial settings. In: Proceedings of the Climbing and Walking Robots and Support Technologies for Mobile Machines (CLAWAR) (2016)
17. Edgington, M., Kassahun, Y., Kirchner, F.: Dynamic motion modelling for legged robots. In: 2009 IEEE/RSJ International Conference on Intelligent Robots and Systems, pp. 4688–4694 (2009)
18. Bishop, C.M.: Neural Networks for Pattern Recognition. Oxford University Press, New York (1995)
19. Keras: Deep Learning library for Theano and TensorFlow. https://keras.io/
20. Kingma, D.P., Ba, J.L.: Adam: a method for stochastic optimization. In: International Conference on Learning Representations (ICLR) (2015)

The Effect of Rotation in the Navigation of Multi-level Buildings: A Pilot Study

Giulia Mastrodonato[1(✉)], Domenico Camarda[1], Caterina De Lucia[2], and Dino Borri[1]

[1] Politecnico di Bari, Bari, Italy
julie.mastrodonato@gmail.com, d.camarda@poliba.it
[2] University of Foggia, Foggia, Italy

Abstract. The aim of the present paper is to investigate user's perception of buildings' layouts with particular emphasis on navigation of multi-level buildings. Up to date, research seems to pay more attention to wayfinding in two-dimensional environments, investigating it in public buildings such as hospitals, airports or university departments where it is more common to experience disorientation. The present work deepens this issue and focuses on the effect of rotation – due to staircases – on people's cognitive maps. The study consists of a pilot work based on two cases: one qualitative, conducted at the University of Bremen, and the other one quantitative, conducted at the Technical University of Bari. Main results suggests that staircases affect somehow people's perception of layout during navigation of multi-level buildings.

Keywords: Spatial frame of reference · Indoor orientation · Rotation problem · Multi-level buildings · Wayfinding

1 Introduction

In cognition studies spatial environment is largely considered not per se, but from the standpoint of agents' spatial behaviours. Large and inclusive conceptualizations of spatial environments, for their representation and management, are a critical stage in building intelligent ontology-based devices [1]. Space organization is an important part of human agents' spatial prerogatives, which suggests intricate interplays between sensorial and cognitive attitudes.

This work is rooted on a research network on intelligent models and system architectures to support and enhance intelligent navigation, organization and design of space. The paper explores the conceptualization and mental representation ability of human agents toward space, particularly toward reaching spatial objectives. The research investigates agents' cognitive behaviours in movement orientation (lower-level behaviours) and memories and fantasies (higher-level behaviours) while ·interacting with spatial environments.

Authors are particularly grateful to prof. M. Bhatt from University of Bremen, for his precious scientific support of the research activity behind this work.

© Springer International Publishing AG 2017
S. Benferhat et al. (Eds.): IEA/AIE 2017, Part I, LNAI 10350, pp. 553–558, 2017.
DOI: 10.1007/978-3-319-60042-0_61

While designing an indoor or outdoor environment, designers, architects or planners must take into account several elements. The way in which users move through it is highly dependent on environment perception [2]. Perception and representation of space are very important for urban planning aims, as urban agents' cognitive feedbacks from their neighbourhoods may induce the success or the failure of planning policies [3]. Rotation has not been given structural importance in the increasing interest put on spatial cognition, as translational movements. Yet, several studies in supporting urban route learning and infrastructure (particularly transportation) design have spurred applied research on rotation [4].

In literature it is widely recognized that the pointing ability is not affected either by physical or by imagined translations but it worsens after physical rotation, even increasing if rotations are only imagined [2, 5, 6]. In fact people have to imagine a different perspective with respect to that from which they had learned the environment and then to align it to the position where they imagine themselves, rotating the spatial frame of reference (SFR) [7, 8]. This process implies a reduction of pointing tasks accuracy whereas the time required to align the two SFRs increases. Translational motions do not involve this cognitive effort.

Elements involving rotations imply the use of different SFRs; their superimposition requires a cognitive effort not necessary with simple translations. In fact, in the surrounding environment it is possible to define an allocentric SFR based on prominent local or global landmarks. Objects are positioned relatively to one another creating qualitative relations that improve the environment legibility and navigability even after rotations. Yet navigation, the interaction between our body and the environment gives rise to changeable relations between us and the objects deriving from perceptual, visual and proprioceptive flows. A crucial issue is to understand if the definition of the adopted SFR in spatial representations is limited only to the egocentric experience or it maintains some relations to the elements characterizing the environment as its intrinsic axes. Shelton and McNamara [9] argue that, even referring to egocentric systems, these systems can adopt allocentric nuances being influenced by prominent directions of space. Only if privileged directions are lacking, then people adopt a purely egocentric SFR.

The present study tries to contribute on this issue, by setting up and discussing a comparative on-field experimentation session in two building staircase environments.

2   Rotation Problem in Staircases: An Experimental Approach

Our research works on the influence of rotation on orientation, particularly considering an element involving rotations, i.e., staircase. Hoelcher [10] recognizes some common strategies when moving through 3D buildings.

In two experiments carried out at the University of Bremen (pilot study) and at the Technical University of Bari we have investigated the performance of users when they access stairs directly along their path (case 1) or after performing a 90° turn before encountering them (case 2). The aim is to assess to what extent the position of this element relative to the layout can increase the disorientation.

To evaluate the orientation ability after covering stairs we carried out some pointing tasks, towards both local and global landmarks, in different points of the building.

Both in Bremen and in Bari participants were divided randomly into two groups. The first group had to cover the stairs directly on the pathway, whereas the second had to turn 90° to get to the stairs. After the learning phase, we carried out some large scale pointing tasks, towards local and global landmarks, in different points of the building in order to evaluate the orientation ability after covering stairs. Instructions were to ignore the building vertical dimension considering all the landmarks at the same level.

Our hypothesis, with reference to the literature, is that when stairs are encountered directly along the pathway (case 1), the large scale pointing tasks performance are better than in the case 2. In fact, once on the top of the stairs the walkway direction will be the same as the initial and the egocentric and allocentric SFRs do not conflict.

To establish the possible effects of disorientation stemming from a different approach to stairs we measured both the pointing accuracy and the latency. The first is a measure of the configurational knowledge [11], the second helps to understand if there are differences between landmarks and how easy it is to access the stored information [12].

The pilot study in Bremen, given the small number of participants (15 people per group; 30 in total), was only qualitative. Instead, the experiment conducted in Bari (77 people in total), gave us the possibility to carry out a one-way ANOVA to test the differences on the means of the two groups in terms of degrees and orientation of the stairs (front/side). The two experiments carried out in Bremen and Bari would not be statistically comparable. This goes beyond the scope of this pilot work. The rationale of the quantitative experiment conducted in Bari is to support, somehow, the results found in Bremen.

As for the first pointing task, the qualitative study of Bremen shows the existence of a larger mean error when the stairs are covered after turning (90°). This result is not found in the quantitative experiment conducted in Bari ($p = 0.431 > 0.05$). This means that there is no difference between the two groups in terms of rotation for the first pointing task. Interestingly, in the second pointing task in Bremen the mean error is higher when the stairs are positioned directly on the pathway than when the users had to perform a 90° left turn before undertaking it. In Bari, again the hypothesis is not statistically significant (p-value $= 0.488 > 0.05$) and therefore there is no difference between the two groups. Somehow, those who face the stairs after turning perceive a rotation on their path but fail to integrate it properly. Our explanation for the Bremen experiment is that having to face a left turn to approach the stairs and then a right turn at the top of the stairwell, participants naturally compensate for the two turns performed on the basis of proprioception information. In fact, the situation in Bari is similar but the hypothesized compensation does not happen. We believe that the substantial difference between the two cases depends on the difference between the layouts of the two buildings. While in Bremen the layout differs from floor to floor (Fig. 1), in Bari it is always the same (Fig. 2). This could imply that participants in the pilot study of Bremen, did not recognize the environments as being similar across the floors; therefore, their perception relied only on the elements from their own locomotion.

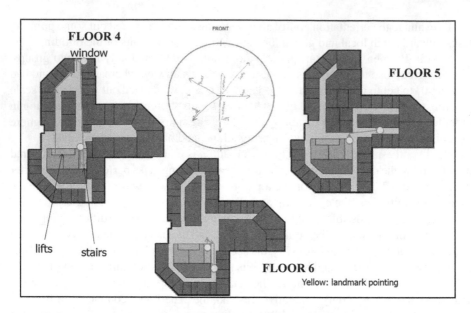

Fig. 1. Floorplans in Bremen: paths for the 1ˢᵗ group

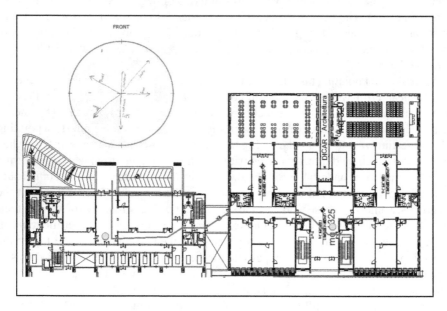

Fig. 2. Floorplan 0 in Bari: paths for the 2ⁿᵈ group

The participants in Bari, on the contrary, when exited from the stairwell, probably recognized the environment and relied more on this fact rather than on their own memory. Therefore, they neglected the position of the stairs relative to their path. Somehow recognizing the environment, they canceled the memory of the rotation accomplished. In the second case, the geometry plays the most important role. The third pointing task in Bari does not provide statistically significant results (p = 0.473 for accuracies > 0.05). That is to say that there is no difference between the two groups. In this case it is noteworthy to note that the mean error appears, larger in the first pointing task, then decreases in the second task - as if crossing the atrium helps to provide stability to the map - and finally increases again during the third pointing task. This could be simply due to the increased cognitive load. During locomotion, mammals and particularly humans activate a navigation process, known as path integration, that allows the integration of rotations and translations in order to provide an estimate of the current position and define the orientation within a wider environment [6, 13, 14]. The subsequent phase is the retrieval. People are able to update relations to objects even after imagining movements, not only after actually performing them. This task is in general more complicated, as it usually requires more time and the positioning accuracy is affected too. However, it may be interesting to assess how the participants rebuild their cognitive maps. For this purpose, after completing the navigation within the building, they are taken into a room with no windows and are asked to imagine themselves standing in a precise location of the building. They have to repeat the pointing task from the imagined position. Once again, we evaluate the accuracy and latency for the comparison between the two groups. Literature reports that the pointing tasks from imagined perspective misaligned with the body are more difficult to perform because the body SFR conflict with the environment SFR [13]. Therefore, as for the first group this conflict should not have occurred because they were asked to imagine themselves, albeit at a different point, being in the same perspective from which the environment had been learned (as if the mental map was aligned with the environment itself). As for the second group such alignment did not exist since the position in which participants were asked to imagine themselves is rotated by 90° with respect to the learning position. In both experiments, the mistakes made by the participants of the second group are almost approximated to rotations of 90°. This clearly indicates that they have not integrated the position of the stairs (which was rotated by the same angle) relative to the learning position. This seems to confirm the hypothesis. However at this point participants knew the procedure and may have used specific strategies to retrieve the spatial information and to identify landmarks.

Latencies are always slightly higher when stairs require a 90° turn. This indicates a certain degree of difficulty when accessing the information stored.

3   Conclusions

This study is part of a research on intelligent models and system architectures to support space navigation and organization, with spatial-cognition approach. In particular, the paper explores cognitive behaviours of agents during their interaction with spatial environments. Results seem to confirm the hypothesis that stair direction plays an important role on the disorientation when navigating complex 3D environments. People seem to be particularly sensitive to disorientation after rotations, because of the presence of stairs. In fact, a preferred environmental direction seems to emerge: moreover, they are unable to point between multiple floors after performing turns. Probably, it is complicated for people to integrate different levels, or people have difficulties in properly updating their location as they perform turns to cover stairs because they are not perceived as rotations. This delicate aspect has to be properly considered in emergency situations. This suggests that spatial memories are based on orientation-dependent representations: instead, when misalignments occur, conflicts trigger between different SFRs. The above findings, coming from experimentations in indoor environments, seem strictly peculiar to indoor environments themselves. This suggests that there is fair interest toward convenient investigation for outdoor generalization.

References

1. Bhatt, M., Hois, J., Kutz, O.: Modular ontologies for architectural design. In: Ferrario, R., Oltramari, A. (eds.) Frontiers in Artificial Intelligence and Applications, vol. 198, pp. 66–77. IOS Press, Amsterdam (2009)
2. Presson, C.C., Montello, D.R.: Updating after rotational and translational body movements: coordinate structure of perspective space. Perception 23(12), 1447–1455 (1994)
3. Zimring, C., Dalton, R.C.: Linking objective measures of space to cognition and action. Environ. Behav. 35(3), 3–16 (2003)
4. Gyselinck, V., Meneghetti, C., Bormetti, M., Orriols, E., Piolino, P., Beni, R.: Considering spatial ability in virtual route learning in early aging. Cogn. Process. 14(3), 309–316 (2013)
5. Rieser, J.J.: Access to knowledge of spatial structure at novel points of observation. J. Exp. Psychol. Learn. Mem. Cogn. 15(6), 1157 (1989)
6. Kelly, J.W., McNamara, T.P.: Spatial memory and spatial orientation. In: Freksa, C., Newcombe, N.S., Gärdenfors, P., Wölfl, S. (eds.) Spatial Cognition 2008. LNCS, vol. 5248, pp. 22–38. Springer, Heidelberg (2008). doi:10.1007/978-3-540-87601-4_5
7. Huttenlocher, J., Presson, C.C.: Mental rotation and the perspective problem. Cogn. Psychol. 4(2), 277–299 (1973)
8. Peruch, P., Lapin, E.A.: Route knowledge in different spatial frames of reference. Acta Physiol. (Oxf) 84(3), 253–269 (1993)
9. Shelton, A.L., McNamara, T.P.: Multiple views of spatial memory. Psychon. Bull. Rev. 4(1), 102–106 (1997)
10. Holscher, C., Brosamle, M., Vrachliotis, G.: Challenges in multilevel wayfinding: a case study with the space syntax technique. Environ. Plann. B: Plann. Des. 39, 63–82 (2012)
11. Richardson, A.E., Montello, D.R., Hegarty, M.: Spatial knowledge acquisition from maps and from navigation in real and virtual environments. Mem. Cogn. 27(4), 741–750 (1999)
12. Montello, D.R.: Spatial orientation and the angularity of urban routes: a field study. Environ. Behav. 23(1), 47–69 (1991)
13. Kelly, J.W., McNamara, T.P., Bodenheimer, B.: Individual differences in using geometric and featural cues to maintain spatial orientation: cue quantity and cue ambiguity are more important than cue type. Psychon. Bull. Rev. 16, 176–181 (2009)
14. Philbeck, J.W., O'Leary, S.: Remembered landmarks enhance the precision of path integration. Psicologica 26, 7–24 (2005)

NAO Robot, Transmitter of Social Cues: What Impacts?

The Example with "Endowment effect"

Olivier Masson[1]([✉]), Jean Baratgin[1,2], and Frank Jamet[1,3]

[1] CHArt (P-A-R-I-S), Paris 8 and University and EPHE, Paris, France
olivier.masson02@univ-paris8.fr
[2] Institut J. Nicod, ENS, Paris, France
[3] University of Cergy-Pontoise, Cergy, France

Abstract. Assuming that social norms are engaged in all human-human inter-actions in an automatic manner, how to program a robot as to activate respect of social norms from humans? We argue that endowment effect, constituting a bias in decision making, could be produced by a "politeness effect" within the exchange paradigm of Knetsch (1989). To test this hypothesis, NAO, a humanoid robot took the place of the human experimenter and was programmed to behave in a neutral way, annihilating all non-verbal social cues emission. In this condi-tion, politeness rules had been respected by minority in contrast with the same methodology lead by a human. Following this experiment, NAO was programmed as to re-activate social norms, using several non-verbal social cues: face tracking, intonations of voice and gestures. First results in this way tend to show the impact of non-verbal social cues, producing an endowment effect again.

Keywords: Perceptual · Robots · Motor · Cognitive · Emotional · Social · Communication · Systems

1 Introduction

When the role of robots becomes more important within humans' environments, current research is only beginning to be extended to the study of its impact on the character of social relationships. Will judgment errors associated with some human interaction contexts persist when individuals interact with a humanoid robot? This study provides a building block to identify non-verbal cues, programmable in a robot, that are able to activate social norms in a human-robot interaction.

1.1 Robots as "Social Beings"

Literature reports of studies showing that human-robot relationships can become social when adequate criteria are met, particularly with humanoid robots. There is also a strong tendency to anthropomorphize robots, which is to say, lending to robots human thoughts and emotions. This is paradoxical in studies as participants know that they interact with

© Springer International Publishing AG 2017
S. Benferhat et al. (Eds.): IEA/AIE 2017, Part I, LNAI 10350, pp. 559–568, 2017.
DOI: 10.1007/978-3-319-60042-0_62

a robot. This robust anthropomorphism would respond to a primary need to recover a satisfactory state of familiarity in the situation of interaction and is independent of technological knowledge [2].

Literature has identified several specific factors that could make a robot appearing more sociable and influencing user's behavior: level of presence - physical or non-physical [3]; the gender of the robot - male or female [32]; modalities of interaction: a discussion between two agents is not a mere result of an exchange of verbal information; the robot must be able to interpret and reproduce the non-verbal cues of his interlocutor (body language, eye contact) [38, 40]; autonomy and interactivity: the robot seems to know how to take decisions in a given situation without the needing a human intermediary. These factors influence many behavioral dimensions in human-robot interactions (HRIs), including: fun [10], cooperation in action [36, 37], trust and respect shown to the agent [12], the general perception of an artificial agent or robot's [10].

Humans' capacity to behave socially with other social individuals makes them able to treat artificial intelligent agents as social entities [33]. As social norms can be defined by interaction rules between people, they can be relevant to interactions between humans and robots [9]. By analyzing factors enabling social norms among humans, we can recreate and control these factors by applying them to a robot.

Another benefit in using a robot is that it could endorse different social roles regarding its programmed behavior, changing the social context of interactions. Then we can further analyze the impact of each behavioral factor involved in HRIs. This last feature offers a new experimental paradigm for studying biases observed in social relations, including the "endowment effect", as a widespread bias observed in every situation involving the exchange of objects.

This bias has been studied with human agents, and we propose here to study it in a new way with NAO robot as an experimenter.

1.2 The "Endowment Effect"

"Endowment effect" was introduced by Thaler in 1980 [30], which defined the "endowment effect" as a tendency to attribute more value to an object when we own it, that when we do not own it.

The endowment effect in situations of exchange of material goods is commonly studied according to the exchange paradigm of Knetsch [27]. This experimental methodology is as it follows:

1. In a first control task, it is ensured that individuals do not have a preference between two objects within a selection task.
2. In the second situation using these two objects, three phases are distinguished:
   a. The donation: The experimenter gives the participant one of these two objects.
   b. The masking step: participants are asked to perform a specific task during around fifteen minutes.
   c. The exchange request: participants are asked if they wish to exchange the first given object against the second one.

In this paradigm, the endowment effect is measured based on the refusal exchange rate. If it is significantly higher than the acceptance rate of exchange acceptation within the two groups, then an endowment effect is observed. Between humans, the results generally show that the trade volume is significantly lower, irrespective of the economic cost, the two objects exchanged comprising intrinsically equivalent values of preference and economic. In literature, two main classes of explanations are brought to account for the endowment effect:

- Loss Aversion. Loss aversion describes asymmetry in values: the uselessness to assign an object is greater than the utility to acquire a property of equivalent value [24]. In this approach the endowment effect is as an application of the "prospect theory", in which values are associated with gains and losses, rather than an absolute value of objects themselves. Loss aversion generally establishes that individuals evaluate losses more heavily than equivalent gains [22, 23, 26].
- Ownership: an Evolutionary Approach. A mere ownership effect also reflects the tendency for people to overestimate the objects that they own. But the explanation is different. Human beings have innately a tendency to possess objects and to appropriate them. [4, 11, 13, 15, 18, 28]. Endowment effect could also be enhanced by a participative feeling of physical possession [14, 16, 20, 21, 27, 28, 31, 32, 34, 39].

1.3 A New Paradigm

Recently, new empirical data observed in populations of different cultures proposes that social rules of individuals can explain the reluctance to exchange an object or to prefer an object already possessed over the same object that these individuals do not possess [1, 5, 6, 17, 19–21, 35, 39].

Baratgin and Jamet suggest an alternative explanation for the source of the endowment effect. The paradigm of exchange implicitly promotes the use of social politeness rules [7]. Indeed, an exchange is a socialized conduct that meets rules. In a group sharing the same culture, we communicate following these standards. For example, when the endowment effect is caused by a "polite" effect, this can lead to the "social ban" to refuse or redeem a "gift". This step of giving is far from neutral. In step of the exchange request, the participants may feel surprise, as this application is a "breach" in the usual politeness rule in Western cultures, dictating that a gift must be kept. Baratgin and Jamet have set up several experiments to validate this hypothesis of politeness effect [7]. Results confirm the hypothesis of Baratgin and Jamet: although a strong endowment effect was observed in the standard condition of Knetsch [25], the endowment effect has completely disappeared in the condition of rudeness, and is highly diminished in the absence of the donor. However, in these conditions it was impossible to control all specific factors activating politeness norms in interactions, for one major reason: experiments between human agents cannot be reproduced identically in the sense that even the experimenter himself can emit clues regardless of his control, which induce within participants a kind of social compliance.

To overpass this issue, Masson, Baratgin and Jamet [29] have implemented a new condition to the exchange paradigm, where the human experimenter was replaced by

NAO, a humanoid robot. The robot was programmed to behave neutrally, by annihilating social nonverbal cues mentioned earlier: voice intonations, gestures, eye movements. In that condition, a reverse effect was revealed. Then, a new pilot session was conducted with a robot programmed in a manner to behave in a social way through the same procedure with 20 participants. In this pilot session: a specific non-verbal cue was implemented to the robot on the base of factors identified in literature: vocal intonations in speech. Results tended to show a production of an endowment effect again. The aim of this new study is to propose an experimental way to test in isolation the impact of one of these factors taken apart: the vocal intonations.

1.4   Issues and Hyptoheses

Basing on the pilot session, we assume that vocal intonations, when recorded in a natural way, are sufficient to activate the respect of politeness rules – defined as an application of social norms – within the exchange paradigm. Operationally, the use of vocal intonations implemented in the robot during the experiment will produce an endowment effect, in contrast with the experiment which used a "neutral" robot.

2   Materials and Methods

2.1   Population

For this experiment, we used a randomly spread sample of 30 students from Paris 8 University (France), 18 females and 12 males aged from 18 to 34, native French or French-speaking and living in France. A link was shared on internet through Paris 8 university networks, allowing students to register for an appointment on an online diary to pass the experiment individually.

2.2   Materials

The Knetsch's paradigm of exchange was led by a "humanoid" NAO robot playing the role of the experimenter (Aldebaran version 4 – "Evolution"). The behavior of the robot was programmed with the Choregraphe software in its version 2 built by Aldebaran (see Annex 1), and stored on a laptop connected to the robot via Wi-Fi, such that it is possible to place the computer next the output of the room, and run the program from there.

Choregraph allows putting some behavior boxes on a visual interface as a way to create an experimental scenario applied to NAO. Moreover, it is possible to make NAO aware of some characteristics of participants thanks to an event programming module. Especially, NAO can hear participant's answers and operate different behaviors regarding to this. Furthermore, come captors on NAO's arms and head is sensitive to the touch. This was particularly important when NAO had to simulate a sleep as long as the participant went through the masking step.

NAO was programmed to lead all the paradigm of exchange methodology in an autonomous way by itself. To produce voical intonations, NAO's discourse was made by prerecording MP3 audio files reproducing all natural intonations present in a between humans dialog. Words of this dialog were recorded in French and were made in a courteous way.

To ensure that preferences of the population was fair to both used objects used, we chose two objects of non-comparable utilities with equivalent and low economic value, accessible for all incomes levels: a bic pen, and a food item – a tiny smarties box. Both objects were selected by referring to a selection task previously performed in which no significant differences in preference between the two objects were revealed. Natural preferences provided choice of these two objects were revealed here as equivalent.

- Object A: a Bic pen "black crystal" model (costing on average € 0.36)
- Object B: smarties box (costing on average € 0.40)

During the experiment, a masking task uses a multiple choice paper form questionnaire with short reasoning questions. A mini-camera was used to record all experimental sessions.

2.3 Experimental Design

Manipulated independent variable is the type of object presented first: Object A ("Condition A"- respectively applied to group A), or object B ("condition B"- respectively applied to group B) and, the major factor observed is the impact of the kind of voice implemented within NAO on the endowment effect level obtained. Though, vocal intonations were added to NAO's voice, in contrast with our previous work, where NAO's speech was built directly from its native vocal synthesis module. This new experiment using adding vocal intonations is made up of two independent groups as mentioned by the exchange paradigm.

Participants are divided as follows:

- Group A: 30 participants (18 females, 12 males)
- Group B: 30 participants (16 females, 14 males)

Answers to the exchange request are rated: yes (acceptance); no (refusal). At the end of the experiment, only two answers were possible: "yes" or "no".

2.4 Procedure

The experiments were conducted at Paris 8 University, at various times of day from 9:00 AM to 8:00 PM, and had an average duration of 15 min. Each session was led individually. Beforehand, in preparation for each session, NAO was placed sitting on a table and positioned as to face the participant. The questionnaire is placed near the robot on the table. The first object (the one which will be given to the participant - object A or object B) is in the right hand of the robot. The left arm of the robot is pulled back his left leg as if he stood on that arm to stabilize its base, which has the effect of masking the second object (object B or object A) at the sight of participant. Also a web is placed on the object, so as to cover it and a part of the left arm of the robot. The participant fill an informed consent form, mentioning that the session will be captured on video, and to ensure that the participant can be left alone with NAO, a brief oral presentation of the robot is given to the participant, reminding him that the robot is a simple tool used to drive the experimentation:

"NAO is a humanoid robot. NAO helps me to collect your answers to the questionnaire."

Also, the participant is reminded that NAO, as a robot, can show some technical limitations, especially regarding its voice recognition module:

"Please, when NAO is asking you something, speak loud enough for it to understand your answer; otherwise it will not capture all the words you say."

If the experience starts with the gift of object B (smarties box), I told the participant: "Here, I lend you this pen, I will use it again to take some notes on end of the experiment", this explanation avoiding participant to appropriate the pen before the proposal to trade the smarties box (object B) against the black pen (object A). If the first object is the pen, participant could use it to answer the questionnaire, this up even more in the direction of an object that he appropriates physically. Regarding the first given object, NAO's discourse is as following:

- Bic pen: "First, I give you this pen. It is yours and you can use it for this experiment. Then you will take it with you when you will leave the room."
- Candy box: "First, I give you this little candy box. It is yours and you could eat it now, but as you will proceed to this experiment first you can put it in our pocket for now."

The participant is then left alone with the robot, after ensuring that the program has started. The handover takes place according to the three main steps of the Knetsch's paradigm of exchange (donation, masking task, exchange request). NAO explain each step of the experiment as the human experimenter would do, excepting that all social non-verbal cues are controlled, so as the robot only operate all useful gestures to lead the experiment. At the end of the experiment, an open question is orally asked to the participant, according to his (her) answer to the exchange request:

"Why did you keep (exchange) the object NAO gave you at first?"

This was an open question to get a maximum of possible reasons on why the participant tend to keep or leave the first given object.

3   Results

In condition A, the number of participants who refused the exchange is: 18 (60% keeping object A). In condition B, the number of participants who refused the exchange is: 21 (70% keeping object B). Though, at the end of the experiment, 27 participants (45%) in total have chosen to keep the object A (pen), and 33 participants (55%) chose to keep the object B. With vocal intonations, refusal rate is significantly and widely higher than acceptance rate.

4   Discussion

The results obtained here show that in both groups, refusal percentages are significantly higher than the acceptance rates ($\square = 0.05$).

These outcomes from the present experiment highlight the production of an endowment effect, in contrast with the "neutral robot" condition. In that latter condition, a reversed endowment effect was observed, individuals redirecting either their choice according to their "natural" preference in presence of the robot, directly related to the utilitarian function of the object, according to the utility theory, or even, in some cases observed, accepted exchange to extend the fun they felt to test the functionality of the robot [29]. These outcomes suggest that, as it was shown in our previous works, some cues are able to annihilate or enhance the level of produced endowment effect from human participants. According to Baratgin's and Jamet's new conditions added to the traditional condition (rudeness and absence of donor), the social context brought by the experimenter's behavior is likely to activate or annihilate social norms regarding politeness rules. Thus, in this present study, vocal intonations seem to be sufficient to produce an endowment effect, regardless all other specific non-verbal cues, neutralized thanks to the use of such a robot as NAO.

So this study shows two important values:

- As the endowment effect can be produced by the use of politeness rules, the observation of endowment effect brought by the paradigm of exchange of Knetsch is a useful tool to indirectly measure the level of social norms activation.
- With this new paradigm consisting of using a traditional experiment lead by a robot, it is possible to identify the programs of behavior that can be implemented in a robot to activate social norms in human-robot interactions.
- Furthermore, vocal intonations seem to be a major non-verbal clue to induce some social interactions in HRIs, regardless of NAO's emotional limitations. For example, NAO cannot smile and its emotional expressions are very limited: only its eyes can show some different colors to express something on its face.

However, endowment effect obtained in the natural vocal intonation condition is not as strong as this is produced with a human experimenter, where, as this is shown in literature, almost the totality of participants refuses to exchange a first given object. These outcomes are a beginning and need to be investigated in additional ways to bring an entire set of useful results for researches in HRIs regarding social and emotional features. Some future work need to be undertaken to investigate the impact of other non-verbal and social clues on endowment effect in exchange situations. For example, some non-verbal cues could reduce or enhance the impact of other cues. In case, outcomes could be different than when they are taken in isolation. Otherwise, this will be needed to lead these experiments within other cultures, as Asia countries – Japan for example – where social norms and relationships between humans and robots are not similar than in western countries.

5 Conclusions

The results obtained in this experiment are consistent with the prediction that vocal intonations constitute an important factor to activate social norms within human-robot interactions. We could further test the other factors in isolation or in combination to compute a whole set of artificial behaviors that are able to activate social norms and social implications in HRIs. We could further investigate the use of a robot with children to test a full battery of theories where social norms seem to play a role, with the aim to understand factors involved in interactions. We could then program robots in a manner to avoid some decision bias from human in interactions. We could thus in a same way improve children's learning by finely adapting the social context to them.

Acknowledgements. Financial support for this work was provided, by a grant from the ANR Chorus 2011(project BTAFDOC), and by a grant of Institut des Sciences Complexes (2014-ISC-PIF petits et moyens équipements).

References

1. Apicella, C.L., et al.: Evolutionary origins of the endowment effect: evidence from Hunter-Gatherers. Am. Econ. Rev. **104**, 1793–1805 (2014)
2. Baddoura, R., Venture, G.: Social vs. useful HRI: experiencing the familiar, perceiving the robot as a sociable partner and responding to its actions. Int. J. Soc. Robot. **5**, 529–547 (2013)
3. Wilma-Bainbridge, A., et al.: The benefits of interactions with physically present robots over video-displayed agents. Int. J. Soc. Robot. **3**, 41–52 (2010)
4. Bakeman, R., Brownlee, J.R.: Social rules governing object conflicts in toddlers and preschoolers. In: Rubin, K.H., Ross, H.S. (eds.) Peer Relationships and Social Skills in Childhood, pp. 99–111. Springer, New York (1982)
5. Baratgin, J.: Effet de dotation et normes sociales: une approche inter-culturelle. In : Symposium on ICAP (2014). http://www.icap2014.com/program-detail_830/effet-de-dotation-et-normes-sociales-une-approche-inter-culturelle?date=8
6. Jamet, F., Baratgin, J., Godin, P.: Don, droit, coutume, cultures. Études expérimentales sur l'effet de dotation. In: Puigelier, C., Tijus, C., Jouen, F. (eds.) Droit, décision et prise de décision. Mare et Martin (Collection Science et Droit), Paris (in press)
7. Baratgin, J.: Le raisonnement humain: Une approche finettienne. Hermann, Paris (in press)
8. Baratgin, J., Jamet, F., Ruggieri, F., Masson, O.: Stupid NAO and Piaget's class inclusion question: a new argument for the relevance-theoretic explanation. In: IEEE Sixth Joint International Conference on Developmental Learning and Epigenetic Robotics (ICDL-EPIROB 2016), Cergy, France, 19–22 September 2016
9. Bartneck, C., Forlizzi, J.: A design centred framework for social human-robot interaction. In: Proceedings of the 13th IEEE International Workshop on Robot and Human Interactive Communication (RO-MAN 2004), pp. 591–594 (2004)
10. Breazeal, C. et al.: Humanoid robots as cooperative partners for people. IJHR (2004, submit)
11. Brosnan, S.F., et al.: Tolerance for inequity may increase with social closeness in chimpanzees. Proc. R. Soc. B. **272**, 253–258 (2005)
12. Cassell, J., et al.: Embodiment in conversational interfaces: rea. In: Proceedings of the CHI 1999 Conference, Pittsburgh, PA, pp. 520–527 (1999)

13. Drayon, L.A., Brosnan, S.F., Carrigan, J., Stoinski, T.S.: Endowment effect in gorillas. J. Comp. Psychol. **127**(4), 365–369 (2013)
14. Dumais, M.-L., Jamet, F., Baratgin, J.: Endowment effect among 6–7 years old children in French Guiana. In: 2nd International Seminar Paradigms in the Social Sciences – Present and Future, PSS 2015. IPP-WPiA UJK, Kielce, 1–2 December 2015
15. Flemming, T.E., et al.: Endowment effects in orangutans. Int. J. Comp. Psychol. **25**, 285–298 (2012)
16. Gelman, S.A., et al.: The nonobvious basis of ownership: preschool children trace the history and value of owned objects. Child Dev. **83**(5), 1732–1747 (2012)
17. Hattori, I., Baratgin, J., Jamet, F., Masasi, H.: Rethinking the endowment effect: an experiment in Japan. 28ème Congrès International de Psychologie appliquée, Paris, France (2014)
18. Huck, S., Kirchsteiger, G., Oechssler, J.: Learning to like what you have: explaining the endowment effect. Econ. J. **505**, 10–21 (2005)
19. Jamet, F., Baratgin, J.: The endowment effect: a cultural and developmental approach. In: Japan-France Joint Workshop on Reasoning, Tennoji, Shirahama, Japan (2014)
20. Jamet, F., Baratgin, J., Bearune, C. : Effet de dotation chez des enfants Kanak. Nouméa. Presse Universitaire de Nouvelle-Caéldonie (in press)
21. Jamet, F., Saïbou-Dumont, M.-S.: Effet de dotation chez l'enfant Saramaca: une approche développementale et culturelle. 28ème Congrès Internationale de Psychology appliquée, Paris, France (2014)
22. Kahneman, D., et al.: Experimental tests of the endowment effect and the coase theorem. J. Polit. Econ. **98**, 1325–1348 (1990)
23. Kahneman, D., Tversky, A.: Prospect theory: an analysis of decision under risk. Econometrica **47**, 313–327 (1979)
24. Kahneman, D., Tversky, A.: Choices, values and frames. Am. Psychol. **39**, 341–350 (1984)
25. Kahneman, D., et al.: Anomalies: the endowment effect, loss aversion, and status quo bias. J. Econ. Perspect. **5**(1), 193–206 (1991)
26. Knetsch, J.L.: The endowment effect and evidence of nonreversible indifference curves. Am. Econ. Rev. **79**(5), 1277–1284 (1989)
27. Knetsch, J.L., Wong, W.-K.: The endowment effect and the reference state: evidence and manipulations. J. Econ. Behav. Organ. **71**, 407–413 (2009)
28. Lakshminarayanan, V., et al.: Endowment effect in capuchin monkeys. Philos. Trans. Roy. Soc. B **363**, 3837–3844 (2008)
29. Masson, O., Baratgin, J., Jamet, F.: NAO robot and the endowment effect. In: IEEE International Workshop on Advanced Robotics and its Social Impacts (ARSO 2015), Lyon, France, pp. 1–6 (2015)
30. Masson, O., Baratgin, J., Jamet, F., Ruggieri, F., Filatova, D.: Use a robot to serve experimental psychology: some examples of methods with children and adults. In: IEEE Information and Digital Technologies 2016, Workshop: Dynamical Systems and Real World Applications, Rzeszow, Poland, 5–7 July 2016 (2016, submitted)
31. Prou, J.-P., Jamet, F., Baratgin, J.: Endowment effect among 3–5 years old Kanak preschoolers. In: 2nd International Seminar Paradigms in the Social Sciences – Present and Future, PSS 2015. IPP-WPiA UJK, Kielce (2015)
32. Reb, J., Connolly, T.: Possession, feelings of ownership and the endowment effect. Judgm. Decis. Making **2**, 107–114 (2007)
33. Reeves, B., Nass, C.: The Media Equation: How People Treat Computers, Television, and New Media like Real People and Places. Cambridge University Press, Cambridge (1996)

34. Saïbou-Dumont, M.-S., Jamet, F., Baratgin, J.: Endowment effect among 7 to 10 years old Awala Yalimapo tribal children. In: 2nd International Seminar Paradigms in the Social Sciences – Present and Future, PSS 2015. IPP-WPiA UJK, Kielce (2015)
35. Shao, J., Jamet, F., Baratgin, J.: Une étude sur l'effet de dotation en Chine. 28ème Congrès Internationale de Psychology appliquée, Paris, France (2014)
36. Siegel, M., et al.: Persuasive robotics: the influence of robot gender on human behavior. In: IEEE/RSJ International Conference on Intelligent Robots and Systems, IROS 2009, pp. 2563–2568. IEEE (2009)
37. Takayama, L., Pantofaru, C.: Influences on proxemic, behaviors in human-robot interaction. In: Proceedings of Intelligent Robots and Systems (IROS) (2009)
38. Thaler, R.: Toward a positive theory of consumer choice. J. Econ. Behav. Organ. **1**(1), 39–60 (1980)
39. Wanguene, M.-L., Jamet, F., Baratgin, J.: Endowment effect and custom among 9 years old Kanka tribal children. In: 2nd International Seminar Paradigms in the Social Sciences – Present and Future, PSS 2015, IPP-WPiA UJK, Kielce (2015)
40. Wilcock, G., et al.: Speech, gaze and gesturing: multimodal conversational interaction with Nao robot. In: ENTERFACE 2012 Summer Workshop, Final Report Project, P1 (2012)

Arduino as a Control Unit for the System of Laser Diodes

Jiri Bradle[1], Jakub Mesicek[1], Ondrej Krejcar[1(✉)], Ali Selamat[1,2], and Kamil Kuca[1,3]

[1] Center for Basic and Applied Research, Faculty of Informatics and Management,
University of Hradec Kralove, Rokitanskeho 62, 500 03 Hradec Kralove, Czech Republic
{jiri.bradle,Jakub.mesicek,kamil.kuca}@uhk.cz,
Ondrej@Krejcar.org
[2] Faculty of Computing, Universiti Teknologi Malaysia, 81310 Johor Baharu, Johor, Malaysia
aselamat@utm.my
[3] Biomedical Research Center, University Hospital Hradec Kralove,
Hradec Kralove, Czech Republic

Abstract. The article describes the possibilities of the Arduino platform when employed as a control unit of laser diode system. Considering the prices of control units for laser diodes that are available it is necessary to search for new and cheaper solutions. Also, there is a requirement to enable control of such a setup using a personal computer. The proposed setup should be provided by the Arduino platform in combination with laser diodes. The aim of this project is to create a device with many options of employment in the lighting field.

Keywords: Laser diode · Arduino · PWM · User interface · Series of communication · Lighting modulation

1 Introduction

Laser diodes are the most common and the most used sort of lasers nowadays. They are used in a wide scale of uses, such as, in telecommunication combined with fiber optics. They are also used for many types of measuring, for distance, temperature or composition of materials. These days, laser diodes are used for many purposes, whether it is in the industrial employment, within scientific activities, or in medicine.

Laser diodes are with their own properties comparable with LEDs (Light Emitting Diodes), both on the level of reliability and failure rate. The difference lies on the fact that the LEDs operate on a higher power take-off and are, therefore, liable to be damaged by a higher current [1]. In most of the cases, it is required to offer the possibility of simple regulation and scanning of the features of laser diodes. Therefore, there is a need to create control units that would facilitate this kind of regulation.

The figures that can be measured on laser diodes are, above all, the power (dBm), temperature (°C), the voltage on the diode (V) and the current flowing through the diode (mA). When it comes to laser diodes, it is possible to regulate effectively only the voltage, which affects the rest of the figures. This article uses small light output diodes so the current flowing through the diode is also relatively small (roughly up to 100 mA). The request for the control unit in this article came from a research team that is dealing

© Springer International Publishing AG 2017
S. Benferhat et al. (Eds.): IEA/AIE 2017, Part I, LNAI 10350, pp. 569–575, 2017.
DOI: 10.1007/978-3-319-60042-0_63

with different areas of biomedicine. In combination with laser diodes, they are trying to solve the possibilities of treatment of cancer cells by the means of light, the source of which is the laser diode. Considering their limited budget, they are searching for a low-cost solution that would enable them to control the laser diodes using a personal computer. Likewise, the current age dictates the control unit to be easily and comfortably configurable using a simple user interface. The way to attain a user friendly control could be the possibility to connect the control unit to a personal computer and the parameters of the diode would be then regulated using a simple program. Therefore, to facilitate this connection, the Arduino platform was assigned.

One of the similar ways of Arduino platform uses in combination with LEDs is described in the article [2] and [3]. These articles are concerned with the human vision research. It is evident that it is possible to use Arduino platform in combination with projects that deal with the control of light elements. The question is how it will perform in combination with laser diodes.

2   Problem Definition and Related Works

There are different types of control units for laser diodes on the market. However, the majority is focused only on one type of issues and they excel in it.

One of the examples of implementation of such a control unit is a product from a company called OptoSci. This company created a control unit for the regulation of the current flowing through the laser diode. The device facilitates connection of different kinds of laser diodes and serves for a constant current supply because of its refresh rate 3 Hz. That implies that it is not suitable for the modulation needs. The details are to be found on the website of the manufacturer [4]. The user interface enabling the regulation of the current and observation of the present figures of laser diodes is one of the components of this control unit. These parameters can be observed and controlled (1) Current, (2) Forward voltage, (3) Temperature, (4) Optical power. The price of this solution rises up to several thousand USD. As another example of control unit implementation can serve products from the company called PicoQuant. One of the product categories this company implements are pulse lasers. The company produces different types of devices on commission with diverse forms of use. One of the devices is the control unit MD 300 for laser diode light modulation [5]. This device can only generate sinusoidal signal at high frequencies. It also lacks the possibility of control using a personal computer. The price of this device ranges in tens of thousands of dollars. As it has been previously mentioned, there is a wide range of commercial control units for laser diodes, but all of them are aimed for a commercial use, therefore their price rises. Owing to this fact, they are not easily accessible for smaller scientific groups and their possibilities of research. The goal of the new solution is to create a control unit that will be inexpensive and simple, but easily extensible or modifiable. Simultaneously, there is a request to have the possibility of controlling more laser diodes on one unit, which is not provided by the above mentioned implementations of control units. The proposed solution should meet the following requirements: (1) Low cost, (2) Possibility to connect more laser diodes, (3) User interface for the control, (4) Luminosity settings, (5) Frequency modulation.

3   New Solution

For the purposes of communication and simple control of the proposed solution, the controlling unit will be connected to a personal computer and it will be handled using a basic user interface. The Arduino UNO board for prototyping [6], is used as a control element. The main component of this panel is a programmable microcontroller ATmega328P, which works on the frequency 16 MHz. It contains 14 digital output and input pins (of which 6 can be used as PWM outputs) and 6 analog inputs that can be used for measuring certain values (in this case, the voltage on the photodiode built in the laser diode body could be measured).

Considering the fact that Arduino can provide signals only for the system of laser diodes, this system must be powered by an auxiliary energy source. Depending on this source, a circuit for LED power supply must be designed. That can be achieved by several RF capacitors and by creating two separate voltage sources (one controlling from Arduino and the other one supplying diodes). The laser diode connection is identical as the classic LEDs and the power circuit must be assembled depending on the type of diodes used for it. The project Ardulink [7] will be used for the communication between personal computer and the control unit. It is an open source project of Mr. Luciano Zu, who created a complete Java implementation for communication and control of the main features between an application and Arduino board. This library shows some demonstrations of protocol and communication on the serial link that will be used for the implementation of new solution. Likewise, it contains also several simple SWING components that serve as a demonstration of the process in the development of the user interface. It will be necessary to create several new components, but the base for their implementation is already designed.

Arduino, as a digital device, offers a very limited variety of options. The basic function will be an on/off switch for the diode. That can be created by configuring the output pin on the value HIGH or LOW, which will open the transistor and allow closing the circuit of the diode.

The second parameter of control is the luminous intensity of diode. For this purpose, it is possible to use Arduino pseudo-analog output that employs PWM [8] (Pulse Width Modulation) technology. As this is a digital device, Arduino can show as the output figures only 1 (+5 V) and 0 (0 V – ground). PWM operates on the principle of pulses with changing width. Only some of the pins enable the employment of PWM. The value setting is executed by the command analogWrite (value).

Since it is not a real analog output, it is not possible to use this method for very demanding applications (e.g. high-frequency measuring). However, the employment of this approach is possible for applications, such as those where it is necessary to affect vision (e.g. laser effects used for entertainment). As it is impossible for the human eye to catch these light changes when first seen, it seems that the intensity is changing, even though it is not true.

The third element for Arduino control is frequency modulation. Again, it is necessary to realize that Arduino is a digital device. Therefore, it is possible to generate only rectangular pulse train signal at the output. For simple implementation, it is possible to use the library Tone [9]. The library is built-in and designated for adjusting the output pin frequency. Thus, it enables, for example, an audio output device to make sounds. In this case, however, it will serve for the diodes to start flashing in the required frequency, from 32 Hz to 65 kHz.

The problem of this basic library is the fact that it is able to generate frequency only for one output at the time. Considering this problem, a third party library will have to be employed. In this case, it will be from Rogue Robotics [10], who created a richer library called Tone. The main advantage of this library is the connection of all the timers in the microcontroller. Thus, it can run different frequencies on several pins at once. ATmega328P includes three timers; therefore, there can be different frequencies on the three different diodes. For that reason, the implementation will comprise of precisely three laser diodes.

4   Implementation

Within the scope of the implementation, a prototype was created to prove the possibilities of the Arduino board as a controlling element for the system of laser diodes. The prototype consists of three laser diodes L-SLD6505A. These diodes were chosen considering the financial range of the implementation of the prototype. They are very inexpensive; the price ranges around 3 USD for a piece. The execution and the light output (5 mW) correspond to the price range. Given the auxiliary supply of voltages, it is possible to change these two diodes for higher-performance diodes.

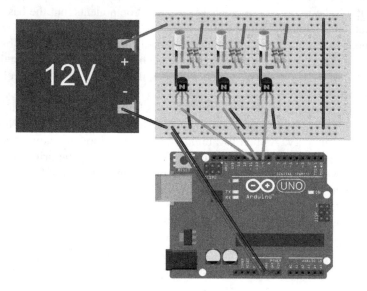

Fig. 1. Prototype connection scheme

The connection of the prototype is depicted in figure (Fig. 1). The outline of the scheme was made in the open source program Fritzing [11].

It is a simple solution where Arduino only opens or closes the circuit using a high-frequency NPN transistor that supplies ground to diode and this way the current can flow through the diode. Considering Arduino being able to work only in two states, this circuit is satisfactory for the demonstration of all the possibilities of laser diode control by this unit. As it has been mentioned in the previous chapter, the aim of the project is to control diodes using a personal computer. The easiest way is to do it by employing the existing project Ardulink. Using core and swing libraries from this project, a simple user interface that covers all possibilities of diode control for the proposed prototype was implemented. The user interface is divided into five tabs where each of them represents the basic functionality.

The first tab is called Connection. It serves for establishing communication with control unit. The user needs to trace back the port that the unit is connected to with USB cable. At the same time, Baud Rate can be set. That has, however, by default, set the maximum value for communication on this line and at the same time it is set on the side of the control unit. Therefore, it should not be changed.

The second tab called Configuration serves for setting the values of the pins that the diodes are connected to. After that, there is the third tab with the name Switch Pane, which enables setting the pins as such. It serves for turning on and turning off the diode. The fourth tab called PWM Panel is more interesting, because it enables to set the luminosity of individual diodes and it offers other possibilities of configuration. It facilitates changes in maximum and minimum value in configuration; it displays the current value not only in the numerical form, but also in the percentage and at the same time, it shows

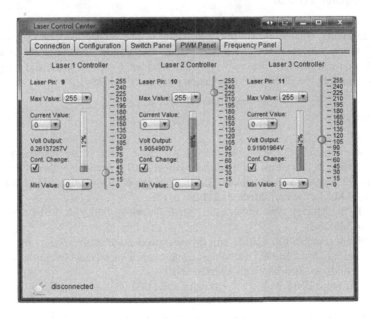

Fig. 2. PWM Panel

the voltage value on the diode. There is a demonstration of the interface for PWM settings in figure (Fig. 2).

Considering the simplicity of the prototype, the testing was done in most of the cases only by human eye. All of the implemented options of settings worked as expected.

During the testing of PWM, it could be noticed how the laser diode reacted to the changes in values, which showed the deceptiveness of a human eye.

The only case of connection of the diodes to an oscilloscope was in the case of frequency testing, because the frequency can be observed only up to 40 Hz, then the diode seems constantly lit. The measured values corresponded to the supposition. The maximum frequency was 65573 Hz, which can be used for some applications.

The price of the proposed solution stands at around 250 USD. That makes a huge difference in comparison with the common control units.

5   Conclusions

The goal of this project was to create an inexpensive control unit, on the Arduino platform, that would serve to control the system of laser diodes. At the same time, it aimed to control diodes using user interface. The result is a prototype that displays all the possibilities of Arduino in combination with laser diodes. The options of turning it off and on, luminosity settings and launching three different frequencies on individual diodes were created. At the same time, these values can be controlled by a personal computer. It works on a general principle that could be used in many circuits. Since the laser diodes are handled the same way as the LEDs, this system could be employed in light control in the rooms of a smart house (turning on and the degree of luminosity) with one computer terminal.

Acknowledgement. This work and the contribution were partially supported by: (1) project "SP-2102-2017 - Smart Solutions for Ubiquitous Computing Environments" Faculty of Informatics and Management, University of Hradec Kralove, Czech Republic and (2) The work was also supported by Czech Science Foundation project 16-13967S.

References

1. Wu, T.-C., Chi, Y.-C., Wang, H.-Y., et al.: Blue laser diode enables underwater communication at 12.4 Gbps. Sci. Rep. 7, 17 January 2017. Article Number: 40480
2. Teikaria, P., Najjara, R.P., Malkkic, H., Knoblaucha, K., Dumortierd, D., Gronfiera, C., Coopera, H.M.: J. Neurosci. Methods **211**(2) (2012)
3. Gildea, K.M., Milburn, N.: Behav. Res. Methods **46**(4), 960–983 (2014). doi:10.3758/s13428-013-0423-1
4. Laser Drivers. OptoSci Ltd. (2015). http://www.optosci.com/category/laser_drivers/
5. Pulsed Lasers and LEDs. PicoQuad. https://www.picoquant.com/products/category/modulated-and-switched-lasers. Cited 3 Oct 2017
6. Arduino. Arduino UNO. https://www.arduino.cc/en/Main/ArduinoBoardUno
7. Ardulink. http://www.ardulink.org/. Cited 3 Oct 2017
8. Arduino. PWM. https://www.arduino.cc/en/Tutorial/PWM. Cited 3 Oct 2017

9. Arduino. Tone. https://www.arduino.cc/en/Reference/Tone. Cited 3 Oct 2017
10. Rogue-code. Arduino Tone Library. https://code.google.com/p/rogue-code/wiki/ToneLibraryDocumentation. Cited 3 Oct 2017
11. Fritzing. http://fritzing.org/home/. Cited 3 Oct 2017

Sentiment Analysis and Social Media

Timeline Summarization for Event-Related Discussions on a Chinese Social Media Platform

Han Wang and Jia-Ling Koh[(✉)]

Department of Computer Science and Information Engineering,
National Taiwan Normal University, Taipei, Taiwan
jlkoh@csie.ntnu.edu.tw

Abstract. In this paper, we proposed an approach to automatically generate timeline summarization for sub-event discussions related to a query event without supervised learning. In order to select event-related sentences, we designed a two-stage method to extract representative entity terms in the event-related discussions and filter out most of the sentences semantically un-related to the query event. A rule-based method was applied to extract sentences which describing sub-events. After that, the discussions are assigned to the corresponding sub-events according to the semantic relatedness measure. Finally, according to the occurring time of each sub-event, the timeline summarization is organized. We evaluated the performance of the proposed method on the real-world datasets. The experiment results showed that each processing step perform effectively. Especially, most noise sentences could be filtered by the proposed method. Moreover, the final timeline summarization graded by users is proven to be useful to well understand the discussion trend of a sub-event.

Keywords: Timeline summarization · Sub-event detection · Text data mining

1 Introduction

The fast growing of the social media platforms makes it easier and popular to get information. It allows users to discuss public issues and express their thinking to the others via posting short messages. The posting messages are not only for users to share their life experience but also to be treated as a kind of social sensors to reflect the sociality opinions. When a social event happens, user's reaction on the social media platforms has become an important information source to reflect the ongoing situation. Interestingly, during the different time periods after an event occurring, people may discuss distinct issues such as what have happened and any derivative incident. For example, there was a powerful typhoon, named Dujuan, hitting Taiwan on September 28, 2015. The typhoon caused serious damage and left much sequela such as the overspreading of dengue and the reservoir sedimentation. It also made drinking water unclean. Before typhoon hit, most people concerned about the route of typhoon and how strong the typhoon was. While typhoon was hitting, people reported what have happened and cared about the announcement from the local government that whether

© Springer International Publishing AG 2017
S. Benferhat et al. (Eds.): IEA/AIE 2017, Part I, LNAI 10350, pp. 579–594, 2017.
DOI: 10.1007/978-3-319-60042-0_64

residents are allowed to take one day off on the next day. After typhoon was gone, many people discussed the effectiveness of reconstruction and the decision making of the mayor based on different issues. The mayor took the wrong decision that only half-day take off was allowed such that the residents suffered heavy rain and strong wind to go out for schools and works.

Accordingly, to automatically summarize the huge amount of event-related posting messages on a social media platform will help people or decision makers to understand the various discussion issues on the event more easily. Moreover, the temporal related issues are crucial to show the development of the sub-events occurring as time goes by. In this paper, we used the data sets collected from a Chinese social media platform. There are two main challenges to tackle the event-related posting data.

(1) Different from news documents, most posting data in a social media platform is short. Therefore, many messages are not semantics complete and meaningful.
(2) The posting messages on social media platforms are usually noisy. A lot of irrelevant entity terms are mentioned in the short messages, regarded as noise, which cause the difficulty of entity extraction and sub-event detection.

This work aims to purpose an approach to investigate the tendency of discussions by discovering the time-related sub-events and the corresponding discussions. For a given query event, such as a typhoon, an earthquake or a nature hazard, the proposed system will generate a timeline summarization of discussions for the corresponding sub-events. How to extract important sub-events and assign the discussion messages to the corresponding sub-events are the main research issues studied in this work.

We start the rest of paper with the discussion of related works in Sect. 2. In Sect. 3, we describe our proposed method for discussion summarization of related sub-events. Section 4 shows the results of performance evaluation. Finally, Sect. 5 concludes our study and presents the direction of future works.

2   Related Work

[1, 2] studied event detection from social media platforms, which were designed to provide an alerting system for earthquake by analyzing data from Twitter. Avvenuti et al. [1] adopted a burst detection algorithm, by calculating the frequency of event related tweets in a short time period, to detect peek of these messages. After confirming the seismic event, the system will alert users in nearby regions immediately. Sakaki et al. [2] took users in social network as social sensors. They utilized the concept of object detection in ubiquitous environment and classified the data collected from Twitter into two classes: relevant or irrelevant to the event by a support vector machine (SVM). According to spatiotemporal information of the event-relevant tweets, a probabilistic model is built to verify the event. Moreover, Chae et al. [3] utilized LDA algorithm to generate a topic list from tweets. For finding the abnormal events, season-trend decomposition loss smoothing, which an algorithm that divide time series into three segments namely: trend, seasonality and remainder, is brought out. Although these works analyzed users' short messages about an event on social medial platforms, their goals were different from ours.

Among the existing works, Pohl et al. [4] and Abhik et al. [5] studied the problem of sub-event detection, which was also considered in our approach. Pohl et al.discovered the metadata from popular social media platforms such as Flicker and You-Tube. They proposed a clustering approach on the posting documents based on Self Organizing Map (SOM), a neural network without hidden layer, where each document is represented by a feature vector according to the contained words. Each resulting map-unit represents a unique sub-event. To identify relevant units, the resulting SOM units are labeled by the most frequent words shown in the codebook vectors. Abhik et al. [5] identified sub-events of nature calamities for awareness of emergency situations. At first, different features of posting documents on a social media platform were extracted, including user-provided annotations and automatically generated information. Then a two-phased clustering approach is performed to cluster the documents and form combined clusters in a weighted manner. Each combined cluster corresponds to a sub-event of the particular event. However, the above tasks did not take temporal information into consideration.

In recent years, many researchers took temporal information into account to find tendency of events. [6, 7] studied timeline summarization using entities and tweets which sharing the same goal as ours. Among these works, Tuan et al. [6] proposed an approach generating timeline summarization of events by finding novelty and salience entities. They extracted predefine-category entities from the contexts of news article where attracted people mostly, and ranked entities based on individual features such as BM25 measure or authority score, using PageRank algorithm [10]. The work focused on the ranking method to select entities for summarizing the sub-events. In contrast, our work mainly studied sentence selection and sub-event related discussions grouping. Moreover, our approach does not need the support of a knowledgebase. Moreovcr, Shou et al. [7] analyzed tweets and summarized large-scale data by using online tweets stream clustering algorithm. They utilized temporal information to extract vectors of each cluster as well. This work focused on designing an approach using tweets to summarize a topic which having similar goal with ours. However, we summarized a sub-event using sentences extracted from short messages on social media platform.

Tual et al. [6] summarized events by inserting ranked entities into the predefined templates. However, the summarized sentences may not be well structured because the inserted entities do not appropriately fit the templates. Therefore, the adopted domain of this work was restricted. On the other hand, Shou et al. [7] represented the summarization of various topics by finding a continuous tweet stream. It is time consuming for users to read over the tweets to understand the topics. In our work, we aimed to find the sentences discussing the same sub-event for summarization. The main contribution of our work is to provide an unsupervised approach to organize the discussions to the corresponding sub-events from noisy sentence data.

3 Approach

In this section, we introduce the proposed approach of timeline summarization for event-related discussions. The framework is shown in Fig. 1, where the three processing modules are entity-term extraction, sentence selection, and discussion

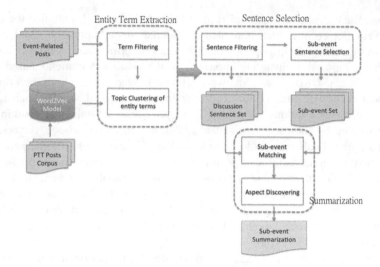

Fig. 1. The proposed framework of timeline summarization for event-related discussions.

summarization. In the following, we will show the strategies designed for each processing module.

3.1 Entity Term Extraction

Given a query term of an event, the Lucene, which is a text search engine library, was used to get the event-related posts from a social media platform. Then two steps are performed to extract event-related entity terms: (1) term filtering, and (2) topic clustering of entity terms.

3.1.1 Term Filtering

At first, each posting data is separated into sentences by comma or period. We use a Chinese nature language processing tool to parse sentences into Chinese semantic terms and their parts of speech (POS tagging). The part of speech taggers will mark nouns as "N" and verbs as "V". Figure 2 shows the POS tagging result of a sentence, where each term is followed by its corresponding POS tag. Then the following 4 steps are performed to extract the candidate entity terms:

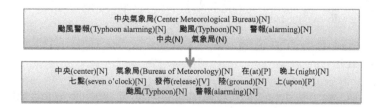

Fig. 2. Result of preprocessing.

(1) The terms labeled as Nouns are picked out.
(2) The terms in the stop-word list are removed.
(3) The single words, temporal or location terms are removed.
(4) The compound Noun phase terms which are combined from continuous Nouns (NN+) are added into the result to be candidate entity terms.

Take Fig. 2 as an example, among the terms labeled as "N". the single words: "陸(Ground)" and "上(Upon)" and the temporal terms: "晚上(night)" and "七點(seven o'clock)" are removed. Then the Noun phase terms "中央(Center)" and "氣象局(Bureau of Meteorology)" are combined to be a compound Noun phase term "中央氣象局(Central Meteorological Bureau)". It is similar to combine "颱風(Typhoon)" and "警報(Alarming)" to be a compound term. Accordingly, there are 6 candidate entity terms extracted from the example sentence.

In order to filter out event irrelevant terms from the candidate terms, we applied the centrality score computing method proposed by Jiaul H. Paik et al. [8] to evaluate the importance of each candidate term in the posts. The centrality score computation [8] has the following assumption. The importance of a term has strong association with the other terms appearing in the same post. In general, the more frequent a term appearing in the corpus is, the more important a term is. Besides, if a term t_i is more frequent relatively to another term t_j, the term t_i should have higher importance than t_j. The importance of terms is passed between each other, and weighted according to the relative frequency for each pair of terms. By using this computation method, the centrality score of each candidate term t_i, denoted as $Cent(t_i)$, is computed. After ranking the candidate terms according to their centrality scores, top n ranked candidate terms are remained for the next step. The other candidate terms are filtered in this step, which are regarded as irrelevant to the query event.

3.1.2 Topic Clustering of Entity Terms

After the process of term filtering, there are still some candidate entity terms irrelevant to the query event although they are often mentioned in the posts. For example, "板主(Administrator of discussion board)" is commonly appears in the posts of PTT. "粉絲團(Fans group)" is also a popular mentioned term. Based on the centrality score, these terms are considered to be representative terms. However, they contribute less semantics related to the query event. We proposed a clustering method to solve this problem. By clustering the terms according to their semantics, the clusters that convey similar semantic concepts are obtained. Then the score of each cluster related to the query event is evaluated. The cluster of terms, which has the lowest event relevant score with the query event, is labeled as the entities with poor semantic quality. The others are labeled as the entities with good semantic quality. The result is consulted when performing sentence selection.

We utilized Word2Vec [9] proposed by Google to construct a feature vector for each term. In our work, about eighty-two thousands posts collected from PTT Bulletin Board System are used to train the word embedding model. Then the similarity between two entity terms is computed according to the cosine similarity of their corresponding vectors. The K-means algorithm was applied to cluster the entity terms into k clusters, in which a strategy was designed to dynamically decide a proper setting of k. The detailed

---

Algorithm 1: Topic clustering of entity term

Input : Candidate entity terms: CT, Number of cluster: k, Query Term: qt

Output: C_l, C_e

1 $//C_l$: the set of entity terms which are not event − related
2 $//C_e$: the set of entity terms which are event − related
3 $C_l \leftarrow \emptyset, C_e \leftarrow \emptyset, k \leftarrow 3$
4 **repeat**
5     $C \leftarrow Kmean(k)//C$ denotes the cluster set
6   **for** each $c \in C$ **do**
7        $n \leftarrow Number\ of\ terms$
8   **for** each $t \in c$ **do**
9           $score_t \leftarrow EAS(t,qt)$ // EAS(t, qt) is the function to measure the degree of an entity term related to the query term
10           $sumAS \leftarrow sumAS + score_t$
11   **end**
12        $ES(c) \leftarrow sumAS/n$
13   **end**
14     $Cs \leftarrow \emptyset$
15     $Cs \leftarrow Sort(ES(c))$ //Sort the clusters according to their ES values in descending order
16   **for** $i = 0$ to k-2 **do**
17        $Gap[i] \leftarrow Cs[i] - Cs[i+1]//$ Compute the difference of ES value between adjacent clusters
18   **end**
19     $avegap \leftarrow GetAverageGap(Gap)//$Get the average difference of ES(c) between adjacent clusters
20   **if** $Gap[k$-$2] \geq avegap$ **then**
21        $C_l \leftarrow Cs[k-1]//$ The cluster with the lowest ES(c) is assigned to C_l
22   **end**
23   **else**
24        $k \leftarrow k+1$
25   **end**
26 **until** $C_l \neq \emptyset$;
27 $C_e \leftarrow \bigcup_{i=1}^{k-2} Cs[i]$
28

Fig. 3. The pseudo code for topic clustering of entity terms.

method is described in the following. Besides, the corresponding pseudo code for topic clustering of entity terms is shown in Fig. 3.

At first, the K-means algorithm with a initial value of k is performed on the candidate entities (line 5) to get a set of clusters: $C = \{c_0, c_1, \ldots, c_{k-1}\}$. The event association score $EAS(ct_i, qt)$ measures the relevance degree of a term with the query event term qt by applying Kullback–Leibler divergence (KL divergence). From line 6 to 13, the event relevant score of each cluster c in C is computed, which is the average event association score $EAS(ct_i, qt)$ for each term ct_i in cluster c. The event association score of a term ct_i is formulated as follows:

$$EAS(ct_i, qt) = P_d(ct_i|qt) \cdot log_2\left(\frac{P_d(ct_i|qt)}{P_d(ct_i|\overline{qt})}\right) \tag{1}$$

Let PD denote the set of documents in the PTT posts corpus. The conditional probability that ct_i appeared in the documents appearing qt, i.e. $P_d(ct_i|qt)$, is computed as follows:

$$P_d(ct_i|qt) = \frac{|\{pd_i|pd_i \in PD \wedge ct_i \in pd_i \wedge qt \in pd_i\}|}{|\{pd_i|pd_i \in PD \wedge qt \in pd_i\}|} \tag{2}$$

Besides, $P_d(ct_i|\overline{qt})$ denotes the conditional probability that ct_i appeared in the documents without appearing qt.

Initially, the number of cluster, k, is set to be 3 as shown in line 3. In Line 15, the clusters are sorted according to their event relevant scores in descending order. In order to evaluate if it is a proper decision to discard the cluster that has the lowest relevant score, the average difference of the relevant scores between each pair of neighbor clusters in the ranked list of clusters is computed (Line 19) to get the average gap.

From line 20 to 25, when the gap between the cluster with the lowest ES score and the previous cluster is larger than the average gap, the cluster with the lowest ES score are assigned to C_l. The terms belongs to this cluster are labeled as the entities with poor semantic quality. Otherwise, the value of k is increased by 1, and the clustering process repeats. Finally, in line 27, the terms in the other clusters are assigned to C_e, which contains the entities with good semantic quality.

3.2   Sentence Selection

In this work, the generated timeline summarization consists of the semantics representative sentences. Accordingly, two stages of processing are performed to select event-related sentences: (1) sentence filtering and (2) sub-event sentence selection.

3.2.1   Sentence Filtering
We adopted three principles to filter the sentences.

(1) The sentence is not completed. It was observed that the length of the sentence is too short to convey enough information.
(2) The sentence is not readable. When the sentence is too long unusually, its readability is poor. It was observed that the sentence has no punctuation or full of repeated words or meaningless symbols.
(3) The sentence is not event-related in semantics. It was observed that the sentence contains more the entities with poor semantics quality than the entities with good quality.

Let $S = \{s_1, s_2, \ldots, s_k\}$ denoted the set of all sentences extracted from the posts in PD. Besides, let T_B and T_G denote the sets of entity terms with poor quality and the ones with good quality, respectively, extracted from C_l and C_e in Sect. 3.1.2.

According to the filtering principles 1 and 2, the corresponding processing is performed as follows. Let $avglen(S)$ denote the average length of the sentences in S. For each sentence s in S, if $|len(s) - avglen(S)| > 10$, s is removed from S. Furthermore, we calculate the average length of passages in the sentences separated by commas and periods. If the length of a passage in a sentence is longer than the average length of passages, the sentence will be discarded. Therefore, the remaining sentences are readable.

According to the third filtering principle, for each sentence s_i in S, the ratio of entity terms with poor semantic quality and the ones with good quality in the sentence is evaluated according to the following function:

$$R(s_i) = \frac{|\{t_j | t_j \in s_i \wedge t_j \in C_l\}|}{|\{t_k | t_k \in s_i \wedge t_k \in C_e\}| + \varepsilon} \tag{3}$$

where ε is a constant to avoid the special case that s_i does not contain any entity with good quality. If $R(s_i)$ is bigger than a gain threshold value (set to be 0.5), the sentence s_i is pruned from the candidate sentence set S.

After performing sentence filtering according to the above three principles, the representative score $SRS(s_i)$ of every sentence s_i in the remaining sentences is evaluated. We assume that if a sentence contains more entity terms which are highly related to the query event, the sentence is more representative for the query event. Therefore, $SRS(s_i)$ is defined to be the weighted sum of the representative score, $TRS(e_i)$, of each entity term e_i in s_i, where the weight uses the centrality score of e_i, i.e. $Cent(e_i)$. Accordingly, the equation of computing $SRS(s_i)$ of s_i is defined as:

$$SRS(s_i) = \sum_{e_i \in s_i} TRS(e_i) \cdot Cent(e_i) \tag{4}$$

The representative score of a term e_i, $TRS(e_i)$, is to compute the semantic importance of an entity term. It is measured by considering both how related the term is to the event and how concentrative the term is to a topic cluster. Therefore, the computation of $TRS(e_i)$ is defined to be the multiplication of two measures: the event association score of ct_i, $EAS(ct_i, qt)$, and its concentration score, $CS(ct_i)$.

$$TRS(ct_i) = CS(ct_i) * EAS(ct_i, qt) \tag{5}$$

Generally, the closer a term is to the centroid of its cluster, the more concentration the term is to a semantic topic. Let c_m denote the centroid of the cluster that the term ct_i belonging to. The concentration score of an entity term ct_i, denoted as $CS(ct_i)$, is measured by computing the cosine similarity between ct_i and c_m as follows:

$$CS(ct_i) = \frac{\vec{ct_i} \cdot \vec{c_m}}{\|\vec{ct_i}\| \|\vec{c_m}\|} \tag{6}$$

$\vec{c_m}$ is computed by averaging the Word2vec vectors of each ct_i. The higher the concentration score is, the higher topic representation the entity term is.

3.2.2 Sub-event Sentence Selection

A rule-based method is proposed to extract sub-event sentences. A sub-event sentence is defined to be a sentence containing an entity term, a verb term, a temporal term and a location term simultaneously. Among the set of extracted sub-event sentences, denoted as *CSE*, the $SRS(s_i)$ score is used to decide the representative score related to the query event for each sentence s_i. Moreover, to prevent from selecting several sentences representing the same sub-event, the diversity of sentences is also considered to select the representative sub-event sentences from *CSE*.

The algorithm for selecting the representative sub-event sentences from *CSE* is as follows. Let *SE* denote the set of selected representative sub-event sentences, where *SE* is an empty set initially. At first, the sentence in *CSE* with the highest $SRS(s_j)$ is selected into *SE*. Then in each iteration, $SelectScore(s_j)$ is computed for each s_j in *CSE* as follow:

$$SelectScore(s_j) = w * SRS(s_j) + (1 - w) * Div(SE, s_j) \qquad (7)$$

where

$$Div(SE, s_j) = \frac{1}{|SE|} \sum_{s_k \in SE} \frac{||\vec{s_j}|| ||\vec{s_k}||}{\vec{s_j} \cdot \vec{s_k}} \qquad (8)$$

For each sentence s_j, its diversity with the selected sentences are measures by averaging the reciprocal of cosine similarity between s_j and each selected sentence s_k in *SE*. The vector of a sentence s_i is obtained by computing the average of the Word2vec vectors of all the entity term e_j in s_i weighted by their centrality score $Cent(e_j)$ as follows:

$$\vec{s_i} = \frac{1}{|s_i|} \sum_{e \in S_i} Cent(e_j) \vec{e_j} \qquad (9)$$

The sentence in *CSE* with the highest $SelectScore(s_j)$ score is the next one selected into *SE*. The process repeats until there is no sentence in *CSE* or the required number of sub-event sentences has been selected into *SE*.

3.3 Summarization

We assumed that most posting messages discuss a certain sub-event. Therefore, the tasks of summarizing the posting messages include matching messages to their sub-events and discovering discussing aspects for each sub-event.

3.3.1 Sub-event Matching

Let $DC = \{dc_1, dc_2, \ldots, dc_m\}$ denote the set of candidate discussion sentences, which are extracted from the posting separated by period. For each dc_i in DC, its similarity with each se_j in *SE* is computed. Here, the similarity between dc_i and se_j is the multiplication of the cosine similarity of their sentence vectors and the Jaccard similarity of their terms:

$$Similarity(se_j, dc_i) = CS\left(\overrightarrow{se_j}, \overrightarrow{dc_i}\right) * JAC(se_j, dc_i) \tag{10}$$

The sub-event sentence se_j which has the highest similarity with dc_i, and $Similarity(se_j, dc_i) \geq t$ for a specified threshold value t is selected to be the matched sub-event of dc_i. However, the sentence dc_i will be discarded if $Similarity(se_j, dc_i) \leq t$. This situation implies that there is no appropriative sub-event se_j matched with the sentence.

3.3.2   Aspect Discovering

Let the set of sentences matched to a sub-event se_j be denoted as $SD_{se_j} = \{sd_1, sd_2, \ldots, sd_m\}$. In general, users discussed a sub-event with different aspects. Therefore, we performed clustering on the sentence in SD_{se_j}. The sentences in SD_{se_j} which belonging to the same cluster are most possible to have similar semantic aspect. Then, the discussing sentences of certain aspect form the sentence pool to summarize a sub-event.

For each SD_{se_j}, the distance between each pair of sentences is measured by the following equation:

$$Dist(sd_i, sd_j) = \sigma\left(1 - CS\left(\overrightarrow{sd_i}, \overrightarrow{sd_i}\right)\right) + (1 - \sigma)(1 - JAC(sd_i, sd_j)) \tag{11}$$

where $JAC(sd_i, sd_j)$ denotes the Jaccard similarity between two sentence according to their terms. According to the distance measure, the agglomerative algorithm by average-link is performed to find the clusters in SD_{se_j}, where the distance threshold 0.5 is set to decide the number of generated clusters.

To generate a timeline summary of certain sub-event, a representative sentence is selected to represent each discussion aspect. From each cluster of certain aspect, the representative sentence is selected among the sentences in the cluster. For each sub-event se_i, let $AC_1, AC_2, \ldots, AC_m$ denote the discovered m clusters of aspects. For each sentence s in AC_i, its CRS score is measured as follows:

$$CRS(s) = cosine(s, se_i) * JAC(s, se_i) \tag{12}$$

where $cosine(s, se_i)$ and $JAC(ac_j, se_i)$ respectively computes the cosine similarity and Jaccard similarity between s and the sub-event sentence se_i. After ranking the sentences in AC_i according to their CRS scores, the top one sentence is selected to represent a discussion aspect.

Finally, for each discussion aspect AC_i, the number of discussion sentences belonging to AC_i is counted for each time interval, which could be a day or a week. Accordingly, for each sub-event, the representative sentence and the popularity of each aspect discussed within a given time interval will be shown in the result of timeline summarization. Take the event of Typhoon Nepartak as an example, two sub-events and the discovered discussing aspects are showing in Table 1.

Table 1. Example of the discovered discussing aspects of sub-events.

Sub-event 1	颱風尼伯特遠離臺灣昨天臺北上午無風無雨 There was no rain and no wind in Taipei this morning because Typhoon Nepartak had leaved away Taiwan.					
Aspect 1	雖然氣象局是說颱風昨天到臺灣，可是昨天感覺無風無雨的，實在不像颱風天，才剛過了12點，風聲有夠大的，雨也開始下，颱風現在才登陸臺灣 Although Center Meteorological Bureau announced that Typhoon arrived Taiwan yesterday, the weather was not like a Typhoon day yesterday due to no rain and no wind. However, after 12 o'clock, wind makes loud sound and rain starts falling. Typhoon just arrived in Taiwan now.					
Popularity	16/07/06	16/07/07	16/07/08	16/07/09	16/07/10	16/07/11
	8	43	44	11	10	1
Aspect 2	尼伯特維持猛烈威力，接近釣魚台群島之後，週五會在臺灣登陸，臺灣預計會出現猛烈的風勢和記錄性的豪雨，需要嚴加防範 Typhoon Nepartak kept strong power. After approaching to Diaoyu Islands, it will land in Taiwan on Friday. There will be strong wind and record-breaking rain in Taiwan. Be prepared.					
Popularity	16/07/06	16/07/07	16/07/08	16/07/09	16/07/10	16/07/11
	1	1	2	-	-	-
Sub-event 2	今天晚上臺北還算是正常上班上課的狀態明天才是颱風假 Everyone still had to go to work and school tonight. However, tomorrow will have a day off because of Typhoon.					
Aspect 1	柯文哲針對明天是否上班上課表示，會與基隆、新臺北討論後，最快在晚上8時、最晚10時宣布 Mayor of Taipei announced that he will discuss with the mayors of Keelung and New Taipei to decide whether it will be one day off tomorrow. There will be a formal announcement between 8 p.m and 10 p.m.					
Popularity	16/07/06	16/07/07	16/07/08	16/07/09	16/07/10	16/07/11
	-	1	2	1	-	-
Aspect 2	今天大家狂報的就是颱風跟爆炸了，不過平常只會報颱風，為什麼突然有人會選在颱風天爆車廂 There were a lot of news talking about Typhoon and the explosion event occurred today. However, it is usually to report the news about Typhoon. Why did someone explode the train on a Typhoon day?					
Popularity	16/07/06	16/07/07	16/07/08	16/07/09	16/07/10	16/07/11
	-	10	8	2	-	-

4   Experiments and Discussion

In this section, two parts of experiments were performed to evaluate the performance of the proposed processing strategies: sentence selection and discussion summarization, where the result was reported in 4.1 and 4.2, respectively. The performance evaluation of sentence selection included experiments on the effectiveness of (1) sentence pruning and (2) sub-event sentence selection. Besides, the experiments of discussion summarization evaluated the effectiveness of (1) sub-event matching, (2) representative sentence selection, and (3) the result of timeline summarization.

In the following experiments, we used a dataset consisting of real-world posting documents. The event-related posts were collected from the PTT Bulletin Board System. Most of the users in PPT were teenagers or college students. Four different query event terms were used to collect the dataset as shown in Table 1. The discussing period, the number of related posts, the number of collected sentences, and the time interval used in timeline summarization are also shown in Table 2. Moreover, 82677 posts collected from June 2005 to September 2016 were used as the training data set to construct the Word2Vec word embedding model.

Table 2. The description of the test dataset.

Query event	Time period	# of posts	# of sentences	Time interval
President election	2015/07–2016/01	2258	15576	A month
Earthquake	2016/02/06–2016/02/13	1151	5551	A day
Typhoon Nepartak	2016/07/06–2016/07/10	914	3262	A day
Typhoon Megi	2016/09/26–2016/09/30	1924	6482	A day

4.1 Performance Evaluation of Sentence Selection

4.1.1 Evaluation of Sentence Pruning

The proposed sentence pruning strategy aims to prune the sentences which represent unclear semantics or noisy information unrelated to the query event. Therefore, this experiment evaluated the precision and the recall of the pruned sentences. 1000 sentences were randomly selected for each query event, where each sentence was manually labeled whether it is a sentence with meaningful semantics or not. The confusion matrix of the pruned and the remaining sentences with respect to the semantic meaningful and semantic unclear sentences is shown in Table 3. The recall of the semantic unclear sentences is 87.48%. The result shows that the effectiveness of the sentence pruning strategy. Most semantically unclear sentences can be pruned by the proposed strategy.

Table 3. The confusion matrix of the pruned and the remaining sentences.

4000 sentences		Ground truth		Total
		Semantic meaningful	Semantic unclear	
System	Remaining sentences	94	481	575
	Pruned sentences	62	3363	3425
Total		156	3844	4000

4.1.2 Evaluation of Sub-event Sentence Selection

In this experiment, we evaluated the precision of the top n sentences chosen by the sub-event sentence selection strategy. For each event, we ask the volunteers to label whether the sentence describes a fact and has no duplicate information with the previous sentences. The precision @n for $n = 3$, 5, or 10 is shown in Table 4.

Table 4. Precision@n of the top sub-event selected sentences.

Event	@3	@5	@10
President Election	66.6%	80%	
Earthquake	100%	80%	50%
Typhoon Nepartak	100%	100%	70%
Typhoon Megi	100%	80%	70%
Average	91.65%	85%	63.33%

The result shows that the top 3 or top 5 selected sub-event sentences met users' expectation very much. It makes sense that the Precision@10 get lower value than Precision@5 because each event usually have less than 10 sub-event occurring. A sample of 5 selected sub-event sentences for the event query Typhoon Nepartak is shown in Table 5. Each sentence describes a fact happened or elaborates a specific incident.

Table 5. A sample of the selected sub-event sentences.

Id	The content in the sentence
s_1	颱風尼伯特逼近臺北市長柯文哲今天上午赴災害應變中心視察 The mayor of Taipei went to NCDR to inspect the progress while Typhoon Nepartak was approaching.
s_2	未來 24 小時颱風將嚴重影響東部及新竹以南地區 Typhoon will affect the east part of Taiwan and south of Hsinchu in coming 24 hours.
s_3	北北基昨天上午沒有明顯風雨信義新光三越各館因颱風都未營業 There was no strong wind and rain in Taipei City yesterday morning. However, Shin Kong Mitsukoshi department store was not open because of typhoon.
s_4	今天晚上臺北還算是正常上班上課的狀態明天才是颱風假 Everyone still has to go to work and school tonight. However, tomorrow will have a day off because of Typhoon.
s_5	颱風尼伯特遠離臺灣昨天臺北上午無風無雨 Typhoon Nepartak has leaved Taiwan. There was no rain and wind in Taipei yesterday morning.

4.2   Performance Evaluation of Discussion Summarization

4.2.1   Evaluation of Sub-event Matching

In this experiment, the top five sub-event sentences are selected for each query event. For each sub-event, the sentences matched to the event were discovered, where the threshold value t was set to be 0.5. The volunteers were asked to label whether the content of the sentences have high association with the sub-event. The precision of sub-event matching for each event query is shown in Table 6.

Table 6. Precision of sub-event matching.

Event query	Selected sentences	Matched sentences	Precision
President election	26	18	69.23%
Earthquake	56	42	75%
Typhoon Nepartak	214	178	83.17%
Typhoon Megi	375	276	73.6%

According to the result shown in Table 6, the average precision is about 75.1%. By observing the properties of the dataset, the event of Taiwanese's president election last a long period, i.e. 7 months. There were not enough focus and significant sub-events happened. That is why the sub-event matching result gets lower precision. To analyze the result in more detailed, the precisions of the matched sentences for each top 5 selected sub-event are shown in Table 7, individually. According to the result, it shows that the better the sub-event sentence is selected, the higher precision of the matched sentences it gets. The matching effectiveness is influenced by the quality of the selected sub-event sentence.

Table 7. Precision of ranked sub-event.

Event query	Rank 1	Rank 2	Rank 3	Rank 4	Rank 5
President election	71.42%	71.42%	60%	-	-
Earthquake	82.14%	75%	80%	62.5%	57.14%
Typhoon Nepartak	90.78%	81.81%	80%	75%	70.58%
Typhoon Megi	82.02%	80.99%	73.33%	60.81%	52.5%

4.2.2   Evaluation of Representative Sentence Selection

In this experiment, we wanted to estimate the performance of representative sentence selection. For each sub-event, several discussion aspects were formed by clustering the matched sentences. For each aspect, the sentence with the highest *CRS* score is selected to be the representative sentence. The volunteers were asked to compare the selected sentence with the other sentences assigned in the same aspect, and label whether this selected sentence is representative enough. According to the result shown in Table 8, the overall precision is higher than 70%, which implies that most of selected represent comments are able to convey an abstract concept or idea of the whole aspect cluster.

Table 8. Precision of picking the representative sentences of discussing aspects.

Event	Number of discovered aspects	Precision
President election	5	60%
Earthquake	6	83.33%
Typhoon Nepartak	7	85.71%
Typhoon Megi	8	62.5%
Overall	26	72.89%

4.2.3   Timeline Summarization

In this experiment, we asked the volunteers to grade the integrated performance of the discovered results of the proposed timeline summarization approach. The volunteers were asked to give an integer grading from 1 to 3. If no information or knowledge count be got from the timeline sub-event summary, score 1 is given. If the result could help users understand the sub-events and the corresponding opinions partially, score 2 is given. If the content could help users understand what sub-events happened and the opinions about the sub-events completely, score 3 is given. According to the grading result shown in Table 9, the average score is 2.3. It indicates that the volunteers could get better understanding about the sub-events and discussing aspects by reading through the sub-event sentences and the representative sentences of various discussing aspects. The timeline summarization is useful for user to understand the discussing trends of sub-events.

Table 9. Overall grading result.

Event	Average grading
President election	2
Earthquake	2.6
Typhoon Nepartak	2.4
Typhoon Megi	2.2
Overall average	2.3

5 Conclusion and Future Work

In this paper, we proposed an approach to automatically generate timeline summarization of sub-event discussions related to the query event without supervised learning. Three main processing modules are proposed in our framework: entity-term extraction, sentence selection, and discussion summarization. A two-stage method was used to extract representative entity terms in the event-related discussions and filter out most of the sentences semantically un-related to the query event. Besides, a rule-based method was applied to extract sentences which describing sub-events. After that, the discussions are assigned to the corresponding sub-events according to the semantic relatedness measure. Finally, according to the occurring time of each sub-event, the timeline summarization is organized. The performance evaluation showed the effectiveness of the proposed methods on the real-world datasets. Especially, most noise sentences could be filtered by the proposed method. Moreover, the final timeline summarization graded by users is proven to be useful to well understand the discussion trend of a sub-event.

In our approach, the discussing aspects in the organized summarization mainly depended on the discovered sub-event sentences. Instead of a rule-based method, how to design a supervised learning approach based a small size of training set to perform well sub-event sentence selection is under our consideration.

References

1. Avvenuti, M., Meletti, C., Cresci, S., Tesconi, M., Marchetti, A.: EARS (earthquake alert and report system): a real time decision support system for earthquake crisis management. In: Proceedings of the 20th ACM SIGKDD International Conference on Knowledge Discovery and Data Mining, KDD 2014, pp. 1749–1758 (2014)
2. Sakaki, T., Okazaki, M., Matsuo, Y.: Earthquake shakes twitter users: real-time event detection by social sensors. In: Proceedings of the 19th International Conference on World Wide Web, WWW 2010, pp. 851–860 (2010)
3. Chae, J., Thom, D., Ebert, D.S., Bosch, H., Ertl, T., Jang, Y., Maciejewski, R.: Spatiotemporal social media analytics for abnormal event detection and examination using seasonal-trend decomposition. In: IEEE, Visual Analytics Science and Technology (VAST), pp. 143–152 (2012)

4. Pohl, D., Bouchachia, A., Hellwagner, H.: Automatic sub-event detection in emergency management using social media. In: Proceedings of the 21st International Conference on World Wide Web (short paper), WWW 2012, pp. 683–686 (2012)
5. Tuan, T., Calaudia, N., Nattiya, K., Ujwal, G., Avishek, A.: Balancing novelty and salience: adaptive learning to rank entities for timeline summarization of high-impact events. In: Proceedings of the 24th ACM International on Conference on Information and Knowledge Management, CIKM 2015, pp. 1201–1210 (2015)
6. Abhik, D., Toshniwal, D.: Sub-event detection during nature hazards using features of social media data. In: Proceedings of the 22nd International Conference on World Wide Web, WWW 2013, pp. 783–788 (2013)
7. Shou, L., Wang, Z., Chen, K., Chen, G.: Sumblr: continuous summarization of evolving tweet streams. In: Proceedings of the 36th International ACM SIGIR Conference on Research and Development in Information Retrieval, SIGIR 2013, pp. 533–542 (2013)
8. Paik, J.H., Oard, D.W.: A fixed-point method for weighting terms in verbose informational queries. In: Proceedings of the 23rd ACM International Conference on Information and Knowledge Management, CIKM 2014, pp. 131–140 (2014)
9. Mikolov, T., Chen, K., Corrado, G., Dean, J.: Efficient Estimation of Word Representations in Vector Space (2013). arXiv:13013781v3
10. Siersdorfer, S., Kemkes, P., Ackermann, H., Zerr, S.: Who with Whom and How? – Extracting large social networks using search engines. In: Proceedings of the 24th ACM International on Conference on Information and Knowledge Management, CIKM 2015, pp. 1491–1500 (2015)

Evidential Link Prediction in Uncertain Social Networks Based on Node Attributes

Sabrine Mallek[1,2]([✉]), Imen Boukhris[1], Zied Elouedi[1], and Eric Lefevre[2]

[1] LARODEC, Institut Supérieur de Gestion de Tunis,
Université de Tunis, Tunis, Tunisia
sabrinemallek@yahoo.fr, imen.boukhris@hotmail.com, zied.elouedi@gmx.fr
[2] EA 3926, Laboratoire de Génie Informatique et d'Automatique
de l'Artois (LGI2A), Univ. Artois, 62400 Béthune, France
eric.lefevre@univ-artois.fr

Abstract. The design of an efficient link prediction method is still an open hot issue that has been addressed mostly through topological properties in recent years. Yet, other relevant information such as the node attributes may inform the link prediction task and enhance performances. This paper presents a novel framework for link prediction that combines node attributes and structural properties. Furthermore, the proposed method handles uncertainty that characterizes social network noisy and missing data by embracing the general framework of the belief function theory. An experimental evaluation on real world social network data shows that attribute information improves further the prediction results.

Keywords: Social network analysis · Link prediction · Uncertain social network · Belief function theory · Node attributes · Structural properties

1 Introduction

The link prediction problem (LP) is gaining considerable attention in various fields, such as sociology, bioinformatics, and computer science. The aim is to infer missing links from partially observed networks, such as uncovering criminals and terrorists, or potential new links like suggesting future friendships or collaborations. Typically, the most basic assumption for link prediction is that the more similar two nodes are, the more likely they connect. That is, the main concern is how to evaluate and compute similarities accurately. Typical methods use topological properties based on local and global graph information. Yet, other information such as group affiliation or node attributes add semantics to connections between the nodes. Frequently, a great deal of information is available at the nodes level. Several real-world social networks (SN) handle nodes with valued attributes. For example, Facebook users have profiles with attributes containing contact information, work, education, family and relationships. This information boosts LP by adding a meaningful semantic to the nodes characteristics.

© Springer International Publishing AG 2017
S. Benferhat et al. (Eds.): IEA/AIE 2017, Part I, LNAI 10350, pp. 595–601, 2017.
DOI: 10.1007/978-3-319-60042-0_65

On the other hand, most link prediction methods lack functionality to properly manipulate and deal with noisy and imperfect SN data, whereas, these latter are very often biased and exposed to errors [3]. More importantly, anonymization techniques, experimental settings and social networks sampling induce high level uncertainty. In that regard, there is increasable interest to uncertain SN [10] where uncertainty relates to nodes and/or links existence. We outlined, in previous works [4,5], the importance of handling uncertainty when analyzing SN. We proposed a graph-based social network model that encapsulates uncertainty at the edges level and we designed methods for LP with uncertainty-handling capabilities. However, none of them take into account semantic similarity, they only consider topological information.

In this work, we develop a novel framework for LP in social networks that combines both network topology and node attributes information in a unified scheme. Furthermore, the novel approach handles uncertain networks and operates fully under uncertainty thanks to the belief function theory (BFT) [1,8] which is a general framework for reasoning under uncertainty that provides convenient tools to deal with imperfect and missing data problems. This paper is organized as follows. In Sect. 2, a brief survey on link prediction related work is presented. In Sect. 3, fundamental concepts of the BFT are defined. Section 4 exposes our proposals: a framework for link prediction in uncertain networks. Section 5 gives the experiments and Sect. 6 concludes the paper.

2   Link Prediction Related Work

Let $G(V, E)$ be a social network graph where V is the set of nodes and E is the set of edges. For two unlinked nodes x and y, most methods compute a similarity score s_{xy} on the basis of their common features. The scores are sorted in a decreasing order, and the pairs with the highest scores are most likely to exist. Typically, the scores are computed from network topology based on local or global information. Local information uses node neighborhoods where popular metrics include Common Neighbors, the Jaccard Coefficient, Preferential Attachment and Adamic/Adar. For example, the common neighbors metric, denoted by CN, counts the common neighbors between (x, y). In contrast, global information methods use topological properties of the global network. Popular scores include Hitting time, SimRank and the shortest path. Indeed, structural metrics present some advantages as they are generic and simple. Yet, they present inconveniences as local methods favor the nodes with the highest degrees whereas global methods suffer from high complexity. Most importantly, the two types of methods only relate to network topology and do not take semantic similarity into account reducing the performances of LP.

Meanwhile, other methods consider different information sources. Yu et al. [12] integrate network proximity and node attributes for LP in weighted SN by boosting the links connecting nodes with similar attributes. However, the method does not scale to large networks. Hasan et al. [2] test node attributes to predict co-authorships. Yet, some features appear to be not suitable to evaluate similarities between the authors. O'Madadhain et al. [7] combine network-based and entity-based features to predict co-participation in events over time under supervised learning. Although semantic attributes enhance LP, they present some limitations like unavailability. Frequently, SN policies do not impose the users to put all their information and content i.e., Facebook allows users to control their privacy settings. Generally, information is hidden because of privacy, legal, ethical or operational concerns. In addition, users information may not be reliable as they can put false and misleading information or even create total fake profiles. To deal with this ambiguity, we incorporate uncertainty in LP by embracing the BFT as it allows to manage and deal with uncertainty.

3   Basic Definitions of the Belief Function Theory

In the belief function theory [1,8], a problem is drawn through a finite set of exhaustive and mutually exclusive events denoted by Θ and called the frame of discernment. 2^{Θ} be its power set. A mass function $m : 2^{\Theta} \to [0,1]$, called basic belief assignment (bba), on 2^{Θ} satisfies:

$$\sum_{A \subseteq \Theta} m(A) = 1. \tag{1}$$

To combine two mass functions m_1 and m_2 derived from reliable and distinct sources of evidence, the conjunctive rule [9] denoted by $\bigcirc$ is applied:

$$m_1 \bigcirc m_2(A) = \sum_{B,C \subseteq \Theta : B \cap C = A} m_1(B) \cdot m_2(C). \tag{2}$$

Evidence may be ambiguous or incomplete. Thus, it may not be equally trustworthy. For that, a discounting operation [8] is applied to m to get the discounted bba denoted by $^{\alpha}m$. Given the reliability degree of the source evaluated by a discounting rate $\alpha \in [0,1]$, the discounting operator is defined by:

$$\begin{cases} ^{\alpha}m(A) = (1 - \alpha) \cdot m(A), \forall A \subset \Theta \\ ^{\alpha}m(\Theta) = \alpha + (1 - \alpha) \cdot m(\Theta). \end{cases} \tag{3}$$

To fuse two bba's m_1 and m_2 defined on two disjoint frames Θ and Ω, a vacuous extension, denoted by $\uparrow$, is applied. The bba's are extended to the product space of the frame of discernment $\Theta \times \Omega = \{(\theta_i, \omega_k), \forall i \in \{1, \ldots, |\Theta|\}, \forall k \in \{1, \ldots, |\Omega|\}\}$. The vacuous extension operation is defined by:

$$m^{\Theta \uparrow \Theta \times \Omega}(C) = \begin{cases} m^{\Theta}(A) & \text{if } C = A \times \Omega, A \subseteq \Theta, C \subseteq \Theta \times \Omega \\ 0, & \text{otherwise} \end{cases} \tag{4}$$

The relation between two disjoint frames Θ and Ω can be fulfilled using a multi-valued mapping mechanism [1] denoted by τ. The function τ ascribes the subsets $B \subseteq \Omega$ that may fit a subset $A \subseteq \Theta$:

$$m_{\tau}(A) = \sum_{\tau(B)=A} m(B). \tag{5}$$

To make decision in the belief function framework, the pignistic probability denoted by $BetP$ is computed from the bba m. It is defined by [9]:

$$BetP(A) = \sum_{B \subseteq \Theta} \frac{|A \cap B|}{|B|} \frac{m(B)}{(1 - m(\emptyset))}, \forall A \in \Theta. \tag{6}$$

4 Evidential Link Prediction in Uncertain Social Networks

We develop a framework for link prediction that handles uncertainty and combines structural properties and node attributes. We consider in this paper, a SN graph model that handles uncertainty at the edges level. This structure was introduced in [4,5]. The uncertainty degree about the existence of a link xy is quantified using a basic belief assignment denoted by m^{xy} defined on $\Theta^{xy} = \{E_{xy}, \neg E_{xy}\}$, where E_{xy} is the event supporting the existence of the link xy and $\neg E_{xy}$ endorses its absence. Based on the intuition of local methods, in this paper, our proposed approach called evidential link prediction (ELP), considers the neighborhood of the nodes and compares their features. For instance, given two unlinked nodes x and y, we compare the features of the neighbors of y to those of x and conversely. The idea is that when an individual is similar to another one's connections then they are likely to connect. Subsequently, the most similar nodes are retained and considered as sources of evidence regarding xy existence. In fact, we did not limit our analysis to only common neighbors in order to overcome the limitation of favoring nodes with highest degrees. However, when similar nodes are also common neighbors they are considered more reliable sources of evidence. Therefore, our method takes into account both node attributes and structural properties. The information gathered from the most similar node to x and that to y is pooled to get an overall evidence about xy. To this end, the steps of our novel framework for predicting a new link xy in an evidential SN are detailed below.

Similarity Assessment. First, the sets of neighbors $\tau(x)$ and $\tau(y)$ of x and y are computed and the attributes of each node and the neighbors of the second are compared such that x is compared to the neighbors $y_n \in \tau(y)$ of y and vice versa. The attributes of the nodes are assumed to have categorical values with no missing values. The similarity is evaluated such that:

$$S_{node_1, node_2} = \frac{\#matched\ attributes}{\#total\ attributes} \tag{7}$$

Next, the most similar node to x denoted by y_s and that to y denoted by x_s are considered. Note that, when there are more than two most similar nodes, the common neighbor with the highest mass on the event "exist" is chosen, otherwise it is chosen randomly.

Reliability Evaluation. Upon getting the similar nodes, we evaluate their reliability through a discounting operation (Eq. 3). When the most similar node is not a common neighbor, it is not considered as a total reliable source. A discount coefficient denoted by $\beta = 1 - S_{node_1, node_2}$ is built according to the similarity score. Actually, when the nodes have all the attributes in common i.e., $S_{node_1, node_2} = 1$, then the most similar node is fully reliable i.e., $\beta = 0$. Hence, m^{xx_s} gives the discounted mass ${}^{\beta}m^{xx_s}$ according to Eq. 3.

Fusion and Prediction. To fuse and propagate information to the query links xy, a vacuous extension (Eq. 4) on the product space $\Theta^{xx_s} \times \Theta^{yy_s}$ is applied first to make the *bba*'s bear on the same referential. The induced *bba*'s are fused using the conjunctive rule to get the global mass $m_{\bigcirc}^{\mathcal{PS}}$ such that:

$$m_{\bigcirc}^{\mathcal{PS}} = m^{xx_s \uparrow \mathcal{PS}} \bigcirc m^{yy_s \uparrow \mathcal{PS}} \tag{8}$$

Upon combination, the obtained *bba*'s are transferred to the frame Θ^{xy} of the query link by a multi-valued mapping (Eq. 5) according to the method presented in [5]. Finally for links selection, pignistic probabilities $BetP^{xy}$ are ranked in a decreasing order of confidence where the top ranked links are the ones having the highest scores on the event "exists".

5   Experimental Evaluation

We examine the validity and soundness of our proposals using a component of 1060 nodes and 10 K edges of a real world SN of *Facebook* friendships [6]. It includes node attributes (such as education, language, school, location, work) that have been anonymized. We proceed by constructing the evidential SN by simulating *bba*'s according to the procedure presented in [4]. A comparative study is made with the classical Common Neighbor (CN) method and the approach from [5], called belief link prediction (BLP), which is inspired from the Common Neighbors method and uses solely structural properties.

The performance is evaluated using the precision-recall (PR) threshold curve as it discussed [11] to provide a fair and consistent tool to analyze LP results. The plot is made by varying the threshold of the top ranked links. At each threshold, we get different decision values given by the links scores e.g., pignistic probabilities for the ELP and BLP, and CN score for the Common Neighbor method. Thus, different pairs of recall and precision are computed. Figure 1 gives the PR curves on the three methods. As shown, the proposed novel approach gives accurate predictions. One can see that the ELP plot is above the BLP and CN curves. Interestingly, taking node attributes information into account improves performances. In addition, one should note that the ELP method takes local and semi-local structural information into account as it considers direct and indirect neighbors. This adds flexibility to the similarity assessment unlike the traditional indices based on common neighbors. All in all, validity of the new approach is approved. Furthermore, node attributes information enhance link prediction accuracy as it adds a semantic meaning to network topology.

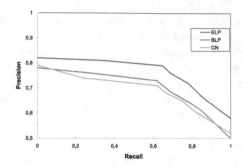

Fig. 1. PR curve of the link prediction methods

6   Conclusion

In this paper, we have developed a method for LP in uncertain SN by combining topological properties and node attributes. Uncertainty is handled thanks to the belief function theory. Similarities are evaluated by matching common attribute values where common neighbors are endorsed as more reliable sources. Evidence regarding new predicted links is estimated through a fusion and mapping procedures. Experiments confirm that semantic information given by the nodes attributes and uncertainty handling in SN enhance LP performance.

References

1. Dempster, A.P.: Upper and lower probabilities induced by a multivalued mapping. Ann. Math. Stat. **38**, 325–339 (1967)
2. Hasan, M.A., Chaoji, V., Salem, S., Zaki, M.J.: Link prediction using supervised learning. In: Proceedings of SDM 2006 Workshop on Link Analysis, Counterterrorism and Security (2006)
3. Kossinets, G.: Effects of missing data in social networks. Soc. Netw. **28**, 247–268 (2003)
4. Mallek, S., Boukhris, I., Elouedi, Z., Lefevre, E.: Evidential link prediction based on group information. In: Prasath, R., Vuppala, A.K., Kathirvalavakumar, T. (eds.) MIKE 2015. LNCS, vol. 9468, pp. 482–492. Springer, Cham (2015). doi:10.1007/978-3-319-26832-3_45
5. Mallek, S., Boukhris, I., Elouedi, Z., Lefevre, E.: The link prediction problem under a belief function framework. In: Proceedings of the IEEE 27th International Conference on the Tools with Artificial Intelligence, pp. 1013–1020 (2015)
6. McAuley, J.J., Leskovec, J.: Learning to discover social circles in ego networks. In: Proceedings of the 26th Annual Conference on Neural Information Processing Systems 2012, pp. 548–556 (2012)
7. O'Madadhain, J., Hutchins, J., Smyth, P.: Prediction and ranking algorithms for event-based network data. SIGKDD Explor. Newslett. **7**(2), 23–30 (2005)
8. Shafer, G.: A Mathematical Theory of Evidence. Princeton University Press, Princeton (1976)

9. Smets, P.: Application of the transferable belief model to diagnostic problems. Int. J. Intell. Syst. **13**(2–3), 127–157 (1998)
10. Svenson, P.: Social network analysis of uncertain networks. In: Proceedings of the 2nd Skövde Workshop on Information Fusion Topics (2008)
11. Yang, Y., Lichtenwalter, R.N., Chawla, N.V.: Evaluating link prediction methods. Knowl. Inf. Syst. **45**(3), 751–782 (2014)
12. Yu, Z., Kening, G., Feng, L., Ge, Y.: A new method for link prediction using various features in social networks. In: Proceedings of the 11th Web Information System and Application Conference, WISA 2014, pp. 144–147 (2014)

Arabic Tweets Sentimental Analysis Using Machine Learning

Khaled Mohammad Alomari[1]([⊠]) [iD], Hatem M. ElSherif[2] [iD], and Khaled Shaalan[2] [iD]

[1] Faculty of Arts and Sciences, Abu Dhabi University, Abu Dhabi, UAE
khaled.alomari@adu.ac.ae
[2] Faculty of Engineering and IT, The British University in Dubai, Dubai, UAE
hatem.m.elsherif@gmail.com, khaled.shaalan@buid.ac.ae

Abstract. The continuous rapid growth of electronic Arabic contents in social media channels and in Twitter particularly poses an opportunity for opinion mining research. Nevertheless, it is hindered by either the lack of sentimental analysis resources or Arabic language text analysis challenges. This study introduces an Arabic Jordanian twitter corpus where Tweets are annotated as either positive or negative. It investigates different supervised machine learning sentiment analysis approaches when applied to Arabic user's social media of general subjects that are found in either Modern Standard Arabic (MSA) or Jordanian dialect. Experiments are conducted to evaluate the use of different weight schemes, stemming and N-grams terms techniques and scenarios. The experimental results provide the best scenario for each classifier and indicate that SVM classifier using term frequency–inverse document frequency (TF-IDF) weighting scheme with stemming through Bigrams feature outperforms the Naïve Bayesian classifier best scenario performance results. Furthermore, this study results outperformed other results from comparable related work.

Keywords: Sentiment analysis · Machine learning · Arabic natural language processing

1 Introduction

There has been limited sentiment analysis research addressing Arabic language, where this limitation attributed to the difficulty of analyzing the composition of Arabic Language as well as its complexity and the multiplicity. In 2016, there were 168,426,690 Arabic speaking people using the internet, representing 4.7% of the global internet population (much greater than contribution of Russian [2.9%] and German [2.3%]). Out of the estimated 388,332,877 persons in the digital world, Arabic speaks only 43.4% across the internet. The number of Arabic speaking internet users has been growing to 6602.5% in the last sixteen years (2000–2016) [1]. There is a rapidly growing rate of comments, feedbacks, ratings and reviews added online by Arabic users, which are gaining greater importance and attention. This trend driven by a rapid increase in the number of social media applications channels and users. MSA is the single formal Arabic script mostly based on Classic Arabic and is different from regional Arabic dialects.

© Springer International Publishing AG 2017
S. Benferhat et al. (Eds.): IEA/AIE 2017, Part I, LNAI 10350, pp. 602–610, 2017.
DOI: 10.1007/978-3-319-60042-0_66

Colloquial versions of Arabic differ widely, which can be categorized by regional forms such as (Khaliji, Mesopotamian, Syro-Palestinian, Egyptian, Maghrebi) [2].

In this paper, we introduce a new Arabic Jordanian annotated twitter corpus that are suitable to sentimental analysis. It also investigates several preprocessing and ML strategies for evaluating their performance aiming at finding best ML strategy for sentimental analysis in multiple domain Arabic corpus. Motivated by superior performance achieved by Support Vector Machines and Naïve Bayes classifiers in English [3] and Arabic sentimental analysis research, this study analyzes both selected algorithms performance using different preprocessing strategies such as (stop words, stemming), N-grams and different weighting schemes. The rest of the paper is organized as follows. Section 2, outlines challenges of Arabic sentiment analysis and summarizes the related work. Section 3, describes our approach in building the corpus. Section 4, presents the used methods and experimentations. Section 5, discusses the obtained results. Finally, the main conclusions are presented.

2   Related Work

Many challenges are associated with Arabic Natural Language Processing (ANLP). In [4], a comprehensive survey is provided which discusses several ANLP challenges, such as Arabic diglossia and regional dialect phenomena. Meanwhile, Arabic sentiment analysis inherits the ANLP challenges, mainly due to the nature of the combinations of syntax, morphology and lexical entities from MSA and classical Arabic [5]. In addition, the absence of Arabic language standardization outside of the media and academia is considered a major challenge for ANLP research especially the use of dialects in social media [6–8].

Sentiment analysis systems are usually designed for languages with a single form, such as English. Meanwhile, international sentiment requires text analysis in multiple different local language forms. In addition, dialectical diversity and richness of the language challenges hinder the text analysis task [9]. In the literature, studies acknowledged nine principal reasons for Arabic language being particularly problematic for sentiment analyses such as complicated morphology and use of Arabic dialects, with poor spelling. Those concerns can be summarized as either a lack of language resources or problems associated with regional dialects [10, 11]. Table 1 presents a summary of major researches in Arabic sentiment analysis adopting Machine Learning approach.

Arabic Sentiment Analysis researchers have built Sentiment Analysis corpus from diverse electronic online data. As far as Arabic Sentiment Analysis researches is concerned [8, 12–14], publicly available Arabic twitter datasets are still limited in size and coverage of Arabic dialects. Meanwhile, available Arabic Jordanian twitter datasets are very limited such as the work of [12].

Table 1. A summary of major Arabic sentiments analyses using ML Approach.

Author	Dataset name	Size	Multi domain	Available	Source	Type[a]
[13]	Twitter Dataset	2591	Yes	Yes	Tweet/Facebook	MSA/DA
[8]	Twitter Corpus	8868	N/A	Yes	Tweet	MSA/DA
[12]	Tweet as string vector	2000	No	Yes	Tweet	MSA/DA
[15]	LABR	63257	No	Yes	Book	MSA/DA
[16]	AWATIF	<10 k	Yes	No	Wikipedia/Talk Pages/Forums/ News wire	MSA/DA
[17]	OCA	500	No	Yes	Movie	MSA
[18]	AOC	1.4 M	No	Yes	Newspapers Arabic Online	MSA/DA
[14]	Tweets	1000	No	Yes	Twitter	MSA/DA

[a]MSA stands for Modern Standard Arabic and DA stands for Dialectal Arabic

3 Arabic Jordanian General Tweets (AJGT) Corpus

This study introduces an Arabic tweets corpus written in Jordanian dialect and MSA annotated for the purpose of sentiment analyses. In the following paragraphs, we describe the method of collecting Arabic tweets through Twitter application programming interface (API), as well the data preprocessing and generation of the AJGT corpus.

Data Collection: In May 2016, a collection of tweets is retrieved using multiple keywords by narrowing down the search domain to Jordanian related general topics. RapidMiner utilized to retrieve and filter tweets. Manual selection process conducted to identify Jordanian dialect or MSA tweets from different topics based on content and expression of feelings [12].

Data Preparation: collected tweets included a blend of English and Arabic characters. Some characters are repeated (e.g. "حلووووو" "rather than the original "حلو"). We used ASAP Utilities[1] (Excel plugin) for data cleaning by filtering the text and removing links, duplicate tweets, hashtags and Foreign characters.

Corpus Generation: tweets manually annotated as either positive or negative by two human experts, a third expert was consulted. Finally, the generated AJGT corpus consists of 1,800 tweets classified as (900 positives, 900 negatives). The AJGT corpus is publicly available as Github project[2].

---

[1] http://www.asap-utilities.com.

[2] https://github.com/komari6/Arabic-twitter-corpus-AJGT.

4 Arabic Sentiment Analysis Experimental Framework

The ML model is developed using RapidMiner software platform because it has powerful text processing tools that support Arabic Language and provide tokenization, filtration of tokens and Arabic stemming, among others. Figure 1 shows the process model applied for each tweet. In our experiments, we applied the SVM and NB classifier to nine scenarios: for each of the three N-gram method (Unigram, Bigrams and Trigrams), we used a full stemming, light stemming, and without stemming. In addition, for each analysis we applied either the term frequency–inverse document frequency (TF-IDF) or term frequency (TF) weighting schemes; thus, generating eighteen distinct analysis processes for each weighting scheme per classifier. In order to test different scenarios, we adopted the 10-fold cross-validation approach with shuffled sampling where it builds random subsets of the Test Set and measures the performance of each scenario by computing the following performance metrics (Accuracy, Precision, Recall and F-Score). The proposed models did not include an Arabic stop word removal process, as the preliminary results indicated that including it reduces all scenarios performance.

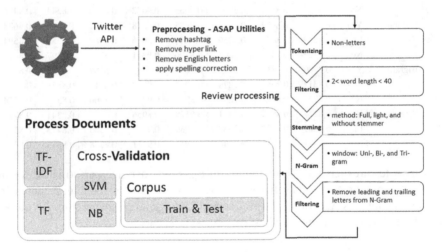

Fig. 1. Steps followed in the generation and validation of the AJGT corpus

5 Results and Discussion

Experiment evaluation results summary shown in Table 2 concluded as follows: (1) SVM classifier using stemmer with TF-IDF weighting scheme through Bigrams achieves the highest Accuracy (88.72%) and F-score (88.27%), (2) NB classifier best scenario results achieved using light stemmer with TF weighting scheme through Trigrams feature (Accuracy: 83.61%) and (F-score: 84.73%), (3) SVM classifier using stemming through Trigrams feature achieved best Precision results (TF-IDF: 92.10%, TF: 91.29%) confirming work of [13], Nevertheless due to the slight lower Precision results in Bigrams feature using TF-IDF weighting scheme (92.08%) and the better Recall results (84.89%) leading to highest F-score (88.27%). Generally, the Trigrams feature achieved the best Precision results in both SVM and NB classifiers, with either TF-IDF or TF weighting schemes, and (4) NB classifier without using stemming through Unigram feature with TF weighting scheme achieved the best Recall result (93.11%) outperforming SVM classifier result.

Table 2. 10-fold cross-validation results using the TF-IDF and TF as weighting schemes.

	N-gram	Stem	Accuracy		Precision		Recall		F	
			NB	SVM	NB	SVM	NB	SVM	NB	SVM
TF-IDF	Unigram	Yes	0.7822	0.8717	0.7546	0.8945	0.8378	0.8444	0.7936	0.8682
		Li	0.8144	0.8783	0.7863	0.9024	0.8644	**0.8489**	0.8233	0.8745
		No	0.8133	0.8678	0.7671	0.8912	0.9011	0.8389	0.8284	0.8638
	Bigrams	Yes	0.8144	**0.8872**	0.7847	0.9208	0.8678	**0.8489**	0.8239	**0.8827**
		Li	0.8200	0.8806	0.7885	0.9175	0.8756	0.8367	0.8295	0.8750
		No	0.8172	0.8606	0.7721	0.9069	0.9011	0.8044	0.8313	0.8523
	Trigrams	Yes	0.8178	0.8861	0.7878	**0.9210**	0.8711	0.8456	0.8271	0.8812
		Li	**0.8228**	0.8789	**0.7916**	0.9195	0.8778	0.8311	0.8321	0.8727
		No	0.8206	0.8583	0.7762	0.9065	**0.9022**	0.8000	**0.8341**	0.8496
TF	Unigram	Yes	0.7917	0.8672	0.7593	0.8885	0.8578	0.8411	0.8047	0.8638
		Li	0.8239	0.8628	0.7839	0.8814	0.8956	0.8389	0.8358	0.8594
		No	0.8222	0.8478	0.7651	0.8790	**0.9311**	0.8078	0.8397	0.8414
	Bigrams	Yes	0.8200	0.8811	0.7798	0.9087	0.8933	**0.8489**	0.8325	0.8771
		Li	0.8317	0.8667	0.7870	0.8954	0.9100	0.8311	0.8439	0.8618
		No	0.8233	0.8467	0.7698	0.8917	0.9233	0.7900	0.8394	0.8374
	Trigrams	Yes	0.8217	**0.8822**	0.7811	**0.9129**	0.8956	0.8467	0.8341	**0.8779**
		Li	**0.8361**	0.8622	**0.7938**	0.8969	0.9089	0.8200	**0.8473**	0.8562
		No	0.8261	0.8411	0.7746	0.8914	0.9211	0.7778	0.8413	0.8302

N-gram features have a different effect in classifiers average performance for the three used stemming approaches. In case of NB classifier, as shown in Fig. 2, increasing the N-gram improves Accuracy and F-score, and TF weighting scheme (Fig. 2b) outperforms TF-IDF (Fig. 2a) achieving best results using Trigram.

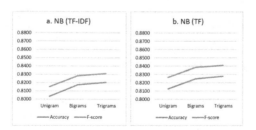

Fig. 2. NB classifier average performance

On the other hand, in case of SVM classifier performance measures (Accuracy and F-score) improvement caused by the increase of N-gram dropped when using the

Trigrams feature as shown in Fig. 3. Although N-gram nearly has the same effect on both weighting schemes. It is clear that SVM classifier performs better using TF-IDF in general and more specifically with the Bigrams feature. Furthermore, results show major differences between both classifiers regarding Accuracy and F-score, while Accuracy average performance is higher than F-score in SVM classifier. As shown in Fig. 3, the NB classifier is the opposite as shown in Fig. 2.

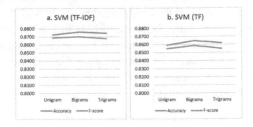

Fig. 3. SVM classifier average performance

As shown in Fig. 4, stemming approaches also have different effect in classifiers average measures performance for the implemented N-grams and weighting schemes. Although the NB results using different stemming approaches approximate, using light stemmer nearly achieved the best result. On the other hand, SVM results of using regular stemmer outperform other approaches.

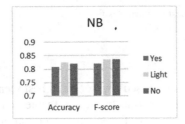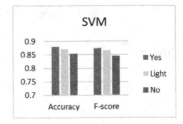

Fig. 4. Classifiers average performance results (Accuracy, F-score) by stemming approaches

Comparing study results with other related work, we observe the following: The work of [14] combining N-grams (Unigrams, Bigrams) on Arabic twitter dataset concludes that SVM classifier performs better than NB. Furthermore, in their extended work [19], results improved using SVM classifier combining N-grams (Unigrams, Bigrams, Trigrams) while investigating different normalization, stop words and stemming approaches. Another enhancement study conducted by same authors [20] confirms that the SVM classifier achieves superior results and using hybrid approaches combining ML and SO further improved the results. This study result shows that our approach through SVM classifier using stemmer with TF-IDF weighting scheme and Bigrams outperforms, in terms of Accuracy and F-score, the best results of [14, 19, 20].

The study results outperformed [12] results and confirms their conclusion, in case of Arabic twitter dataset SVM classifier with light stemmer (without using N-gram)

gives better Accuracy. Nevertheless, using stemmer with TF-IDF weighting scheme through Bigrams gives much better results. Another study [7] used the [12] corpus achieved better results using the rule-based (lexicon-based) approach. However, although rule-based approach achieves superior results comparing to ML in single domain corpus, ML as a supervised approach is domain-independent [14] and more suitable for twitter multi-subject corpus.

The study results summary shown in Fig. 5 illustrates the best scenario. First, SVM classifier using stemmer with TF-IDF weighting scheme through Bigrams achieves the best performance which aligns with the work of [21] in English sentimental analysis. On the other hand, NB classifier achieves best performance results using light stemmer with TF weighting scheme through Trigrams feature. Comparing both classifiers best scenario, we conclude that SVM classifier proposed scenario that outperforms NB classifier results in terms of Accuracy and F-score.

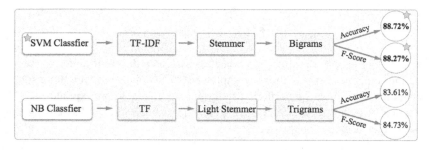

Fig. 5. Summary of best scenario results

6   Conclusions

This study main goal is to investigate the ML supervised approach and best scenario for Arabic sentimental analysis in multiple domain corpora. In order to achieve this goal: First, we introduced a new publicly available Arabic tweets corpus (1,800 annotated tweets) written in Jordanian dialect and MSA from different general topics, namely: AJGT corpus, contributing to the Arabic sentiment analyses research domain limited resources. Second, experiments are conducted comparing two machine learning algorithms (SVM and NB) utilizing different features and preprocessing strategies. We have used several N-grams (Unigram, Bigrams, Trigrams) with different weighting schemes (TF, TF-IDF) and applied alternative stemming techniques (no stemmer, stemmer, light stemmer).

This study concluded that adapting machine learning supervised approaches in Arabic sentimental analysis give promising results. The experiment concludes that SVM classifier using stemmer with (TF-IDF) weighting scheme through Bigrams is the best scenario achieving highest performance results outperforming NB classifier best scenario. Moreover, the proposed system following the best performing scenario using SVM classifier (Accuracy: 88.72% and F-score: 88.27%) outperforms other Arabic sentiment analyses research results. For our further work, we plan to increase the dataset, add third classification (neutral) and consider hashtags. In addition, investigate the proposed approach using other related Arabic regional dialect such as Palestinian Arabic dialect.

References

1. INternet World Stats: Internet World Users by Language. Top 10 Languages. http://www.internetworldstats.com/stats7.htm
2. Al-Kabi, M., Al-Qudah, N.M., Alsmadi, I., Dabour, M., Wahsheh, H. (eds.): Arabic/English Sentiment Analysis: An Empirical Study (2013)
3. Agarwal, B., Mittal, N.: Prominent Feature Extraction for Sentiment Analysis. Springer, Cham (2016)
4. Farghaly, A., Shaalan, K.: Arabic natural language processing: challenges and solutions. TALIP **8**, 1–22 (2009)
5. Ray, S.K., Shaalan, K.: A review and future perspectives of arabic question answering systems. IEEE Trans. Knowl. Data Eng. **28**, 3169–3190 (2016)
6. Bani-Khaled, T.A.: Standard Arabic and Diglossia. A problem for language education in the Arab world. Am. Int. J. Contemp. Res. **4**, 180–189 (2014)
7. Siddiqui, S., Monem, A.A., Shaalan, K.: Towards improving sentiment analysis in Arabic. In: Hassanien, A.E., Shaalan, K., Gaber, T., Azar, A.T., Tolba, M.F. (eds.) Proceedings of the International Conference on Advanced Intelligent Systems and Informatics 2016, pp. 114–123. Springer, Cham (2017)
8. Refaee, E., Rieser, V.: An Arabic Twitter Corpus for subjectivity and sentiment analysis. In: Proceedings of the Ninth International Conference on Language Resources and Evaluation (LREC-2014), Reykjavik, Iceland, 26–31 May 2014, pp. 2268–2273 (2014)
9. Shaalan, K.: A survey of Arabic named entity recognition and classification. Comput. Linguist. **40**, 469–510 (2014)
10. El-Makky, N., Nagi, K., El-Ebshihy, A., Apady, E., Hafez, O., Mostafa, S., Ibrahim, S.: Sentiment analysis of colloquial Arabic Tweets (2015)
11. Al-Twairesh, N., Al-Khalifa, H., Al-Salman, A.: Subjectivity and sentiment analysis of Arabic: trends and challenges. In: 2014 IEEE, Doha, Qatar, 10–13 November 2014, pp. 148–155. IEEE, Piscataway (2014)
12. Abdulla, N.A., Ahmed, N.A., Shehab, M.A., Al-Ayyoub, M. (eds.): Arabic sentiment analysis: Lexicon-based and corpus-based. In: 2013 IEEE Jordan Conference on Applied Electrical Engineering and Computing Technologies (AEECT) (2013)
13. Duwairi, R.M., Qarqaz, I. (eds.) Arabic sentiment analysis using supervised classification. In: 2014 International Conference on Future Internet of Things and Cloud (FiCloud) (2014)
14. Shoukry, A., Rafea, A.: Sentence-level Arabic sentiment analysis. In: International Conference on Collaboration Technologies and Systems (CTS), 21–25 May 2012, Denver, Colorado; Proceedings, pp. 546–550. IEEE, Piscataway (2012)
15. Aly, M., Atiya, A.: LABR: large scale arabic book reviews dataset. In: Meetings of the Association of Computational Linguistics (ACL) (2013)
16. Abdul-Mageed, M., Diab, M.T.: AWATIF: a multi-genre corpus for modern standard arabic subjectivity and sentiment analysis and evaluation. In: Calzolari, N., Choukri, K., Declerck, T., Dogan, M.U., Maegaard, B., Mariani, J., Odijk, J., Piperidis, S. (eds.) Proceedings of the Eighth International Conference on Language Resources and Evaluation (LREC-2012), Istanbul, Turkey, 23–25 May 2012, pp. 3907–3914. European Language Resources Association (ELRA) (2012)

17. Rushdi-Saleh, M., Teresa, M.-V.M., Ureña-López, A.L., Perea-Ortega, J.M.: OCA: opinion corpus for Arabic. J. Am. Soc. Inf. Sci. **62**, 2045–2054 (2011)
18. Zaidan, O.F., Callison-Burch, C.: The Arabic online commentary dataset: an annotated dataset of informal Arabic with high dialectal content. In: Proceedings of the 49th Annual Meeting of the Association for Computational Linguistics: Human Language Technologies: short papers, vol. 2, pp. 37–41. Association for Computational Linguistics, Portland, Oregon (2011)
19. Shoukry, A., Rafea, A.: Preprocessing Egyptian Dialect Tweets for sentiment mining. In: Fourth Workshop on Computational Approaches to Arabic, AMTA 2012, pp. 47–59 (2012)
20. Shoukry, A., Rafea, A.: A hybrid approach for sentiment classification of Egyptian Dialect Tweets. In: Gelbukh, A., Shaalan, K. (eds.) Advances in Arabic Computational Linguistics. First International Conference on Arabic Computational Linguistics: ACLing 2015, 17–20 April 2015, Cairo, Egypt: Proceedings, pp. 78–85. IEEE, Piscataway (2015)
21. Rushdi Saleh, M., Saleh, R., Martín-Valdivia, M.T., Montejo-Ráez, A., Ureña-López, L.A.: Experiments with SVM to classify opinions in different domains. Expert Syst. Appl. **38**, 14799–14804 (2011)

Getting Frustrated: Modelling Emotional Contagion in Stranded Passengers

C. Natalie van der Wal[(⊠)], Maik Couwenberg, and Tibor Bosse

Department of Computer Science,
Vrije Universiteit Amsterdam, Amsterdam, Netherlands
c.n.vander.wal@vu.nl

Abstract. Train passengers can get stranded due to a variety of events, such as a delay, technical malfunctioning or a natural disaster. Stranded passengers can get frustrated, which could escalate in misbehaviours. Examples are verbal and physical violence or dangerous behaviours such as opening emergency exits and walking in unauthorized areas. In this work, an agent-based model of stranded passengers was created to analyse and predict the dynamics of frustration and misbehaviours. It was determined how age, gender, emotional contagion, social identity and traveller type influence the frustration dynamics and number of misbehaviours. Important findings are that emotional contagion, age and gender can have an amplifying effect on frustration and misbehaviours, while traveller type seemed to have no influence. This model can be used by transport operators in preparing for stranded passengers scenarios.

Keywords: Crowd · Emotional contagion · Frustration · Passengers

1 Introduction

Imagine yourself being stranded on your train journey for four hours! What would you do and how would you feel? A lot of times passengers get frustrated and angry and start to yell or intimidate other passengers or the personnel on the train. Sometimes, passengers break out the train while that is not allowed and could start walking on the train tracks or other dangerous areas. On November 24th 2015 for example, passengers on the train towards Utrecht Central Station, Netherlands, got stranded for four hours without any clear threat and repeated misinformation. Several passengers decided to break free and open the emergency exit without permission and despite warnings of the conductor. Luckily nobody got hurt.

The problem in these situations is that many stranded passengers need to be kept within a confined space, without electricity, working toilet, food and in very warm or cold conditions. How long will the stranded passengers follow the orders of the personnel? When does the frustration lead to a dangerous level, so that passengers start to perform misbehaviours such as verbal and psychical violence or opening emergency doors without permission? To investigate these questions, computer models can be used, since real world experiments with humans are difficult to perform for these situations. With computer simulations, many different scenarios can be investigated.

© Springer International Publishing AG 2017
S. Benferhat et al. (Eds.): IEA/AIE 2017, Part I, LNAI 10350, pp. 611–619, 2017.
DOI: 10.1007/978-3-319-60042-0_67

The research question is: what is the effect of (1) age, (2) gender, and (3) traveller type, on: (a) the group frustration level and (b) the number and (c) type of misbehaviours in a scenario with stranded passengers on a train. Factors important for the level of frustration and for answering the research question were modelled in an agent-based model. The rest of this paper is organized as follows. First, the proposed stranded passengers model and literature background is presented in Sect. 2. Then, in Sect. 3 the hypotheses and simulation results are shown, followed by a summary and discussion in Sect. 4.

2   Stranded Passengers Model

In this Section: (1) it is described which theories and concepts from the literature have been translated into modelling concepts for the agent-based model; (2) which scenario is modelled and (3) the conceptual model and formalisation are described briefly.

2.1   Socio Cultural Modelling Concepts

Different socio-cultural factors were chosen for modelling: age, gender, traveller type, emotional contagion and social identity. Here, it is explained how they are based upon the literature and how they are modelled. Social contagion of frustration takes place, based on social identity [4, 9]. Every passenger compares him/herself to other passengers. Passengers that are similar to him/herself (based on age, gender, traveller type) can infect their frustration level stronger than passengers not similar to him/herself. This influence is causing a strengthening or diminishing of the frustration experienced. This mechanism is based on social identification theory [10] and emotional contagion [2].

The agent's age and gender affect the selection of actions. According to literature, young men are more prone to exert aggressive behaviour compared to any other age group or gender. [5]. Aggressive actions undertaken by other agents are attributed a negative valence, further increasing the passenger's own frustration.

There are two traveller types: commuters versus tourists, representing different experiences of travelling. These travellers have different goals based on their travel experiences: arriving on time versus arriving in itself (not necessarily on time).

Based on the frustration level in combination with the characteristic of the passenger (age, gender, traveller type) an action is chosen (do nothing, ask questions, yell, intimidate or apply force). This is based on the literature: the higher the frustration level, the more aggressive the behaviour and men are more likely than women to express aggression. [1, 3]. This is modelled with different thresholds for behaviours for each passenger type.

Every passenger has a frustration level that will increase or decrease based on: 1. the events (public service announcements with information about the delay or speed of the train), 2. the frustration of others around the passenger, 3. the goal(s) of the passenger. The frustration level increases when the estimated arrival time (based on the delay) is later then the scheduled arrival time. The larger this difference, the higher the frustration level becomes. The public service announcements and speed of train can increase or decrease the frustration level. (increase: information about a delay or train standing still, decrease: train starts to move, new information on arrival time). This is combined with the goals of the passenger. A passenger that wants to arrive instead of arriving on time won't increase its frustration level in case of a delay, but does increase its frustration level if a new estimated arrival time can't be given (arrival is unsure). Finally, it's combined with the social contagion of frustration levels of other passengers similar to the passenger in focus.

2.2 Scenario of Stranded Passengers in a Train

The model simulates passengers that are in a train that is stranded outside of a train station, whereby passengers are not allowed to exit the train without clear instructions. All agents in the model are either passengers or railway staff. Passengers can be either commuters (assumed to be in a rush to arrive at a location on time) or tourists (assumed to be more relaxed and less worried about arriving on time). Public service announcements (PSA's) are made on the train and all agents can perceive them. At the initialisation of the model (before the first PSA is made), passengers have a belief on their arrival time and location of arrival. A passenger will update his/her beliefs based on the first public service announcement broadcasted through the entire train. After the broadcast, the agent will believe it will arrive at a new time X on location Y. After initialisation, a first announcement about the delay is made. Beliefs are also dependent on the movement of the train. At the start of the simulation, the train is moving and all passengers and staff are at a certain location in the moving train. All passengers notice the movement of the train and will be able to notice that the train moves, or is standing still. Should the train stand still, passengers start to update their beliefs and attribute negative valence to this event, since it is in conflict with prior held beliefs about their supposed arriving time. Commuters will keep getting frustrated at PSA's indicating there is no movement yet and often check if the train has already started moving. Tourists on the other hand overcome the initial negative valence associated with the violation of their beliefs, because they are less in a rush than the commuters. Passengers are experiencing the increasing levels of frustration and are also expressing it towards other passengers. Passengers that are resembling each other closely (in gender, age and traveller type), can influence each other's level of frustration more than people that do not resemble each other. This influence is causing a strengthening or diminishing of the frustration experienced. The level of frustration also indicates which intentions for subsequent behaviours each passenger has. When frustration reaches a certain threshold, then a passenger might get up and start asking questions to the conductor regarding the delay, it can start to yell or can perform physical violence. Otherwise the passenger does nothing (keeps enjoying the journey). The quality of information received might be positive and alleviate the frustration a little or it might also be 'bad' information leading to more frustration. In the case that frustration is reaching high levels, the passenger starts to become aggressive and has a higher chance of acting aggressively, by spitting, punching or vandalizing. Whether or not the passenger will partake in such drastic actions is based on the makeup of the agent. The agent's age and gender are influencing the selection of actions, according to literature. Aggressive actions undertaken by other agents are attributed a negative valence further increasing the passenger's own frustration.

2.3   Conceptual Model

The agent-based model was created with a belief-desire-intention (BDI) modelling approach. [8] The modelling concepts with their dynamical relations between them are shown in Fig. 1. Concepts on the left of the box are input states: environmental factors (*events*) and observations (*group emotion, perception*). The internal agent concepts inside the box are: *beliefs, frustration, goals, intentions* and *the agents' make-up*. The output concepts at the right of the box are *action* and *expression*. The arrows depict which concept(s) influence another concept. In Table 1 these concepts are explained in more detail.

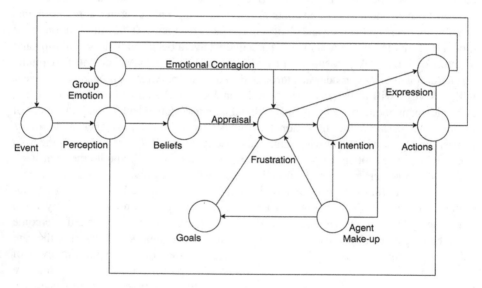

Fig. 1. Conceptual model.

Table 1. Description of agent concepts.

Concept type	Concept	Description
Perception; Agent Input State	Observation train speed	The passenger observes I the train is moving or standing still
Perception; Agent Input State	Observation public announcement	The passenger can perceive the public announcement
Perception; Agent Input State	Observation other passengers	The passenger can observe the actions and emotions of other passengers

(*continued*)

Table 1. (*continued*)

Concept type	Concept	Description
Belief; Agent Internal State	Belief arrival time	The belief of the passenger of arriving at a certain time
Belief; Agent Internal State	Belief arrival location	The belief of the passenger of the arriving location
Goal; Agent Internal State	Goal reach destination Goal reach destination on time Goal happy to travel	Each passenger has one of this three goals
Emotion; Agent Internal State	Frustration level	Each passenger has a frustration level that can increase or decrease
Own Characteristics; Agent Internal State	Age	Passengers to one of these age groups: kids, adolescents, adults, elderly
Own Characteristics; Agent Internal State	Gender	Passengers are either male or female
Intentions; Agent Internal State	Intention enjoy trip Intention ask questions Intention become aggressive	The passenger has one of these three intentions based on his frustration level
Actions; Agent Output State	Action do nothing Action ask questions Action yelling Action intimidation Action apply force	Based on the passenger's intention and own characteristics, the passenger selects one of these actions.
Actions: Agent Output State	Action express frustration	The passenger expresses his frustration level to other passengers

The model combines contagion mechanisms from the ASCRIBE model [2] (social contagion of emotion) with appraisal mechanisms (individual emotion) from the OCC model [7]. This fits the goal of modelling frustration dynamics in stranded passengers best. The current Stranded Passengers model differs from the ASCRIBE model in that it includes new agent mental states and agent characteristics to model the effects of culture on the processes during emergency situations and it includes appraisal mechanisms. The model was implemented in the Netlogo language [6]. For lack of space only an example rule for of the agent's behaviour (a decision rule for a female traveller to start yelling) and the pseudo-code are shown below.

```
to action_selection [example rule of agent behaviour]
  set fem_threshold .7
  ask passengers with [intention = 3 and action = false and
gender = 0 and frustrated > fem_threshold] [set chance random
100 ifelse chance < 20[set action true set yelling yelling + 1]
  ...
end

Initialisation [pseudo-code]
  Broadcast Public Service Announcement (PSA)
  For each passenger set: type of traveller, goal, gender, age,
belief
To go
  While current time < end time: update train movement
  For every 20 time steps:  broadcast PSA
  For each passenger perceive world, update internal states,
perform actions
end
```

3   Simulation Results

To determine the effect of (1) Age, (2) Gender, (3) Traveller Type on: (a) the level of frustration of the passengers and (b) the type of (mis)behaviours, multiple simulations were performed whereby these factors were systematically varied.

Hypotheses. (1) Adolescents and adults are expected to be most frustrated compared to children and elderly, because adults and adolescents have travel goals to arrive on time, while children and the elderly do not; (2) when there are more male passengers, there will be more misbehaviours than when there are less male passengers. It is assumed that men are more assertive and take more risk, together with emotional contagion this will lead to a faster increase in the group frustration level; (3) when most passengers are commuters, there will be more misbehaviours when there are an equal number of commuters as tourists. It is assumed commuters become more frustrated and faster than tourists. There were no a priori hypotheses on the effect of emotional contagion on the frustration level, because this is an emergent effect.

Simulation Results: Scenario. When comparing the actions performed by frustrated passengers in two scenarios (indefinite delay and long delay), passengers choose to yell or ask questions above intimidation or physical violence. See Fig. 2.

Simulation Results: Emotional Contagion. In Table 2 it is shown that emotional contagion has an effect on the choice of action. When social contagion is off, asking questions is the most performed action. When social contagion is on, yelling is the main chosen action and applying intimidation or force are relatively chosen more frequently than when social contagion is off. An explanation could be that the spreading of emotions through social contagion speeds up the group frustration level,

Table 2. Number of passenger actions in simulation experiment.

Actions	Scenario 1: Indefinite delay		Scenario 2: Long delay	
	Emotional contagion ON	Emotional contagion OFF	Emotional contagion ON	Emotional contagion OFF
Questions	1780	2265	712	783
Yelling	2330	1233	1381	914
Intimidation	1293	661	738	469
Force	441	235	259	156
Passive	37156	38606	39910	40678

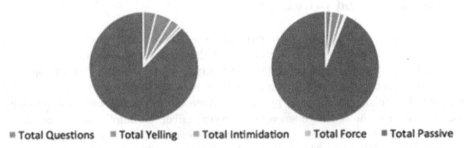

■ Total Questions   ■ Total Yelling   ■ Total Intimidation   ■ Total Force   ■ Total Passive

Fig. 2. Passenger actions during an indefinite delay (left) or long delay (right).

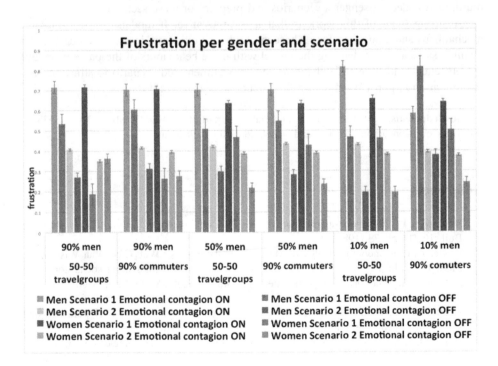

Fig. 3. Level of frustration by gender, traveller type and emotional contagion

which in turn leads to more intense misbehaviours. The other way around, decrease in group frustration is also spread through emotional contagion when the train starts riding in the long delay scenario, which in turns leads to no aggressive actions quickly.

Simulation Results: Gender, Age, Traveller Type. When most passengers are male, group frustration level is larger than when are more or an equal number of female passengers. This supports hypothesis 2. See Fig. 3. Mainly the adolescents and adults have a larger amplifying effect on the group frustration level compared to the children and elderly. This supports hypothesis 1. Traveller type does not seem to influence the group frustration level. Surprisingly, this is different than expected in hypothesis 3.

4 Conclusion and Discussion

An agent-based model of group frustration level and number and type of misbehaviours of stranded passengers on a train was created. The main research question was: what is the effect of (1) age, (2) gender, and (3) traveller type on: (a) the group frustration level and (b) the number and (c) type of misbehaviours in stranded passengers train scenario. Structured simulations supported two out of three a-priori hypotheses. Furthermore, social contagion showed an interesting emergent effect: an amplifying effect on the group frustration level. These results are of interest to emergency prevention and management stakeholders. This model will be further developed and used by transport operators and other emergency prevention and management professionals to run multiple stranded passenger's scenarios and prepare for these scenarios.

A strong point of this work is that it is innovative. It models social contagion mechanisms and cultural factors. These are both still quite rare in crowd models. Next planned steps are (1) extending the model with more behaviours of the passengers and the presence of facilities; (2) changing the environment and scenario to stranded passengers at an airport (3) validating this model with real world data.

Acknowledgments. This research was undertaken as part of EU H2020 IMPACT GA 653383. We thank our Consortium Partners and stakeholders for their input.

References

1. Berkowitz, L.: Frustration-aggression hypothesis: examination and reformulation. Psychol. Bull. **106**(1), 59–73 (1989)
2. Bosse, T., Hoogendoorn, M., Klein, M.C., Treur, J., Van Der Wal, C.N., Van Wissen, A.: Modelling collective decision making in groups and crowds: integrating social contagion and interacting emotions, beliefs and intentions. Auton. Agent. Multi-Agent Syst. **27**(1), 52–84 (2013)
3. Challenger, R., et al.: Understanding crowd behaviours, vol. 1: Practical guidance and lessons identified. The Stationery Office (TSO), London (2010)
4. Hogg, M.A., Jackson, R.L.: Encyclopedia of identity. SAGE, Los Angeles (2010)

5. Mileti, D.S.: Factors related to flood warning response. In: Paper for the US-Italy Workshop on the Hydrometeorology, Impact, and Management of Extreme Floods, Perugia, Italy, November 1995

6. Netlogo. https://ccl.northwestern.edu/netlogo/

7. Ortony, A., Clore, G., Collins, A.: The Cognitive Structure of Emotions. Cambridge Unviersity Press, Cambridge (1998)

8. Rao, A.S., Georgeff, M.P.: BDI agents: from theory to practice. In: ICMAS, vol. 95, pp. 312–319 (1995)

9. Reicher, S.D.: 'The battle of Westminster': developing the social identity model of crowd behaviour in order to explain the initiation and development of collective conflict. Eur. J. Soc. Psychol. 26(1), 115–134 (1996)

10. Tajfel, H.: Social Identity and Intergroup Relations. Cambridge University Press, Cambridge (2010)

An Agent-Based Evacuation Model with Social Contagion Mechanisms and Cultural Factors

C. Natalie van der Wal[✉], Daniel Formolo, and Tibor Bosse

Department of Computer Science, Vrije Universiteit, Amsterdam, The Netherlands
{c.n.vander.wal,d.formolo,t.bosse}@vu.nl

Abstract. A fire incident at a transport hub can cost many lives. To save lives, effective crisis management and prevention measures need to be taken. In this project, the effect of cultural factors in managing and preventing emergencies in public transport systems is analysed. An agent–based model of an evacuating crowd was created. Socio-cultural factors that were modelled are: familiarity with environment, response time and social contagion of fear and beliefs about the situation. Simulation results show that (1) familiarity and social contagion decrease evacuation time, while increasing the number of falls; (2) crowd density and social contagion increase evacuation time and falls. All three factors show different effects on the response time. This model will be used by transport operators to estimate the effect of these socio-cultural factors and prepare for emergencies.

Keywords: Crowd model · Evacuation simulation · Social contagion

1 Introduction

In crisis management and prevention, one prepares for many different emergency situations. In this work, the focus lies on an immediate evacuation scenario. Current prevention approaches can include risk assessment, drills and real-life or desktop scenario training. Computer evacuation modelling is becoming integrated in emergency prevention and management more and more as well. Crowd evacuation simulations have been used to analyse different phenomena, such as exit selection, queuing, herding behaviour, panic propagation, fluid behaviour, decision behaviour, escape behaviour, pushing behaviour, competitive and collaborative behaviours, kin behaviour, jamming, clogging and following behaviour [11]. Most of these models do not incorporate psychological and social factors [9, 11]. Observations of actual emergencies show that people tend to be slow to respond to evacuation alarms (taking up to 10 min) and take the familiar route out instead of the nearest exit [2–4, 6]. These risky behaviours stem from being unfamiliar with the environment, not seeing immediate signs of danger and following others' (unsafe) behaviour. Evacuation simulation models could become more realistic by incorporating these realistic human behaviours, as currently they do not. In this innovative work, we model social and cultural factors in an evacuation simulation, namely familiarity, response time and social contagion. These factors were stated as the most important and most interesting factors to study in stakeholder's meetings with transport

© Springer International Publishing AG 2017
S. Benferhat et al. (Eds.): IEA/AIE 2017, Part I, LNAI 10350, pp. 620–627, 2017.
DOI: 10.1007/978-3-319-60042-0_68

operators and other professionals working in emergency prevention and management in transport hubs. The main research question is: how do (1) familiarity with the environment, (2) social contagion of emotions and beliefs and (3) crowd density affect: (a) the evacuation time, (b) response time and (c) number of falls in an immediate evacuation from a building?

The rest of the paper is organised as follows. Section 2 starts with a short literature review followed by introducing the conceptual and formal model. This is followed by the simulation results in Sect. 3 and a summary and discussion in Sect. 4.

2   Socio-Cultural Evacuation Model

2.1   Background Literature: Crowd Evacuation Models

There are many different approaches for crowd evacuation simulations. Zheng and colleagues describe seven approaches for computer evacuation models: (1) cellular automata, (2) lattice gas, (3) social force, (4) fluid dynamics, (5) agent-based, (6) game theory, (7) animal experiments [11]. In microscopic models (e.g. cellular automata, lattice gas, social force, agent-based models), the pedestrian is modelled as a particle. However, in macroscopic models (e.g. fluid dynamic models), a crowd of pedestrians is modelled as a fluid. It is concluded that in further research: (1) different approaches should be combined to study crowd evacuation and (2) psychological and physiological elements should be incorporated into the evacuation models.

Templeton and colleagues also conclude that current crowd simulations don't include psychological factors and therefore cannot accurately simulate large collective behaviour that has been found in extensive empirical research on crowd events [9]. The authors argue that crowd members should be able to identify with each other in crowd simulations.

Santos and Aguirre have reviewed the integration of social and psychological factors incorporated in evacuation simulation models [7]. They describe how social dimensions are incorporated in three evacuation simulation models: FIRESCAP, EXODUS and Multi-Agent Simulation for Crisis Management (MASCM). EXODUS includes 22 social psychological attributes and characteristics for each agent, including age, name, sex, breathing rate, running speed, dead/alive, familiarity with building, agility and patience. Agents can also perform tasks before evacuating the building, such as picking up a purse or searching for a lost child. Still, the agents in EXODUS cannot have social micro-level interactions that would create a collective definition of the situation for the group. MASCM includes the social interaction in the way of evacuation leaders. For example, evacuation leaders can communicate 'please follow me' and start to walk along the evacuation route or find an evacuee at the distance or wait for the evacuee to approach. FIRESCAP implements the social theory of 'collective flight from a perceived threat'. The egress is a result of a socially structured decision making process guided by norms, roles and role relations. Agents also have a level of familiarity with the location of the exits, difference in perceived time available and perceived time needed and the ability to avoid congestion and to take turns in the exiting process. Other models that Santos and Aguirre review do not model social dimensions, such as group decision making, but focus more on the physical constraints and factors such as walking speed, walkways, stairways etcetera to find the optimal flow of the evacuation process. Agents are rational in these simulations: they can find the optimal escape route and can avoid physical obstructions and in some models, even overtake another person that would obstruct their way. Even though these models do have parameters like gender, age, individual walking speeds and different body dimensions, they lack the social interactive characteristics, such as monitoring others.

2.2   The Socio-Cultural Crowd Evacuation Model

Based on the lack of psychological, social and cultural factors in evacuation models, it was decided to create our proposed model based on earlier work called the ASCRIBE model [1]. In ASCRIBE, group-decision making is modelled as social contagion of mental and emotional states in combination with individual decision making as the effect of beliefs and emotions upon each other as well as how these both influence a person's intentions. The proposed evacuation model adds new social and cultural factors: familiarity and response time. The response time during an evacuation is a combination of deciding to evacuate and then performing the physical action of evacuation. The first part can take a very long time. This is partly based on bystander apathy and informational social influence, whereby passengers do 'nothing' or wait a long time before responding to the alarm, simply because others around them are doing the same. The second part of the response time is based on the familiarity a passenger has with the environment: the less familiar, the more dependent on the intentions and beliefs of other passengers and the familiar route.

The evacuation dynamics were modelled using an agent-based belief-desire-intention (BDI) and network-oriented modelling approaches [10]. An overview of the agent modules is shown in Fig. 1. The model was implemented in the Netlogo multi-agent language [5]. For lack of space, only part of the formal model is presented here. In formula 1 below, the calculation of the aggregated impacts of fear levels from other agents on a specific agent is shown. Each passenger is influenced by the level of fear of others at every time step (emotional contagion). Thereafter, the fear level of each passenger is calculated, see formula 2. This is based on the fear level of the previous time step (persistence), the levels of intentions to evacuate (amplifying fear) and walk randomly (decreasing fear) and the other passengers' levels of fear (social contagion).

$$others\_fear(t) = ssum_\lambda(\omega_{y1x} \cdot fear_{y1}, \dots, \omega_{kx} \cdot fear_k) = ssum_\lambda(\omega_{y1x} \cdot fear_{y1} + \dots + \omega_{kx} \cdot fear_k)$$

$$= \frac{\sum_k^{y1} \omega_{y1x} \cdot fear_{y1}(t)}{\sum_k^{y1} \omega_{y1x}}; \text{ where by } \lambda = \sum_k^{y1} \omega_{y1x}. \tag{1}$$

$$fear(t + \Delta t) = fear(t) + \eta_{mental} \cdot (max(\omega_{persistence} \cdot fear(t),$$
$$alogistic(aggfears(t), \omega_{amplifyfeeling} \cdot desire\_evacuate(t),$$
$$\omega_{inhibitfeeling} \cdot desire\_walkrand(t), \omega_{decreasefear} \cdot observation\_staf\_instr(t),$$
$$\omega_{decreasefear} \cdot observation\_pa(t))) - fear(t)) \cdot \Delta t. \tag{2}$$

$$\text{Whereby, } \quad alogistic_{\sigma\tau}(V_1, \dots, V_k) = (\frac{1}{1 + e^{-\sigma(V_1 + \dots + V_k - \tau)}}) - \frac{1}{1 + e^{\sigma\tau}})(1 + e^{-\sigma\tau})$$

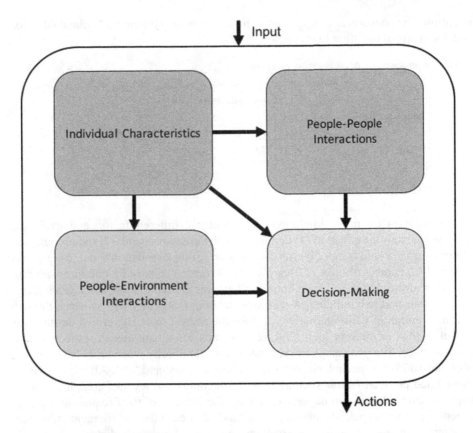

Fig. 1. Agent modules of the socio-cultural evacuation model

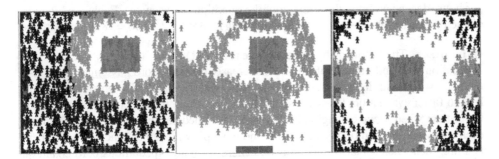

Fig. 2. Screenshots of Socio-cultural Evacuation Simulation Left: start of simulation. Middle: most people take the familiar exit. Right: Everybody takes nearest exit.

In formula 3 it is shown how the intention to evacuate is calculated. A logistic function is used to decide if the intention to evacuate or keep walking randomly is larger. This outcome is then multiplied by the desire to evacuate to represent the strength of the intention. The intention is a number between $(0,1)$, whereby 0 means a minimal intention and 1 a maximal intention to evacuate.

$$intention\_evacuate(t + \Delta t) = intention\_evacuate(t) + \eta_{body} \cdot$$
$$(desire\_evacuate(t) \cdot logistic((\omega_{amplifyintention} \cdot desire\_evacuate(t),$$
$$\omega_{inhibitintention} \cdot desire\_walkrand(t)) \cdot \Delta t.$$

Whereby, $logistic = logistic_{\sigma\tau}(V_1, \ldots, V_k)$

$$= \frac{1}{1 + e^{-\sigma(V_1 + \ldots + V_k - \tau)}}$$

(3)

3   Simulation Results

Experimental Design.   A simulation experiment with different factors and levels was designed to study the effects of (1) familiarity with the environment, (2) social contagion of emotions and beliefs and (3) crowd density on (a) the evacuation time, (b) response time and (c) number of falls. A square (20×20 meters) layout of a building with four exits (top, down, left, right; main entrance: left) was chosen to represent a general layout of a transport hub building. A passenger without familiarity will evacuate through the main entrance; with familiarity will take the nearest exit. The crowd density was varied as low, medium or high (2, 4, or 8 persons per square meters respectively, at initialisation). The percentage of passengers with familiarity was varied between 0%, 50% and 100%. Social contagion was varied between 'on' and 'off'. All other environmental and personal factors such as width of the doors and level of compliance were kept constant between simulations, except for the location of the fire and the walking speeds. The fire was placed randomly in the 'middle' area of the environment (minimum 2 meters away from the exits). The walking speeds were randomly distributed between 3,6 and 5.4 kilometres per hour. The running speed was between 7.2 and 10.8 kilometres per hour (dependent upon the strength of the intention to evacuate). Each combination of Factors and Levels was run 100 times, resulting in: $3 \times 3 \times 2 \times 100 = 1800$ simulations.

Hypotheses.   The following hypotheses were tested: (1) when familiarity increases, the evacuation time and number of falls will decrease, because more passengers will take the nearest exit and therefore there will be less congestion and falls which in turn will lead to faster evacuation; (2) when social contagion is on, the evacuation time will be lower than when social contagion is off. This is assumed because when people 'infect' each other with their emotions and beliefs, more people will start to evacuate when there is a fire, then when social contagion is off. There were no expectations beforehand on the effects of familiarity and social contagion on the response time and of social contagion on the number of falls, since these are mainly emergent effects.

Tuning and Model Assumptions.   The model was tuned manually by two modellers (authors CNvdW and DF). Agreement was reached about realistic settings for the steepness and threshold parameters based on inspecting the outcome patterns, by comparing it with theory from [10] and social and cultural psychological theories. The egress flowrate (people evacuating the building) was set to 82 people per meter per minute, in line with international data-supporting rates of passage for pedestrian movements in public assembly places [8]. Passengers move 'freely' up to 4 passengers per square meter [8]. Crowd congestion happens between 5 to 8 people per square meter, which reduces the speed and facilitates a 10% chance of falling. When there are 8 or more passengers on the next position, the passenger can't move forward.

Simulation Results Social Contagion. In Fig. 3 it is shown that the evacuation time decreases when social contagion is ON versus when it is switched off. This supports hypothesis 2. Interestingly, the number of falls and response time increase when social contagion is ON, this points to a negative effect of social contagion, even though the total evacuation time does decrease.

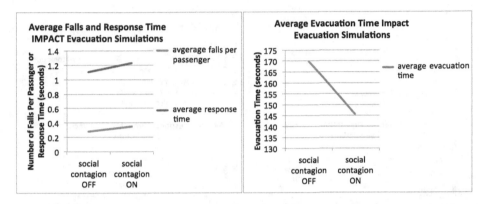

Fig. 3. Evacuation Time, Falls and Response Time versus Social Contagion

Simulation Results Familiarity. The left column of Fig. 4 shows how evacuation time and number of falls per passenger decrease when familiarity increases. This supports hypothesis 1. Evacuation time decreases linearly for both models with or without social contagion. The number of falls decrease steeply from 0 to 50% familiarity and thereafter less steep. Again, a similar pattern of familiarity on response time, in case of social contagion is noticed. Not a big difference between 50% and 100% familiarity, but a big change between 0 and 50% familiarity. This could mean that if only a small number of people do not take the main entrance/familiar route as exit, already a lot less falls are gained and response time is faster. When social contagion is off, the response time increases from 0 to 50% familiarity and then decreases when familiarity is 100%. This could indicate the only gain in response time when people can't affect each other's beliefs and emotions, is when everybody takes the nearest exit instead of just half of the people or nobody.

Simulation Results Crowd Density. The right column of Fig. 4 shows that the higher the crowd density, the higher the evacuation time and number of falls for both models, with or without social contagion. Especially from a medium to high crowd density the evacuation time and falls increase steeper that from low to medium density. For response time, there is a different pattern showing: when there is social contagion the response

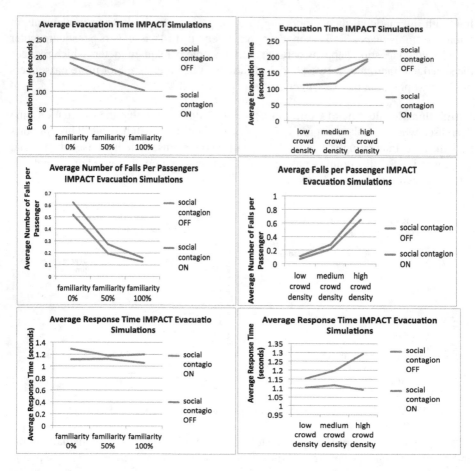

Fig. 4. Evacuation Time, Falls and Response Time versus Familiarity (left column) or crowd density (right column)

time increases with crowd density, but without social contagion it stays more or less the same. This actually seems to point to a negative effect of social contagion for the response time. (Fig. 2)

4   Conclusions

Based on the lack of psychological, social and cultural factors in evacuation models, this innovative work proposed a socio-cultural evacuation simulation. Social and cultural factors modelled are: familiarity, response time and social contagion. These socio-cultural factors were targeted as the most important and interesting factors to study by emergency management stakeholders. The main research question was: how do (1) familiarity with the environment, (2) social contagion of emotions and beliefs and (3) crowd density affect: (a) the evacuation time, (b) response time and (c) number of falls in an immediate evacuation from a building. Simulation results support the hypotheses that: (1) when familiarity increases, the evacuation time and number of falls will decrease; (2) when social contagion is on, the evacuation time will be lower than when social contagion is off. Interestingly, the main effect of social contagion, shows that response time and number of falls were higher, although overall evacuation time was faster when social contagion was on. After investigating the effects of familiarity and crowd density, it seems that this is mainly due to a high crowd density, since familiarity let response time decrease in case of social contagion and not when social contagion is off. In summary: (1) familiarity and social contagion have a positive effect on evacuation time; (2) crowd density and social contagion have a negative effect on number of falls and (3) familiarity, crowd density and social contagion have an interaction effect on response time: beneficial for response time are high familiarity and social contagion or high crowd density with no social contagion.

The strong points of this work are: (1) it is innovative, including socio-cultural factors, (2) it is supported by stakeholders in emergency prevention and management; (3) the simulation results support the a priori hypotheses and (4) interesting emergent effects were found. Points for improvement are: (1) the pathfinding algorithm (now a straight line) will be improved in a next version, (2) more socio-cultural factors that are important in evacuation modelling will be included in a next version: gender, prosocial behaviour and compliance and (3) the model will be validated against real-world data from a planned experiment and data of previous evacuation experiments.

Acknowledgments. This research was undertaken as part of EU H2020 IMPACT GA 653383. We thank our Consortium Partners and stakeholders for their input.

References

1. Bosse, T., Hoogendoorn, M., Klein, M.C., Treur, J., Van Der Wal, C.N., Van Wissen, A.: Modelling collective decision making in groups and crowds: integrating social contagion and interacting emotions, beliefs and intentions. Auton. Agent. Multi-Agent Syst. **27**(1), 52–84 (2013)
2. Challenger, R., et al.: Understanding crowd behaviours, Volume 1: Practical guidance and lessons identified. The Stationery Office (TSO), London (2010)
3. Grosshandler, W.L., et al.: Draft report of the technical investigation of The Station nightclub fire. US Dept Comm Report (2005)
4. Kobes, M., et al.: Building safety and human behaviour in fire: a literature review. Fire Saf. J. **45**(1), 1–11 (2010)
5. Netlogo. https://ccl.northwestern.edu/netlogo/
6. Proulx, G., Fahy, R.F.: The time delay to start evacuation: review of five case studies. Fire Saf. Sci. **5**, 783–794 (1997)
7. Santos, G., Aguirre, B.: A critical review of emergency evacuation simulation models (2004)
8. Still, G.K.: Introduction to Crowd Science. CRC Press (2014)
9. Templeton, A., Drury, J., Philippides, A.: From mindless masses to small groups: conceptualizing collective behavior in crowd modeling (2015)
10. Treur, J.: Network-Oriented Modeling: Addressing Complexity of Cognitive, Affective and Social Interactions. Springer, Switzerland (2016)
11. Zheng, X., Zhong, T., Liu, M.: Modeling crowd evacuation of a building based on seven methodological approaches. Build. Environ. **44**(3), 437–445 (2009)

A Consensus Approach to Sentiment Analysis

Orestes Appel[1,2]([✉]), Francisco Chiclana[1], Jenny Carter[1], and Hamido Fujita[3]

[1] Centre for Computational Intelligence (CCI),
De Montfort University, Leicester, UK
orestes.appel@my365.dmu.ac.uk, {chiclana,jennyc}@dmu.ac.uk
[2] Bissett School of Business, Mount Royal University, Calgary, AB, Canada
oappel@mtroyal.ca
[3] Iwate Prefectural University (IPU), Iwate, Takizawa, Japan
issam@iwate-pu.ac.jp

Abstract. There are many situations where the opinion of the majority of participants is critical. The scenarios could be multiple, like a number of doctors finding commonality on the diagnosing of an illness or parliament members looking for consensus on a specific law being passed. In this article we present a method that utilises Induced Ordered Weighted Averaging (IOWA) operators to aggregate a majority opinion from a number of Sentiment Analysis (SA) classification systems, where the latter occupy the role usually taken by human decision-makers. Previously determined sentence intensity polarity by different SA classification methods are used as input to a specific IOWA operator. During the experimental phase, the use of the IOWA operator coupled with the linguistic quantifier 'most' ($IOWA_{most}$) proved to yield superior results compared to those achieved when utilising other techniques commonly applied when some sort of averaging is needed, such as arithmetic mean or median techniques.

Keywords: Hybrid sentiment analysis method · Naïve Bayes · Maximum entropy · Consensus · Majority support · Sentiment aggregation · IOWA · OWA

1 Introduction

Group decision making (GDM) is a task where a number of agents get involved in a decision process to generate a value that represents their individual decisions in the group process [4]. The *arithmetic mean* and the *median* are central tendency values widely used in homogeneous GDM where experts are equally important [9]. In heterogeneous GDM, Yager's Induced Ordered Weighted Averaging (IOWA) operator [10] is widely used because it allows for different importance degrees to be implemented but also because it allow for the implementation of the concept of 'majority'. In the Sentiment Analysis (SA) context, any of the possible SA classification methods available can be considered an agent. The aim is to obtain a collective classification value that reflects *the opinion of the majority* of the SA classification methods. Experiments have been conducted using

© Springer International Publishing AG 2017
S. Benferhat et al. (Eds.): IEA/AIE 2017, Part I, LNAI 10350, pp. 628–634, 2017.
DOI: 10.1007/978-3-319-60042-0_69

the IOWA operator coupled with the linguistic quantifier 'most' (IOWA$_{most}$) to implement the concept of majority with three SA classification methods: Naïve Bayes [6], Maximum Entropy [2], and the Hybrid Approach to the SA problem devised in [1].

The remainder of this paper is organised as follows: Sect. 2 covers the basic concept of IOWA operator and the derivation of its associated weighting vector. Section 3 addresses the role of IOWA operators in the achieving of fuzzy majority in collective decision-making. In order to provide context, Sect. 4 covers the hybrid method introduced by the authors in [1], as the approach presented in this article represents an enhancement to this method in terms of obtaining a majority sentiment classification opinion. Section 5 covers the experimental results obtained when applying the proposed majority based methodology, and section 6 closes the paper with some conclusions and a brief discussion of possible further work.

2   IOWA Operators

Yager's IOWA operator [10] has been proved to be extremely useful in group decision making problems because it allows to implement the concept of *fuzzy majority* [11].

Definition 1 (IOWA Operator). *An IOWA operator of dimension n is a mapping IOWA: $(\mathbb{R} \times \mathbb{R})^n \longrightarrow \mathbb{R}$, which has an associated set of weights $W = (w_1, \cdots, w_n)$ to it, verifying $w_i \in [0, 1]$, $\sum_{i=1}^{n} w_i = 1$, such that*

$$IOWA\left(\langle u_1, a_1 \rangle, \ldots, \langle u_n, a_n \rangle\right) = \sum_{i=1}^{n} w_i \cdot a_{\sigma(i)}, \tag{1}$$

and $\sigma : \{1, \ldots, n\} \longrightarrow \{1, \ldots, n\}$ is a permutation function such that $u_{\sigma(i)} \geq u_{\sigma(i+1)}$, $\forall i = 1, \ldots, n-1$.

In the above definition the reordering of the set of values to aggregate, $\{a_1, \ldots, a_n\}$, is induced by the reordering of the set of values $\{u_1, \ldots, u_n\}$ associated to them. In [11], Yager proposed the following approach to obtain the IOWA associated weighting vector: Let $Q : [0, 1] \to [0, 1]$ be a function such that $Q(0) = 0$, $Q(1) = 1$, and $Q(x) \geq Q(y)$ for $x > y$ corresponding to a fuzzy set representation of a proportional monotone quantifier. Then,

$$w_i = Q\left(i/n\right) - Q\left((i+1)/n\right) \tag{2}$$

Some examples of linguistic quantifiers are *"at least half", "most of"* and *"as many as possible"*, which have been proposed [11] to be represented by using function:

$$Q(r) = \begin{cases} 0 & \text{if } 0 \leq r < a \\ \frac{r-a}{b-a} & \text{if } a \leq r \leq b \\ 1 & \text{if } b < r \leq 1 \end{cases} \tag{3}$$

with the values $(0, 0.5)$, $(0.3, 0.8)$ and $(0.5, 1)$ for (a, b), respectively [5].

3   IOWA Based Fuzzy Majority in GDM

In [7], Pasi and Yager elaborate that one of the possible semantics of IOWA operators is that of being drivers of a *majority opinion*. What is required is an operator that computes an average-like aggregation of the "**majority** of values that are similar". In [7], the authors establish that "similar values must have close positions in the induced ordering in order to appropriately be aggregated". Hence, the final output of an IOWA operator should reflect the opinion of the majority *if* similar values are closer to each other in the induced vector. Then, what is required is the ability to calculate the similarities between the values to be aggregated in order to compute "the values of the inducing variable of the IOWA operator" [7]. In order to support this, a binary support function, *Sup*, is introduced, where $Sup_\alpha(a, b)$ expresses the support from b for a at an α level of desired tolerance based on the concept that "the more similar two values are, the more they support each other":

$$Sup_\alpha(a_i, a_j) = \begin{cases} 1 & \text{if} \quad |a_i - a_j| < \alpha \\ 0 & \text{otherwise} \end{cases} \tag{4}$$

The higher the tolerance is, the less it is imposed that the two values *have to be closer to each other to support each other*. If we were to aggregate a set of values and we wanted to order them in increasing order of support, then for each value the sum of its support values is computed with respect to the rest of the values to be aggregated [7]. These overall supports are utilised as the values of the order inducing variable. Thus, the use of an adequate support function will enable the induction of an ordering based on proximity, which is key to understanding how IOWA operators generate a *majority-based aggregation* of the values to be aggregated via the linguistic quantifier *most* (as presented in Eq. (3) with values $(a, b) = (0.3, 0.8)$). Also, Pasi and Yager's strategy implies that the construction of the weighting vector appropriately implements more *influence* in the aggregation result from the most supported individual values. Consequently the following process for the construction of the weighting vector from the induced support values is proposed:

1. Include in the definition of the overall support for a_i the similarity of the value a_i with itself:

$$t_i = s_i + 1. \tag{5}$$

2. On the basis of the t_i values, the weights of the weighting vector are computed as follow:

$$w_i = Q\left(\frac{t_i}{n}\right) \bigg/ \sum_{j=1}^{n} Q\left(\frac{t_j}{n}\right) \tag{6}$$

"The value $Q(t_i/n)$ denotes the degree to which a given member of the considered set of values represents the *majority*" when the linguistic quantifier Q is used.

4   A Hybrid Approach to the SA Problem at the Sentence Level Aimed to Opinion Consensus

In [1], we describe a hybrid model for the SA (HSC/HAC) problem at the sentence level that is based on semantic rules, smart NLP techniques and fuzzy sets. The IOWA approach for aggregation presented in this article will be used to complement the aforementioned HSC/HAC model with the aim to arrive at a consensus sentiment classification opinion in SA [3] representing the opinion of the majority of approaches available to address the SA problem, as depicted in Fig. 1. Formally, the problem to address is how to determine the subjectivity intensity polarity for a given sentence S_k using the outputs of several classification systems. In a way, each method to be used and applied to the aforementioned sentence S_k, can be seen as an 'agent/person' giving her opinion on whether the sentence S_k is positive or negative. In our context, we would like to *aggregate the polarity intensity* value of sentence S_k measured by using different classification methods. Hence, the final polarity value will be the 'induced aggregation of the majority' of the subjectivity intensity polarity of sentence S_k when one takes into consideration all the different contributions of all the participating classification methods. The different applied classification methods will issue their individual *opinions*, just as individual agents use their own judgement.

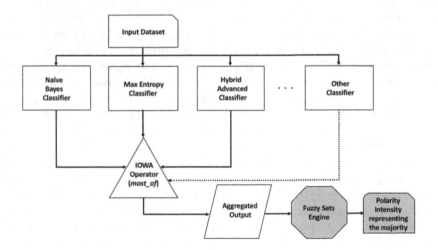

Fig. 1. *IOWA_{most}* operator aggregating classifier methods outputs

5   Experimental Results Obtained Applying $IOWA^{\alpha}_{most}$ aggregation

The $IOWA^{\alpha}_{most}$ operator performance was evaluated against both the *Arithmetic mean* and the *Median* performances (see Table 1). Experiments have been performed for both the Movie Review Dataset (http://www.cs.cornell.edu/people/pabo/movie-review-data/) and the Twitter Dataset *Sentiment140* (http://help.sentiment140.com/for-students). In order to use the output of all classifiers as an input to the $IOWA^{\alpha}_{most}$ process all participating scores have been converted to the interval $[0, 1]$, where S_k corresponds to any sentence in the test dataset and $\{m_1, m_2, \ldots, m_n\}$ represents the different classification methods being aggregated $(n \geq 2)$, then:

$$IOWA^{\alpha}_{most}[S_k](m_1, m_2, \ldots, m_n) = \Theta^{S_k} \tag{7}$$

Once the aggregation with the semantic representing the *opinion of the majority* has been computed, then Eq. (7) corresponds to the intensity level in which the value Θ belongs. The aggregated value Θ^{S_k} will take on the value x in $\mu_{\tilde{A}}(x)$ and in consequence a proper linguistic label belonging to set $G = \{Poor, \ Slight, \ Moderate, \ Very, \ Most\}$ will be generated to represent the polarity intensity (how positive or how negative) of a given sentence S_k [1]. The datasets used in the proof of concept count each (positive occurrences and negative occurrences) with 5,331 sentences. We have annotated 500 sentences, approximately 10%, assigning each of them a value $v_k \in G$. These were estimated by looking at the classification outcomes of the three classifiers we are utilising as inputs and estimating a linguistic label in G that is representative of the opinion of the majority. However, before we applied the IOWA$_{most}$ operator, we combined directly the results of the three chosen methods using the *Arithmetic mean* and the *Median*. The outcomes, which are summarised in Table 1 below, are not as good as those obtained by using the IOWA operator. This fact, shows that the IOWA operator does a much better job at aggregating the individual outcomes of the three aforementioned techniques, by giving more weight to the leaning opinion of the majority. In essence, by properly weighting the advise of the three methods (NB, ME and the HSC/HAC approach) we do obtain a more realistic aggregation effect that represents the thinking of the majority. The main difference between the results obtained when using different tolerance values (0.3 and 0.5) when IOWA$^{\alpha}_{most}$ is applied, is not in whether the outcome will distance itself from representing the opinion of the majority, but rather to which *linguistic label* (Poor, Slight, Moderate, etc.) a specific sentence will be assigned. Depending on the majority value calculated a sentence classified as 'Moderate' with a tolerance of 0.3 could now be labelled as 'Very' in terms of intensity, when the tolerance value changes to 0.5. In reality, the lower the *tolerance*, the more demanding the IOWA operator is on how closely the values in the aggregation support each other (see Table 1 for the experiments results).

Table 1. All aggregation methods compared

Semantic	Median	Mean	IOWA$_{most}^{\alpha=0.3,\ 0.5}$
Represents opinion of the majority	337	388	500
Does **not** represent opinion of the majority	163	112	0
% of success	67.40	77.60	100

6   Conclusions and Further Work

IOWA operators can certainly play a significant role in aggregating the opinions of a number of sentiment classification systems. The aforementioned operator works by producing a value that gets significantly closer to the collective opinion of the participants. The IOWA$_{most}^{\alpha}$ used in this article conveys the semantic of the opinion of the majority ('most'). Its performance in identifying the *intensity of the opinion of the majority*, according to our experiments, surpassed the one exhibited by *Arithmetic Mean* and *Median* techniques. In essence, IOWA$_{most}^{\alpha}$ produces a larger pull towards the values that support each other, driving the results in the direction of what the majority reflects. In terms of further work, we believe there are some avenues that could be pursued in the short-term: (a) Investigate other OWA operators that could potentially produce a better aggregation representing the semantic *majority opinion* and (b) Utilise the OWA measure of *dispersion*, which calculates the degree to which all aggregates are used in the resulting final aggregation [8].

References

1. Appel, O., Chiclana, F., Carter, J., Fujita, H.: A hybrid approach to the sentiment analysis problem at the sentence level. Knowl. Based Syst. **105**, 110–124 (2016). doi:10.1016/j.knosys.2016.05.040
2. Bishop, C.M.: Pattern Recognition and Machine Learning, 1st edn. Springer Science + Business Media, New York (2006). LLC
3. Cabrerizo, F.J., Chiclana, F., Al-Hmouz, R., Morfeq, A., Balamash, A.S., Herrera-Viedma, E.: Fuzzy decision making and consensus: challenges. J. Intell. Fuzzy Syst. **29**(3), 1109–1118 (2015)
4. F. Herrera and E. Herrera-Viedma. Linguistic decision analysis: steps for solving decision problems under linguistic information. Fuzzy Sets and Systems, 115: 67–82, 2000.
5. J. Kacprzyk. Group decision making with a fuzzy linguistic majority. Fuzzy Sets and Systems, 18: 105–118, 1986.
6. Pang, B., Lee, L., Vaithyanathan, S.: Thumbs up? Sentiment classification using machine learning techniques. In: Proceedings of the Association for Computational Linguistics (ACL-2002) Conference on Empirical Methods in Natural Language Processing (EMNLP), vol. 10, pp. 79–86 (2002)
7. Pasi, G., Yager, R.R.: Modeling the concept of majority opinion in group decision making. Inf. Sci. **176**(4), 390–414 (2006)

8. J. Peláez, J. M. Doña, and J. Gómez-Ruiz. Analysis of OWA operators in decision making for modelling the majority concept. Applied Mathematics and Computation, 186: 1263–1275, 2007.

9. Perkins, J.: Python Text Processing with NLTK 2.0 Cookbook. Packt Publishing, Birmingham (2010)

10. Yager, R., Filev, D.: Induced ordered weighted averaging operators. IEEE Transactions on Systems, Man and Cybernetics, Part B: Cybernetics **29**(2), 141–150 (1999)

11. Yager, R.R.: Quantifier guided aggregation using OWA operators. Int. J. Intell. Syst. **11**(1), 49–73 (1996)

Way of Coordination of Visual Modeling and Mental Imagery in Conceptual Solution of Project Task

P. Sosnin[✉] and M. Galochkin

Ulyanovsk State Technical University, Severny Venetc str. 32, 432027 Ulyanovsk, Russia
{sosnin,m.galochkin}@ulstu.ru

Abstract. In designing the software-intensive systems (SISs), one of the basic reasons for the extremely low degree of success is a gap between natural and artificial forms of human interactions with a computerized environment. Controlled coordinating a mental imagination and visual modeling can facilitate increasing the degree of success by the more effective interacting the designers with natural experience and its models as in predictable so in unpredictable situations. For achieving these effects, we have developed and tested a way of operative creating the necessary interfaces during conceptual solutions of project tasks.

Keywords: Conceptual designing · Human-computer interaction · Mental imagery · Question-answering · Software intensive system · Visual modeling

1 Preliminary Bases

Position. If in the real-time, any designer will have a possibility to create interactive visual models disclosing for understanding the unpredictable situations that take place during solving the project tasks, then such version of artificial interactions will be similar to natural interactions with the physical world. In similar situations, interactions of the designer with built interactive models will consist of intertwined compositions including the natural and artificial components that will be more correspondent each to another or, by another word, the gap between them will be decreased. In these conditions, specially built models will help the designer interacting with the situations to understand them.

Purpose. In the context of problems [1] with successful designing the SISs, to develop a way-of-working that will help the designer to create necessary interfaces with an operational environment in situations of a high complexity or self-interruptions caused by appearing a useful idea or a new task. Any of such situations require its understanding. For understanding the situation, the designer must activate a mental imagination that is better to register by adequate visual model beyond the brain.

This work was supported by the Russian Fund for Basic Research (RFBR), Grant #15-07-04809a and Russian Ministry of Education (State Contract № 2.1534.2017/ПЧ).

S. Benferhat et al. (Eds.): IEA/AIE 2017, Part I, LNAI 10350, pp. 635–638, 2017.
DOI: 10.1007/978-3-319-60042-0_70

Mental imagery is one of the basic intellectual phenomena [2], activating of which are incited by the intelligence of the designer if for this is the reasons. Effects caused by these phenomena can be increased, when imagination will be supported by artificial objects perceived by senses [3]. In the offered way aimed at automating the mental imagination, visual models will fulfill this function.

Methodology. In achieving the understanding, the imagination fulfills a subordinated role, because the designer must express the verified result of understanding at the language of the project. In our approach to conceptual designing the SYSs, the designer uses conceptual experiments [4] for achieving the reusable results of understanding. Moreover, results of such experimenting are included to a theory of the corresponding project. In fulfilling all these works, designers can use a question-answer approach and precedent-oriented approach that are applied in coordination [4]. Implementing the question-answer approach is schematically shown in Fig. 1.

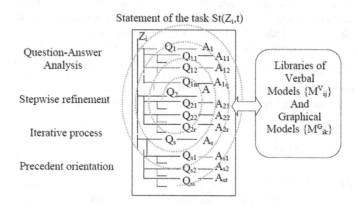

Fig. 1. Features of question-answer approach

The right column of the scheme indicates that the designer creates the statement of the task with the use of the question-answer analysis, the iterative process of which is implemented by the stepwise refinement. Operative creating and using visual models accompanies this process-oriented on its reuse as a precedent. The designer can use and apply models of precedents, creating of which support the specialized toolkit WIQA (Working In Questions and Answers) intended for conceptual solving the task [4].

2   A Set of Visual Models Affected on Mental Imagery

The basic aims of conceptual solving the task are following:

1. To present the statement $St(Z_i, t)$ in the understandable form for which is verified achieving the algorithmic realizability of the task solution.
2. To develop and test a conceptually algorithmic solution in conditions corresponding the place of the task in the project of SIS.

For achieving the first aim, the designer includes the necessary textual and graphical models from $\{M^V_{ij}\}$ and $\{M^G_{ik}\}$ in the construct $St(Z_i, t)$, and embedded components will provide reuse of understanding in the process of which these models will repeatedly activate the mental imagery. Without such activation, the needed understanding is impossible. It should be noted, in a stimulation of the mental imagery, visual items of any text will participate as special graphics, but, in understanding, the use of models $\{M^G_{ik}\}$ is more effective. The toolkit WIQA supports creating and transforming the visual models for types presented in Fig. 2.

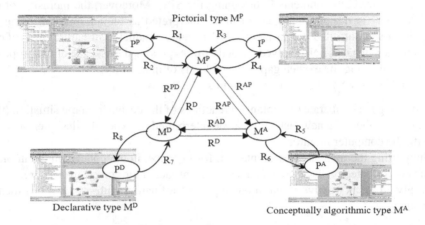

Fig. 2. Normative types of visual models

A set of types include:

- Pictorial type M^P, models of which helped to express the structure of the requested graphical construct as an interactive model I^P or not. For both versions of models, the used graphical editor automatically create programmatic versions, changing of which reflected on graphical models. Such opportunity is also realized for other types of models.
- Declarative type M^D intended for visualizing the semantics of textual models $\{M^V_{ij}\}$ that are important for the achievement of understanding. The main cause for using of this type is the check of $St(Z_i, t)$ and its verbal components via mechanisms of declarative programming. Therefore, the version P^D has a Prolog-like description.
- Conceptually algorithmic type M^A provides visual modeling of the algorithmic components of the task being solved. For this, the designer can use a pseudo code language L^{WIQA} that is built for the semantic memory of the toolkit WIQA. In the current state of WIQA, the type M^A supports the work with Use-Case diagrams, Activity diagrams, and diagrams of Classes. For the transition to the version P^A, the model-driven approach provides the automatic transition to the version P^A.

The scheme in Fig. 2 includes not only types but also relations among them. The set of relations consist of pairs presenting the transitions between corresponding models of different types (transitions $[R^{PD}, R^{DP}]$, $[R^{PA}, R^{AP}]$, $[R^{DA}, R^{AD}]$) and between models and their programmatic versions ($[R_1, R_2]$, $[R_3, R_4]$, $[R_5, R_6]$, $[R_7, R_8]$). Each of these transitions is realized either automatically or automated, including behavioral action.

3 Conclusion

Coordinating the use of described visual models with the mental imagination facilitates decreasing the gap between natural and artificial forms of designer's interactions with the computerized environments in designing the SISs. Moreover, the inclusion of the proposed way in designer's practice can be interpreted as the automation of mental imagery in its controlled use in mental experiments conducted in natural or artificial interactions with tasks being solved. Exactly this expresses the essence of the proposed version of reducing the existed gap between kinds of interactions.

The proposed way has the following features:

- Providing the deliberate or unplanned reactions of the designer on the situation (that signalizes about the new task, or it can be interpreted so) when the designer interacts with the computer monitor;
- Supporting the mental experimentation, for instance, in the conceptual solution of the task oriented on the reuse managed by the model of the corresponding precedent;
- Applying the normative visual modeling in coordination with processes of mental imagery.

In its realized version, this way support the work of a designer with conceptual objects mapped in the semantic memory of the toolkit WIQA.

Among the offered innovations, there are: a typology of interactive visual models including the specifications of types (pictured, declarative and conceptually algorithmic types); method of iterative creating the visual models in the context of developing the model of the precedent for the corresponding task; method of iterative achieving the sufficient level of understanding the perceived situations. To work with indicated findings, we developed the specialized graphical editor

References

1. Chaos reports 1994–2016. http://www.standishgroup.com
2. Moulton, S.T., Kosslyn, St.M.: Imagining predictions: mental imagery as mental emulation Phil. Trans. R. Soc. B 2009, **364**, 1273–1280 (2009)
3. Petre, M.: Mental imagery and software visualization in high-performance software development teams. J. Vis. Lang. Comput. **21**(3), 171–183 (2010)
4. Sosnin, P.: Conceptual experiments in automated designing. In: Zuanon, R. (ed.) Projective Processes and Neuroscience in Art and Design, pp. 155–181. IG-Global (2016)

Author Index

nited States